# ACHIEVEMENT IN AMERICAN SOCIETY

# ACHIEVEMENT IN AMERICAN SOCIETY

*Edited by*
BERNARD C. ROSEN, *Cornell University*
HARRY J. CROCKETT, Jr. and CLYDE Z. NUNN, *University of Nebraska*

*with* FOREWORD
by JAMES S. COLEMAN, *Johns Hopkins University*

SCHENKMAN PUBLISHING COMPANY, INC.
CAMBRIDGE, MASSACHUSETTS

Library of Congress Catalog Card #67-29330

Copyright © 1969
SCHENKMAN PUBLISHING COMPANY, INC.
*Cambridge, Massachusetts 02138*

PRINTED IN THE UNITED STATES OF AMERICA

# FOREWORD

Individual achievement, like the economic growth of nations, is not an easy matter to understand. It may be said to depend upon ability; yet how is ability defined except as the capacity to achieve under some standard conditions? Thus the concept of "ability" itself must be regarded as a catch-all for our ignorance about the relatively stable individual factors that lead to achievement, and how they combine to do so. It is a way of separating the individual determinants from those outside the individual that affect the result, that is, the achievement. Yet the division is not quite so gross: certain individual factors affecting achievement are in fact distinguished from ability. Such affective elements as the value accorded achievement by the individual, his motivation to achieve in this particular direction, and other personality factors that make possible the organization of abilities toward achievement. Yet what is "ability" itself other than an organization of more elementary tools toward a task? In short, our knowledge of the individual determinants of achievement, cognitive and affective (if such a classification is even appropriate) is in its infancy.

One direction toward developing that knowledge is to move explicitly outside the individual, to the social environment in which achievement occurs. For the social environment, whether in the individual's present or his past, comprises the determinants, not only of achievement, but also of all the non-biological *individual* determinants of achievement: those factors which we call motivation, values, personality, drive, and even developed abilities. Thus these social factors, acting as determinants of achievement, or as determinants of determinants of achievement, constitute one window through which the process of achievement may be seen, a window which allows a view of the way various elements conjoin to produce a result.

This book provides such a window. The papers of which it is composed give some idea of the way the social environment in which an individual finds himself, or the environment which surrounded him at an earlier time, affect his achievement. Certain aspects of this environment, such as his family or his immediate peer environment, are variable from individual to individual, while others are alike over

v

a whole culture. Some have their effect through shaping his personality, others through affecting his interest or desire to achieve, still others in affecting the external obstacles to achievement. Altogether, they provide a basis for a social view of achievement, a view which shows promise of illuminating even the individual dynamics by which an individual organizes his physical self to arrive at a goal.

JAMES S. COLEMAN

# TABLE OF CONTENTS

**FOREWORD** by James S. Coleman                                                    v

**INTRODUCTION**                                                                     1

Part I.    *ACHIEVEMENT: THE SOCIAL CONTEXT*                                          9

      **INTRODUCTION**                                                         3

         Robin M. Williams, Jr.
         **ACHIEVEMENT AND SUCCESS AS VALUE ORIENTATIONS**        13

         Robert E. L. Farls
         **REFLECTIONS ON THE ABILITY DIMENSION IN HUMAN
         SOCIETY**                                                18

         John W. Gardner
         **THE GREAT TALENT HUNT**                                 33

Part II.   *ORIGINS OF ACHIEVEMENT: PERSONALITY AND STRUCTURAL
       FACTORS*                                                         43

      **INTRODUCTION**                                                        45

    A.   *THE IMPACT OF MICRO-SOCIAL STRUCTURES: THE FAMILY*                 52

         Bernard C. Rosen and Roy G. D'Andrade
         **THE PSYCHOSOCIAL ORIGINS OF ACHIEVEMENT MOTI-
         VATION**                                                 55

         Ernest A. Haggard
         **SOCIALIZATION, PERSONALITY AND ACADEMIC ACHIEVE-
         MENT IN GIFTED CHILDREN**                                85

         Virginia C. Crandall
         **ACHIEVEMENT BEHAVIOR IN YOUNG CHILDREN**               95

         Ralph H. Turner
         **SOME FAMILY DETERMINANTS OF AMBITION**                112

    B.   *THE IMPACT OF MACRO-SOCIAL STRUCTURES: RACE AND
       ETHNICITY*                                                      129

         Bernard C. Rosen
         **RACE, ETHNICITY, AND THE ACHIEVEMENT SYNDROME**       131

         Albert J. Reiss, Jr. and A. Lewis Rhodes
         **ARE EDUCATIONAL NORMS AND GOALS OF CONFORM-
         ING, TRUANT AND DELINQUENT ADOLESCENTS INFLU-
         ENCED BY GROUP POSITION IN AMERICAN SOCIETY?**          154

Martin Deutsch
MINORITY AND CLASS STATUS AS RELATED TO FACTORS
IN ACHIEVEMENT                                                        174

C.  *THE IMPACT OF MACRO-SOCIAL FACTORS: SOCIAL CLASS*      181

William H. Sewell, Archie O. Haller, and Murray A. Straus
SOCIAL STATUS AND EDUCATIONAL AND OCCUPA-
TIONAL ASPIRATION                                                     183

Robert D. Hess and Virginia C. Shipman
EARLY EXPERIENCE AND THE SOCIALIZATION OF COG-
NITIVE MODES IN CHILDREN                                              193

Jackson Toby
ORIENTATION TO EDUCATION AS A FACTOR IN THE
SCHOOL MALADJUSTMENT OF LOWER-CLASS CHILDREN    212

Part III.  *ACHIEVEMENT IN ACADEMIC SETTINGS*                  227

INTRODUCTION                                                          229

A.  *THE IMPACT OF MACRO-SOCIAL STRUCTURES: THE SCHOOL
AS A SOCIAL SYSTEM*                                                   237

Talcott Parsons
THE SCHOOL CLASS AS A SOCIAL SYSTEM: SOME OF ITS
FUNCTIONS IN AMERICAN SOCIETY                                         239

Barbara Biber and Patricia Minuchin
THE ROLE OF THE SCHOOL IN THE SOCIALIZATION OF
COMPETENCE                                                            260

Natalie Rogoff Ramsoy
LOCAL SOCIAL STRUCTURE AND EDUCATIONAL SELECTION    283

B.  *THE IMPACT OF MICRO-SOCIAL STRUCTURES: THE PEER GROUP*    295

Theodore M. Newcomb
STUDENT PEER-GROUP INFLUENCE                                          297

C. Norman Alexander, Jr. and Ernest Q. Campbell
PEER INFLUENCE ON ADOLESCENT ASPIRATIONS AND
ATTAINMENTS                                                           312

James S. Coleman
ABILITY AND SCHOOL ACHIEVEMENT                                        323

C.  *THE IMPACT OF MICRO-SOCIAL STRUCTURES: THE STUDENT-
TEACHER RELATIONSHIP*                                                 329

Jules Henry
DOCILITY, OR GIVING TEACHER WHAT SHE WANTS                 331

Howard S. Becker
SOCIAL CLASS VARIATIONS IN THE TEACHER-PUPIL RE-
LATIONSHIP                                                            342

**Part IV. ACHIEVEMENT IN OCCUPATIONAL SETTINGS: PERSONALITY AND STRUCTURAL FACTORS**    357

**INTRODUCTION**    359

**A. ACHIEVEMENT IN ORGANIZATIONS: CONSTRAINTS AND ADAPTATIONS**    365

Victor H. Vroom
**EGO-INVOLVEMENT, JOB SATISFACTION AND JOB PERFORMANCE**    367

Wilbert E. Moore
**CLIMBERS, RIDERS, TREADERS**    384

Arthur K. Davis
**BUREAUCRATIC PATTERNS**    391

Donald Roy
**EFFICIENCY AND "THE FIX": INFORMAL INTERGROUP RELATIONS IN A PIECEWORK MACHINE SHOP**    407

**B. ACHIEVEMENT AND CREATIVITY**    425

Donald W. MacKinnon
**WHAT MAKES A PERSON CREATIVE?**    427

Jerome S. Bruner
**THE CONDITIONS OF CREATIVITY**    435

**C. ACHIEVEMENT AND WOMEN**    451

Florence Rockwood Kluckhohn
**AMERICAN WOMEN AND AMERICAN VALUES**    453

Alice S. Rossi
**WOMEN IN SCIENCE: WHY SO FEW?**    470

**Part V. ACHIEVEMENT AND SOCIAL MOBILITY: PERSONALITY AND STRUCTURAL FACTORS**    487

**INTRODUCTION**    489

**A. FACTORS DETERMINING INTERGENERATIONAL MOBILITY**    495

Peter M. Blau and Otis Dudley Duncan
**SOME PRELIMINARY FINDINGS ON SOCIAL STRATIFICATION IN THE UNITED STATES**    497

**B. INTERACTION OF PERSONALITY AND STRUCTURAL FACTORS IN DIFFERENTIAL MOBILITY**    519

Harry J. Crockett, Jr.
**SOCIAL CLASS, EDUCATION AND MOTIVE TO ACHIEVE IN DIFFERENTIAL OCCUPATIONAL MOBILITY**    521

Bruce K. Eckland
ACADEMIC ABILITY, HIGHER EDUCATION AND OCCU-
PATIONAL MOBILITY                                          533
Robert A. Ellis and W. Clayton Lane
STRUCTURAL SUPPORTS FOR UPWARD MOBILITY          552
W. Lloyd Warner and James C. Abegglen
EXECUTIVE CAREERS TODAY: WHO GETS TO THE TOP?    564

C.  STRUCTURAL FACTORS IN DIFFERENTIAL MOBILITY         579

Richard L. Simpson and Ida Harper Simpson
SOCIAL ORIGINS, OCCUPATIONAL ADVICE, OCCUPA-
TIONAL VALUES AND WORK CAREERS                    581

Part VI.  DEVELOPING ACHIEVEMENT                            597

INTRODUCTION                                      599

A.  THE PROBLEM OF METHODS                              601

Martin Deutsch
FACILITATING DEVELOPMENT IN THE PRE-SCHOOL CHILD:
SOCIAL AND PSYCHOLOGICAL PERSPECTIVES            603

B.  THE PROBLEM OF GOALS                                621

David C. McClelland
ENCOURAGING EXCELLENCE                            623

SELECTED ANNOTATED REFERENCES                               637

INDEX                                                       645

# INTRODUCTION

# INTRODUCTION

This is a book of essays and research reports about achievement: its origins, distribution and manifestations in American society. But let us be clear at the outset — we are not concerned with every kind of achievement in every conceivable social context. For the most part the materials included in this book focus upon *occupational* achievement in more or less conventional spheres. The successful gangster, the popular entertainer, the creative poet — all are examples of achievement in their own arenas, but they do not fall with the purview of this volume. Studies of academic achievement are included, but primarily because scholastic performance is generally viewed as a factor in eventual occupational success. In the same vein, it will be noted that the selections on creativity deal primarily with exceptional performance in conventional occupations; and the papers on achievement among women are concerned with the factors which affect, usually adversely, the ability of women to achieve success in work outside of the home.

This emphasis upon work is an explicit response to the high valuation placed upon occupational achievement in American society. We are aware, of course, that there are other arenas in which achievement is esteemed. After all, friendship and marital harmony may also be considered values in our society. But it is fair to say that in no other sphere are the social rewards for achievement as great as in the area of work. As Williams in the first selection of this book so correctly notes, "The comparatively striking feature of American culture is its tendency to identify standards of personal excellence with competitive occupational achievement."

Though limited in the kinds of achievement they consider, the selections in this book all address themselves to much the same kinds of questions: Who achieves, what contributes to achievement, what hinders it — and why?

These are not uniquely American questions, but they are familiar ones in a society which has made achievement and success a part of the national dream. For in a society such as ours, it cannot help but be noticed that some persons "make it" while others do not. Though

3

the reasons are often obscure, some people never seem to get started, others falter and "run out of gas," only a few amply fulfill their early promise. Even in cases where there appears to be no marked difference in ability and where the starting point is roughly the same, there may be differences in eventual achievement. Almost everyone whose hair is time-flecked with gray has observed this phenomenon among his circle of friends and acquaintances. The range from success to failure is probably not great in most cases, but it is there. And its existence has long intrigued Americans.

Consider the plaintive query of Willy Loman. "What is the secret?" he asked a highly successful young man in the play, "Death of a Salesman." No one answered the distraught salesman, but surely not because no answers were available. For speculation about the causes of achievement is as much a part of American culture as is the emphasis upon it. In point of fact, almost every conceivable factor has been offered to account for achievement. For example, some persons view achievement as largely due to chance and look for clues to the future in the stars. Others have been attracted to the notion that physiological factors provide the answer to the puzzle of achievement. It was once widely believed that the bumps on our heads were what really counted, and for a time phrenology enjoyed great vogue.

In this country, the greatest attention has been directed to what might be called moralistic and intellective factors. Perhaps it would be instructive to briefly examine the history of the perspectives provided by these factors, because they point up major differences between the kinds of studies reported in this book and much previous discussion of achievement.


## THE MORALISTIC PERSPECTIVE

The maxims of Poor Richard are typical of the approach taken in discussions of achievement throughout much of our history. In a sense the injunctions of Franklin to be thrifty, honest, and sober are as much explanations of achievement as they are directions for its attainment. Success was thought to be one's reward for the development of a highly valued character structure. The individual was exhorted to develop qualities of character which would inevitably contribute to his success: "Early to bed, early to rise *makes* one healthy, wealthy and wise." It was felt that social rewards naturally belonged to the frugal and moral; the self-indulgent non-conformist could only expect, and rightly deserved, inevitable failure. This approach was, of course, very satisfying to the wealthy and privileged, who were able not only to enjoy the fruits of power and affluence but to feel morally superior as well. The moralistic school produced a voluminous inspirational literature which probably reached its apogee in Horatio Alger's stories. The prescriptions for success which repeatedly occur in these books stress the importance of sobriety, thrift, a respectful attitude towards authority and the wisdom of marrying the boss's daughter.

In the late nineteenth century, interest in understanding achievement received impetus and support from a rather surprising quarter: the theory of evolution, or more precisely its social derivative — Social Darwinism. The successful person, the Social Darwinist argued, had achieved his position because he was the most fit. The qualities which made him fit had evolved over time through natural selection. But what were these qualities? The early answers to this question were primarily moralistic in the value-laden way typical of early Social Darwinian thinking. That is, the most successful were thought to be hard-working, thrifty, punctual, God-fearing and the like.

In time, however, Darwin's scientific approach had the effect of producing discontent with such explanations, particularly when the suspicion arose that the traits so highly praised were in fact rationalizations for class dominance. More objective efforts to study achievement coincided with the development of the social sciences which introduced new constructs and techniques that seemed to hold great promise. One construct which early caught the attention of scientists was intelligence.

THE INTELLECTIVE PERSPECTIVE

There is something very logical in the notion that intelligence is related to achievement. Surely, achievement requires intelligence. Hence, it seems reasonable to argue that the more intelligent the individual the more likely he is to become successful. The research which the introduction of ways to measure intelligence made possible seemed to confirm this conclusion. For example, during the First World War intelligence tests administered to inductees revealed that the scores of Negroes were on the average lower than those for whites.

Could there be any question that the whites had achieved a higher standard of living and greater status than Negroes? And was it not true that the white man had achieved more because of his greater intelligence? The tests seemed to answer in the affirmative.

The next two decades produced an avalanche of studies reporting I.Q. differences between groups with dissimilar levels of achievement. Perhaps the most characteristic of these studies were those reporting higher scores among persons in the middle class than in the lower class. Again the conclusion seemed obvious. Middle class persons were more successful because they were more intelligent.

A closer examination of these studies revealed some facts which had passed unnoticed. It was found that some Negroes had higher I.Q. scores than some whites, and that urban Northern Negroes as a group tended to perform better in the test than rural Southern whites. A search for the cause of this surprising finding showed the I.Q. test to be heavily biased in favor of urban, middle class subjects. The question arose: Does the test measure intelligence or does it largely reflect differences in cultural opportunities; and is not the latter factor a more accurate explanation of differential race and class achievement? Furthermore, it was discovered that the relationship of I.Q. scores to performance was not without its ambiguities. Although intelligence as measured by the I.Q. test is positively correlated with academic achievement, the correlation is far from perfect: some persons achieve more than their I.Q. test would indicate was possible, while others achieve less. Research has shown that two persons with very similar I.Q. scores may differ greatly in their performance in school.

Perhaps more troubling were the findings of Terman and his associates. In a longitudinal study of individuals with very high I.Q. scores, Terman found great differences in occupational achievement. It was expected that this group of gifted individuals would in time occupy positions of importance and display their talents in a wide variety of creative activities. This was true in some cases, but for a significant number it was not. Despite I.Q. levels described as being of the order of genius, some members of Terman's sample ultimately ended in quasi-skilled occupations, while others achieved far less than their I.Q. scores would suggest was possible. These differences between potential and actual achievement made it clear that the search for an understanding of achievement could not end in a study of intellective factors alone. The search, of course, did not end.

And in a sense it was Terman who helped point the way when he suggested that the personalities of some of his subjects might explain the discrepancies between I.Q. scores and eventual achievement.

## THE PERSONALITY-SOCIAL STRUCTURE PERSPECTIVE

What the moralistic-intellective approaches have in common is the notion that there is a simple and sovereign factor which explains achievement and accounts for its effects and distribution in society. This is not our position. It seems clear to us that achievement is a complex phenomenon; no single explanatory factor will suffice to explain it. Hence this book will not single out one factor for exclusive attention. On the other hand, any attempt to evaluate all the factors which might conceivably be related to achievement would inevitably be doomed to failure.

Our strategy is to operate between these two extremes by focusing upon a limited number of factors. But, these factors are neither moralistic nor intellective, though we grant that such factors may influence achievement. The essays and researches reported in this volume were deliberately selected because their approach *is* neither intellective nor moralistic. They focus upon social structural, and psychological variables. At the psychological level, some selections examine the relationship of such personality variables as motivation, values, and aspirations to achievement. Other selections view achievement socially, examining the effects of various social structures upon the individual's opportunity to compete successfully for occupational (or academic) achievement in American society.

These structures may be small, as in the case of the family or peer group, or large, as in the case of the bureaucratic organization. But whatever their size, the structure of relationships which develop within a social system is viewed as affecting the individual's perception of his environment, influencing what he strives to achieve, and determining to some degree how successful he will be in reaching his goal. The individual's perceptions, values and motives in turn influence his relationships with others. In so doing, they affect the structure of the group and thus feed back upon the achievement process.

The selections which make up this book address themselves in some way to the problem of how personality or social structure affect achievement. Some selections are discursive, though we hope provocative. Most are reports of empirical research. Our preference has been for reports of original research, though occasionally we have included an article which reviews a portion of the field and summarizes general findings. We have sought to keep not only the "spirit," but also, insofar as space permits, the "letter" of each author's contribution. Abridgments in most cases are slight; often virtually the entire article is included. Neither individually nor collectively do they examine all the personality or structural factors which might be related to achievement. But cumulatively they present impressive evidence of the relevance of these factors to achievement.

# PART I

Achievement: The Social Context

# PART I

## Achievement, The Social Context

## INTRODUCTION

A widespread concern with achievement is a familiar phenomenon on the American scene. Though the frantic efforts to upgrade our school system and encourage talent that followed the disclosure of Russian priority in space technology might suggest it all began in response to Communist competition, the fact is that a marked stress on personal achievement has characterized American society from the beginning. Foreign observers of the American scene, from Tocqueville to Laski and Brogan, have long been struck by the high valuation Americans place upon personal achievement, particularly as it is expressed in status striving and social mobility. Americans, implicitly assenting to this appraisal of their culture, devote considerable time and energy to measuring achievement, searching for its origins, assessing its distribution in society and evaluating its effects. Support for this statement can be found in the ubiquitous achievement tests employed in schools at all levels, the many researches into the antecedents and social correlates of achievement and the numerous studies of social mobility.

What *is* new is a growing recognition of the social importance of achievement, and a greater willingness to examine the social context in which it is expressed. There is, for example, a better understanding today of the *social* meaning of human ability. It is easy to see that an individual's talents and skills will be of value to him in most societies, and particularly in those prepared to reward individual initiative and enterprise. What is not so readily apparent is that human ability is more than an individual asset — it is a social resource as well. Faris maintains in a selection in this section that the skills and talents of its members are a major source of a society's strength. This is especially true in modern societies. It is becoming increasingly clear that industrial societies require large numbers of highly trained, achievement-oriented people to perform the numerous specialized roles found in a complex social system.[1] Indeed, a nation's survival in a competitive world may depend upon its ability to identify talent, encourage its development and direct it into socially useful channels — a fact which may help explain why the United States is currently engaged in

11

what Gardner in the third selection calls "The Great Talent Hunt." Whether our society will function smoothly, or perhaps continue to operate at all for very long, will depend in part on our willingness and ability to provide talented and motivated people with adequate training and sufficient opportunity to utilize their skills and achieve their goals.

The nature of these goals will vary of course with the individual. For notwithstanding the pressures in contemporary society towards uniformity and conformity, we do not all have the same aspirations.[2] Yet in most cases an individual's goals will reflect to some degree the norms and values of the society in which he lives. Two values which are relevant to goal striving are achievement and success. Achievement refers to exceptional accomplishment; success emphasizes social rewards. Though they are analytically different values, as Williams makes clear in his selection, they are often empirically inextricably interconnected. When we examine specific cases, it is not always clear what it is that Americans are applauding — achievement or success, or both. This is particularly likely to be the case as regards achievement in conventional areas of work. For occupational achievement in American society is often measured by the amount of social rewards it earns — that is, success.[3] Still, notwithstanding this difficulty, it is reasonably clear that Americans would like to believe that achievement and success, though different, are related and that one will follow the other. Which is to say, that achievement will be recognized and bring with it the social rewards associated with success.

### REFERENCES

1. Bert F. Hoselitz and Wilbert E. Moore, *Industrialization and Society*, UNESCO; Mouton, 1963.
2. Jose Ortega y Gasset, *Revolt of the Masses*, New York: New American Library, 1950.
3. Geoffrey Gorer, *The American People; A Study in National Character*, New York: Norton, 1958. Max Lerner, *America as a Civilization: Life and Thought in the United States Today*, New York: Simon and Schuster, 1957.

# ACHIEVEMENT AND SUCCESS AS VALUE ORIENTATIONS

## ROBIN M. WILLIAMS, JR.

American culture is marked by a central stress upon personal achievement, especially secular occupational achievement. The "success story" and the respect accorded to the self-made man are distinctly American, if anything is. Our society has been highly competitive — a society in which ascribed status in the form of fixed, hereditary social stratification has been minimized. It has endorsed Horatio Alger and has glorified the rail splitter who becomes president: "Periodic public opinion polls are not needed to justify the selection of Abe Lincoln as the culture hero who most fully embodies the cardinal American virtues. . . . Even the inevitable schoolboy knows that Lincoln was thrifty, hard-working, eager for knowledge, ambitious, devoted to the rights of the average man, and eminently successful in climbing the ladder of opportunity from the lowermost rung of laborer to the respectable heights of merchant and lawyer. . . ."[1]

Emphasis upon achievement must be distinguished from the broader valuation of personal excellence. All societies have standards of character and proficiency, and accord rewards to those best meeting whatever standards are most highly appraised, whether of military prowess, ritual knowledge, asceticism, piety, or what not. The comparatively striking feature of American culture is its tendency to identify standards of personal excellence with competitive occupational achievement. In the pure type, the value attached to achievement does not comprehend the person as a whole, but only his accomplishments, emphasizing the objective results of his activity. Because of the preoccupation with business, the most conspicuous achievements have been those centered in business enterprise. We can say, with Laski and many others, that the "values of the business man" dominate and permeate national life. Yet achievement has never been completely identified with sheer business success; for example, such an assumption does not account

Reprinted from Robin M. Williams, Jr. American Society, second edition (New York: Alfred A. Knopf, Inc., 1960), by permission of the publisher and the author.

for the respect and prestige accorded to the professions. Seen in the context of other major value themes,[2] business success seems to be a dominant focus, but not the dominant value-pattern, in American society.

However, as already noted, economic success has been so heavily stressed in certain parts of our society as to impose a widespread and persistent strain upon institutional regulation of means used to attain this goal. At the extreme, only questions of technical effectiveness enter into the choice of means — thus, the "Robber Barons," "business is business," and much organized crime, vice and racketeering. Perhaps the apogee of largely unrestrained economic acquisition was reached in the period of "business baroque" from about 1890 to 1912, when the leaders of business "exulted openly in power and riches, won by national centralization. . . ."[3]

Adequate research evidence is not as yet available to allow an accurate appraisal of the extent to which success rather than achievement has moved to the center of the values of our culture. Such evidence is greatly needed, for the question thus raised is fundamental to any real diagnosis of the current value-system. Whereas achievement refers to valued accomplishments, success lays the emphasis upon rewards. Amoral success-striving may not have gone to the lengths suggested by some observers,[4] but the important point is that once success goals are divorced from the ultimate values of society, the way is opened for a corrosion of regulative norms.[5] In the United States, the available evidence suggests that, even though success is often regarded as an end in itself and sometimes there is almost no positive relation between success and moral virtue, yet the success pattern is still linked to achievement, achievement is still associated with work, and work is still invested with an almost organic complex of ethical values. Thus, success is still not a primary criterion of value in its own right, but rather a derivative reward *for* active, instrumental performance. There is growing evidence that performance in consumption is partly replacing performance in work: how one spends his income, rather than what he did to earn it appears increasingly to be a mark of "achievement."[6] Nevertheless, as Wecter has suggested, the American heroes are not merely successful — they must be successful within a certain ethical framework: they must be, or appear to be, "self-respecting, decent, honorable, with a sense of fair play; no Machiavelli nor Mussolini need apply."[7] The belief that virtue will be rewarded and that success attends upon effort dies hard; and in our culture failure is still more likely to be charged to defect of character than to blind fate, capricious accident, or impersonalized social and economic forces, and the wealthy and powerful still either desire or find it expedient to justify their position in the name of "service" and "stewardship."

The dimensions of success values may perhaps be clarified by an examination of the place of wealth and its attainment in the culture. Many foreign and native observers have viewed American society as grossly acquisitive and materialistic, as naïvely impressed by bigness, speed, wealth, and power. Such a view is too simple, as an examination of American attitudes toward money will illustrate.

We may begin by eliminating any interpretation such as "of course money is wanted because it is the universal agency for satisfying any desires that can be met by purchasable goods."[8] For many profitable activities are socially condemned and not widely carried on; and people strive intensely for wealth long after their basic physical needs have been met or even after they have achieved nearly every conceivable means for satisfying their desires. Santayana's insight has more accurately indicated the central function of money in the American value system: "It is the symbol and measure he (the American) has at hand for success, intelligence, and power; but as to money itself he makes, loses, spends and gives it away with a very light heart."[9] In a society of relatively high social mobility, in which position in the scale of social stratification basically depends upon occupational achievement, wealth is one of the few obvious signs of one's place in the hierarchy. Achievement is difficult to index, in a highly complex society of diverse occupations, because of the great differences in abilities and effort required for success in various fields. At the same time, the central type of achievement is in business, manufacturing, commerce, finance; and since traditionalized social hierarchies, fixed estates, and established symbols of hereditary rank have had only a rudimentary development, there is a strong tendency to use money as a symbol of success. Money comes to be valued not only for itself and for the goods it will buy, but as symbolic evidence of success and, thereby, of personal worth.

Much the same type of analysis applies to the so-called American love of bigness. It is said that Americans are impressed by size *qua* size; "bigger and better" is a childish love of quantity as such. Actually the important thing is that "better" is presumed to be *implied* by "bigger." Things are good not so much because they are big, but because goodness is assumed and bigness therefore means more of something already considered valuable. Again Santayana has well expressed the essential point: "Respect for quantity is accordingly more than the childish joy and wonder at bigness; it is the fisherman's joy in a big haul, the good uses of which he can take for granted."[10] Unquestionably, we are dealing here with a culture that values action and the mastery of the physical world, [11] and its whole history has been, in the main, an experience of expansionism and mastery: increasing population, increasing territory, increased levels of living, and so on indefinitely. Given the definition of such things as good, respect for quantity directly follows.

## REFERENCES

1. Robert K. Merton, "The Self-Fulfilling Prophecy," *The Antioch Review* (Summer 1948), p. 199.

2. The so-called success philosophy attains its full cultural meaning only along with a particular kind of moral individualism. See Cuber and Harper, *Problems of American Society*, p. 356: "The basic premise of this philosophy is that individuals, not classes, are the real competing units. A man is said to reap his reward by 'his own' efforts, skills, and perseverance."

3. Miriam Beard, *A History of the Business Man* (New York, 1938), p. 641. For a similar period in the ancient world see Gilbert Murray, *Five Stages of Greek Religion* (London, 1935), p. 79. Compare also pp. 115 ff. for an analysis of the way in which the Good becomes assimilated to success (wealth and power) in a certain type of social order.

4. Geoffrey Gorer, *The American People: A Study in National Character* (New York, 1948), pp. 169 and 172.

5. Some of the more important personality strains engendered by high levels of aspiration in a competitive order have been compactly analyzed by Karen Horney in several works; see, for example, *The Neurotic Personality of Our Time* (New York, 1937).

6. See, for example: Eli Chinoy, *Automobile Workers and the American Dream* (Garden City, N. Y., 1955); David Riesman, "The Suburban Sadness," in William M. Dobriner (ed.), *The Suburban Community* (New York, 1958).

7. Dixon Wecter, *The Hero in America* (New York, 1941), p. 482. (This comment has to be qualified to take into account a Huey Long and an Al Capone, as well as the hero worship of the movie stars who are presented as

living in opulent success as the result of pure accident — unrelated to personal virtues.)

8. The American sociologist Charles Horton Cooley pointed out as long ago as the turn of the century that "wealth as an object of ambition and a measure of success owes its ascendency to its social implications, and the pursuit of it is by no mean a proof of materialism or sensuality. . . . The fact that a man desires it, throws little or no light upon the real object of his ambition." — *Sociological Theory and Social Research* (New York, 1930), p. 222; the quotation is from the essay "Personal Competition," which first appeared as an article in 1899.

9. *Character and Opinion in the United States* (New York, 1920), p. 185. Cf. Gorer: *The American People*, p. 177: "It can be said that, as a general rule, the acquisition of money is very important to Americans, but its retention relatively unimportant."

10. *Character and Opinion in the United States*, p. 182.

11. Cf. Laski, *The American Democracy*, p. 42. "No attempt to grasp the nature of the American spirit can be complete which does not emphasize the degree to which action is of its essence."

# REFLECTIONS ON THE ABILITY DIMENSION IN HUMAN SOCIETY

## ROBERT E. L. FARIS

The survival and welfare of every person on earth rests on organization. In simple organizations, as in prehistoric societies, only small populations can exist. Our immense contemporary civilization survives luxuriously only by virtue of a base of elaborate organization.

More extensive organization can support more population at high standards of living. As Ogburn has shown, among modern nations differences in living standards are related not so much to inequality of resources as to differences in complexity of organization.[1]

We cannot have intricate systems without a supply of high and conspicuous ability in the population. Scarcity of abilities is palpably a major and conspicuous obstacle to progress in some of the currently developing nations.[2]

It also appears that, in our own economy, the supply of ability is a factor in its potential growth rate. The present concern about automation bears on the point. Assuming that we do not elect to arrest further automation, the solution to technological unemployment must lie in the growth rate of the Gross National Product, and this in turn obviously requires an augmented supply of the various kinds of ability involved in inventing and organizing. There will have to be new products if we are to employ the persons no longer needed on farms and unskilled laboring jobs. These new devices will have to be developed at a greater rate than the already high pace of invention.

The current tempo, which we must outrun, is illustrated by the observation that eighty per cent of the sales of the Radio Corporation of America are of products unknown a little over a decade ago, and by a recent forecast of the Du Pont Company that at least 60 per cent of its 1975 sales revenue will be from products now in their introductory

Reprinted from the *American Sociological Review* (Vol. 26, No. 6, December 1961, pp. 835–843) by permission of the American Sociological Association and the author.

stages or still to be invented. It has also been predicted that within the next three years, in the transportation industry, almost 30 per cent of its sales dollar will come from products either new or so changed as to be considered new. Chemical research, an immensely important component of all inventive activity, measured by published volume, has doubled from 1950 to 1960. While these selected examples may over-represent the present pace of technical innovation, they give a useful impression that the needed acceleration is from an already swift-moving rate of development.

Present population trends do not give a prospect of an early automatic increase in the proportion of productive persons, for the U.S. population is now bulging at the young and old ages. We will have 16 per cent more population in the United States by the end of the present decade, but only a three per cent increase in the most creative ages of 25–44. This fact clearly intensifies the urgency of artificial stimulation of capacities in the part of the population that must bear the mental burdens.

It does not suffice to have a limited stock of geniuses at the top of the productive organization. The need is equally great for a wide distribution, throughout the society, of personal characteristics favorable to the operation of elaborate technology and organization. While mankind has always correctly sought for able leaders, we have chronically over-emphasized the importance of a few great men in the growth of civilization, and have failed to appreciate the importance of distributed ability. Advanced achievements, we now realize, rest not only on the shoulders of generals, statesmen, and inventors, but importantly on the skills, muscles, and morale of the common soldier, the curiosity and optimism of minor technicians, and also the inconspicuous crescive processes of custom and law-building which underlie all governmental structure.

Elaborate technology is not alone capable of upholding a civilization. It fails without a wise distribution of machine skills. The ingenious products of the inventor's mind must be continually maintained, improved, repaired, and properly use. The pre-industrial peasant who has never known gasoline engines may acquire a tractor and learn to drive it, but unless he has also a supply of generalized comprehension of such matters as the effects of overheating, the necessity of lubrication, the function of spark plugs, he will not long till his fields by machinery.

Deficiency of technical ability contributes to the fact that in 1961 the unemployment rate is the highest among the unskilled and uneducated workers. Many of these workers, at their present levels of ability, are not qualified for the new jobs created by technical advance. Simple retraining for more skilled tasks will not suffice, for recent studies have revealed a lack of general aptitude in the majority of those with long-term unemployment. Many are in fact on the edge of illiteracy, and their deficiencies are in important part matters of basic schooling.

Ogburn's conception of the three factors determining the rate of invention, proposed a third of a century ago in his notable book *Social Change*, still appears to be sound. These factors are (a) a supply of inventive ability, (b) a demand for inventions, and (c) the existing body of knowledge, which he called the cultural base. Ogburn argued that the influence of the first two is less crucial to the rate of inventive progress than that of the third, holding that large populations generally have an adequate supply of individuals of high potential mental ability and that the need factor fails at crucial times, as in the case of the Black Death, and makes no contribution at all to ingenious but unneeded devices, such as hula hoops.

The most significant element in Ogburn's theory is the statement of the way in which the accumulated store of knowledge, the cultural base, becomes almost self-nourishing. When all of the elements needed for a flying machine were present, the steps of making the final working combination were so small and so obvious that they were taken independently by more than one inventor. We know, therefore, that had the Wright brothers died in childhood we would still have had airplanes and at about the same time.

Our hero-admiring habits have beguiled us into overlooking the significance of the thousands of contributors to the development of every complex machine in favor of the person who made the small step in the middle of the stage that marked the transition from a merely promising device to a functioning but unperfected machine. The jet monster we ride in today is a product of the combined thought of great numbers of uncelebrated innovators, many probably equal in mental capability to the Wright brothers. The point applies also to more commonplace products — a nylon garment, for example, is based on a long series of chemical discoveries, and on an unmeasured amount of anonymous ingenuity involved in the design of the machines that extrude filaments and stretch them into fibers, dye and spin the threads, and fabricate them into serviceable garments. The important brain power responsible for all this is not a possession of a few giants, but is a funded mental wealth which is a characteristic of any civilized population, but is lacking in varying degrees in less developed societies.

The above argument suggests a concept of *collective ability*, denoting the supply and organization within a society of all the relevant abilities which give the society its creativeness and power. This *collective ability* is not only a matter of technical knowledge, but also of general comprehension of social wisdom, as well as of popular aspiration toward excellence in a variety of fields of mental activity. A high level of collective ability produces not only science and machinery, but also efficient organizational behavior; this in turn allows effective complex governmental, economic, and social organization.[3] Responsibility for research in this superorganic form of creative potential must of course be accepted by the science of sociology.

The relative security and power of advanced nations thus lie not in buried gold but mainly in the accumulated capital of collective ability. The statement also applies to the great world society, and to subdivision within nations. Thus our best defense against discouragement in our flooding tide of troubles would be an acceleration in the development of our collective mental power. This, of course, does not automatically produce a stable Utopia; new problems will erupt forever. To handle them we will need ever further exponential growth of collective ability.

Not long ago the prospect of such a growth seemed hopeless, for ability was generally held to be fixed in biological inheritance, and improvable, if at all, only by a glacially slow and impractical eugenics program. The present argument, however, is that, in a literal sense, and to an important degree, a society generates its level of ability, and further, that the upper limit is unknown and distant, and best of all, that the processes of generation of ability are potentially subject to intentional control.

The foregoing statement is not a new thought. It was familiar to some prominent Nineteenth Century European scholars. But a half-century or so ago a miniature Dark Age descended over the field of human psychology and the doctrines of the mental testers convinced an impressed public with a secular variant of an infant damnation doctrine.

A single illustration is here offered to symbolize the whole movement. The able and distinguished psychologist, Carl E. Seashore, spent much of his research career investigating musical ability, which he analyzed into a few measured elements. Among the most basic of these, he believed, was the ability to discriminate accurately small differences in musical pitch. He held as follows:[4]

> [Pitch discrimination is] an immediate impression . . . dependent upon the presence or absence in various degrees of the sensitive mechanism in the inner ear. . . . A good test in the hands of an expert may properly establish the physiological limit of pitch discrimination. . . . The physiological limit for hearing pitch does not improve with training. . . . What a blessing to a girl of the age of eight if the music teacher would examine her, and, if necessary say, "much as I regret it, I must say that you would find music dull and difficult, and I would advise you to take up some other art."

This is, of course, to say that either the ability was there or not, and if not, nothing could be done about it. This view was and still is widely held by educators and the public.

Seashore's conviction was strengthened by the fact that he had made unsuccessful efforts to train persons to improve pitch discrimination. The trouble turned out to be that he apparently did not know how to apply such training — possibly his heart was not in the task. Eventually, however, training did succeed in reversing Seashore's results and the concept of that particular type of fixed innate ability was flatly overthrown.[5]

The same delayed revolution has been, and is now, going on in the field of abilities in general. We no longer heed the doctrinaire testers who pronounce specific individual limits for potentialities in mechanical ability, language ability, artistic ability, and mathematical ability. Their ceilings have all been discovered to be penetrable. Slow readers are being retrained. The linguistic near-imbecility of college students is treated by new teaching methods and motivational stimulation. Barriers in many fields of knowledge are falling before the new optimism, which holds that anybody can learn anything.[6]

In sum, we have turned away from the concept of human ability as something fixed in the physiological structure, to that of a flexible and versatile mechanism subject to great improvement. Upper physiological limits of performance may eventually be shown to exist, but it seems certain that these are seldom if ever reached in any person, and in most of the population the levels of performance actually reached have virtually no relation to innate capacities.[7]

Thus the amount of ability in each person is created in the course of experience, and the supply of ability in any society is at present a consequence mainly of impersonal social processes rather than of intentional control.[8]

Any society tends automatically to reproduce its level of achieved ability among its members. The most obvious factor in this continuity is the richness of the social heritage. As we learn in our first course in sociology, a preliterate society can have a culture only as complex as can be carried in the minds of the living generation. With the acquisition of writing this limit is removed, and civilization of unlimited complexity is made possible. The fund of knowledge stored in print and accessible to the population is a major component of the framework of collective ability.

Another variable of obvious importance is the breadth of distribution of advanced knowledge within a population. It makes a difference whether the advanced knowledge is possessed only by a small minority or distributed widely in a population by formal education. Institutionalized schooling viewed variously as having the purposes of child-tending, job-qualifying, and mate-finding, is above all a potent instrument for raising the ability level of the population. This is done at the lower grades by transmitting important basic aspects of the general heritage, and in the higher levels by developing versatile capacity to face novel problems. Graduate schools in the various fields of science concentrate on this latter capacity by training students for independent and original research, and, to the extent that they succeed in their principal function, constantly and exponentially add to the supply of the most generative type of human ability in the population.

Aware as we all are of the educational boom in the United States, we may still overlook its spectacular implications for the future. What is happening at the present time is that the nation is quietly lifting itself by its bootstraps to an importantly higher level of general ability — an achievement which, though less dramatic than a space voyage to the moon and less measurable than the Gross National Product, may mean more to the national future than either.

A few statistical items may help us to assess the extent and possible consequences of the contemporary educational surge. It was only forty years ago, according to the U.S. Census, that less than 27 per cent of the age group 25–35 completed a high school education or more. The percentage reached 58 in 1950, over 70 in 1960, and is expected to exceed 78 by 1970. College enrollment is of course rising to a similar flood level. A little over 30 years ago the undergraduate enrollment of the United States population ages 18 to 21 was 21 per cent. In 1961, it is over 30 per cent. If intentions could be accepted as reliable for forecasting they would indicate a 1970 percentage at least twice as large.[9]

Graduate school enrollments in the same period have increased from about 200,000 to 330,000, and the prediction for 1970 is 560,000 — thus approaching the tripling of the most important source of advanced research ability in only twenty years. Most of this is a net gain in educational achievement, for the majority of the fathers of contemporary graduate students, 62 per cent, never even attended college, and only 13 per cent of the fathers ever had any graduate study. No comparable quantitative expansion in formal education has occurred in all history. Any qualitative improvements, of course, add further to the effects of these trends.

The consequences of such an educational prosperity to the pace of basic research and, therefore, our ability to meet new perils are incalculably great. Our present accomplishments in science arise from the activities of a relatively limited number of trained persons. An estimate by the National Science Foundation indicates that academic research manpower today is not large for a nation of 180 million. In 1953 the full-time equivalent number of faculty members engaged in research was only 16,500. Incidentally, of these only 1,700 were in psychology and the social sciences, which may help to explain why our nation has more success in handling technical problems than human affairs.

It has been estimated that the United States Ph.D. output in all fields of knowledge will nearly double in the decade 1960–70. Any such increase, if maintained, will automatically continue to add to the ability level of the population as the highly trained generation advances through the age levels and replaces the older and less-educated people — thus the force of the present increase alone may not be fully experienced until forty years have passed. Allowing for various uncertainties in all the above statistics, all signs point to a half century of immensely fruitful development in the national supply of formally educated people.

Formal education, for all its importance, is not the only producer of talent in the population. We have abundant reason to recognize the importance of other contributing influences which are less conspicuous and controlled.

Among the most effective of these is the informal influence of the family on the intelligence of children. We have long recognized a relation between abilities of father and son, but here again too much credit has traditionally been given to heredity. Sociologists have had reason to become aware of the fact that mind itself arises in a social process, and this knowledge should suggest a search for intellectual differences resulting from varying qualities of influence from parent to child.

There is now a large and growing body of convincing research which indicates that a factor of central importance in this family transmission of ability is size of vocabulary. Children normally acquire their speech initially within the family, and in harmonious families the degree of richness in parental language becomes a major determiner of the quality and quantity of the child's vocabulary during his growing years. We know that intelligence tests and school success are heavily influenced by verbal facility, and it must follow that the size and precision of the vocabulary used by parents before their children would be a major factor in achieved and measured intelligence.

Size of parental vocabulary is not the whole story, however, and we may be sure that research directed toward subtle influences within the family will yield applicable knowledge. Among the promising objects of such study we may list: the degree of richness and warmth of relation between parents and children, variations in clarity and orderliness of communication, amount of encouragement of the child to take initiative in talking and relating experience, the development of early familiarity and ease with handling quantities and measurements, acquisition of advanced motivation for reading and school learning, the creation of a broad appetite for orientation to the world and a hunger for knowledge of all kinds, a delight in novel thoughts, and the development of a sense of confidence that answers to questions are not hard to find.[10] We may also look within family processes to find how it comes about that some children gain a self concept of a person who expects to be able to do whatever he decides to undertake.

Another research lead of promise is in the field of sources and effects of aspiration. We have much reason to believe that aspiration is a controlling variable of importance within family, peer groups, communities, and other social groupings, and that these groups may affect intelligence upward or downward through supplying or limiting aspiration among its members.

Among the well-known institutionalized obstructions to learning is the informal complex of attitudes long embedded in the special culture of school children. This attitude complex may be the major explanation of the notorious inefficiency of the instructional process in the schools. Experiments of many kinds have abundantly shown that children can learn far more efficiently, and can handle much more complex materials, than they actually do in the schools. There is a minor scandal and mystery in the fact that a child can spend three years in school study of a foreign language and know little of it, while the same child placed in a school abroad may acquire speaking ability within a few months.

A part of the explanation of the disappointing product of the schools thus must lie in the existence among school children of an informal culture that constitutes a destructive influence on aspiration for learning. In general, our schools are burdened by an ancient pupil tradition which defines lessons and study as unpleasant and also as unimportant to the life the children see about them. Probably most children acquire this concept in the first or second grade and never lose it completely even through the college years.

In general, the assurances of teachers that mathematics, languages, history, and science will be of interest and importance in the student's future life is successfully opposed by the child's experience in athletics, activities, and social intercourse. Coleman has recently described the operation of informal prestige systems in a group of public high schools, and has shown how these systems direct energy and aspiration away from scholarship.[11] In each of the schools studied the students who were accepted as members of the "leading crowd" held attitudes involving less emphasis on scholarship than those held by the consensus of all students, and in most schools the leaders differed from the other students in the direction of even greater emphasis on athletics. In each school, athletics appeared to be more influential than scholarship — that is, most students stated that they would generally prefer to be remembered as athletic stars than as brilliant scholars. Of course all this has long been known, and since the days of Woodrow Wilson at Princeton has been a matter of much concern to educators. Our formal educational system, powerful as it is, operates against a heavy braking effect from an informally organized aspect of juvenile society.

The above is only one among various ways in which our society and culture inhibit abilities. Research has shown that one of the most direct of these influences operates through the control of aspiration by the primary groups of school-age children and youth. Abundant evidence supports the principle that primary groups tend to form on the basis of homogeneity in almost every respect observed — age, sex, socio-economic status, activity interests, and intellectual qualities. Furthermore, once established, these primary groups exert pressure on their members to maintain their similarities. This force operates to hold the achievement and aspiration level toward the approved mode for the group.[12]

Such a pull toward mediocrity is of course not limited to school children — it occurs at all ages at which primary groups are spontaneously formed. A potentially superior member comes to realize that he faces the choice between concealing his intellectual interests or finding himself losing his position in the group.[13]

Social life opposes superiority in still another way, through a constant social pressure to communicate intelligibly. Original individual thought develops most readily in privacy, and can be inhibited by a felt need to make sense to others at all times. A rich social life in primary groups allows little opportunity for such mental privacy, and includes an atmosphere of disapproval of the person who at any time expresses a thought difficult for his friends to grasp. This atmosphere may involve implications of conceit and even a touch of mental abnormality.

There is a parallel, though not identical, process which allows for social influences in broader categories of society to limit aspirations. The large family and neighborhood community has been shown to influence attitudes and expectations toward education and mental development. Occupational status of fathers is statistically related to vocational ambitions of sons.[14] Even sons who aspire to a level above that of their fathers usually tend to limit their goals to a moderate ascent above the achievements of their fathers.

At the top limit of performance for some persons there seems to be an additional aspiration barrier, as if a demon were establishing a line beyond which performance could not possibly go. Few persons can summon their maximum effort against what they conceive to be an absolute impossibility, but their powers may be released if they are shown, by the example of achievement by a person they view to be comparable, that the thing can be done. Such an *aspiration boundary* probably accounts for the long delay of track athletes in performing a four-minute mile run. For years great runners had come close but failed to beat the clock across the magic line. Extrapolations from world records over shorter and longer distances indicated that comparable running ability should make the feat possible, but there were athletes and sports experts who questioned that it would ever be done. In 1954, however, Roger Bannister achieved it, breaking not only the record but also the aspiration boundary for many talented athletes. By the end of 1960 the four-minute mile had been performed 66 times.

It appears probable that a similar aspiration boundary effect operates with reference to mental achievements, and that many persons of high ability have to wait for Newtons and Einsteins to show that the looming redoubts are not invulnerable. Persons of lower ability, of course, cannot so readily be inspired by the genius at the top, but the same effect may occur at their level. In the days when all great American writers appeared to be in New England, General Lew Wallace inspired a sequence of worthy Indiana writers by his production of *Ben Hur*. It would seem that we sociologists could learn much, and profitably apply the knowledge, from the study of the effect of successful achievements on lifting the aspiration boundaries of the colleagues of the achiever.

The foregoing discussion is meant only as a sample of some of the ways in which the society, and its subgroups, may regulate in a variety of inconspicuous ways the general level of aspiration and performance among its members. It appears that immense potentialities of human abilities are being smothered by systematic social influences which tend to hold achievement toward the medial level of a group or a community. Only a few escape from such influences — the rest aim and achieve at a level near that of their closest social groups.

The central implication of the present argument is that attractive potentialities of increase in collective ability are possible if we advance our knowledge of the sociological influences that stimulate and limit aspiration and achievement, and find strategic points at which we may establish some control over them. No great difficulties appear to stand in the way. It appears that we only need to apply a massive research effort in the field of the relation of social factors to abilities. Fortunately there exists today a nation-wide enthusiasm for the development of talent resources; a milling crowd is stirring into action even in advance of academic sociological leadership.

Public support of facilities for formal education has never been more enthusiastic, and money for paying teachers has never been easier to find. There is more support than ever before for stimulating a higher proportion of students to pursue advanced education. Trials abound of new approaches to teaching methods, some with spectacular implications of the unused powers in our children. Of these, two merit special mention here. At Stanford University, Patrick Suppes has recently been conducting an experiment with first grade children, in which the approach to arithmetic is made through set theory, which the children appear to grasp easily. At Yale, Omar K. Moore has successfully arranged to have an experimental group of thirty-five preschool children learn reading, writing, printing, and typing. One of his subjects at the age of 2 years and 11 months has been filmed in the act of reading a first-grade story.

Also significant, if less bold, are such new developments as the ferment of Honors Plans in the colleges, the increase in the supply of fellowships to draw the best students into advanced study, the development of methods of testing and identifying potentially superior students, and various plans for enrichment and acceleration of instruction.

All of this school effort is to the good, and vigorous support of it will surely produce rewards. Even greater benefit, however, may in time result from the discovery and application of knowledge in the influence of other aspects of social life on ability. The schools, however improved, will not perform the tasks which belong to the family and the community. It is not enough to know how to offer a subject, say a foreign language, by the most advanced instructional methods if the subject is meaningless to the student. We have not yet faced the question of what the significance of academic study of the Spanish language is to the daughter of a Minneapolis dentist who plans to marry a farm-implement salesman of Norwegian descent. Nor have we learned to bring students to college with an effective appetite for the types of knowledge most useful to themselves and the nation. At present business training, home economics, and physical education outnumber mathematics, physics, sociology, and philosophy in the expressed academic intentions of high school students.

In the present opera on the nature and destiny of man's genius, we have heard only the opening bars of the overture, but the music suggests that the production will some day be a success, and that the amount of effort we put into it will make a difference in the time required. Biology and genetics, while not entirely irrelevant to the cause, promised more than they could deliver in the early years of the century. Individual psychology has taught much, but now we perceive evidence that an important part of the relevant causation of abilities is essentially sociological in nature, and that control is most likely to come through penetration of this aspect of the subject. Research in the sociology of collective ability thus promises to give us an unmatched opportunity to apply advanced techniques of discovery to a matter of critical human importance.

Men of wealth, position, and responsibility wishing to provide security for their children find that there is actually no way of having absolute assurance that a fortune can survive. Currency can fluctuate in value and deteriorate through war and inflation. Gold and diamonds have arbitrary worth which can vanish with economic disorganization. Land can be taxed away or confiscated by agrarian reformers. No kind of material wealth is more secure than the social organization which stands back of it. The most favorable chance of survival, therefore, eventually goes to persons of highest general ability and wisdom who can deal with problems of complexity in a time of change. Effective intelligence, then, is a richer legacy than acres of diamonds, not only to the heirs of a tycoon, but also to the posterity of a nation. To learn how to expand the heritage of collective intelligence would create the best legacy we could leave to the children of our children.

## REFERENCES

1. William F. Ogburn, "Population, Private Ownership, Technology, and the Standard of Living," *American Journal of Sociology*, 56 (January, 1951), pp. 314–319.

2. Brazil, for example, has immense wealth of resources, in arable land, hydro-electric potential, forest, fish, rubber, iron, bauxite, and possibly oil. Sixty-seven million persons inhabit the country, but half are barefoot, undernourished, and illiterate. Two-thirds of the children get no schooling. *Time*, June 30, 1961.

3. Recent studies show that there is a high relation between level of education and tendency to join voluntary associations. See, for example, Charles R. Wright and Herbert H. Hyman, "Voluntary Association Memberships of American Adults: Evidence from National Sample Surveys," *American Sociological Review*, 23 (June, 1958), pp. 284–294.

4. Ruth F. Wyatt, "Improvability of Pitch Discrimination," *Psychological Monographs*, 58 (1945), passim.

5. *Ibid.*, pp. 51–53. Wyatt used a stroboscope which permitted subjects to see which of two sounds had the higher pitch. The subjects were trained in twelve 50-minute sessions, and all improved. The group as a whole gained more than a third of the maximum possible.

6. See Jerome S. Bruner, *The Process of Education.* Cambridge: Harvard University Press, 1961. Bruner holds that "any subject can be taught effectively in some intellectually honest form to any child at any stage of development."

7. If it appears illogical to claim that physiological differences exist, but do not produce differences in performance, consider the rates of speed of automobiles on crowded metropolitan streets. The vehicles differ in horsepower, and in observed speeds, but the speeds may depend entirely on factors other than horsepower — openness of the way ahead, urgency of the trip, nerves of the driver, and disposition of back-seat passengers. On a road race, of course, the factor of horsepower could become the principal determiner of speed.

8. In the case of mental calculators, and perhaps some other prodigious performers, the processes are unsystematic and accidental. A number of calculating prodigies developed their ability as a consequence of circumstances that required frequent counting, and an abundance of solitude. See R. E. L. Faris, "Sociological Causes of Genius," *American Sociological Review,* 5 (October, 1940), pp. 689–699.

9. In April, 1961 a national sample of parents of children of precollege age was asked by the American Institute of Public Opinion if they thought their children would go to college. Seventy-one per cent of parents replied yes, and only 16 per cent no.

10. The present discussion obviously concerns not only the type of intelligence measured by IQ, but whatever mental capacities have value for human purposes. Current research, for example, succeeds in drawing a distinction between a high IQ and a certain type of creativity which would appear to be related to inventiveness. See Jacob W. Getzels and Philip W. Jackson, "Family Environment and Cognitive Style: A Study of the Sources of Highly Intelligent and of Highly Creative Adolescents," *American Sociological Review,* 26 (June, 1961), pp. 351–359.

11. James S. Colemàn, "The Adolescent Subculture and Academic Achievement," *American Journal of Sociology,* 55 (January, 1960), pp. 337–347.

12. See Matilda W. Riley and S. H. Flowerman, "Group Relations as a Variable in Communications Research," *American Sociological Review,* 16 (April, 1951), pp. 174–180. The authors find that membership in school children's peer groups implies mediocrity ". . . since basically all peer oriented youths aspire to be like each other, on a level which the majority can reach."

13. Some choose the second course and accept loneliness and unpopularity as an unavoidable price for the satisfactions of mental achievement. A fortunate few may find comrades of their own level and have the best of both

mental adventure and group life, but for the extremely superior this is seldom possible. Norbert Wiener, for example, during his "square peg" period at Harvard, ". . . tried at one time to unite the five of us (all prodigies) into a sort of prodigy club, but the attempt was ridiculous. . ." Norbert Wiener, *Ex-Prodigy*. New York: Simon and Schuster, 1953, p. 139.

14. See Seymour M. Lipset and Reinhard Bendix, *Social Mobility in Industrial Society*. Berkeley: University of California Press, 1959. Chapter IX, "Intelligence and Motivation" (pp. 227–259) reviews the evidence on this point.

# THE GREAT TALENT HUNT

## JOHN W. GARDNER

Speaking on the campus of Stanford University in 1906, William James said, "The world . . . is only beginning to see that the wealth of a nation consists more than in anything else in the number of superior men that it harbors."[1]

James was generous in suggesting that the world shared his own prophetic understanding. Actually, he was half a century ahead of his time. We are just now coming to grasp the profound truth of his remark.

The fact is that we are witnessing a revolution in society's attitude toward men and women of high ability and advanced training. For the first time in history, such men and women are very much in demand on a very wide scale. Throughout the ages, human societies have always been extravagantly wasteful of talent. Today, as a result of far-reaching social and technological developments in our society, we are forced to search for talent and to use it effectively. Among the historic changes which have marked our era, this may in the long run prove to be one of the most profound.

In recent years the need for men of high ability and advanced training has often been so pressing in one field or another as to claim national attention. Such attention has frequently ignored broader educational and social goals in favor of "crash" programs to meet the crisis of the moment. When the shortage of engineers first became acute, some people behaved as though no other educational goal could be as important as turning out more engineers. After the Russians put the first satellite into orbit, some of our leaders seemed to be saying that the only conceivable purpose of American education was to pour human material into defense activities. And the human material came to be talked of in much the same terms we use in speaking of our oil or uranium reserves.

All of this has annoyed a good many thoughtful people. And it has led some to suppose that the whole recent emphasis on talent is the work of men whose concern for the Cold War has unhinged their judgment. This view calls for correction. The demand for highly trained talent is, of course, affected by international crises. But its roots lie deeper, and its consequences reach out into every phase of our national life. The demand for talent is an inevitable consequence of our stage of development as a society. As such, it has been rising for a long time. It is not a recent trend. We can observe societies in the world today at every stage of development from the most primitive to the most advanced, and nothing is easier to demonstrate than that every step toward the latter involves a heavier demand for educated talent. As Alfred North Whitehead put it, "In the conditions of modern life the rule is absolute, the race which does not value trained intelligence is doomed."[2]

The demand for high-talent manpower is firmly rooted in the level of technological complexity which characterizes modern life, and in the complexity of modern social organization. And more important than either of these is the *rate of innovation and change* in both technological and social spheres. In a world that is rocking with change we need more than anything else a high capacity for adjustment to changed circumstances, a capacity for innovation. The solutions we hit on today will be outmoded tomorrow. Only high ability and sound education equip a man for the continuous seeking of new solutions. We don't even know what skills may be needed in the years ahead. That is why we must train our ablest young men and women in the fundamental fields of knowledge, and equip them to understand and cope with change. That is why we must give them the critical qualities of mind and the durable qualities of character which will serve them in circumstances we cannot now even predict.

It is not just technical competence which is needed. A society such as ours is dependent upon many kinds of achievement, many kinds of complex understanding. It requires large numbers of individuals with depth of judgment, perspective and a broad comprehension of the problems facing our world.

And the importance of education in modern society is not limited to the higher orders of talent. A complex society is dependent every hour of every day upon the capacity of its people to read and write, to make complex judgments and to act in the light of fairly extensive information. When there is not this kind of base on which to build, modern social and economic developments are simply impossible. And if that base were to disappear suddenly in any complex society, the whole intricate interlocking mechanism would grind to a halt.

The chief means of carrying on the talent hunt is the educational system. Schools not only educate youngsters — they sort them out. When the need for talent is great — as it is today — this sifting tends to become fairly rigorous.

There was a time — a fairly recent time — when education was *not* a rigorous sorting-out process. The demand for individuals of high ability is now so familiar to us as to seem wholly unremarkable, but it constitutes a profound change in human affairs. Throughout the millennia of history, it has been the normal experience of mankind that only a few of the gifted individuals in a population have had the chance to develop their gifts. Generally speaking, individuals whose gifts have been discovered and cultivated have been as chance outcroppings of precious rock, while the great reserves of human talent lay undiscovered below.

In 1900 only about 4 per cent of the college-age population went to college. For every youngster who went on with his schooling, there were many just as bright who did not. The boy without an education could look around and see plenty of able and ambitious young fellows in the same condition. Large numbers of children grew up in areas where schools were poor or nonexistent. Many energetic boys broke off schooling to pull their weight on the family farm or to go West.

Most Americans approved of such decisions. The Horatio Alger heroes rarely held advanced academic degrees. In every machine shop and executive suite at the turn of the century stories were swapped about the kid who went to college, learned a lot of hifalutin theory and then made a mess of his first job.

Lord Palmerston, the British statesman, once said of Cornelius Vanderbilt that it was a pity a man of his ability had not had the advantage of formal schooling. When a friend passed this on to Vanderbilt, the latter snapped, "You tell Lord Palmerston from me that if I had learned education I would not have had time to learn anything else."[3]

At the turn of the century it was assumed that the only fields which required advanced training were medicine, law, the ministry and the scholarly fields, and even in those fields the requirements were exceedingly flexible. Only a tiny proportion of leaders in other fields could boast college degrees.

Despite the foresight of men such as William James, the critical importance of human resources in modern society did not force itself to public attention until very recently, when the nation began to experience dramatic shortages in strategic professions such as medicine, teaching, engineering and physics.

As each profession faced shortages, each laid cool and aggressive plans to capture a bigger share of the oncoming stream of talent. Then it became apparent that the total stream was limited, and studies were initiated to determine whether we were making proper use of our human resources.

The studies revealed that we were making very poor use of these resources and that there was inefficiency and waste in our whole approach to the development of talent. The problems which came to light are not ones which we shall solve easily. Many bright young people do not continue their schooling; others are being ill-trained. Too high a proportion of Negro children grow up in circumstances which are such as to smother talent rather than to nourish it. We make wholly inadequate use of the talents of women in our society.

The educational reforms of the past few years have tackled some of these problems fairly effectively, and others ineffectively. The reforms will continue. Our kind of society must make maximum use of the talent available. It needs desperately to find and train able individuals at many levels, and to an increasing degree modern educational systems are designed to accomplish that result. To the extent that they are not well fitted to achieve that end, they are not modern.

As a result, today's student faces problems of which his great-grandfather never dreamed. He knows that his aptitudes and performance are being measured and predicted from the early grades of school. Every day's performance contributes its score to the inexorable summation that will decide his fate. He sees the brightest youngsters move into the most desirable colleges. He sees industry's recruiters on the college campus asking for the A and B students. He sees the able youngsters heading off into the best jobs. Don't try to tell him how tough it was in the old days. Grandpa had it easy.

VESTIGES OF STRATIFICATION

One of the obstacles to the full development of talent in our society is that we still have not achieved full equality of opportunity.

In stratified societies, the amount of education received by a child depended upon his status in the society. If he was born to rank and wealth he had access to a good education. If he was born in the lower strata he usually did not. In this way, the educational system confirmed and held in place differences in status which were hereditarily determined. Thus was the class war, as well as other wars, won on the playing fields of Eton.

The history of American education has been one long campaign to get as far away from that kind of system as effort and ingenuity could take us. "Geniuses will be raked from the rubbish . . ." wrote Thomas Jefferson.[4] But despite the efforts of generations of Americans to nullify the principle of stratification in our educational system, it still has a good deal of vitality. Most of the obvious positive steps toward true equality of opportunity have been taken; yet major inequalities of opportunity stemming from birth remain. And it will be a formidable task to eradicate these. Being born a Negro, for example, involves obvious limitations on educational opportunity in some parts of the country, and less obvious limitations in all parts of the country.

Despite our system of free schools, poverty can still be a profound handicap and wealth a clear advantage. The families at the lowest economic level must all too often live in a slum or near-slum area where the schools do not attract the best teachers. The prosperous citizen can afford a house in an expensive suburb which has a fine school. The good suburban schools are sociologically not unlike the good independent prep schools. The chief difference is that in the suburb, establishing residence is a part — and a very expensive part — of the price of admission (the other part being heavy school taxes). In a way the private prep school is more democratic because it takes in a number of scholarship students of truly impoverished parents. There is no possibility of such an arrangement in Scarsdale. A youngster cannot attend the Scarsdale schools unless his parents live in Scarsdale; and that is something that impoverished parents do not commonly do.

Some of the problems associated with poverty are well illustrated in a case which was brought to my attention several years ago. When

Tom B. was a senior in high school, the principal told him his grades were high enough to get him to a good college. Tom took a job in an aircraft factory instead. The principal couldn't understand it, but most of Tom's family and friends would not have understood any other decision. Tom's father, an invalid whose own education ended with the fourth grade, was genuinely — if profanely — proud of Tom's attainments ("The kid talks like a ——— dictionary!"), but thought the boy was already overeducated. His mother, a clerk in the five-and-ten, liked the idea of his going to college but needed his help to support the family. The wages offered by the factory looked like a fortune to Tom. He had worked part time since he was eight, but this was a man's job for a man's pay. He took it.

Actually, poverty is usually accompanied by other complicating factors, and this was so in Tom's case. If he had had a fierce determination to go on to college, he might have found a way. But his diet was deficient in other things besides money. There were virtually no books in Tom's home. No one ever talked about ideas. No one ever mentioned educational goals. Most of Tom's pals in the run-down part of town where he lived had quit school long since. He had literally never had an informal out-of-school chat with anyone who reminisced about his own college years or recommended college to him. It is not surprising, then, that he had no awareness of what college could mean, no motivation to use his fine mind, no aspirations that involved intellectual performance. The image of a fat pay check from the aircraft company was very real; and the image of college was very pale.

Only in recent years have we come to the realization that these deficiencies are as damaging as any monetary handicap. The son of the city's leading lawyer had financial resources that Tom did not have; but even more important, he had an awareness of intellectual values and educational goals. This awareness was passed on to him as a hereditary advantage — in much the same way that money and a title of nobility are passed on. Jacques Barzun says:

> There is no mystery about it: the child who is familiar with books, ideas, conversation — the ways and means of the intellectual life — before he begins school, indeed, before he begins consciously to think, has a marked advantage. He is at home in the House of Intellect just as the stableboy is at home among horses, or the child of actors on the stage.[5]

Differences in educational opportunity will never be completely eradicated, but they must be reduced in scope and significance. Amer-

icans rightly resent the disparities of social background and the prejudices which limit the recognition of talent wherever it occurs. They
will continue to do so as long as such disparities and prejudices exist.

But it would be wrong to leave the impression that stratification of
educational opportunity is still a dominant feature of our system. It
is not. The vestiges of stratification still exist, but the great drama of
American education has been the democratization of educational opportunity over the past century. This has been one of the great social
revolutions. In emphasizing that much ground remains to be won, we
must not belittle the victories already achieved.

## THE MARKET FOR TALENT

We have said that talent is very much in demand in our own society
today. But it is not in demand in all societies today. It was not always
in demand in our own society. And not all kinds of talent are in
demand at any one time.

An earnest young student from a South Asian country said to me,
"You talk of the need for education in underdeveloped societies, but
my problem is to find a job when I get back. Half my friends are
unemployed intellectuals."

His problem is not unique. Part of the difficulty is that his country
does not have the broad base of education at lower levels which makes
a modern society possible. The young men they send abroad receive
first-class modern educations, and come back to a society which is not
prepared to use their talents.

Another difficulty is that the fields in which these young men are
educated are often chosen without regard to the needs of the society.
In some Latin-American countries, for example, very large numbers
of young men do the fashionable and traditional thing of preparing
themselves in law, even though the last thing their country may need
is another lawyer. Similarly in many underdeveloped countries the
urge toward industrialization leads more young men into engineering
than a pre-industrial society could possibly support.

But the greatest problem is the view taken by the educated man in
these countries that his education fits him for (and entitles him to) a
job at a certain level of prestige. If such a job is not available, he will
often refuse to work. He will not put his superior knowledge to work
on whatever tasks the society requires. He does not want to dirty his

hands. A European living in Guatemala once said, "There will always be opportunities for able foreigners in this country — as long as the best-educated Guatemalans refuse to live outside the capital city."

It was once widely believed in this country that there would never be more than a limited market for educated talent. As recently as the 1930's, learned treatises were being written to warn against the overproduction of highly educated people. One still hears echoes of this theme. But in recent years we have reached a stage of development in which these fears have less basis. The demand is so great that there is little likelihood of unemployment of highly trained people.

But even in our own society there may be overproduction of educated talent in specific lines. Indeed, on many occasions in the future there will be an imbalance between the number of men trained for a given line of work and the number of jobs available. Attempts will be made to minimize this through accurate forecasts of manpower needs, but experience with such forecasts has been discouraging. The alternative — and the wiser course — is to educate men and women who are capable of applying excellent fundamental training to a wide range of specific jobs.

Nothing contributes more damagingly to the unemployment of educated talent than rigid specialization and rigid attitudes supporting this specialization. The future is necessarily hazardous for the individual who trains himself to do a specific job, receives an advanced degree for that line of work and believes that society owes him a living doing it. If technological innovations reduce the demand for his specialty, he has nowhere to go. On the other hand, if he is broadly trained in fundamental principles, and knows that he may have to apply those principles in varying contexts over the years, he is in a position to survive the ups and downs of the job market.

There has been a curious shift in the nature of our anxieties concerning the lower end of the spectrum of ability. For many years, when we were steadily upgrading the lower strata of society in terms of literacy and conditions of life, thoughtful people were inclined to say, "This is all very well, but when everyone gets educated, who's going to do the dirty work?" That is a rather old-fashioned question today. There has been a dramatic reduction in the amount of "dirty work" in our society, and we are paying quite high wages for the dirty work that remains. The fear now is that automation may reduce unskilled jobs so substantially that there will be serious unemployment.

This leads to some interesting social questions, but they are not ones which we can explore in this context.

Although a modern society is wise to foster talent on as wide a scale as possible, no society, modern or traditional, can promise every talented individual the opportunity to earn a living in the exercise of his talent. Some years ago I wrote an article describing the need for talent in modern society and shortly thereafter received an aggrieved letter from a correspondent who described his own talent along a certain line and asserted that he could not market it. He believed that society owed him a living for the exercise of this talent, and he was deeply embittered by the treatment he had received.

But the truth is that no society will ever provide a living for every kind of talent. We need not dwell on the fact that some kinds of talent — for picking pockets, let us say — have to be discouraged; nor that other kinds — the capacity to imitate birdcalls, for example — are trivial. Even in the case of genuinely important gifts — the gifts of the artist, writer, composer, architect or sculptor — the individual can never assume that society will support him in the exercise of his talent. Talent is one thing and the marketability of talent is something else. The latter will depend upon the kind and degree of talent involved, the attitudes of society toward that talent, the prosperity of the society and many other things. It will never be easy for the gifted individual who is ahead of his time (or behind the times) or who exercises his talent in a way that does not coincide with the fashion of the moment.

Talented young people should not be misled in these matters. They must not be led to assume that there is always a market for talent. But while the individual must be realistic, all who care about excellence in a society must be vigilant concerning the waste of talent. Teachers, curators, deans, critics, art dealers, editors, foundation officers, publishers — in short, all who are in a position to encourage talent — should continuously ask themselves whether the society is providing sufficient opportunities for its varied resources of talent. If important kinds of talent are withering on the vine, they had better know why.

## REFERENCES

1. "Stanford's Ideal Destiny," Founders Day Address, 1906, *Memories and Studies*, Longmans, Green & Company, 1934.

1

2. *Aims of Education,* The Macmillan Company, 1929.

3. Irvin G. Wyllie, *The Self-Made Man in America,* Rutgers University Press, 1954, pp. 104–105.

4. William Peden (ed.), *Notes on The State of Virginia* (1782), University of North Carolina Press, 1955.

5. Jacques Barzun, *The House of Intellect,* Harper and Brothers, 1959, p. 142.

# PART II

Origins of Achievement:
Personality and Structural Factors

## INTRODUCTION

Personality is commonly believed to be an important factor in achievement, as the traits often ascribed to successful people clearly emphasize. It is commonplace to hear the achieving person in our culture described as competitive, ambitious, persistent, independent, aggressive and so on. But even assuming that this characterization is correct, it is not clear why some people possess these traits while others do not. Why is one person ambitious, while another is not? What, after all, determines the goals toward which the individual will strive? And what influences how energetic he will be in their pursuit? The selections in this section suggest that the answers to these and related questions may be sought, at least in part, in the individual's socialization experiences during his early years. They also indicate that what the individual learns, what motives, values, aspirations and skills he will acquire as he moves toward adulthood, is associated with the groups to which he belongs.

MICRO-SOCIAL STRUCTURE: THE FAMILY

No group is more influential in shaping the personality of individuals in our society than the family. The reasons for this can be found in the family's strategic role in the socialization process, for it is in the family that the individual first makes contact with the social world. Hence familial agents of socialization are able to affect the individual when he's most plastic and susceptible to social influence.

The experiences of the child in the family reflects the complex patterns of interaction which develop over time between family members. These patterns may be thought of as forming a structure in that they tend to produce stable relationships within the family unit. Family structure influences the socialization process by affecting the patterns of authority and support between parent and child, by influencing the degree of parental involvement in the child, and by helping shape the expectations parents and children have of one another.

Recent researches have shown that family structure affects the development of certain personality traits related to achievement. The selection by Rosen and D'Andrade points up, for example, the crucial importance of parental involvement and warmth for the development of achievement motivation in boys. Of particular interest is the finding that boys need greater autonomy in their relationships with their fathers than with their mothers. Haggard's article on the socialization of gifted child and Crandall's review of researches on the origins of achieving behavior in children provide other examples of how parent-child relationships affect the formation of personality in ways which influence the child's achievement in a variety of situations.

Often parent-child relationships are delineated by reference to demographic factors, such as family size, birth order, sex and number of years separating each child and the ages of parents. The most frequently studied demographic factors are those of family size and birth order. Some data indicate that family size is a variable affecting the socialization process in ways that are relevant to the development of achieving behavior. Bossard, for example, described the small family as a planned unit driven by ambition.[1] Evidence of achievement in this type of family is likely to be lavishly applauded while failure elicits marked parental disappointment and displeasure. The stress on competition and achievement in a small family probably heightens the sense of rivalry between siblings and increases the importance of parental approval. Intense competition is a characteristic which Mead maintained is often found in small families, particularly in the middle class.[2]

The relationship of ordinal position to achievement is more ambiguous, although studies in this area have been very numerous. Parents are said to train their first born child (oldest or only) early in mastering his environment, in part because he is the sole object of parental attention and expectations. Thus, it has been noticed that the first born child tends to talk earlier than the latter born. Koch[3] found that first born children are more competitive than latter born. Perhaps this in part explains Schachter's[4] finding that first born and only children are over-represented among men of eminence.

The selection by Turner tends to confirm the notion that positional factors are related to ambition, and hence possibly in the long run to achievement. His study of high school seniors revealed that the subjects from small families tend to have higher levels of ambition than those from large families. The relationship of sibling position to ambition, however, disappeared when size of family was held constant. His finding corresponds closely with those reported in a study by Rosen who found that the effect of birth order on the development of achievement motivation is ambiguous unless family size and social class are taken into account.[5]

## MACRO-SOCIAL STRUCTURES

Family structure is influenced by the broader social structure in which it is embedded. The social structure acts upon the system of family relationships in diverse ways: it delineates functions for the family; it sets familial goals and defines appropriate means for their attainment; it helps shape the form and quality of interaction between parent and child, thus affecting the learning of normative behavior patterns, values and other aspects of culture which parents regard as appropriate and desirable for the child.

Social structure influences the socialization process by affecting the resources which society places at the parents' disposal. The amount and quality of food, shelter, education and recreational facilities which parents provide the child is related to the family's position in the class structure in most societies, and in some societies to their religious and racial identity as well.

An individual's position in the social structure also affects his perception of the character of the larger social system in which he lives. Whether society is perceived as hostile or friendly, open or closed, expanding, static or constricting will depend to some degree on one's access to society's resources. These perceptions in turn influence the manner in which the parent will rear the child. Many parents seek to prepare the child to take his place in the world as they know it. The more foresighted will try to train their offspring to perform adequately in the world as they expect it to be.

Structural factors will help form the socialization process when position in a social structure is associated with membership in groups containing idiosyncratic belief systems and value orientations. For example, differences between societies and sometimes among subgroups within a society in their socialization practices may reflect essentially different conceptions of the nature of man. Thus, the parents' conceptions of the child's innate goodness, malleability and capabilities will influence their expectations of, and goals for, the child.

Parental expectations and goals reflect to some extent what society regards as desirable or obligatory in the performance of important institutional roles within and outside the family. No society permits its members complete freedom in their performance of vital social roles. More or less broad guidelines are laid out to direct the individual's interaction with other members in a role structure. As normatively sanctioned expectations, these guidelines influence the kinds of behavior parents will elicit and reward, and what will be punished and suppressed. Whether a parent will reward achievement, self-reliance, and assertiveness, or prefer dependence, docility, and obedience in children will depend in part on how society defines the roles of parent and child, what roles the child is being trained to play and the location of these roles in the broader social structure.

The factors most often cited in studies of the impact of social structure on socialization and achievement are social class, race and ethnicity. Two recent publications contain extensive reviews of the literature dealing with the relationship of these structural variables to achievement and social mobility.[6] Hence there is no point in covering the same ground again in any extensive fashion. But it would be useful to sample the studies and summarize their conclusions.

## SOCIAL CLASS

A number of investigators have suggested that social classes in the United States tend to be characterized by somewhat different values.[7] Thus, it has been reported that middle class persons in general are more oriented toward achievement and success, particularly as it is expressed through status striving, than individuals in the lower class. For example, differences in the educational aspirations of youngsters from the several social classes have been reported by Bordua who found that parents in the middle class place more stress on their children entering college than do lower class parents.[8]

The socialization of the child in American society reflects this class orientation towards achievement. Mothers in the middle class, as the selection by Rosen shows, tend to train their sons earlier in independent mastery than do mothers in the lower social strata. The selection by Hess and Shipman is of particular interest in that it provides data obtained through observation. In an experimental study, they found that middle class Negro mothers are more likely than Negro mothers from the lower class to train their children in thinking habits most conducive to good performance in school, and presumably also in later life.

The areas in which the individual seeks to compete and excel and the degree to which this activity is successful will depend in part on his values and aspirations. For even when the individual is highly motivated to achieve, motivation alone is not sufficient to ensure success. That is, achievement motivation may provide the internal impetus to excel, but it does not impel the individual to take the necessary supplementary steps to achieve success. Such steps include, among others, hard work in association with a belief that the external environment can be mastered through rational effort, careful planning, and a willingness to defer gratification and be physically mobile. Whether or not the individual will understand the importance of these steps and implement them will depend in part upon his values.

In two studies with different samples, Rosen found that middle class persons were more likely to possess the kinds of values which influence the individual's willingness to mobilize his energies toward achievement than were respondents in the lower social strata.[9] A study by Straus involving a sample of Wisconsin high school boys found a positive relationship between social class and the willingness to postpone self-gratification.[10] The selection by Sewell, Haller and Straus reports that Midwestern high school students from high school status families have higher educational and occupational aspirations than students from lower status families, even when intelligence is held constant. Moreover, as the selection by Toby so ably illustrates, the experiences and values associated with lower class life poorly prepare, and inadequately motivate, the adolescent to compete in an academic milieu.

RACE AND ETHNICITY

Even the casual observer cannot help but notice the marked differences in affluence and status attained by various racial and ethnic groups in American society. Some groups moved into middle class positions rapidly, although their arrival in this country is of relatively recent origin. Other groups with a history of far longer presence in the United States have hardly began to enjoy the fruits of a prosperous and rapidly burgeoning society. The Greeks and Jews are examples of ethnic groups which found adjustment to American society relatively easy, and have on the whole prospered. The Negro, the American Indian, and the Mexican-American, on the other hand, are examples of groups whose access to society's resources is still highly limited.

It has been argued that the relatively rapid mobility of Jews in the United States is related to certain aspects of the group's culture which stresses achievement and learning, and thus facilitated their adjustment to an industrial, achievement-oriented society.[11] The selection by Rosen tends to support this argument empirically by reporting stronger achievement values and higher vocational-educational aspirations among Jews than most other ethnic groups examined in his study. The Jewish sample was also found to have higher levels of achievement motivation than any other group excepting the Greeks.

The situation of the Negro in the United States is a poignant example of how a repressive social structure affects the socialization process in ways which inhibit the development of an interest in achievement. There can be no question that the opportunity structure is virtually closed to the Negro in many parts of the country. As a much discriminated against group it is difficult to imagine how most Negroes, particularly those in the lower class, can see the larger social system as being anything other than essentially hostile, closed and restrictive. In such an environment it is psychologically functional for the individual to restrict his aspirations and resist those values which direct him toward goals that society will eventually deny him anyway. It is not surprising that lower class parents in this racial group tend not to train their children in achievement, nor inculcate belief systems and value orientations which facilitate the attainment of success. But these are by no means the only consequences of poverty and discrimination on the outlook of young Negroes. The selections by Deutsch and by Reiss and Rhodes describe some of the painful effects an impoverished physical and intellectual environment have on Negro children living in our urban slums.

## REFERENCES

1. James H. Bossard, *Parent and Child,* Philadelphia: University of Pennsylvania Press, 1953.
2. Margaret Mead, *And Keep Your Powder Dry,* New York: William Morrow and Co., 1943.

3. Helen L. Koch, "Some Personality Correlates of Sex, Sibling Position and Sex of Siblings Among Five and Six-Year-Old Children," *Genetic Psychology Monographs,* 52 (August, 1955), pp. 3–50.

4. Stanley Schachter, "Birth Order, Eminence, and High Education," *American Sociological Review* 28 (October, 1963), 1963, pp. 757–767.

5. Bernard C. Rosen, "Family Structure and Achievement Motivation," *American Sociological Review,* 26 (August, 1961), pp. 374–385.

6. Leonard Berkowitz, *The Development of Motives and Values in the Child,* New York: Basic Books, 1964. Harry J. Crockett, Jr. "Psychological Origins of Mobility," in N. J. Smelser and S. M. Lipset, Editor, *Social Structure and Mobility in Economic Development,* Chicago: Aldine, 1966.

7. Herbert Hyman, "The Value Systems of Different Classes: A Social Psychological Contribution to the Analysis of Stratification" in R. Bendix and S. Lipset (Editors), *Class, Status and Power,* Glencoe: The Free Press, 1953; Talcott Parsons, "A Revised Analytical Approach to the Theory of Social Stratification," in Bendix and Lipset, *op. cit.*

8. David J. Bordua, "Educational Aspirations and Parental Stress on College," *Social Forces,* 38 (March, 1960), pp. 262–269.

9. Bernard C. Rosen, "The Achievement Syndrome: A Psychocultural Dimension of Social Stratification," *American Sociological Review,* 21 (April, 1956), pp. 203–211.

10. Murray A. Straus, "Deferred Gratification, Social Class and the *Achievement Syndrome,*" *American Sociological Review,* 27 (June, 1962), pp. 326–335.

11. Nathan Hurvitz, "Sources of Middle-Class Values of American Jews," *Social Forces,* 37 (December, 1958), pp. 117–123.

# A:

# THE IMPACT OF MICRO-SOCIAL STRUCTURES: THE FAMILY

# THE PSYCHOSOCIAL ORIGINS OF
# ACHIEVEMENT MOTIVATION

## BERNARD C. ROSEN
## ROY G. D'ANDRADE

The keystone around which studies of the origins of achievement motivation ($n$ Achievement) have been built is the notion that training in independent mastery is an antecedent condition of the motive. This approach grew out of McClelland's and his associates' theory of the nature and origins of motivation. They argue that all motives are learned, that "they develop out of repeated affective experiences connected with certain types of situations and types of behavior. In the case of achievement motivation, the situation should involve 'standards of excellence,' presumably imposed on the child by the culture, or more particularly by the parents as representatives of the culture, and the behavior should involve either 'competition' with those standards of excellence or attempts to meet them which, if successful, produce positive affect or, if unsuccessful, negative affect. It follows that those cultures or families which stress competition with standards of excellence or which insist *that the child be able to perform certain tasks well by himself* . . . should produce children with high achievement motivation."[3]

Two distinctly different kinds of child-training practices are implicit in this theory. The first is the idea that the child is trained to do things "well"; the second, the notion that he is trained to perform tasks "by himself." The former has been called *achievement training*[2] in that it stresses competition in situations involving standards of excellence; the latter has been called *independence training* in that it involves putting the child on his own. The failure to disentangle these two

Reprinted with abridgment from *Sociometry* (Vol. 22, No. 3, September 1959, pp. 185–218) by permission of the American Sociological Association and the authors.

This research was supported by a grant to the senior author from the National Institute of Mental Health.

concepts has resulted in a focus of attention upon independence training largely to the exclusion of achievement training, although the
former is primarily concerned with developing self-reliance, often in
areas involving self-caretaking (e.g., cleaning, dressing, amusing, or
defending oneself). Although both kinds of training practices frequently occur together, they are different in content and consequences
and needed to be examined separately. We believe that of the two
training practices, achievement training is the more effective in generating n Achievement.

There is another component of independence training — one which
is explicit in the idea of independence — that needed further exploration: *autonomy*. By autonomy, we mean training and permitting the
child to exercise a certain amount of freedom of action in decision
making. The operation of both components, we believe, tends to
increase the power of independence training to generate n Achievement, since in itself high parental expectations for self-reliance may
cause rebellion, feelings of rejection, or of apathy on the part of the
child, while autonomy without parental expectations for self-reliance
and achievement may be perceived as mere permissiveness or indifference. In association with parental demands that the child be self-
reliant, autonomous, and show evidence of high achievement, there
must be sanctions to see that these demands are fulfilled. Winterbottom[7] found that mothers of children with high n Achievement gave
somewhat more intense rewards than mothers of children with low n
Achievement. Little was known about the role of negative sanctions,
or of the relative impact of sanctions from either parent. Further study
was required of the degree and kind of sanctions employed by both
parents to see that their demands are met.

This study departed from two practices common in studies of the
origins of n Achievement. The first practice is to derive data exclusively from ethnographic materials; the second, to obtain information
through questionnaire-type interviews with mothers. Interviews and
ethnographies can be valuable sources of information, but they are
often contaminated by interviewer and respondent biases, particularly
those of perceptual distortion, inadequate recall, and deliberate in-
accuracies. There was a need for data derived from systematic observation of parent-child relations. It is not enough to know what parents
*say* their child-rearing practices are; these statements should be
checked against more objective data, preferably acquired under controlled experimental conditions, that would permit us to *see* what they

do. In this study, experiments were employed which enabled a team of investigators to observe parent-child interaction in problem-solving situations that were standardized for all groups and required no special competence associated with age or sex.

An equally strong objection can be raised against the tendency to ignore the father's role in the development of the child's need to achieve. Apart from an earlier study of father-son power relations, no efforts had been made to determine the father's contribution to achievement and independence training — a surprising omission even granted the mother's importance in socializing the child in American society. Although we were not prepared to take a position on the nature of the role relationships between father, mother, and son with respect to this motive, we deliberately created experimental conditions which would enable us to observe the way in which the three members of the family interacted in a problem-solving situation.

EXPERIMENTAL PROCEDURE

The subjects selected to provide data needed for the testing of these hypotheses about the origins of achievement motivation were 120 persons who made up 40 family groups composed of a father, mother, and their son, aged nine, ten, or eleven. The selection of the family groups began with testing the boy. Seven schools in three northeastern Connecticut towns were visited by the same field worker who administered a Thematic Apperception Test individually and privately to 140 boys, aged nine, ten, or eleven. As is customary in the TAT procedure, the subject was presented with a set of four ambiguous pictures and asked to tell a story about each. His imaginative responses were then scored according to a method developed by Mc-Clelland and his associates which involves identifying and counting the frequency with which imagery about evaluated performance in competition with a standard of excellence appears in the thoughts of a person when he tells a brief story under time pressure. Experience has shown that this imagery can be identified objectively and reliably. It is the assumption of this test that the more the individual shows indications of evaluated performance connected with affect in his fantasy, the greater the degree to which achievement motivation is part of his personality. The stories were scored by two judges; the Pearsonian coefficient of correlation between scorers was .87, a level of reliability similar to those reported in earlier studies with this measure.

Subjects with scores of plus 2 to minus 4 (approximately the bottom quartile) were labeled as having a low *n* Achievement, those with scores of plus 9 to plus 22 (approximately the top quartile) as having high *n* Achievement. Any boy with an I.Q. score below 98, with physical defects, whose parents were separated, or who had been raised during part of his life by persons or relatives other than his parents (e.g., grandparents) was eliminated from the sample. Forty boys, matched by age, race, I.Q., and social class, were chosen for further study. All were white, native born, and between nine and eleven years of age; the average was ten years. Half of the boys had high *n* Achievement scores, half had low scores. In each achievement motivation category, half of the boys were middle class, half were lower class.

A pair of observers visited each family group, usually at night. There were two teams of observers, each composed of a man and woman. Both teams had been trained together to ensure adequate intra- and interteam reliability. Once in the home, the observers explained that they were interested in studying the factors related to success in school and eventually to a career, and that the son was one of many boys selected from a cross-section of the community. When rapport had been established, the parents and their son were placed at a table — usually in the kitchen — and it was explained that the boy was going to perform certain tasks.

EXPERIMENTAL TASKS

The observers wanted to create an experimental situation from which could be derived objective measures of the parents' response to their son as he engaged in achievement behavior. Tasks were devised which the boy could do and which would involve the parents in their son's task performance. The tasks were constructed so that the subjects were often faced with a choice of giving or refusing help. At times they were permitted to structure the situation according to their own norms; at other times the experimenters set the norms. In some situations they were faced with decision conflicts over various alternatives in the problem-solving process. The observation of the parents' behavior as their son engaged in these experimental tasks provided information about the demands the parents made upon him, the sanctions employed to enforce these demands, and the amount of independence the child had developed in relations with his parents. A category system, similar to the Bales system,[1] was devised to permit scoring interaction between parents and son so that the amount and form of each subject's participation could be examined. The investigators were able to learn from these interaction data how self-reliant the parents expected their son to be, how much autonomy they permitted him in decision-making situations, and what kind and amount of affect was generated in a problem-solving situation.

In creating the experimental tasks an effort was made to simulate two conditions normally present when boys are solving problems in the presence of their parents: (1) tasks were constructed to make the boys relatively dependent upon their parents for aid, and (2) the situation was arranged so that the parents either knew the solution to the problem or were in a position to do the task better than their son. In addition, tasks were created which tapped manual skills as well as intellectual capacities, although intelligence is a factor in any problem-solving situation. It was for this reason that the experimenters controlled for I.Q.

Pretesting had shown that no single task would provide sufficient data to test all hypotheses. Hence, five tasks were constructed, each designed to attack the problem from a somewhat different angle and yet provide certain classes of data that could be scored across tasks. The five tasks used in this study are as follows:

1. *Block Stacking.* The boys were asked to build towers out of very irregularly shaped blocks. They were blindfolded and told to use only one hand in order to create a situation in which the boy was relatively dependent upon his parents for help. His parents were told that this was a test of their son's ability to build things, and that they could *say* anything to their son but could not touch the blocks. A performance norm was set for the experiment by telling the parents that the average boy could build a tower of eight blocks; they were asked to write down privately their estimate of how high they thought their son could build his tower. The purposes of this experiment were (a) to see how high were the parents' aspirations for and evaluations of their son, e.g., if they set their estimates at, above, or below the norm; (b) to see how self-reliant they expected or permitted their son to be, e.g., how much help they would give him.

There were three trials for this task. The first provided measures of parental evaluations and aspirations not affected by the boy's performance; the second and third trial estimates provided measures affected by the boy's performance. The procedure for the third trial differed from the first two in that the boy was told that he would be given a nickel for each block he stacked. Each member of the family was asked to estimate privately how high the boy should build his tower. No money would be given for blocks stacked higher than the estimate nor would the subject receive anything if the stack tumbled before he reached the estimate. Conservative estimates, hence, provided security but little opportunity for gain; high estimates involved more opportunity for gain but greater risk. The private estimates were then revealed to all and the family was asked to reach a group decision. In addition to securing objective measures of parental aspiration-evaluation levels, the observers scored the interaction between subjects, thus obtaining data as to the kind and amount of instructions the parents gave their son, the amount of help the son asked for or rejected, and the amount and kind of affect generated during the experiment.

2. *Anagrams.* In this task the boys were asked to make words of three letters or more out of six prescribed letters: G, H, K, N, O, R. The letters, which could be reused after each word was made, were printed on wooden blocks so that they could be manipulated. The parents were given three additional lettered blocks, T, U, and B, and a list of words that could be built with each new letter. They were informed that they could give the boy a new letter (in the sequence T, U, B) whenever they wished and could say anything to him, short of telling him what word to build. There was a ten-minute time limit for this experiment. Since this is a familiar game, no efforts were made to explain the functions of the task.

The purposes of this experiment were: (a) to see how self-reliant the parents expected their son to be, e.g., how soon they would give him a new letter, how much and what kind of direction they would give him, if they would keep him working until he got all or most of the words on the list or "take him off the hook" when he got stuck; and (b) to obtain, by scoring interaction between the subjects, measures of the affect generated by the problem-solving process, e.g., the amount of tension shown by the subjects, the positive and negative remarks directed toward one another.

3. *Patterns.* In this experiment the parents were shown eight patterns, graduated in difficulty, that could be made with Kohs blocks. The subjects were informed that pattern 1 was easier to make than pattern 2, pattern 3 was more difficult than 2 but easier than 4, and so forth. The subjects were told that this was a test of the boy's ability to remember and reproduce patterns quickly and accurately. Each

parent and boy was asked to select privately three patterns which the boy would be asked to make from memory after having seen the pattern for five seconds. All three patterns were chosen *before* the boy began the problem solving so that his performance in this task would not affect the choices of the patterns. Where there were differences of choice, as inevitably they were, the subjects were asked to discuss their differences and make a group decision. Insofar as possible the observers took a verbatim account of the decision-making process, scoring for three kinds of variables: (a) the number of acts each subject contributed to the decision-making process, (b) the number of times each individual initiated a decision, and (c) the number of times each subject was successful in having the group accept his decision or in seeing to it that a decision was made.

The purposes of this experiment were: (a) to obtain another measure of the parents' evaluations of and aspirations for the boy, e.g., whether they would pick easy or difficult tasks for him to do; (b) to get a measure of the autonomy permitted the boy, e.g., whether they would let him choose his own patterns or impose their choices upon him; and (c) to see how much help they would give him and what affect would be generated by the experiment.

4. *Ring Toss*. In this experiment each member of the group was asked to choose privately ten positions, from each of which the boy was to throw three rings at a peg. The distance from the peg was delineated by a tape with 1-foot graduations laid on the floor. The subjects were told that this was a test of discrimination and judgment and that after each set of three tosses they would be asked to make a judgment as to the best distance from which to make the next set of tosses. Group decisions were made as to where the boy should stand. The purposes of this experiment were: (a) to see whether the parents imposed standards of excellence upon a task for which no explicit standard has been set, e.g., whether the parents would treat this as a childish game or see it as a task which could and should be done well. Would they choose easy or difficult positions? (b) to determine how much autonomy they permitted their son, e.g., would they let him choose his own position?

5. *Hatrack*. The Maier Hatrack Problem was used in this experiment. The boy was given two sticks and a C-clamp and instructed to build a rack strong enough to hold a coat and hat. His parents were told that this was a test of the boy's ability to build things. In this task no one was given the solution at the beginning of the experiment. For

the first time the parents had no advantage over the boy — a most uncomfortable position for many parents, particularly the fathers. This stress situation was created deliberately to maximize the possibility of the problem generating affect, as was often the case, with some hostility being directed at the observers. After seven minutes the parents were given the solution to the problem. The purposes of this experiment were: (a) to see how self-reliant the parents expected their son to be. After receiving the solution what kind of clues would the parents give the boy? How hard would they expect him to work on his own? (b) to obtain measures of the affect created in an unusually frustrating situation. How would the parents handle their frustration? Would they turn it against the boy?

CATEGORY SYSTEM

References have been made to the use of a category system for scoring interaction between subjects. A brief discussion of this system, shown in Diagram 1, is in order. Most of the subjects' verbal and some of their motor behavior (e.g., laughing, hand-clapping, scowling) was scored in one of twelve categories. In eight of these categories were placed acts involving relatively strong affect. Four additional categories were used to distinguish between various kinds of statements — either giving, requesting, or rejecting directions — which contained very little or no affect. A distinction was made between negative and positive affective acts. Affective acts associated with explicit or implicit evaluations of the boy's performance which aimed at motivating or changing his behavior were scored differently from affective acts which involved reactions to the boy and only indirectly to his performance.

An act was defined as the smallest segment of verbal or motor behavior which could be recognized as belonging to one of the twelve categories in the system. The actor rather than the target of the acts was used as the observer's frame of reference.

This category system involves a good deal of inference on the part of the observer — a factor which can make for low observer reliability. To ensure adequate reliability, the interaction in each family was scored by two observers who had been trained to work as a team. In the early stages of the field work tape recordings were taken of family interaction. After the experiments the observers rescored the inter-

DIAGRAM 1

*The System of Categories Used in Scoring Parent-Child Interaction*

| +X | Expresses approval, gives love, comfort, affection |
| +T | Shows positive tension release, jokes, laughs |
| +E | Gives explicit positive evaluation of performance, indicates job well done |
| +P | Attempts to push up performance through expression of enthusiasm, urges cheers on |
| N | Gives nonspecific directions, gives hints, clues, general suggestions |
| S | Gives specific directions, gives detailed information about how to do a task |
| aa | Asks aid, information, or advice |
| ra | Rejects aid, information, or advice |
| —P | Attempts to push up performance through expressions of displeasure; urges on indicating disappointment at speed and level of performance |
| —E | Gives explicit negative evaluation of performance, indicates job poorly done |
| —T | Shows negative tension release, shows irritation, coughs |
| —X | Expresses hostility, denigrates, makes sarcastic remarks |

action protocols and discussed scoring differences in order to increase interobserver reliability. Tape recordings were discontinued when the scorers felt that their scores were substantially the same. Each team of observers visited 20 families. The reliability of observers for the gross number of acts scored is high. The Pearsonian coefficient of correlation between the first pair of scorers is plus .93, and for the second pair plus .97. No significant differences between pairs of observers has been discovered.

ACHIEVEMENT TRAINING

Measures of achievement training were obtained from the estimates and choices made by the parents in three tasks: Block Stacking, Patterns, and Ring Toss. Each task provided measures of achievement training which, though positively related to one another, were sufficiently independent to require their being treated as separate scores. This situation was a result of intended fundamental differences between the tasks. Thus, in one task (Block Stacking) the parents were asked how well their son would do, in a second situation (Patterns) they were asked to choose a task for him to perform, while on the last problem (Ring Toss) they were given on open-ended situation which they could structure in a number of ways.

PARENTAL ASPIRATIONS AND EVALUATIONS

The parents' estimates of how well their son would do in the Block Stacking task are considered measures of their aspiration for and evaluations of him. In this case the estimates were made against a stated norm. The parents' first estimate, unaffected by any previous performance in this task, is conceived to be primarily a measure of parental aspirations for the boy. Undoubtedly, this estimate is somewhat affected by the parents' evaluation of the boy's competence, for aspiration and evaluation levels are often intricately mixed. Nonetheless, since presumably the parents had never seen their son perform a block-stacking test with one hand while blindfolded, we believe the element of aspiration level to be dominant in this measure.

## EXPERIMENTAL FINDINGS

We began by comparing the fathers of boys with high $n$ Achievement with the fathers of boys with low $n$ Achievement and the mothers of high $n$ Achievement boys with the mothers of boys with low $n$ Achievement. It had been predicted that the parents of the boys with high $n$ Achievement scores would give higher estimates than parents of boys with low scores. And in fact the data are in the predicted direction; the fathers and mothers of boys with high $n$ Achievement scores on the average give higher estimates, but the differences are not statistically significant. However, when father's and mother's scores are summed together the differences between parental groups is significant ($F = 4.09$, $P < .05$).

Parental estimates for the second and third trials of this task were combined to form a single score. Since the means and standard deviations of both estimates were about the same, no transformation into standard scores was necessary. Both estimates had been influenced considerably by the boy's performance. The combined score was considered as a measure of the parents' aspiration-evaluation of the boy as affected by his performance against a given standard of excellence. The data show that the mothers of boys with high $n$ Achievement scores give considerably higher estimates for the second and third trials of this task than do the mothers of boys with low scores ($F = 10.28$, $P < .005$). The differences between the fathers, although in the predicted direction in that the fathers of boys with high $n$ Achievement scores tend to give higher estimates, are not statistically significant.

The Patterns task was designed to provide additional and supplemental measures of parental aspiration-evaluation levels. In this situation the parents were not asked to estimate how well their son would do, but actually to select three tasks, graded in difficulty, for their son to perform. Since all three choices were made before their son began the problem, these scores could be considered as performance-free measures of the parents' evaluation of the boy's capacity to do the task, plus their aspiration for him to do the more difficult task in a situation structured by degree of difficulty with no stated norm or group average.

Each subject's three choices were combined by simple addition (no transformation of scores was necessary) to provide a single score for each person. We had expected that the parents of boys with high achievement motivation scores — in keeping with their tendency to have higher aspirations for and evaluations of their boys — would choose the more difficult patterns for their sons. The data indicate a difference in this direction, but the differences are small and not significant for either fathers or mothers.

PARENTAL STANDARDS OF EXCELLENCE

In the two experiments just described some parents would very likely have imposed standards of excellence upon the tasks even if the experimenters had not done so. However, since they had been asked to make their estimates or choices in situations where standards were explicit (as in the Block Stacking task where a group performance norm had been given, or in the Patterns task where the complexity of the patterns had been clearly graded by the experimenters) it could not be clearly seen from these experiments whether parents differed in their tendencies to impose standards upon the problems their children were expected to solve. The Ring Toss experiment was devised for this purpose. In this experiment no norm or group standard of excellence was set by the investigators. Each parent was asked to make ten choices of "the best place for your son to stand." After each choice the boy threw three rings at the peg. A measure of the height of the standard of excellence each parent set for the boy was derived by summing the choices (number of feet the boy is asked to stand from the peg) of each parent.

We hypothesized that parents who imposed standards of excellence upon this normless task would be most likely to structure tasks generally in these terms. Our expectation was that the parents of boys with high motivation scores would be more likely to impose standards of excellence upon this task in that they would place their sons farther from the peg than would parents of boys with low scores. The data tend to support this expectation: the fathers and mothers of high $n$ Achievement boys, on the average, chose positions further from the peg than the parents of children with low achievement motivation. The differences, however, are significant only in the case of the mothers ($F = 5.47$, $P < .025$). Combining the scores for fathers and mothers increases the differences between parental groups ($F = 6.99$, $P < .01$).

The Anagrams experiment involved another task for which the investigators had set no explicit standard of excellence, the parents and boy merely being provided with lettered blocks out of which words could be made. This experiment had been designed primarily to provide measures of independence training. The sum of the time at which new letters (the parents shared three letters) were given by both (or either) parents was treated originally as a measure of self-reliance training, i.e., the longer the parents delayed in giving the boy new letters the more indication that they expected him to work longer and harder at a problem on his own. This experiment revealed a clear difference between parental groups but not in the direction we had predicted: the parents of high $n$ Achievement boys gave new letters *sooner* than the parents of boys with low $n$ Achievement ($F = 6.28$, $P < .025$).

This finding, so different from what had been expected, prompted a re-evaluation of the task and a further (albeit ex post factum) interpretation of the data. We believe, now, that we were mistaken in assuming that this task would only measure self-reliance training. Rather, our observations indicate that this experiment elicited from some parents a type of achievement training in which the element of competition with a standard of excellence was very strong. The parents (especially the mothers) of boys with strong achievement motivation, it appeared, tended to perceive the task not so much as one which their son should do on his own, *but as a challenge to do well*. They reacted to this experiment with more emotion and competitiveness than displayed toward any other problem. The mother, in particular, was eager for her son to do well and often became anxious when he stopped making words. Both parents typically showed keener pleasure and disappointment at the boy's success or failure than was ordinarily displayed by the parents of boys with weak achievement motivation. The boy with strong motivation tended to receive letters sooner, we believe, because his parents were eager to see him make words and because of their reluctance to frustrate him to a point where his motive to excel in this important area would be destroyed.

In choosing to structure this task in terms of achievement training rather than self-reliance training — a decision congruent with our theoretical position that the former is the more important in the development of achievement motivation, the parents of high *n* Achievement boys are nonetheless exhibiting less self-reliance training than the parents of low *n* Achievement boys. This is contrary to our theoretical expectations, but is similar, as we shall see below, to other empirical data which indicate that the mothers of high *n* Achievements score low on self-reliance training — and typically the mother played her most prominent role in the Anagrams experiment.

ACHIEVEMENT TRAINING AND PERFORMANCE LEVELS

The behavior of people with high achievement motivation is characterized by persistent striving and general competitiveness. It would follow from this, other things being equal, that boys with high achievement motivation would perform better than those with low motivation — and in fact this proved to be the case. Boys with high *n* Achievement tend to build higher towers of blocks, construct patterns faster, and make more words in the Anagrams task. The differences are significant in the case of the Block Stacking task ($F = 8.16$, $P < .005$), but not for the Patterns and Anagrams experiments. In the latter two tasks the individual's performance is very greatly affected by his intelligence. Since I.Q. score was one of the variables controlled in this study (there were no differences between the mean I.Q. scores of boys with high $n$ Achievement and their peers with low achievement motivation), even these small differences are surprising. The superior performance of high $n$ Achievement boys appears to be more a function of greater self-reliance and zest in competitive activity than of intelligence. Thus, boys with high achievement motivation tend to ask for less aid (aa), are more likely to reject offers of help from their parents (ra), and appear to get more pleasure out of participating in the experiments — they show less evidence of negative affect ($-$T) and more of positive feelings ($+$T). Although for only one of these variables — asks aid ($F = 5.76$, $P < .05$) — is there a significant difference between groups, the direction of the differences in all four cases consistently points to greater self-reliance and self-assurance on the part of boys with high need for achievement.

The question arises, then, whether the higher estimates of the parents of boys with high $n$ Achievement are not a natural response to his superior performance, rather than a measure of their aspirations for and evaluations of him. In two tasks, Block Stacking and Anagrams, where there were significant differences between parental groups, the analysis of covariance technique was used to control the effect of the boy's performance upon parental estimates. This technique enabled us to compute what the parents' estimates of the boy's performance, or their willingness to give him a new letter, would be if the performance of high and low $n$ Achievement boys were made comparable. An analysis of covariance of the mother's estimates for the second and third trials in the Block Stacking task — there had been no significant difference between fathers — provided an adjusted F ratio for the mother's estimates which, although reduced, is still statistically significant ($F = 6.17$, $P < .05$).

In order to see whether the speed with which the parents give their sons new letters in the Anagrams task is merely a function of the rate at which the boy builds words — it will be remembered that high $n$ Achievement boys made more words during the ten-minute time limit for this task than boys with low achievement motivation — an analysis of covariance was computed with the number of words controlled. The adjusted F ratio not only remained significant but increased very slightly from 6.28 to 6.45, both ratios being significant at the .05 level.

In the Ring Toss experiment there was no question of whether superior performance by high $n$ Achievement boys had influenced their parents to make significantly higher choices, because in this task high $n$ Achievement boys were less successful in placing rings around the peg than their low $n$ Achievement peers. The reason for this is simple: the parents of high $n$ Achievement boys tended to place their sons farther away from the peg and consequently the number of their successes was smaller; the tetrachloric correlation between the number of successes and the distance away from the peg is — .31.

These data clearly indicate that the parents were not responding *merely* to the boy's performance, but this is not to say his ability had no influence on their estimates and choices. In the Block Stacking experiment, for example, the parents' aspirations and evaluations tend to go up as the boy's performance improves. This is particularly true for the mothers of high $n$ Achievement boys, who are more affected by the boy's performance than the fathers. Thus, for the first trial of the Block Stacking task the F ratio for fathers of high $n$ Achievement boys is larger than mothers, but for the second and third trials the mothers' F ratio jumps from 1.24 to 10.12, while the fathers' F increases only slightly, from 2.78 to 3.45. This is particularly interesting in view of the fact that fathers were more active in this task than mothers, who seemed to feel that this was the sort of task about which males were more informed. Nonetheless, even though the mothers of high $n$ Achievement boys did not generally perceive this task as falling under their area of parental training, they responded quite strongly to their sons' performance in their aspirations and evaluations. From a longer developmental point of view, of course, these data do not permit us to state with certainty as to which came first, the higher aspiration-evaluation levels of the parents, or the boy's superior performance; the data strongly suggest that they very probably interact.

INDEPENDENCE TRAINING, SANCTIONS, AND ACHIEVEMENT MOTIVATION

Earlier we distinguished between achievement training and independence training; the latter was broken down into two components: self-reliance training and the granting of relative autonomy in decision making. Associated with *both* independence and achievement training are sanctions — rewards and punishments — administered by the parents to reinforce appropriate behavior in the child. The data to index these variables were obtained by examining the interaction between parents and child as they engaged in the experimental tasks, and by observing the decision-making process in those instances where the subjects were asked to make a group estimate or choice of what the boy should do.

The scoring of parent-child interaction produced a voluminous amount of data: hundreds of acts were scored during the average three-hour experimental session. It was necessary, therefore, to combine scores where possible. Three clusters resulted from this analysis which appear to be conceptually and theoretically meaningful:[6]

1. *Warmth.* A combination of positive tension ($+T$) and positive evaluational acts ($+E$), indicating generally pleasant, happy, anxiety-relieving, laughing-joking behavior. This cluster provides a measure of the amount of positive affect the parents put out while the boy is working.

2. *Rejection.* A combination of negative tension ($-T$) and hostile acts ($-X$), indicating generally unpleasant, irritated, unhappy behavior. This cluster provides a measure of the negative affect the parent gives out while the boy is working.

3. *Pushing.* A combination of friendly ($+P$) and irritated ($-P$) statements by the parents urging the boy to work hard, to get on with the task. This cluster provides a measure of one kind of pressure parents put on the boy to meet their expectations.

SELF-RELIANCE TRAINING

Directional statements (S and N) were used as measures of self-reliance training; a large number of N type acts in which the child is *not told exactly* what to do, but merely given a clue would indicate independence training; while a high incidence of specific directions (S) would be a sign of little such training. We had predicted that the parents of high need Achievement boys would generate more "N" acts and fewer "S" acts than the parents of boys with low achievement motivation. The data show that the fathers and mothers of high $n$ Achievement boys give out *proportionately* more "N" acts and fewer "S" acts, but the differences are not significant. For total number of acts, the fathers of high $n$ Achievement boys score higher on "N" acts and lower on "S" acts; the mothers of high $n$ Achievement boys also score lower on "S" acts, but unlike the fathers they also score lower on "N" type acts. Although in all but one case — the lower N score for mothers of high $n$ Achievement boys — the differences are in the direction predicted, in none of these cases are the differences statistically significant.

Pushing statements (+P and −P) are acts aimed at motivating the boy to work harder. An argument can be made for considering this type of act as reflecting either independence *or* achievement training, but in the context in which we observed this type of behavior it seemed to us to be primarily an index of independence training. We believe that a large number of pushing statements indicates *low* self-reliance training, for such statements often came from parents who appeared unable to sit back and let their boy work at his own speed but felt impelled to make him do well by urging or shouting him on. This type of parent seemed to assume that the boy had little internal need to excel, and that without external pressure he would soon run out of gas. As had been predicted, the fathers of high $n$ Achievement boys gave fewer pushing statements than the fathers of boys with low achievement motivation. However, the reverse was true for the mothers: in this case it was the mothers of high $n$ Achievement boys who had the higher score for pushing type statements. In none of these cases, however, are the differences statistically significant.

AUTONOMY

An index of the autonomy permitted the boy in decision making, another aspect of independence training, was derived by observing the family decision-making process in three tasks: Block Stacking (third trial), Patterns, and Ring Toss. The observers scored three types of behavior in this process: (1) the number of acts each subject contributed to the decision making, (2) the number of times each subject initiated the decision process by being the first to present a choice for consideration, (3) the number of times an individual made the decision for the group or stated the final judgment. In all these decision-conflict situations somebody must state the final resolution, whether authoritatively or only as the summation of consensus. This final summation or statement was scored as "deciding." Intercorrelations between these three types of acts were computed; all correlations were sufficiently high to permit their being combined into a single score labeled "autonomy." The transformation of raw scores into standard scores was not necessary. It should be remembered that in this experiment the lower the parental autonomy score, the greater the autonomy permitted the boy.

We expected that the parents of high need Achievement boys would give their son more autonomy in the decision-making process than would be granted boys with low $n$ Achievement. The data are in the direction predicted with respect to the fathers, but quite the reverse is true in the case of the mothers: the mothers of low $n$ Achievement boys tend to grant greater autonomy to their sons. Unfortunately, none of these differences is statistically significant.

SANCTIONS

Typically, positive and negative reinforcements are associated with any learning situation — rewards for success and punishment for failure. We had predicted that the parents of boys with high achievement motivation would score higher on Warmth (positive affect) and lower on Rejection (negative affect) than the parents of low $n$ Achievement boys. *The data show that the mothers of high n Achievement boys score significantly higher on Warmth than the mothers of low n Achievement boys* ($F = 8:87$, $P<.01$). The differences between fathers, although in the predicted direction, are not significant ($F = 4.13$, $P<.10$).

Fathers of boys with high $n$ Achievement tend to score lower on Rejection. The reverse is true for the mothers: *the Rejection scores are higher for mothers of high n Achievement motivation boys than for the mothers of low n Achievement boys.* None of these differences in Rejection, however, are statistically significant.

PARENTAL PROFILES AND MOTIVATION

In the analysis of data so far the relationship of each variable to achievement motivation was examined separately. The Split Plot type of analysis of variance was next employed to permit the examination of all variables simultaneously for each parent.[4] All scores were transformed into standard scores, and in the case of four variables (S, Pushing, Rejection, and Autonomy) where low parental scores for parents had been hypothesized as producing high $n$ Achievement

CHART 1

*Profiles for Father: High n Achievement Group and Low n Achievement Group*

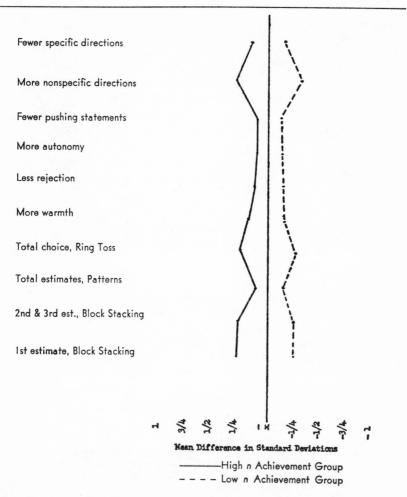

Fewer specific directions

More nonspecific directions

Fewer pushing statements

More autonomy

Less rejection

More warmth

Total choice, Ring Toss

Total estimates, Patterns

2nd & 3rd est., Block Stacking

1st estimate, Block Stacking

Mean Difference in Standard Deviations

———————High *n* Achievement Group

– – – – Low *n* Achievement Group

the direction of the scores was reversed. Hence, we have labeled these as "Fewer Specific Statements," "Less Pushing," "Less Rejection"; a high score for Autonomy means that the parents have given their son a relatively high amount of autonomy. This was done in order to make it possible to sum across all variables and arrive at a meaningful figure for each parent. A mean score for each variable

CHART 2

*Profiles for Mothers: High* n *Achievement Group and Low* n *Achievement Group*

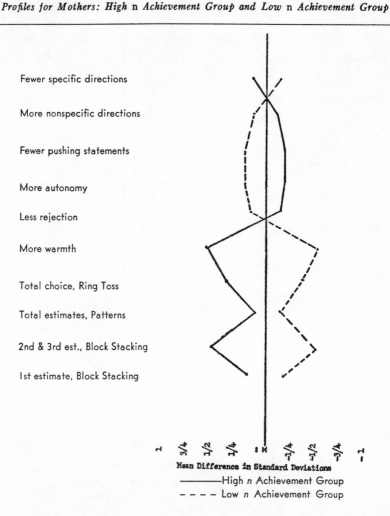

Fewer specific directions

More nonspecific directions

Fewer pushing statements

More autonomy

Less rejection

More warmth

Total choice, Ring Toss

Total estimates, Patterns

2nd & 3rd est., Block Stacking

1st estimate, Block Stacking

Mean Difference in Standard Deviations

——————High *n* Achievement Group

– – – – Low *n* Achievement Group

for fathers and mothers was computed and the distance from the mean in standard deviations was plotted; the profiles for fathers are shown in Chart 1, for mothers in Chart 2.

A Split Plot analysis of variance reveals that there are significant differences *in levels* between the profiles of the parents of boys with high achievement motivation and the parents of boys with low *n* Achevement. The differences in levels for fathers is greater ( F = 10.09,

$P < .005$) than for mothers ($F = 4.77$, $P < .05$). By difference in level we mean that when the scores for each variable are summed for each parent, the parents of high $n$ Achievement boys have a significantly higher *total* score than the parents of low $n$ Achievement boys. Thus, although some variables are not significant when tested separately, and others only barely significant, when the scores of all the variables are pooled together each contributes something to the total variance and the result is a significant difference between groups. This is most apparent in Chart 1 where the fathers' profiles are compared. It can be seen that the mean scores for the fathers of boys with high achievement motivation are higher for every variable, where "highness" was predicted as being positively related to high $n$ Achievement. It should be remembered that the scores for S, P, Rejection, and Autonomy were reversed so that what appears as a "high" score in the chart is in fact a low score. In the case of these four variables, low parental scores were predicted as tending to produce high $n$ Achievement. The difference between the two groups of fathers is not great; it is the *consistency* of the direction of these differences which when summed together make for a significant difference between the two groups. Another way of saying this is to point out that since the profiles of the two groups are almost parallel, there is no significant interaction between $n$ Achievement groups and test variables when the level differences are taken out of the profiles.

The profiles for mothers are not parallel so that even when level differences are taken out the profiles for the mothers of high $n$ Achievement boys remains significantly different from that of the mothers of low $n$ Achievement boys ($F = 2.30$, $P < .025$). The fact that there are interaction differences for mothers is not surprising when we remember that some of the variables which discriminate between groups for fathers do not do so for mothers, while other variables which are not significant for fathers are highly significant for mothers (e.g., Warmth). There are even some reversals in that mothers of high $n$ Achievement boys give fewer nonspecific directions, more pushing statements, and are more dominant than the mothers of low $n$ Achievement boys.

Another way of examining the differences between the parents of high and low $n$ Achievement boys is shown in Chart 3. On this chart there is a profile for fathers and a profile for mothers. Each profile is obtained by computing the mean difference between the scores of the fathers, and then of the mothers, of high and low $n$ Achievement

CHART 3

*Profiles for Fathers and Mothers: Mean Difference between Fathers of "Highs" and Fathers of "Lows"; Mothers of "Highs" and Mothers of "Lows"*

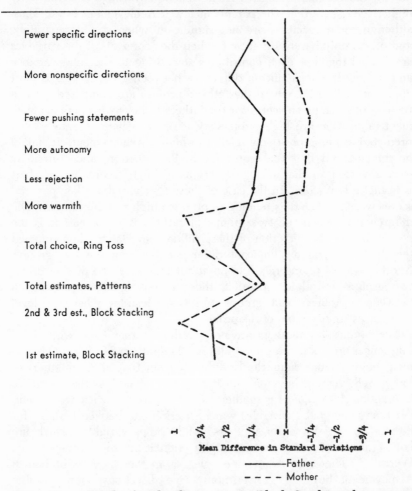

Mean Difference in Standard Deviations

——————— Father

– – – – Mother

boys. For example, for the first estimate Block Stacking the average standard score of the fathers of low *n* Achievement boys is subtracted from the average standard score of the fathers of boys with high achievement motivation. The difference is positive; that is, on the average the father of a high *n* Achievement boy had a higher score than the average father of a boy with low *n* Achievement. If the difference had been negative the point would have been plotted below the zero line, indicating that the average father of a low $n$ Achievement boy had made the higher estimate. If there had been no difference, the point would have been on the zero line; the farther the point is plotted away from the zero line, the greater the difference between groups. Thus, for mothers with respect to the variable Warmth the difference between $n$ Achievement groups is more than plus ¾ indicating that the average score for the mothers of high $n$ Achievement boys is more than three quarters of a standard deviation higher than that of the mothers of low $n$ Achievement boys.

Chart 3 shows that the fathers of high $n$ Achievement boys when compared with the fathers of low $n$ Achievement boys tend to give higher estimates and choices for the Block Stacking and Pattern tasks, place their sons farther away from the peg in the Ring Toss experiment, are more warm, less rejecting, give their boy more autonomy, are less pushing, and give more nonspecific directions and fewer specific ones. The two groups of mothers when compared with one another present a somewhat different picture. The mothers of high $n$ Achievement boys also tend to give higher estimates and choices for the Block Stacking and Patterns tasks, place their sons farther away from the peg in the Ring Toss experiment, give fewer specific directions, and are more warm. However, they are more rejecting, give the boy less autonomy, are more pushing, and give fewer nonspecific directions.

PARENTAL ROLE RELATIONSHIPS AND ACHIEVEMENT MOTIVATION

The relationships of achievement motivation to certain training practices employed by *fathers and mothers considered separately* have now been described. But we know that the boy is subject to the influence of both parents, and that he belongs to a family unit in which the expectations and role behavior of both parents may have important consequences for his motivation. We know also that the parental pairs in this study did not always have the same expectations of the boy or the same reactions to his performance. The question then arises: Is there a difference between the parents of high and low $n$ Achievement boys *when the parents are considered as a family pair?* Specifically, are the scores of the parents of high $n$ Achievement boys more likely to be similar or dissimilar to one another than are the scores of the parents of boys with low achievement motivation? And what are the consequences of these similarities or dissimilarities for the development of achievement motivation?

The correlation technique made it possible to determine the relationship between the scores of fathers and mothers *considered as pairs*. Two sets of Pearsonian coefficients of correlation were computed for each variable: one set for the fathers and mothers of boys with high motivation, the other for the parents of the low motivation group. These correlations are taken as measures of the role relationships between parental pairs. A positive correlation is considered as indicating a *similar* role relationship; i.e., the parental scores tend to be high or low together. A negative correlation is considered as indicating a *dissimilar* role relationship, with parental scores moving in opposite directions. It must be stressed that these correlations tell us nothing about how high or low the scores are, merely that they are similar or dissimilar. To discover if there were any significant differences between the parents of high and low *n* Achievement boys the correlation coefficients were transformed into Z scores and the Standard Error of Difference computed. The ratio of the difference between Z's and the Standard Error of Difference was then computed and tested for significance. Table 1 presents the correlation for each measure, first for parents of high *n* Achievement boys and second for parents of low *n* Achievement boys. The probability of difference between these two groups is shown in column 3.

Achievement motivation has been defined in terms of affective arousal over evaluated performance in connection with standards of excellence. Such standards are imparted to the individual typically by the parents, who indicate that he is expected to perform well in relation to these standards of excellence. In time he comes to have the same expectations of himself. Learning to respond to such standards and expectations of high performance can be conceived of as learning a cognitive map of the world in which these standards and expectations are, so to speak, a relevant part of the terrain. It seems reasonable to assume that a strong set of standards is most likely to be learned when both parents agree on standards of excellence and have high aspirations and expectations for achievement. Where agreement between parents is lacking the boy is more likely to be confused and the probability of the standards becoming cues for affective arousal is lowered.

For the tasks performed in this study the optimal learning situation would be one in which the parental aspirations and choices are in

TABLE 1

Correlation Analysis of Pairs of Parents of High n Achievement Boys Compared with Pairs
of Parents of Low n Achievement Boys

|  | F x M | F x M |  |
| --- | --- | --- | --- |
| Achievement Training | (Highs) | (Lows) | P |
| 1st estimate, Block Stacking | .50 | .36 | .308 |
| 2nd estimate, Block Stacking | .57 | .31 | .171 |
| 3rd estimate, Block Stacking | .36 | .35 | .480 |
| 1st choice, Patterns | .36 | —.09 | .087 |
| 2nd choice, Patterns | .37 | —.27 | .026 |
| 3rd choice, Patterns | —.01 | .06 | .496 |
| Ring Toss | .83 | .86 | .500 |
| Independence Training |  |  |  |
| Self-reliance Training: |  |  |  |
| No. of specific directions | .28 | .31 | .460 |
| No. of nonspecific directions | .01 | .33 | .159 |
| No. of pushing statements | —.02 | .12 | .348 |
| Autonomy: |  |  |  |
| No times "initiator" | —.248 | —.728 | .026 |
| No. times "decider" | —.258 | —.276 | .480 |
| No. acts in decision process | .086 | —.149 | .245 |
| Sanctions |  |  |  |
| No. of Warmth responses | —.39 | .23 | .030 |
| No. of Rejection responses | .23 | .70 | .032 |

agreement or, in terms of the correlation analysis of parental pairs, one in which the parents play similar roles. The data show that for several achievement training measures (estimates and choices in Block Stacking and Patterns) the parents of high $n$ Achievement boys tend to play more similar roles than do the parents of low $n$ Achievement boys. That is, six of the seven correlations are positive and five are higher for the parents of the "highs" than for the parents of the "lows." The extremely high correlations for Total Choices, Ring Toss, is a result of the fact that each parent was asked to make a series of successive choices with both parents basing each choice on the previous position of the boy. There is one significant difference between the correlations of the parents of high and low $n$ Achievement groups: the second choice in the Patterns task. This is interesting when we remember that the patterns chosen by the parents of the "highs" were not significantly more difficult than those chosen by the parents of the "lows." There is, however, greater agreement between the parents of high $n$ Achievement boys as to how difficult the task should be, and in general this is more likely to be the case among parents of high than of low $n$ Achievement boys.

The situation is reversed for the measures of self-reliance training, i.e., S, N, and P type statements. For these variables, the parents of low $n$ Achievement boys tend to have the more similar roles. Thus, for all three variables the correlations are positive and are higher between parents of the "lows," although the differences between the two groups are not statistically significant. This finding lends additional credence to our hypothesis that self-reliance training, when not associated with high achievement training, is not a sufficient cause of $n$ Achievement. The consistency with which both parents of low $n$ Achievement boys put their sons on their own is especially significant in the light of the greater dissimilarity in their willingness to let the boy assert himself in the decision-making process. The correlations between fathers and mothers of low $n$ Achievement boys for the three measures of autonomy are all negative and higher than the correlations for the parents of the "highs." For one measure, "number of times initiator," the difference between high or low groups is statistically significant at the .026 level. This greater dissimilarity in parental roles indicates a tendency for one person to dominate the decision-making process and suggests a greater loss of autonomy for low $n$ Achievement boys. Where both parents try to affect the decision-making process the boy has some freedom of movement, and can, in the terminology of Simmel, even play the role of the "third who enjoys," but where one parent lays down the law the boy has fewer alternatives. It should be noted that in two of the measures of autonomy the parents of high $n$ Achievement boys also play somewhat dissimilar roles, and that for the measure "number of times decider" there is virtually no difference between "high" and "low" groups, which is probably a function of this aspect of the decision-making process where only one person wins.

The affect given out by the parents is considered to be the basic factor determining the child's affective arousal to standards of excellence. We believe that the child's sensitivity to parental affect is increased when he is faced with a situation where there is a difference between parents in the amount and kind of affect they display, or where a single parent is both warm and rejecting. Positive affect (Warmth), in particular, becomes more valued as it is both given and withheld; thus a parent who is both warm and rejecting will have more effect on the child than one who is uniformly warm. Hence, both dissimilarity between parents, or dissimilar affect from one parent, will result in a greater value placed upon warmth by the child. This notion is supported by a finding by Sears, Maccoby, Levin, et al.[5] who note that the child who has "high conscience" has a mother who is relatively warm and uses withdrawal of love fairly often; neither warmth nor withdrawal of love when used alone is effective in producing "high conscience."

This finding has particular relevance for the data on positive sanctions shown in Table 1 where it can be seen that the parents of the "highs" play more dissimilar roles than the parents of the "lows"; the correlation between the fathers and mothers of high $n$ Achievement boys for Warmth is —.39, as compared with .23 for the parents of low $n$ Achievement boys. This difference between groups is significant at the .03 level. It should be remembered that both parents of the "highs" were above average for Warmth, although this difference was not significant for fathers, and that the mothers of high $n$ Achievement boys were more warm and rejecting than the mothers of the "lows." We believe that this dissimilarity between parents and variations in the affect given out by the mother sensitizes the high $n$ Achievement boy to the need for approval and increases his willingness to internalize the standards and expectations of his parents.

The role relationships of parents with respect to Rejection is unlike that found for Warmth. Correlations for this variable are positive for both groups, but the correlation is higher for the parents of the "lows" (.70) than for the parents of the "highs" (.23): the difference is significant at the .032 level. These data indicate that when the low $n$ Achievement boy experiences rejection he is far more likely to receive it from both parents than is the high $n$ Achievement boy. Negative affect, then, when not associated with compensating warmth from one or both of the parents, seems not likely to generate high need achievement.

### DISCUSSION AND SUMMARY

The question of how achievement training, independence training, and sanctions are related to achievement motivation may be rephrased by asking, How does the behavior of parents of boys with high *n* Achievement differ from the behavior of parents whose sons have low *n* Achievement?

To begin with, the observers' subjective impressions are that the parents of high *n* Achievement boys tend to be more competitive, show more involvement, and seem to take more pleasure in the problem-solving experiments. They appear to be more interested and concerned with their son's performance; they tend to give him more things to manipulate rather than fewer; on the average they put out more affective acts. More objective data show that the parents of a boy with high *n* Achievement tend to have higher aspirations for him to do well at any given task, and they seem to have a higher regard for his competence at problem solving. They set up standards of excellence for the boy even when none is given, or if a standard is given will expect him to do "better than average." As he progresses they tend to react to his performance with warmth and approval, or, in the case of the mothers especially, with disapproval if he performs poorly.

It seems clear that achievement training contributes more to the development of *n* Achievement than does independence training. Indeed, the role of independence training in generating achievement motivation can only be understood in the context of what appears to be a division of labor between the fathers and mothers of high *n* Achievement boys.

Fathers and mothers both provide achievement training and independence training, but the fathers seem to contribute much more to the latter than do the mothers. Fathers tend to let their sons develop some self-reliance by giving hints (N) rather than always telling "how to do it" (S). They are less likely to push (P) and more likely to give the boy a greater degree of autonomy in making his own decisions. Fathers of high *n* Achievement boys often appear to be competent men who are willing to take a back seat while their sons are performing. They tend to beckon from ahead rather than push from behind.

The mothers of boys with high achievement motivation tend to stress achievement training rather than independence training. In fact, they are likely to be more dominant and to expect less self-reliance than the mothers of boys with low *n* Achievement. But their aspirations for their sons are higher and their concern over success greater. Thus, they expect the boys to build higher towers and place them farther away from the peg in the Ring Toss experiment. As a boy works his mother tends to become emotionally involved. Not only is she more likely to reward him with approval (Warmth) but also to punish him with hostility (Rejection). *In a way, it is this factor of involvement that most clearly sets the mothers of high* n *Achievement boys apart from the mothers of low* n *Achievement boys:* the former score higher on every variable, expect specific directions. And although these mothers are likely to give their sons more option as to exactly (fewer Specifics) what to do, they give them less option about doing something and doing it well. Observers report that the mothers of high *n* Achievement boys tend to be striving, competent persons. Apparently they expect their sons to be the same.

The different emphasis which the fathers and mothers of high *n* Achievement boys place upon achievement and independence training suggests that the training practices of father and mother affect the boy in different ways. Apparently, the boy can take and perhaps needs achievement training from both parents, but the effects of independence training and sanctions, in particular Autonomy and Rejection, are different depending upon whether they come from the father or mother. In order for high *n* Achievement to develop, the boy appears to need more autonomy from his father than from his mother. The father who gives the boy a relatively high degree of autonomy provides him with an opportunity to compete on his own ground, to test his skill, and to gain a sense of confidence in his own competence. The dominating father may crush his son (and in so doing destroys the boy's achievement motive), perhaps because he views the boy as a competitor and is viewed as such by his son. On the other hand, the mother who dominates the decision-making process does not seem to have the same effect on the boy, possibly because she is perceived as *imposing her standards* on the boy, while a dominating father is perceived as *imposing himself* on the son. It may be that the mother-son relations are typically more secure than those between father and son, so that the boy is better able to accept higher levels of dominance and rejection from his mother than his father without adverse effect on his need to achieve. Relatively rejecting, dominating fathers, particularly those with less than average warmth — as tended to be the case with the fathers of low *n* Achievement boys — seem to be a threat to the boy and a deterrent to the development of *n* Achievement. On the other hand, above-average dominance and rejection, coupled with above-average warmth, as tends to be the case with mothers of high *n* Achievement boys, appear to be a spur to achievement motivation. It will be remembered that the fathers of high *n* Achievement boys are on the average less Rejecting, less Pushing, and less Dominant — all of which points to their general hands-off policy.

It is unlikely that these variables operate separately, but the way in which they interact in the development of achievement motivation is not clear. Possibly the variables interact in a manner which produces cyclical effects roughly approximating the interaction that characterized the experimental task situations of this study. The cycle begins with the parents imposing standards of excellence upon a task and setting a high goal for the boy to achieve (e.g., Ring Toss, estimates and choices in Block Stacking and Patterns). As the boy engages in the task, they reinforce acceptable behavior by expressions of warmth (both parents) or by evidences of disapproval (primarily mother). The boy's performance improves, in part because of previous experience and in part because of the greater concern shown by his parents and expressed through affective reaction to his performance and greater attention to his training. With improved performance, the parents grant the boy greater autonomy and interfere less with his performance (primarily father). Goals are then reset at a higher level and the cycle continues.

## REFERENCES

1. Bales, R. F., *Interaction Process Analysis*, Cambridge, Mass.: Addison-Wesley, 1951.
2. Child, I. L., T. Storm, and J. Veroff, "Achievement Themes in Folk Tales Related to Socialization Practice," in J. W. Atkinson, *Motives in Fantasy, Action and Society*, Princeton, N. J.: Van Nostrand, 1958.
3. McClelland, D. C., J. W. Atkinson, R. Clark, and E. Lowell, *The Achievement Motive*, New York: Appleton-Century-Crofts, 1953.
4. Sakoda, J. M., "Directions for a Multiple-Group Method of Factor Analysis," mimeographed paper, University of Connecticut, June, 1955.
5. Sears, R. R., E. E. Maccoby, and H. Levin in collaboration with E. L. Lowell, P. S. Sears, and J. W. M. Whiting, *Patterns of Child Rearing*, Evanston, Ill.: Row, Peterson, 1957.
6. Tryon, R. C., *Cluster Analysis*, Ann Arbor, Mich.: Edwards Brothers, 1939.
7. Winterbottom, M. R., "The Relation of Need for Achievement to Learning Experiences in Independence and Mastery," in J. W. Atkinson, *Motives in Fantasy, Action, and Society*, Princeton, N. J.: Van Nostrand, 1958.

# SOCIALIZATION, PERSONALITY, AND ACADEMIC ACHIEVEMENT IN GIFTED CHILDREN

ERNEST A. HAGGARD

Children grow up, as everyone knows, to become members of their society, and in the process they develop most of the skills and values prized by adults. Since this "socialization process" is going on around us all the time, it is generally taken as a matter of course. We adults constantly exert pressures which mold the behavior and attitudes of our children. Presumably, the more we understand human behavior, the better able we shall be to teach our children the many diverse skills necessary to become effective adults in our society.

The attempt to increase our understanding of human behavior is hindered by subtle restrictions which we can never entirely escape. These restrictions include our inability to comprehend the full complexity of human behavior. Of more importance, perhaps, is the fact that, as we become socialized, we develop rather stable pictures of ourselves and of our world. We are used to our world as we have come to see it, and we resist seeing it differently; our cultural and intellectual heritage not only enables us to view our world with meaning but also tends to restrict our view of it. For example, in educational circles the view has been held that human learning can be explained by a few "laws of learning," such as the laws of effect, recency, and frequency. And since children learn in school, some persons recommend that we teach in terms of these "laws."

The writer of this report believes that the so-called classical laws of learning — or, more generally, stimulus-response theories of psychology — do not offer an adequate explanation of human learning.[1] Furthermore, there is strong reason to believe that educational practices based on a stimulus-response theory will not be adequate to meet present-day demands for educating our youth and will be practically useless (if not a hindrance) in helping to develop the intellectual resources found in our gifted children.

Up to the present, no general theory of behavior and learning has been worked out well enough to justify its systematic application in educational practice. Rather, we have a variety of promising insights that have been proposed by workers in such fields as cultural anthropology, sociology, psychoanalysis, and Gestalt and clinical psychology. When brought together, these insights seem to offer fruitful leads to a better understanding of human learning or, broadly speaking, of the socialization process. One of the purposes of the research project has been to use some of these leads in a setting concerned with the education of gifted children. In so doing, we hoped to learn more about the conditions related to the ways in which children come to utilize their energies and abilities in achieving various intellectual and interpersonal skills during preadolescence and adolescence.

In this research an attempt was made to study academic learning, to be sure, but we tried, at the same time, to consider such learning in relation to the totality of the individual's personality and experience. To do this required study of such factors as patterns of socialization pressures; the developing personality structures of the children doing the learning, as well as their patterns of academic achievement; and any possible interrelationships among these factors. Considering all these factors together, we hoped to gain a clearer picture of the place and meaning that academic learning has in the lives of gifted children. It might be well, therefore, to present briefly some of our major working assumptions regarding the child's behavior, the socio-cultural context in which it occurs, and the meaning of academic achievement in this context.

First, we assume that all behavior is motivated, that behavior is a function of how the individual sees his world at the time and of how he can satisfy his needs and realize his goals within the limits of what is possible for him. From this point of view, the individual's behavior is adaptive for him at the moment. Over time, such behavior patterns will become stabilized and tend to regulate his subsequent perceptions, motivations, and behaviors.

We also assume that all behavior occurs in some physical-social-cultural context, which also tends to regulate the individual's behavior, and that his behavior must be appraised in terms of this context. The most important aspect of this context includes the persons who exert pressures and constraints on the child, who encourage or require him to learn to do tasks upon which they place value. The extent to which the individual has acquired the valued skills and attitudes of his group will indicate the extent to which he has become a socialized member of the group. Incidentally, socialization always places more or less stress on the person being socialized, since it necessarily requires his doing some things he may not want to do, and not doing other things that he may want to do. This is the price that must be paid in order to develop stable, "socially acceptable" patterns of behavior.

A high level of proficiency in linguistics, arithmetic, and other academic skills is a greatly prized value of the parents and teachers of the children whom we studied (almost all the children are from upper-middle-class professional families, and most of them are children of university faculty members). Under such conditions we assume that, if the socialization process proceeds smoothly, the children will learn to channel much of their energy toward high academic achievement — much more than would children from a cultural group not holding these values or not holding them so strongly.

Academic achievement, then, is seen as one of many expressions of the extent to which the children studied are responsive to socialization pressures and are in the process of acquiring the skills, attitudes, and so on which are prized in their socio-cultural group. It is true, of course, that differences in such factors as innate potentials (for example, ability, temperament, energy level) or differences in the degrees and patterns of socialization pressures and experiences will always exist and will complicate the picture of how any given child uses his energies to achieve academically. Because of such differences, the children will differ; in more technical language, they will develop different personality structures.

If personality structure is largely a function of the socialization process, it follows that academic achievement is also related to personality structure. More specifically, we assume that the general level of academic achievement will be related to the degree of pressure put on these children to develop academic skills and also that certain personality factors will accompany the general level of academic achievement. We also assume that, other things being equal, relatively low academic achievement will occur when the child has run into difficulties with respect to the socialization process. Finally, if such factors as innate ability are held constant, we assume that children showing different patterns of academic achievement will likewise tend to have different personality structures.

On the basis of such assumptions a seven-year project of research on socialization, personality, and mental processes was begun in the Laboratory School of the University of Chicago. We studied an entire class of seventy-six children in Grade III, and the interrelationships among a variety of variables were traced until the children had finished Grade IX. Our purpose in this article is to indicate the general nature of our procedures and findings, particularly as they apply to questions of educational theory and practice. . . .

. . . This research was initiated because of our interest in how children learn to channel their energies and, in the process, develop various abilities and skills as they become socialized members of their cultural group. A study of how children develop high-level proficiency in linguistic and arithmetic skills seemed to be a good starting point in seeking answers to this more general question. By and large, the findings reported below are statistically significant, and the various characteristics and relationships either were stable throughout the five-year period which we studied or tended to shift systematically during this period.

In the presentation of our findings, comparative statements will be used to indicate the variable, factor, or trait that was found to characterize each of the achievement groups. That is to say, if the high general achievers usually show some personality trait which is not found among the low achievers or the opposite of which is shown by low achievers, such a trait will be used to describe the high academic achievers. Thus these results do not describe any particular child so much as they indicate the traits which tend to be found in the children in the various achievement groups. It should also be kept in mind that the personality variables frequently refer to the children's underlying attitudes and feelings, which may or may not be expressed openly in their everyday behavior.

By the time they arrived in Grade III, the *high general achievers* (pupils who performed at a high level on all the tests) were sensitive and responsive to socialization pressures, had largely accepted adult values, and were striving to live up to adult expectations. They saw their parents as being somewhat overprotective, pressuring for achievement, and lacking in emotional warmth (frequently they were correct). Insofar as they accepted many of the adult values as their own, their conformity in this respect seems to have given them a high degree of security and confidence in their relations with adults, even though they expressed some underlying resentment toward authority figures. In general, however, they showed a high degree of inner harmony, being rather adept at emotional control and at organizing and integrating their experiences, ideas, and feelings. In their behavior with others, they were somewhat more tense, competitive, and aggressive; had developed good work habits and were persistent in them; got along better with their parents, teachers, and peers; and showed a higher level of overall adjustment than did the low academic achievers. (Incidentally, the designation "low achievers" must be taken in a relative sense, as the low achievers in this group would be "superior" achievers in most classrooms.)

By Grade VII, various changes had taken place in the children who remained high academic achievers. Although they continued to respond to the socialization pressures of adults and to strive toward adult standards of behavior, they had developed strong antagonistic attitudes toward adults and often pictured adults as being inadequate and ineffective. Such attitudes were not expressed by the low achievers. Thus, although the high achievers had accepted adult norms and expectations and had shown increased surface conformity, they increasingly rejected adults as persons. At the same time, they showed a marked increase in the level of their anxiety and a corresponding decrease in their intellectual originality and creativity. Although there was no such difference in anxiety and creativity between high and low achievers in Grade III, a marked difference existed between these groups by Grade VII. The high achievers were able, however, to control and channel their anxiety in various ways, for example, through the intellectualization of their experiences or the mastering of new knowledges and intellectual skills. They also became more aggressive, persistent, hard driving, and competitive, and they showed signs of willingness to be aggressive and destructive in order to defeat and win over other persons. But, withal, they retained a high degree of mental flexibility and spontaneity, particularly in their ability to manipulate abstract symbol systems.

Interestingly enough, by the time they reached Grade VII, the high achievers began to emerge as the social leaders of their peers; they served on the important class committees and held the important class offices, and so on. Actually, they were respected more than liked by their peers. The fact that the high academic achievers became the social leaders also suggests an important characteristic of the school's atmosphere, since in most classrooms these children would probably be snubbed as "grinds" and "bookworms." In this school setting, however, where all the children are concerned about doing well academically, many of them come to idealize intellectual prowess and consider it an essential ingredient to justify self-esteem and acceptance. . . .

. . . More often than not, however, children with the same intelligence quotients showed widely different patterns of academic achievement. Consequently, with respect to such questions as the prediction of academic achievement and the selection of persons for training in particular fields, it seems clear that the non-intellectual personality factors, as well as their intellectual correlates, must be considered in order to distinguish between those who can, and those who do, achieve in particular areas of endeavor.

If we think of academic achievement as a by-product of the socialization process, the question arises why learning difficulties occur in a cultural setting in which intellectual accomplishment is so highly prized. An explanation which follows from our general assumption — that the level and the pattern of academic achievement are related to how an individual perceives his world and relates to it — is that difficulties in the acquisition of the valued skills should result when the socialization process does not progress smoothly. Thus learning difficulties should occur when the conditions which normally facilitate the child's acceptance of the essential aspects and norms of his culture somehow goes awry. And, since the parents are the primary socializing agents, one would expect that disjointed parent-child relationships play a role in such learning difficulties.

Although learning problems occur in all academic subjects, linguistic difficulties may be used to illustrate the existence of disturbed socialization patterns, partly because language is one of the most significant and universal aspects of any culture and also because it seems to be learned without difficulty under normal conditions. Granted the absence of real incapacities, if a child develops marked linguistic difficulties, it may be assumed that his doing so results from conflicts in the pattern of socialization pressures imposed upon him, or is a symptom of rebellion against excessive pressures to acquire the valued linguistic skills or against related pressures which have become intolerable, or is caused by inner conflicts resulting from the pressures. In any case, it is often observed that children who develop linguistic blocks or related learning difficulties characteristically have concurrent "emotional problems," which must be dealt with in order to alleviate the learning difficulty. A child who develops marked learning problems also provides himself with an ingenious means of self-defense and of frustrating and embarrassing his parents and teachers — particularly if they place primary emphasis on intellectual achievement. Furthermore, the development of such symptoms leaves the child immune from the usual punishments or other retributions that would probably result if he were to express openly his hostility toward the socializing agents. On the contrary, his development of such symptoms serves to satisfy certain emotional needs by giving the child added personal attention and sympathy, as well as relaxation of pressures to achieve.

Our findings clearly indicate that, in the setting of this study, it is not only the parents and, to a lesser extent, the teachers who exert pressures on a particular child to achieve academically. The other children, coming from similar backgrounds, also exert strong pressures which frequently are not openly observable but nonetheless add to the pressures imposed by adults. We observed, for example, that the children chose the high academic achievers to be the class leaders, apparently because of admiration for the intellectual prowess of the achievers, the pervasive competition among the children for the top marks, and their articulate awareness of the standing of all members of the class in the various subjects. A child would find it difficult to adjust to such a setting without responding to the peer-imposed pressures.[2]

The findings of this research raise a number of important questions concerning the possible relations between socialization pressures upon children to achieve academically and our stated educational values and objectives. We have already considered some of the apparent effects of such pressures on the development of character structure and the effect of character structure, in turn, on the extent to which gifted children acquire proficiency in such culturally valued skills as those required for high-level academic achievement. We have seen that, in some respects at least, academic achievement was furthered when parents, teachers, and peers exerted strong pressures on the children to utilize their energies in the interest of intellectual pursuits. But it appears that the consequences of such pressure were not wholly positive, and some of the negative side effects of exceptional academic achievement in preadolescents might easily be brushed away because of the positive aspects which are so highly prized by the adults in the cultural group which we studied.

Perhaps the first question that should be raised is whether it is at all necessary for these parents to exert strong pressures upon their children to achieve academically. Our knowledge to date suggests that, if the parents are themselves intellectually oriented and are not ambivalent about the value of intellectuality as a way of life, the child, as a matter of course, will accept the same value system and acquire the appropriate behavior patterns. We are not surprised, for example, that a child normally learns to speak English (or American) or Chinese or French, depending on the cultural context in which he is reared, in due time and without effort. But parents and teachers usually are not content to have their children acquire academic skills "normally" and "in due time" but have rather definite ideas regarding the degree of proficiency desired by certain ages. It becomes necessary, then, to exert pressures on children to get them to meet the schedules.

Let us grant (with some misgivings) that children must meet certain arbitrary time schedules in order to acquire the many diverse skills necessary to function as competent adults in our society. Even if we could list the number of skills and facts that they need to learn, we should still be faced with some fundamental but unanswered questions. Among these questions are: When should adults apply socialization pressure, and how much, to accomplish their notions of the desired behaviors? What consequences result from the application of such pressures? Although psychologists and educators do not have answers to these questions, some of the findings of this research offer interesting comments on them.

Take the question of when and how much pressure should be applied. In many cases we found that the strong pressures exerted by parents to have their children excel academically were full blown by the time the children were in Grade III. Furthermore, by that time some of the children were responding to their parents' wishes in the desired manner. But it should be emphasized that not every child was a high academic achiever. Of the children who were exposed to roughly equivalent pressures to achieve, only a small number did so with relative ease and dispatch. Other children became tense, anxious, guilty, or rebellious and performed less well than they might have under more relaxed conditions. Some of the latter children seemed to be on the way to becoming academic casualties of their parents' excessive ambitions for them.

Some children can stand up well under pressures which seem to crush some of their classmates. It would be interesting to know the extent to which such factors as parental love and support, or permission for self-realization, interact with such factors as natural ability, temperament, and energy level to enable a child to respond favorably to strong pressures for academic achievement — and to do so without showing undue strain at the time or without laying the groundwork for later personality disturbances. It would be interesting to know also the most appropriate time periods for imposing such pressures in order to obtain the maximal learning of the desired skills and to insure their availability for adaptive use in the future. But we know only that all children should not be treated alike and that any one child should not be treated the same way at all times. The art that parents and teachers need to perfect involves the applying of socialization pressures compatible with the child's current perception of his world and of himself in relation to it, and with his emotional and intellectual capabilities at the time.

The question of possible undesirable side effects which might result from pushing a child to excel in all academic areas seems not to have been asked by some of the parents who exerted such pressures. Partial answers to this question are provided, however, by the children who by Grade VII began to show the possible consequences of their parents' pressure on them. In some of the children these consequences include, of course, a remarkable degree of intellectual proficiency and accomplishment in both the extent and the depth of their learning and in the extent to which they took over adult-like behaviors and value systems. Without question, such consequences satisfy the wishes of the parents of these children.

It is much less likely that these same parents would appraise so favorably various other characteristics which also seem to result from excessive socialization pressures. For example, by Grade VII the high general achievers seemed to have devoted themselves to intellectual accomplishment with a vengeance and to have become over-intellectualized, almost to the exclusion of other interests and activities. In arriving at this point, they had become somewhat disdainful of adults and hostile toward, and competitive with, their peers in order to maintain the position of intellectual superiority in the group.

They also experienced a mounting level of anxiety (which apparently fed back to help them in their drive toward further accomplishments) and a decline in free creative thinking.

Assuming that the high general achievers in this sample are representative of countless others from similar backgrounds, we may well ask: Does very high academic accomplishment at this age level always tend to have such side effects? If so, can this pattern of preadolescent socialization and its consequences be considered desirable? It remains to be seen how these children will fare as they continue to mature. . . .

## REFERENCES

1. E. A. Haggard, "Learning: A Process of Change," *Educational Leadership*. XIII (December, 1955), 149–56.

2. In a related study it was found that the children who attended this school showed shifts in the obtained intelligence quotients in the direction of the average of the children in their class, and that the longer the children were in attendance, the more nearly their intelligence quotients approximated the average of their classmates. The usual finding is, of course, that on repeated testings a child's intelligence quotient will tend to "regress toward the mean" of the national average of 100. (D. Heftel, "An Investigation of the Hypothesis that There Is a Tendency for Intelligence Quotient To Regress toward the Subground Mean." Unpublished Master's thesis, University of Chicago, 1951.)

# ACHIEVEMENT BEHAVIOR IN YOUNG CHILDREN

VIRGINIA C. CRANDALL

No one knows exactly why or when children begin to want to do something *well*. Although observers often note that the infant of a year or less struggles to turn himself over, to pull himself up, to walk, to grasp an object, and to acquire speech, most investigators concerned with "achievement motivation" or "achievement behavior" would not classify these early efforts as motivated by a desire to "achieve." What criteria, then, distinguish certain purposeful behaviors as achievement behaviors? Crandall, Katkovsky and Preston (1960a) suggest that "achievement behavior is behavior directed toward the attainment of approval or the avoidance of disapproval [from oneself or from others] for competence of performance in situations where standards of excellence are applicable." Somewhat similarly, in describing achievement *motivation,* McClelland and his colleagues (1953) state: "The child must begin to perceive performance in terms of standards of excellence" and to experience pleasant or unpleasant feelings about meeting or failing to meet these standards. Early efforts at locomotion, prehension and speech are not usually categorized as achievement behavior because children of such very young ages do not yet have the cognitive ability to apply "standards of excellence" to their own behavior. Psychologists would generally agree that the child must be able to note a discrepancy between his present level of competence and a higher level of skill and to predict that more proficiency will produce greater pleasure, pride or approval from others than his present skill will now permit. Thus, it is at the point when the child attempts to *perfect* a skill, to accomplish some-

Reprinted with abridgment from *Young Children* (Vol. 20, No. 2, November 1964, pp. 77–90) by permission of the National Association for the Education of Young Children and the author.

The preparation of this paper was supported in part by research grant M-2238 from the National Institute of Mental Health, United States Public Health Service.

thing *more efficiently* or *quickly,* to produce a *better* product, to do something *well,* that his efforts are defined as achievement behavior.

Achievement motivation would seem to have its origin in learning experiences during early childhood. McClelland, et al. (1963) maintain that feelings of pleasure originally attendant upon mild changes in sensory stimulation become associated with early efforts at independent mastery. That is, the child learns to anticipate that certain levels of skill will produce feelings of pleasure if they are perceived as moderately above his present performance level just as he tends to enjoy moderate increments in kind, quality, intensity, and patterning of other forms of stimulation. But these authors state further that "stronger achievement motives probably required for most (though not necessarily all) children some structuring of performance standards, some *demands* by the parents and the surrounding culture" (1953, p. 78; see also 1958, pp. 437–452). Crandall, Preston and Rabson (1960) place primary, rather than secondary, emphasis on such demands, rewards and punishments when considering the genesis of the achievement need. They argue that direct social reinforcement of the child's accomplishment is necessary if the child is to learn to value achievement activities as potential sources of satisfaction and security. Only later, and for some children, do approval from others for good performance become unnecessary and feelings of pride or self-approval constitute sufficient reinforcement to maintain or increase their achievement behaviors.

Individual differences have been found (Crandall, Preston & Rabson, 1960) among three-, four- and five-year-olds in the frequency and persistence with which tasks requiring skill and effort are attempted. Sears and Levin (1957) also report that four- and five-year-old children varied in their aspirations to tackle succeeded or failed tasks, and Tyler, Rafferty and Tyler (1962) found individual differences among nursery school children in their attempts to get recognition for achievement behavior. Finally, McClelland (1958) reports that individual differences in achievement motivation (measured with a test involving the drawing of "doodles") had appeared by the age of five. These studies suggest that the desire to achieve must have been established to some degree by the time these children were tested or observed, but that it is more fully developed in some preschool children than in others. No research, however, has attempted to investigate the approximate age or conditions under which achievement behavior *begins* to emerge.

First-, second-, and third-grade children spend more time and strive more intensely in some kinds of achievement activities than in others (Crandall, 1961). Thus, achievement efforts of young grade school children not only vary from child to child, but also vary for any one child from one achievement area to another (i.e., intellectual, physical skills, mechanical and artistic activities). It is possible that similar differentiation occurs even earlier, but no research of this nature has been reported.

## EARLY ENVIRONMENTAL STIMULATION

Recent investigations have focused on stimulation in the preschool child's physical and social environment as a possible determinant of intellectual achievement (Bruner, 1961; Deutsch, 1964; Hunt, 1961; Hunt, 1963).

A group of researchers under the direction of Martin Deutsch (e.g., Deutsch, 1962; Deutsch, 1964; Deutsch & Brown, 1964; John, 1963; John, 1964) have studied Negro and white children on the edge of a large slum area in New York. These investigators found concept formation, auditory and visual discrimination, language acquisition and IQ scores related to such factors as race, social class, nursery school or kindergarten attendance, and father's presence or absence from the home. One of the elements common to all these factors, they reason, is the social and physical stimulus deprivation or enrichment concomitant to the child's status on each of these dimensions.

Forgays (1963) presented four-year-old children with discrimination problems in which their only incentive was the opportunity to obtain tactual, visual or auditory stimulation. Middle class children learned these problems more rapidly than lower class subjects, presumably because of their early exposure to more stimulating surroundings.

Most of the researchers associated with these studies have recommended that environmental intervention might increase the achievement of children from deprived backgrounds. The idea is not new. As early as 1907, Montessori (1912; 1959), in her work with three-to-six-year-old children from the slums of Rome, provided her pupils with a wide variety of materials to play with and tasks of graded difficulty to choose from at will. By the time these children were five years of age, many of them were reading and writing. Fowler (1962;

1963) demonstrated that two, three- and four-year-old children can be taught to read by providing a very shallow gradient of stimuli consisting primarily of printed verbal and pictorial material. In his excellent review (1962) of earlier attempts to teach children of preschool ages to read, Fowler states ". . . of 25 children who learned to read before the age of 3 . ., 72 per cent had definitely enjoyed a great deal of unusually early intellectual stimulation. . . . There was no evidence of a child reading early where stimulation was absent."

Nursery school attendance is an obvious source of enrichment of the child's environment and, thus, of his intellectual achievement. Results from studies of preschool attendance are too complex, however, to be reviewed here. In general, they seem to indicate that substantial increases in IQ cannot be expected from nursery school attendance unless the child has come from an environment which is unusually static and unstimulating (e.g., an orphanage). Even then, results attributed to the environmental stimulation of nursery school may have been artifacts of test unreliability, practice effects of repeated testing, and/or the greater rapport of nursery school children with adult examiners who tested them. Wellman's summary (1943) of studies conducted at the Iowa Child Welfare Research Station and the reviews of Hunt (1961), Jones (1954), and Swift (1964) are recommended to the interested reader. Now let us focus directly on the achieving child himself.

ACHIEVING CHILDREN PERSONALITY CHARACTERISTICS

What are the personality attributes of children who display more achievement behavior than their peers? A longitudinal study (Sontag, Baker & Nelson, 1958) based on ratings of children's behavior in nursery and elementary school, as well as in the home, showed that both boys and girls whose IQs increased during the preschool years were independent of adults and competitive with peers. In addition, the girls were less "feminine" in their behavior than girls with decreasing IQs and did not need immediate rewards for good behavior, but could delay gratification until some more distant time. Later, during the elementary school years, both male and female IQ "ascenders" were again found to be competitive in the scholastic situation and independent, initiating more activities on their own and more frequently attempting to overcome obstacles by themselves. Boys with increasing IQs were also more aggressive and more anxious than boys whose IQs declined. "Ascending" girls displayed more sibling rivalry, had parents who emphasized the importance of school achievement and, at the preschool ages, these girls were able to delay gratification. This ability to delay rewards for more long-term goals has also been shown to be associated with higher achievement motivation scores (Mischel, 1961).

Independence, then, was a consistent characteristic of children who showed increases in IQ scores. Such independence was also present in the three-to-five-year-old achieving children of another study (Crandall, Preston & Rabson, 1960). That is, the more time these children chose to spend in achievement activities during nursery school, the less they sought emotional support and instrumental help from the staff or from their mothers in the home.

In spite of the fact that independence is related to achievement, a similar sample of children who displayed more achievement efforts in nursery school were found to be compliant to the requests and demands of the adult staff (Crandall, Orleans, Preston & Rabson, 1958). Haggard (1957) also reports that compliance to adult pressures and values was found among children at the elementary age level who were high academic achievers. In this longitudinal study of gifted children, Haggard investigated a variety of personality characteristics associated with academic achievement and reports that to some degree these factors change with age.

. . . [He found] that achieving children, in contrast to peers who perform less well, do not need to depend upon adults but are somewhat compliant and conforming to their demands and accept and incorporate adults' high evaluations of the importance of achievement. They are also able to work without being immediately rewarded for their efforts, show initiative, self-reliance, and emotional control. While achieving children of preschool and early elementary age are somewhat aggressive and competitive, their social relationships are generally good. Achievement, however, seems to be exacting its toll. By later elementary school or junior high age, aggression and competition have become accentuated, relationships with siblings, peers and adults show some disruption, and the children are less creative and more anxious. Research on high school students, beyond the scope of this paper, indicates that these attributes become increasingly pronounced at later ages. Does this mean that the effort to achieve "produces" the less desirable personality attributes? Or does it mean that only if children have acquired such a personality constellation will they then be able to achieve in our highly competitive, post-Sputnik educational system? Cause and effect relationships cannot be determined from these data, but it is obvious that our "education for excellence" is accompanied by certain psychological costs.

ACHIEVEMENT MOTIVATION AND ATTITUDES
DIRECTLY RELATED TO ACHIEVEMENT ACTIVITIES

In addition to general personality attributes which have been found to distinguish achieving from nonachieving children, some studies have also shown that achieving children score higher on measures of achievement motivation. Usually an index of achievement motivation is obtained by asking the child to tell stories about pictures or about dolls or to complete a story after a situation has been described to him. Winterbottom (1958) found that eight-to-ten-year-old boys who obtained the highest achievement motivation scores on a story-telling measure were rated by their teachers as showing more motivation to achieve in general, and in sports and schoolwork in particular. Achievement motivation scores, however, did not differentiate the boys who were rated as actually performing more successfully in those activities from the boys who were rated as less successful in their attempts. In a longitudinal study of six-to-ten-year-old children, higher achievement motivation scores were obtained by children whose IQ scores had increased over that age period, while those children with decreasing IQ scores had lower scores on the motivational measure (Kagan, Sontag, Baker & Nelson, 1958). High achievement motivation also characterized nine-to-eleven-year-old boys (Rosen & D'Andrade, 1959) who displayed greater proficiency on achievement tasks consisting of block stacking, anagrams and constructing patterns. Finally, Cox (1962) reports that fourth- and fifth-grade Australian children with higher achievement motivation scores were superior on school examination performance and were more often in the "superior stream" than in the "inferior stream" (comparable to ability groups in this country).

On the other hand, Crandall, Katkovsky and Preston (1962) did not find achievement motivation scores to be any higher among early elementary school children who performed more adequately on reading and arithmetic achievement tests and IQ tests. Nor did children with high achievement motivation scores choose to spend more time or strive harder in intellectual achievement activities than did children with lower scores. Murstein and Collier (1962) also report that seventh-grade children with higher motivation scores did not perform better on arithmetic problems or a canceling task than did children with lower motivation scores.

These disparities may arise in part from difficulty in the method by which achievement motivation has been assessed. That is, among very young children the stories told to pictures or doll play situations are often so meager as to allow for only the crudest scoring. Or it may be that findings vary by such situational factors as whether or not motivation has been "aroused," and the probability of reward which the situation offers. Little work of this nature has been done, however, with subjects under college age.

It may be that more specific attitudes, beliefs and expectations concerning achievement activities of different kinds would also contribute to the understanding of achievement behavior. For example, the degree to which children expect that they will be successful in intellectual achievement attempts has generally been found to influence their actual intellectual achievement performance. In studies conducted at the Fels Institute, junior high students who expected to obtain good grades in mathematics and English were, in fact, those students who did perform better in these courses, particularly where high success-expectancy was combined with high IQ. But, when IQ and expectancy were in conflict, the children's expectations of success were even more highly related to their grades than were their intelligence test scores! Children who were confident about being successful also actually performed more competently on standardized achievement tests, and Battle (in press) found that if a child expected to do well in mathematics he persisted longer on a difficult mathematics problem.

It should be pointed out, however, that among the junior high students studied by the Fels group and the first- and second-grade pupils studied by Sears (1964), the positive relationship of expectancy to performance was somewhat weaker for the poor students than for those who were doing well in school, thus leading to the conclusion that some of the poorer students were giving unrealistically high estimates of their own ability.

Sex Differences

Girls seem to have more difficulty than boys in evaluating their ability accurately. Additional findings from the Sears study (1964) indicate that fifth- and sixth-grade girls' concepts of their own mental ability are rather inconsistently related to their performance on intelligence and achievement tests, and the author also states that "girls generally show *less good* self-concepts than boys." Brandt (1958) also finds that girls are less accurate or realistic than boys in their self-concepts. Crandall, Katkovsky and Preston (1962) even report that among first-, second- and third-grade girls, the brighter the girl, the less successful she expected to be on intellectual tasks, and the lower her IQ score, the more successfully she expected she would perform in intellectual activities!

In the same study, the authors also observed the children in free play. They report that the girls who spent most time and were striving hardest in intellectual activities had received higher scores on a measure of their desire to be good at intellectual activities. Thus, the extent of their effort seemed to be determined by their *wish* to do well. Among the boys, however, expectancy of intellectual success was closely and realistically related to IQ scores, and boys who thought they could do well were those who were observed to strive hardest in intellectual activities in free play. In addition, these boys held higher standards for their own performance and thought that they, rather than fate, luck or other people, caused their own intellectual successes and failures. This belief in self-responsibility for, or control over, intellectual successes and failures was also found in elementary children who had higher report card grades and achievement test scores (Crandall, Katkovsky & Crandall, in press).

An investigation (Crandall & Rabson, 1960) of both nursery school and early elementary school children revealed that there were no differences between boys and girls in the *amount* of achievement efforts they displayed at either age level, but among the elementary children boys chose more often than girls to return to a previously failed task in an attempt to master it. The girls, however, avoided returning to the previously failed task and were more dependent on both peers and adults for help and approval and more often withdrew from threatening situations in free play.

There is some possibility that girls achieve for different reasons than boys. A number of studies suggest that girls' achievement efforts may more often be directed at obtaining affection or approval from others than from the self-approval attendant upon successful task accomplishment. For example, Sears (1962) found that among elementary school boys there were consistent, moderate relationships between achievement motivation and the boys' scholastic achievement test scores. Among the girls of that study, however, *affiliative* motives, rather than their achievement motivation, related most directly to their academic achievement test scores.

Tyler, Rafferty and Tyler (1962) demonstrated that girls who made more attempts in nursery school to obtain recognition for achievement also made more attempts to obtain love and affection. Boys' behavior, however, showed no such relationships. Similarly (Crandall, Dewey, Katkovsky & Preston, 1964), elementary-school girls who displayed more achievement efforts were those who sought the most approval from the staff of the Day Camp where they were being observed, while achievement efforts and approval-seeking showed no such relationship among the boys.

Thus, young girls may be using achievement striving to obtain love and approval from others. If this is the case, it is not surprising that in our culture which values achievement so highly, girls have become anxious regarding achievement, attempt to obtain approval for their achievement efforts, are prone to avoid the risk of failing, are dependent on adult help, and cannot rate their own competence accurately, often "underselling" it. For girls, the effort to achieve seems to exact fairly strong psychological penalties as the necessary price of affection and approval.

## PARENTAL INFLUENCES ON CHILDREN'S ACHIEVEMENT BEHAVIOR

While there are many aspects of the social environment which contribute to children's achievement behavior, perhaps the most crucial of these for the very young child is found in interaction with his parents. Since it has already been noted that achieving children are also independent, it might be assumed that parents of these children make early and strong demands for independent behavior. Studies on this point, however, show inconsistent results. On the one hand, high achievement motivation was found in eight-to-ten-year-old boys whose mothers reported on a questionnaire that they had expected early independent behavior (Winterbottom, 1958), and high intelligence and achievement test scores were obtained by third-grade boys whose mothers had expected early or moderately early independence (Siss & Wittenborn, 1962). Yet Chance (1961) reports first-grade children performed more proficiently on academic achievement tests if their mothers expected independent behaviors to occur relatively *late* in childhood. When Rosen and D'Andrade (1959) observed parents as their boys (nine-to-eleven) worked on achievement tasks, they discovered that fathers of boys with high achievement motivation allowed their sons more independence, but mothers allowed them less. Still another study (Crandall, Preston & Rabson, 1960) did not find independence training, as observed in the home, to be related in either direction to the children's achievement efforts in nursery school.

Part of the disparity in these findings may lie in the differences between mothers' retrospective reports on written questionnaires (Chance, 1961; Siss & Wittenborn, 1962; Winterbottom, 1958) and the direct observation of mothers' current independence training techniques used in the latter two studies. Part of the difference may be due to the ages of the children studied. In addition, a recent investigation (Rosen, 1964) has found that boys who received early independence training evidence greater incorporation of their mothers' achievement values — whether these values are strong or weak, positive or negative. Thus, if, by chance, the groups of mothers tested in the foregoing investigations happened to vary from study to study in the achievement orientations they held, the relationships found between independence training and the achievement motivation or behavior of their sons might well be affected. It is interesting to note, however, that mothers' direct reinforcement of achievement attempts (i.e., training specifically aimed at encouraging achievement behavior) was effective in producing higher achievement motivation (Rosen & D'Andrade, 1959) and more achievement efforts (Crandall et al., 1960).

Mothers' attempts to accelerate their children's cognitive and motor development have also been investigated. Moss and Kagan (1958) found that mothers who "pushed" their children's development had sons whose intelligence test scores at three years of age were higher than those of less acceleratory mothers, and IQ ascenders in the elementary years also had more acceleratory mothers (Sontag, Baker & Nelson, 1958).

Investigations by Crandall, Katkovsky and Preston (1960b) indicate that parental influences differ greatly depending on the sex of parent and child and the area of achievement behavior under consideration. For example, children's efforts to achieve in the mechanical area were most often associated with attitudes the parents held toward their children of the *same* sex, while parental influences in the physical skills area seemed to come from both the same-sex and the opposite-sex parent. That is, both boys and girls spent more time and worked harder at sports and gross motor activities if their parents of the same sex had participated frequently with them and instigated them toward these pursuits. The physical skills efforts, however, of both boys and girls were also associated with the importance fathers placed on their children's competence in this area, and high achieving boys had mothers who were rejecting and non-nurturant while girls had fathers who were low in affection.

In the intellectual area the children's efforts were most often associated with attitudes held by parents of the opposite sex and with the context of the child's relationship to that parent. The intellectually striving boys had *mothers* who considered intellectual competence highly important for their sons and whose relationships with them were ones of active involvement. That is, these mothers not only praised their sons' intellectual achievement efforts and were especially nurturant and affectionate, but they were also overtly rejecting and punitive. Conversely, girls who displayed such intellectual efforts in the free-play situation had *fathers* who were generally affectionate and nurturant but criticized, as well as praised, their daughters' achievement efforts. The girls' fathers were also more satisfied than dissatisfied with their daughters' efforts and they, as well as the mothers, evaluated the girls' intellectual competence as high. However, like the boys' mothers, these girls' mothers were also overtly rejecting.

The Rosen and D'Andrade (1959) study found that both parents of those boys with high achievement motivation scores held high standards for their sons and were more competitive, more interested, and demonstrated more involvement during the sons' performance. The mothers (but not the fathers) were likely to reward their sons with warmth and approval and showed some tendency, also, to punish with hostility and rejection. The authors conclude, "In a way, it is this factor of involvement that most clearly sets the mothers of high *n* Achievement boys apart from the mothers of low *n* Achievement boys."

In sum, the foregoing studies suggest that high levels of active parental involvement, particularly along cross-sex, parent-child lines, provide the basis for achievement motivation, performance on intelligence tests, and intellectual achievement behaviors evidenced in free play. It should be noted that in each case, part of that involvement was reflected in negatively-valued parental behaviors or attitudes such as rejection, criticality, hostility, or "pushing" the child beyond his ability, and that this was particularly true of *mothers* of achieving children of either sex.

Other investigations of the parental behaviors associated with high academic achievement in children have also found proficiency in the classroom associated with parent-child relationships usually characterized as undesirable. For example, mothers of achieving girls were less affectionate and less nurturant (Crandall, Dewey, Katkovsky & Preston, 1964) and mothers of achieving boys were less accepting (Barwick & Arbuckle, 1962) and more coercive (Hoffman, Rosen & Lippitt, 1958) than were those of other children who performed more poorly. Haggard (1957), too, reports that high achieving children in the early elementary years "saw their parents as being somewhat overprotective, pressuring for achievement and lacking in emotional warmth (frequently they were correct)."

The attitudes which parents hold about their own personal achievements have been found to affect their attitudes toward their children's achievements and to influence their own behavior with their children in achievement activities. Since neither of these analyses is directly concerned with the *children's* achievement behavior, they will not be discussed here. The interested reader is referred to Katkovsky, Preston & Crandall, 1964a; 1964b.

The salience of early maternal behaviors to achievement development was demonstrated in a longitudinal study by Kagan and Moss (1962). Intellectual achievement in adult males was strongly related to high maternal protection and low maternal hostility during the first three years of the boy's life, followed by acceleration of the child's achievement efforts during ages three to ten. The achieving adult women, however, had had mothers who were hostile toward them and lacking in protectiveness during the first three years of life while they simultaneously accelerated their daughters' achievement development during that period and again during the ages six to ten. Thus, variations in maternal behavior in the very early years have effects so far-reaching as to produce differences in achievement behavior many years later in adulthood.

## CONCLUSION

This discussion has not attempted to present a comprehensive picture of all the social and cultural, peer, sibling and school factors which have been found to relate to children's achievement behavior. This summary has focused principally on the achieving child himself since it is ultimately the orientations he has developed which determine whether he will attempt to achieve when he is faced with a potential achievement situation. External forces can have impact only indirectly as they influence his motivations and attitudes.

Similarly, in studying the determinants of children's achievement behavior, it seems imperative that we must eventually establish the specific orientations the young child holds which promote, guide or limit his achievement efforts. Then the link can be established between social and environmental factors and these orientations and we will better understand how and why such external forces are influencing his behavior. While research of this kind has been done with older subjects, almost none has been attempted with preschool children. The difficulty here is primarily one of measurement, and does not reflect indifference to the developmental aspects of achievement attitudes. Attitudes and motivations have previously been assessed almost exclusively through verbal measures, and very young children lack the necessary verbal skills. In addition, our real attack on the origins of achievement orientations, facilitating or impeding effects on their emergence, and their specificity or generality across kinds of activity as they make their initial appearance cannot really be investigated until nonverbal measures are developed.

This report has reflected the almost-exclusive emphasis on behaviors of an intellectual nature which characterizes research in achievement. Some few research attempts reveal that many children seek approval for, or feel proud of, their competence in sports, crafts, leadership ability, art and many other fields of endeavor. We know very little about the determinants of these kinds of achievement efforts. The paucity of research in these domains of behavior is probably a reflection of the overweaning emphasis on intellectual achievement which has grown out of present international rivalries; it is indeed unfortunate that such exigencies have turned our attention away from such important aspects of achievement development.

## REFERENCES

Barwick, Janice, & Arbuckle, D. The study of the relationship between parental acceptance and the academic achievement of adolescents. *J. educ. Res.*, 1962, 56, 148–151.

Battle, Esther. Motivational determinants of academic task persistence. *J. abnorm. soc. Psychol.*, in press.

Brandt, R. M. The accuracy of self-estimate: a measure of self-concept. *Genet. psychol. Monogr.*, 1958, 58, 55–99.

Bruner, J. S. The cognitive consequences of early sensory deprivation. In P. Solomon (Ed.), *Sensory Deprivation*. Cambridge: Harvard Univer. Press, 1961.

Chance, June E. Independence training and first graders' achievement. *J. consult. Psychol.* XXV, 1961, 149–154.

Cox, F. N. An assessment of the achievement behavior system in children. *Child Develpm.*, 1962, 33, 907–916.

Crandall, V. Parents as identification models and reinforcers of children's achievement behavior. Progress report, NIMH Grant M-2238, January, 1961 (mimeographed).

Crandall, V., Dewey, Rachel, Katkovsky, W., & Preston, Anne. Parents' attitudes and behaviors and grade school children's academic achievements. *J. genet. Psychol.*, 1964, 104, 53–66.

Crandall, V., Katkovsky, W., & Preston, Anne. A conceptual formulation of some research on children's achievement development. *Child Develpm.*, 1960, 31, 787–797. (a)

Crandall, V., Katkovsky, W., & Preston, Anne. Parent behavior and children's achievement development. Paper read at American Psychol. Assn., Chicago, 1960. (b)

Crandall, V., Katkovsky, W., & Preston, Anne. Motivational and ability determinants of young children's intellectual achievement behaviors. *Child Develpm.*, 1962, 33, 643–661.

Crandall, V., Orleans, Sonya, Preston, Anne, & Rabson, Alice. The development of social compliance in young children. *Child Develpm.*, 1958, 29, 429–443.

Crandall, V., Preston, Anne, & Rabson, Alice. Maternal reactions and the development of independence and achievement behavior in young children. *Child Develpm.*, 1960, 31, 243–251.

Crandall, V., & Rabson, Alice. Children's repetition choices in an intellectual achievement situation following success and failure. *J. genet. Psychol.*, 1960, 97, 161–168.

Crandall, Virginia, Katkovsky, W., and Crandall, V. J. Children's beliefs in their own control of reinforcements in intellectual-academic situations. *Child Develpm.*, in press.

Deutsch, Cynthia. Auditory discrimination and learning: social factors. Paper presented at Arden House Conference on Preschool Enrichment of Socially Disadvantaged Children, December, 1962.

Deutsch, M. Facilitating development in the preschool child: social and psychological perspectives. *Merrill-Palmer Quarterly*, in press.

Deutsch, M., & Brown, B. Social influences in Negro-white intelligence differences. *J. soc. Issues*, in press.

Forgays, D. G. Subject characteristics and the selective influence of enriched experience in early life. Symposium paper presented at American Psychol. Assn., Philadelphia, August, 1963.

Fowler, W. Cognitive stimulation, IQ changes and cognitive learning in three-year-old identical twins and triplets. *Amer. Psychologist*, 1961, 16, 373. (Abstract)

Fowler, W. Teaching a two-year-old to read: An experiment in early childhood learning. *Genet. Psychol. Monogr.*, 1962, 66, 181–283.

Fowler, W. Structural dimensions of the learning process in early reading. Symposium paper presented at American Psychol. Assn., Philadelphia, August, 1963.

Grimes, J., & Allinsmith, W. Compulsivity, anxiety and school achievement. *Merrill-Palmer Quarterly*, VII, 1961, 247–271.

Haggard, E. A. Socialization, personality, and achievement in gifted children. *Sch. Rev.*, Winter Issue, 1957, 318–414.

Hoffman, Lois, Rosen, S., & Lippett, R. Parental coerciveness, child autonomy, and child's role at school. Paper read at American Psychol. Assn., Washington, August, 1958.

Hunt, J. McV. *Intelligence and Experience*. New York: Ronald Press, 1961.

Hunt, J. McV. The epigenesis of intrinsic motivation and the stimulation of early cognitive learning. Paper read at American Psychol. Assn., Philadelphia, August, 1963.

John, Vera P. The intellectual development of slum children: some preliminary findings. *Amer. J. Orthopsychiat.*, 1963, 33, 813–822.

John, Vera. The social context of language acquisition. *Merrill-Palmer Quarterly*, in press.

Jones, H. E. The environment and mental development. In L. Carmichael (Ed.), *Manual of Child Psychology*. New York: Wiley, 1954. Pp. 631–696.

Kagan, J., & Moss, H. A. *Birth to Maturity: A Study in Psychological Development.* New York: John Wiley, 1962.

Kagan, J., Sontag, L. W., Baker, C. T., & Nelson, Virginia L. Personality and IQ change. *J. abnorm. soc. Psychol.*, 1958, 56, 261–266.

Katkovsky, W., Preston, Anne, & Crandall, V. J. Parents' attitudes toward their personal achievements and toward the achievement behaviors of their children. *J. genet. Psychol.*, 1964, 104, 67–82. (a)

Katkovsky, W., Preston, Anne, & Crandall, V. J. Parents' achievement attitudes and their behavior with their children in achievement situations. *J. genet. Psychol.*, 1964, 104, 105–121. (b)

McClelland, D. C. The importance of early learning in the formation of motives. In J. Atkinson (Ed.), *Motives in Fantasy, Action and Society.* Princeton: D. Van Nostrand Co., Inc., 1958. Pp. 437–452.

McClelland, D. C. Risk taking in children with high and low need for achievement. In J. Atkinson (Ed.), *Motives in Fantasy, Action and Society.* Princeton: D. Van Nostrand Co., Inc., 1958. Pp. 306–321.

McClelland, D., Atkinson, J., Clark, R., & Lowell, E. *The Achievement Motive.* New York: Appleton-Century-Crofts, Inc., 1953.

Mischel, W. Delay of gratification, need for achievement, and acquiescence in another culture. *J. abnorm. soc. Psychol.*, 1961, 62, 543–552.

Montessori, Maria. *The Montessori Method.* New York: Frederick A. Stokes, 1912.

Montessori, Maria. *Education for a New World.* Wheaton, Ill.: Theosophical Press, 1959.

Moss, H. A., & Kagan, J. Maternal influences on early IQ scores. *Psychol. Rep.*, 1958, 4, 655–661.

Murstein, B. I., & Collier, H. The role of the TAT in the measurement of achievement as a function of expectancy. *J. proj. Tech.*, 1962, 26, 96–101.

Rosen, B. C. Family structure and value transmission. *Merrill-Palmer Quarterly*, Jan. 1964, 59–76.

Rosen, B. C., & D'Andrade, R. The psychosocial origins of achievement motivation. *Sociometry*, 1959, 22, 185–218.

Ruebush, B. K. Interfering and facilitating effects of test anxiety. *J. abnorm. soc. Psychol.*, 1960, 66, 205–212.

Sears, Pauline S., & Levin, H. Level of aspiration in preschool children. *Child Develpm.*, 1957, 28, 317–326.

Sears, Pauline S. Correlates of need achievement and need affiliation and classroom management, self-concept and creativity. Unpublished manuscript, Laboratory of Human Development, Stanford University, 1962.

Sears, Pauline S. Self-concept in the service of educational goals. *Calif. J. Instructional Improvement*, Spring, 1964.

Siss, R., & Wittenborn, J. R. Motivational attitudes of mothers and teachers and their influence upon the educational achievement of third grade boys. Paper read at American Psychol. Assn., St. Louis, August, 1962.

Sontag, L. W., Baker, C. T., & Nelson, Virginia. Mental growth and personality development: a longitudinal study. *Child Develpm. Monogr.*, 1958, No. 2 (Whole No. 68).

Swift, Joan W. Effects of early group experiment: the nursery school and day nursery. In M. L. Hoffman & L. W. Hoffman (Eds.), *Review of Child Development Research.* New York: Russell Sage, 1964.

Tyler, F. B., Rafferty, Janet, & Tyler, Bonnie. Relationships among motivations of parents and their children. *J. genet. Psychol.*, 1962, 101, 69–81.

Wellman, Beth L. The effects of preschool attendance upon intellectual development. In R. G. Barker, J. Kounin, & H. F. Wright (Eds.), *Child Behavior and Development.* New York: McGraw-Hill, 1943. Pp. 229–243.

Winterbottom, Marian. The relation of need for achievement to learning experiences in independence and mastery. In J. Atkinson (Ed.), *Motives in Fantasy, Action and Society.* Princeton: Van Nostrand, 1958.

# SOME FAMILY DETERMINANTS OF AMBITION

RALPH H. TURNER

That a child's level of ambition is related to his socioeconomic background has been abundantly demonstrated. There is still much to be learned about the crucial aspects of class position and about the degree of class difference in ambition relative to starting point. But the average working class child clearly has lower horizons than the middle class child.[1]

Within each class, however, there is much variation. The concept of social class is a useful research fiction or a genuine unit of social experience only because there is usually consistency between such variables as way of life, advantages and disadvantages of life situation, subjective sense of standing in society, and social characteristics of one's most accessible associates. When a child's ambitions are atypical for his class background, it is reasonable to suppose that the convergence among the components of his class position has been incomplete. The child fails to hold the ambitions which are characteristic of his class background because the impact of that background is compromised by inconsistent elements. Carson McGuire has suggested that families be classified with respect to socioeconomic position as *conforming, mobile,* and *divergent.* The mobile family, in which "both parents are oriented to a life style consciously or unconsciously held by them to be 'better' than their present mode of living" is hypothesized to be a principal source of mobility aspiration in children.[2]

*Nature of family determinants.* It is useful to think of two ways in which the family mediates the impact of social class position upon the child. First, the family either faithfully creates the typical life situa-

Reprinted from *Sociology and Social Research* (Vol. 46, No. 4, July 1962, pp. 397–411) by permission of the publisher and the author.

Collection and processing of these data were facilitated by grants from the Social Science Research Council and UCLA. The cooperation of officials of the Los Angeles and Beverly Hills Schools made administration of the questionnaire possible.

tion[3] for each member, or it creates a situation which is atypical for members of the social stratum. Second, the family transmits a sub-culture which either corresponds to the family's position or deviates from it.

The typical middle class situation, for example, is often thought to be one in which the members experience relative economic security, receive a good deal of sustained attention and affection from their parents, experience a stable family life, and which in other ways reflects the constellation of the small family in economic sufficiency. When this constellation is altered by family breakup or by the un-usually large family, some of the important conditions which make the middle class child into the typical adult from his class background may be missing. On the other hand, when the constellation is found in the lower level families, some of the conditions which help to create the middle class child are present. Hence, there is reason to hypothesize that the highest ambitions among working class children will appear in families which come closest to placing the child in a life situation characteristic of a higher socio-economic level.

There is also considerable basis for supposing that the most am-bitious children in lower level families have been exposed to attitudes within the home that are characteristic of higher level families. Joseph Kahl found that among a small group of boys from craftsman and minor white collar backgrounds, all of whom had high I.Q.'s, the ambitions in most cases reproduced the parents' attitudes toward mobility and their present position.[4] Hilde Himmelweit reported that the parents of a group of upwardly mobile boys from working class backgrounds in London exhibited more consistently middle class atti-tudes than even a comparable group of middle class parents.[5] David Bordua found that among a group of ninth- and twelfth-graders in Massachusetts, parental stress on college had much to do with the childrens' plans to attend college and also helped to account for the apparent relationships of sex, religion, and socio-economic status to the decision on whether to attend college.[6]

In the present paper we shall report the relationships between ambi-tion and a number of family variables, as found in a study of high school seniors in Los Angeles, California. In addition, we shall con-sider a systematic variation in the aspect of ambition which the child emphasized, and observe its relationship to the family variables.

*Nature of the data.* The data for this report are the questionnaire responses of 1057 male and 1118 female native white "anglo" seniors in ten high schools in the Los Angeles metropolis. The high schools were selected so as to represent the range from low to high socioeconomic neighborhoods. The questionnaires were administered in required classes by the investigator and his assistants under carefully controlled conditions. The larger investigation was principally concerned with the relationship of class values to ambition, but certain items of information dealing with family background were included in the questionnaire.[7]

Level of ambition was tapped by several questions. Both men and women were asked what level of schooling they expected to complete and with what material level they would be satisfied. Men were also asked what occupation they planned to make their life work and whether they expected to be self-employed or employees. Women were asked two questions about their future husbands: with what occupational and what educational level they could be completely satisfied. A composite index of ambition level was computed by assigning arbitrary weights to the individual ambition items. For men, weights of from zero to three were assigned for occupational, educational, and material ambition, and a weight of zero or one for independent or employee status. For women the same weights were used for educational and material ambition. But husband occupation and education were each weighted from zero to two. For both men and women the index values ranged from zero to ten and produced reasonably normal distributions.

Ambition is not all of one kind, and an effort was made to recognize some difference in the aspects of ambition which students might emphasize. Ambition may be largely striving for wealth or it may be principally the quest for a way of life which is aesthetically and intellectually rich. The theory of social class links these goals together, and they are undoubtedly equated to a considerable degree in the ambitions of most. But it is important to distinguish the tendency to stress either aspect disproportionately. A crude index of such emphasis can be developed by comparing the educational and material ambitions of each individual. The two types of ambition were converted into standard scores, and the score on educational ambition subtracted from the score on material ambition. With the addition of a constant, the index (*MEPI*) ranged from zero, for extremely disproportionate educational ambition, to four, for balanced ambition, to nine for extremely disproportionate material ambition. The value implication of the index was indicated by its correlation with a value question asking for a choice between making "a very good living," and "enjoying art, music, and books." Students from high socioeconomic backgrounds tended to score lower on the index (i.e., emphasize education more) than students from low backgrounds.

In this report we are chiefly concerned with the relationship between these two indices and characteristics of the family situation which may create an atypical socialization environment for the child.

PARENTAL EDUCATION

Perhaps the simplest hypothesis to account for mobility orientation is that some member of the family represents a higher level and inculcates its point of view in the child. A slight indication of involvement in the subculture of a class different from the family's objective position is supplied by a discrepancy between education and occupation of the breadwinner. Students were asked to report the levels of education reached by both their mothers and fathers. Such reports undoubtedly contain much inaccuracy. There is also some danger of contamination — that the student's high ambition may lead him to augment the schooling attributed to his parents. By examining educational background in relation to other background characteristics attributed by the child we have probably reduced the effect of such contamination.

*Father's education.* The relationship between a man's occupation and his education may be taken as an indication of the degree to which his perspective fits his objective station. If a man has less education than is customary in his occupation it is likely that he does not have the background to comprehend and employ the value system of his occupational level. If he has more education than is customary, it is likely that his value system will contain elements characteristic of persons in higher ranked occupations than his own. These discrepant values should be reflected in the home life and communicated to the child, affecting his ambition level and his ambition emphasis.

In order to test the hypothesis that the breadwinner's education has an effect on the child's ambition apart from objective family station, relationships were tested within eight categories of breadwinner's occupation. Mean ambition indices and material-educational polarization indices were computed so as to compare the group whose education was above the median with the group whose education was below the median for each occupation. The hypothesis that high parental education would be associated with a high level of ambition was confirmed by the direction of mean differences in seven out of eight occupational categories for men and seven out of eight categories for women. The hypothesis that material-educational polarization index values are negatively associated with education was likewise confirmed in seven of eight occupational categories for men and for women. For men the exception in both instances fell in the unskilled-semi-skilled labor grouping. For women the exception with regard to ambition level applied to semi-professionals and the exception regarding ambition emphasis applied to business agents and managers. Most of the relationships were not statistically significant. Since a reversal occurred each time in one cell it was not permissible to sum the chi-square values to secure a test of overall significance. Hence we conclude that fairly impressive but not decisive evidence for the hypotheses has been secured.

*Mother's education.* If some member is to represent a class position higher than the family's objective station, the mother may be more readily able to serve in this fashion than the father. As the person actively responsible for the family position, the father has difficulty representing a higher level without disparaging himself and his own efforts. The mother, on the other hand, escapes responsibility and can be less ambivalent. When the mother herself has "married down," or when she has had higher aspirations before marriage than she has been able to realize within marriage, a special relationship to her children appears likely. It is reasonable to suppose that in a large proportion of the instances when the mother has more schooling than her husband she represents a higher status level than the husband has achieved for the family. Hence we can test the hypothesis that high ambition is associated with the family situation in which the mother has more education than the father.

If the mother sometimes brings a different class element into the family than is represented by its objective position, the effect may be revealed upon the emphasis as well as the extent of ambition. We have observed that a disproportionate emphasis upon material ambition in relation to the educational ambition probably characterizes students from lower backgrounds. If the mother imports the point of view of a higher level into the home, then she should also offset this tendency. By enabling the child to learn his ambition in a family

TABLE I
AMBITION IN RELATION TO SUPERIOR MOTHER'S EDUCATION*

| Type of ambition | P | Observed percentage of high ambition | | Adjusted expected percentage of high ambition | |
|---|---|---|---|---|---|
| | | Mother's education >father's | Mother's education ≤father's | Mother's education >father's | Mother's education ≤father's |
| Men | | | | | |
| Ambition index | .001 | 43 | 43 | 35 | 47 |
| Occupation amb. | .025 | 41 | 42 | 35 | 44 |
| Educational amb. | .001 | 46 | 46 | 37 | 49 |
| Material amb. | — | 31 | 31 | 28 | 31 |
| M. E. P. I. | — | 55 | 56 | 61 | 54 |
| Women | | | | | |
| Ambition index | .001 | 42 | 39 | 30 | 42 |
| Educational amb. | .001 | 50 | 43 | 39 | 47 |
| Material amb. | — | 52 | 51 | 46 | 53 |
| M. E. P. I. | — | 59 | 59 | 64 | 58 |

* all figures are given in percentages

where some of the attitudes of a higher level are already at work she should stimulate the less readily understood educational emphasis in ambition. Accordingly we shall test the hypothesis that ambition emphasis, as measured by the material-educational polarization index, is negatively associated with higher mother- than father-education.

In order to test these hypotheses we have first removed all cases in which the father is not either principal or cobreadwinner, and classified the remainder into two groups. Students whose mothers have more schooling than their fathers constitute the first group; students whose mothers have the same or less schooling than their fathers constitute the second. Each of the relevant ambition measures has been dichotomized as near the median as possible and the percentages of high and low ambition computed for the two groups. The percentages of high ambition are reported in Table 1.

The percentages by themselves are not, however, an accurate indication of the possible effect of mother's education. Any degree of randomness in the relation between mother's education and father's education creates a negative relationship between the proportion of mothers who have more schooling than their husbands, and the education of the husband. Since there are positive relationships between father's education and certain measures of ambition, the effect of

superior mother's education will be nullified. While there is considerable educational homogamy in the parents of our subjects, the average father's education in the first group (mother's education greater
than father's) is markedly less than in the second group.

Two procedures have been employed to correct for this difficulty.
The first procedure supplies a ready description of the relationship,
but no test of significance. It is possible to predict for each of the
two groups the proportion of students who would have high ambitions
on the basis of their father's education alone. This is accomplished
by a simple standardization procedure, multiplying the over-all father's
education-specific rate of high ambition by the number of students in
the group whose fathers have the respective amounts of education,
and summing the products separately for the two groups. Translated
into percentages, these figures provide an adjusted model against
which to compare the observed frequencies in the two groups. The
adjusted percentages appear in the final columns of the Table. Interpretation can be illustrated by reference to the ambition index for
men students. Initially, the observation that the two groups do not
differ in the proportion of students having high ambition might have
led to the conclusion that superior mother's education is unrelated to
son's ambition. However, the adjusted expected percentages show
that when due allowance is made for the differences in the distribution of father's education, the 43 per cent of Group I who have high
ambition should be compared with an expected 35 per cent. There
is apparent support for the hypothesis that boys whose mothers have
more schooling than their fathers are more likely to have high ambition than other boys from equivalent levels.

The second procedure was employed to allow tests of significance.
Separate fourfold tabulations between the two groups and ambition
were made within three levels of father's education. Thus, a simple
fourfold relationship could be tested with father's education held relatively constant. When the three relationships were in the hypothesized
direction the chi-squares could be summed and their significance determined with three degrees of freedom assumed. In those instances
in which all relationships were not in the same direction, they were
also not of sufficient magnitude to be significant, so that interpretation
was simplified. Significance figures appear in the first column of the
table.

For both men and women the first hypothesis is supported with respect to the ambition index. Occupational ambition for men also appears to afford support. The second hypothesis likewise appears to be confirmed, though there is less basis for confidence here. For both men and women the relationship between superior mother's education and educational ambition is clear while the relationship with material ambition is not large enough for significance. However, use of the material-educational polarization index supplies a more demanding test, and the relationship in both instances falls a little short of a minimum criterion of significance. The relationships in all of the fourfold tables are in the hypothesized direction. Furthermore, father's education is only incompletely controlled by the necessary condensation of six categories into three. Consequently, while we cannot claim confirmation of the second hypothesis, we are probably justified in suspecting that a more refined test would show that superior mother's education is a small factor accounting for a tendency to stress the educational side of ambition rather than the material side.

It was implied in the discussion that mother's education might be an even more important factor than father's education when added to the impact of father's occupation. Coefficients of partial correlation can supply measures of the comparative extent to which father's and mother's education add to the determination of ambition by father's occupation. After all cases in which the father was not the principal or cobreadwinner and in which any of the relevant items were coded "not answered" were eliminated, a balance of 919 males and 984 females supplied the basis for the analysis. The coefficients reported in Table 2 show that both father's and mother's education make significant additions to father's occupation in predicting the child's ambition level and in predicting his ambition emphasis. The addition is somewhat greater for ambition level than for ambition emphasis, but only because all correlations between family level and ambition level are higher than those with ambition emphasis. The correlations with mother's education are only trivially larger than the correlations with father's education. The hypothesis that the mother's education is a more important additional predictor than father's education fails to receive support.

The correlation analysis also allows us to measure the influence of mother's education with both occupation and education of the father controlled. Here the partial correlation coefficients are small but highly significant. For those who prefer to treat father's education together

120    *Some Family Determinants of Ambition*

TABLE II
CORRELATION OF FATHER'S AND MOTHER'S EDUCATION
WITH AMBITION*

| Independent variable and variable held constant | Correlated with ambition index | | Correlated with material-educational polarization index | |
|---|---|---|---|---|
| | Male | Female | Male | Female |
| Zero-order coefficients | | | | |
| Father's education | +.19 | +.25 | —.14 | —.16 |
| Mother's education | +.35 | +.34 | —.17 | —.14 |
| Father's occupation | +.30 | +.36 | —.19 | —.18 |
| Father's occupation held constant: | | | | |
| Father's education | +.27 | +.34 | —.18 | —.20 |
| Mother's education | +.16 | +.24 | —.12 | —.13 |
| Father's education and education held constant: | | | | |
| Mother's education | +.14 | +.17 | —.11* | —.11 |
| (Total number) | (919) | (984) | (919) | (984) |

* All coefficients are significant at the .001 level by the t-test unless marked by an asterisk, in which case P<.01.

with occupation as a more comprehensive measure of family position there is evidence that the characteristic of the mother also makes its own independent impact.

FAMILY STRUCTURE

If the education of mother and father are taken as indicators of the extent to which atypical values are being transmitted to the child, there are other indicators of the degree to which the family faithfully reproduces the life situation typical of the family's objective position. In this investigation we have secured evidence on two such indicators.

*Family stability.* Family stability, completeness, and organization about the father as breadwinner have often been part of the image of the conventional middle class family. Relevant questions included in the questionnaire are the following:

53. Have you lived with your father (or step-father) most of your life?

54. Have you lived with your mother (or step-mother) most of your life?
55. In your family, who has earned *most* of the money to pay most of the bills during your lifetime?

The hypotheses were as follows: "yes" answers to the first two questions are associated with high ambition and relative emphasis on educational ambition; father as principal breadwinner is associated with high ambition and relative emphasis on educational ambition; and the relationship with presence or absence of the mother should be greater than with presence or absence of the father.

Although the assumptions regarding the effect of the normal stable family in facilitating ambition and an appreciation of the nonmaterial forms of attainment are commonplace, they are not free from challenge. Dynes, Clarke, and Dinitz observe that high ambition is often viewed in psychoanalytic literature as a consequence of special kinds of stress in the family of orientation. Employing the Reissman scale to measure the ambition of 153 male and 197 female university students, they discovered that high aspirers had more often felt rejection and favoritism from their parents, more often expressed little attachment to their parents, and less often stated that their childhoods had been happy.[8] In contrast to such psychoanalytic theory, we have assumed that the development of ambition is a matter of cultural learning which is facilitated by the stable middle class family.

Simple comparisons of mean ambition indices supported all of the hypotheses concerning level of ambition in the case of both men and women students. However, none of the differences reached the minimum requirements for statistical significance. Combining items did not improve the results. When relationships were tested separately within high, middle, and low neighborhoods, employing fourfold tabulations, a significant relationship between complete family ("yes" on both questions 53 and 54) and high ambition appears in the high neighborhoods, but not elsewhere. The data supply no consistent support for the hypotheses regarding ambition emphasis.

It is apparent that these questions supply no convincing clue to the family determinants of ambition. The evidence of six correlations in the predicted direction out of six relationships examined is impressive but not compelling. Neighborhood variation suggests that the incomplete family inhibits ambition only in areas where middle class values

TABLE III
AMBITION AND FAMILY SIZE

| Number of siblings | Mean ambition index | | Material-educational polarization index | | Number of persons | |
|---|---|---|---|---|---|---|
| | Male | Female | Male | Female | Male | Female |
| Only child | 5.41 | 5.01 | 3.54 | 3.83 | 144 | 138 |
| One sibling | 5.25 | 5.09 | 3.83 | 3.75 | 338 | 377 |
| Two siblings | 4.71 | 4.87 | 3.94 | 3.87 | 236 | 254 |
| Three siblings | 4.77 | 4.59 | 4.13 | 3.97 | 123 | 136 |
| Four siblings | 3.97 | 4.45 | 4.45 | 4.22 | 71 | 72 |
| Five or more siblings | 4.38 | 3.87 | 4.11 | 4.12 | 65 | 87 |

are most fully entrenched, but supplies no clue to upward mobility aspiration in lower neighborhoods. However, a single significant correlation is insufficient to justify any positive conclusion. More sensitive indicators are required before confident conclusions can be reached regarding this group of hypotheses.

*Family size.* Family size has been shown to be related to ambition by other investigators. A British study, for example, reported that the children from larger families were more likely to drop out of school than equally intelligent students from smaller families.[9]

The present data (Table 3) show the anticipated negative relationship between family size and the ambition index in the case of both men and women students. The relationships are quite modest and the mean ambition scores progress irregularly, but there appears little doubt that the product-moment coefficients measure genuine relationships. Since family size is also negatively correlated with the background index, the extent to which family size is independently correlated with ambition must be determined. The partial correlation of $-.13$ ($P < .001$) between family size and the ambition index when the background index is held constant shows that boys from large families are less likely than those from small families to have high ambitions, regardless of background. The insignificant coefficient of $-.05$ for women fails to support the same conclusion, however. Why the relationship should not apply to women students as well as to men our data do not clarify.

There is likewise a relationship between family size and the relative stress on educational or material ambition. Students from small families aspire to relatively more educational than material achievement, while students from larger families set relatively higher material than educational goals. The relationship is clear and linear for men, except at the upper end of the distribution. The relationship is similar for the women, except that it is weaker and fails to apply between the only child and the child with a single sibling. The reversal for five or more siblings which characterizes both males and females suggests that the very large family may have distinctive characteristics. A larger number of cases would be required in order to judge whether a genuine departure from linearity is indicated. Since students from high socioeconomic backgrounds resemble those from small families in laying greater stress on the educational component of ambition, it is again necessary to correct for family background level. The findings are similar to those for ambition level; the partial correlation coefficient for males is significant while the coefficient for women is not.

## POSITION IN THE FAMILY

While we usually think of the class position as being equally an attribute of each of the members of the family, it is quite likely that both the transmission of the subculture and relevant aspects of the life situation vary from individual to individual within the family. Because of his unique position within the family, one member may be more effectively exposed to the circumstances which determine the goals typical of his class position than another. Hence, certain positions among one's siblings and certain constellations of siblings may foster higher ambition than others.

*Sibling position.* Just as the large family is thought sometimes to deprive the child of some of the "advantages" of his middle class origin, the first, middle, and youngest children may share unequally in these advantages. The first child has a period of exclusive attention that others do not have, at a time when the novelty of a child's behavior enhances parental interest. In addition, the practice of primogeniture has left its traces in contemporary culture, so that more responsibility for the future station of the family is placed on the oldest son. Psychological studies have also suggested relevant differences according to family position. Robert Sears has produced evidence that first children are more dependent than others,[10] which might render them more subject to parental influence and affect their ability to pursue high ambition. Stanley Schachter reports greater anxiety in first-born children and a greater need for affiliation under stress.[11] The cultural evidence leads us to predict highest ambition for the oldest child; the psychological evidence is subject to alternative interpretations which preclude a specific prediction.

Initially the mean ambition indexes show a relationship favoring the oldest son, with the youngest son next and sons who are middle children last. However, there is a correlation between family size and position, and the results may be spurious. All "middle children" must by definition have two or more siblings, while oldest and youngest children need have only one to qualify. For a more refined analysis, "only children" were omitted from the tabulation, the ambition index was dichotomized near the fifty per cent point into high and low ambition, and the three categories of oldest, youngest, and middle child were used to reflect sibling position. The relationship between ambition and sibling position produced a simple chi-square of 10.172, significant at the one per cent level with two degrees of freedom. The data were then further subdivided according to number of siblings, and the relationship between sibling position and ambition examined separately within each such division. Chi-square tests were made and were in no instance significant. Furthermore, the apparent relationship was in the predicted direction in three instances and in the opposite direction in two.

The same analysis was repeated for the relative emphasis on education or material ambition, with much the same results. An apparent relationship between emphasis on education and being the first child is an artifact of the distribution of family position by family size. For women, likewise, apparent relationships between both variables and siblings position disappeared when family size was held constant. Our findings regarding ambition, then, are fully in accord with the negative conclusions of Harold Jones[12] regarding intelligence and sibling position when appropriate controls are exercised.

The negative evidence regarding sibling position may not in itself be decisive, however. In the sample at large, 36 per cent of the males and 35 per cent of the females are eldest children, as compared with 25 per cent who are youngest children. Since the probabilities of being eldest and youngest children are equal, a priori, the possibilities of selection or misreporting cannot be overlooked. If students tended not to report elder siblings who were no longer living at home, some such effect would have been observed. Or if sibling differences in ambition had already been reflected in disproportionate drop-out rates among younger siblings, a disproportion of older children would have remained in the sample. We have no basis on which to select from among these and other interpretations of the peculiarity of the sample, and hence must leave the issue with this note of uncertainty.

*Sex of siblings.* One further facet of sibling relationships was explored. Orville Brim has shown some differences between the attitudes of boys who have sisters and those who do not. When opposite sex siblings are present the child may learn some of his attitudes from them, with the result that his own attitudes conform less sharply to his sex identification than they otherwise would.[13] West, on the other hand, found no relationship between sex of siblings and the tendency to become a scientist.[14]

Hypotheses were formulated on the basis of the same kind of assumption made by Brim. If ambition can be regarded as something of a masculine attitude, the boy without sisters should be more ambitious than the boy with sisters. Likewise, the girl with brothers should be more ambitious than the girl without brothers. All of our subjects who had one or more siblings were classified according to whether all siblings were male, all were female, or both sexes were represented. Initially it appeared that there might be some relationships, such as a tendency for boys with sisters only to have lower ambition than boys with one or more brothers. However, when the sample was redivided according to family size and the relationships of ambition and emphasis with sex of siblings reexamined, none large enough to be significant emerged. Furthermore, the direction of apparent relationships from one sized family to the next varied, so no summation procedure could be justified.

So long as we assume that the effect of sibling position and sex of siblings should be the same for different sized families, we can fairly confidently employ our data in order to deny any relationships with ambition. However, small group research is beginning to indicate the extent to which different sized groups are governed by different principles in the establishment of coalitions and in many other respects. We find, for example, no difference in ambition according to sex of sibling in the two-child family. In the three-child family we find the highest ambition for both boys and girls when both siblings are of the same sex as the subject and the lowest ambition when both are of the opposite sex. These differences are small and are not significant for the number of three-child families in our sample. But on the assumption that there can be coalitions among siblings in the three-child family but not in the two-child family, the observations can find support from a theory stressing the organization of like values or of antithetical values among one's siblings. In larger families the coalition patterns become more complex and the children who have siblings all of one sex become too few in number to allow the same sort of analysis. Relative size of each sex group would have to be the basis for analysis.

We are led to suggest that the negative findings regarding sibling position and sex may indicate less an absence of relationship than the inadequacy of assuming that a given position has the same consequence for its occupant in families of different size. Since our subsamples by different size of family are not large, the negative findings must remain inconclusive.

SUMMARY

It has often been suggested that the establishment of ambitions which are atypical for a child from a given class background occurs because in some fashion the family conveys an atypical set of values or creates an atypical life situation. In order to test some hypotheses derived from this assumption, measures of level of ambition and of relative polarization of ambition toward educational or material goals were secured from 1057 male and 1118 female native white "anglo" high school seniors in the Los Angeles metropolitan area. It was found, as predicted, that ambition was likely to be high and emphasis placed on the educational component of ambition when the breadwinner's education was high relative to his occupation and when the education of the mother exceeded that of the father. A partial correlation analysis further indicated that the influence of mother's education and father's education was about the same, when father's occupation was held constant. It also showed that mother's education made a small but significant addition to father's occupation and education combined.

The hypothesis that the complete family with the father as breadwinner would produce the highest ambition received consistent support, but not of sufficient magnitude for statistical significance. A breakdown by neighborhood level supplied suggestive evidence that the relationship exists only in higher socioeconomic areas. No relationships with ambition emphasis were found.

Our findings are consistent with those of other investigators in showing that both level of ambition and relative emphasis on education are associated with the small family. When partial correlation analysis was employed in order to discount the correlation between family size and family background level, the large family still exhibits a small but significant association with low ambition and relative emphasis on the material component of ambition in the case of boys. For girls, however, the relationship between background level and family size seems largely to account for the relationships between size and ambition.

A final set of hypotheses regarding sibling position and sex of siblings as determinants of ambition was tested. Apparent relationships disappeared in all instances when size of family was held constant. However, the negative findings may not be decisive because we probably should have predicted different relationships within families of different size. With this qualification, our data point to the characteristics of the total family rather than objective sibling position in accounting for the character of a child's ambition.

## REFERENCES

1. Seymour M. Lipset and Reinhard Bendix, *Social Mobility in Industrial Society* (Berkeley & Los Angeles: University of California Press, 1959).

2. Carson McGuire, "Conforming, Mobile, and Divergent Families," *Marriage and Family Living*, 14 (May, 1952), 109–115.

3. Ralph H. Turner, "Life Situation and Subculture: A Comparison of Merited Prestige Judgments by Three Occupational Classes in Britain," *British Journal of Sociology*, 9 (December, 1958), 299–320.

4. Joseph Kahl, "Educational and Occupational Aspirations of 'Common Man' Boys," *Harvard Educational Review*, 23 (Summer, 1953), 186–203.

5. Hilde T. Himmelweit, "Socio-Economic Background and Personality," *International Social Science Bulletin*, 7 (1955), No. 1, 29–34.

6. David J. Bordua, "Educational Aspirations and Parental Stress on College," *Social Forces*, 38 (March, 1960), 262–269.

7. For a full account of the larger study and a more detailed explanation of procedures see Ralph H. Turner, *The Social Context of Ambition*, forthcoming.

8. Russell R. Dynes, Alfred C. Clarke, and Simon Dinitz, "Levels of Occupational Aspiration: Some Aspects of Family Experience as a Variable," *American Sociological Review*, 21 (April, 1956), 212–215.

128 Some Family Determinants of Ambition

9. Jean E. Floud, A. H. Halsey, and F. M. Martin, *Social Class and Educational Opportunity* (London: Heineman, Ltd., 1956), 90–91.

10. Robert R. Sears, "Ordinal Position in the Family as a Psychological Variable," *American Sociological Review*, 15 (June, 1950), 397–401.

11. Stanley Schachter, *The Psychology of Affiliation* (Stanford: Stanford University Press, 1959).

12. Harold E. Jones, "The Environment and Mental Development," in Leonard Carmichael, ed., *Manual of Child Psychology*, Second Edition (New York: Wiley, 1954), 667–668.

13. Orville Brim, Jr., "Family Structure and Sex Role Learning by Children: A Further Analysis of Helen Koch's Data," *Sociometry*, 21 (March, 1958), 1–16.

14. S. Stewart West, "Sibling Configurations of Scientists," *American Journal of Sociology*, 66 (Nov., 1960), 268–274.

# B.

## THE IMPACT OF MACRO-SOCIAL STRUCTURES: RACE AND ETHNICITY

# RACE, ETHNICITY, AND THE ACHIEVEMENT SYNDROME

## BERNARD C. ROSEN

The upward mobility rates of many racial and ethnic groups in America have been markedly dissimilar when compared with one another and with some white Protestant groups. For example, among the "new immigration" groups which settled primarily in the Northeast, the Greeks and Jews have attained middle class status more rapidly than most of their fellow immigrants. In general, ethnic groups with Roman Catholic affiliation have moved up less rapidly than non-Catholic groups. And the vertical mobility of Negroes, even in the less repressive environment of the industrial Northeast, has been relatively slow.[1]

The reasons offered to explain these differences vary with the group in question. Thus, differences in group mobility rates have sometimes been interpreted as a function of the immigrant's possession of certain skills which were valuable in a burgeoning industrial society. In this connection, there is some evidence that many Jews came to America with occupational skills better suited to urban living than did their fellow immigrants. Social mobility seems also to be related to the ability of ethnic and racial groups to organize effectively to protect and promote their interests. Both the Greeks and the Jews were quicker to develop effective community organizations than were other immigrants who had not previously faced the problem of adapting as minority groups. For the Jews, this situation grew out of their experiences with an often hostile gentile world; for the Greeks, out of their persecutions by the Turks. The repressiveness of the social structure or the willingness of the dominant groups to permit others to share in the fruits of a rich, expanding economy has also been given as an explanation of differential group mobility. This argument has merit in the case of Negroes, but it is less valid in a comparison of the Jews with Southern Italians or French-Canadians. Finally, it has been suggested that groups with experiences in small

Reprinted from the *American Sociological Review* (Vol. 24, No. 1, February 1959, pp. 47–60) by permission of the American Sociological Association and the author.

town or urban environments were more likely to possess the cultural values appropriate to achievement in American society than were ethnic and racial groups whose cultures had been formed in rural, peasant surroundings. Here, again, it has been noted that many Jews and a small but influential number of Levantine Greeks had come from small towns or cities, while most of the Roman Catholic immigrants from Eastern and Southern Europe (and Southern Negroes before their migration to the North) came from rural communities.[2]

As valid as these explanations may be — and we believe they have merit — they overlook one important factor: *the individual's psychological and cultural orientation towards achievement;* by which we mean his psychological need to excel, his desire to enter the competitive race for social status, and his initial possession of, or willingness to adopt, the high valuation placed upon personal achievement and success which foreign observers from Tocqueville to Laski have considered an important factor in the remarkable mobility of individuals in American society.

Three components of this achievement orientation are particularly relevant for any study of social mobility. The first is a psychological factor, *achievement motivation,* which provides the internal impetus to excel in situations involving standards of excellence. The second and third components are cultural factors, one consisting of certain *value orientations* which implement achievement-motivated behavior, the other of culturally influenced *educational-vocational aspiration levels.* All three factors may affect status achievement; one moving the individual to excel, the others organizing and directing his behavior towards high status goals. This motive-value-aspiration complex has been called the *Achievement Syndrome.*[3]

It is the basic hypothesis of this study that many racial and ethnic groups were not, and are not now, alike in their orientation toward achievement, particularly as it is expressed in the striving for status through social mobility, and that this difference in orientation has been an important factor contributing to the dissimilarities in their social mobility rates. Specifically, this paper examines the achievement motivation, values, and aspirations of members of six racial and ethnic groups. Four of these are "new immigration" ethnic groups with similar periods of residence in this country who faced approximately the same economic circumstances upon arrival: the French-Canadians, Southern Italians, Greeks, and East European Jews. The fifth is the Negro group in the Northeast, the section's largest "racial" division.

The last, and in some ways the most heterogeneous, is the native-born white Protestant group. Contributing to the fact that these six groups have not been equally mobile, we suggest, are differences in the three components of the achievement syndrome: their incidence is highest among Jews, Greeks, and white Protestants, lower among Southern Italians and French-Canadians, and lowest among Negroes.

RESEARCH PROCEDURE

The data were collected from a purposive sample of 954 subjects residing in 62 communities in four Northeastern states: 51 in Connecticut, seven in New York, three in New Jersey, and one in Massachusetts. The subjects are 427 pairs of mothers and their sons; 62 pairs are French-Canadians, 74 are Italians, 47 are Greeks, 57 are Jews, 65 are Negroes and 122 are white Protestants. Most subjects were located through the aid of local religious, ethnic, or service organizations, or through their residence in neighborhoods believed to be occupied by certain groups. The subject's group membership was determined ultimately by asking the mothers in personal interviews to designate their religion and land of national origin. The interviewers, all of whom were upper-classmen enrolled in two sociology classes, were instructed to draw respondents from various social strata.[4] The respondent's social class position was determined by a modified version of Hollingshead's Index of Social Position, which uses occupation and education of the main wage-earner, usually the father, as the principal criteria of status. Respondents were classified according to this index into one of five social classes, from the highest status group (Class I) to the lowest (Class V).[5] Most of the mothers and all of the sons are native-born, the sons ranging in age from eight to 14 years (the mean age is about 11 years). There are no significant age differences between the various groups.

Two research instruments were used: a projective test to measure achievement motivation and a personal interview to obtain information on achievement value orientations and related phenomena. Achievement motivation has been defined by McClelland and his associates as a redintegration of affect aroused by cues in situations involving standards of excellence. Such standards usually are imparted to the individual by his parents, who impart the understanding that they expect him to perform well in relation to these standards of excellence, rewarding him for successful endeavor and punishing him for failure. In time he comes to have similar expectations of himself when exposed to situations involving standards of excellence and re-experiences the affect associated with his earlier efforts to meet these standards. The behavior of people with high achievement motivation is characterized by persistent striving and general competitiveness.

Using a Thematic Apperception Test, McClelland and his associates have developed a method of measuring the achievement motive that involves identifying and counting the frequency with which imagery about evaluated performance in competition with a standard of excellence appears in the thoughts of a person when he tells a brief story under time pressure. This imagery now can be identified objectively and reliably. The test assumes that the more the individual shows indications of connections between evaluated performance and affect in his fantasy, the greater the degree to which achievement motivation is part of his personality.[6] This projective test, which involves showing the subject four ambiguous pictures and asking him to tell a story about each, was given privately and individually to the sons in their homes. Their imaginative responses to the pictures were scored by two judges; the Pearson product moment correlation between the two scorings was .86, an estimate of reliability similar to those reported in earlier studies using this measure.

Following the boys' testing, their mothers were interviewed privately. The interview guide included several standardized questions designed to indicate the mother's achievement value orientations, her educational and vocational aspirations for her son, and the degree to which she had trained him to be independent.

FINDINGS AND INTERPRETATION

*Achievement Motivation.* Empirical studies have shown that achievement motivation is generated by (at least) two kinds of socialization practices: (1) *achievement training*, in which the parents, by imposing standards of excellence upon tasks, by setting high goals for their child, and by indicating their high evaluation of his competence to do a task well, communicate to him that they expect evidences of high achievement; (2) *independence training*, in which the parents indicate to the child that they expect him to be self-reliant and, at the same time, grant him relative autonomy in decision-making situations where he is given both freedom of action and responsibility for success or failure. Essentially, achievement training is concerned with getting the child to *do things well,* while independence training seeks to teach him to do things *on his own.* Although both kinds often occur together and each contributes to the development of achievement motivation, achievement training is the more important of the two.[7]

Two bodies of information — ethnographic studies of the "old world" or non-American culture and recent empirical investigations of the training practices used by Americans of various ethnic backgrounds — strongly indicate that the six groups examined here, in the past and to some extent today, differ with respect to the degree to which their members typically emphasize achievement and independence training. Ethnic differences in these matters were first studied by McClelland, who noted that the linkage between independence training and achievement motivation established by recent empirical studies suggests an interesting parallel with Weber's classic description of the characterological consequences of the Protestant Reformation. Weber reasoned, first, concerning salvation, that an important aspect of the Protestant theological position was the shift from reliance on an institution (the Church) to a greater reliance upon self; it seemed reasonable to assume that Protestant parents who prepared their children for increased self-reliance in religious matters would also tend to stress the necessity for the child to be self-reliant in other aspects of his life. Secondly, Weber's description of the personality types produced by the Reformation is strikingly similar to the picture of the person with high achievement motivation; for example, the hard-working, thrifty Protestant working girl, the Protestant entrepreneur who "gets nothing out of his wealth for himself except the irrational sense of having done his job well."[8]

The hypothesis deduced from these observations was put to the test by McClelland, who questioned white Protestant, Irish-Catholic, Italian-Catholic, and Jewish mothers about their independence training practices. He found that Protestants and Jews favored earlier independence training than Irish and Italian Catholics.[9] These findings are supported and enlarged upon by data derived from questioning the 427 mothers in this study about their training practices. The mothers were asked, "At what age do you expect your son to do

TABLE 1. MEAN AGE OF INDEPENDENCE TRAINING BY
ETHNICITY AND SOCIAL CLASS

| Ethnicity | Social Class * | | | | |
|---|---|---|---|---|---|
| | I-II-III | IV | V | $\bar{x}$ | N |
| French-Canadian | 8.00 | 7.69 | 8.08 | 7.99 | 62 |
| Italian | 6.79 | 7.89 | 8.47 | 8.03 | 74 |
| Greek | 6.33 | 8.14 | 7.52 | 7.67 | 47 |
| Jew | 6.37 | 7.29 | 6.90 | 6.83 | 57 |
| Negro | 6.64 | 6.98 | 7.39 | 7.23 | 65 |
| Protestant | 5.82 | 7.44 | 7.03 | 6.87 | 122 |
| $\bar{x}$ | 6.31 | 7.64 | 7.59 | | |

Ethnicity:    $F = 8.55$   $P < .01$
Social Class:    $F = 21.48$   $P < .001$
Ethnicity × Class:    $F = 6.25$   $P < .01$

* The three-class breakdown was used in an earlier phase
of the analysis. An examination of the means of cells using a
four-class breakdown revealed no change in pattern and did
not warrant new computations.

the following things?" and to note the appropriate items from the
following list (taken from the Winterbottom index of training in independence and mastery):[10]

1. To be willing to try things on his own without depending on his mother
   for help.
2. To be active and energetic in climbing, jumping, and sports.
3. To try hard things for himself without asking for help.
4. To be able to lead other children and assert himself in children's
   groups.
5. To make his own friends among children of his own age.
6. To do well in school on his own.
7. To have interests and hobbies of his own. To be able to entertain
   himself.
8. To do well in competition with other children. To try hard to come
   out on top in games and sports.
9. To make decisions like choosing his own clothes or deciding to spend
   his money by himself.

An index of independence training was derived by summing the
ages for each item and taking the mean figure. The data in Table 1
show that the Jews expect earliest evidence of self-reliance from their
children, followed by the Protestants, Negroes, Greeks, French-
Canadians, and Italians. Both primary sources of variation — ethnicity
and social class — are significant.

Data on the relative emphasis which racial and ethnic groups place upon achievement *training* (that is, imposing standards of excellence upon tasks, setting high goals for the child to achieve, and communicating to him a feeling that his parents evaluate highly his task-competence) are much more difficult to obtain. Achievement training as such, in fact, is rarely treated in studies of ethnic socialization practices. Hence, inferences about achievement training were drawn primarily from ethnographic and historical materials, which are usually more informative about achievement as such than about relevant socialization practices.

The groups about which the most is known concerning achievement training, perhaps, are the Protestants, the Jews, and, to a lesser extent, the Greeks. These groups traditionally have stressed excellence and achievement. In the case of the Protestants, this tradition can be located in the Puritan Ethic with its concept of work as a "calling" and the exhortation that a job be done well. Of course, not all Protestants would be equally comfortable with this tradition; it is much more applicable, for example, to Presbyterians and Quakers than to Methodists and Baptists. Nonetheless, the generally longer residence of Protestants in this country makes it probable that they would tend to share the American belief that children should be encouraged to develop their talents and to set high goals, possibly a bit beyond their reach. The observation that Jews stress achievement training is commonplace. Zyborowski and Herzog note the strong tendency among *shtetl* Jews to expect and to reward evidences of achievement even among very young children. The image of the Jewish mother as eager for her son to excel in competition and to set ever higher goals for himself is a familiar one in the literature of Jewish family life.[11] Careful attention to standards of excellence in the Greek home is stressed by the parents: children know that a task which is shabbily performed will have to be re-done. In this country, the Greek is exhorted to be "a credit to his group." Failure to meet group norms is quickly perceived and where possible punished; while achievement receives the approbation of the entire Greek community.

Among the Southern Italians (the overwhelming majority of American-Italians are of Southern Italian extraction), French-Canadians, and Negroes the tradition seems to be quite different. More often than not they came from agrarian societies or regions in which opportunities for achievement were strictly curtailed by the social structure and where habits of resignation and fatalism in the face of social and environmental frustrations were psychologically functional. Under such conditions children were not typically exhorted to be achievers or urged to set their sights very high. Of course, children were expected to perform tasks, as they are in most societies, but such tasks were usually farm or self-caretaking chores, from which the notion of competition with standards of excellence is not excluded, but is not ordinarily stressed. As for communicating to the child a sense of confidence in his competence to do a task well, there is some evidence that in the father-dominant Italian and French-Canadian families, pronounced concern with the child's ability might be perceived as a threat to the father.[12]

On the whole, the data indicate that Protestants, Jews, and Greeks place a greater emphasis on independence and achievement training than Southern Italians and French-Canadians. The data on the Negroes are conflicting: they often train children relatively early in self-reliance, but there is little evidence of much stress upon achievement training. No doubt the socialization practices of these groups have been modified somewhat by the acculturating influences of American society since their arrival in the Northeast.[13] But ethnic cultures tend to survive even in the face of strong obliterating forces, and we believe that earlier differences between groups persist — a position supported by the present data on self-reliance training. Hence, the hypothesis that the racial and ethnic groups considered here differ with respect to achievement motivation. We predicted that, on the average, achievement motivation scores would be highest among the Jews, Greeks, and white Protestants, lower among the Italians and French-Canadians, and lowest among the Negroes. Table 2 shows that the data support these predictions, indicated by the following mean scores: Greeks 10.80, Jews 10.53, Protestants 10.11, Italians 9.65, French-Canadians 8.82, and Negroes 8.40.

A series of "t" tests of significance between means (a one-tail test was used in cases where the direction of the difference had been predicted) was computed. The differences between Greeks, Jews, and Protestants are not statistically significant. The Italian score is significantly lower than the score for the Greeks, but not for the Jews and Protestants. The largest differences are between the French-Canadians and Negroes on the one hand and the remaining groups on the other: the French-Canadian mean score is significantly lower than those of all other groups except Italians and Negroes; the mean score for all Negroes is significantly lower than the scores for all other groups except French-

BERNARD C. ROSEN    139

TABLE 2. MEAN ACHIEVEMENT MOTIVATION SCORES
BY ETHNICITY AND SOCIAL CLASS

| Ethnicity | Social Class | | | | | |
| | I-II | III | IV | V | $\bar{x}$ | N |
| --- | --- | --- | --- | --- | --- | --- |
| French-Canadian | 10.00 | 10.64 | 8.78 | 7.75 | 8.82 | 62 |
| Italian | 8.86 | 12.81 | 7.54 | 10.20 | 9.65 | 74 |
| Greek | 9.17 | 12.13 | 10.40 | 8.75 | 10.80 | 47 |
| Jew | 10.05 | 10.41 | 10.94 | 11.20 | 10.53 | 57 |
| Negro | 11.36 | 9.00 | 8.23 | 6.72 | 8.40 | 65 |
| Protestant | 11.71 | 10.94 | 9.39 | 7.31 | 10.11 | 122 |
| $\bar{x}$ | 10.55 | 11.26 | 9.01 | 8.32 | | |

Ethnicity:  $F = 1.23$  $P > .05$
Social Class:  $F = 5.30$  $P < .005$
Ethnicity × Class:  $F = 1.32$  $P > .05$

Canadians. A "Roman Catholic" score was obtained by combining Italian and French-Canadian scores, and scores for all non-Negro groups were combined to form a "White" score. The differences between group means were tested for significance (by a one-tail "t" test) and it was found that the "Catholic" score is significantly lower than the scores for Protestants, Greek Orthodox, and Jews. The Negro mean score is significantly lower than the combined score of all white groups.

A comparison of ethnic-racial differences does not tell the whole story. There are also significant differences between the social classes. In fact, analysis of Table 2 indicates that social class accounts for more of the variance than ethnicity: the F ratio for ethnicity is 1.23, for class 5.30. The small number of cases in Classes I and II greatly increases the within-group variance; when these two classes are combined with Class III the variance is decreased and the F ratio for ethnicity increases sharply to 2.13. Social class, however, remains more significantly related to achievement motivation than ethnicity. This finding is especially important in this study since the proportion of subjects in each class varies for the ethnic groups. There are relatively more middle class than lower class subjects among the Jews, Greeks, and Protestants than among Italians, French-Canadians, and Negroes. To control for social class it was necessary to examine the differences between cells as well as between columns and rows. A series of "t" tests of differences between the means of cells revealed that for the most part the earlier pattern established for total ethnic means persists, although in some instances the differences between groups are decreased, in others increased, and in a few cases the direction of the differences is reversed. Neither ethnicity nor social class alone is sufficient to predict an individual's score; both appear to contribute something to the variance between groups, but on the whole social class is a better predictor than ethnicity. Generally, a high status person from an ethnic group with a low mean achievement motivation score is more likely to have a high score than a low status person from a group with a high mean score. Thus, the mean score for Class I-II Negroes is higher than the score for Class IV-V white Protestants: a "t" test revealed that the difference between these two means is significant at the .05 level, using a two-tail test. This relatively high score for Class I-II Negroes, the third highest for any cell in the table, indicates, perhaps, the strong motivation necessary for a Negro to achieve middle class status in a hostile environment. Generally, the scores for each group decrease as the class level declines, except for the Jews whose scores are inversely related to social status — a finding for which we can offer no explanation.

*Achievement Value Orientations.* Achievement motivation is one part of the achievement syndrome; an equally important component is the achievement value orientation. Value orientations are defined as meaningful and affectively charged modes of organizing behavior — principles that guide human conduct. They establish criteria which influence the individual's preferences and goals. Achievement values and achievement motivation, while related, represent genuinely different components of the achievement syndrome, not only conceptually but also in their origins and, as we have shown elsewhere, in their social correlates.[14] Value orientations, because of their conceptual content, are probably acquired in that stage of the child's cultural training when verbal communication of a fairly complex nature is possible. Achievement motivation or the need to excel, on the other hand, has its origins in parent-child interaction beginning early in the child's life when many of these relations are likely to be emotional and unverbalized. Analytically, then, the learning of achievement oriented values can be independent of the acquisition of the achievement motive, although empirically they often occur together.

Achievement values affect social mobility in that they focus the individual's attention on status improvement and help to shape his behavior so that achievement motivation can be translated into successful action. The achievement motive by itself is not a sufficient condition of social mobility: it provides internal impetus to excel, but it does not impel the individual to take the steps necessary for status achievement. Such steps in our society involve, among other things, a preparedness to plan, work hard, make sacrifices, and be physically mobile. Whether or not the individual will understand their importance and accept them will depend in part upon his values.

Three sets of values[15] were identified as elements of the achievement syndrome, as follows:

1. *Activistic-Passivistic Orientation* concerns the extent to which the culture of a group encourages the individual to believe in the possibility of his manipulating the physical and social environment to his advantage. An activistic culture encourages the individual to believe that it is both possible and necessary for him to improve his status, whereas a passivistic culture promotes the acceptance of the notion that individual efforts to achieve mobility are relatively futile.

2. *Individualistic-Collectivistic Orientation* refers to the extent to which the individual is expected to subordinate his needs to the group. This study is specifically concerned with the degree to which the society expects the individual to maintain close physical proximity to his family of orientation, even at the risk of limiting vocational opportunities; and the degree to which the society emphasizes group incentives rather than personal rewards. The collectivistic society places a greater stress than the individualistic on group ties and group incentives.

3. *Present-Future Orientation* concerns the society's attitude toward time and its impact upon behavior. A present oriented society stresses the merit of living in the present, emphasizing immediate gratifications; a future oriented society encourages the belief that planning and present sacrifices are worthwhile, or morally obligatory, in order to insure future gains.[16]

Examination of ethnographic and historical materials on the cultures of the six ethnic groups revealed important differences in value orientation — differences antedating their arrival in the Northeast. The cultures of white Protestants, Jews, and Greeks stand out as considerably more individualistic, activistic, and future-oriented than those of the Southern Italians, French-Canadians, and Negroes. Several forces — religious, economic, and national — seem to have long influenced the Protestants in this direction, including, first, the Puritan Ethic with its stress upon individualism and work; then the impact of the liberal economic ethic (Weber's "Spirit of Capitalism") emphasizing competitive activity and achievement; and finally, the challenge of the frontier, with its consequent growth of a national feeling of optimism and manifest destiny. All of these factors tended very early to create a highly activistic, individualistic, future-oriented culture — the picture of American culture held by foreign observers since Tocqueville.[17]

The Jews, who for centuries had lived in more or less hostile environments, have learned that it is not only possible to manipulate their environment to insure survival but even to prosper in it. Jewish tradition stresses the possibility of the individual rationally mastering his world. Man is not helpless against the forces of nature or of his fellow man; God will provide, but only if man does his share. Like Protestantism, Judaism is an intensely individualistic religion and the Jews an intensely individualistic people. While the family was close knit, it was the entire *shtetl* which was regarded as the inclusive social unit; and in neither case was loyalty to the group considered threatened by physical mobility. The Jews typically have urged their children to leave home if in so doing they faced better opportunities. *Shtetl* society, from which the vast majority of American Jewry is descended, vigorously stressed the importance of planning and working for the future. A *shtetl* cultural tradition was that parents save for many years, often at great sacrifice to themselves, in order to improve their son's vocational opportunities or to provide a daughter with a dowry.[18]

In some respects, Greek and Jewish cultures were strikingly similar at the turn of the century. The ethos of the town and city permeated the Greek more than most other Mediterranean cultures, although only a small proportion of the population was engaged in trade — with the important exception of the Levantine Greeks, who were largely merchants. The image of the Greek in the Eastern Mediterranean area was that of an individualistic, foresighted, competitive trader. Early observers of the Greek in America were impressed by his activistic, future-oriented behavior. E. A. Ross, a rather unfriendly observer, wrote as early as 1914 that "the saving, commercial Greek climbs. From curb to stand, from stand to store, from little store to big store, and from there to branch stores in other cities — such are the stages in his upward path."[19]

Though separated by thousands of miles, French-Canadian and Southern Italian cultures were similar in many respects. Both were primarily peasant cultures, strongly influenced by the Roman Catholic Church. Neither could be described as activistic, individualistic, or future-oriented. In Southern Italian society the closed-class system and grinding poverty fostered a tradition of resignation — a belief that the individual had little control over his life situation and a stress upon the role of fate (*Destino*) in determining success. The living conditions of French-Canadians, although less harsh, were sufficiently severe to sharply limit the individual's sense of mastery over his situation. In neither group was there a strong feeling that the individual could drastically improve his lot; for both groups the future was essentially unpredictable, even capricious. Extended family ties were very strong in both groups: there is the Southern Italian saying, "the family against all others"; the French-Canadian farmer in need of help will travel many miles to hire a kinsman rather than an otherwise convenient neighbor.[20]

Ironically, although Negroes are usually Protestant (however, not ordinarily of the Calvinistic type) and have been exposed to the liberal economic ethic longer than most of the other groups considered here, their culture, it seems, is least likely to accent achievement values. The Negro's history as a slave and depressed farm worker, and the sharp discrepancy between his experiences and the American Creed, would appear to work against the internalization of the achievement values of the dominant white group. Typically, the Negro life-situation does not encourage the belief that one can manipulate his environment or the conviction that one can improve his condition very much by planning and hard work.[21] Generally, family ties have not been strong among Negroes, although traditionally the mother was an especially important figure and ties between her and her children, particularly sons, may still be very strong.[22]

Another and more direct way of studying ethnic values is to talk with group members themselves; thus our personal interviews with the mothers. (Their sons in many cases were too young to give meaningful answers.) They were asked whether they agreed or disagreed with the following statements, listed here under the appropriate value orientation categories.

(1) *Activistic-Passivistic Orientation.*
   Item 1. "All a man should want out of life in the way of a career is a secure, not too difficult job, with enough pay to afford a nice car and eventually a home of his own."
   Item 2. "When a man is born the success he is going to have is already in the cards, so he might just as well accept it and not fight against it."
   Item 3. "The secret of happiness is not expecting too much out of life and being content with what comes your way."

144     Race, Ethnicity, and the Achievement Syndrome

TABLE 3. MEAN VALUE SCORES BY ETHNICITY AND SOCIAL CLASS

| Ethnicity | Social Class | | | | | |
|---|---|---|---|---|---|---|
| | I-II | III | IV | V | $\bar{x}$ | N |
| French-Canadian | 4.00 | 4.21 | 4.60 | 2.46 | 3.68 | 62 |
| Italian | 5.86 | 4.00 | 3.96 | 3.40 | 4.17 | 74 |
| Greek | 6.33 | 5.52 | 4.80 | 3.25 | 5.08 | 47 |
| Jew | 5.94 | 5.47 | 5.41 | 4.80 | 5.54 | 57 |
| Negro | 6.00 | 5.00 | 4.90 | 4.67 | 5.03 | 65 |
| Protestant | 5.86 | 5.50 | 4.97 | 3.54 | 5.16 | 122 |
| $\bar{x}$ | 5.91 | 5.08 | 4.78 | 3.49 | | |

Ethnicity:      F = 11.62   P < .001
Social Class:   F = 33.80   P < .001
Ethnicity × Class:   F = 2.43   P < .01

(2) *Individualistic-Collectivistic Orientation.*
Item 4. "Nothing is worth the sacrifice of moving away from one's parents."
Item 5. "The best kind of job to have is one where you are part of an organization all working together even if you don't get individual credit." [23]

(3) *Present-Future Orientation.*
Item 6. "Planning only makes a person unhappy since your plans hardly ever work out anyway."
Item 7. "Nowadays with world conditions the way they are the wise person lives for today and lets tomorrow take care of itself."

Responses indicating an activistic, future-oriented, individualistic point of view (the answer "disagree" to these items) reflect values, we believe, most likely to facilitate achievement and social mobility. These items were used to form a value index, and a score was derived for each subject by giving a point for each achievement-oriented response. In examining the mothers' scores two assumptions were made: (1) that they tend to transmit their values to their sons, and (2) that the present differences between groups are indicative of at least equal, and perhaps even greater, differences in the past.

The ethnographic and historical materials led us to expect higher value scores for Jews, white Protestants, and Greeks than for Italians, French-Canadians, and Negroes. In large measure, these expectations were confirmed. Table 3 shows that Jews have the highest mean score followed closely by Protestants, Greeks and Negroes (surprisingly). The Italians' score is almost a point lower, and the French-Canadian score is the lowest for any group. The scores for Jews, Protestants, and Greeks do not significantly differ when the two-tail test is used (we were not able to predict the direction of the o. ferences), but they are all significantly higher than the scores for Italians and French-Canadians. When Italian and French-Canadian scores are combined to form a "Roman Catholic" score, the latter is significantly lower than the scores for Jews, Protestants, or Greeks.

The prediction for the Negroes proved to be entirely wrong. Their mean score is significantly higher than the scores for Italians and French-Canadians. Nor is the Negro score significantly different from those for Protestants and Greeks, although it is significantly lower than the Jewish score when the one-tail test is used. The skeptic may regard the relatively high Negro value score as merely lip-service to the liberal economic ethic, but it may in fact reflect, and to some extent be responsible for, the economic gains of Negroes in recent years.[24]

Social class also is significantly related to achievement values and accounts for more of the variance than ethnicity. Almost without exception, the mean score for each ethnic group is reduced with each decline in status. *Social class, however, does not wash out the differences between ethnic groups.* A series of "t" tests between cells across each social class reveals that Greek, Jewish, and Protestant scores remain significantly higher than Italian and French-Canadian scores. Negro scores also remain among the highest across each social class. Ethnicity and social class interact and each contributes something to the differences between groups: the individual with high social status who also belongs to an ethnic group which stresses achievement values is far more likely to have a high value score than an individual with low status and membership in a group in which achievement is not emphasized. Neither variable is sufficient to predict an individual's score; and for some groups social class seems to be the more significant factor, for others ethnicity appears to play the greater role. Thus, for Jews and Negroes the mean scores remain relatively high for each social class; in fact, Class V Jews and Negroes have larger mean scores than many French-Canadians and Italians of higher social status.

*Aspiration Levels.* Achievement motivation and values influence social mobility by affecting the individual's need to excel and his willingness to plan and work hard. But they do not determine the areas in which such excellence and effort take place. Achievement motivation and values can be expressed, as they often are, through many kinds of behavior that are not conducive to social mobility in our society, for example, deviant, recreational, or religious behavior. Unless the individual aims for high vocational goals and prepares himself appropriately, his achievement motivation and values will not pull him up the social ladder. Increasingly, lengthy formal education, often including college and post-graduate study, is needed for movement into prestigeful and lucrative jobs. An educational aspiration level which precludes college training may seriously affect the individual's chances for social mobility.

Their cultures, even before the arrival of the ethnic groups in the Northeast, were markedly different in orientation towards education.[25] The Protestants' stress upon formal education, if only as a means of furthering one's career, is well known. Traditionally, Jews have placed a very high value on educational and intellectual attainment; learning in the *shtetl* society gave the individual prestige, authority, a chance for a better marriage. Contrariwise, for Southern Italians, school was an upper class institution, not an avenue for social advancement for their children, booklearning was remote from everyday experience, and intellectualism often regarded with distrust. French-Canadians, although not hostile to education and learning, were disinclined to educate their sons beyond the elementary level. Daughters needed more education as preparation for jobs in the event they did not marry, but sons were destined to be farmers or factory workers, in the parents' view, with the exception at times of one son who would be encouraged to become a priest. Greeks — generally no better educated than Italians or French-Canadians — on the whole were much more favorably disposed towards learning, in large part because of their intense nationalistic identification with the cultural glories of ancient Greece.[26] This identification was strengthened by the relatively hostile reception Greeks met on their arrival in this country, and is in part responsible for the rapid development of private schools supported by the Greek community and devoted to the teaching of Greek culture — an interesting parallel to the Hebrew School among American Jews. Finally, Negroes, who might be expected to share the prevalent American emphasis upon education, face the painfully apparent fact that positions open to educated Negroes are scarce. This means that most Negroes, in all likelihood, do not consider high educational aspirations realistic. And the heavy drop-out in high school suggests that the curtailment of educational aspirations begins very early.

To test whether and to what degree these differences between groups persist, the mothers were asked: "How far do you *intend* for your son to go to school?" It was hoped that the term *intend* would structure the question so that the reply would indicate, not merely a mother's pious wish, but also an expression of will to do something about her son's schooling. The data show that 96 per cent of the Jewish, 88 per cent of the Protestant, 85 per cent of the Greek, 83 per cent of the Negro (much higher than was anticipated), 64 per cent of the Italian, and 56 per cent of the French-Canadian mothers said that they expected their sons to go to college. The aspirations of Jews, Protestants, Greeks, and Negroes are not significantly different from one another, but they are significantly higher than the aspirations of Italians and French-Canadians.

Social class, once more, is significantly related to educational aspiration. When class is controlled the differences between ethnic groups are diminished — particularly at the Class I-II-III levels — but they are not erased: Jews, Protestants, Greeks, and Negroes tend to have aspirations similar to one another and higher than those of Italians and French-Canadians for each social class. The differences are greatest at the lower class levels: at Class V, 85 per cent of the Protestants, 80 per cent of the Jews, and 78 per cent of the Negroes intend for their sons to go to college as compared with 63 per cent of the Greeks, 50 per cent of the Italians, and 29 per cent of the French-Canadians.

The individual, to be socially mobile, must aspire to the occupations which society esteems and rewards highly. An individual, strongly motivated to excel and willing to plan and work hard, who sets his heart on being the best barber will probably be less vertically mobile than an equally endowed person who aspires to become the best surgeon. Moreover, the individual who aspires to a high status occupation is likely to expend more energy in competitive striving — and in so doing improve his chances for social mobility — than someone whose occupational choice demands relatively little from him.

Since many of the boys in this study were too young to appraise occupations realistically, we sought to obtain a measure of ethnic group vocational aspiration by questioning the mothers about their aspirations for their sons, once again assuming that they would tend to communicate their views of status levels and their expectations to their sons. Ten occupations were chosen which can be ranked by social status; seven of our ten occupations (marked below by asterisks) were selected from the N.O.R.C. ranking.[27] The occupations, originally presented in alphabetical order, are given here in the order of status: Lawyer*, Druggist, Jewelry Store Owner, Machinist*, Bank Teller, Insurance Agent*, Bookkeeper*, Mail Carrier*, Department Store Salesman*, and Bus Driver*. The mothers were asked: "If things worked out so that your son were in the following occupations, would you be satisfied or dissatisfied?" To obtain aspiration scores for each mother, her responses were treated in three ways:

1. The number of times the mother answered "satisfied" to the ten occupations was summed to give a single score. In effect this meant giving each occupation a weight of one. Since the subject must inevitably select lower status occupations as she increases her number of choices, the higher the summed score, the lower the aspiration level. The basic limitation of this method is that it is impossible to know from the summed score whether the occupations chosen are of low or high status.

2. To correct for this, a second index was derived by assigning weights to the seven occupations taken from the N.O.R.C. study according to their position in the rank order. Thus the highest status position, lawyer, was given a rank weight of 1.0 and the lowest a weight of 6.5 (store salesman and bus driver were tied for last place). Here again, the higher the score, the lower the aspiration level.

3. A third method of weighting the occupations was devised by taking the percentage of the entire sample of mothers who said that they would be satisfied with a particular occupation, and using the reciprocal of each percentage as the weight for that occupation. (The reciprocal was first multiplied by one thousand to eliminate decimals.) The mothers ranked the occupations somewhat differently than the N.O.R.C. ranking (assigning a higher status to bookkeeper and insurance agent and lower status to machinist and mail carrier). The assumption here is that the higher the percentage who answered "satisfied," the higher the status of the occupation. A score for each mother was obtained by summing the reciprocal weights for each occupation chosen. With this method, the highest status occupation is lawyer (score of 11.0), the lowest bus driver (48.0). All ten occupations were used in this index. The higher the subject's score, the lower her aspiration level.

Although these indexes differ somewhat, they provide very similar data on ethnic group vocational aspirations. Table 4 shows the same rank ordering of groups for all three indexes, in descending order as follows: Jews, Greeks, Protestants, Italians, French-Canadians, and

TABLE 4. MEAN SCORES AND RANK POSITION OF SIX
ETHNIC GROUPS USING THREE INDEXES
OF VOCATIONAL ASPIRATION *

| | Index of Vocational Aspiration | | | |
|---|---|---|---|---|
| Ethnicity | Number Satisfied | Rank Weight | Reciprocal Weight | N |
| French-Canadian | 6.60 (5) | 14.43 (5) | 119.90 (5) | 62 |
| Italian | 5.96 (4) | 12.66 (4) | 104.55 (4) | 74 |
| Greek | 4.70 (2) | 7.78 (2) | 73.51 (2) | 47 |
| Jew | 3.51 (1) | 6.02 (1) | 59.48 (1) | 57 |
| Negro | 6.95 (6) | 16.18 (6) | 138.74 (6) | 65 |
| Protestant | 5.28 (3) | 10.12 (3) | 88.19 (3) | 122 |

* Rank positions are shown by figures in parentheses.

Negroes. A series of "t" tests of differences between group mean
scores revealed differences and similarities much like those found for
achievement motivation. Thus the Jews, Greeks, and Protestants
show significantly higher mean scores (that is, they tend to be satisfied with fewer occupations and indicate satisfaction with only the
higher status positions) than the Roman Catholic Italians and French-
Canadians. The mean score for Jews is significantly higher than the
scores for Protestants and Greeks, but there are no significant differences between Greeks and Protestants, or between Italians and French-
Canadians. The mean score for Negroes is significantly lower than the
scores for all other groups except French-Canadians. In examining
the aspirations of Negroes it should be remembered that most of these
occupations are considered highly desirable by many Negroes, given
their severely limited occupational opportunities, so that their aspiration level may appear low only by "white" standards. There are, however, these problems: are the Negro mothers (83 per cent) in earnest
in saying that they intend for their sons to go to college? And, if so,
how is this to be reconciled with their low vocational aspirations?

Social class, too, is significantly and directly related to vocational
aspiration — a familiar finding — but it is not as significant as ethnicity. Analysis of variance of data for each of the three indexes reveals that ethnicity accounts for more of the variance than social class.
For example, when the number of occupations with which the mother
would be satisfied for her son is used as an index of vocational aspiration, the F ratio for ethnicity is 12.41 as compared with a ratio of 9.92

for social class. The same pattern holds for data derived from the other two indexes. Although ethnicity and class interact, each contributing to the differences between groups, the effects of class are more apparent at the middle class (Classes I-II-III) than at the working and lower class (Classes IV-V) levels.

As the question was worded in this study, in one sense it is misleading to speak of the "height" of vocational aspirations. For all groups have "high" aspirations in that most mothers are content to have their sons achieve a high status. The basic difference between groups is in the "floor," so to speak, which they place on their aspirations. For example, at least 80 per cent of the mothers of each ethnic group said that they would be satisfied to have their sons be lawyers, but only two per cent of the Greeks and seven per cent of the Jews were content to have their sons become bus drivers, as compared with 26 per cent of the French-Canadians and 43 per cent of the Negroes. Again, 12 per cent of the Jewish, 22 per cent of the Protestant, and 29 per cent of the Greek mothers said that they would be satisfied to have their sons become department store salesmen, as compared with 48 per cent of the Italians, 51 per cent of the Negro, and 52 per cent of the French-Canadian mothers.

SUMMARY

This paper examines differences in motivation, values, and aspirations of six racial and ethnic groups which may explain in part their dissimilar social mobility rates. Analysis of ethnographic and attitudinal and personality data suggests that these groups differed, and to some extent still differ, in their orientation toward achievement. The data show that the groups place different emphases upon independence and achievement training in the rearing of children. As a consequence, achievement motivation is more characteristic of Greeks, Jews, and white Protestants than of Italians, French-Canadians, and Negroes. The data also indicate that Jews, Greeks, and Protestants are more likely to possess achievement values and higher educational and vocational aspirations than Italians and French-Canadians. The values and educational aspirations of the Negroes are higher than expected, being comparable to those of Jews, Greeks, and white Protestants, and higher than those of the Italians and French-Canadians. Vocational aspirations of Negroes, however, are the lowest of any group in the sample. Social class and ethnicity interact in influencing motivation, values, and aspirations; neither can predict an individual's score. Ethnic differences persist when social class is controlled, but some of the differences between ethnic groups in motivation, values, and aspirations are probably also a function of their class composition.

## REFERENCES

1. Cf. W. L. Warner and L. Srole, *The Social Systems of American Ethnic Groups*, New Haven: Yale University Press, 1945; F. L. Strodtbeck, "Jewish and Italian Immigration and Subsequent Status Mobility," in D. McClelland, A. Baldwin, U. Bronfenbrenner and F. Strodtbeck, *Talent and Society*, Princeton: Van Nostrand, 1958; M. Davie, *World Migration*, New York: Macmillan, 1936.

2. Cf. N. Glazer, "The American Jew and the Attainment of Middle-Class Rank: Some Trends and Explanations," in M. Sklare, editor, *The Jews: Social Patterns of an American Group*, Glencoe, Ill.: Free Press, 1958; W. L. Warner and L. Srole, *op. cit.*; T. Burgess, *Greeks in America*, Boston: Sherman, French, 1913; T. Saloutos, "The Greeks in the U. S.," *The South Atlantic Quarterly*, 4 (January, 1945), pp. 69–82; T. Kalijarvi, "French-Canadians in the United States," *Annals, American Academy of Political and Social Science* (September, 1942); G. Myrdal, *An American Dilemma*, New York: Harper, 1944.

3. B. C. Rosen, "The Achievement Syndrome: A Psychocultural Dimension of Social Stratification," *The American Sociological Review*, 21 (April, 1956), pp. 203–211.

4. The interviewers were trained by the writer; efforts were made to control for interviewer biases. It should be remembered that the sample is not random at any point in the selection process. Hence, the reader is cautioned to regard the data presented here as tentative and suggestive.

5. A. B. Hollingshead and F. C. Redlich, "Social Stratification and Psychiatric Disorders," *American Sociological Review*, 18 (April, 1953), pp. 163–169.

6. D. C. McClelland, J. Atkinson, R. Clark, and E. Lowell, *The Achievement Motive*, New York: Appleton-Century-Crofts, 1953.

7. M. Winterbottom, "The Relation of Need for Achievement to Learning Experiences in Independence and Mastery," in J. Atkinson, editor, *Motives in Fantasy, Action and Society*, Princeton: Van Nostrand, 1958; B. C. Rosen, "The Psychosocial Origins of Achievement Motivation," mimeographed progress report to the National Institute of Mental Health, 1957.

8. D. C. McClelland, "Some Social Consequences of Achievement Motivation," in M. R. Jones, editor, *Nebraska Symposium on Motivation, 1955,* Lincoln: University of Nebraska Press, 1955.

9. D. C. McClelland, A. Rindlisbacher, and R. C. deCharms, "Religious and Other Sources of Parental Attitudes Towards Independence Training," in D. C. McClelland, editor, *Studies in Motivation,* New York; Appleton-Century-Crofts, 1955.

10. Winterbottom, *op. cit.*

11. M. Zyborowski and E. Herzog, *Life Is With People,* New York: International University Press, 1952.

12. P. H. Williams, *South Italian Folkways in Europe and America,* New Haven: Yale University Press, 1938; H. Miner, *St. Dennis: A French-Canadian Parish,* Chicago: University of Chicago Press, 1939.

13. It does not necessarily follow that the impact of American culture has reduced the differences between groups. An argument can be made that for some groups life in America has accentuated differences by allowing certain characteristics of the groups to develop. We have in mind particularly the Greeks and Jews whose need to excel could find little avenue for expression through status striving in Europe.

14. Rosen, "The Achievement Syndrome," *op. cit.,* pp. 208–210.

15. The values, but not the items which index them, represent a modification of Kluckhohn's schema. See, F. Kluckhohn, "Dominant and Substitute Profiles of Cultural Orientations," *Social Forces,* 28 (May, 1950), pp. 376–393.

16. For the most part, the value orientations examined in this study, their description, and the items used to index them, are identical with those which appear in Rosen, "The Achievement Syndrome," *op. cit.*

17. For a history of the development of the liberal economic ethic and its manifestation on the American scene, see J. H. Randall, *The Making of the Modern Mind,* Boston: Houghton Mifflin, 1926; J. K. Galbraith, *The Affluent Society,* Boston: Houghton Mifflin, 1958.

18. Zyborowski and Herzog, *op. cit.;* B. C. Rosen, "Cultural Factors in Achievement," mimeographed, 1952.

19. Quoted in Saloutos, *op. cit.,* p. 71. The writer is indebted to J. Gregoropoulos, a native of Athens, for many helpful comments on European and American Greek communities.

20. Miner, *op. cit.* See also Williams, *op. cit.*

21. We recognize that to infer a group's values from its life-situation and then to use these values to explain an aspect of that situation is to reason circularly. However, the temporal sequence between values and mobility has a chicken-egg quality which is difficult to avoid because values and

life-situation interact. To some extent, knowledge of ethnic cultures prior to their arrival in the United States helps to establish the priority of values to mobility. In the case of the Negroes, however, relatively little is known about their several cultures before their transportation to this country.

22. E. F. Frazier, *The Negro Family in the United States*, Chicago: University of Chicago Press, 1939; see also Frazier's *The Negro in the United States*, New York: Macmillan, 1957, especially Chapters 13 and 24.

23. Of course, if Whyte is correct about the growth of the organization man and the importance of the "social ethic," agreement with this statement may indicate an asset rather than a handicap to social mobility. See W. H. Whyte, Jr., *The Organization Man*, New York: Simon and Schuster, 1957.

24. The relatively high value score for Negroes supports our contention that achievement motivation and achievement values are genuinely different components of the achievement syndrome. It will be remembered that the Negroes had the lowest mean motivation score. If achievement motivation and values are conceptually and empirically identical, there should be no difference between the two sets of scores.

25. For a comparison of ethnic group education and vocational aspirations, see R. M. Williams, Jr., *American Society*, New York: Knopf, 1951, Chapter 8; F. J. Woods, *Cultural Values of American Ethnic Groups*, New York: Harper, 1956, Chapters 5 and 7.

26. Attempts by Mussolini to create a similar bond between his people and ancient Rome, or even the more recent Renaissance, were unsuccessful. French-Canadians for the most part have long refused to be impressed by the "secular" achievement of European anti-clerical French society.

27. National Opinion Research Center, "Jobs and Occupations: A Popular Evaluation," *Opinion News*, 9 (September 1, 1947). We substituted store salesman for store clerk and bus driver for streetcar motorman. The position of the three occupations which did not appear in the N.O.R.C. survey are ranked according to their similarity to occupations in the survey.

# ARE EDUCATIONAL NORMS AND GOALS OF CONFORMING, TRUANT AND DELINQUENT ADOLESCENTS INFLUENCED BY GROUP POSITION IN AMERICAN SOCIETY?

ALBERT J. REISS, JR.
A. LEWIS RHODES

This paper describes the educational achievement goals and the value placed on schooling by an adolescent population, considers their aspirations in relation to these goals, and examines differences among conforming, truant and delinquent adolescents in relation to these goals. The question then examined is, are these relationships independent of the adolescent's group position in society as represented by his race, sex, I.Q., socio-economic status and age?

Most sociological theories of deviant behavior emphasize that the major value goals in American Society are those of ascetic Protestantism. This ethic is most apparent in the middle class stratum of American Society, but it permeates all of our major institutions such as our schools, the work-place and other "success-oriented" institutions. In respect to the schools, it is said that the dominant orientation is to strive for higher education and to achieve scholastically. Education is valued both for itself, and for its means to other ends or goals in society.

The working class boy, it is maintained, often is exposed to situations in which achievement is measured by the dominant middle class norms but his ability to compete successfully is limited by his working class origins. Cohen, for example, reasons that the working class child is often denied *status* in conventional society because of his inability to compete successfully in the larger status system and the institu-

Reprinted from the *Journal of Negro Education* (Summer 1959, pp. 252-267) by permission of the publisher and the authors.

The research reported herein was performed pursuant to a contract with the United States Office of Education, Department of Health, Education, and Welfare.

tional organizations generated by it. This creates a reality adjustment for him and places him in the market for a solution.[1] In general, Cohen maintains there are three possible solutions to this status problem: the *college boy solution* where the working class boy accepts the middle-class status system and conforms to the expectations of that system, the *stable-corner boy solution* which offers substitute goals to those of the middle-class status system — substitutes which make class achievements improbable (for example, truancy is valued as an end in itself),[2] and the *subcultural delinquent solution* which represents the repudiation of middle class standards and the adoption of its antithesis.[3]

At a more general level of theory, Merton, Cloward and others have suggested that deviant behavior results from the degree of disjuncture between values and the opportunities provided by social positions in society.[4]

We are not directly examining these hypothetical approaches to the problem of goal orientation in our society and their relation to deviant behavior in this paper, although we plan to do so later. Here we are concerned with a number of related and important questions on which these approaches rest. We shall indicate our interest by a series of questions: (1) In general, what are the cultural expectations or goals with respect to going to school and educational achievement in American society? (2) Do truants and delinquents perceive the dominant norms relating to "going to school" and "getting an education" in about the same way as conforming adolescents in their group position? (3) Are truants and delinquents more likely than conforming adolescents to show constricted aspiration levels and to perceive their parents as holding a similar constricted view? (4) Are truants and delinquents more likely than conforming adolescents to want to quit school in response to the coercive pressures of the compulsory school attendance norms *or* because they wish to implement alternative conforming goals in the society? Each of these relationships is investigated to see whether it is independent of the adolescent's group position in society as represented by his race, sex, I.Q., socio-economic status and age.

STUDY DESIGN

The data for the study were gathered from pupils in grades 7 through 12 in public, private and parochial schools of the Nashville,

Tennessee Standard Metropolitan Area. We have some information from a questionnaire survey on 21,720 such boys and girls of whom 15 per cent are Negroes in segregated schools. The data were gathered in 58 separate school administrations, 17 of which were either city public, parochial or private schools and 41 of which were county public schools. We estimate that these schools provide us with about four-fifths of the population of this age group.

We undoubtedly were more successful in getting all conformers than we were deviant boys and girls since deviants were more likely to be absent when questionnaires were administered, more likely to have dropped out of school or to be inaccessible for other reasons. These provide obvious limitations to the study — limitations, however, which may be more apparent than real limitations when the study population is large. In any event, we are not so much interested in precise estimates of deviant behavior or of population norms as we are in examining specific relationships under the model of partial association. Under these conditions our failures are perhaps less restricting than they might otherwise be.

We have a number of measures for conforming and deviant behavior. For purposes of economy of presentation we limit the discussion of deviant behavior in this paper to official and unofficial cases known to the Davidson County Juvenile Court and to cases of truancy known to the attendance divisions of the respective city and county school systems. All nontruants and nondelinquents are residual groups of conforming adolescents.

The legal norms of American Society generally require that boys and girls in cities attend school until they are 16 or 17 years of age. Tennessee law requires compulsory school attendance, at least on a part time basis, until age 17. Enforcement of this law creates a special class of deviants — truants, persons who fail to attend school in compliance with the norm. Not all failures to comply with the law, acts of truancy, lead to a definition of the person who deviates as a truant. There are at least four classes of truants which are recognized informally by the attendance officers in the Nashville and Davidson County School systems. There is the child who persistently violates the compulsory school attendance law so that legal action is taken to file an habitual truant petition with the Davidson County Juvenile Court (Habitual Truant). There is the child for whom persistent truancy is a part of a delinquency pattern so that truancy is not perceived as the principal problem (Delinquent Truant). Truancy may also manifest itself in the form of sporadic periods of absence from school; often this form of truancy is a consequence of the parent's failure to enforce the norm (Sporadic Truancy). Finally some truancy occurs as patterned evasion either on particular days designated for skipping school or in response to occasional peer or adult pressures. These acts of truancy, however, do not lead to quasi-official definitions of the acts as a persistent problem, and therefore of the violator as a "truant." For most of our detailed analysis it is necessary to treat the first three classes as a single class of truants, although in some cases we summarize information for the separate subgroups. The residual group of nontruants, including adolescents who violate other norms of society and are officially defined as delinquent, are treated as conformers in comparisons involving truants. They conform to the norm of compulsory school attendance even though they violate other norms of the society.

The general approach to analysis followed in this paper is to examine zero order relationships under the model of partial association. We have five measures of normative evaluation and aspiration which we will consider: a general population norm of how much education most people ought to get in our society, adolescents' evaluations of how important schooling is to them, their perceptions of mother's expectations and their own expectations as to how far they ought to go in school, and the desire to quit school as measured by a quit school scale. We also examine whether the adolescent's desire to quit school is related to a feeling of compulsion to attend or to an alternative conforming goal of wanting to go to work. These seven relationships are presented in Table 1 as zero order relationships. We then examine each of these for variation by race, sex, I.Q., socioeconomic status and in some cases age, with two categories for race, sex, and socio-economic status and three for I.Q.[5] Table 1 also presents the zero order relationship for each attribute of group position with the seven educational norms and goals. The relation of the norms and goals to conforming, delinquent and truant behavior then is examined under the model of partial association. Each of the four factors, race, sex, I.Q., and socio-economic status (and in some cases, a fifth, age), is successively introduced as a test factor so that we have first, second, third and fourth order partials for all relationships. The one-tailed sign test is employed with respect to the series of comparisons created by higher order partialing. Relationships are only reported for sign distributions which are at the .05 confidence level. Let us now turn to examine these relationships.

Table I  *Deviant Behavior and Group Position Indicators by Educational Norms and Goals*

| Educational norms and goals | Juv. Court % Rec. | Juv. Court % No Rec. | Truancy % Rec. | Truancy % No Rec. | Race % White | Race % Negro | Sex % Males | Sex % Females | I.Q. % Low | I.Q. % Middle | I.Q. % High | Socioeconomic % Blue Collar | Socioeconomic % White Collar | Per cent Total Population |
|---|---|---|---|---|---|---|---|---|---|---|---|---|---|---|
| **Norm: people ought to:** | | | | | | | | | | | | | | |
| go to college | 42 | 46 | 35 | 46 | 44 | 52 | 52 | 41 | 40 | 46 | 59 | 42 | 57 | 45 |
| finish h. s., or less | 58 | 54 | 65 | 54 | 56 | 48 | 48 | 59 | 60 | 54 | 41 | 58 | 43 | 55 |
| Total cases (city) | 354 | 6216 | 332 | 7570 | 4816 | 1754 | 3254 | 3316 | 1081 | 3455 | 2034 | 1869 | 4701 | 7902 |
| **Value: School most impt.:** | | | | | | | | | | | | | | |
| Agree | 60 | 70 | — | — | 67 | 88 | 67 | 73 | 76 | 70 | 64 | 71 | 67 | 70 |
| Disagree | 40 | 30 | — | — | 33 | 12 | 33 | 27 | 24 | 30 | 36 | 29 | 33 | 30 |
| *Total (city & county) | 607 | 17562 | 469 | 17752 | 15704 | 2517 | 8939 | 9282 | 3424 | 7831 | 3960 | 6820 | 11401 | 18221 |
| **Aspiration of Mother:** | | | | | | | | | | | | | | |
| go to college | 23 | 49 | 16 | 48 | 48 | 42 | 52 | 44 | 24 | 43 | 73 | 35 | 69 | 48 |
| finish high school | 77 | 51 | 84 | 52 | 52 | 58 | 48 | 56 | 76 | 57 | 27 | 65 | 31 | 52 |
| **Subject's Aspiration:** | | | | | | | | | | | | | | |
| go to college | 42 | 67 | 28 | 69 | 67 | 62 | 74 | 62 | 44 | 63 | 82 | 53 | 81 | 67 |
| finish high school | 58 | 33 | 72 | 31 | 33 | 38 | 26 | 38 | 56 | 37 | 18 | 47 | 19 | 33 |
| Total (county only) | 142 | 7798 | 155 | 10547 | 7827 | 293 | 3781 | 4339 | 1190 | 4175 | 2756 | 4415 | 3705 | 8120 |
| **Quit School Scale:** | | | | | | | | | | | | | | |
| Want to quit most | 57 | 33 | 61 | 33 | 34 | 30 | 42 | 26 | 40 | 34 | 25 | 36 | 29 | 34 |
| Want to quit least | 43 | 67 | 39 | 67 | 66 | 70 | 58 | 74 | 60 | 66 | 75 | 64 | 71 | 66 |
| **Quit school, forced to go:** | | | | | | | | | | | | | | |
| Agree | 23 | 8 | 28 | 8 | 9 | 7 | 11 | 6 | 12 | 8 | 4 | 10 | 5 | 9 |
| Disagree | 77 | 92 | 72 | 92 | 91 | 93 | 89 | 94 | 88 | 92 | 96 | 90 | 95 | 91 |
| **Quit school, go to work:** | | | | | | | | | | | | | | |
| Agree | 42 | 17 | 48 | 17 | 18 | 17 | 22 | 14 | 29 | 17 | 8 | 22 | 11 | 18 |
| Disagree | 58 | 83 | 52 | 83 | 82 | 83 | 78 | 86 | 71 | 83 | 92 | 78 | 89 | 82 |

*The city and county total is for all groups unless reported for city only or county only.

158

FINDINGS

How do adolescents perceive the cultural expectations with respect to educational achievement in our society? Our indicator here is the statement "Most people ought to go to college, or finish high school, or go to high school until 16 years old, or finish grade school, or get some schooling." It should be noted that the item is worded so as to try to make it independent of the adolescent's own norm or that of his membership or reference groups by generalizing it to "most people."

Our adolescents split roughly fifty-fifty at the finish high school-ought to go to college cutting point. The large majority of subjects perceive the norm as either to finish high school or go to college. Negroes, males, white-collars and high I.Q. adolescents are more likely to see the norm as requiring that one go to college than are their counterparts. The differences are particularly substantial for I.Q. and socio-economic status comparisons. From these zero order relationships we would predict that blue-collar, white girls with low I.Q.'s would be least likely to see the norm as requiring one to have some college education, and this is in fact the case. Only one of every four girls in this sub-group sees the norm as requiring that one get some college education, a figure which incidentally is about the level of education achieved by persons 25 to 29 years old in the U.S. population in 1950. We also would predict that white-collar Negro boys with high I.Q.'s would be most likely to perceive the norm as that of a college education. We fail to confirm this prediction because we find that white-collar Negro girls with high I.Q.'s require a somewhat higher level of education for the population than this subgroup of Negro boys who require about as much education as do the white-collar, high I.Q. white boys. Interestingly enough, these white-collar, high I.Q. groups perceive the norm as being that where three out of every four persons ought to go to college. Looked at in terms of group theory, we find that the perception of the norm varies considerably with one's position in race, sex and socioeconomic status groups, and perhaps one's perception of being a "bright" student.

There is only a very small difference between our juvenile court deviants and conformers in their perception of the general norm of how much education most people ought to get in our society. Given our large number of cases, however, this small difference of 5 per cent (in which delinquents have somewhat lower expectations about educational goals in the society) is statistically significant. Let us, therefore, see whether or not the introduction of our test factors will show that this difference holds even though the difference between the two aggregates is small. For the race, sex, I.Q. subgroup comparisons, the predicted relationship holds in all but two of the 11 groups in which it can be tested. Using the sign test we cannot reject the null hypothesis at this third order of partial analysis. When we control on socio-economic status as well as race, sex, and I.Q., however, we conclude that the original relationship is not independent.

There is a somewhat larger difference between our truants and conformers in their perception of the general norm of how much education most people ought to get in American society. Only 35 per cent of the truants as compared with 46 per cent of the conformers perceive the general norm as requiring one to get some college education. This relationship does not hold for Negroes, since Negro truants are as likely as Negro nontruants to require a college education. Negroes of course are more likely to require a course in education than are whites in our population. The relationship is independent of sex but not I.Q. and socioeconomic status for whites.

We are inclined to conclude that delinquents and truants are really quite similar to conformers in their perception of the general norm of how much education a person ought to get in American Society. There is, on the whole, much greater variation in the perception of this norm by race, sex, I.Q. and socioeconomic status than there is for the conforming-deviant group comparisons.

Are deviants as likely as conformers to place a high value on schooling? We asked our students a six-choice, Likert type, agree-disagree question: "Schooling is the most important thing in life for me." This statement, we felt, gets at the general question of how important the school and the major values associated with *going to school* are to the subject. It requires a specific evaluation of the primacy of schooling with respect to other values of the subject. We find that 70 per cent of our subjects agreed with this statement, although they differ in intensity: 19 per cent strongly agreed with it, 26 per cent agreed with it, and 25 per cent agreed a little with it. Disregarding intensity differences we find that Negroes agreed with this item by roughly 20 per cent more than did whites. In fact, they were more likely to strongly agree with it. We also find that girls, low I.Q. subjects and blue-collars were more likely to place a high value on schooling.

Comparing the adolescent's perceptions of how much education

most people ought to get with the exclusive value placed on schooling,
we find some very important differences for our sub-groups. These can
be summarized briefly.

1. Negroes require a somewhat higher level of educational attainment
for the general population and place a substantially greater value on schooling than do whites.

2. Girls place greater emphasis on the exclusive value of schooling than
do boys, even though boys require higher attainment levels for the general population.

3. Blue collars value schooling more than do white collars even though
white collars perceive that most people ought to go farther in school.

4. Low I.Q. boys and girls feel that schooling is the most important
thing in life to them more often than do high I.Q. boys and girls, but
their perception of how far people ought to go in school is more restricted.

We, of course, would predict on the basis of these zero order relationships that low I.Q., blue-collar, Negro females would value schooling the most. They do, for 92 per cent of the 489 girls in this group
agree with the statement. Correlatively, we would expect that high
I.Q., white-collar, white boys would value it least and in fact this is
the case — only 61 per cent of the 1108 boys in this subgroup agree
with this statement. There are substantial differences in intensity
as well. While 48 per cent of the low I.Q., blue-collar, Negro girls
strongly agree with the statement, only 10 per cent of the high I.Q.,
white-collar, white boys strongly agree with it. And 77 percent of
the former as compared with 34 per cent of the latter strongly agree
or agree with the statement. High I.Q., white-collar, white boys then
are most likely to either agree just a little with the statement or to
disagree with it. It is an anomaly of our society that the adolescent
subgroup which is most likely to finish college places the lowest
*exclusive* value on schooling, while that adolescent sub-group which
is least likely to go to college places the greatest exclusive value on
it. Lest one regard this finding as altogether trivial since it explores
schooling as the most important value in life, one might recall that
many college teachers complain that the white-collar boy in their
classes, often a "bright" student, is poorly motivated, content to be
a "Gentleman's 'C'" student, and so on. They may in fact, express a
preference for teaching the boy from working class origins, praising
him for his motivation to learn.

Now how should we account for these seemingly incongruent findings, remembering that one can value schooling at any aspiration or attainment level? We would reason somewhat as follows:

1. Negroes should value schooling more than whites since schooling is the only major avenue of social mobility open to Negroes in our society, particularly southern Negroes as are our subjects. Furthermore, the school is increasingly perceived as an equality institution by Negroes.

2. Similarly, it is well known that girls in our society are more achievement oriented in school, that teachers consider them to be better motivated as students, and that adolescent boys are less likely to identify with women teachers than are girls. These and other related factors may account for the fact that girls consider it a more important value than boys on the average.

3. The surprise to us is that blue-collar and low I.Q. adolescents are more likely to consider schooling as the most important thing to them than are white-collar and high I.Q. adolescents. From other data in the study, we know that white collars are less likely to endorse the statement: "The best way to get ahead in life is to get a good education," and that they are likely to choose alternative statements about the best way to get ahead in life, such as "The best way to get ahead in life is to work hard" or, "The best way to get ahead in life is to have a pleasing personality." We suspect middle class children are more likely to take a college education for granted — it is then that the other values such as working hard and having a pleasing personality are most important. Lower class children must put first things first and an education cannot be taken for granted. Hence schooling may be the most important thing in life for them on the average.

4. Exactly why low I.Q. boys and girls should find schooling the most important thing in life for them is less easy to explain. Since the relationship was unexpected, we sought an *ex post facto* explanation. But how to choose among them: I.Q. of course is class related, but only some and not all of the relationship is explained on this basis in our study. I.Q. appears to exert an important and independent influence on valuing schooling as the *most important thing in life*. It might be suggested that the low I.Q. boy and girl face status inequality both in and out of school. Given this status inequality, the school perhaps is the more democratic of the inequality situations in which he participates. Low I.Q. adolescents perhaps are, after all, given more attention — even if in a special education course — in the school than they are accorded by their family or peers who often reject them. If this is the case, and we do not know that it is, it might account for some of the greater value they place on schooling.

Turning to the relationship of the exclusive value placed on schooling with deviant behavior, we find a small but statistically significant difference between the value placed on schooling and delinquent behavior. Delinquents place less value on schooling. The relationship holds for both race groups, within race-sex groups and the third order partial for race, sex and I.Q. But the relationship is clearly not independent of socio-economic status since it disappears for all but the white male subgroup. Nonetheless, this finding is of some importance. White male delinquents in our society probably have a greater propensity to reject the school as a controlling organization than do delinquents in the other subgroups. Yet, the white delinquent boy from white-collar origins is *more* likely to disagree that schooling is the most important thing in life for him than is the white delinquent from blue-collar origins.

If we think of the social system as controlling individuals through the internalization of the expectations of others or by bringing self expectations in conformity with the expectations of significant others, we would expect that subject's behavior would be related to these expectations. One measure of the expectation of significant others we used is the subjects' perceptions of how far mother and father expected they should go in school. We report here only the data for subject's mother. There of course is an extremely high correlation between the perceived expectations of mother and father.

We would not expect that all parents would have clearly formed goals for their children and had communicated these goals to them. Nor would we expect that even though they had such goals that their children would clearly perceive them as expectations. We would for these reasons expect that there might be variation among our subjects by race, sex, I.Q., and socio-economic status in the degree to which they know the specific educational goal their mother wishes they would reach. Since the opportunity to obtain a college education is more restricted for Negroes than whites we would expect that fewer Negroes than whites would report that their mother expected them to reach a specific educational goal. And that is in fact the case. One-third of all Negroes as contrasted with 15 per cent of all whites report that they did not know their mothers' educational expectations. This relationship appears to hold independent of the sex, I.Q. and socio-economic status level of subjects. We also would expect that parents of high I.Q. subjects would be more likely to project definite educational goals for their children and this is in fact the case; while 30 per cent of all low I.Q. subjects do not know their mother's expectations, this is true for only 8 per cent of high I.Q. subjects. Boys are less likely than girls and blue-collar subjects less likely than white-collar subjects to know their mothers' educational goals for them, but these differences are much smaller than those by race and I.Q. of subject. Interestingly enough truants and delinquents are no less likely than conformers to know their mother's expectations about educational achievement. Our discussion below about the relation of perception of mothers' educational aspirations to conforming-deviant class of subject is based only on those cases where subjects report they perceive a definite educational goal for their mother.

We shall begin by noting that about one-half (49 per cent) of the subjects perceived their mothers as wanting them to go to college — an expectation one would hardly anticipate being fulfilled even given large structural chances in opportunity in American society. This expectation was perceived as higher in white (49%) than Negro (42%), boys (52%) than girls (44%), white-collar (69%), than blue-collar (35%) and high I.Q. (73%) than low I.Q. (24%) subjects. On the basis of these zero order relationships, we would predict that most white-collar white boys with high I.Q.'s would perceive their mothers' expectations to be that of a college education. And this is the case — 89 per cent of all white-collar, white boys with high I.Q.'s say their mothers want them to go to college. The only subgroups with expectation levels close to this are those of white-collar Negro high I.Q. boys and girls where 72 and 67 per cent respectively believe their mothers hold such expectations. On the other hand, we would expect that the perceptions blue-collar Negro girls with low I.Q.'s have of their mothers' educational expectations would be the lowest of that for any subgroup. This is not the case, for race is more important than sex in accounting for relationship. Negro mothers are perceived as holding lower expectations regarding educational achievement than white mothers only by their sons, while the reverse is the case for Negro girls. The perceptions of blue-collar, low I.Q. white girls, therefore, are the lowest: only 13 per cent of these girls perceive their mothers as wanting them to go to college. It also is apparent from our data that white mothers in the lower stratum of American society are less likely than Negro mothers to project high aspirations on to their children if they are low rather than high I.Q.

children. Disregarding the possibility the white and Negro I.Q. groups are not altogether comparable test groups, we suggest that the importance of schooling to the Negro family makes their members more likely than those of the white family to project unrealistic educational goals in the low I.Q. child.

Deviant behavior in the forms of delinquency and truancy bear a substantial relationship to subject's perception of educational expectations. While roughly one-half of the conforming mothers expect their sons to go to college, only 15 per cent of the mothers of truants and 23 per cent of the mothers of juvenile court cases are perceived as holding college expectations. This relationship is independent of race, sex, I.Q. and socio-economic status for both the juvenile court and truancy comparisons. Clearly the mothers of delinquents and truants regardless of the race, sex, I.Q. and socio-economic status of the deviant are less likely to project college expectations on to their children than are mothers of conforming children.

We inquired about subject's educational aspirations. Unfortunately we secured information on subject's aspirations only for the county school segment of our population. This segment has a higher proportion of white-collar and of white subjects than the total sample. We cannot assume therefore that the county proportions represent norms for the entire population. Under these circumstances we shall report only the relative differences between subgroups. Our adolescents were much more likely to report an educational expectation for themselves than they were to report a definite educational expectation being held by their mother. Seventeen per cent of our subjects failed to report a definite educational expectation which they perceived mother as holding for them while only an estimated four per cent of our subjects failed to report an educational goal for themselves.

There is only a small race difference in subject's educational aspirations such that Negroes are somewhat less likely to aspire toward a college education. Boys are more likely than girls to aspire to college, just as their mothers were more likely to have college aspirations for them. We find a substantial socio-economic differential as we did for mother's aspiration — white collars are more likely to want to go to college. And, we find a substantial I.Q. differential as we did for mother's aspiration — high I.Q. subjects are more likely to want to go to college. On the basis of these zero order relationships we would predict that white-collar Negro boys with high I.Q.'s are most likely to want to go to college. This particular subject is a rare occurrence in our county school population. There is only one of them and he wants to go to college. We find however, that our 5 blue-collar, high I.Q. Negro boys all also want to go to college. Among Negro boys, in fact, high I.Q. seems to be a decisive influence on college aspiration. Correlatively we would expect that white, blue-collar, low I.Q. girls would rank lowest in aspiration level, and this is very clearly the case. There is considerable variation then in subject's aspiration by race, sex, I.Q. and socio-economic status so that if we think of these as membership groups, there is considerable variation by subject's membership group.

Juvenile delinquents and truants are somewhat less likely to report a definite educational goal for themselves than are conforming adolescents. The differences are small, however. Roughly eight per cent of the deviant adolescents failed to report a definite goal as contrasted with about four per cent for the conformers in our county school population. Considering only those cases where subjects report a definite educational goal, let us see whether truants and delinquents differ from conformers in the level to which they aspire. Truants and delinquents are much less likely than conformers to aspire to a college education. The difference between truants and conformers is considerably greater in fact than that between delinquents and conformers. Truants have the lowest aspiration level with only one in four of the truants in the county school population aspiring to enter college. This can be contrasted with two of every five delinquents and two of every three conformers in the county school population aspiring to enter college. This substantial relationship is independent of the race, sex, I.Q. and socio-economic status level of the adolescent for both the truant-conformer and delinquent-conformer comparisons. The relationship holds without attenuation in almost all of the subgroup comparisons so that there seems little question that the fairly large relationship between subjects aspiration and deviant behavior is independent of race, sex, I.Q. and socio-economic status.

Are deviants, particularly truants and delinquents, more likely than conformers to want to quit school? Truants, at least, if given the opportunity to carry out the desire to quit school would no longer be defined as deviant with respect to the norm if they quit. For many delinquents and truants the opportunity to quit school makes possible a consideration of alternative conforming goals such as the opportunity to work full time. It therefore seemed desirable to gain some idea of how the desire to quit school was related to conformity. An ordinal scale (Guttman) was developed to assess the desire to quit school. The scale meets the major criteria of scalability for the total population and has been replicated in six independent tests with large populations. A low scale score indicates little desire to quit school and a high scale score a strong desire to quit school. There are four items in the scale providing five scale types. These five scale types were combined into two classes to permit higher order levels of partial analysis. The category including scale types four and five is defined as "desire to quit school" and it contains 33.7 per cent of all cases.

The desire to quit school shows a substantial relationship with sex and I.Q. and somewhat smaller relationships with race and socio-economic status. There are no age differences. White persons, boys, low I.Q. subjects, and blue-collar subjects are more likely to want to quit school. On the basis of these zero order relationships we would predict that low I.Q., blue-collar, white males would be most likely to want to quit school and that they would be most likely to fall into scale types four and five. Fifty-four per cent of boys in this subgroup are in these scale types as compared with 34 per cent of all adolescents. Correlatively, we would predict that high I.Q. white-collar Negro females would be least likely to be in scale types four and five and this is the case as only 8 per cent of this subgroup falls into these scale types.

Delinquents (57%) and truants (61%) are more likely than conforming adolescents (33%) to be in scale types four and five — those most likely to want to quit school. This relationship is independent of race, sex, I.Q. and socio-economic status for both the delinquent-conformer and truant-conformer comparisons. The relationship is somewhat attenuated for Negroes but not whites and it is stronger among females than males. It should be noted that the quit school scale is a poor predictor of either delinquency or truancy since there are many more conforming adolescents who want to quit school than there are delinquent or truant adolescents. Yet it is apparent that delinquents and truants are more likely to want to quit school than are conforming adolescents even when age, race, sex, I.Q. and socio-economic status are taken into account.

Violation of the norm of compulsory school attendance leads to a special class of deviants — the truants. At the same time the act of truancy frequently becomes an element in a more generalized delinquency pattern. Aggression is directed against the school norms as well as other norms in society. Cohen hypothesizes that rejection

of the school is an element in the definition of the delinquent subculture and one would expect these boys to be truants. Cohen and Whyte
also consider truancy as an element in the patterned activity of corner
boys. Violation of the norm of compulsory school attendance suggests,
then, that there is active rebellion against the norm, particularly when
it is part of the corner boy or delinquent subcultural patterns. We
attempted to assess the extent to which rebellion against the norm is
an element in deviant behavior with a simple yes-no choice to the
item "I want to quit school because I am forced to go." Only 28 per
cent of all truants agree with this statement, suggesting that rebellion
against the law, while an element in truancy, is not a major element.
The relationship is even smaller between all delinquents and non-
delinquents; only 23 per cent of all delinquents feel the coercive pressure of the norm as contrasted with 8 per cent for non-delinquents.
We find that the per cent who want to quit school because they feel
the coercive pressure of the norm varies by type of truancy, however.
The delinquent truant is most likely (39 per cent), the habitual truant
(30 per cent) less so, and the sporadic truant (23 per cent) least likely
to want to quit because they feel the coercive pressure of the norm.
Still, if we accept this item as a valid measure of rebellion against the
norm, none of our classes of truants could be said to be primarily in
rebellion against it.

There is only a very small race difference in the per cent who want
to quit school because they feel the coercive pressure of the norm;
whites are somewhat more likely to want to quit. The differences are
to some extent larger for sex, I.Q. and socio-economic status with boys;
low I.Q. and blue-collar subjects more likely to want to quit. There
are no differences by age. On the basis of these zero order relationships we might expect that blue-collar, low I.Q. white boys would be
the most likely to want to quit school because they are forced to go,
although we would not be too confident of confirming the prediction
since the differences are not great. We do find that the 935 low I.Q.
blue-collar white boys are most likely (19.7 per cent) to want to quit
school because they feel the coercive pressure of the norm. Correlatively we would expect that high I.Q., white-collar, Negro girls would
be least likely to want to quit and this is the case; none of the 25
girls in this subgroup wanted to quit. But it also is true that none
of 42 high I.Q., blue-collar, Negro girls wanted to quit because they
felt the coercive pressure of the norm thus suggesting that I.Q. is more
important than socio-economic status for Negro girls. While 8.5 per

cent of all adolescents want to quit school because they feel the pressure of the norm, our range is from none wanting to quit for this reason among high I.Q. Negro girls to 20 per cent for the low I.Q., blue-collar, white boys.

We have noted that truants (28 per cent) and delinquents (23 per cent) are more likely than conformers (8 per cent) to want to quit school because they are forced to attend school. The question arises as to whether the relationship is independent of the race, sex, I.Q. and socio-economic status of adolescents. The norm appears to be less salient for delinquents as a sub-group than for truants as a sub-group given their relative differences in desire to quit school from a feeling of rebellion. For the delinquent and truant versus conformer comparisons, the relationship is not independent of race, sex, I.Q., and socio-economic status. The difference does not hold for the Negro sub-group comparisons although it holds for the white sub-group comparisons. The relationship is larger and not attenuated for the truant-conformer comparison (as compared with the delinquent-conformer comparison). Looked at another way, while the difference between the *delinquents* and conformers is not maintained at the first order partial for race, it does not disappear in the *truant* and conformer comparisons until the fourth order partial for race, sex, I.Q. and socio-economic status. Nonetheless the difference between truants and non-truants is markedly attenuated in the race and sex comparisons for Negro sub-groups. Although age bears no relationship to the dependent variable, its introduction at the fifth order of partial association seems relevant since older subjects do have the legal opportunity to quit school even though they may be forced to attend for nonlegal reasons such as parent pressures. When we introduce age in addition to race, sex, I.Q. and socio-economic status and disregard the Negro sub-groups since the relationship already has disappeared for Negroes, we find that the relationship holds by age but that it is considerably attenuated for subjects who are over 16 years of age but that it remains strong for whites under 16 years of age. It appears, then, that white truants are more likely than white non-truants to want to quit school because they are forced to attend and that this relationship is independent of sex, I.Q., socio-economic status and age, although somewhat attenuated for the age group 16 years of age and over. We do not have a sufficient number of truants for each type of truant to test the relationship by type. There are rather large numbers of white blue-collar males under 16 years of age by type of truant. Within this group about three-fifths of the delinquent truants feel the coercive pressure of the norm as compared with two-fifths of the habitual truants and 27 per cent of the sporadic truants. This relationship is probably true only for blue-collar, white males, however.

We have observed that most delinquent and truant boys do not respond to the norm of compulsory school attendance out of a wish to quit school because they are forced to go even though their actual behavior, at least in the case of truants, can be defined as rebellion against the norm. We wished to see whether or not this actual rebellion in the form of truancy might be more closely related to alternative conforming goals in the society. We chose here the alternative conforming goal of going to work and asked our adolescents to say whether they wanted to quit school and go to work. "Work" in this sense might be considered a conforming alternative to the deviant behavior — a resolution of the conflict experienced in being forced to attend school. We find that about twice as many of our adolescents would like to quit school and go to work as quit school because they are forced to go (8 per cent). The desire to quit school and go to work is somewhat stronger with truancy than was the desire to quit school because of the coercive pressure of the norm. Almost half (48 per cent) of our truants want to quit school and go to work as compared with 17 per cent of the non-truants. There is not too much difference by type of truancy. The delinquent truant is somewhat more likely (55 per cent) to want to quit school and go to work than is the sporadic truant (46 per cent) and the habitual truant (44 per cent). It is of some interest here to note that the boy or girl for whom truancy represents the major act of rebellion is least likely to want to quit school for a more conforming goal. It should be kept in mind too that the conforming goal is not equally available to all adolescents since the opportunities for work are age related.

There is almost no race difference in the desire to quit school and go to work and only a small age difference such that older boys are more likely to want to quit school and go to work. There are substantial differences by sex, I.Q. and socio-economic status, however. Boys, low I.Q. and blue-collar adolescents are more likely to want to quit school and go to work. We would expect on the basis of these zero order relationships that low I.Q., blue-collar, white males should be most likely to want to quit school and go to work and this is true. Forty-one per cent of the white boys in this sub-group want to quit school and go to work. Correlatively, we would expect that high I.Q., white-collar, Negro girls would be least likely to want to quit school and go to work and this is the case; only one of the 25 girls in this sub-group wants to quit school and go to work.

We have observed that 48 per cent of all truants as compared with 18 per cent of non-truants want to quit school and go to work. We also note that 42 per cent of all delinquents as compared with 17 per cent of all non-delinquents want to quit school and go to work. For both deviant groups, work may represent a conforming solution. Is this relationship independent of the race, sex, I.Q. and socio-economic status of the adolescent? The relationship is independent, but it is attenuated for Negroes. And in fact, if Negroes are considered separately the results are not statistically significant for Negro sub-groups. Interestingly enough the relationship holds with fewer exceptions for the delinquent-conformer than the truant-conformer comparisons.

The *opportunity* to quit school and go to work is age related. After age 16 the legal norms permit our adolescent group to quit school. There is some restriction of job opportunity for this group, however, since the child labor laws and company policies restrict employment to certain kinds of jobs. Yet one would predict that the relationship is not as strong in this group since many of those who once wanted to quit school and go to work presumably dropped out of school when the law permitted them to do so and are not included in our school population. We would expect our relationship to be strongest therefore in the group that is compelled to remain in school and this is the case.

CONCLUSIONS

The perception of how much education most people ought to get in American society and adolescent evaluations of how important schooling is to them, how far their mothers expect them to go in school, how far they want to go in school, their desire to quit school, to quit school because one is forced to go, and to quit school and go to work all vary substantially with race, sex, I.Q. and socio-economic status, but little by age. If we think of race, sex, I.Q. and socio-economic status as indicators of the adolescent's group position or his membership groups, then we can see that norms and goals vary considerably by group position. In the case of subject's perception of mother's aspiration there is as much as 80 per cent difference between subjects in some race-sex-I.Q.-socio-economic group positions.

There is a much stronger relationship between deviant behavior and subject's perception of mother's or his own aspirations than there is between deviant behavior and subject's assessment of the norm of education for the general population or the value he places on schooling. One might interpret this finding in several ways. One might infer that self perceptions are more indicative of behavior than are assessments about the general cultural norms impinging on behavior. Or, one might conclude that delinquent and truant perceptions of the cultural norms are much the same as those of conformers. What matters is the way the delinquent or truant relates to these general norms.

Delinquents and truants are more likely to want to quit school and accept the conforming goal of getting a job than they are to want to quit school because they regard the norm of compulsory school attendance as coercive. This suggests that rebellion against the norm as represented at least by truancy might be ameliorated at least for a large number of truants and delinquents by an opportunity to undertake a productive role in the labor force.

Negro adolescents value schooling more than white adolescents and are more achievement oriented in terms of their educational aspirations. The age, sex, I.Q. and socio-economic status position of the Negro is of less influence on his behavior than is his race position when comparison is made with the white adolescents. In some cases this group position is so important that it specifies the more general relationships between truancy and delinquency and educational norms and goals so that they hold only for white adolescents, and therefore are not independent of the group position designated by race.

## REFERENCES

1. See Albert K. Cohen, *Delinquent Boys,* Glencoe, Illinois: The Free Press, 1955, Chapter 4.

2. See also William F. Whyte, *Street Corner Society,* Chicago: The University of Chicago Press, 1937, pp. 98–104.

3. *Ibid.,* pp. 127–130.

4. The most recent statement of this position can be found in Robert K. Merton, "Conformity, Deviation and Opportunity Structures" and Richard A. Cloward, "Illegitimate Means, Anomie and Deviant Behavior," *American Sociological Review*, 24: 177–189, 147–164, April 1959.

5. White collar includes professional, managerial, proprietory, official, sales, clerical and kindred occupations. Low I.Q. includes scores of 89 and below, middle I.Q. scores of 90 to 109 and high I.Q. scores of 110 and above.

# MINORITY AND CLASS STATUS AS RELATED
# TO FACTORS IN ACHIEVEMENT

MARTIN DEUTSCH

It can be assumed that the social context of a child's life is crucial to his particular growth of consciousness and the unique role he perceives himself playing in the world. In an affluent society whose goal is success and whose measurement is consumption, the lower-class child starts the race to the goal with an assortment of disadvantages. Economic uncertainty, slum living, crowded homes, and small value given to intellectual activity are not an adequate foundation for achievement. It is another problem that the struggle against poverty sometimes leads to deepened understanding and maturity: scores of unique individuals are only exceptions to the rule and do not alter the effects of these conditions on the aggregate. The majority of Negroes is found in the lower socio-economic groups and consequently is subjected to the whole array of deleterious factors associated with such social status.

To avoid confounding social with racial status, a number of studies attempted to equate middle-class Negroes with similar white groups. It is doubtful if such an equation can be validly made. The results of the present study, and of other studies, delineate some of the negative psychological attributes associated with self-awareness of Negro status, or any racial status deviating from the valued white norm. But even if this could be controlled for, middle-class identification is more than simply socio-economic position. The great majority of Negro middle-class members is at most one or two generations removed from lower-class status, and in order to achieve truly comparable populations for social psychological research, comparable class stability is essential.

Excerpted from "Minority Group and Class Status as Related to Social and Personality Factors in Scholastic Achievement," by Martin Deutsch, *Society for Applied Anthropology Monograph* (No. 2, 1960, pp. 26–29), by permission of the Society for Applied Anthropology and the author.

In planning the present study, it had been considered also desirable to have a population of both Negro and white middle-class children, as it was felt that it would then be possible to measure more accurately some of the effects of being Negro in a white society. The criterion of class stability, though, makes it extremely difficult to find in a small area a sufficient Negro population.

As a result, in the present study, the Negro children are differentiated from the white majority by the cumulative effects of having inferior status as members of a racial minority, as well as social class handicaps, while the white children in the study have only the class handicap. In the classroom process records, there are frequent remarks by the teachers to the effect that if the Negro child is to achieve he must be twice as good and capable as his white counterpart. It was noticed on field trips that the Negro children were admonished continually to be on their best behavior so they would not bring disgrace (sic) on themselves or their race. This and the anxiety it produced in the children became one of the basic discussions in the teachers' seminar. The groups of children with whom the writer met often insisted he must be Negro, and when this was explored they said that someone who was nice to them and did not criticize them must be Negro. Their expectations, reinforced by the anxiety of their middle-class teachers, were that the larger white world would fundamentally be rejecting and critical. It must be remembered that this is a world with which they had practically no personal contact (with the exception of the principal and a few teachers). It is undoubtedly this experience of a segregated life with the consequent anxieties reinforced by the school that plays a vital role in the development of the negative self-image of these children.

It is for these reasons that a study such as the present one is a study of the effects of chronic social stress on personality development, motivation, and subsequent school achievement. This chronic stress is what is probably seen in the increasing divergence between the experimental-group boys and control-group girls over successive school years. In addition, in median tests of longitudinal achievement data between the high and low achievers in the experimental group, the low achievers showed no progress, and, in fact, had a slight decline (not statistically significant), while the high achievers show a flattening in progress curves. Unfortunately, there are no comparable longitudinal data for the control group. The important fact here is that even the more advanced experimental children do not show significant progress; while the national norm expectation is one year's progress in one school year, it would be expected that the advanced children would even exceed this norm. Seemingly, the weight of the whole complex of negative factors which have been delineated here is depressing the scholastic functioning of these children, as well as distorting personality growth. While the data as collected here do not give specific causal information, the internal relationships in them make this a compelling conclusion.

In this flattening of progress there must be some nullifying of the expected effect of the school. Further, if there is some nullification of the school's academic influence, it is likely that its socializing effects are also partially vitiated. A partial parallel to this situation may be found in Gordon's[1] study of canal-boat and gypsy children, in which he discovered that the IQ's of these children declined as they got older. He related this to the infrequent school attendance of the children, and to the fact that a poor environment is more stimulating for a younger than for an older child, inasmuch as there is proportionately less prior knowledge or experience. This may relate rather closely to the present data, as the canal-boat children attended approximately 5 percent of the normal school time, the gypsy children approximately 35 percent while the process records in the present study indicate that a good percentage of time in the experimental school classes was given over to non-academic and often disorganized activity. It might be that for children from nonintellectually stimulating environments the school must offer proportionately more stimulation. This would be particularly true for children who came from a broken home or one in which parents work such long hours that little time is left at home. However, the poor cultural environment which increases the child's need for stimulation in school does little to prepare the child to accept his school experience. So the children who most need the socialization influence of the school may well be those who are the least amenable to it because of their previous narrow range of experience. It would seem, therefore, that it should properly become society's responsibility, through the school, to provide not only schooling but also the preparation for it.

Coming from an intact home is significantly correlated with achievement, and the achievement scores of the total experimental group were influenced by the large proportion of children from broken homes. Again, here it might be that the school should supply some of the support and stimulation that are absent in the broken home. In the classroom process records, it was observed that some of the teachers would be quite critical of the children when they answered incorrectly. This might not only affect motivation negatively, but it might also reinforce the negative self-image of the child. It is interesting that one of the most frequently used negatively-toned words with which the children described themselves was "stupid."

Special training in group processes and on the effects of social deprivation might be helpful for teachers in these schools. These children require considerably more reinforcement than do others, possibly because absent, missing, and excessively burdened parents cannot supply it. One student observer put it aptly in describing the classroom as a continual competitive battle among the children to gain the teacher's attention. In a sense, the children are trying to gain the attention of a parental substitute and are extremely responsive to any encouragement or warmth (although the responsiveness rarely includes any prolonged periods of self-control or orderliness). Although approval was important to the children, the teachers agreed in the seminars that attention was more important even if it was a severe reprimand. It is probably this factor which in good measure leads to classroom chaos which is responsible for the limited percentage of time actually going into academic work. With middle-class children the problem is usually different, with parents tending to be over-indulgent, families more intact, and subsequent decrease in the need for the attention of the teacher.

A cross-racial class factor, the crowding variable, is a major one in both populations, and because of this its effects could not adequately be measured in this study. It is possible, though, that it is playing a major role in depressing the levels of performance of the total populations, and would be worth further investigation. Some relationship was found between crowding and reading achievement in this study, as reported earlier, and there are also some qualitative data to support this finding.

An anecdotal corroboration of this relationship might be interesting. In one of the experimental classes there was a boy who after school habitually went into a large closet and closed the door. With the prevalence of psychoanalytic assumptions about such behavior, he was put on the "urgent" waiting list for an evaluation by the school psychologist without further ado — and without further investigation. The process recorder in the class meanwhile discovered that the boy left the light on in the closet — surely a modification of intra-uterine conditions. When asked why he went into the closet and what he did there, the boy replied, after urging and quite hesitantly, that it was the only place he knew of to be alone, and that he usually read while he was there. In the course of the study, it was found that this child came from a home which consisted of a three-room apartment shared by 14 people. The anomaly both here and in other cases is that this child, obviously bright, was functioning on a relatively low scholastic level, and was quite embarrassed at acknowledging the fact that he read. Under questioning, he explained that at home there were always some people sleeping, so he could never leave a light on and would be laughed at anyway if caught reading.

In the popular literature in post-sputnik America there has been a torrential criticism of our school system and its apparent failure to fulfill its goals. Teachers, administrators, physical plant and equipment have all been held responsible. In the experimental school dealt with here, there were competence and sincerity in the vast majority of personnel, and the physical plant was adequate. But the orientation of our schools at present is almost entirely toward middle-class values and way of life, which sometimes have no concrete meaning for the lower-class child. In addition to the more general ones raised earlier, the problem here appeared to be one of a standard curriculum, tailored to our pervasive middle-class value system and to the over-all norms of child development. But norms after all are mathematical averages, and it is crucial here to keep in mind that we are dealing with children who come from among the poorest home environments; who have the poorest nutritional status; who have the least parental support and reward; and who are most subject to premature birth, para-natal complications and accidents, all of which may lead to a higher proportion of central nervous system damage. It is unrealistic *a priori* to expect such children to perform at the norm. In other words, a proportion of the retardation here could be expected. Both the segregated nature of their lives and the encapsulation of the school in a minority group living area are serious handicaps, as the broad experiences reflected in modern curricula are not shared by these children.

As has been shown, these children from lower-class and culturally deprived environments are more limited in access to new knowledge and in opportunities for new experience, and this is even more true in a racially encapsulated community. The teachers in the seminar felt that the curriculum was unrealistic in terms of the experiences of the children in the school, and they had many concrete suggestions for changes in teaching method and content. Unfortunately, they did not feel free to channel these suggestions and felt that the special problems of their children were not understood by the educational hierarchy. For example, an early grade primer presents country situations, and yet the vast majority of these children have never been to the country. Similarly, the primers are not bi-racial, and often have meaningless story content, and fail to present situations with which these children can become involved, or to picture children with whom they can identify. This is a further extension of the alienating experiences these children have in a segregated community, in segregated schools, surrounded by the majority racial group. Instead of making school a more meaningful experience for these children who most need it, such instructional materials serve only to turn to them another of society's unsmiling faces.

The principle drawn from the foregoing is that when the home is a proportionately less effective socializing force, the school must become a proportionately more effective one; further, the deficiencies of the home and immediate environment create deficiencies in the children's experiences which make it more difficult for them to deal with a curriculum which presupposes a variety of experience which they cannot enjoy. The question to be dealt with in this context is how the school can become a more potent socializing force for these children.

The data of the current study could offer some suggestions. For example, the inferior performance of the Negro boy relative to the Negro girl and the not infrequent absence of the father from the home lead to a consideration of the potentially beneficial role which male teachers could play. Similarly the instability of the broken home might be somewhat compensated by children having the same teacher over a longer period of time. A set of rewards might be worked out to channel the attention needs into the scholastic areas, and somehow intellectual activity and the child's confidence in himself could be consciously reinforced. Also, the apparent greater facility with numbers rather than words might be put to more extensive use in the teaching situation, and perhaps an expanded remedial reading program around story content which has intrinsic interest and familiarity for the children would be helpful in overcoming a basic deficiency. In addition, the child can be offered broadening experiences which must include integrated schooling and after-school activities: he must no longer feel that visiting another neighborhood is tantamount to a trip to a foreign country.

However, if the schools are to compensate meaningfully for the impoverished intellectual background of these children, it is necessary to know scientifically the specific effects of their impoverished environment on their cognitive and language development. When the parameters of these deficits have been delineated, then it will become possible for the school to offer an effective enrichment program in the early years to stimulate the intellectual maturation of these children, so that the gap between their actual functioning and average grade expectations can be closed. This is a major task for social scientists, and no effective enrichment can be possible until these more microscopic effects of environment have been understood and their implications systematically tested in the actual school situation. Also, if the school is to be the comprehensive socializing institution, the all-day school program should be expanded, as it is one of the most successful current attempts to increase the influence of the school and to develop constructive behavioral alternatives for the children.

This discussion has centered mainly on the role of the school in helping to compensate for the deficiencies of the home. The fact of these deficiencies, however, and their close relationship to overcrowded, encapsulated, and economically marginal living conditions cannot be ignored. Society must solve these social problems, but in the meantime there is an important role here for the social scientist and particularly the social psychologist and the cultural anthropologist, who could study extensively the dynamic relationships between environmental and social circumstances and personality and intellectual performance.

The lower-class child, and especially the lower-class minority group child, lives in a milieu which fosters self-doubt and social confusion, which in turn serves substantially to lower motivation and makes it difficult to structure experience into cognitively meaningful activity and aspirations. As Erich Fromm consistently points out, one of the social characteristics of modern man is his increasing alienation from both his work and his fellow man. The dynamics of this psychological process in a technological society might be best understood through the study of the progressive alienation of the Negro child in a white world.

## REFERENCE

1. Gordon, H. *Mental and Scholastic Tests Among Retarded Children,* Board of Education Pamphlet, No. 44, London, 1923.

C.

# THE IMPACT OF MACRO-SOCIAL
# FACTORS: SOCIAL CLASS

# SOCIAL STATUS AND EDUCATIONAL AND OCCUPATIONAL ASPIRATION

WILLIAM H. SEWELL
ARCHIE O. HALLER
MURRAY A. STRAUS

Much of the research on the mechanisms determining the individual's occupational prestige position has been concentrated upon social factors influencing achievement motivation.[1] A number of studies show a positive correlation between the youth's levels of educational and occupational prestige status aspirations on the one hand and various measures of the social status of his family.[2] On the whole, sociologists have attributed this correlation to educational and occupational achievement values that are presumed to be directly influenced by the family's position in the status structure.[3] That is, it is supposed that the level of achievement motivation is greatly influenced by the educational and occupational values specific to the status milieu in which he is reared.

Nevertheless, the research evidence in support of this claim is weak in that it has not been based on adequate samples from large populations nor have certain important variables, known to be related to status and aspiration levels, been controlled. In particular, a number of studies have shown that educational and occupational aspiration levels are positively correlated with intelligence,[4] and others have shown that intelligence is similarly related to social status.[5] On the basis of such studies, it may be reasoned that the apparent effects of parental social status on the youth's levels of aspiration may be due to the common relationship of these variables to intelligence. The democratic ethos notwithstanding, careful studies have shown that in general those of lower intelligence tend to be disproportionately concentrated in the lower social classes; and those of lower intelligence

Reprinted from the *American Sociological Review* (Vol. 22, No. 1, February 1957, pp. 67–73) by permission of the American Sociological Association and the authors.

have been shown to have lower levels of educational and occupational aspiration. Thus, the apparent relationship of the youth's educational and occupational prestige aspirations to the value of his social status situation may in reality be a simple reflection of differences in intelligence. Moreover, it is a well known fact that there are gross differences in the occupational and educational aspirations of males and females in our society. Consequently, it would seem necessary to test the relationship between status and aspiration separately for the sexes with intelligence controlled.

The purpose of the present article is to present the results of a study testing the general hypothesis that levels of educational and occupational aspiration of youth of both sexes are associated with the social status of their families, when the effects of intelligence are controlled.

## PROCEDURE

The general hypothesis was broken down into four specific null hypotheses for testing, as follows:

1. Among females, there is no significant association between level of educational aspiration and social status when measured intelligence is controlled.

2. Among females, there is no significant association between level of occupational aspiration and social status when measured intelligence is controlled.

3. Among males, there is no significant association between level of educational aspiration and social status when measured intelligence is controlled.

4. Among males, there is no significant association between level of occupational aspiration and social status when measured intelligence is controlled.

Any tests of the general hypothesis must logically meet a number of conditions. First, they should be restricted to older youth so that the subjects' statements of their aspirations derive from impending decisions, thus omitting the fantasy aspirations of younger persons. Second, they should be limited to youth who have not entered the labor market so as to measure aspirations rather than rationalizations of actual behavior. Finally, they should be performed upon a sample drawn from a large and diverse population, so as to include subjects who vary widely in status and in educational and occupational aspiration.

The data for this study were taken from a one-sixth random sample of all nonfarm seniors in public and private high schools in Wisconsin in 1947–1948.[6] Students whose parents were farmers were excluded from the analysis because the available information would not permit their classification by status level. Since the 4,167 persons included in the study are all high school seniors, it may be assumed that their statements of aspirations are more nearly devoid of fantasy than at any other time previous to actual labor market entry. Because the sample was randomly drawn from a population in a state with a complex occupational and social structure, it may be assumed that a wide range of status positions and occupational and educational aspirations is represented.

Two dependent variables are used in the analysis: level of educational aspiration and level of occupational aspiration. Data for the dependent variable, educational aspiration, were taken from responses to a series of questions concerning education the student planned to obtain after graduation. The questions asked whether and when the student planned to attend college, and, if any, the name of the college. All students definitely planning to enter a regular four-year college program or its equivalent were classified as having high educational aspirations. All others were classified as having low educational aspirations. Data for the second dependent variable, level of occupational aspiration, were taken from a question concerning the vocation the student planned to enter. The responses to this question were assigned actual or interpolated North-Hatt occupational prestige values.[7] Using the prestige value of the public school teachers (78 N-H points) as the cutting point, the occupational prestige scores were dichotomized into high and low categories. Persons choosing occupations equal to or higher than public school teachers were considered to have high occupational aspirations, and all others, low occupational aspirations.

Social status, as measured by the prestige of parental occupation, is the independent variable. Data for the assessment of this variable were taken from a question regarding the present occupation of the student's parent. These responses were assigned North-Hatt occupational prestige values, actual or interpolated. The students were then arranged into five equal-sized rank-ordered parental occupational pres-

TABLE 1. PER CENT WITH HIGH-LEVEL EDUCATIONAL ASPIRATIONS BY PARENTAL OCCUPATIONAL PRESTIGE
STATUS AND INTELLIGENCE: FEMALES

| Intelligence Quintiles | Parental Occupational Prestige Status Quintiles | | | | | Total Per Cent (N) |
|---|---|---|---|---|---|---|
| | V (N–H: 93–72) | IV (N–H: 72–67) | III (N–H: 67–60) | II (N–H: 60–55) | I (N–H: 55–37) | |
| V (IQ: 139–118) | 84 | 70 | 60 | 47 | 40 | 65 (463) |
| IV (IQ: 118–112) | 72 | 53 | 37 | 48 | 34 | 49 (463) |
| III (IQ: 112–107) | 46 | 42 | 36 | 33 | 26 | 36 (463) |
| II (IQ: 107–101) | 50 | 35 | 28 | 23 | 23 | 30 (463) |
| I (IQ: 101–65) | 23 | 27 | 21 | 13 | 8 | 18 (463) |
| Total Per cent (N) | 62 (463) | 45 (463) | 36 (463) | 28 (463) | 27 (463) | 40 (2315) |

tige categories. The control variable, measured intelligence, was
treated similarly. Data for the latter were taken from scores on the
Henmon-Nelson Test of Mental Ability.[8] The subjects were each
placed in one of five equal-sized categories rank-ordered from highest
to lowest intelligence. Because there was variation in the number of
cases for which there were pertinent data on the several variables involved, rankings on social status and intelligence were made separately
for each null hypothesis tested. The IQ and N-H quintiles for each
table have overlapping values; persons with these values were proportionately assigned to the appropriate quintile.

RESULTS

The first null hypothesis, that among females there is no significant
association between level of educational aspiration and social status
when intelligence is controlled, is tested by data presented in Table 1.
The entry in each cell of the table is the percentage of females of a
specific level of measured intelligence and a specific social status level
who have high level educational aspirations, i.e., that intend to go to
college. As the table shows, the proportion intending to go to college varies systematically both with social status (reading row-wise)
and with measured intelligence (reading column-wise). The hypothesis is tested by computing and summing five independent chi-square
values and the degrees of freedom from the data presented in Table

1, on chi-square with four degrees of freedom within each of the five intelligence categories.[9] The effects of intelligence on levels of aspirations are thus statistically controlled by an over-all test based upon chi-square values calculated for each level of intelligence. This procedure is illustrated by the data in Table 1. For Intelligence Quintile V (IQ V), the chi-square of parental occupational prestige status on level of educational aspiration is $\chi^2_{o(4)} = 52.80$; for IQ IV, $\chi^2_{o(4)} = 38.05$; for IQ III, $\chi^2_{o(4)} = 10.39$; for IQ II, $\chi^2_{o(4)} = 13.61$; and IQ I, $\chi^2_{o(4)} = 18.02$. Summing these component $\chi^2$ values, $\chi^2_{o(20)} = 132.87$. Comparing this with the critical value of $\chi^2$ at the .05 probability level, $\chi^2_{o(2)} = 132.87 > \chi^2_{t(20)}.05 = 31.41$. This means that the first null hypothesis must be rejected. The direction of the relationship as indicated by the changes in the percentages of each row, shows that at all intelligence levels females from high status families are more likely to have high level educational aspirations than are those from lower status families. It is concluded that among females, there is a significant positive relationship between level of educational aspiration and parental social status. This relationship is independent of any correlation between intelligence and either of these variables.

The same routine is used to test the second null hypothesis that among females there is no significant association between level of occupational aspiration and social status with intelligence controlled. (See Table 2.) The results indicate that there is no significant relationship between level of occupational aspiration and social status when intelligence is controlled: $\chi^2_{o(20)} = 29.95 < \chi^2_{t(20)}.05 = 31.41$.

TABLE 2. Per Cent with High-Level Occupational Aspirations by Parental Occupational Prestige Status and Intelligence: Females

| Intelligence Quintiles | Parental Occupational Prestige Status Quintiles | | | | | Total Per Cent (N) |
|---|---|---|---|---|---|---|
| | V (N–H: 93–72) | IV (N–H: 72–67) | III (N–H: 67–60) | II (N–H: 60–55) | I (N–H: 55–39) | |
| **V** (IQ: 139–118) | 49 | 40 | 35 | 32 | 33 | 40 (371) |
| **IV** (IQ: 118–113) | 39 | 36 | 33 | 35 | 30 | 35 (371) |
| **III** (IQ: 113–108) | 28 | 35 | 27 | 25 | 13 | 26 (370) |
| **II** (IQ: 108–102) | 35 | 19 | 24 | 21 | 20 | 23 (370) |
| **I** (IQ: 102–65) | 25 | 21 | 13 | 15 | 11 | 16 (370) |
| **Total** Per cent (N) | 39 (371) | 31 (371) | 27 (370) | 24 (370) | 20 (370) | 28 (1852) |

However, the table indicates that this may be due to the fact that there is little difference in the occupational aspiration level of the girls of a given intelligence level in each of the three lower status categories. This has the effect of using up 15 degrees of freedom without accounting for much variation. For this reason the highest two and the lowest three status quintiles were combined and the hypothesis was retested. In this case, $\chi^2_{o(5)} = 16.95 > \chi^2_{t(5)}.05 = 11.07$. On the basis of this evidence the null hypothesis may be rejected. Again the direction of the relationship indicates that females from high status families more frequently choose high level occupations than do those from families of lower status, but the relationship is not so consistent as was the relationship between status and aspiration to attend college. However, it may be concluded tentatively that among females there is a positive relation of level of occupational aspiration to parental social status when intelligence is controlled.

The third null hypothesis is tested by data on males presented in Table 3. Here again high level educational aspirations or college plans are most characteristic of those from high status families and of those of high intelligence. Ninety per cent of the subjects of high status and high intelligence plan to attend college, and 32 per cent of the subjects of low status and low intelligence plan to attend college. The null hypothesis is tested in the same way as before. In this case, $\chi^2_{o(20)} = 65.51 > \chi^2_{t(20)}.05 = 31.41$, which indicates that the hypothesis of no association between educational aspiration level and social status must be rejected when the educational aspiration effects of in-

TABLE 3. PER CENT WITH HIGH-LEVEL EDUCATIONAL ASPIRATIONS BY PARENTAL OCCUPATIONAL PRESTIGE STATUS AND INTELLIGENCE: MALES

| Intelligence Quintiles | Parental Occupational Prestige Status Quintiles | | | | | Total Per Cent (N) |
|---|---|---|---|---|---|---|
| | V (N-H: 93–72) | IV (N-H: 72–67) | III (N-H: 67–60) | II (N-H: 60–55) | I (N-H: 55–39) | |
| V (IQ: 139–119) | 90 | 79 | 79 | 71 | 66 | 79 (384) |
| IV (IQ: 119–113) | 71 | 70 | 53 | 57 | 61 | 63 (384) |
| III (IQ: 113–109) | 58 | 62 | 51 | 55 | 43 | 54 (383) |
| II (IQ: 109–102) | 66 | 45 | 32 | 41 | 24 | 40 (383) |
| I (IQ: 102–59) | 34 | 35 | 23 | 26 | 32 | 30 (383) |
| Total Per cent (N) | 68 (384) | 59 (384) | 47 (383) | 48 (383) | 43 (383) | 53 (1917) |

TABLE 4. Per Cent with High-Level Occupational Aspirations by Parental
Occupational Prestige Status and Intelligence: Males

| Intelligence Quintiles | Parental Occupational Prestige Status Quintiles | | | | | Total Per Cent (N) |
|---|---|---|---|---|---|---|
| | V (N–H: 93–73) | IV (N–H: 73–67) | III (N–H: 67–60) | II (N–H: 60–55) | I (N–H: 55–39) | |
| V (IQ: 139–119) | 84 | 48 | 55 | 64 | 45 | 63 (278) |
| IV (IQ: 119–113) | 54 | 51 | 51 | 37 | 35 | 45 (278) |
| III (IQ: 113–109) | 41 | 42 | 43 | 29 | 32 | 37 (278) |
| II (IQ: 109–103) | 45 | 36 | 21 | 27 | 22 | 29 (278) |
| I (IQ: 103–59) | 25 | 19 | 16 | 18 | 17 | 18 (277) |
| Total Per cent | 57 | 38 | 36 | 33 | 27 | 39 |
| (N) | (278) | (278) | (278) | (278) | (277) | (1389) |

telligence are controlled. Examination of each row from left to right, column by column, shows that the high status categories consistently have the highest proportion of those planning to attend college. Thus, with the present data, it is not possible to refute by controlling intelligence the hypothesis of a direct positive relationship of educational aspiration level with social status among males.

The fourth hypothesis is tested by the data in Table 4. Testing the null hypothesis as before, $\chi^2_{o(20)} = 53.73 > \chi^2_{t(20)}.05 = 31.41$. According to the standard followed in the present study, the null hypothesis must be rejected. In this table, as in earlier ones, a study of the direction of percentage changes in each intelligence category shows that those from families of higher social status are more likely to have high level occupational aspirations than are those of lower status families. Therefore, it must be concluded that among males the apparent positive relationship of level of occupational aspiration to parental social status cannot be accounted for by controlling measured intelligence.

## Summary and Conclusions

In summary, four tests have been made of the hypothesis that levels of educational and occupational aspiration of youth are not associated with the social status of their families when the effects of measured intelligence are controlled. On the basis of these tests, it must be concluded that the apparent effects of social status on levels of educational and occupational aspiration are not simply due to the common relationship of these variables to intelligence, although intelligence is related to both types of aspirations.[10] This conclusion is specific to persons from nonfarm families. Within this group, however, the relationship of level of aspiration to social status with intelligence controlled holds for both sexes and for both educational and occupational aspirations. Because the sample was drawn randomly from a broad population of high school seniors (the entire state of Wisconsin), and because the effects of measured intelligence and sex were controlled, the present tests lend support to the sociological claim that values specific to different status positions are important influences on levels of educational and occupational aspiration. This does not deny the importance of intelligence to educational and occupational aspirations, but suggests that status makes an independent contribution to these aspirations.

## REFERENCES

1. See, for example, Russell R. Dynes, *et al.*, "Levels of Occupational Aspiration: Some Aspects of Family Experience as a Variable," *American Sociological Review*, 21 (April, 1956), pp. 212–215; Robert J. Havighurst and Robert R. Rodgers, "The Role of Motivation in Attendance at Post High School Educational Institutions," in Byron S. Hollingshead, *Who Should Go To College*, New York: Columbia University Press, 1952, pp. 135–165; Herbert H. Hyman, "The Value Systems of Different Classes: A Psychological Contribution to the Analysis of Stratification," in Reinhard Bendix and Seymour Martin Lipset (editors), *Class, Status and Power: A Reader in Social Stratification*, Glencoe: The Free Press, 1953, pp. 426–442; Harold F. Kaufman, *et al.*, "Problems of Theory and Method in the Study of Social Stratification in Rural Society," *Rural Sociology*, 18 (March, 1953), pp. 12–24; Seymour Martin Lipset, "Social Mobility and Urbanization," *Rural Sociology*, 20 (September–December, 1956), pp. 220–228; Sverre Lysgaard, "Social Stratification and the Deferred Gratification Pattern," *Transactions of the Second World Congress of Sociology*, II, London: The International Sociological Association, 1953, pp. 364–377; Leonard Reissman, "Levels of Aspiration and Social Class," *American Sociological Review*, 18 (June, 1953), pp. 233–242.

2. William Arthur Bradley, Jr., "Correlates of Vocational Preferences," *Genetic Psychology Monographs*, 28 (1943), pp. 99–169; Harold D. Carter,

"Vocational Interests and Job Orientation," *Applied Psychology Monographs,* 2, Stanford: Stanford University Press, 1944; Hyman, *op. cit.;* Joseph A. Kahl, "Educational and Occupational Aspirations of 'Common Man' Boys," *Harvard Educational Review,* 23 (Summer, 1953), pp. 186–203; Robert Kroger and C. M. Louttit, "The Influence of Father's Occupation on the Vocational Choices of High School Boys," *Journal of Applied Psychology,* 19 (April, 1935), pp. 203–212; Raymond A. Mulligan, "Socioeconomic Background and College Enrollment," *American Sociological Review,* 16 (April, 1951), pp. 188–196; J. Richard Porter, "Predicting Vocational Plans of High School Senior Boys," *Personnel and Guidance Journal,* 33 (December, 1954), pp. 215–218; Joseph Stubbins, "The Relationship Between Level of Vocational Aspiration and Certain Personal Data," *Genetic Psychology Monographs,* 41 (1950), pp. 327–408.

3. Hyman, *op. cit.;* Lipset, *op. cit.*

4. Ralph F. Berdie, "Why Don't They Go To College," *Personnel and Guidance Journal,* 31 (March, 1953), pp. 352–356; Bradley, *op. cit.;* Carter, *op. cit.;* Kahl, *op. cit.;* T. E. Livesay, "Test Intelligence and College Expectation of High School Seniors in Hawaii," *Journal of Educational Research,* 35 (January, 1942), pp. 334–337; T. E. Livesay, "Test Intelligence and Future Vocation of High School Seniors in Hawaii," *Journal of Applied Psychology,* 25 (December, 1941), pp. 679–686; Porter, *op. cit.;* Stubbins, *op. cit.*

5. Barbara Stoddard Burks, "The Relative Influence of Nature and Nurture on Mental Development," *National Society for the Study of Education Yearbook,* 27 (1928), pp. 219–316; J. E. Collins, "Relation of Parental Occupation to Intelligence of Children," *Journal of Educational Research,* 17 (March, 1928), pp. 157–169; James F. Duff and Godfrey H. Thomson, "Social and Geographic Distribution of Intelligence in Northumberland," *British Journal of Psychology,* 14 (October, 1923), pp. 192–198; M. E. Haggerty and Harry B. Nash, "Mental Capacity of Children and Parental Occupation," *Journal of Educational Psychology,* 15 (December, 1924), pp. 559–572; Robert J. Havighurst and Fay H. Breese, "Relations Between Ability and Social Status in a Midwestern Community, III. Primary Mental Abilities," *Journal of Educational Psychology,* 38 (April, 1947), pp. 241–247; T. M. Livesay, "The Relation of Test Intelligence of High School Seniors in Hawaii to the Occupation of Their Fathers," *Journal of Applied Psychology,* 25 (August, 1941), pp. 369–377; T. M. Livesay, "Relation of Economic Status to 'Intelligence' and Racial Derivation of High School Seniors in Hawaii," *American Journal of Psychology,* 57 (January, 1944), pp. 77–82; S. L. Pressey and Ruth Ralston, "The Relation of the General Intelligence of School Children to the Occupation of Their Fathers," *Journal of Applied Psychology,* 3 (December, 1919), pp. 336–373; Peter Standiford, "Parental Occupation and Intelligence," *School and Society,*

23 (January 23, 1926), pp. 117–119; William H. Sewell and Bertram L. Ellenbogen, "Social Status and the Measured Intelligence of Small City and Rural Children," *American Sociological Review*, 17 (October, 1952), pp. 612–616; L. M. Terman and M. A. Merrill, *Measuring Intelligence*, Boston: Houghton Mifflin Co., 1937.

6. The data were gathered from the high schools by the Wisconsin Student Counseling Center as a part of a regular program of intelligence testing. The years 1947–1948 were chosen because they are the earliest for which data are available for a projected longitudinal study of educational and occupational behavior.

7. National Opinion Research Center, "Jobs and Occupations: A Popular Evaluation," *Opinion News*, 9 (September, 1947), pp. 3–13.

8. V. A. C. Henmon and M. J. Nelson, *The Henmon-Nelson Test of Mental Ability*, Chicago: Houghton Mifflin Company (1942).

9. George W. Snedecor, *Statistical Methods*, 4th ed. Ames: Iowa State College Press, 1946, pp. 188–189; G. Udny Yule and M. G. Kendall, *Introduction to the Theory of Statistics*, 13th ed., rev. London: Charles Griffin and Company, 1948, p. 426.

10. Following the procedure in testing the hypotheses in the body of this article, chi-square values were computed so as to test within each sex category the association of levels of educational and occupational aspiration to measured intelligence with social status controlled.

# EARLY EXPERIENCE AND THE SOCIALIZATION
# OF COGNITIVE MODES IN CHILDREN

ROBERT D. HESS and VIRGINIA C. SHIPMAN

One of the questions arising from the contemporary concern with the education of culturally disadvantaged children is how we should conceptualize the effects of such deprivation upon the cognitive faculties of the child. The outcome is well known: children from deprived backgrounds score well below middle-class children on standard individual and group measures of intelligence (a gap that increases with age); they come to school without the skills necessary for coping with first grade curricula; their language development, both written and spoken, is relatively poor; auditory and visual discrimination skills are not well developed; in scholastic achievement they are retarded an average of 2 years by grade 6 and almost 3 years by grade 8; they are more likely to drop out of school before completing a secondary education; and even when they have adequate ability are less likely to go to college (Deutsch, 1963; Deutsch & Brown, 1964; Eells, Davis, Havighurst, Herriels, & Tyler 1951; John, 1963; Kennedy, Van de Riet, & White, 1963; Lesser, 1964).

For many years the central theoretical issues in this field dealt with the origin of these effects, argued in terms of the relative contribution of genetic as compared with environmental factors. Current interest in the effects of cultural deprivation ignores this classic debate; the more basic problem is to understand how cultural experience is translated into cognitive behavior and academic achievement (Bernstein, 1961; Hess, 1964).

Reprinted with abridgment from *Child Development* (Vol. 36, No. 4, December 1965, pp. 869–886) by permission of The Society for Research in Child Development, Inc., © 1965, and the authors.

This research is supported by the Research Division of the Children's Bureau, Social Security Administration; Department of Health, Education, and Welfare; Ford Foundation for the Advancement of Learning; and grants-in-aid from the Social Science Research Committee of the Division of Social Sciences, University of Chicago.

The focus of concern is no longer upon the question of whether social and cultural disadvantage depress academic ability, but has shifted to a study of the mechanisms of exchange that mediate between the individual and his environment. The thrust of research and theory is toward conceptualizing social class as a discrete array of experiences and patterns of experience that can be examined in relation to the effects they have upon the emerging cognitive equipment of the young child. In short, the question this paper presents is this: what *is* cultural deprivation, and how does it act to shape and depress the resources of the human mind?

The arguments we wish to present here are these: first, that the behavior which leads to social, educational, and economic poverty is socialized in early childhood — that is, it is learned; second, that the central quality involved in the effects of cultural deprivation is a lack of cognitive meaning in the mother-child communication system; and, third, that the growth of cognitive processes is fostered in family control systems which offer and permit a wide range of alternatives of action and thought and that such growth is constricted by systems of control which offer predetermined solutions and few alternatives for consideration and choice.

In this paper we will argue that the structure of the social system and the structure of the family shape communication and language and that language shapes thought and cognitive styles of problem-solving. In the deprived-family context this means that the nature of the control system which relates parent to child restricts the number and kind of alternatives for action and thought that are opened to the child; such constriction precludes a tendency for the child to reflect, to consider and choose among alternatives for speech and action. It develops modes for dealing with stimuli and with problems which are impulsive rather than reflective, which deal with the immediate rather than the future, and which are disconnected rather than sequential.

This position draws from the work of Basil Bernstein (1961) of the University of London. In his view, language structures and conditions what the child learns and how he learns, setting limits within which future learning may take place. He identifies two forms of communication codes or styles of verbal behavior: *restricted* and *elaborated*. Restricted codes are stereotyped, limited and condensed, lacking in specificity and the exactness needed for precise conceptualization and differentiation. Sentences are short, simple, often unfinished; there is little use of subordinate clauses for elaborating the content of the sentence; it is a language of implicit meaning, easily understood and commonly shared. It is the language form often used in impersonal situations when the intent is to promote solidarity or reduce tension. Restricted codes are nonspecific clichés, statements, or observations about events made in general terms that will be readily understood. The basic quality of this mode is to limit the range and detail of concept and information involved.

Elaborated codes, however, are those in which communication is individualized and the message is specific to a particular situation, topic, and person. It is more particular, more differentiated, and more precise. It permits expression of a wider and more complex range of thought, tending toward discrimination among cognitive and affective content.

The effects of early experience with these codes are not only upon the communication modes and cognitive structure — they also establish potential patterns of relation with the external world. It is one of the dynamic features of Bernstein's work that he views language as social behavior. As such, language is used by participants of a social network to elaborate and express social and other interpersonal relations and, in turn, is shaped and determined by these relations.

The interlacing of social interaction and language is illustrated by the distinction between two types of family control. One is oriented toward control by *status* appeal or ascribed role norms. The second is oriented toward *persons*. Families differ in the degree to which they utilize each of these types of regulatory appeal. In status- (position-) oriented families, behavior tends to be regulated in terms of role expectations. There is little opportunity for the unique characteristics of the child to influence the decision-making process or the interaction between parent and child. In these families, the internal or personal states of the children are not influential as a basis for decision. Norms of behavior are stressed with such imperatives as, "You must do this because I say so," or "Girls don't act like that," or other statements which rely on the status of the participants or a behavior norm for justification (Bernstein, 1964).

In the family, as in other social structures, control is exercised in part through status appeals. The feature that distinguishes among families is the extent to which the status-based control maneuvers are modified by orientation toward persons. In a person-oriented appeal system, the unique characteristics of the child modify status demands and are taken into account in interaction. The decisions of this type of family are individualized and less frequently related to status or role ascriptions. Behavior is justified in terms of feelings, preference, personal and unique reactions, and subjective states. This philosophy not only permits but demands an elaborated linguistic code and a wide range of linguistic and behavioral alternatives in interpersonal interaction. Status-oriented families may be regulated by less individuated commands, messages, and responses. Indeed, by its nature, the status-oriented family will rely more heavily on a restricted code. The verbal exchange is inherent in the structure — regulates it and is regulated by it.

These distinctions may be clarified by two examples of mother-child communication using these two types of codes. Assume that the emotional climate of two homes is approximately the same; the significant difference between them is in style of communication employed. A child is playing noisily in the kitchen with a assortment of pots and pans when the telephone rings. In one home the mother says, "Be quiet," or "Shut up," or issues any one of several other short, peremptory commands. In the other home the mother says, "Would you keep quiet a minute? I want to talk on the phone." The question our study poses is this: what inner response is elicited in the child, what is the effect upon his developing cognitive network of concepts and meaning in each of these two situations? In one instance the child is asked for a simple mental response. He is asked to attend to an uncomplicated message and to make a conditioned response (to comply); he is not called upon to reflect or to make mental discriminations. In the other example the child is required to follow two or three ideas. He is asked to relate his behavior to a time dimension; he must think of his behavior in relation to its effect upon another person. He must perform a more complicated task to follow the communication of his mother in that his relationship to her is mediated in part through concepts and shared ideas; his mind is stimulated or exercised (in an elementary fashion) by a more elaborate and complex verbal communication initiated by the mother. As objects of these two divergent communication styles, repeated in various ways, in similar situations and circumstances during the preschool years, these two imaginary children would be expected to develop significantly different verbal facility and cognitive equipment by the time they enter the public-school system.

A person-oriented family allows the child to achieve the behavior rules (role requirements) by presenting them in a specific context for the child and by emphasizing the consequences of alternative actions. Status-oriented families present the rules in an assigned manner, where compliance is the *only* rule-following possibility. In these situations the role of power in the interaction is more obvious, and, indeed, coercion and defiance are likely interactional possibilities. From another perspective, status-oriented families use a more rigid learning and teaching model in which compliance, rather than rationale, is stressed.

A central dimension through which we look at maternal behavior is to inquire what responses are elicited and permitted by styles of communication and interaction. There are two axes of the child's behavior in which we have a particular interest. One of these is represented by an *assertive, initiatory* approach to learning, as contrasted with a *passive, compliant* mode of engagement; the other deals with the tendency to reach solutions impulsively or hastily as distinguished from a tendency to *reflect,* to compare alternatives, and to choose among available options.

These styles of cognitive behavior are related, in our hypotheses, to the dimensions of maternal linguistic codes and types of family control systems. A status-oriented statement, for example, tends to offer a set of regulations and rules for conduct and interaction that is based on arbitrary decisions rather than upon logical consequences which result from selection of one or another alternative. Elaborated and person-oriented statements lend themselves more easily to styles of cognitive approach that involve reflection and reflective comparison. Status-oriented statements tend to be restrictive of thought. Take our simple example of the two children and the telephone. The verbal categoric command to "Be quiet" cuts off thought and offers little opportunity to relate the information conveyed in the command to the context in which it occurred. The more elaborated message, "Would you be quiet a minute? I want to talk on the phone" gives the child a rationale for relating his behavior to a wider set of considerations. In effect, he has been given a *why* for his mother's request and, by this example, possibly becomes more likely to *ask* why in another situation. It may be through this type of verbal interaction that the child learns to look for action sequences in his own and others' behavior. Perhaps through these more intent-oriented statements the child comes to see the world as others see it and learns to take the role of others in viewing himself and his actions. The child comes to see the world as a set of possibilities from which he can make a personal selection. He learns to role play with an element of personal flexibility, not by role-conforming rigidity.

RESEARCH PLAN

For our project a research group of 163 Negro mothers and their 4-year-old children was selected from four different social status levels: Group A came from college-educated professional, executive, and managerial occupational levels; Group B came from skilled blue-collar occupational levels, with not more than high-school education; Group C came from unskilled or semiskilled occupational levels, with predominantly elementary-school education; Group D from unskilled or semiskilled occupational levels, with fathers absent and families supported by public assistance.

These mothers were interviewed twice in their homes and brought to the university for testing and for an interaction session between mother and child in which the mother was taught three simple tasks by the staff member and then asked to teach these tasks to the child.

One of these tasks was to sort or group a number of plastic toys by color and by function; a second task was to sort eight blocks by two characteristics simultaneously; the third task required the mother and child to work together to copy five designs on a toy called an Etch-a-Sketch. A description of various aspects of the project and some preliminary results have been presented in several papers (Brophy, Hess, & Shipman, 1965; Jackson, Hess, & Shipman, 1965; Meyer, Shipman, & Hess, 1964; Olim, Hess, & Shipman, 1965; Shipman & Hess, 1965).

RESULTS

The data in this paper are organized to show social-status differences among the four groups in the dimensions of behavior described above to indicate something of the maternal teaching styles that are emerging and to offer examples of relations between maternal and child behavior that are congruent with the general lines of argument we have laid out.

## Social-Status Differences

*Verbal codes: restricted versus elaborated.* — One of the most striking and obvious differences between the environments provided by the mothers of the research group was in their patterns of language use. In our testing sessions, the most obvious social-class variations were in the total amount of verbal output in response to questions and tasks asking for verbal response. Mothers from the middle-class gave protocols that were consistently longer in language productivity than did mothers from the other three groups.

Taking three different types of questions that called for free response on the part of the mothers and counting the number of lines of typescript of the protocols, the tally for middle-class mothers was approximately 82 contrasted with an average of roughly 49 for mothers from the three other groups.

These differences in verbal products indicate the extent to which the maternal environments of children in different social-class groups tend to be mediated by verbal cue and thus offer (or fail to offer) opportunities for labeling, for identifying objects and feelings and adult models who can demonstrate the usefulness of language as a tool for dealing with interpersonal interaction and for ordering stimuli in the environment.

In addition to this gross disparity in verbal output there were differences in the quality of language used by mothers in the various status groups. One approach to the analysis of language used by these mothers was an examination of their responses to the following task: They were shown the Lion Card of the Children's Apperception Test and asked to tell their child a story relating to the card. This card is a picture of a lion sitting on a chair holding a pipe in his hand. Beside him is a cane. In the corner is a mouse peering out of a hole. The lion appears to be deep in thought. These protocols were the source of language samples which were summarized in nine scales, two of which we wish to describe here.

The first scale dealt with the mother's tendency to use abstract words. The index derived was a proportion of abstract noun and verb types to total number of noun and verb types. Words were defined as abstract when the name of the object is thought of apart from the cases in which it is actually realized. For example, in the sentence,

"The lion is an *animal*," "animal" is an abstract word. However, in the sentence, "This animal in the picture is sitting on his throne," "animal" is not an abstract noun.

In our research group, middle-class mothers achieved an abstraction score of 5.6; the score for skilled work levels was 4.9; the score for the unskilled group was 3.7; for recipients of Aid to Dependent Children (ADC), 1.8.

The second scale dealt with the mother's tendency to use complex syntactic structures such as coordinate and subordinate clauses, unusual infinitive phrases (e.g., "To drive well, you must be alert"), infinitive clauses (e.g., "What to do next was the lion's problem"), and participial phrases (e.g., "Continuing the story, the lion . . ."). The index of structural elaboration derived was a proportion of these complex syntactic structures, weighted in accordance with their complexity and with the degree to which they are strung together to form still more complicated structures (e.g., clauses within clauses), to the total number of sentences.

In the research group, mothers from the middle class had a structure elaboration index of 8.89; the score for ADC mothers was 6.46. The use of complex grammatical forms and elaboration of these forms into complex clauses and sentences provides a highly elaborated code with which to manipulate the environment symbolically. This type of code encourages the child to recognize the possibilities and subtleties inherent in language not only for communication but also for carrying on high-level cognitive procedures.

*Control systems: person versus status orientation.* — Our data on the mothers' use of status- as contrasted with person-oriented statements comes from maternal responses to questions inquiring what the mother would do in order to deal with several different hypothetical situations at school in which the child had broken the rules of the school, had failed to achieve, or had been wronged by a teacher or classmate. The results of this tally are shown in Table 1.

As is clear from these means, the greatest differences between status groups is in the tendency to utilize person-oriented statements. These differences are even greater if seen as a ratio of person-to-status type responses.

The orientation of the mothers to these different types of control is seen not only in prohibitive or reparative situations but in their instructions to their children in preparing them for new experiences. The data on this point come from answers to the question: "Suppose your

TABLE 1

PERSON-ORIENTED AND STATUS-ORIENTED UNITS
ON SCHOOL SITUATION PROTOCOLS (MOTHERS)
A. MEAN NUMBER

| Social Class | Person-Oriented | | Status-Oriented | | P/S Ratio | N |
|---|---|---|---|---|---|---|
| Upper middle... | 9.52 | (1–19) | 7.50 | (0–19) | 1.27 | 40 |
| Upper lower.... | 6.20 | (0–20) | 7.32 | (2–17) | 0.85 | 40 |
| Lower lower.... | 4.66 | (0–15) | 7.34 | (2–17) | 0.63 | 35 |
| ADC........... | 3.59 | (0–16) | 8.15 | (3–29) | 0.44 | 34 |

B. MEAN PER CENT

| Social Class | Person-Oriented | Status-Oriented | N |
|---|---|---|---|
| Upper middle... | 36.92 | 27.78 | 40 |
| Upper lower.... | 31.65 | 36.92 | 40 |
| Lower lower.... | 26.43 | 40.69 | 35 |
| ADC.......... | 20.85 | 51.09 | 34 |

child were starting to school tomorrow for the first time. What would you tell him? How would you prepare him for school?"

One mother, who was person-oriented and used elaborated verbal codes, replied as follows:

"First of all, I would remind her that she was going to school to learn, that her teacher would take my place, and that she would be expected to follow instructions. Also that her time was to be spent mostly in the classroom with other children, and that any questions or any problems that she might have she could consult with her teacher for assistance."

"Anything else?"

"No, anything else would probably be confusing for her at her particular age."

In terms of promoting educability, what did this mother do in her response? First, she was informative; she presented the school situation as comparable to one already familiar to the child; second, she offered reassurance and support to help the child deal with anxiety; third, she described the school situation as one that involves a personal relationship between the child and the teacher; and, fourth, she presented the classroom situation as one in which the child was to learn.

A second mother responded as follows to this question:

"Well, John, it's time to go to school now. You must know how to behave. The first day at school you should be a good boy and should do just what the teacher tells you to do."

TABLE 2

INFORMATION MOTHERS WOULD GIVE TO CHILD ON HIS FIRST DAY AT SCHOOL

| Social Status | Imperative | Instructive | Support | Preparation | Other | N |
|---|---|---|---|---|---|---|
| | | | % of Total Statements | | | |
| Upper middle... | 14.9 | 8.7 | 30.2 | 8.6 | 37.6 | 39 |
| Upper lower.... | 48.2 | 4.6 | 13.8 | 3.8 | 29.6 | 41 |
| Lower lower.... | 44.4 | 1.7 | 13.1 | 1.2 | 39.6 | 36 |
| ADC.......... | 46.6 | 3.2 | 17.1 | 1.3 | 31.8 | 37 |
| | | | % of Mothers Using Category | | | |
| Upper middle... | 48.7 | 38.5 | 76.9 | 33.3 | 87.2 | ... |
| Upper lower.... | 85.4 | 17.1 | 39.0 | 19.5 | 70.7 | ... |
| Lower lower.... | 75.0 | 5.6 | 36.1 | 8.3 | 77.8 | ... |
| ADC.......... | 86.5 | 16.2 | 43.2 | 8.1 | 86.5 | ... |

In contrast to the first mother, what did this mother do? First, she defined the role of the child as passive and compliant; second, the central issues she presented were those dealing with authority and the institution, rather than with learning; third, the relationship and roles she portrayed were sketched in terms of status and role expectations rather than in personal terms; and, fourth, her message was general, restricted, and vague, lacking information about how to deal with the problems of school except by passive compliance.

A more detailed analysis of the mothers' responses to this question grouped their statements as *imperative* or *instructive* (Table 2). An imperative statement was defined as an unqualified injunction or command, such as, "Mind the teacher and do what she tells you to do," or "The first thing you have to do is be on time," or "Be nice and do not fight." An instructive statement offers information or commands which carry a rationale or justification for the rule to be observed. Examples: "If you are tardy or if you stay away from school, your marks will go down"; or "I would tell him about the importance of minding the teacher. The teacher needs his full cooperation. She will have so many children that she won't be able to pamper any youngster."

*Status differences in concept utilization.* — One of the measures of cognitive style used with both mothers and children in the research group was the S's mode of classificatory behavior. For the adult version (Kagan, Moss & Sigel, 1963) S is required to make 12 consecutive sorts of MAPS figures placed in a prearranged random order on a large cardboard. After each sort she was asked to give her reason for putting certain figures together. This task was intended to reveal her typical or preferred manner of grouping stimuli and the level of abstraction that she uses in perceiving and ordering objects in the environment. Responses fell into four categories: descriptive part-whole, descriptive global, relational-contextual, and categorical-inferential. A descriptive response is a direct reference to physical attributes present in the stimuli, such as size, shape, or posture. Examples: "They're all children," or "They are all lying down," or "They are all men." The subject may also choose to use only a part of the figure — "They both have hats on." In a relational-contextual response, any one stimulus gets its meaning from a relation with other stimuli. Examples: "Doctor and nurse," or "Wife is cooking dinner for her husband," or "This guy looks like he shot this other guy." In categorical-inferential responses, sorts are based on nonobservable characteristics of the stimulus for which each stimulus is an independent representative of the total class. Examples: "All of these people work for a living" or "These are all handicapped people."

As may be seen in Table 3, relational responses were most frequently offered; categorical-inferential were next most common, and descriptive most infrequent. The distribution of responses of our status groups showed that the middle-class group was higher on descriptive and categorical; low-status groups were higher on relational. The greater use of relational categories by the working-class mothers is especially significant. Response times for relational sorts are usually shorter, indicating less reflection and evaluating of alternative-hypotheses. Such responses also indicate relatively low attention to external stimuli details (Kagan, 1964). Relational responses are often subjective, reflecting a tendency to relate objects to personal concerns in contrast with the descriptive and categorical responses which tend to be objective and detached, more general, and more abstract. Categori-

TABLE 3

MEAN RESPONSES TO ADULT SIGEL SORTING TASK (MAPS)

| | SOCIAL STATUS | | | |
| CATEGORY | Upper Middle $N = 40$ | Upper Lower $N = 42$ | Lower Lower $N = 39$ | ADC $N = 41$ |
|---|---|---|---|---|
| Total descriptive..... | 3.18 | 2.19 | 2.18 | 2.59 |
| Descriptive part-whole........ | 1.65 | 1.33 | 1.31 | 1.49 |
| Descriptive global.... | 1.52 | 0.86 | 0.87 | 1.10 |
| Relational-contextual. | 5.52 | 6.79 | 7.38 | 6.73 |
| Categorical-inferential | 3.30 | 3.00 | 2.23 | 2.66 |

TABLE 4

CHILDREN'S RESPONSES TO SIGEL SORTING TASK (MEANS)

| | SOCIAL STATUS | | | |
|---|---|---|---|---|
| CATEGORY | Upper Middle $N = 40$ | Upper Lower $N = 42$ | Lower Lower $N = 39$ | ADC $N = 41$ |
| Descriptive part-whole........ | 2.25 | 0.71 | 0.20 | 0.34 |
| Descriptive global.... | 2.80 | 2.29 | 1.51 | 0.98 |
| Relational-contextual. | 3.18 | 2.31 | 1.18 | 1.02 |
| Categorical-inferential | 2.02 | 1.36 | 1.18 | 0.61 |
| Nonscorable verbal responses... | 5.75 | 6.31 | 6.64 | 7.24 |
| Nonverbal.......... | 3.00 | 6.41 | 7.08 | 8.76 |
| No sort............. | 1.00 | 0.62 | 2.21 | 1.05 |

cal responses, in particular, represent thought processes that are more orderly and complex in organizing stimuli, suggesting more efficient strategies of information processing.

The most striking finding from the data obtained from the children's Sigel Sorting Task was the decreasing use of the cognitive style dimensions and increasing nonverbal responses with decrease in social-status level. As may be seen in the tables showing children's performance on the Sigel Sorting Task (Tables 4 and 5), although most upper middle-class children and a majority of the upper lower-class children use relational and descriptive global responses, there is no extensive use of any of the other cognitive style dimensions by the two lower lower-class groups. In looking at particular categories one may note the relative absence of descriptive part-whole responses for other than the middle-class group and the large rise in nonverbal responses below the

TABLE 5

PERCENTAGE OF FOUR-YEAR-OLD CHILDREN
RESPONDING IN EACH OF THE CATEGORIES

| | SOCIAL STATUS | | | |
|---|---|---|---|---|
| CATEGORY | Upper Middle $N = 40$ | Upper Lower $N = 42$ | Lower Lower $N = 39$ | ADC $N = 41$ |
| Descriptive part-whole........ | 40.0 | 28.6 | 18.0 | 14.6 |
| Descriptive global.... | 70.0 | 54.8 | 53.8 | 31.7 |
| Total descriptive..... | 80.0 | 66.7 | 59.0 | 39.0 |
| Relational-contextual. | 77.5 | 66.7 | 41.0 | 43.9 |
| Categorical-inferential | 52.5 | 45.2 | 30.8 | 24.4 |
| Nonscorable verbal... | 85.0 | 88.1 | 92.3 | 85.4 |
| Nonverbal.......... | 52.5 | 66.7 | 82.0 | 87.8 |
| No sort............. | 12.5 | 7.1 | 25.6 | 19.5 |

middle-class level. These results would seem to reflect the relatively undeveloped verbal and conceptual ability of children from homes with restricted range of verbal and conceptual content.

Relational and descriptive global responses have been considered the most immature and would be hypothesized to occur most frequently in pre-school children. Relational responses are often subjective, using idiosyncratic and irrelevant cues; descriptive global responses, often referring to sex and occupational roles, are somewhat more dependent upon experience. On the other hand, descriptive part-whole responses have been shown to increase with age and would be expected to be used less frequently. However, these descriptive part-whole responses, which are correlated with favorable prognostic signs for educability (such as attentiveness, control and learning ability), were almost totally absent from all but the upper middle-class group. Kagan (1964) has described two fundamental cognitive dispositions involved in producing such analytic concepts: the tendency to reflect over alternative solutions that are simultaneously available and the tendency to analyze a visual stimulus into component parts. Both behaviors require a delayed discrimination response. One may describe the impairment noted for culturally disadvantaged children as arising from differences in opportunities for developing these reflective attitudes.

The mothers' use of relational responses was significantly correlated with their children's use of nonscorable and nonverbal responses on the Sigel task and with poor performance on the 8-Block and Etch-a-Sketch tasks. The mothers' inability or disinclination to take an abstract attitude on the Sigel task was correlated with ineffectual teaching on the 8-Block task and inability to plan and control the Etch-a-Sketch situation. Since relational responses have been found (Kagan, Moss, & Sigel, 1963) to be correlated with impulsivity, tendencies for nonverbal rather than verbal teaching, mother-domination, and limited sequencing and discrimination might be expected and would be predicted to result in limited categorizing ability and impaired verbal skills in the child.

## ANALYSIS OF MATERNAL TEACHING STYLES

These differences among the status groups and among mothers within the groups appear in slightly different form in the teaching sessions in which the mothers and children engaged. There were large differences among the status groups in the ability of the mothers to teach and the children to learn. This is illustrated by the performance scores on the sorting tasks.

Let us describe the interaction between the mother and child in one of the structured teaching situations. The wide range of individual differences in linguistic and interactional styles of these mothers may be illustrated by excerpts from recordings. The task of the mother is to teach the child how to group or sort a small number of toys.

The first mother outlines the task for the child, gives sufficient help and explanation to permit the child to proceed on her own. She says:

"All right, Susan, this board is the place where we put the little toys; first of all you're supposed to learn how to place them according to color. Can you do that? The things that are all the same color you put in one section; in the second section you put another group of colors, and in the third section you put the last group of colors. Can you do that? Or would you like to see me do it first?"

Child: "I want to do it."

This mother has given explicit information about the task and what is expected of the child; she has offered support and help of various kinds; and she has made it clear that she impelled the child to perform.

A second mother's style offers less clarity and precision. She says in introducing the same task:

"Now, I'll take them all off the board; now you put them all back on the board. What are these?"

Child: "A truck."

"All right, just put them right here; put the other one right here; all right put the other one there."

This mother must rely more on nonverbal communication in her commands; she does not define the task for the child; the child is not provided with ideas or information that she can grasp in attempting to solve the problem; neither is she told what to expect or what the task is, even in general terms.

A third mother is even less explicit. She introduces the task as follows:

"I've got some chairs and cars, do you want to play the game?" Child does not respond. Mother continues: "O.K. What's this?"

Child: "A wagon?"

Mother: "Hm?"

Child: "A wagon?"

Mother: "This is not a wagon. What's this?"

The conversation continues with this sort of exchange for several pages. Here again, the child is not provided with the essential information he needs to solve or to understand the problem. There is clearly some impelling on the part of the mother for the child to perform, but the child has not been told what he is to do. There were marked social-class differences in the ability of the children to learn from their mothers in the teaching sessions.

Each teaching session was concluded with an assessment by a staff member of the extent to which the child had learned the concepts taught by the mother. His achievement was scored in two ways: first, the ability to correctly place or sort the objects and, second, the ability to verbalize the principle on which the sorting or grouping was made.

Children from middle-class homes were well above children from working-class homes in performance on these sorting tasks, particularly in offering verbal explanations as to the basis for making the sort. Over 60 per cent of middle-class children placed the objects correctly on all tasks; the performance of working-class children ranged as low as 29 per cent correct. Approximately 40 per cent of these middle-class children who were successful were able to verbalize the sorting principle; working-class children were less able to explain the sorting principle, ranging downward from the middle-class level to one task on which no child was able to verbalize correctly the basis of his sorting behavior. These differences clearly paralleled the relative abilities and teaching skills of the mothers from differing social-status groups.

The difference among the four status levels was apparent not only on these sorting and verbal skills but also in the mother's ability to regulate her own behavior and her child's in performing tasks which require planning or care rather than verbal or conceptual skill. These differences were revealed by the mother-child performance on the Etch-a-Sketch task. An Etch-a-Sketch toy is a small, flat box with a screen on which lines can be drawn by a device within the box. The marker is controlled by two knobs: one for horizontal movement, one for vertical. The mother is assigned one knob, the child the other. The mother is shown several designs which are to be reproduced. Together they attempt to copy the design models. The mother decides when their product is a satisfactory copy of the original. The products are scored by measuring deviations from the original designs.

These sessions were recorded, and the nonverbal interaction was described by an observer. Some of the most relevant results were these: middle-class mothers and children performed better on the task

TABLE 6

PERFORMANCE ON ETCH-A-SKETCH TASK (MEANS)

| | SOCIAL STATUS | | | |
|---|---|---|---|---|
| | Upper Middle<br>N = 40 | Upper Lower<br>N = 42 | Lower Lower<br>N = 40 | ADC<br>N = 41 |
| Total score<br>(range 0–40)...... | 14.6 | 9.2 | 8.3 | 9.5 |
| Average number<br>of attempts....... | 12.7 | 17.2 | 12.2 | 15.1 |
| Complete figures<br>rejected.......... | 2.3 | 3.6 | 3.5 | 3.4 |
| Child's total score.... | 5.9 | 4.0 | 3.4 | 4.0 |
| Child's contribution<br>to total score<br>(per cent)........ | 40.4 | 43.5 | 41.0 | 42.1 |

(14.6 points) than mothers and children from the other groups (9.2; 8.3; 9.5; [Table 6]). Mothers of the three lower-status groups were relatively persistent, rejecting more complete figures than the middle-class mothers; mothers from the middle class praised the child's efforts more than did other mothers but gave just as much criticism; the child's cooperation as rated by the observer was as good or better in low-status groups as in middle-class pairs (Table 7), there was little difference between the groups in affect expressed to the child by the mother (Brophy et al., 1965).

In these data, as in other not presented here, the mothers of the four status groups differed relatively little, on the average, in the affective elements of their interaction with their children. The gross differences appeared in the verbal and cognitive environments that they presented.

TABLE 7

MOTHER-CHILD INTERACTION ON ETCH-A-SKETCH TASK (MEANS)

| | SOCIAL STATUS | | | |
|---|---|---|---|---|
| | Upper Middle<br>N = 40 | Upper Lower<br>N = 41 | Lower Lower<br>N = 39 | ADC<br>N = 39 |
| Praises child........ | 4.6 | 6.9 | 7.2 | 7.5 |
| Criticizes child...... | 6.4 | 5.5 | 6.4 | 5.9 |
| Overall acceptance<br>of child.......... | 2.2 | 3.2 | 3.4 | 3.6 |
| Child's cooperation... | 5.6 | 5.3 | 4.5 | 5.1 |
| Level of affection<br>shown to child..... | 4.8 | 5.4 | 5.2 | 5.8 |

*Ratings made by observer; low number indicates more of the quality rated.

Against this background I would like to return for a moment to the problem of the meaning, or, perhaps more correctly, the lack of meaning in cultural deprivation. One of the features of the behavior of the working-class mothers and children is a tendency to act without taking sufficient time for reflection and planning. In a sense one might call this impulsive behavior — not by acting out unconscious or forbidden impulses, but in a type of activity in which a particular act seems not to be related to the act that preceded it or to its consequences. In this sense it lacks meaning; it is not sufficiently related to the context in which it occurs, to the motivations of the participants, or to the goals of the task. This behavior may be verbal or motor; it shows itself in several ways. On the Etch-a-Sketch task, for example, the mother may silently watch a child make an error and then punish him. Another mother will anticipate the error, will warn the child that he is about to reach a decision point; she will prepare him by verbal and nonverbal cues to be careful, to look ahead, and to avoid the mistake. He is encouraged to reflect, to anticipate the consequences of his action, and in this way to avoid error. A problem-solving approach requires reflection and the ability to weigh decisions, to choose among alternatives. The effect of restricted speech and of status orientation is to foreclose the need for reflective weighing of alternatives and consequences; the use of an elaborated code, with its orientation to persons and to consequences (including future), tends to produce cognitive styles more easily adapted to problem-solving and reflection.

The objective of our study is to discover how teaching styles of the mothers induce and shape learning styles and information-processing strategies in the children. The picture that is beginning to emerge is that the meaning of deprivation is a deprivation of meaning — a cognitive environment in which behavior is controlled by status rules rather than by attention to the individual characteristics of a specific situation and one in which behavior is not mediated by verbal cues or by teaching that relates events to one another and the present to the future. This environment produces a child who relates to authority rather than to rationale, who, although often compliant, is not reflective in his behavior, and for whom the consequences of an act are largely considered in terms of immediate punishment or reward rather than future effects and long-range goals.

When the data are more complete, a more detailed analysis of the findings will enable us to examine the effect of maternal cognitive environments in terms of individual mother-child transactions, rather than in the gross categories of social class. This analysis will not only help us to understand how social-class environment is mediated through the interaction between mother and child but will give more precise information about the effects of individual maternal environments on the cognitive growth of the young child.

## REFERENCES

Bernstein, B. Social class and linguistic development: a theory of social learning. In A. H. Halsey, Jean Floud, & C. A. Anderson (Eds.), *Education, economy, and society.* Glencoe, Ill.: Free Press, 1961.

Bernstein, B. Family role systems, communication, and socialization. Paper presented at Conf. on Develpm. of Cross-National Res. on the Education of Children and Adolescents, Univer. of Chicago, February, 1964.

Brophy, J., Hess, R. D., & Shipman, Virginia. Effects of social class and level of aspiration on performance in a structured mother-child interaction. Paper presented at Biennial Meeting of Soc. Res. Child Develpm., Minneapolis, Minn., March, 1965.

Deutsch, M. The disadvantaged child and the learning process. In A. H. Passow (Ed.), *Education in depressed areas.* New York: Columbia Univer. T.C., 1963. Pp. 163–180.

Deutsch, M., & Brown, B. Social influences in Negro-white intelligence differences. *J. soc. Issues,* 1964, 20 (2), 24–35.

Eells, K., Davis, Allison, Havighurst, R. J., Herrick, V. E., & Tyler, R. W. *Intelligence and cultural differences.* Chicago: Univer. of Chicago Pr., 1951.

Hess, R. D. Educability and rehabilitation: the future of the welfare class. *Marr. fam. Lvg,* 1964, 26, 422–429.

Jackson, J. D., Hess, R. D., & Shipman, Virginia. Communication styles in teachers: an experiment. Paper presented at Amer. Educ. and Res. Ass., Chicago, February, 1965.

John, Vera. The intellectual development of slum children: some preliminary findings. *Amer. J. Orthopsychiat.,* 1963, 33, 813–822.

Kagan, J., Moss, H. A., & Sigel, I. E. Psychological significance of styles of conceptualization. *Monogr. Soc. Res. Child Develpm.,* 1963, 28, No. 2.

Kagan, J. Information processing in the child: significance of analytic and reflective attitudes. *Psychol. Monogr.,* 1964, 78, No. 1 (Whole No. 578).

Kennedy, W. A., Van de Riet, V., & White, J. C., Jr. A normative sample of intelligence and achievement of Negro elementary school children in the southeastern United States. *Monogr. Soc. Res. Child Develpm.,* 1963, 28, No. 6.

Lesser, G. Mental abilities of children in different social and cultural groups. New York: Cooperative Research Project No. 1635, 1964.

Meyer, Roberta, Shipman, Virginia, & Hess, R. D. Family structure and social class in the socialization of curiosity in urban preschool children. Paper presented at APA meeting in Los Angeles, Calif. September, 1964.

Olim, E. G., Hess, R. D., & Shipman, Virginia. Relationship between mothers' language styles and cognitive styles of urban preschool children. Paper presented at Biennial Meeting of Soc. Res. Child Develpm., Minneapolis, Minn., March, 1965.

Shipman, Virginia, & Hess, R. D. Social class and sex differences in the utilization of language and the consequences for cognitive development. Paper presented at Midwest. Psychol. Ass., Chicago, April, 1965.

# ORIENTATION TO EDUCATION AS A FACTOR IN THE
# SCHOOL MALADJUSTMENT OF LOWER-CLASS CHILDREN

## JACKSON TOBY

Even taking an extremely crude index of school achievement, that of grade placement, *for every age level* the average grade of middle-class urban children is higher than that of lower-class children. (See Tables 1, 2, and 3.) These differences can be observed at 7 and 8 years of age as well as at 17. Apparently whatever produces the difference starts operating to differentiate lower-class from middle-class children from the early grades. Another way of looking at class selectivity of the educational process is to observe the proportion of

TABLE 1. MEDIAN YEARS OF SCHOOL COMPLETED BY NATIVE WHITE BOYS BY MONTHLY RENTAL VALUE OF HOME AND BY AGE IN CITIES OF 250,000 INHABITANTS OR MORE, 1940

| Age | Monthly Rental Value of Home | | | | | | |
|---|---|---|---|---|---|---|---|
| | Under $10 | $10–$14 | $15–$19 | $20–$29 | $30–$49 | $50–$74 | $75 and over |
| 7 years | 1.3 | 1.5 | 1.6 | 1.7 | 1.7 | 1.7 | 1.7 |
| 8 years | 2.1 | 2.4 | 2.4 | 2.5 | 2.6 | 2.6 | 2.7 |
| 9 years | 2.8 | 3.2 | 3.3 | 3.4 | 3.5 | 3.7 | 3.7 |
| 10 years | 3.6 | 4.0 | 4.2 | 4.4 | 4.5 | 4.6 | 4.7 |
| 11 years | 4.4 | 4.9 | 5.1 | 5.3 | 5.5 | 5.6 | 5.6 |
| 12 years | 5.4 | 5.7 | 6.0 | 6.2 | 6.5 | 6.6 | 6.7 |
| 13 years | 6.0 | 6.7 | 7.1 | 7.2 | 7.5 | 7.7 | 7.8 |
| 14 years | 7.2 | 7.8 | 7.9 | 8.2 | 8.5 | 8.7 | 8.8 |
| 15 years | 8.3 | 8.5 | 8.8 | 9.2 | 9.4 | 9.6 | 9.8 |
| 16 years | 8.6 | 9.3 | 9.6 | 9.8 | 10.3 | 10.5 | 10.6 |
| 17 years | 9.4 | 9.9 | 10.2 | 10.7 | 10.7 | 11.3 | 11.5 |

*Source:* Bureau of the Census, *Sixteenth Census of the United States* (*1940*), *Monograph on Population Education: Educational Attainment of Children by Rental Value of Home* (Washington: Government Printing Office, 1945), p. 3.

Reprinted from *Social Forces* (Vol. 35, 1957, pp. 259–266) by permission of the University of North Carolina Press and the author.

TABLE 2. DISTRIBUTION OF RETARDED AND NONRETARDED PUPILS
ACCORDING TO OCCUPATIONAL STATUS OF FATHER (SIMS' SCALE)
IN THE NEW YORK CITY PUBLIC SCHOOLS, 1931–32

| Father's Occupational Status | Total | Slow Prog-ress | Normal Prog-ress | Rapid Prog-ress |
|---|---|---|---|---|
| Total ............... | 100.0 | 100.0 | 100.0 | 100.0 |
| Professional ........... | 3.7 | 1.3 | 4.4 | 6.2 |
| Clerical ............... | 19.8 | 11.2 | 19.4 | 31.9 |
| Artisan ............... | 24.0 | 22.0 | 19.4 | 24.8 |
| Skilled laborer ......... | 36.9 | 43.8 | 35.1 | 29.8 |
| Unskilled laborer ....... | 15.6 | 21.7 | 15.6 | 7.3 |

lower-class boys in high school a generation ago (Tables 4 and 5) or in college today.[1]

Why are middle-class children more successful in their studies? Why do lower-class children drop out at younger ages and complete fewer grades? One hypothesis is that school teachers are middle-class in their values, if not in their origins, and penalize those students who do *not* exhibit the middle-class traits of cleanliness, punctuality, and neatness or who *do* exhibit the lower-class traits of uninhibited sexuality and aggression.[2] Some social scientists believe that lower-class children, even though they may have the intellectual potentialities for high levels of academic achievement, lose interest in school or never become interested because they resent the personal rejection of their teachers. Such rejection is, they say, motivated by the teachers' mistaken notion that lower-class children are deliberately defy-

TABLE 3. PERCENTAGE DISTRIBUTION OF PUPILS ACCORDING TO
FATHER'S OCCUPATIONAL STATUS AND PUPILS'
PROGRESS STATUS, 1931–32

| Father's Occupational Status | Pupils' Progress Status | | | |
|---|---|---|---|---|
| | Total | Slow | Normal | Rapid |
| Professional ........... | 100.0 | 13.2 | 39.7 | 47.1 |
| Clerical ............... | 100.0 | 21.3 | 32.7 | 46.0 |
| Artisan ............... | 24.0 | 22.0 | 25.5 | 24.8 |
| Skilled laborer ......... | 100.0 | 45.0 | 31.9 | 23.1 |
| Unskilled laborer ....... | 100.0 | 53.0 | 33.6 | 13.4 |

*Source for Tables 2 and 3:* Eugene A. Nifenecker, *Statistical Reference Data Relating to Problems of Overageness, Educational Retardation, Non-Promotion, 1900–1934* (New York: Board of Education, 1937), p. 233.

TABLE 4. HIGH SCHOOL ATTENDANCE OF THE CHILDREN OF
FATHERS FOLLOWING VARIOUS OCCUPATIONS, SEATTLE,
ST. LOUIS, BRIDGEPORT, AND MOUNT VERNON, 1919–1921

| Parental Occupation | Number in High School for Every 1,000 Men 45 Years of Age or Over |
|---|---|
| Proprietors | 341 |
| Professional service | 360 |
| Managerial service | 400 |
| Commercial service | 245 |
| Building trades | 145 |
| Machine trades | 169 |
| Printing trades | 220 |
| Miscellaneous trades | 103 |
| Transportation service | 157 |
| Public service | 173 |
| Personal service | 50 |
| Miners, lumber workers, and fishermen | 58 |
| Common labor | 17 |

TABLE 5. PERCENTAGE OF STUDENTS IN EACH OF TWO HIGH
SCHOOL YEARS FROM EACH OF THE OCCUPATIONAL
GROUPS, 1919–1921

| Parental Occupation | Freshman Class | Senior Class |
|---|---|---|
| Proprietors | 17.7 | 22.9 |
| Professional service | 7.7 | 12.5 |
| Managerial service | 15.4 | 19.1 |
| Commercial service | 8.6 | 11.1 |
| Clerical service | 5.9 | 5.9 |
| Agricultural service | 2.3 | 2.3 |
| Artisan-proprietors | 4.4 | 3.5 |
| Building trades | 8.8 | 5.3 |
| Machine trades | 8.3 | 4.6 |
| Printing trades | 1.0 | 0.8 |
| Miscellaneous trades | 4.8 | 2.3 |
| Transportation service | 6.2 | 3.6 |
| Public service | 1.7 | 1.1 |
| Personal service | 1.4 | 0.9 |
| Miners, lumber workers, and fishermen | 0.5 | 0.3 |
| Common labor | 1.8 | 0.6 |
| Unknown | 3.5 | 3.2 |

*Source for Tables 4 and 5:* George S. Counts, *The Selective
Character of American Secondary Education* (Chicago: University of Chicago Press, 1922), pp. 33, 37.

ing them. Davis and Havighurst show that children are the prisoners of their experience and that lower-class children behave the way they do, not because of any initial desire to defy school authorities, but rather because of their lower-class childhood training.[3]

According to this hypothesis, teacher rejection makes the lower-class boy resentful and rebellious. His attitude is, "If you don't like me, I won't cooperate." Unfortunately for him, however, school achievement is related to later occupational advancement. Failure to cooperate with the teacher cuts off the lower-class boy from a business or professional career. Professor August Hollingshead describes what happens to lower-class boys from a small town in Illinois who withdraw from school to escape the psychic punishment meted out by the teachers and upper-class children.

> The withdrawees' job skills are limited to what they have learned from contact with parents, relatives, friends, and through observations and personal experience, largely within the community; no withdrawee has any technical training for any type of job; furthermore, few have plans to acquire it in the future. . . . The boys have some acquaintance with working on farms, washing cars, loading and unloading grain, repairing cars, driving trucks, doing janitor work, clerking in stores, and odd jobs, but their lack of training, job skills, and experience combined with their youth and family backgrounds severely limit their job opportunities. These factors, along with need, force them to take whatever jobs they can find. . . . Menial tasks, long hours, low pay, and little consideration from the employer produces discontent and frustration, which motivate the young worker to seek another job, only to realize after a few days or weeks that the new job is like the old one. This desire for a more congenial job, better pay, shorter hours, and a better employer gives rise to a drift from job to job.[4]
>
> The association between education, job levels, and prestige in the social structure is so high that the person with more education moves into the high-ranking job and the person with little education into the low-ranking job. Furthermore, and this is the crucial fact from the viewpoint of the person's relation to the social structure, each tends to remain in the job channel in which he starts as a young worker. This is especially true if he has less than a high school education; then he starts as an unskilled menial and has few opportunities in later years to change to skilled labor, business, or the professions. Therefore, his chances to be promoted up through the several levels of the job channel in which he functions are severely limited. As the years pass, his position in the economic system becomes fixed, and another generation has become stable in the class structure.[5]

In other words, Professor Warner and his colleagues point out that the American public school teacher is suspicious of lower-class children and unwilling to give them a chance. If they withdraw from school to escape the pressures, they must surrender their chance to realize the American dream: social mobility.

Another hypothesis attributes the inferior performance of lower-class children at school *directly* to the economic disabilities of their families. John is a poor student because he lacks the nourishing food for sustained effort or because he is compelled to work after school instead of doing his homework; or he is a truant because he is ashamed to appear at school in ragged clothes or torn shoes. Like the rejecting teacher hypothesis, the economic disability hypothesis treats the child as essentially passive. According to both, he is victimized by a situation over which he has no control, in the one case by teachers who reject him, in the other by an economic system which does not allow him the opportunities to realize his ambitions.

But it is not at all clear that the average lower-class child has academic aspirations which are thwarted by his teachers or his economic circumstances. Studies of withdrawees from high school show that the majority leave school with no regrets; some volunteer the information that they hate school and are delighted to get through with it.[6] These data suggest that some lower-class children view the school as a burden, not an opportunity. Perhaps it is not only teacher preudice and his parents' poverty that handicap the lower-class child at school. *He* brings certain attitudes and experience to the school situation just as his teacher does.

> Whereas the middle-class child learns a socially adaptive fear of receiving poor grades in school, of being aggressive toward the teacher, of fighting, of cursing, and of having early sex relations, the slum child learns to fear quite different social acts. His gang teaches him to fear being taken in by the teacher, of being a softie with her. To study homework seriously is literally a disgrace. Instead of boasting of good marks in school, one conceals them, if he ever receives any. The lower-class individual fears not to be thought a street-fighter; it is a suspicious and dangerous social trait. He fears not to curse. If he cannot claim early sex relations his virility is seriously questioned.[7]

Of course, not all lower-class children have a hostile orientation to the school. As a matter of fact, the dramatic contrast between the educational attainments of drafted enlisted men in the two World Wars show that the public schools are being used more and more;

and some of this increase undoubtedly represents lower-class youths who eagerly take advantage of educational opportunities.[8] Still, many lower-class children do *not* utilize the educational path to social advancement.[9] Apparently, one reason for this is a chronic dissatisfaction with school which begins early in their academic careers. Why should middle-class children "take to" school so much better?

To begin with, it should not be taken for granted that any child, whatever his socio-economic origin, will find school a pleasant experience from the very first grade. On the contrary, there is reason to believe that starting school is an unpleasant shock. The average child cannot help but perceive school as an invasion of his freedom, an obligation imposed on him by adults. Forced to come at set times, to restrain his conversation so that the teacher may instruct the class as a group, he may not see any relationship between what she asks him to learn and what he might be interested in doing. And in terms of maximizing his pleasure at the time, he is quite right. Except for kindergarten and ultra-progressive schools, the curriculum is a discipline imposed on the pupil rather than an extension and development of his own interests. This is not to condemn the school system. But it does point up the problematic nature of school adjustment.

Middle-class parents make it quite clear that school is nothing to be trifled with. They have probably graduated at least from high school, and their child is aware that they *expect* him to do the same or better. If he has difficulty with his studies, they are eager (and competent) to help him. And not only do his *parents* expect him to apply himself to his studies, so do his *friends* and *their* parents. He is caught in a neighborhood pattern of academic achievement in much the same way some lower-class boys are caught in a neighborhood pattern of truancy and delinquency. This concern with education is insurance against the child's fall in social status. Middle-class parents convey to their children subtly or explicitly that they must make good in school if they want to go on being middle-class. This may be phrased in terms of preparation for a "suitable" occupation (an alternative to a stigmatized occupation such as manual labor), in terms of a correlation between a "comfortable" standard of living and educational level, or in terms of the honorific value of education for its own sake.

Middle-class parents constantly reinforce the authority and prestige of the teacher, encouraging the child to respect her and compete for her approval. The teacher makes a good parent-surrogate for him because his parents accept her in this role.[10] They urge him to value the gold stars she gives out and the privilege of being her monitor. But although the middle-class child's initial motivation to cooperate with the teacher may spring from his parents, motivation functionally autonomous of parental pressure usually develops to supplement it.[11] Part of this new motivation may be the intrinsic interest of the subject matter, or at least some of it, once he has gotten well along in his course. *Learning* to read may be a disagreeable chore; but the time soon comes when interesting stories are made accessible by the development of reading skill. An even more important source of motivation favorable to school is the recognition he gets in the form of high marks. He learns that scholastic competition is somewhat analogous to the social and economic competition in which his parents participate. The object of scholastic competition is to win the approving attention of the teacher, to skip grades, and to remain always in the "bright" classes. (In grade school the "bright" and the "dull" classes take approximately the same work, but pupils and teachers have no difficulty in separating the high prestige groups. In high school, "commercial," "trade," and "general" courses have different curricula from the high prestige "college" course. Again, there is consensus among the students as well as the teachers that the non-college courses are for those who are not "college material.")[12]

Of course it is not competition alone that gives the middle-class child an emotional investment in continued scholastic effort; it is the *position* he achieves in that competition. Apparently his pre-school training prepares *him* much better for scholastic competition than his lower-class classmate.[13] His parents mingle with lawyers, accountants, businessmen, and others who in their day-to-day activities manipulate symbols. In the course of conversation these people use a sizeable vocabulary including many abstractions of high order. He unconsciously absorbs these concepts in an effort to understand his parents and their friends. He is stimulated in this endeavor by the rewards he receives from his parents when he shows verbal precociousness. These rewards are not necessarily material or conscious. The attention he receives as a result of a remark insightful beyond his years, the pride his mother shows in repeating a bright response of his to her friends, these are rewards enough. This home background is valuable preparation for successful competition in school. For, after all, school subjects are designed to prepare for exactly the occupational level to which his parents are already oriented. Hence he soon *achieves* in school a higher than average status. (See Tables 1, 2, and 3.) To maintain this status intact (or improve it) becomes the incentive for further effort, which involves him deeper and deeper in the reward and punishment system of the school. Thus, *his success cumulates and generates the conditions for further success.*

A similar conclusion was reached after a study of the success and failure of children in certain nonacademic activities. Dr. Anderson concluded that success and practice mutually reinforce one another, producing remarkable differentiations in performance.

> . . . a child is furnished from early life with the opportunity to hammer nails. In the course of the next ten or fifteen years, the child has 100,000 opportunities to hammer nails, whereas a second child in the same period of time has only ten or fifteen opportunities to hammer nails. At the age of twenty, we may be tremendously impressed with the ease and accuracy with which the first child hammers nails and likewise with the awkwardness and incapacity of the second child. We speak of the first child as an expert and the second child as a boob with respect to the nail hitting situation, and we may naively ascribe the ability of the first child to an inherited ability because its appearance is so inexplicable in comparison with the lack of ability of the second child.[14]
>
> The most significant fact which comes out of these observations is the fact that if we take a particular child and record his relationship to the group, we find that in ninety-five percent of the situations with which he is presented in the play situation, he is the dominating or leading individual, whereas another child under the same conditions is found to be in the leading position only five percent of the time.
>
> . . . the social reactions of these particular children . . . may be the product of hereditary factors, environmental factors, more rapid rate of development, or a large number of factors combined. The important fact for our discussion is that within a constant period one child is getting approximately twenty times as much specific practice in meeting social situations in a certain way as is a second child. Life is something like a game of billiards in which the better player gets more opportunity for practice and the poorer player less.[15]

For the average middle-class child, the effective forces in his life situation form a united front to urge upon him a favorable orientation to school. Of course, this may not be sufficient to produce good school adjustment. He may not have the native intelligence to perform up to the norm. Or he may have idiosyncratic experiences that alienate him from scholastic competition. But, apparently, for the *average* middle-class child, this favorable orientation, combined with the intellectual abilities cultivated in his social milieu, results in satisfactory performance in the school situation.

The other side of the coin is the failure of some lower-class children to develop the kind of orientation which will enable them to overcome the initial frustration of school discipline.[16] To begin with, the parents of the lower-class child may not support the school as do middle-class parents. His parents probably do not have much education themselves, and, if not, they cannot very well make meaningful to him subjects that they do not themselves understand. Neither are they able to help him surmount academic stumbling blocks. Even more important, they lack the incentive to encourage him in and praise him for school accomplishment at that critical early period when he finds school new and strange and distasteful. Almost the same reasoning can be applied to the inculcation of a cooperative attitude toward school in the child as has been applied to an acceptant attitude toward toilet training. If the parents convey to the child their eagerness to have him adjust to irksome school discipline, he will probably accept it to please them and retain their love just as he learned to urinate and defecate at appropriate times and places. But toilet training and school adjustment training differ in an important particular. Parents *must* toilet train the child because permitting him to soil himself at will is a constant and immediate nuisance.

The consequences of a child's disinterest in school may also be unpleasant, both for him and for his parents, but it is not immediate. In the short run, allowing him to neglect school may be the least troublesome course for his parents to take. If they are neutral or antagonistic toward school, a result (1) of the esoteric nature of the curriculum from the point of view of skills cultivated and appreciated in the lower-class milieu and (2) of their failure to see the relevance of education to occupational advancement into a higher socioeconomic class, they do not *have* to give the kind of support to the school given by middle-class parents. There is no reason to assume that the value of education is self-evident. For those lower-class people who have lost hope in social mobility, the school is a symbol of a competition in which they do not believe they can succeed. If they themselves have given up, will they necessarily encourage their children to try to be better?

Moreover, coming as he does from a social stratum where verbal skills are not highly developed, the lower-class child finds school more difficult than does his middle-class contemporary. His father, a carpenter or a factory worker, manipulates concrete objects rather than symbols in his occupational role. In so far as he learns from his father, he is more likely to learn how to "fix things" than the importance of a large vocabulary.[17] This learning does not help him with his school work, for school tends to give a competitive advantage to those with verbal facility.

This disadvantage with respect to verbal skills may account for the poorer showing of lower-class children on standard intelligence tests.[18]

> . . . the cultural bias of the standard tests of intelligence consists in their having fixed upon only those types of mental behavior in which the higher and middle socio-economic groups are superior. In those particular areas of behavior, the tests might conceivably be adequate measures of mental differences among individual children within the more privileged socio-economic groups. But they do not measure the comparative over-all mental behavior of the higher and lower socio-economic groups, because they do not use problems which are equally familiar and motivating to all such groups.[19]

In other words, middle-class children have an advantage because they are more familiar with the sort of problems that occur on the tests. This does not necessarily mean that the intelligence tests are invalid. It depends upon what the investigator thinks he is measuring. If he believes he is getting at "innate" ability, abstracted from cultural milieu and idiosyncratic learning, he is naive. An intelligence test is a valid measure of the native intellectual ability of an individual only under special circumstances, one of these being that the respondent's experience is similar to that of the group on which the test was standardized. Thus, a Navaho boy who scores 80 on the Stanford-Binet (Revised Form) may be unusually intelligent. Until a test is designed to tap the experiences of Navahos, there exists no reference point about which to assess superiority and inferiority.[20]

However, it is not only the *content* of the intelligence test that gives middle-class urban children a better chance at high scores. It is the *structure* of the test situation. Even if we could find items equally familiar or unfamiliar to everyone taking the test, differential interest in solving abstract problems would work against the lower-class student.

> . . . finding completely unfamiliar problems is not a possible choice, because such problems (namely, those involving some relationship between esoteric geometrical figures) do not arouse as great interest or as strong

a desire to achieve a solution among low socio-economic groups as among high groups. The reason is clear: such an unrealistic problem can arouse the child's desire to achieve a solution only if the child has been trained to evaluate highly any and all success in tests. No matter how unreal and purposeless the problem may seem, the average child in a high socio-economic group will work hard to solve it, if his parents, his teacher, or other school officers expect him to try hard. The average slum child, however, will usually react negatively to any school test, and especially to a test whose problems have no relation to his experience.[21]

However justified the criticisms of the intelligence test as an instrument measuring native intellectual ability, it is highly predictive of academic accomplishment. A student with a high I.Q. score does better in his studies, on the average, than one with a low I.Q. score.[22] Hence the discrepancy between the scores of lower-class students and of middle-class students is an index of the former's disadvantage in the school situation.

One possible response of the lower-class child to his disadvantages in the school situation is to increase his efforts. But his initial orientation drives him in the opposite direction. He is more likely to respond to competitive failure by going on strike psychologically, neglecting his homework, paying no attention in class, annoying the teacher. Uninterested in the curriculum, he learns as little as he can. Instead of a situation where the student and the teacher work toward a common goal, the development of the student's understanding of certain ranges of problems, he and his teacher are oriented antagonistically to one another. The teacher tries to stuff into his head as much of the curriculum as possible; he tries to absorb as little as is consistent with his own safety, in terms of sanctions mobilized by the school and his parents.

*But school subjects are cumulative.* Within a few years he is retarded in basic skills, such as reading, absolutely necessary for successful performance in the higher grades. Whether he is promoted along with his age-mates, "left back," or shunted into "slow" programs makes relatively little difference at this point. For whatever is done, he finds himself at the bottom of the school status hierarchy. He is considered "dumb" by the more successful students and by the teachers. This makes school still more uninteresting, if not unpleasant, and he neglects his work further. Eventually he realizes he can never catch up.

Without realizing what he was doing, he had cut himself off from the channels of social mobility. In those crucial early grades where the basis for school adjustment was being laid, he had not yet known that he wanted more out of life than his parents. Or, if he knew, he did not realize that school achievement and high occupational status are related. And he was not lucky enough to have parents who realized it for him and urged him on until he was old enough to identify with the school through choice. There is a certain irreversibility about school maladjustment. The student can hardly decide at 18 that he wants to become a lawyer if he is five years retarded in school. It is no longer possible for him to "catch up" and use school as a means to realize his ambitions. Sometimes lower-class men will rue their failure to take advantage of the opportunities presented by the school. James T. Farrell captures the flavor of this regret in the following passage from one of his novels:

> Walking on, seeing the lights of Randolph Street before him, he won-dered if they were college football players [referring to the young men walking in front of him]. That was what Studs Lonigan might have been. Even if he did admit it, he had been a damn good quarterback. If he only hadn't been such a chump, bumming from school to hang around with skunky Weary Reilley and Paulie Haggerty until he was so far behind at high school that it was no use going. It wouldn't have been so hard to have studied and done enough homework to get by, and then he could have set the high school gridiron afire, gone to Notre Dame and made himself a Notre Dame immortal, maybe, alongside of George Gipp, the Four Horsemen, Christie Flannagan and Carideo. How many times in a guy's life couldn't he kick his can around the block for having played chump.[23]

If, on the other hand, the social milieu of the lower-class boy sup-ported the school and encouraged him to bend every effort to keep up with his work, he would finish high school whether he enjoyed it or not — the way middle-class boys do. At graduation he might decide that he would like to become a plumber. That is, he might not crave middle-class status enough to suffer the discipline of continued educa-tion. But if he were not content with a lower-class status, if he wanted above all things to "be somebody," the educational route to high status would still be open. He would still have a *choice;* he would not be forced to accept a menial occupational role whether he liked it or not. As it is, the crucial decision is made before he is old enough to have a voice in it; it is made by his parents, his neighbors, and his friends.

To sum up, the middle-class child has the following advantages in school compared with the lower-class child: (1) his parents are probably better educated and are therefore more capable of helping him with his school work if this should be necessary; (2) his parents are more eager to make his school work seem meaningful to him by indicating, implicitly or explicitly, the occupational applications of long division or history; (3) the verbal skills which he acquires as part of child training on the middle-class status level prepare him for the type of training that goes on in school and give him an initial (and cumulating) advantage over the lower-class child in the classroom learning situation; and (4) the coordinated pressure of parents, friends, and neighbors reinforce his motivation for scholastic success and increase the probability of good school adjustment.

## REFERENCES

1. Helen B. Goetsch, *Parental Income and College Opportunities* (New York: Teachers College, Columbia University, Contributions to Education, No. 795, 1940).

2. W. L. Warner, R. J. Havighurst, and M. B. Loeb, *Who Shall Be Educated?* (New York: Harper & Brothers, 1944).

3. Allison Davis and Robert J. Havighurst, *Father of the Man* (Boston: Houghton Mifflin, 1947).

4. August B. Hollingshead, *Elmtown's Youth* (New York: John Wiley & Sons, 1949), p. 369.

5. *Ibid.*, p. 388.

6. Howard C. Seymour, The Characteristics of Pupils Who Leave School Early — A Comparative Study of Graduates with Those Who are Eliminated Before High School Graduation, unpublished Ph.D. dissertation, Harvard University, 1940; Harold J. Dillon, *Early School Leavers* (New York: National Child Labor Committee, 1949).

7. Allison Davis, *Social Class Influences on Learning* (Cambridge, Massachusetts: Harvard University Press, 1949), p. 30.

8. 41 percent of the selectees of World War II were high school graduates or better, as contrasted with only 9 percent in World War I. Samuel A. Stouffer and others, *The American Soldier* (Princeton: Princeton University Press, 1949), I, 59. Compulsory school attendance laws may have something to do with this difference, but the average age of high school graduation is beyond the age of compulsory attendance in most states.

9. The assumption here is that the goal of success is sufficiently widespread in the American ethos and the penalties for criminal deviance sufficiently

great that the failure to utilize a legitimate channel of social mobility can usually be explained as due (1) to a failure on the part of the individual to *perceive* that channel as feasible for him and to define it as an opportunity, (2) to objective disabilities which cannot be overcome by effort, or (3) to his perception of other and better opportunities. We assume, therefore, that the lower-class subculture (uncongenial to social mobility) has its roots in a sour-grapes reaction. This does *not* mean that every lower-class boy yearns for higher socioeconomic status at some time or other in his life. Some of them have been socialized into the sour grapes tradition before having the experience on which they might personally conclude that the grapes are sour.

10. Professor Green maintains that the middle-class boy is more closely supervised by his mother than the lower-class boy and that this "personality absorption" creates a dependence on adult authority much greater than that of the less well supervised lower-class boy. If this theory were accepted, we would thus find additional reason for the relative tractability and cooperativeness of the middle-class boy in school. Arnold W. Green, "The Middle Class Male Child and Neurosis," *American Sociological Review*, XI (1946), 31–41.

11. See Gordon W. Allport, *Personality* (New York, Henry Holt and Company, 1937), pp. 191–206, for a discussion of functional autonomy.

12. George S. Counts, *The Selective Character of American Secondary Education* (Chicago: University of Chicago Press, 1922), shows the middle-class orientation of the "college" course; see also R. E. Eckert and T. O. Marshall, *When Youth Leaves School* (New York: The Regents' Inquiry, McGraw-Hill, 1938), p. 67.

13. Millie C. Almy, *Children's Experiences prior to First Grade and Success in Beginning Reading* (New York: Teachers College, Columbia University, Contributions to Education, No. 954, 1949); Dorris M. Lee, *The Importance of Reading for Achieving in Grades Four, Five, and Six* (New York: Teachers College, Columbia University, Contributions to Education, No. 556, 1933).

14. John E. Anderson, "The Genesis of Social Reactions in the Young Child," *The Unconscious: A Symposium*, ed. by E. S. Dummer (New York: Alfred A. Knopf, 1928), pp. 83–84.

15. *Ibid.*, pp. 81–82.

16. At this point we are abstracting from such situational considerations as teacher rejection, the economic resources of the family and native capacity. We are considering only the orientations of the boy himself.

17. Of course this is a matter of degree. The lower-class boy acquires verbal skills but not on so high a level as the middle-class boy.

18. Walter S. Neff, "Socio-economic Status and Intelligence: a Critical Survey," *Psychological Bulletin*, XXXV (1938), 727–757.

19. Allison Davis, *op. cit.*, p. 48.

20. Dorothy Leighton and Clyde Kluckhohn, *Children of the People* (Cambridge, Massachusetts: Harvard University Press, 1947), pp. 148–155.

21. *Ibid.*, pp. 68–69.

22. Eugene A. Nifenecker, *Statistical Reference Data Relating to Problems of Overageness, Educational Retardation, Non-Promotion, 1900–1934* (New York: Board of Education, 1937), p. 111.

23. James T. Farrell, *Judgment Day* (New York: Vanguard Press, 1935), p. 24.

# PART III

Achievement in Academic Settings

# INTRODUCTION

The present section views the child as he experiences the school, an organization which expects and demands individual efforts to achieve in terms of more universalistic standards than those of his family. Indeed, as the selection by Parsons indicates, the major criterion governing the differentiation of individuals in the school setting is academic accomplishment. Receiving or forfeiting rewards according to his performance, each child is impressed indelibly with the importance of achievement.

## The Impact of Macro-Social Structures

Although the school imparts to all children this awareness of the fundamental importance of achievement behavior in American life, the school cannot and does not develop impartially in each student the maximum achievement-relevant skills commensurate with his or her ability. Forces operating both within and without the school prevent such an outcome. A major issue presents itself at this point. To what extent is the school an agency for sorting and selecting its members into life-paths which lead invariably to the propagation and maintenance of the previously established status structure of the larger society?

Looking first at external factors influencing the acquisition of achievement skills in school, many studies have shown family socio-economic status to be a prime variable. Students from families lower in social status, other things equal, do less well in school and develop their achievement skills to lesser degrees than do students from families higher in social status.[1] Rogoff's paper in this section, drawing data from a national sample, presents evidence supporting this conclusion, and also shows that factors varying across communities (such as community size and relation to metropolitan area) affect school achievement.[2] Without denying the importance of family and school experiences as predictors of academic accomplishments, Rogoff deflects a portion of our attention to the increasing relevancy of community structures in our search for comprehension of achievement in the academic setting.

Before discussing factors at work within the school which affect the acquisition of achievement skills, let us consider briefly the meaning of achievement in the academic setting. It is useful to distinguish between intra-level achievement — exemplary performance in specific courses — and inter-level achievement — meeting the minimal requirements for promotion or graduation at various points in the education process. We suggest that students oriented more toward intra-level achievement, in comparison with students more oriented toward inter-level achievement, will be satisfied more frequently by day-to-day successes in problem-solving and creative academic work. If this is true, then personality variables may be more closely associated with intra-level achievement, while social structural variables may be more closely associated with inter-level achievement. For example, many more students from Middle class backgrounds than from Working class backgrounds learn to value inter-level achievement, and to exhibit the kinds of extra-academic behaviors (in manners, dress, morals, and so on) conducive to such achievement. But the qualities underlying exemplary accomplishment within a given grade-level — such as intelligence, curiosity, and persistence — are less determined by social class background. Hence, such personality characteristics may here assume considerable importance.[3]

Turning now to factors operating within the school, we note at once how the development of personality characteristics relevant to academic achievement may be nurtured or stunted by differences of school social organizations. Such results are particularly evident in the Biber and Minuchin paper presented in this section. Their delineation of schools by clearly specified criteria into "modern" and "traditional" structures denotes expectations of different kinds of achievement behavior of those students in the respective schools. A variety of differences were observed by Biber and Minuchin. It was found, for instance, that children in the "modern" school showed inquisitiveness and concern for depth of understanding, while children in the "traditional" school displayed more concern with efficient and speedy activity which resulted in the "correct" answer. The reader may agree that the "modern" school system described by these authors should fit its students for more exemplary performances in adult occupational roles than should the "traditional" systems. Longitudinal research documenting or disconfirming this outcome is sorely needed.

## THE IMPACT OF MICRO-SOCIAL STRUCTURES

We consider here two interactional systems which may exert strong influence on the acquisition of achievement skills and the quality of academic performance: student peer group relations, and student-teacher relations.

### The Student Peer Group

A mounting body of evidence affirms the power of the student peer group to raise or lower achievement aspirations and to enhance or obstruct academic performance. This situation results from the lengthy period of formal education demanded by the conditions of modern industrial society. Because most youths must be trained in myriad ways impossible for the family or kin-group to accomplish, and entry into responsible adulthood must be delayed while formal training outside the home is acquired, familial influence on the young is weakened and peer group influence grows.[4] The peer group becomes an especially effective socializing agent during adolescence, when it serves as a "buffer group" between the secure but dependent status provided youths by the family and the impersonal, anxiety-laden but independent status awaiting them in the adult world.[5]

A basic framework for understanding peer group relations as they impinge on academic concerns is provided by Newcomb (selection 17). Although his discussion refers to college students, the theoretical principles are appropriate to understanding peer relations at most school levels. Nevertheless, it should be noted that the *content* of peer group influence may well be different between the elementary school level and higher grade levels. For example, at the elementary level, sociometric status (one's standing in the group's rank of interpersonal "liking" or attractiveness) is positively related to academic performance.[6] Still, in elementary school powerful peer pressures may subdue the extraordinary or creative child.[7] In the latter school years, on the other hand, sociometric status is frequently associated with mediocre academic performance rather than exemplary performance.

The potent influence of the peer group on several kinds of academic outcomes has been demonstrated at the high school,[8] college,[9] and post-college levels.[10] In addition, the selection by Alexander and Campbell indicates that peer group influence in high school has consequences for post-high school behavior. Their research shows that, whatever the educational attainments of parents, students are both more likely to expect to attend college and to actually enter college if their high school friends expected to go to college. The weight of the evidence on peer group effects, particularly the longitudinal data of Alexander and Campbell, makes one skeptical of those challenges asserting that peer groups do not have adverse effects on academic concerns or that such effects are at most only moderate and temporary.[11]

Peer group influence on academic achievement which is not directly mediated by interpersonal interaction may also occur. That is, even though all persons in a social system do not interact directly, the system may be pervaded by powerful norms, explicit or implicit, regarding what members *should* do, and these norms may strongly affect what members *actually* do. Such normative effects are established in the selection by Coleman. His research shows that the most able students earn the highest grades *if* academic performance is highly valued by the student peer culture; among schools in which the student culture devalues academic performance, the more typical pattern, the relationship between ability and performance is blunted.[12]

It must be stressed that both relations between peers and the norms of the student culture may either promote or retard both intra- and inter-level achievement. The importance of such variations may be grasped by noting several of the possible combinations of student norms in different schools. Thus, there are schools in which neither type of achievement is highly valued; schools in which inter-level achievement but not intra-level achievement is valued; schools in which both types of achievement are equally valued; and schools in which intra-level achievement is more highly valued than inter-level achievement. Clearly, vast differences in levels of academic performance and achievement skills will be manifest among these diverse types of schools.

## Teacher-Student Relations

Knowledge of the teacher-student relationship as it affects achievement is meager, research having been guided more by the concerns of educational practitioners than by the urge to develop general theoretical explanations.[13] Although effects stemming from community social structure, the social system of the school, and the student peer group may each be more powerful than effects arising from teacher-student relationships, nearly everyone will recall one or another type of teacher-student experience as having enhanced his own learning and achievement skills. No doubt the elements in any such situation enhancing learning for some persons are unimportant or even detrimental to learning for other persons; but this signifies only that the phenomenon is complex — an ubiquitous circumstance in social research. Discoveries in this area should be made an immediate goal.

We present two studies here, each illustrating the subtle, deleterious effects of one variable (social class background of the participants) on the development of achievement skills among the students.[14] Henry's analysis of teacher-student interaction in a Middle class elementary school setting finds the promotion of academic interests and accomplishments subordinated to the "social adjustment" values of the Middle class teacher. Above all, the students learn that docility in the classroom is rewarding.

In Becker's paper, incongruence in values between the Middle class teacher and her Lower class students is shown to produce much misunderstanding and conflict between the participants. The outcome is low academic performance, negative feelings toward school, and scarcely any development of achievement skills among the students.

## REFERENCES

1. Outstanding among the many community studies documenting this fact is that of August B. Hollingshead, *Elmtown's Youth* (New York: John Wiley and Sons, 1949). Among the first of the demographic analyses supporting the assertion is that of Elbridge Sibley, "Some Demographic Clues to Social Stratification," *American Sociological Review*, 7 (June, 1942), 322–330. And the full power of social status background in determining academic achievement is revealed by Terman's longitudinal study of gifted children, showing that even among persons with very high intelligence (I.Q. above 150), academic performance is significantly affected by family status background. See Lewis M. Terman and Melita H. Oden, *The Gifted Child Grows Up: Twenty-five Year's Follow-up of a Superior Group* (Stanford: Stanford University Press, 1947).

2. See also Alan B. Wilson, "Residential Segregation of Social Classes and Aspirations of High School Boys," *American Sociological Review*, 24 (December, 1959), 836–845. He reports that the educational aspirations of high school boys are significantly influenced by the social class and racial

compositions of a school's student body, even when such variables as I.Q. and grade average are statistically controlled.

3. To be sure, the family structures and socialization practices which encourage the development of intelligence, curiosity, diligence and concern for learning as an end in itself are more frequently found in the Middle class setting than in the Working class setting. But present evidence suggests that if we take as a base the numbers of students who are positively oriented toward inter-level achievement, and as a numerator the numbers of students who are also positively oriented toward intra-level achievement, the resulting ratios for the two social class backgrounds would not be markedly dissimilar.

4. For examples, see: Edward L. McDill and James Coleman, "Family and Peer Influences in College Plans of High School Students," *Sociology of Education*, 38 (Winter, 1965), 112–126; Bernard C. Rosen, *Adolescence and Religion* (Cambridge: Schenckman Publishing Company, 1966), 102–104; Clay Brittain, "Adolescent and Parent-Peer Cross-Pressures," *American Sociological Review*, 28 (June, 1963), 385–391; Urie Bronfenbrenner, Edward C. Devereux, George J. Succi and Robert R. Rodgers, "Response to Pressure from Peers Versus Adults among Soviet and American School Children" (paper presented at the Symposium of Social Factors in Personality Development, XIX International Congress of Psychology, Moscow, USSR, August, 1966).

5. Research on peer group influence in personality development is surveyed in Richard A. Schmuck and Anita Lohman, "Peer Relations and Personality Development" (Ann Arbor: Institute for Social Research, University of Michigan, 1966).

6. Richard A. Schmuck, "Sociometric Status and Utilization of Academic Ability," *Merrill-Palmer Quarterly*, 8 (July, 1962), 165–172.

7. E. Paul Torrance, "Laboratory Studies of Peer Pressures Against Highly Creative Group Members," in E. P. Torrance, *et al.*, The Minnesota Studies of Creative Thinking in the Early School Years. *Research Memo.* BER-60-1 (Minneapolis: University of Minnesota, 1960), 22–23.

8. Edward L. McDill and James S. Coleman, "High School Social Status, College Plans, and Interest in Academic Achievement: A Panel Analysis," *American Sociological Review*, 28 (December, 1963), 905–918; Robert E. Herriott, "Some Social Determinants of Educational Aspiration," *Harvard Educational Review*, 33 (Spring, 1963), 157–177; James S. Coleman, *The Adolescent Society* (Glencoe, Illinois: The Free Press, 1961).

9. Walter L. Wallace, "Institutional and Life-Cycle Socialization of College Freshman," *American Journal of Sociology*, 70 (November, 1964), 303–318; Desmond S. Cartwright and Richard J. Robertson, "Membership in

Cliques and Achievement," *American Journal of Sociology*, 66 (March, 1961), 441–445.

10. Everett C. Hughes, Howard S. Becker and Blanche Geer, "Student Culture and Academic Effort," in Nevitt Sanford, editor, *The American College* (New York: John Wiley and Sons, 1962), 515–530.

11. See Ralph H. Turner, *The Social Context of Ambition* (San Francisco: Chandler Publishing Company, 1964).

12. Coleman's study was made in ten northern Illinois high schools selected for the diversity of their characteristics. The predominant pattern of the value systems of the schools was one heavily weighted in the direction of athletic and popularity success rather than scholastic achievement, even though some schools differed to some extent in their relative emphasis on the various values as prerequisites to being popular or in the "leading crowd."

13. For summaries of research in this area see N. L. Gage, editor, *Handbook of Research on Teaching* (Chicago: Rand McNally and Company, 1963), 700–710; John C. Glidewell, Mildred B. Kantor, Louis M. Smith and Lorene A. Stringer, "Social Structure and Socialization in the Elementary School Classroom (Clayton, Missouri: The St. Louis County Health Department, 1965); David E. Lavin, *The Prediction of Academic Performance* (New York: Russell Sage Foundation, 1965), 138–145.

14. Of course teacher-student relationships may also raise the level of academic performance and achievement skills. For studies reporting such positive effects, see the annotated references at the end of this section.

# A.

# THE IMPACT OF MACRO-SOCIAL STRUCTURES: THE SCHOOL AS A SOCIAL SYSTEM

# THE SCHOOL CLASS AS A SOCIAL SYSTEM:
# SOME OF ITS FUNCTIONS IN AMERICAN SOCIETY

## TALCOTT PARSONS

This essay will attempt to outline, if only sketchily, an analysis of the elementary and secondary school class as a social system, and the relation of its structure to its primary functions in the society as an agency of socialization and allocation. While it is important that the school class is normally part of the larger organization of a school, the class rather than the whole school will be the unit of analysis here, for it is recognized both by the school system and by the individual pupil as the place where the "business" of formal education actually takes place. In elementary schools, pupils of one grade are typically placed in a single "class" under one main teacher, but in the secondary school, and sometimes in the upper elementary grades, the pupil works on different subjects under different teachers; here the complex of classes participated in by the same pupil is the significant unit for our purposes.

### THE PROBLEM: SOCIALIZATION AND SELECTION

Our main interest, then, is in a dual problem: first of how the school class functions to internalize in its pupils both the commitments and capacities for successful performance of their future adult roles, and second of how it functions to allocate these human resources within the role-structure of the adult society. The primary ways in which these two problems are interrelated will provide our main points of reference.

First, from the functional point of view the school class can be treated as an agency of socialization. That is to say, it is an agency through which individual personalities are trained to be motivationally

Reprinted with abridgement from the *Harvard Educational Review* (Vol. 29, No. 4, Fall 1959, pp. 297-318) by permission of the publisher and the author.

and technically adequate to the performance of adult roles. It is not the sole such agency; the family, informal "peer groups," churches, and sundry voluntary organizations all play a part, as does actual on-the-job training. But, in the period extending from entry into first grade until entry into the labor force or marriage, the school class may be regarded as the focal socializing agency.

The socialization function may be summed up as the development in individuals of the commitments and capacities which are essential prerequisites of their future role-performance. Commitments may be broken down in turn into two components: commitment to the implementation of the broad *values* of society, and commitment to the performance of a specific type of role within the *structure* of society. Thus a person in a relatively humble occupation may be a "solid citizen" in the sense of commitment to honest work in that occupation, without an intensive and sophisticated concern with the implementation of society's higher-level values. Or conversely, someone else might object to the anchorage of the feminine role in marriage and the family on the grounds that such anchorage keeps society's total talent resources from being distributed equitably to business, government, and so on. Capacities can also be broken down into two components, the first bing competence or the skill to perform the tasks involved in the individual's roles, and the second being "role-responsibility" or the capacity to live up to other people's expectations of the interpersonal behavior appropriate to these roles. Thus a mechanic as well as a doctor needs to have not only the basic "skills of his trade," but also the ability to behave responsibly toward those people with whom he is brought into contact in his work.

While on the one hand, the school class may be regarded as a primary agency by which these different components of commitments and capacities are generated, on the other hand, it is, from the point of view of the society, an agency of "manpower" allocation. It is well known that in American society there is a very high, and probably increasing, correlation between one's status level in the society and one's level of educational attainment. Both social status and educational level are obviously related to the occupational status which is attained. Now, as a result of the general process of both educational and occupational upgrading, completion of high school is increasingly coming to be the norm for minimum satisfactory educational attainment, and the most significant line for future occupational status has come to be drawn between members of an age-cohort who do and do not go to college.

We are interested, then, in what it is about the school class in our society that determines the distinction between the contingents of the age-cohort which do and do not go to college. Because of a tradition of localism and a rather pragmatic pluralism, there is apparently considerable variety among school systems of various cities and states. Although the situation in metropolitan Boston probably represents a more highly structured pattern than in many other parts of the country, it is probably not so extreme as to be misleading in its main features. There, though of course actual entry into college does not come until after graduation from high school, the main dividing line is between those who are and are not enrolled in the college preparatory course in high school; there is only a small amount of shifting either way after about the ninth grade when the decision is normally made. Furthermore, the evidence seems to be that by far the most important criterion of selection is the record of school performance in elementary school. These records are evaluated by teachers and principals, and there are few cases of entering the college preparatory course against their advice. It is therefore not stretching the evidence too far to say broadly that the primary selective process occurs through differential school performance in elementary school, and that the "seal" is put on it in junior high school.[1]

The evidence also is that the selective process is genuinely assortative. As in virtually all comparable processes, ascriptive as well as achieved factors influence the outcome. In this case, the ascriptive factor is the socio-economic status of the child's family, and the factor underlying his opportunity for achievement is his individual ability. In the study of 3,348 Boston high school boys on which these generalizations are based, each of these factors was quite highly correlated with planning college. For example, the percentages planning college, by father's occupation, were: 12 per cent for semi-skilled and unskilled, 19 per cent for skilled, 26 per cent for minor white collar, 52 per cent for middle white collar, and 80 per cent for major white collar. Likewise, intentions varied by ability (as measured by IQ), namely, 11 per cent for the lowest quintile, 17 per cent for the next, 24 per cent for the middle, 30 per cent for the next to the top, and 52 per cent for the highest. It should be noted also that within any ability quintile, the relationship of plans to father's occupation is seen. For example, within the very important top quintile in ability as measured, the range in college intentions was from 29 per cent for sons of laborers to 89 per cent for sons of major white collar persons.[2]

The essential points here seem to be that there is a relatively uniform criterion of selection operating to differentiate between the college and the non-college contingents, and that for a very important part of the cohort the operation of this criterion is not a "put-up job" — it is not simply a way of affirming a previously determined ascriptive status. To be sure, the high-status, high-ability boy is very likely indeed to go to college, and the low-status, low-ability boy is very unlikely to go. But the "cross-pressured" group for whom these two factors do not coincide[3] is of considerable importance.

Considerations like these lead me to conclude that the main process of differentiation (which from another point of view is selection) that occurs during elementary school takes place on a single main axis of *achievement*. Broadly, moreover, the differentiation leads up through high school to a bifurcation into college-goers and non-college-goers.

To assess the significance of this pattern, let us look at its place in the socialization of the individual. Entering the system of formal education is the child's first major step out of primary involvement in his family of orientation. Within the family certain foundations of his motivational system have been laid down. But the only characteristic fundamental to later roles which has clearly been "determined" and psychologically stamped in by that time is sex role. The post-oedipal child enters the system of formal education clearly categorized as boy or girl, but beyond that his *role* is not yet differentiated. The process of selection, by which persons will select and be selected for categories of roles, is yet to take place.

On grounds which cannot be gone into here, it may be said that the most important single predispositional factor with which the child enters school is his level of *independence*. By this is meant his level of self-sufficiency relative to guidance by adults, his capacity to take responsibility and to make his own decisions in coping with new and varying situations. This, like his sex role, he has as a function of his experience in the family.

The family is a collectivity within which the basic status-structure is ascribed in terms of biological position, that is, by generation, sex, and age. There are inevitably differences of performance relative to these, and they are rewarded and punished in ways that contribute to differential character formation. But these differences are not given the sanction of institutionalized social status. The school is the first socializing agency in the child's experience which institutionalizes a differentiation of status on nonbiological bases. Moreover, this is not an ascribed but an achieved status; it is the status "earned" by differential performance of the tasks set by the teacher, who is acting as an agent of the community's school system.

## THE STRUCTURE OF THE ELEMENTARY SCHOOL CLASS

In accord with the generally wide variability of American institutions, and of course the basically local control of school systems, there is considerable variability of school situations, but broadly they have a single relatively well-marked framework.[4] Particularly in the primary part of the elementary grades, *i.e.*, the first three grades, the basic pattern includes one main teacher for the class, who teaches all subjects and who is in charge of the class generally. Sometimes this early, and frequently in later grades, other teachers are brought in for a few special subjects, particularly gym, music, and art, but this does not alter the central position of the main teacher. This teacher is usually a woman.[5] The class is with this one teacher for the school year, but usually no longer.

The class, then, is composed of about 25 age-peers of both sexes drawn from a relatively small geographical area — the neighborhood. Except for sex in certain respects, there is initially no formal basis for differentiation of status within the school class. The main structural differentation develops gradually, on the single main axis indicated above as achievement. That the differentiation should occur on a single main axis is ensured by four primary features of the situation. The first is the initial equalization of the "contestants'" status by age and by "family background," the neighborhood being typically much more homogeneous than is the whole society. The second circumstance is the imposition of a common set of tasks which is, compared to most other task-areas, strikingly undifferentiated. The school situation is far more like a race in this respect than most role-performance situations. Third, there is the sharp polarization between the pupils in their initial equality and the *single* teacher who is an adult and "represents" the adult world. And fourth, there is a relatively systematic process of evaluation of the pupils' performances.

From the point of view of a pupil, this evaluation, particularly (though not exclusively) in the form of report card marks, constitutes reward and/or punishment for past performance; from the viewpoint of the school system acting as an allocating agency, it is a basis of *selection* for future status in society.

Two important sets of qualifications need to be kept in mind in interpreting this structural pattern, but I think these do not destroy the significance of its main outline. The first qualification is for variations in the formal organization and procedures of the school class itself. Here the most important kind of variation is that between relatively "traditional" schools and relatively "progressive" schools. The more traditional schools put more emphasis on discrete units of subject-matter, whereas the progressive type allows more "indirect" teaching through "projects" and broader topical interests where more than one bird can be killed with a stone. In progressive schools there is more emphasis on groups of pupils working together, compared to the traditional direct relation of the individual pupil to the teacher. This is related to the progressive emphasis on co-operation among the pupils rather than direct competition, to greater permissiveness as opposed to strictness of discipline, and to a de-emphasis on formal marking.[6] In some schools one of these components will be more prominent, and in others, another. That it is, however, an important range of variation is clear. It has to do, I think, very largely with the independence-dependence training which is so important to early socialization in the family. My broad interpretation is that those people who emphasize independence training will tend to be those who favor relatively progressive education. The relation of support for progressive education to relatively high socio-economic status and to "intellectual" interests and the like is well known. There is no contradiction between these emphases both on independence and on co-operation and group solidarity among pupils. In the first instance this is because the main focus of the independence problem at these ages is vis-à-vis adults. However, it can also be said that the peer group, which here is built into the school class, is an indirect field of expression of dependency needs, displaced from adults.

The second set of qualifications concerns the "informal" aspects of the school class, which are always somewhat at variance with the formal expectations. For instance, the formal pattern of nondifferentiation between the sexes may be modified informally, for the very salience of the one-sex peer group at this age period means that there is bound to be considerable implicit recognition of it — for example, in the form of teachers' encouraging group competition between boys and girls. Still, the fact of coeducation and the attempt to treat both sexes alike in all the crucial formal respects remain the most important. Another problem raised by informal organization is the question of how far teachers can and do treat pupils particularistically in violation of the universalistic expectations of the school. When compared with other types of formal organizations, however, I think the extent of this discrepancy in elementary schools is seen to be not unusual. The school class is structured so that opportunity for particularistic treatment is severely limited. Because there are so many more children in a school class than in a family and they are concentrated in a much narrower age range, the teacher has much less chance than does a parent to grant particularistic favors.

Bearing in mind these two sets of qualifications, it is still fair, I think, to conclude that the major characteristics of the elementary school class in this country are such as have been outlined. It should be especially emphasized that more or less progressive schools, even with their relative lack of emphasis on formal marking, do not constitute a separate pattern, but rather a variant tendency within the same pattern. A progressive teacher, like any other, will form opinions about the different merits of her pupils relative to the values and goals of the class and will communicate these evaluations to them, informally if not formally. It is my impression that the extremer cases of playing down relative evaluation are confined to those upper-status schools where going to a "good" college is so fully taken for granted that for practical purposes it is an ascribed status. In other words, in interpreting these facts the selective function of the school class should be kept continually in the forefront of attention. Quite clearly its importance has not been decreasing; rather the contrary.

## THE NATURE OF SCHOOL ACHIEVEMENT

What, now, of the content of the "achievement" expected of elementary school children? Perhaps the best broad characterization which can be given is that it involves the types of performance which are, on the one hand, appropriate to the school situation and, on the other hand, are felt by adults to be important in themselves. This vague and somewhat circular characterization may, as was mentioned earlier, be broken down into two main components. One of these is the more purely "cognitive" learning of information, skills, and frames of reference associated with empirical knowledge and technological mastery. The *written* language and the early phases of mathematical thinking are clearly vital; they involve cognitive skills at altogether new levels of generality and abstraction compared to those commanded by the pre-school child. With these basic skills goes assimilation of much factual information about the world.

The second main component is what may broadly be called a "moral" one. In earlier generations of schooling this was known as "deportment." Somewhat more generally it might be called responsible citizenship in the school community. Such things as respect for the teacher, consideration and co-operativeness in relation to fellow-pupils, and good "work-habits" are the fundamentals leading on to capacity for "leadership" and "initiative."

The striking fact about this achievement content is that in the elementary grades these two primary components are not clearly differentiated from each other. Rather the pupil is evaluated in diffusely general terms; a *good* pupil is defined in terms of a fusion of the cognitive and the moral components, in which varying weight is given to one or the other. Broadly speaking, then, we may say that the "high achievers" of the elementary school are both the "bright" pupils, who catch on easily to their more strictly intellectual tasks, and the more "responsible" pupils, who "behave well" and on whom the teacher can "count" in her difficult problems of managing the class. One indication that this is the case is the fact that in elementary school the purely intellectual tasks are relatively easy for the pupil of high intellectual ability. In many such cases, it can be presumed that the primary challenge to the pupil is not to his intellectual, but to his "moral," capacities. On the whole, the progressive movement seems to have leaned in the direction of giving enhanced emphasis to this component, suggesting that of the two, it has tended to become the more problematical.[7]

The essential point, then, seems to be that the elementary school, regarded in the light of its socialization function, is an agency which differentiates the school class broadly along a single continuum of achievement, the content of which is relative excellence in living up to the expectations imposed by the teacher as an agent of the adult society. The criteria of this achievement are, generally speaking, undifferentiated into the cognitive or technical component and the moral or "social" component. But with respect to its bearing on societal values, it is broadly a differentiation of *levels* of capacity to act in accord with these values. Though the relation is far from neatly uniform, the differentiation underlies the processes of selection for levels of status and role in the adult society. . . .

## SOCIALIZATION AND SELECTION IN THE ELEMENTARY SCHOOL

To conclude this discussion of the elementary school class, something should be said about the fundamental conditions underlying the process which is simultaneously (1) an emancipation of the child from primary emotional attachment to his family, (2) an internalization of a level of societal values and norms that is a step higher than those he can learn in his family alone, (3) a differentiation of the school class in terms both of actual achievement and of differential *valuation* of achievement, and (4) from society's point of view, a selection and allocation of its human resources relative to the adult role system.[8]

Probably the most fundamental condition underlying this process is the sharing of common values by the two adult agencies involved — the family and the school. In this case the core is the shared valuation of *achievement*. It includes, above all, recognition that it is fair to give differential rewards for different levels of achievement, so long as there has been fair access to opportunity, and fair that these rewards lead on to higher-order opportunities for the successful. There is thus a basic sense in which the elementary school class is an embodiment of the fundamental American value of equality of opportunity, in that it places value *both* on initial equality and on differential achievement.

As a second condition, however, the rigor of this valuational pattern must be tempered by allowance for the difficulties and needs of the young child. Here the quasi-motherliness of the woman teacher plays an important part. Through her the school system, assisted by other agencies, attempts to minimize the insecurity resulting from the pressures to learn, by providing a certain amount of emotional support defined in terms of what is due to a child of a given age level. In this respect, however, the role of the school is relatively small. The underlying foundation of support is given in the home, and as we have seen, an important supplement to it can be provided by the informal peer associations of the child. It may be suggested that the development of extreme patterns of alienation from the school is often related to inadequate support in these respects.

Third, there must be a process of selective rewarding of valued performance. Here the teacher is clearly the primary agent, though the more progressive modes of education attempt to enlist classmates more systematically than in the traditional pattern. This is the process that is the direct source of intra-class differentiation along the achievement axis.

The final condition is that this initial differentiation tends to bring about a status system in the class, in which not only the immediate results of school work, but a whole series of influences, converge to consolidate different expectations which may be thought of as the children's "levels of aspiration." Generally some differentiation of friendship groups along this line occurs, though it is important that it is by no means complete, and that children are sensitive to the attitudes not only of their own friends, but of others.

Within this general discussion of processes and conditions, it is important to distinguish, as I have attempted to do all along, the socialization of the individual from the selective allocation of contingents to future roles. For the individual, the old familial identification is broken up (the family of orientation becomes, in Freudian terms, a "lost object") and a new identification is gradually built up, providing the first-order structure of the child's identity apart from his originally ascribed identity as son or daughter of the "Joneses." He both transcends his familial identification in favor of a more independent one and comes to occupy a differentiated status within the new system. His personal status is inevitably a direct function of the position he achieves, primarily in the formal school class and secondarily in the informal peer group structure. In spite of the sense in which achievement-ranking takes place along a continuum, I have put forward reasons to suggest that, with respect to this status, there is an important differentiation into two broad, relatively distinct levels, and that his position on one or the other enters into the individual's definition of his own identity. To an important degree this process of differentiation is independent of the socio-economic status of his family in the community, which to the child is a prior ascribed status.

When we look at the same system as a selective mechanism from the societal point of view, some further considerations become important. First, it may be noted that the valuation of achievement and its sharing by family and school not only provides the appropriate values for internalization by individuals, but also performs a crucial integrative function for the system. Differentiation of the class along the achievement axis is inevitably a source of strain, because it confers higher rewards and privileges on one contingent than on another within the same system. This common valuation helps make possible the acceptance of the crucial differentiation, especially by the losers in the competition. Here it is an essential point that this *common* value on achievement is shared by units with different statuses in the system. It cuts across the differentiation of families by socio-economic status. It is necessary that there be realistic opportunity and that the teacher can be relied on to implement it by being "fair" and rewarding achievement by whoever shows capacity for it. The fact is crucial that the distribution of abilities, though correlated with family status, clearly does not coincide with it. There can then be a genuine selective process within a set of "rules of the game."

This commitment to common values is not, however, the sole integrative mechanism counteracting the strain imposed by differentiation. Not only does the individual pupil enjoy familial support, but teachers also like and indeed "respect" pupils on bases independent of achievement-status, and peer-group friendship lines, though correlated with position on the achievement scale, again by no means coincide with it, but cross-cut it. Thus there are cross-cutting lines of solidarity which mitigate the strains generated by rewarding achievement differentially.[9]

It is only *within* this framework of institutionalized solidarity that the crucial selective process goes on through selective rewarding and the consolidation of its results into a status-differentiation within the school class. We have called special attention to the impact of the selective process on the children of relatively high ability but low family status. Precisely in this group, but pervading school classes generally, is another parallel to what was found in the studies of voting behavior.[10] In the voting studies it was found that the "shifters" — those voters who were transferring their allegiance from one major party to the other — tended, on the one hand, to be the "cross-pressured" people, who had multiple status characteristics and group allegiances which predisposed them simultaneously to vote in opposite directions. The analogy in the school class is clearly to the children for whom ability and family status do not coincide. On the other hand, it was precisely in this group of cross-pressured voters that political "indifference" was most conspicuous. Non-voting was particularly prevalent in this group, as was a generally cool emotional tone toward a campaign. The suggestion is that some of the pupil "indifference" to school performance may have a similar origin. This is clearly a complex phenomenon and cannot be further analyzed here. But rather than suggesting, as is usual on common sense grounds, that indifference to school work represents an "alienation" from cultural and intellectual values, I would suggest exactly the opposite: that an important component of such indifference, including in extreme cases overt revolt against school discipline, is connected with the fact that the stakes, as in politics, are very high indeed. Those pupils who are exposed to contradictory pressures are likely to be ambivalent; at the same time, the personal stakes for them are higher than for the others, because what happens in school may make much more of a difference for their futures than for the others, in whom ability and family status point to the same expectations for the future. In particular for the upwardly mobile pupils, too much emphasis on school success would pointedly suggest "burning their bridges" of association with their families and status peers. This phenomenon seems to operate even in elementary school, although it grows somewhat more conspicuous later. In general I think that an important part of the anti-intellectualism in American youth culture stems from the *importance* of the selective process through the educational system rather than the opposite.

One further major point should be made in this analysis. As we have noted, the general trend of American society has been toward a rapid upgrading in the educational status of the population. This means that, relative to past expectations, with each generation there is increased pressure to educational achievement, often associated with parents' occupational ambitions for their children.[11] To a sociologist this is a more or less classical situation of anomic strain, and the youth-culture ideology which plays down intellectual interests and school performance seems to fit in this context. The orientation of the youth culture is, in the nature of the case, ambivalent, but for the reasons suggested, the anti-intellectual side of the ambivalence tends to be overtly stressed. One of the reasons for the dominance of the anti-school side of the ideology is that it provides a means of protest against adults, who are at the opposite pole in the socialization situation. In certain respects one would expect that the trend toward greater emphasis on independence, which we have associated with progressive education, would accentuate the strain in this area and hence the tendency to decry adult expectations. The whole problem should be subjected to a thorough analysis in the light of what we know about ideologies more generally.

The same general considerations are relevant to the much-discussed problem of juvenile delinquency. Both the general upgrading process and the pressure to enhanced independence should be expected to increase strain on the lower, most marginal groups. The analysis of this paper has been concerned with the line between college and non-college contingents; there is, however, another line between those who achieve solid non-college educational status and those for whom adaptation to educational expectations at *any* level is difficult. As the acceptable minimum of educational qualification rises, persons near and below the margin will tend to be pushed into an attitude of repudiation of these expectations. Truancy and delinquency are ways of expressing this repudiation. Thus the very *improvement* of education standards in the society at large may well be a major factor in the failure of the educational process for a growing number at the lower end of the status and ability distribution. It should therefore not be too easily assumed that delinquency is a symptom of a *general* failure of the educational process.

DIFFERENTIATION AND SELECTION IN THE SECONDARY SCHOOL

It will not be possible to discuss the secondary school phase of education in nearly as much detail as has been done for the elementary school phase, but it is worthwhile to sketch its main outline in order to place the above analysis in a wider context. Very broadly we may say that the elementary school phase is concerned with the internalization in children of motivation to achievement, and the selection of persons on the basis of differential capacity for achievement. The focus is on the *level* of capacity. In the secondary school phase, on the other hand, the focus is on the differentiation of *qualitative types* of achievement. As in the elementary school, this differentiation cross-cuts sex role. I should also maintain that it cross-cuts the levels of achievement which have been differentiated out in the elementary phase.

In approaching the question of the types of capacity differentiated, it should be kept in mind that secondary school is the principal springboard from which lower-status persons will enter the labor force, whereas those achieving higher status will continue their formal education in college, and some of them beyond. Hence for the lower-status pupils the important line of differentiation should be the one which will lead into broadly different categories of jobs; for the higher-status pupils the differentiation will lead to broadly different roles in college.

My suggestion is that this differentiation separates those two components of achievement which we labelled "cognitive" and "moral" in discussing the elementary phase. Those relatively high in "cognitive" achievement will fit better in specific-function, more or less technical roles; those relatively high in "moral" achievement will tend toward diffuser, more "stoically" or "humanly" oriented roles. In jobs not requiring college training, the one category may be thought of as comprising the more impersonal and technical occupations, such as "operatives," mechanics, or clerical workers; the other, as occupations where "human relations" are prominent, such as salesmen and agents of various sorts. At the college level, the differentiation certainly relates to concern, on the one hand, with the specifically intellectual curricular work of college and, on the other hand, with various types of diffuser responsibility in human relations, such as leadership roles in student government and extracurricular activities. Again, candidates for post-graduate professional training will probably be drawn mainly from the first of these two groups.

In the structure of the school, there appears to be a gradual transition from the earliest grades through high school, with the changes timed differently in different school systems. The structure emphasized in the first part of this discussion is most clearly marked in the first three "primary" grades. With progression to the higher grades, there is greater frequency of plural teachers, though very generally still a single main teacher. In the sixth grade and sometimes in the fifth, a man as main teacher, though uncommon, is by no means unheard of. With junior high school, however, the shift of pattern becomes more marked, and still more in senior high.

By that time the pupil has several different teachers of both sexes[12] teaching him different subjects, which are more or less formally organized into different courses — college preparatory and others. Furthermore, with the choice of "elective" subjects, the members of the class in one subject no longer need be exactly the same as in another, so the pupil is much more systematically exposed to association with different people, both adults and age-peers, in different contexts. Moreover, the school he attends is likely to be substantially larger than was his elementary school, and to draw from a wider geographical area. Hence the child is exposed to a wider range of statuses than before, being thrown in with more age-peers whom he does not encounter in his neighborhood; it is less likely that his parents will know the parents of any given child with whom he associates. It is thus my impression that the transitions to junior high and senior high school are apt to mean a considerable reshuffling of friendships. Another conspicuous difference between the elementary and secondary levels is the great increase in high school of organized extracurricular activities. Now, for the first time, organized athletics become important, as do a variety of clubs and associations which are school-sponsored and supervised to varying degrees.

Two particularly important shifts in the patterning of youth culture occur in this period. One, of course, is the emergence of more positive cross-sex relationships outside the classroom, through dances, dating, and the like. The other is the much sharper prestige-stratification of informal peer groupings, with indeed an element of snobbery which often exceeds that of the adult community in which the school exists.[13] Here it is important that though there is a broad correspondence between the prestige of friendship groups and the family status of their members, this, like the achievement order of the elementary school, is by no means a simple "mirroring" of the community stratification scale, for a considerable number of lower-status children get accepted into groups including members with higher family status than themselves. This stratified youth system operates as a genuine assortative mechanism; it does not simply reinforce ascribed status.

The prominence of this youth culture in the American secondary school is, in comparison with other societies, one of the hallmarks of the American educational system; it is much less prominent in most European systems. It may be said to constitute a kind of structural fusion between the school class and the peer-group structure of the elementary period. It seems clear that what I have called the "human relations" oriented contingent of the secondary school pupils are more active and prominent in extracurricular activities, and that this is one of the main foci of their differentiation from the more impersonally- and technically-oriented contingent. The personal qualities figuring most prominently in the human relations contingent can perhaps be summed up as the qualities that make for "popularity." I suggest that, from the point of view of the secondary school's selective function, the youth culture helps to differentiate between types of personalities which will, by and large, play different kinds of roles as adults.

The stratification of youth groups has, as noted, a selective function; it is a bridge between the achievement order and the adult stratification system of the community. But it also has another function. It is a focus of prestige which exists along side of, and is to a degree independent of, the achievement order focussing on school work as such. The attainment of prestige in the informal youth group is itself a form of valued achievement. Hence, among those individuals destined for higher status in society, one can discern two broad types: those whose school work is more or less outstanding and whose informal prestige is relatively satisfactory; and vice versa, those whose informal prestige is outstanding, and school performance satisfactory. Falling below certain minima in either respect would jeopardize the child's claim to belong in the upper group.[14] It is an important point here that those clearly headed for college belong to peer groups which, while often depreciative of intensive concern with studies, also take for granted and reinforce a level of scholastic attainment which is necessary for admission to a good college. Pressure will be put on the individual who tends to fall below such a standard.

In discussing the elementary school level it will be remembered that we emphasized that the peer group served as an object of emotional dependency displaced from the family. In relation to the pressure for school achievement, therefore, it served at least partially as an expression of the lower-order motivational system *out* of which the child was in process of being socialized. On its own level, similar things can be said of the adolescent youth culture; it is in part an expression of regressive motivations. This is true of the emphasis on athletics despite its lack of relevance to adult roles, of the "homosexual" undertones of much intensive same-sex friendship, and of a certain "irresponsibility" in attitudes toward the opposite sex — *e.g.*, the exploitative element in the attitudes of boys toward girls. This, however, is by no means the whole story. The youth culture is also a field for practicing the assumption of higher-order responsibilities, for conducting delicate human relations without immediate supervision and learning to accept the consequences. In this connection it is clearly of particular importance to the contingent we have spoken of as specializing in "human relations."

We can, perhaps, distinguish three different levels of crystallization of these youth-culture patterns. The middle one is that which may be considered age-appropriate without clear status-differentiation. The two keynotes here seem to be "being a good fellow" in the sense of general friendliness and being ready to take responsibility in informal social situations where something needs to be done. Above this, we may speak of the higher level of "outstanding" popularity and qualities of "leadership" of the person who is turned to where unusual responsibilities are required. And below the middle level are the youth patterns bordering on delinquency, withdrawal, and generally unacceptable behavior. Only this last level is clearly "regressive" relative to expectations of appropriate behavior for the age-grade. In judging these levels, however, allowance should be made for a good many nuances. Most adolescents do a certain amount of experimenting with the borderline of the unacceptable patterns; that they should do so is to be expected in view of the pressure toward independence from adults, and of the "collusion" which can be expected in the reciprocal stimulation of age-peers. The question is whether this regressive behavior comes to be confirmed into a major pattern for the personality as a whole. Seen in this perspective, it seems legitimate to maintain that the middle and the higher patterns indicated are the major ones, and that only a minority of adolescents comes to be confirmed in a truly unacceptable pattern of living. This minority may well be a relatively constant proportion of the age cohort, but apart from situations of special social disorganization, the available evidence does not suggest that it has been a progressively growing one in recent years.

The patterning of cross-sex relations in the youth culture clearly foreshadows future marriage and family formation. That it figures so prominently in school is related to the fact that in our society the element of ascription, including direct parental influence, in the choice of a marriage partner is strongly minimized. For the girl, it has the very important significance of reminding her that her adult status is going to be very much concerned with marriage and a family. This basic expectation for the girl stands in a certain tension to the school's curricular coeducation with its relative lack of differentiation by sex. But the extent to which the feminine role in American society continues to be anchored in marriage and the family should not be allowed to obscure the importance of coeducation. In the first place, the contribution of women in various extra-familial occupations and in community affairs has been rapidly increasing, and certainly higher levels of education have served as a prerequisite to this contribution. At the same time, it is highly important that the woman's familial role should not be regarded as drastically segregated from the cultural concerns of the society as a whole. The educated woman has important functions *as wife and mother*, particularly as an influence on her children in backing the schools and impressing on them the importance of education. It is, I think, broadly true that the immediate responsibility of women for family management has been increasing, though I am very skeptical of the alleged "abdication" of the American male. But precisely in the context of women's increased family responsibility, the influence of the mother both as agent of socialization and as role model is a crucial one. This influence should be evaluated in the light of the general upgrading process. It is very doubtful whether, apart from any other considerations, the motivational prerequisites of the general process could be sustained without sufficiently high education of the women who, as mothers, influence their children.

CONCLUSION

With the general cultural upgrading process in American society which has been going on for more than a century, the educational system has come to play an increasingly vital role. That this should be the case is, in my opinion, a consequence of the general trend to structural differentiation in the society. Relatively speaking, the school is a specialized agency. That it should increasingly have become the principal channel of selection as well as agency of socialization is in line with what one would expect in an increasingly differentiated and progressively more upgraded society. The legend of the "self-made man" has an element of nostalgic romanticism and is destined to become increasingly mythical, if by it is meant not just mobility from humble origins to high status, which does indeed continue to occur, but that the high status was attained through the "school of hard knocks" without the aid of formal education.

The structure of the public school system and the analysis of the ways in which it contributes both to the socialization of individuals and to their allocation to roles in society is, I feel, of vital concern to all students of American society. Notwithstanding the variegated elements in the situation, I think it has been possible to sketch out a few major structural patterns of the public school system and at least to suggest some ways in which they serve these important functions. What could be presented in this paper is the merest outline of such an analysis. It is, however, hoped that it has been carried far enough to suggest a field of vital mutual interest for social scientists on the one hand and those concerned with the actual operation of the schools on the other.

## REFERENCES

1. The principal source for these statements is a still unpublished study of social mobility among boys in ten public high schools in the Boston metropolitan area, conducted by Samuel A. Stouffer, Florence R. Kluckhohn, and the present author.

2. See table from this study in J. A. Kahl, *The American Class Structure,* New York, Rinehart & Co., 1953, p. 283. Data from a nationwide sample of high school students, published by the Educational Testing Service, show similar patterns of relationships. For example, the ETS study shows variation, by father's occupation, in proportion of high school seniors planning college, of from 35 per cent to 80 per cent for boys and 27 per cent to 79 per cent for girls. (From *Background Factors Related to College Plans and College Enrollment among High School Students,* Princeton, N.J., Educational Testing Service, 1957.)

3. There seem to be two main reasons why the high-status, low-ability group is not so important as its obverse. The first is that in a society of expanding educational and occupational opportunity the general trend is one of upgrading, and the social pressures to downward mobility are not as great as they would otherwise be. The second is that there are cushioning mechanisms which tend to protect the high status boy who has difficulty "making the grade." He may be sent to a college with low academic standards, he may go to schools where the line between ability levels is not rigorously drawn, etc.

4. This discussion refers to public schools. Only about 13 per cent of all elementary and secondary school pupils attend non-public schools, with this proportion ranging from about 22 per cent in the Northeast to about 6 per cent in the South. U.S. Office of Education, *Biennial Survey of Education in the United States, 1954–1956,* Washington, U.S. Government

Printing Office, 1959, Chap. ii, "Statistics of State School Systems, 1955–56," Table 44, p. 114.

5. In 1955–56, 13 per cent of the public elementary school instructional staff in the United States were men. *Ibid.*, p. 7.

6. This summary of some contrasts between traditional and progressive patterns is derived from general reading in the literature rather than any single authoritative account.

7. This account of the two components of elementary school achievement and their relation summarizes impressions gained from the literature, rather than being based on the opinions of particular authorities. I have the impression that achievement in this sense corresponds closely to what is meant by the term as used by McClelland and his associates. Cf. D. C. McClelland *et al.*, *The Achievement Motive*, New York, Appleton-Century-Crofts, Inc., 1953.

8. The following summary is adapted from T. Parsons, R. F. Bales, *et al.*, *Family, Socialization and Interaction Process*, New York, The Free Press of Glencoe, 1955, esp. Chap. IV.

9. In this, as in several other respects, there is a parallel to other important allocative processes in the society. A striking example is the voting process by which political support is allocated between party candidates. Here, the strain arises from the fact that one candidate and his party will come to enjoy all the perquisites — above all the power — of office, while the other will be excluded for the time being from these. This strain is mitigated, on the one hand, by the common commitment to constitutional procedure, and, on the other hand, by the fact that the nonpolitical bases of social solidarity, which figure so prominently as determinants of voting behavior, still cut across party lines. The average person is, in various of his roles, associated with people whose political preference is different from his own; he therefore could not regard the opposite party as composed of unmitigated scoundrels without introducing a rift within the groups to which he is attached. This feature of the electorate's structure is brought out strongly in B. R. Berelson, P. F. Lazarsfeld and W. N. McPhee, *Voting*, Chicago, University of Chicago Press, 1954. The conceptual analysis of it is developed in my own paper, " 'Voting' and the Equilibrium of the American Political System" in E. Burdick and A. J. Brodbeck (eds.), *American Voting Behavior*, New York, The Free Press of Glencoe, 1959.

10. *Ibid.*

11. J. A. Kahl, "Educational and Occupational Aspirations of 'Common Man' Boys," *Harvard Educational Review*, XXIII (Summer, 1953), pp. 186–203.

12. Men make up about half (49 per cent) of the public secondary school instructional staff. *Biennial Survey of Education in the United States, 1954–56, op. cit.*, Chap. ii, p. 7.

13. See, for instance, C. W. Gordon, *The Social System of the High School: A Study in the Sociology of Adolescence*, New York, The Free Press of Glencoe, 1957.

14. M. W. Riley, J. W. Riley, Jr., and M. E. Moore, "Adolescent Values and the Riesman Typology" in S. M. Lipset and L. Lowenthal (eds.), *Culture and Social Character*, New York, The Free Press of Glencoe, 1961.

# THE ROLE OF THE SCHOOL IN THE
# SOCIALIZATION OF COMPETENCE

## BARBARA BIBER AND PATRICIA MINUCHIN

## I. *Introduction*

Societies have long regarded their schools as primary institutions for the socialization of competence, created and sustained for the express purpose of inducting the child into his culture as a competent and skillful human being. As a crucial socializing force, the school shares its function with the family, the peer group, sometimes other institutions such as the church, but even more than the others its function is described directly in the realm of "competence": to educate means, at the very least, to make competent.

Within the consensus that the school's function lies in this realm, however, there is a range of viewpoint among educators and in the environments and methods they have created. If we approach education with a research stance, we need to begin with the understanding that schools vary in their vision of what they are trying to accomplish for the child — the scope of what they wish to undertake, the hierarchy of their goals, their cognizance of psychological development as it affects functioning, and the extent of their concern for the propensities, heritage and equipment the child brings with him into the learning situation.

In this paper we will be considering the school's role in the socialization of competence from a vantage point relevant to the recent explorations in education but rooted in trends which have been evolving over a period of several decades. We will present the basic tenets of a changing conception and methodology of education, and we will use the approach and findings of a research project,[1] assessing the impact of such changes, as a way of exploring problems and implications in this area.

An original article printed for the first time in this volume.

It is not pertinent for our purposes to describe the study at length, but a general background description may prove useful: [2]

The research was designed as an intensive field located study, using existing situations for the comparative assessment of educational effects. Four schools — three public and one private — were selected as the settings. They were equivalent in several important respects: they were urban schools serving relatively homogeneous, middle class populations; their administrations were stable; they were reputed to be "good" schools, benign in their attitudes toward children; and they all perceived the task of teaching as a serious professional responsibility. They differed, however, in their basic educational viewpoints and methods — in the extent to which they had been influenced by the growing knowledge of learning processes and personality development. Two of the schools were considered essentially traditional in this respect and two essentially modern; the modern private school most closely represented the values and viewpoint of changing education, as described in Section II to follow.

Research centered on 105 fourth grade children — nine year old boys and girls from upper middle class, well educated families. To serve the multiple purposes of the project, the schools were studied as social institutions, the fourth grade classrooms were observed intensively through the school year, the parents of the study children were interviewed, and the children were observed in their classrooms and individually tested in a series of six sessions. The testing and interviewing of the children constituted the basic source of assessment data, tapping, presumably, the internalized effects of different school experiences. The scope of the testing was broad. It involved a variety of techniques (IQ and Achievement testing, problem solving tasks, projectives, play sessions, self-scaling techniques, etc.), and was geared to understanding and comparing the children on varied aspects of psychological functioning in the areas of intellectual mastery, interpersonal relationships, and aspects of self-concept. Some of these measures are relevant to the concept of competence and will be reported in subsequent sections of the paper.

It should be noted that the independent variable — the modern or traditional quality of school experience — is taken as a total influencing experience, in this study, with cumulative impact on the child's development. This approach reflects the conviction that the many factors making up the total experience are interwoven and are experienced by the child as a complex atmosphere rather than as a series of discrete experiences. The component parts can be identified conceptually, however, and described discretely.

The following section, Theory and Assumptions of Educational Change, presents the important elements of traditional and changing education in terms that have particular meaning for the concept of competence and to the concern for how it is socialized. The final section, Research Findings and Problems, weighs the research evidence and raises some of the implications and issues in these areas.

## II. *Theory and Assumptions of Educational Change*

### THE PROVINCE OF EDUCATION

In redefining its role as an educating and socializing force, the changing school has first of all broadened its scope. It has taken explicit responsibility for fostering growth in areas of child functioning that were not traditionally part of the school's self-defined province. One would include among these areas: 1) the school's concern with the child's intellectual functioning in a group context, where he must pool his work and ideas toward achievements that are cooperative in process and mutual in product; 2) the school's concern with vitality, depth and effectiveness in interpersonal relationships, defining this as interpersonal competence or as effective interaction with the human environment; 3) the school's concern with the child's capacity to express what is personal, fantasy-rooted and unique, to handle without constriction relatively open situations as well as those requiring finite problem solution, mastery of structured material, and impersonal skills; 4) the school's concern for the child's self-knowledge, and for the extent to which this knowledge gains in differentiation, reality and usefulness as the child grows.

### INTELLECTUAL MASTERY

Within the clearly acknowledged province of the school — the sphere of intellectual growth — the school has also been changing its viewpoint and practices. Intellectual mastery is conceived less in terms of fact acquisition, more in terms of the organization of knowledge and a complex, active stance toward learning.

In such schools high priority is placed upon stimulating as great a degree of organization of experience as is suitable to the stage of cognitive maturity. According to the developmental theorists, Werner (1957) and Piaget (1958), cognitive maturing is seen as a progression from diffuse, global awareness to an increasingly differentiated condition, until a new level of integration is attained. This progression is related to chronological stages but occurs as well on exposure to new, complex experience or ideas at any age.

In the last few years there has been a felicitous convergence of the modern school's approach to learning in this respect and the work of psychologists — Bruner (1961), Hilgard (1964), Suchman (1961), Ojemann (1961) and others — in emphasis on learning through active discovery, organization of knowledge by governing principles, inductive reasoning and the basic stance of vital questioning and probing search.

The changing schools and those psychologists whose work is syntonic with their methods have a common orientation concerning the stance the child will need to take toward a changing world. They look upon the kind of learning in which the child must be an active and consolidating thinker as a way of equipping him with tools for analysis and decision making and with propensities for the adaptation and flexibility essential for competence in the unforeseeable, much-changed world of his adult years. Having been helped to perceive all knowledge as moving and changing, never coming to finality, the child may be readier to conceive of and utilize knowledge as an instrument for change. Ideally, the facts he acquires will come under disciplined cognitive control and his intellectual mastery will serve toward making an impact on his changing world.

## KNOWLEDGE AND INDIVIDUAL MEANING

The growing recognition of the need to educate for greater competence in terms of hard core intellectual mastery and independent thinking has been paralleled by concern that we develop individuals in whom propensities for divergent thinking are also highly developed (Getzels and Jackson, 1962; Guilford, 1959; Torrance, 1962). If one uses the stock phrases — creativity, originality — all schools will consider these to be worthwhile goals, except perhaps those that have been bludgeoned into eliminating all "frills." For the traditional school, however, the meaning of these terms is circumscribed. Creative activities are a subject matter domain and the style of teaching for this subject matter shares the dominant approach to mastery in the traditional school — curtailed exploration, premature imposition of standards of technical proficiency and precision, focus of interest and evaluation on the final product rather than on the multiple processes out of which it emerges, and application of formalized standards that encourage uniformity rather than diversity.

For the changing school, originality and creativity, as they appear in the end products of learning experience, are seen as evidence that an integrative process has taken place — that some part of the child's perception of objective reality has filtered through his own existing pattern of meanings and feelings and reappears, in his expressive output, as a new blend of the personal and the impersonal.

## The Sequence of Education

In the modern school there is basic investment in individuality — its uniqueness, complexity and malleability. But there are important commonalities in the sequence of growth of all children; every design for schooling — modern or traditional — is conditioned by its conceptual framework for projecting individuality against the patterns of advancing maturity. For the modern school neither normative chronological descriptions nor the deviation of achievement from IQ scores is suitable. Instead, the concept of stages of development, delineated by important qualitative shifts in interests, motivation and productive capacity — according to the models of Erikson (1959), Piaget (1958) and Werner (1957) — has proved a more useful theoretical tool.

Drawing on many sources, the modern school builds curriculum on a broad, inclusive purview of each stage of development, asking: What are the known capacities? Are they being fully exercised? What are the key confusions and conflicts? What are the major sources of gratification? Where are the areas of greatest vulnerability? What are the crucial learning idioms and the specific directions of the urge to master?

The question of how best to facilitate progression from stage to stage — to educate — can become an issue between acceleration and fulfillment. The changing school has not accepted the meaning of acceleration which is vested in earliest possible mastery of specific skills.

It is aligned with the psychodynamic concept of fulfillment for each stage of development. It is equally concerned, however, with preparatory experiences geared toward future competence.

## THE GENERALITY OF COMPETENCE

Perhaps it is useful to conceptualize the idea of general competence in two ways. The first is a matter of performance adequacy over a wide range of tasks; it might be described as a *high plurality of skills.* The second is a matter of resourcefulness in many situations — an active, flexible, generally effective stance; it might be described as a *high generality of competence.* These are alternative ways of being effective, sometimes co-existent and sometimes not, and the school has some role in relation to each of them.

In relation to the first aspect — the high plurality of skills — the changing school shares with the more traditional school a self assignment to educate for basic skills and information over a wide variety of subject matter. This induction of the child into the symbol systems, skills, basic facts and ideas of his culture and era represents a basic charge to the school in its role as a socializing force for competence, and all schools strive to fulfill this charge.

In the teaching of skills, however, the modern school may be said to differ from its more traditional counterpart in several ways:

It strikes a different balance between rehearsing specific content and skills, and offering learning at more integrated and cross-sectional levels. The traditional curriculum is apt to be relatively fragmented; the school teaches and expects learning to occur predominantly through specific rehearsal and in pockets of content. The modern school ties its teaching of skills and basic content into more complex units, though it uses practice and rehearsal as well.

The modern school is apt to highlight a somewhat different roster of skills. It places greater stress, for instance, on the skills of communication. Further, the modern school has a less standardized conception of adequate progress in general. The expectation and acceptance of individual patterns is greater; uneven performance across areas is taken, at least in part, as an expression of legitimate variation rather than as evidence that effort has not been applied.

It is in relation to the second concept of generality, however, that the changing schools have departed most from the traditional. They place great value on the kind of competence that is expressed in a general resourcefulness, a resilience, a predisposition to assess a situation and find one's way in it. These schools have geared much of their theory and practice to developing such attitudes and effectiveness.

## COMPETENCE MOTIVATION

Traditional education has been geared primarily to the effectiveness of performance. It has tended to ask few questions about how strong the child's learning drive is — unless to wonder why he is "not trying" — but it has built its learning climate on certain assumptions.

It has been traditionally assumed, for instance, that the child's motivation for effective performance is rooted primarily in his strong dependence on adults. He works and learns in order to win approval and avoid trouble or pain, and that pleasure or pain follow directly from the reactions of adults to his efforts. It has been further assumed that the competitive drive is strong, vis-à-vis other children, and that effort can be mobilized in the interest of surpassing competitors and garnering the lion's share of praise and approval. This effort has been so mobilized, without particular concern either for its side effects or for its possible alternatives. Lastly, it has been assumed that self-discipline and other superego virtues enable the child to apply himself persistently to his work and that it is not the work itself that has major compelling power; this is, in some instances, a self-fulfilling prophecy. By this concept of competence motivation, the setting of clear and extrinsic standards is essential; grades, teacher approval and disapproval, comparison with the group, etc. are the mobilizers of motivation.

The changing school system has worked and taught on the basis of other assumptions. Psychologists have come only lately to dealing with the urge to explore and to master, arguing its place in dynamic theory and the origins of its energy (White, 1959). Educators have been little concerned with these theoretical problems, but they have a somewhat longer history of central contact with this energy and curiosity. At least from the time of Dewey, a whole wing of American education has systematically built its teaching methods on the assumption that the child has a strong and intrinsic drive to explore, to extend his world, to gain in understanding and to make an impact. They have assumed that this exploration and learning is inherently pleasurable and that it is the business of education to offer such experiences as will keep this force alive. The changes in education have built on competence motivation conceived in terms of the pleasure and power that are inherent in mastery.

Beyond the intrinsic motivation to master, the changing schools have built on two other sources of motivation, as they conceive them: the identification with learning goals developed through the teacher-child relationship, and the identification with group work goals developed through peer group interaction.

The aim of the teacher in the modern school is partly to provide a model for intensive and zestful attitudes toward learning and for a vigorous approach to gathering and organizing knowledge. More specifically, however, he attempts to establish a personalized and differentiated relationship to each child as an individual, hoping to make it possible thereby for the child to internalize the teacher's particular goals for his learning — to understand and adopt their relevance to himself. The quality of the teacher-child relationship changes in the form and extent of closeness as the child grows older, but it always aims for communication that will enhance internalization of meaningful learning goals rather than for reinforcement of specific behavior through approval and disapproval.[3]

It is assumed in these schools, further, that peer group ties are deeply important to the school age child, and that there is considerable motivational impetus to perform well when effective functioning has implications for peer relationships. These schools provide for learning in varying group combinations as well as in individual work and study.

FEELINGS OF COMPETENCE

The difference between traditional and changing schools in their attitudes toward self-feeling is not, perhaps, a sheer matter of difference in conceptions or assumptions; it is a basic difference in the extent to which such a construct enters into the teaching philosophy or system. The traditional school is concerned with the confidence with which the child performs and presents himself, and the child who is competent within this system often feels pride and satisfaction with himself as a by-product of his performance, but deep feelings about capacity and self-image as a learner are not, in themselves, within the province of the traditional school.

For the changing school, self-concept and feeling is a pivotal factor. The school is concerned that the child know himself well, to the extent possible at his age level, and that he feel adequate and capable at any age. Self contact, realistic evaluation of oneself, and feelings of confidence and competence are assumed to mediate effective functioning — the child's capacity to learn, to meet the environment and to act on it. The modern school actually assumes an interconnected triumvirate of feeling, motivation and performance, all of which affect each other, and the school maintains a teaching alertness toward all levels.

If one were to summarize the theory and assumptions of traditional and changing education, then, in the terms by which we have described them, one might say that traditional education has concerned itself with competent performance, rooted in subject matter mastery, drawing on motivation that is competitive and approval-oriented in nature, and concerning itself only in part with the child's feeling of competence or adequacy. Changing education has also concerned itself with competent performance, but has defined this differently, through a broader range of life areas, a more personalized quality of impact, and through a definition of meaningful cognition that stresses the tools and principles for intellectual exploration, the organization of knowledge and the breadth and flexibility of its application. It has assumed and drawn on a different motivational system — intrinsic curiosity and the internalization of learning goals — and has given to feelings of competence and adequacy the status of a key mediating factor in the socialization of competence.

## III. *Research Findings and Problems: The Study of Competence in the School Context*

### THINKING PROCESSES

In our study the thinking processes were a central area of interest. We were concerned with some of the questions that would grow naturally from the contrasting methods and goals of traditional and changing schools. How would the children respond to problem-solving situations, to situations requiring search and exploration? How would they respond when the demand was for cooperative rather than for individual solving? What would their thinking style be when personal rather than impersonal content was the material for cognitive organization? We drew data relevant to these questions from a variety of techniques, individual and group problem-solving and semi-projective techniques, as well as from classroom observations.[4] Our formulation of measures for the techniques stemmed from our interest in several goals of the changing school: its general emphasis on a probing, differentiating style of thought; its central valuing of the knowing and known individual self; its efforts to bring about integration of subjective and objective experience, etc.

From the analysis of classroom observations it was established that the teaching in study classrooms of the changing schools was significantly different from that in the traditional schools, with respect to intellectual stimulation and style, in ways that were congruent with the schools' postulated goals and assumptions. These clear differences in method and climate, as established by the teachers, were reflected in the way the children functioned in relation to their learning activities. Though this material was inappropriate for measurement of the *internalized* effects[5] of school experience, it documented the fact that the children in the changing schools utilized the classroom as a vehicle for the expression of a different kind of thinking process. They took initiative in asking questions, offering comments that opened up the search for explanations and for understanding relationships. This contrasted with the intellectual activities of children in the traditional classrooms, who concentrated on efficient, rapid closing-in on facts that would serve as correct answers. Further, the children in the changing schools were more intrinsically involved in their school work, as evidenced in a quality of intentness, focused participation and a higher proportion of school time spent in actual work. An interesting difference appeared also in the content of children's contacts with each other. In the traditional schools, the interchange was more often personal or social in nature; in the changing schools it was more often connected with work at hand, in contrast to a common impression that modern education offers a playful and less work-oriented school life.

If we turn now to the measures of internalization, we are in a position to examine our findings concerning thinking processes, with respect to our expectations. The pattern of these findings is complex and irregular, varying with the nature of the task and the situational context, and was not always consistent with our expectations.

We did not find, as we had expected, that the children from the changing schools engaged in more varied, exploratory search for problem implications and solutions. There are a series of possible explanations for this negative finding. They include the possibility that educational goals have not been realized, as well as the possibility that methodological problems of sample size, measurement of complex variables, etc., have obscured distinctions. It has seemed to us, however, that an interpretation of these findings in terms of a test-taking syndrome is among the most plausible.

The children of the most modern school lacked experience in taking tests. This was partly due to the school's preferred modes of evaluation and partly to its exemption, as a private school, from the jurisdictional requirements of a public school system. Certain attitudinal elements were at least as important as lack of concrete practice. Only in this school were there children who regarded the sessions as interruptions, not welcomed, to their classroom activities. They were not set to "do as well as possible" in response to adults who were unknown to them. They responded selectively to the elements of the testing and interviewing procedure, with differing degrees of involvement and effort. To the extent that this pattern represents autonomy as to where and toward whom one expends one's energies, it matches their school experience and might be regarded as an effect consonant with the goals of the school. At the same time, it opens up a question: Is the sphere of their optimal responsiveness too restricted? Is it important that children be able to meet the kind of reality demands implicit in test-taking at this stage of development? On the other hand, is this expectation one that has been built in to concepts of measurement intrinsic to traditional education, without much analysis of the problem of optimal balance between adaptation and autonomy in relation to stages of maturing?

It should be noted that on the group problem solving test, which was timed and impersonal, but distinct in that the problem was presented to the group as a whole, the findings were reversed.[6] Here, as anticipated, ability to work through a problem together was in direct alignment with differences in the schools. The children in the most modern school were both most efficient and successful, in timing and accuracy.

The failure to solve the problem in the allotted time by the children in the traditional schools has less significance than the play of motivational forces that were brought to the surface by the occasion of the test.

In the traditional school groups there was more evidence of aggression, a need to be "best," projection of blame in response to frustration, and dependence on evaluation delegated to outside authority. The pattern reflects an investment in successful performance for the sake of status in a competitive hierarchy; the children's school experience had not prepared them for effective modes of cooperative behavior.

In the children of the modern school, cooperative functioning was competent and gratifying. But here again the fundamental issue rests with the processes involved in the course of solving, more than with the success. That the school had developed capacity for mutually supporting group behavior toward a goal showed in the energy directed toward planning and carrying through the work together and in the spontaneous expressions of pleasure. Behind these behavioral patterns of constructive interaction one assumes a dynamic group process — a flow of deeply felt allegiances, conflicts, pleasures — so meaningful to the children that it can supersede the inevitable undercurrent of rivalrous, competitive feeling that must also be part of their school lives, though comparatively benign. The gains for competence, or one aspect of it, are obvious.

Still, there is room for further questioning. The performance of children from the most modern school on the four problem situations did not meet our expectations. The sharp contrast in approach to those problems and to the one just reviewed leads to new conjectures. Is it possible that they have become dependent, for their best functioning, on the intellectual potency derived from this group process so that, when confronted alone, they feel less adequate, less stimulated to bring forth equivalent efforts, as individuals? There is a further conjectural step. Should we view such dependence, if that is what it is as a restricting influence, interfering with upstanding, competent performance on one's own? Or is there some merit in looking at this dependence developmentally, as one does in other areas of maturing at earlier stages of the growth sequence?

It was from the questions we put to the children about themselves through the two techniques mentioned earlier, the Stick Figure Scale and the Dictated Letter, that we gained insight into another aspect of the thinking process. Though the techniques differed in degree of structure, they were both drawing on personal material, giving a quite different prismatic view of how the children were thinking.

As expected, the children from the modern schools were clearly more differentiated in their knowledge of themselves than were the children from the traditional schools.[7] They projected finer gradations in their judgments of themselves on the Stick Figure Scale, and their self-perceptions varied according to the particular preference, mood or quality about which they were introspecting. In the letters they dictated they showed themselves, again, to be in contact with more complex self-images and able to communicate verbally about them. Their letters dealt with more kinds of content, extending beyond factual material such as name, address, and the sequence of lessons in the school day, to include, for example, such personal material as the love of horses and stuffed animals, the feeling that the little brother is a "brat," and the added comment, "not really."

Furthermore, the letters were rated as more personalized not only in terms of substantive content but in the way the children expressed their own individualized perceptions, feelings and meanings. The traditional school children handled the task very effectively, at one level, but their letters had a more stereotyped, non-spontaneous quality.

In this much, the modern school appears to be accomplishing its goal to help the child sustain individuality through the integration of objective ideas and subjective meanings. Other facts about these same letters, however, raise questions that have concerned educators of this persuasion and are close to our concern with questions of competence. The children of the most modern school showed high variability. It was in this group that the most spontaneous, integrated letters were produced, but it was also mostly in this group that children were found who could not cope with the task at all.

Educationally, there are other problems to consider. Is there an inevitable choice for the school and the teacher between the development of exploratory, personally meaningful, probing modes of thought, applied either to knowledge of the self or mastery of impersonal knowledge, and the development of workmanlike, efficient functioning, less individualized and less searching in its style of ordering experience? If, indeed, the one is inevitably at the cost of the other, the question of values enters in. At the present stage, however, such a conclusion would be premature. There has not been, as yet, enough investment on a large scale in the study of how to balance the enactment of these goals in curriculum design; nor has there been enough work, empirically or in systematic research form, on considering what balances are suitable for which children.

## MOTIVATION AND SELF-FEELING

If we consider motivation and feelings of competence in the context of the child learning in school, what questions might we wish to answer from a research framework? Basically, there appear to be two:

1. Do the changing schools produce more positive self-feelings, a greater sense of competence? Do their children show a higher motivation to learn? Or motivation of a different, more internalized and less extrinsic, kind?

2. In general, is there evidence from school-related research that high motivation, positive self-feeling, and competent functioning are related? Do they move together? To what extent are they dependent on each other?

We have approached the evaluation of the *motivation* to learn and perform effectively at several levels: 1) through measures of attitudes and identification with school, drawn from interviews, sentence completion, projectives, etc.; 2) through evaluation of attitudes and effectiveness of performance in the several test sessions; 3) through conventional scoring of "achievement motivation" obtained through a version of the TAT and measured by a slight modification of the McClelland system (McClelland *et al.*, 1953); and 4) through a measure of the extent to which the children stressed external and tangible criteria (adults as judges, tests, formal marking systems) in this same projective material for the evaluation of learning adequacy and academic accomplishment.

In the extent to which these children were invested in their schools, thoughtful about its workings, enthusiastic and positive in their evaluations, our findings followed the clear lines of the modern-traditional distinction, with the children of the modern private school most intensely and positively involved; this was, in fact, the only school where the boys were strongly identified. If investment in the learning situation is part of the motivation for effective learning, then these modern schools, particularly the most modern, have apparently mobilized their children well. It is also true, however, that it was among children of the modern private school that we found the motivation to perform effectively and with concentration in our testing situations to be most variable. As noted in the previous section, they seemed, as a group, less geared to perform for us, more prone to reject items of our test battery, and this was particularly true of the boys. One takes the impression of children highly motivated to live and work in situations they have found meaningful, but not automatically mobilized to perform well in situations that have been set for them.

On the conventional measures of achievement need, from our modified TAT, the modern and traditional groups were not different. They did differ, however, in the extent to which their themes highlighted the presence of external criteria for judging the adequacy of accomplishment; children from traditional schools projected significantly more of such content, and the children from the modern private school the least of any group.

From these data on motivation, then, there is evidence that children educated by more modern methods are more invested in the school situation; that motivation to perform effectively is more unevenly mobilized by children from the most modern educational environment; and that, though there is no clear evidence of differences in "achievement need," as between children from modern and traditional schools, there is evidence of greater externalization of standards in the traditionally educated, with the judgment of adequacy more readily seen as outside themselves.

Our measures of the *feeling* of competence and adequacy are relatively modest, and confound positive feeling with the accuracy of self-evaluation in a way that one can be cognizant of but not easily unravel. We found no differences between children from modern and traditional schools either on a specific measure, in which they were asked to evaluate their academic effectiveness, nor on a more combinatory measure assessing different aspects of self-evaluation.

Did we expect greater feelings of competence and adequacy from the children of the changing schools? Certainly, their schools hold this as an important, even crucial, goal and attempt to build toward it. The fact that we did not find such evidence raises two possible explanations, not mutually exclusive. One lies in the familiar problem of measurement, particularly troublesome for variables where the connection between the underlying phenomenon and the behavioral indicators requires much inference. The other lies in the inherent complexity of what is being measured. Educators who have tried to influence the development of adequacy feelings have been aware of the complexity, and that the outcome is apt to be a long time building. Further, it seems possible that for the children the sources of uncertainty in the modern atmosphere are different in quality but not necessarily easier to integrate. Schools of this kind present fewer experiences of closure, less concretization of standards, implicit pressure toward the internalization of standards and toward meeting one's own best level. This may be no less a burden, even with adult support, than an atmosphere which demands that external and arbitrary standards be met. Yet the educators involved — not unmindful of the problem — have tended to stay with the judgment that the feeling of adequacy and competence consolidates, eventually, at a level that is more stable for more children than the feeling of adequacy that comes by a different kind of education. This feeling may come earlier, within the traditional rubric, but primarily for the highly successful child and with continuing dependence on an "other directed" set of reinforcements.

Aside from checking this general assumption, the job for further exploration lies in two directions: 1) exploration of the balance of experiences and reinforcements, extrinsic-intrinsic, that support positive self-feeling, with attention to the needs of different age levels, and 2) identification of children who thrive best in different kinds of environments or require different experiences and handling within a particular environment. The work of Grimes and Allinsmith (1961), who found that especially anxious or compulsive children function better in structured than unstructured school environments, is a relevant line of research.[8]

We come now to the second question, considered at a general level and without reference to the educational philosophy of the schools. Do motivation, self-feeling and competent performance appear interdependent, moving along together?

We see no empirical evidence of interrelationship among these variables in the data from our total sample. The intercorrelations among our measures are uniformly low, and data from a substudy of high and low achieving children in the three public schools bear out this finding (Minuchin and Shapiro, 1964).

In this substudy we found no distinguishing features in motivation or feelings of academic adequacy, as we measured them, between the more and less academically effective children. Here the sex differences, albeit based on small numbers, were provocative and worthy of further checking. Effective *boys* were extremely competent in goal directed intellectual situations, popular with their peers, but constricted in their approach to unstructured situations and resentful toward school adults;

effective *girls* not only showed high skills in goal directed intellectual situations and in interaction with peers, but also far surpassed the boys in free and imaginative functioning in the face of more personalized intellectual situations, and in the active, effective adaptation they made to the total school environment, including adult authorities. Yet the boys evaluated themselves confidently in terms of their effectiveness, while the girls evaluated themselves with greater diffidence and lesser reality. Whether this is a deep and consistent sex linked pattern or an artifact of verbal measures is an important research question.

Other investigators have also explored the extent to which motivation, feeling and performance move together for the child in the school situation, though this is recognized as still a young field of investigation.[9] Among them, Haggard in particular has pointed to the negative aspects that may accompany effective and highly motivated performance, a factor that we have also noted among the high achieving boys of our own substudy.

By some definitions children such as these are models of socialization — highly motivated, confident of their capacity and effective in their efforts. If we broaden the definition of competent performance or consider the total pattern, however, there are crucial and less soothing implications. Under the accumulating impact of pressure to achieve, the motivation stays very high in these competent children, but performance actually constricts, staying at "pay off" levels, with an apparent atrophy of creative, flexible and personalized competence; feelings of competence take on a brittle and complex quality since they must be fed through reaffirmation and the defeat of others, and are accompanied by anxiety and anger. We are led to question the cost of socialization in these terms, the role of school and home values in what is elicited from children who are probably capable of a different kind of development, and to a general question of whether we can consider the relationship of motivation, feeling and performance without honoring the complexities and alternate conceptions of each factor.

To recapitulate: There is some evidence that different philosophies of socialization in the schools affect children's competence motivation and feelings differentially, though the lines of effect are complex and still not totally clear. The changing schools appear to affect different children in different ways, mobilizing some to broad and desirable effectiveness, perhaps burdening and inhibiting others in ways they cannot easily manage. There is some evidence, further, that competent performance, competence motivation and feelings of competence can and do move independently, at least when we test their interrelationships on a group basis. Basic capacity levels and sex differences appear relevant to the ways in which these factors combine, for the school child.

If we wish to advance our understanding of the relationships among performance, motivation and feeling, we may need more differentiated analysis of each of these factors, more sensitive measures, and consideration of the concomitant effects of alternate courses of socialization. We might also want to give more attention to the effect of changing school practices on individuals. We might want to consider children who represent success and failure in the different educational environments, studying intensively the nature of their motivation and self-feeling as it relates to the form and quality of their performance in school and as they grow.

## REFERENCES

1. The Psychological Impact of School Experience, supported by the National Institute of Mental Health, USPHS, grant M-1075.

2. The report of this study is being prepared and will be published in book form. See also interim report: Biber, Barbara; Zimiles, H.; Minuchin, Patricia; and Shapiro, Edna. The Psychological Impact of School Experience: a series of papers on selected findings (mimeo), November, 1962.

3. See the detailed description of two teachers, fifth and sixth grade levels, in Sears and Sherman (1964). They represent a "modern" and a relatively "traditional" teacher, in our terms, and exemplify in part the distinction described here.

4. It might be noted that in our own study the schools were selected, and later systematically assessed, with respect to their variation along the modern-traditional continuum. The schools each had unique characteristics, obviously, and these are important at times in considering the study's findings, but the most modern school was representative in most respects of the changing values described here; the other schools differed from it in varying degrees, with the study school at the other extreme representing traditional values.

The four individual problem-solving techniques offered a range of cognitive challenge. They required differentiated analysis of the stimulus situation, processing and utilization of information, the organization of similarities and differences toward solution by an abstract principle, the flexibility to overcome functional fixedness, and fluid processes of association and thought. The four techniques were: the Cylinder problem, adapted from Saugstad (1959), the Meaning Context problem, adapted from Werner and Kaplan (1950), Uncommon Uses, adapted from Guilford (1956) and the Spies problem, developed by Edna Shapiro of the Bank Street research staff and similar in principle to the Vigotsky Concept Formation Test.

The group problem-solving technique, the Russell Sage Social Relations Test (Damrin, 1959), was included for another purpose. It tested the children's ability to plan and work cooperatively with their peers toward problem solution. Within a time limit, the children were required to plan their procedure and to build an object, as a group, that would exactly match a previously constructed model. Here both verbal and non-verbal elements, analytic and reconstitutive processes, were involved. Time solution scores were amply supplemented by analysis of observations which had been taken concurrently and had recorded the structure of participation, task concentration, follow-through of planning, affective tone, etc.

Two semi-projective techniques tapped the children's thinking processes in relation to self-image: the Stick Figure Scale, a self-scaling technique, based on a technique developed by Mary Engel (1963) and the Dictated Letter, a self-descriptive letter.

5. Sechrest (1964) has recently criticized the procedure of drawing inferences concerning "generalized" effects from classroom observations. In this study such observations are complementary but not central to inferences concerning what we call "internalized" and what Sechrest calls "generalized" effects.

6. See Minuchin, 1965.

7. See Minuchin, 1962.

8. There has been little direct work by other investigators concerning the effects of different school atmospheres on motivation or feelings of competence, but the recent work of Sears (1963) and Spaulding (1963), has bearing. Sears explored a series of classrooms, rating teacher variability along dimensions somewhat parallel to those described earlier in this paper, and related these two "target" variables in fifth and sixth grade children; Spaulding extended this work to additional classrooms and to fourth grade children as well. Sears found that task oriented work and circumscribed application — what she describes as "the quiet, industrious classroom, honored for centuries as a sign of teaching efficiency" — was related to teaching methods that involved direct giving of information, teaching to the class as a unit, much evaluation by the teacher, little personalized interest or communication. The finding suggests that relatively traditional teaching mobilizes high motivation for this kind of industrious application.

Sears found no systematic relationship between self-concept variables and teaching philosophy and style, but Spaulding found positive self-concept related to teacher behavior that was acceptant and individualized, and which facilitated task oriented behavior and avoided negative evaluation. In the Sears study, teachers' favorable reactivity and perception of the child appeared to play a greater role in the self-concepts, the competence feelings, of less bright children than those of children with higher ability. There is general evidence from her work that different educational methods and styles may have differential effects on brighter and less gifted children, and on boys and girls.

9. A number of studies have explored the relation of anxiety to performance in school, anxiety seen here as the feeling of uncertainty and doubt about one's competence (Grimes and Allinsmith, 1961; Keller and Rowley, 1962; Sarason et al., 1960; etc.). Findings have varied, but they go in the direction of suggesting a functional range: higher anxiety does not necessarily imply lower performance, at least defined through the ability to score well on tests, but above a certain point high anxiety appears to become clearly crippling for performance, not only in individual terms but in comparative ones. There remain the questions to which some investigators have pointed of the interdependence of anxiety and the structure and demands of the situation: What factors build anxiety in the school situation? What are the conditions under which the relatively vulnerable child functions poorly?

Other studies have considered the relation between performance and positive feelings of confidence. Here some connections have been established between expectations of success and actual performance (Crandall, 1964). It has been suggested, however, that the relationship of feelings of competence to performance is weaker for those who function poorly than for the successful child (Sears, 1963), with the obvious implication that more defensive and complicated mechanisms tend to enter in for those who do not function well.

Further, there has been an association suggested between performance level, feelings of confidence, and the sex of the child, much along the lines found in our substudy of high and low achievers (Brandt, 1958; Crandall et al., 1962; Sears, 1962, etc.). Girls tend to have less high and accurate self-concepts in general (at least as they express them to psychologists), bright and effective girls tending to underestimate their functioning. The point has been raised by various people that for girls competent intellectual functioning may conflict with elements of the self-image related to an acceptable social sex role; they tend to refrain from what might be taken as bragging or, at a deeper level, to deny their competence as a threat to acceptable femininity. Competent boys are found in most research to be more realistic and outspoken in their self-evaluation, to radiate an accepting, non-guilty enjoyment of their ability to work well and achieve.

Research on achievement *motivation* has pointed up the sex difference factor again, but in different terms. Research relating achievement motivation to actual performance, while not extensive for children, has included some important studies (Cox, 1962; Crandall, 1963; Crandall *et al.*, 1962; Rosen and D'Andrade, 1959; Sears, 1962; Winterbottom, 1958). Some have established a connection between high achievement motivation and effective functioning while others have not. The problems of age level, choice of measures, sex of child, area of functioning, etc. are interwoven in the discrepant findings. There is some accumulation of evidence, however, that the motivational components of competent performance in boys and girls may be quite different, with the suggestion that boys' achievement is more directly reflective of the motivation to achieve, while the academic achievement of girls may more often occur in the service of social and affiliative needs. The girls' wish to do well is seen as instrumental to the approval and personal recognition it brings (though, if we are to judge by the self-feeling data, not without uncertainty and conflict). For boys, the syndrome of effective functioning is more often of a piece, accompanied or sparked by strong achievement motivation, realistic appraisal of ability, and confidence about the capacity to do well.

The work of Haggard (1957) in particular, however, brings us back to a sober appraisal of the possible mechanisms involved where pressure and standards are high and the capable, confident, highly motivated child meets them with energy and room to spare. He found that the most effective of the gifted children he studied were highly motivated, as third graders, to live up to adult expectations; they tended to be secure, confident and independent, though competitive and somewhat tense. By seventh grade, they were still highly effective achievers, still striving toward adult standards, still apparently confident, but they showed a decrease in intellectual originality and creativity, antagonism and rejection toward adults, higher anxiety, and a hard driving willingness to defeat and win over others.

# REFERENCES

Biber, Barbara, Zimiles, H., Minuchin, Patricia, & Shapiro, Edna. The psychological impact of school experience: a series of papers on selected findings (mimeo), November, 1962.

Brandt, R. M. The accuracy of self-estimate: a measure of self-concept. *Genet. psychol. Monogr.*, 1958, *58*, 55–99.

Bruner, J. The act of discovery. *Harvard Educ. Rev.*, 1961, *31*, 21-32.

Cox, F. N. An assessment of the achievement behavior system in children. *Child Develpm.*, 1962, *33*, 907–916.

Crandall, V. J. Achievement. In Stevenson, H. W. (Ed.) Child Psychology. *Yearb. nat. Soc. Stud. Educ.*, 1963, *62*, Part I, 416–459.

Crandall, Virginia. Achievement behavior in young children. *Young Child.*, November, 1964, *20* (2), 77–90.

Crandall, V. J., Katkovsky, W., & Preston, Anne. Motivational and ability determinants of young children's intellectual achievement behaviors. *Child Develpm.*, 1962, *33*, 643–661.

Damrin, Dora, E. The Russell Sage Relations Test: a technique for measuring group problem solving skills in elementary school children. *J. exp. Educ.*, 1959, *28* (1), 85–99.

Engel, Mary, & Raine, W. J. A method for the measurement of the self-concept of children in the third grade. *J. genet. Psychol.*, March, 1963, *102*, 125–137.

Erikson, Erik, H. Identity and the life cycle. *Psych. Issues,* 1959, *1* (1).

Getzels, J. W., & Jackson, P. *Creativity and Intelligence.* New York: Wiley, 1962.

Grimes, J. W., & Allinsmith, W. Compulsivity, anxiety, and school achievement. *Merrill-Palmer Quart.*, October, 1961, 7 (4), 247–271.

Guilford, J. P. The structure of intellect. *Psychol. Bull.*, 1956, *53*, 267–293.

Guilford, J. P. Three faces of intellect. *Amer. Psychologist,* 1959, *8*, 469–480.

Haggard, E. A. Socialization, personality, and achievement in gifted children. *Sch. Rev.*, Winter Issue, 1957, 318–414.

Hilgard, E. R. Issues within learning theory and programmed learning. *Psychol. in Schs.*, April, 1964, *1* (2), 129–139.

Keller, E. D., & Rowley, V. N. Anxiety, intelligence and scholastic achievement in elementary school children. *Psychol. Rep.*, 1962, *11*, 19–22.

McClelland, D. C., Atkinson, J. W., Clark, R. A. & Lowell, E. L. *The Achievement Motive.* New York: Appleton-Century-Crofts, 1953.

Minuchin, Patricia. Self-differentiation in children of varying backgrounds. Paper presented at the Amer. Orthopsychiat. Ass., March, 1962 (mimeo).

Minuchin, Patricia. Solving problems cooperatively: a comparison of three classroom groups. *Childh. Educ.*, May, 1965, 480–484.

Minuchin, Patricia & Shapiro, Edna. Patterns of mastery and conflict resolution at the elementary school level. New York: Bank Street College of Education (U. S. Office of Educ. Coop. Res. Project No. 1401), 1964.

Ojemann, R. H. Investigations on the effects of teaching an understanding and appreciation of behavior dynamics. In Caplan, G. (Ed.), *Prevention of Mental Disorders in Children.* New York: Basic Books, 1961.

Piaget, J. *The Growth of Logical Thinking in the Child.* New York: Basic Books, 1958.

Rosen, B., & D'Andrade, R. The psychosocial origins of achievement motivation. *Sociometry,* 1959, *22*, 185–218.

Sarason, S., Davidson, K., Lighthall, F., Waite, R., & Ruebush, B. *Test Anxiety in Elementary School Children.* New York: Wiley, 1960.

Saugstad, P. Incidental memory and problem solving. *Psychol. Rev.,* 1959, 59.

Sears, Pauline S. Correlates of need achievement and need affiliation and classroom management, self-concept and creativity. Unpublished manuscript, Laboratory of Human Development, Stanford Univer., 1962.

Sears, Pauline S. The effect of classroom conditions on the strength of achievement motive and work output on elementary school children. Stanford Univer. (U. S. Office of Educ. Coop. Res. Project No. 873), 1963.

Sears, Pauline S., & Sherman, Vivian S. *In Pursuit of Self Esteem.* Belmont, Calif.: Wadsworth Publishing, 1964.

Sechrest, L. Studies of classroom atmosphere. *Psychol. in Schs.,* April, 1964, *1* (2), 103–118.

Spaulding, R. L. Achievement, creativity, and self-concept correlates of teacher-pupil transactions in elementary schools. Univer. of Illinois (U. S. Office of Educ. Coop. Res. Project No. 1352), 1963.

Suchman, R. Inquiry training: building skills for autonomous discovery. *Merrill-Palmer Quart.,* July, 1961.

Torrance, E. P. *Guiding Creative Talent.* Englewood Cliffs, N.J.: Prentice-Hall, 1962.

Werner, H. *Comparative Psychology of Mental Development.* New York: International Univer. Press, 1957.

Werner, H., & Kaplan, Edith. The acquisition of word meanings: a developmental study. *Mongr. Soc. Res. Child Develpm.,* 1950, *1.*

White, R. W. Motivation reconsidered: the concept of competence. *Psychol. Rev.,* September, 1959, *66,* 297–333.

Winterbottom, Marian. The relation of need for achievement to learning experiences in independence and mastery. In Atkinson, J. W. (Ed.), *Motives in Fantasy, Action and Society.* Princeton: Van Nostrand, 1958, 453–478.

# LOCAL SOCIAL STRUCTURE AND
# EDUCATIONAL SELECTION

## NATALIE ROGOFF RAMSOY

This paper is concerned with the way young people are allocated to positions in the social-class structure and the part played by education in the allocating process.

Numerous studies in America, Britain, and western Europe document the fact that youngsters who start life in a given social class vary in the class status they achieve as adults in proportion to the amount of formal schooling they obtain. The more education, the more advantaged the class status. Depending on the starting point, education facilitates either upward social mobility or the maintenance of a favored class position; lack of education brings on downward social mobility, or stability in a disadvantaged class position.

But what are we to make of these facts? Particularly, what is it that sets some youngsters on a path leading ultimately to graduation from college, while others never even complete their secondary education? As usually stated, the facts convey little of a sense of social process, of one thing occurring before another in an identifiable social location, or of one event or status affecting a later event or status through the advent of specific social mechanisms. It is possible that any one or any combination of at least three disparate sets of happenings might bring about the observed relationships. Each of the three to be proposed here, emphasizes a different key process — one stemming from the effect of schools on individual differences in ability, another from the effect of individual family differences in motivation, and the third from differences in community and school environments. In each case, the social process has a specified mechanism operating in a specified context. That these are extremely divergent interpretations of the observed correlation should be evident by the following discussion of each.

First, schools, like all formal organizations, develop a system of rewards and punishments as one way of implementing their goals. The acquisition of skills and knowledge by students is clearly one of the goals of schools. It is certainly not improbable that students who demonstrate the greatest success in acquiring skills and knowledge should most frequently receive the rewards that schools have at their disposal — promotion, high grades, prizes, and scholarships. Since the distribution of marked scholastic ability cuts across the social classes to at least some degree, the reward and punishment system of the schools would lead to a rearrangement of students with respect to their potential social achievement: the more able youngsters, motivated by scholastic rewards, would move further ahead in school, continue their education longer, and eventually move into more prestigeful occupational and social positions than the less able. Moreover, at the end of the school years, a certain amount of social mobility, upward and downward, could be attributed to the encouragement given by schools to the capable, no matter what their social origins, as well as to the discouragement given the less able of all social classes. The observed relationship between educational attainment and adult social-class position might, therefore, be due to the interaction between individual differences in ability and the reward system of schools.

A second process that would lead to the observed results has its locus in the family, rather than the school, and hinges on attitudes rather than aptitude. Some families, valuing achievement, discipline, and social-economic success, encourage their children to do as well as possible in school; the youngster's ability, this interpretation runs, sets only the broadest of bounds on his school performance. More determining than ability is the family's attitude toward education — and the distribution of favorable attitudes toward education again cuts across the class structure to some degree. The education and, ultimately, the social-class achievement of youngsters represent family aspirations come true. Note that the school in this process, plays essentially a passive role, or at least takes something of a secondary part. The school actually rewards, not necessarily those who merit it, but those who *want* to be rewarded, whether or not, in some abstract sense of equitable arrangements, they do merit it. The real locus of social mobility is the living room, not the classroom.

Finally, the possibility exists that educational attainment and adult class status are correlated because of processes arising from community and school structures. Because this idea is less familiar than the others and because the processes it highlights differ in certain formal ways from the others, it will be developed here at somewhat greater length. First, let it be granted that the various social classes are not randomly distributed among the diverse sizes and types of communities in the United States today. (We defer for the moment the evidence for this assertion.) It follows that each of the social classes will be more heavily concentrated in some kinds of community environments than in others, and that communities will vary in the predominant or average social-class affiliation of their residents. Such structural differences may set in motion both formal arrangements — such as school, library, and general cultural facilities in the community — and informal mechanisms, such as normative climates or modal levels of social aspiration, which are likely to affect *all* members of the community to some extent — parents and children, upper, middle, and working classes.

Many of the studies whose general findings are at issue here have, in fact, covered a wide variety of communities. By pooling the behavior of youngsters living in diverse communities, one of the sources of social mobility may be hidden from view, for it is possible that the formal arrangements and informal norms of the community set both a floor and a ceiling on the ultimate achievements in educational and social-class status of their young residents. For example, when we observe that youngsters from the more favored social origins end up on the average with greater educational attainment we may in fact be observing the results of the greater concentration of such youngsters in communities that facilitate academic achievement through better schools and through prevailing climates of opinion that nurture and sustain high educational aspiration. Upward social mobility, under these conditions, would result for the lucky minority of working-class youngsters whose families live, by accident or design, in predominantly middle-class communities; and downward social mobility for the unlucky middle-class youngsters living in less favored environments; while stability of class position would be the typical outcome for the majority of youngsters living in towns, villages, or cities where their class status is not a deviant one.

One of the intriguing implications of this idea is that it proposes a continuing but ever-changing link between ecological processes that lead to spatial patterns of residence and work, on the one hand, and the processes through which persons are allocated to positions in the social-class structure, on the other. Socio-economic position influences the type of community or neighborhood where families will live; their ecological status then affects the life chances of their children, some of whom will maintain the social-class status of the parents, while others will shift in status. Both individual and net shifts of class status in the second generation lead to further changes in ecological patterns, and so on, possibly until some kind of equilibrium is reached.

In sum, three variant interpretations have been offered for a recurrent empirical observation: that young people from given social origins vary in their educational attainment; such variations eventually leading to differences in the social-class status achieved in adulthood. Educational attainment thereby leads to upward or downward social mobility, or to maintenance of parental class status. In effect, the three interpretations can be ordered with respect to the importance they attach to events transpiring in the classroom itself. According to the first, the classroom is the central stage, for it is there that youngsters are rewarded or punished for their scholastic ability and performance, and it is the rewards and punishments they experience that lead to their academic and social attainments. According to the second interpretation, youngsters are carriers of aspirations and attitudes acquired from their families, and it is these states of mind that prevail, although they may be reinforced (unwittingly?) by the reward-and-punishment system of the school. The last interpretation calls attention to the community setting of both schools and families, and suggests that the ecological environment leads to formal and informal arrangements within and outside of the schools, affecting the educational attainment of residents.

None of these interpretations excludes the others. It is not necessary to demonstrate that only one of the social processes can be observed, the others being absent. Instead, a research design is called for that permits us to see whether all three are operative and, if possible, to gauge their relative significance. An empirical study with such a design is currently in process at the Bureau of Applied Social Research of Columbia University. We are fortunate enough to be given access to information gathered by the Educational Testing Service, concerning the college-going and career plans of over thirty-five thousand American high-school seniors, who constituted the entire senior class of 1955 of over five hundred public secondary schools. Concerning the schools, which provide a fairly representative sample of the twenty thousand-odd senior public high schools in the United States, information was collected, at the time of the field work, from their principals. This has now been supplemented by consulting national and state school directories, other published surveys, and census sources describing the towns and counties where the schools are located.

What kinds of information are needed to provide empirical tests of the ideas advanced here? We need to know something about the social origins of the youngsters, something about their future orientations, and their scholastic ability. Finally, we need to introduce some principle for classifying the communities where they attend high school. Specifically, here are the indicators to be used in attempting to compare the proposed types of social processes with the factual evidence. First, we shall see how youngsters who vary in scholastic ability — indicated by their performance on a twenty-item test devised especially for this study by the Educational Testing Service — compare with respect to their plans for going on to college. This will provide the evidence for seeing whether or not the reward-and-punishment system of the schools helps to channel the more capable youngsters into the route of higher education. Moreover, we shall simultaneously trace the effect of the youngster's social background on his college-going orientation. Several criteria have been used to classify the families of orientation of the high-school seniors: their fathers' occupational status, fathers' educational attainment, and the college experience of their older siblings. Combining these three properties of the families with the average college-going propensities of the high-school seniors who belonged to such family types permitted us to construct a set of ranked socio-educational classes, ranging from well-educated professional and managerial families, who clearly imbue their offspring with a desire to go to college, to poorly or uneducated unskilled manual and farm families who are far more indifferent to higher education as a desirable goal. Five such classes were finally discerned, each containing approximately 20 per cent of the thirty-five thousand high-school seniors, so that they may be referred to as the socio-educational status quintiles.

One further word about classifying the students according to their scholastic ability. At some of the high schools studied, the vast majority of seniors scored well above the mean, while at other schools, the bulk of the senior class did extremely poorly on the test. While this is in itself a significant result, it also has the following implication: if we were to classify individual seniors according to their absolute scholastic aptitude score, we should be comparing the behavior of youngsters who actually stood at just about all possible relative positions within their own school. Almost any given score represents the top, the middle, and the bottom relative position at one or more of the 518 high schools observed. Therefore, the scores were converted into school-specific quartiles for all those who were in a senior class of 15 or more. (This eliminates about 20 per cent of the schools, but less than 3 per cent of the 35,000 students.) Since we want to observe the effect of allocating rewards and punishments by school authorities, we clearly need to compare those who are at the top in their own school with those at the bottom, no matter what the absolute level of scholastic ability is at the school.

Finally, we have used the expressions "scholastic ability" and "scholastic performance" as though they were interchangeable, despite the fact that they are clearly disparate. Fortunately, the principals of about one hundred of the high schools were asked to check the school records of each of their seniors and indicate what his class standing was. The correlation between ability, as indicated by the short written test, and class standing, which summarizes the student's performance over a four-year period, is extremely high, although it does vary somewhat among the high schools. We use this evidence as a justification for taking the student's performance on the aptitude test as a fairly good indicator of his behavior in the classroom.

Scholastic ability plays a decisive role in students' plans to continue with their education. Some 61 per cent of all high-school seniors in the top quarter of their class planned to go to college; in successive quartiles, the proportion drops to 44 per cent, 33 per cent and 24 per cent. The preliminary evidence suggests that the high school in effect *does* allocate rewards and punishments in such a way as to encourage the competent and discourage the incompetent. At the same time, there is a marked tendency for students' further educational plans to be influenced by the socio-educational status of their families. Seventy-two per cent of those from professional or managerial families plan to attend college; the proportion decreases to 47 per cent, 35 per cent, 26 per cent, and finally 24 per cent through the succeeding socio-educational status categories. And, as many other studies have shown, the two social processes reinforce one another. The full picture is given in Table 1, where the proportions planning to attend college are shown at every level of scholastic ability and from each of the five types of social origins simultaneously. College-going propensities vary greatly

TABLE 1

**Per Cent of High-School Seniors Planning to Attend College,
According to Scholastic Ability (in Quartiles) and
Socio-Educational Status of the Family**

| Scholastic-ability quartile | FAMILY-STATUS QUINTILE | | | | | All quintiles | No. of cases |
|---|---|---|---|---|---|---|---|
| | (Top) 5 | 4 | 3 | 2 | (Bottom) 1 | | |
| (Top) 4 | 83 | 66 | 53 | 44 | 43 | 61 | (8,647) |
| 3 | 70 | 53 | 37 | 29 | 29 | 44 | (8,709) |
| 2 | 65 | 41 | 31 | 20 | 21 | 33 | (8,696) |
| (Bottom) 1 | 53 | 30 | 22 | 16 | 18 | 24 | (8,509) |
| All quartiles | 72 | 47 | 35 | 26 | 24 | 40 | |
| No. of cases | (6,520) | (6,647) | (6,465) | (8,116) | (6,811) | | (34,561) |

Notes: Students are classified here according to their scholastic-aptitude quartile in their own high school. Family status position, however, is constant for all students coming from a given family background, no matter what the social composition of their high school.
The number of cases on which each of the percentages is based ranges from 963 to 2,505.

among the twenty categories of high-school seniors: 83 per cent of the brightest youngsters from the most advantaged families plan to attend college, but only 16 per cent of the least competent children of skilled and semiskilled workers (category 2) are college-oriented. Both the school and the family play a part in determining who is to gain education beyond high school. Among previous studies, the relative importance of the two has varied greatly; Kahl's study in the suburbs of Boston[1] shows the family to be almost twice as influential as the school, while Sewell's Wisconsin data[2] suggest the school to be almost three times as important as the family; our own nation-wide sample falls squarely between the two, with each of the sources playing about an equal role.

So much, then, for the first two social processes leading to the observed correlation between educational attainment and social mobility or stability. What of the third? With the first two, it was clear, both from the logic of the argument and from the guidelines provided by past research, just what indicators to use in order to test the validity of our ideas. The third set of social processes are, we suggested, generated by conditions in the community, which affect the type of educational and cultural facilities the town can provide and which presumably also shape the average social and education aspiration level of the residents. But what types of indicators would most accurately portray such environmental states? This is clearly a major sociological problem and one to which we can make only a limited contribution. Furthermore, we have only begun to probe the data in this study for tentative leads and therefore offer the following evidence with the appropriate reservations.

We start with a principle of classifying communities that derives from a set of frequently used descriptive terms, employed by laymen, educators, social scientists, and just about everyone who has ever given a moment's thought to the varieties of educational experience: the size and type of community — village or small town, suburban or metropolitan — where the schools are located. The temptation is strong to clothe this idea in polysyllabic sociological garb, but in fact the impulse to use such a classification scheme arose from the fact that it is one of the very few environmental properties used frequently enough and over a long enough period of time to warrant a systematic empirical test.

Nine types of communities were discerned, varying in population size and their relationship to a metropolitan area. Table 2 identifies the types and presents the salient results concerning the college-going propensities of youngsters attending high school in each environment. It is up to the reader to decide whether or not the results confirm his expectations. For example, who would have predicted that the college-going propensities of youngsters attending high school in the very largest cities is almost as low as that of youngsters residing in the

TABLE 2

## College-Planning Rates and Social Composition of High-School Senior Classes in Diverse Community Contexts

| Type of Community | Number of high schools | Number of seniors | Per cent planning to attend college | PER CENT OF SENIORS IN EACH FAMILY-STATUS QUINTILE (Top) 5 | 4 | 3 | 2 | (Bottom) 1 | Total |
|---|---|---|---|---|---|---|---|---|---|
| Small independent towns: | | | | | | | | | |
| Less than 2,500 | 270 | 6,991 | 33 | 9 | 17 | 12 | 20 | 42 | 100% |
| 2,500–9,999 | 85 | 5,451 | 39 | 16 | 20 | 16 | 24 | 24 | 100% |
| 10,000–49,999 | 42 | 5,591 | 48 | 21 | 20 | 19 | 24 | 16 | 100% |
| Suburbs: | | | | | | | | | |
| Less than 2,500 | 36 | 1,768 | 37 | 17 | 18 | 18 | 26 | 21 | 100% |
| 2,500–9,999 | 15 | 1,085 | 46 | 30 | 18 | 19 | 23 | 10 | 100% |
| 10,000–49,999 | 22 | 3,116 | 50 | 34 | 18 | 19 | 21 | 8 | 100% |
| Large towns and cities: | | | | | | | | | |
| 50,000–99,999 | 10 | 2,176 | 45 | 22 | 20 | 22 | 23 | 13 | 100% |
| 100,000–499,999 | 19 | 3,669 | 37 | 17 | 18 | 24 | 30 | 11 | 100% |
| 500,000 or more | 19 | 5,589 | 39 | 20 | 22 | 23 | 24 | 11 | 100% |
| All communities | 518 | 35,436 | 40 | 19 | 19 | 19 | 23 | 20 | 100% |

smallest towns and villages and is surpassed by that of youngsters from the larger towns and, of course, the suburbs? College-going is apparently affected by the size and type of community where the decision to attend college is made — but hardly in a simple, linear fashion. One note of caution. We were able to observe only those young people who remained in school until the twelfth grade, and the tendency to stay in school that long varies among the diverse types of communities. The college-going proportions need to be corrected, therefore, by taking into account those youngsters who will not attend college because they have not completed a secondary education. Community educational-retention rates are positively correlated both with urbanization and with community wealth (median family income), and much more markedly with the latter than the former. Therefore, the wealthy suburbs should have their college-going proportions reduced the least, since most of their youngsters do stay in school through the twelfth grade, followed by the larger cities, and finally small towns and rural villages. This would keep the three main types of communities in the same rank order but would increase the gap between the smallest and largest places.

The second part of Table 2 describes the social composition of the student body attending high school in the various types of communities. Note the marked degree of social segregation implied by these distributions — the children of farmers (category 1) concentrated in the smallest villages and towns, the children of professionals and managers in the larger suburbs, and the children of industrial workers (category 2) most heavily concentrated in cities of 100,000–500,000. We cannot here mention more than a few of the major consequences of such ecological segregation.

One of the most interesting consequences concerns the scholastic aptitude of youngsters attending schools situated in diverse community contexts. Table 3 presents the trends, showing median aptitude scores of students coming from families of each of the five socio-educational status types and living in each type of community. Here, of course, we describe students according to their absolute scores on the aptitude test, since we want to evaluate the effect of the environment on scholastic ability. Test scores ranged from 0 to 20; the mean for all 35,000 seniors to whom it was given is 8.9; the standard deviation, 4.7.

Again, the suburbs stand out as most conducive to pronounced scholastic achievement. For convenience, an unweighted average aptitude score is given for all students attending schools in each community

## TABLE 3

### *Scholastic Ability and College-Planning Rates, by Social Origins and Community Context*

**A.   Median Aptitude Scores**

**FAMILY–STATUS   QUINTILE**

| Type of Community | (Top) 5 | 4 | 3 | 2 | (Bottom) 1 | Unweighted mean of all quintiles |
|---|---|---|---|---|---|---|
| Small independent towns: | | | | | | |
| Less than 2,500 | 11.2 | 9.2 | 8.3 | 7.7 | 6.9 | 8.7 |
| 2,500–9,999 | 11.6 | 9.7 | 8.6 | 8.1 | 7.4 | 9.1 |
| 10,000–49,999 | 12.7 | 10.1 | 9.0 | 9.1 | 7.3 | 9.6 |
| Suburbs: | | | | | | |
| Less than 2,500 | 11.9 | 9.8 | 9.0 | 8.2 | 7.2 | 9.2 |
| 2,500–9,999 | *13.0+ | 10.8 | 9.4 | 8.2 | 7.2 | 10.0 |
| 10,000–49,999 | 13.0 | 11.3 | 10.5 | 9.9 | 8.5 | 10.6 |
| Large towns and cities: | | | | | | |
| 50,000–99,999 | 12.0 | 8.8 | 8.0 | 7.1 | *5.0— | 8.0 |
| 100,000–499,999 | 11.8 | 9.5 | 8.4 | 7.7 | 7.0 | 8.9 |
| 500,000 or more | 11.7 | 9.6 | 8.8 | 8.6 | 7.2 | 9.2 |

\* Medians were computed from grouped data, using four score intervals. In these two cases, the medians fell in one of the extreme intervals, and interpolation was not carried out.

**B.   Per Cent Planning to Attend College**

**FAMILY–STATUS   QUINTILE**

| Type of Community | (Top) 5 | 4 | 3 | 2 | (Bottom) 1 | Unweighted mean of all quintiles |
|---|---|---|---|---|---|---|
| Small independent towns: | | | | | | |
| Less than 2,500 | 66 | 45 | 35 | 25 | 25 | 39 |
| 2,500–9,999 | 73 | 50 | 33 | 25 | 27 | 42 |
| 10,000–49,999 | 78 | 55 | 42 | 32 | 32 | 48 |
| Suburbs: | | | | | | |
| Less than 2,500 | 69 | 50 | 35 | 25 | 15 | 39 |
| 2,500–9,999 | 74 | 51 | 38 | 22 | 29 | 43 |
| 10,000–49,999 | 77 | 51 | 40 | 26 | 22 | 43 |
| Large towns and cities: | | | | | | |
| 50,000–99,999 | 67 | 44 | 36 | 35 | 37 | 44 |
| 100,000–499,999 | 69 | 45 | 32 | 22 | 20 | 37 |
| 500,000 or more | 64 | 46 | 31 | 28 | 24 | 39 |

context. This enables us to see the effect that schools exert on their students' academic capacity, without that effect being obscured by the advantages or disadvantages individual students enjoy by virtue of their family background. It appears that all students, whether in the majority or the minority in the school they attend, enjoy the blessings or pay the price their school affords. From those at the top to those at the bottom of the social-class hierarchy, all students attending large suburban schools emerge from their educational experience relatively better equipped in academic skills, while youngsters who attend school in small villages or large industrial cities emerge from their educational environments less adequately prepared. Note how these trends account for some of the heterogeneity in scholastic aptitude *within* a given social class by the diversity in formal academic training received by the youngsters originating in that class.

The second part of Table 3 shows parallel trends for plans to attend college, according to young people's social origins and the type of community where they attend high school. On the face of it, small towns and suburbs appear to be at a par in producing college-oriented youngsters — but again, we should recall the difference between them in the school retention rates through the twelfth grade. After making the appropriate corrections, the suburbs will again rank first in productivity of college students.

The last word has hardly been said on the variety of ways young people may be affected by the community setting where they frame their career and educational goals. Quite the contrary — only after considerably more research effort has been expended will we be ready to make assertions with confidence on the whole matter of broad structural influences on individual behavior.

Specifically, when it comes to schools and social stratifications, the kind of analysis proposed here is carried out in the following spirit: heretofore, when sociologists have investigated the way education and social-class structure relate to one another, relatively scant attention has been accorded the fact that education is a long-term social process, occurring microscopically in the schoolroom and macrosopically in a definite and describable community context. Until now, the challenge of observing these processes has been evaded by the phrase: "Education is the high road to social mobility." No expression could more successfully divert us from the sociological point. The evasion has also directed sociologists to say that the heart of the matter is in the nuclear family, where all of the behavior and all of the attitudes and values are engendered that lead to scholastic achievement, and subsequent social-class achievement, by the members of each new generation. Nothing in our study belies the crucial role of the nuclear family, whose significance is so well recognized that we hardly feel the need to do any proselytizing in its behalf. But that this is all that counts in a bureaucratized, achievement-oriented society, where education is controlled by local communities each with its formally organized school system, is too much to believe. The more we turn in these other directions, the more will we learn about the social structure of our society.

## REFERENCES

1. J. A. Kahl, "Education and Occupational Aspirations of 'Common Man' Boys," *Harvard Educational Review*, XXIII (1953), 186–203.
2. W. H. Sewell, *et al.*, "Social Status and Educational and Occupational Aspiration," *American Sociological Review*, XXI (1956), 203–11.

# B.

## THE IMPACT OF MICRO-SOCIAL STRUCTURES: THE PEER GROUP

# STUDENT PEER-GROUP INFLUENCE

## THEODORE M. NEWCOMB

Students, like other people, are members of groups, and all groups (as distinguished from arbitrary categories) have power over their members. This paper deals, in necessarily oversimplified ways, with the nature, the sources, and the effects of such power, and also with the general problem of relationships between those effects and the presumed objects of college experience. I shall not for present purposes distinguish between formal groups (like a fraternity, or a freshman class) and informal ones (like a loosely defined set of students who, in a given dormitory in a given year, share a couple of classes and an interest in folk music). Nor shall I in any formal way attempt to define the term *peer group,* by which I shall mean simply any set of two or more students whose relationships to one another are such as to exert influence upon them as individuals.

### THEORETICAL AND EMPIRICAL BASES

The theoretical argument for assuming that the effects of a student peer group *should* be rather considerable runs essentially as follows. People respond to a situation not necessarily as it "really" is but as they perceive it to be. And they perceive all but the simplest situations — especially human ones — not as they have been preordained, by their physiological make-up, to perceive them but as they have learned to do so. The matter of learning to perceive — of acquiring habits of perceiving in one way things that might be perceived differently (and often are, especially by other people) is very complex indeed, but nearly all psychologists would agree that such habits are learned as a result of the successes and failures that follow from actions based upon

Reprinted with abridgement from Nevitt Sanford, ed., *The American College* (New York: John Wiley & Sons, Inc., 1962) by permission of the publisher and the author.

"right" and "wrong" ways of perceiving situations. The notions of success and failure assume, of course, that individuals have motives — whether standard, universal, or idiosyncratic — in terms of which success and failure are experienced.

There are powerful reasons why groups have much to do with individuals' successes and failures, and thus with the kinds of perceptual habits that they acquire. This is true, first, because groups so often have it in their power to reward and to punish — as by applause or shame, or by the according or withholding of social status or of worldly goods. Group standards often seem arbitrary to members of other groups — and indeed they are and must be, in the literal sense, for in many areas of life it is the *fact* of consensuality, not its content, that matters. One needs to know, dependably and in advance, what kinds of behavior will and will not be rewarded. Such standards come to have the psychological impact of ineluctability, and are sometimes referred to as "social reality." Successes and failures are matters of group life, second, because human beings want and need each other. If we want and need other people, then their responses to us are potentially rewarding or punishing — regardless of whether our wants represent spontaneous affiliativeness or the calculated instrumental use of others. In either case, group members develop sets of consensual expectations about each other (e.g., husband, wife, and child all want and expect husbandlike, wifelike, and childlike behavior from the appropriate family members, as well as wanting and expecting certain similar, rather than differentiated, kinds of behavior from all).

For the purposes of the present argument, the outcomes of these two bases of group power over its individual members are the same: individual members develop attitudes toward each other — most commonly favorable ones,[1] and they develop consensual sets of expectations regarding each other's behavior and regarding important aspects of their common environment, by which their individual expectations of success and failure are guided. Such consensual expectations about each other's behavior are known as *norms*. Baldly put, groups have power over their members because the same processes of interaction that result in members' feeling favorably toward each other also result, simultaneously, in their adopting norms that enable them to aim at success rather than failure.

The final step of the argument, of course, is that student peer groups, as a special case of a general phenomenon, are subject to the general rules. A plausible case can in fact be made for the assumption that most of the general rules should apply *a fortiori* to student groups. College students (particularly in this country, perhaps) meet each other with a ready-made consensuality compounded of needs for independence from parents in a setting where independence is relatively possible, and of strivings for adult status in a world that treats them half as children. These initial bases of consensus, together with the fact that students are inevitably thrown together in dining rooms, classes, and dormitories, inevitably result — and often rather quickly — in the joint processes according to which groups acquire influence over their members.[2]

The empirical grounds for concluding that substantial peer-group effects *in fact* occur in contemporary American colleges are not as solid as many of us would like to believe. Within the bounds of student peer-group studies, the following conclusions seem justified. (1) Under certain conditions there have been several demonstrations of marked changes in attitude, of consensual nature, during college or professional-school years. (Cf. Jacob, 1957; Newcomb, 1943; Sanford, 1956; Merton *et al.*, 1957.) (2) A much larger set of studies fails to show significant amounts of such changes (see, in particular, Jacob's review, 1957). Almost without exception, however, these studies have made no attempt to study differentiated peer groups. Their data have generally come from samples (more rarely, whole populations) of certain college classes, with no attention to group membership beyond the assumption that entire classes, or even entire student bodies, constitute membership groups. (3) Many and probably most of this larger body of studies have, quite understandably, concentrated upon the kinds of attitude changes that educators consider desirable.

In sum, I believe that the theoretical reasons for expecting important peer-group effects within American colleges are very convincing, and that the expectations have been well supported when they have been put to the proper tests. I shall later suggest certain conditions of peer-group influence that have emerged, or hypothetically would emerge, from such "proper tests."

*A framework for the problem.* It often happens, particularly in the world of human affairs, that the consequences of an event are best understood if viewed in the light of the circumstances of which that event itself is a consequence. The study of peer groups is a case in point: peer-group formation is an outcome of antecedent events; the nature of members' experiences, and thus the effects of those experiences, may be profoundly influenced by the circumstances attending

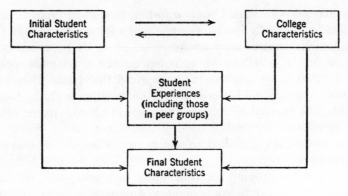

Schematic Diagram Illustrating Interdependent
Influences upon Final Student Characteristics

**Figure 1.** The diagram suggests the framework within which I shall examine some student peer-group phenomena. Within such a framework, at the heart of which are "student experiences" and in particular peer-group experiences, I shall look into the question of how peer-group membership arises and how it comes to have effects.

the group's emergence. And so (in the language of contemporary social scientists) it is necessary to consider peer groups alternately as dependent and as independent phenomena.

More specifically, the nature of student peer-group experience is sure to be influenced by the various factors having to do with student selection, and these in turn are influenced by and (in time) also influence both the actual and the perceived nature of the college itself. In very direct ways, furthermore, various kinds of institutional arrangements — e.g., student living arrangements — influence peer-group formation. The schematic diagram (Figure 1) in which arrows indicate presumed directions of influence, will suggest the kinds of interaction effects which must be taken into account.

SOME CONDITIONS OF PEER-GROUP FORMATION

It is of course "natural" for people with common interests to associate with one another, and it is a truism that, in our own society at least, not only early but also late adolescents (including most college students) seem to have strong needs for acceptance by age and sex peers. The truism leaves unexplained, however, the entire matter of selection. Even in very small colleges, not every one associates with equal frequency or with equal intensity with all of his peers. There are, moreover, wide differences among individuals; some are under-involved and some overinvolved, in terms of local norms. Furthermore, there are many possible bases for peer-group formation, ranging from chance propinquity through more or less casual common interest to shared concerns of great moment. And so, in order to gain our primary objective of understanding the effects of peer-group experience, we must examine such specific questions as why it is that particular peer groups get formed in the first place. I am, of course, making the social scientist's usual assumption that things happen in orderly rather than in "uncaused" ways, and that, in any college community at any given time, if certain conditions had been different the consequences for peer-group formation would have been different.

The following discussion of conditions under which influential peer groups are likely to develop (like the subsequent discussion of their effects) is necessarily a general one. Colleges in this country vary enormously, in almost every conceivable respect; moreover, peer groups of the most diverse forms arise within all but the tiniest colleges. It often happens, for example, that a total student body is an influential group for many of its members; the stamp of the Bryn Mawr girl or the Harvard man may be unmistakable — and quite consciously so, in many instances. At the other extreme, a tiny clique — whose members are bonded together, perhaps, by dissident values or beliefs — may be an influence group par excellence; probably such groups are of more importance in large than in very small colleges. In virtually all colleges, regardless of size and other characteristics, there are roommate pairs or triads, interest and activity groups, and informal circles of friends whose impact upon their members is often decisive. Associated with such variations in the nature of peer groups are of course wide differences among the kinds of motives that lead individuals to join or remain in them, as well as differences in individual personality, and differences in degree and kind of impact the groups have on their various members. The rather general considerations noted below do not apply with equal force, or in constant ways, to all these kinds of groups, but in one way or another I believe that the generalizations are none the less relevant.

In any case, there are three kinds of factors that may be considered of primary importance as independent variables, that is, as variables contributing to the formation of particular peer groups.

*Precollege acquaintance.* Particularly during early college experience, previous acquaintance — especially as established in secondary schools — may form the basis of college peer groups. One study of high school seniors' preferences among colleges (Coleman and Rossi, 1960) found that a small proportion of high school friends hoped to attend the same college. Neither this study nor any other known to me, however, provides much information as to the subsequent fate of precollege friendships.[3] It seems probable that many if not most of them are superseded by others developed in college with previously unknown persons. In the presumably rare cases where they do persist through a significant proportion of the college years, it seems more likely that they re-enforce existing attitudes and values of the individuals involved than that they mediate new ones acquired through college experience.

*Propinquity.* One cannot very well develop peer-group relationships with persons whom one has never met. Neither does one develop them with all of the persons whom one has met. But propinquity determines the probability of any two persons' meeting and, in particular, early propinquity in college — when most other individuals are relatively indistinguishable, since most of them are strangers — determines the probability of early meeting. This basic statement of statistical probabilities, together with a rather basic psychological consideration, has important consequences for peer-group formation. This consideration is that a currently known source of reward is not likely to be valued less than an alternative whose reward value is less certain (cf. G. Murphy, 1947, on "canalization"). Existing sources of reward enjoy a kind of squatter's right and peer-group acceptance is likely to be rewarding. This principle, the consequences of which are in a certain sense conservative, must of course compete with other and sometimes over-riding principles and therefore describes a probable rather than a required state of affairs. But the two kinds of probabilities, together, result in a considerably greater than chance frequency of persisting peer-group relationships that originated in "chance" encounters facilitated by propinquity, as in dormitory residence or classroom attendance.

In view of the fact that marriage rates — even within a single city — vary directly with residential propinquity of marriage partners (cf. Bossard, 1932), we should scarcely expect that the formation of less intimate peer-group relationships would be immune to the same considerations, and the known facts support the expectation. Festinger, *et al.* (1950), for example, have shown that in a housing project for married students the closest interpersonal relationships (in a statistical sense) developed not merely on the part of those whose apartment entrances faced the same court, but also, in particular, among those who used the same stairways and other facilities. A more recent investigation (Newcomb, 1961) shows that, even within a small, two-floor house accommodating only seventeen students, there were at first (but not following intimate acquaintance) significantly more close relationships among the eight men on one floor and among the nine men on the other than between men on the different floors. Roommates, whose proximity to each other was greatest of all, were particularly prone to develop close relationships.[4]

The evidence concerning propinquity, and its attendant probability of interpersonal contact, has obvious implications for peer-group formation as related to the size of college populations. In small colleges, of course, where all students have frequent contacts with nearly all others, the student body as a whole is likely to have more important effects, as a peer group, than in larger institutions. But this does not mean that the totality of peer-group influence is likely to be greater in small than in large colleges. Other things equal, the more intimate kinds of interpersonal relationships that characterize smaller rather than larger groups have relatively great impact upon group members; and subgroup formation is quite as characteristic (if not more so) of very large populations as of smaller ones. At any rate the essential significance of the factor of propinquity is, I think, somewhat as follows. For any individual there are many others, potentially, with whom he might form significant relationships. Those with whom he does in fact develop them are limited by opportunities for contact and reciprocal exploration, which in turn are influenced by physical propinquity. And, other things equal, he is most apt to maintain close relationships with those with whom he first develops them (as determined in part by propinquity). Thus the proper generalization concerning college size is not that peer-group influence is more effective, but that it is of more diverse nature, in larger than in smaller colleges.

Insofar as we are interested in the study of formal peer groups (which are easier to identify than informal ones) it seems clear, from the available evidence, that they are likely to be found wherever local arrangements — of living, dining, studying, engaging in student activities — result in very frequent associations among a given group of students. Not all individuals whose associations with each other are

frequent will necessarily be subject — and certainly not in equal degrees — to the effects of the norms that inevitably develop under such
conditions, but a large proportion of those who are influenced by such
norms can probably be thus discovered.

*Similarity of attitudes and interests.* Birds of a feather do flock together, and the kind of feathering that seems to be most essential for
the human species is clearly marked by common interests. This truism
both rests upon and illustrates some crucial principles concerning
human interaction. People are most likely to interact — and thus, in
terms of probabilities, to develop close relationships — when shared
interest in some aspect of their common environment brings them
together. The earlier principle that interaction tends to *create* consensual attitudes should not obscure the equally important one that
interaction tends to *begin* on the basis of existing interests that are
shared. The two principles, together, imply that interaction may lead
to new (and often widening) kinds of shared interests. Also, of
course, it may merely reinforce existing ones without leading to new
ones. These matters are discussed in the following section.

Contiguity and common interests (or at least those assumed as common) together would seem to account for the beginning of most peer-
group relationships. An initial basis may of course be provided by
the common features of the shared environment, but the selective association that usually occurs within large groups, all of whose members have an environment in common, is likely to be based upon
shared interests that are not inherent in the immediate situation —
like preferred sports, hobbies, or tastes in music or sex partners. In
my own study of the process of acquaintance on the part of small
populations of college men, common interests in sports or college majors often served as a basis for early clique formation, but these did
not necessarily persist; changes tended to occur with further opportunity to explore each others' interests. Closeness of interpersonal
relationships after four months of acquaintance was in many (though
not all) cases determined more by sharing of general values (religious,
perhaps, or aesthetic) than by more specific interests held in common.

Common interests include common problems, of course, insofar as
the latter are not too private to be communicable. The problems of
the late adolescent in our society may not be harder to bear than those
of other ages, but many of them are such as to invite college students
to share them with each other. The struggle for independence is apt
to be one of these, and such a problem is more shareable with peers

than with parents or teachers. In college, moreover, most students for the first time find themselves cut off from intimacies with adults; they probably see little of their parents, and their teachers neither invite intimacies nor welcome students into faculty society. Such a combination of circumstances is hardly calculated to aid the student in his search for identity — precisely at the time when he is least certain about it. Small wonder, then, that students tend to be thrown upon each other: their common problems together with their relative isolation from nonstudents make them ripe for peer-group formation.

The common interests (including common problems) that are so essential to the formation of peer groups may or may not extend beyond those which students bring with them to college, or beyond those which they share with their contemporaries outside of college. If not, the consequences of membership in such groups may be quite unrelated, or even opposed, to the distinctive objectives of higher education, as educators commonly assume. I suppose no one really knows how generally it is true that peer-group effects are essentially irrelevant, in this sense, on the contemporary American scene. In the following section I shall discuss some of the conditions under which such irrelevant outcomes most probably occur.

Meanwhile, to pursue the question of how common interests contribute to the formation of student peer groups, it is well to remember that the interests of groups, like those of individuals, may change. There is a well-known principle in psychology according to which motives initially instrumental to the gratification of some other, overriding motive may take on a life of their own, independently of the goal to which it was at first subsidiary.[5] Means often become ends. An analogous principle may be applied to groups. A group already characterized by consensuality of interests and attitudes, and by interpersonal attitudes that are favorable, may persist as a group on the basis of the latter set of attitudes even though the former set has become dissipated. A group that has acquired considerable interpersonal solidarity may prove to be autonomous, in this sense, but it does not follow that a subsequent basis of consensuality can be dispensed with entirely. If the originally common interests have disappeared, they tend to be replaced by others; if not, interpersonal solidarity is likely to decline, leaving nothing to hold the group together. The social-psychological fact seems to be that group continuity is fostered by high levels of consensuality of both of two kinds: favorable attitudes toward each other, and similar attitudes toward things of common importance — though most groups can tolerate less than a perfectly solid front.

In any case, the educator who despairs at the irrelevancies of student peer-group influences may take heart over the fact that yesterday's poisonous irrelevancy may, in the same group, become today's relevant meat. He may even anticipate that, as students reassort themselves, old groups giving way to new, some of the emerging groups will form around his favorite relevancies. He may, in fact, regard such possibilities as special challenges to his educational skills.

### SOME CONDITIONS OF PEER-GROUP INFLUENCES

As I have already tried to show, it is students' attitudes — rather than their general skills, or specific capacities, or basic personality characteristics — that are most likely to be directly influenced by peer-group membership. Let me first indicate a little more clearly what I mean by attitude and then point to some conditions under which attitudinal effects are most likely to take place.

Attitudes, as social psychologists commonly use the term, refer to the ways in which an individual has learned to assess things with which he is more or less familiar. "Things" include any entity — cabbages or kings or concepts — that he recognizes and distinguishes from other entities. Assessment refers both to the attribution of qualities to the thing in question and to the evaluation of it in view of these qualities — evaluation, that is, in ways such as liking, fearing, approving, or their opposites. We generally think of attitudes as varying in intensity, or strength, in sign (favorable vs. unfavorable), and in generality (i.e., the inclusiveness of the entity to which they refer; one may have attitudes toward a specific man, toward men in general, or toward human beings in general). We often refer to highly generalized attitudes, especially toward nonconcrete entities, as values.

Insofar as groups have power over their members, I have argued, it is because two processes tend to occur together, as group members continue to interact. Members become more favorably disposed to each other, and they come to adopt as their own certain group-shared attitudes, or norms, and to feel that those norms are right and proper. Both of these consequences involve, in important ways, the yielding of power over oneself to others. But it is the second — which I have

described as the sharing in group norms — that is of primary interest
as an outcome of educational experience.

The import of these considerations seems to me to be as follows.
Insofar as we are interested in what college experience does to students' attitudes we must, because of the nature of attitude formation
and change, be interested in the groups to which students (wittingly
or not) yield power over their own attitudes. Most attitudes — and
particularly those in which educators are interested — are, as social
psychologists like to say, anchored in group membership. This statement, let me hasten to add, in no way represents an advocacy of conformity, as opposed to personal independence and critical-mindedness.
The latter, too, represents a kind of value orientation (highly prized
by most social psychologists, incidentally) that, like most others, is
nourished by group support, however narrowly selective. The assertion that, as a matter of empirical observation, values and other kinds
of attitudes are nourished and even created through group membership, carries no implication that any given type or instance of the
general phenomenon is to be applauded or decried.

Insofar as the proposition is correct, however, it is heavy with implications for educators: How can we direct peer-group influences in
accordance with — rather than irrelevantly or in opposition to — our
educational objectives? This question is really a double-headed one.
It invites both scientific and "applied" replies — i.e., both statements
of conditions under which the presumed effects are most likely to
occur and prescriptions for creating those conditions.

At least four conditions that facilitate student peer groups' influence
upon their members' attitudes appear to be well enough established
to deserve mention. No one of them is an essential condition; perhaps any single one of the conditions, under exactly the right circumstances, might prove effective in the absence of all of the others.
Most commonly, however, several or all of these conditions exist together when marked effects have been noted.

*Size of groups.* Perhaps the most obvious of these conditions has
to do with group size. Membership in very large populations is not
likely, of itself, to bring about the strong interpersonal attitudes that
are so important an ingredient in peer-group effects upon attitudes.
Small groups, in which such interpersonal relationships can be established, often mediate the attitudes for which a larger population
(like "the college") stands, but membership in the latter without the

former's mediation would probably not be very effective. From the point of view of formal arrangements which result in group formation, however, relatively large groups have the advantage of making it possible for individuals to be selective in their more intimate associations. From this point of view, the formal group should not be so large that most of its members cannot recognize one another, nor yet so small as to discourage the formation within it of spontaneously formed, congenial subgroups. The combination of strong interpersonal attitudes engendered by the latter, and the strength of support provided by the most inclusive group of which the subgroup is a representative, is often an effective one.[6]

*Homogeneity.* A second condition involves relative homogeneity of group members. Homogeneity of age, sex, social class, or religious affiliation contributes to effective peer-group influence primarily because of the homogeneity of attitudes that tends to go along with such similarities. The more readily observable forms of similarity without their attitudinal counterparts will hardly suffice for the formation of effective groups. The fact that existing homogeneity of attitudes is so important to group solidarity has, of course, implications of conservatism: if group solidarity depends upon the similarity of members' attitudes, its continuing solidarity is likely to be threatened by lessened similarity in those attitudes. But the same fact also provides the possibility of exactly the reverse. As the late Professor Kurt Lewin used to say, apropos of the effectiveness of "group decision" under certain conditions, "it is sometimes easier to change the attitudes of an entire group than of a single individual" — simply because group support may be mobilized for change as well as against it. At any rate, if a group is not relatively homogeneous with regard to some existing attitudes of importance to its members, it will not have much power to change its members' attitudes.

*Isolation.* A third condition, relative isolation from groups having divergent group norms, is closely related to the second. Either the fact or the illusion of a membership homogeneous in attitudes may serve to strengthen the conviction that those attitudes are "right." It is communicative rather than physical isolation, however, that I have in mind. In a college community which I once studied from the point of view of freshman-to-senior attitude changes (1943), I found no students so untouched by the prevalent patterns of decreasing political conservatism as those, who, together with tiny groups of close friends, were so insulated from the majority of their fellows that they were quite unaware of the dominant trend that was so conspicuous to others . . . let me add, again, that to point to a condition of group effectiveness is not necessarily to approve of it. But whether one approves or not, there are many institutions of higher education, and many kinds of formal student groups within still more of them, whose policies of admission together with their selective drawing power result both in attitudinal homogeneity and communicative isolation. The effects of the combination are indubitably conservative, and also indubitably effective.

There is a particularly wry aspect of this condition of isolation from other groups in rendering peer groups effective. We faculty members who so often bemoan what we take to be the undesirable directions in which peer-group effects are expressed do a good deal to contribute to the insulation of students' isolation from ourselves. And then we wonder why student norms are not more thoroughly permeated with our own.

*Importance to individuals of attitudes that are group-supported.* A final facilitating condition for peer-group effectiveness is also an obvious one — the importance to individual members of the group-supported attitudes. Other things being equal, the greater the importance to them of the attitudes for which the group stands the greater is the solidarity of the group, regardless of whether the sense of importance preceded or has been engendered by group membership. Again, the implications appear to be conservative, but again they are not necessarily so. It does not necessarily follow, from the fact that group members feel that something is very important, that existing attitudes (even consensual ones) toward it are immutable. It may follow, from the same fact, that its very importance requires accurate assessment of it, and group power may be mobilized toward recognizing new facts or widened perspectives from which changed attitudes follow. If so, the same group influence which previously resisted change now comes to support it.

In sum, groups become more effective influencers of their members under some sets of conditions than under others. The effective combinations of conditions are not infrequently present in contemporary American colleges, whether or not by design of their educational architects. Very often, too, they are not met — and perhaps fortunately so. The educator's objective is not necessarily that of maximizing peer-group influence, but rather that of understanding how, when, and why it occurs in order that its effects may be consonant with his purposes.

## REFERENCES

1. The prevalence of favorable over unfavorable interpersonal attitudes, as outcomes of interaction, is by no means limited to voluntarily associating group members; witness the very common fact that most parents and children, the world around, have predominantly favorable attitudes toward one another, though they had nothing to do with choosing each other in the first place. Professor George Homans' observation (1950) that interaction and interpersonal attraction tend to increase together is, in general terms, a very dependable one.

2. More substantial bases for the general position outlined above may be found in Asch (1952), Cartwright and Zander (1960), Festinger *et al.* (1950), Gardner and Thompson (1956), Hare *et al.* (1955), Newcomb (1950), Schachter (1959), Sherif and Sherif (1956), Tagiuri and Petrullo (1958), Thibaut and Kelley (1959).

3. Relevant findings will appear in my forthcoming report of a 20-year follow-up of students whose undergraduate attitudes were reported in *Personality and Social Change* (1943).

4. The finding concerning same-floor and different-floor relationships holds even when roommates, whose relationships were generally close, were excluded from consideration. . . . It should be added that all of these 17 men were total strangers to each other on entering the house, and they had nothing at all to do with the choice of their own roommates.

5. Among various formulations of this principle, that of Professor G. W. Allport (1937) has perhaps been most influential; he uses the term "functional autonomy."

6. Witness, for example, the colleges within Cambridge and Oxford Universities, the Houses at Harvard and Yale, and several small colleges in which formal arrangements have resulted in groups of a few hundred that have proven capable of arousing effective group loyalties.

## REFERENCES

Allport, G. W. *Personality: A psychological interpretation.* New York: Holt, Rinehart, and Winston, 1937.

Asch, S. E. *Social psychology.* New York: Prentice-Hall, 1952.

Bossard, J. H. S.  Residential propinquity as a factor in marriage selection. *Amer. J. Sociology*, 1932, **38**, 219–224.

Cartwright, D., and Zander, A.  *Group dynamics: research and theory.* (Rev. ed.) Evanston, Ill.: Row, Peterson, 1960.

Coleman, J. S., and Rossi, P.  How high school seniors choose their colleges. Study in progress, National Opinion Research Center, University of Chicago, 1960.

Festinger, L., Back, K., Schachter, S., Kelley, H. H., and Thibaut, J. *Theory and experiment in social communication.* Ann Arbor: Institute for Social Research, University of Michigan, 1950.

Gardner, E. F., and Thompson, G. G.  *Social relations and morale in small groups.* New York: Appleton-Century-Crofts, 1956.

Hare, A. P., Borgatta, E. F., and Bales, R. F. (Eds.). *Small groups: studies in social interaction.* New York: Knopf, 1955.

Homans, G. C.  *The human group.* New York: Harcourt, Brace, 1950.

Jacob, P. E.  *Changing values in college.* New York: Harper Bros., 1957.

Merton, R. K., Reader, G., and Kendall, Patricia (Eds.).  *The student physician: introductory studies in the sociology of medical education.* Cambridge, Mass.: Harvard University Press, 1957.

Murphy, G.  *Personality: a biosocial approach to origins and structure.* New York: Harper Bros., 1947.

Newcomb, T. M.  *Personality and Social Change.* New York: Dryden, 1943.

Newcomb, T. M.  *Social Psychology.* New York: Dryden, 1950.

Newcomb, T. M.  *The Acquaintance Process.* New York: Holt, Rinehart, and Winston, 1961.

Newcomb, T. M., and Wilson, E. K. (Eds.).  *The study of college peer groups: problems and prospects for research.* New York: Social Science Research Council, in press.

Sanford, N. (Ed.).  Personality development during the college years. *J. of soc. Issues,* 1956, **12** (4), 1–71.

Schachter, S.  *The psychology of affiliation.* Stanford: Stanford University Press, 1959.

Sherif, M., and Sherif, Carolyn W.  *An outline of social psychology.* New York: Harper Bros., 1956.

Tagiuri, R., and Petrullo, L. (Eds.).  *Person perception and interpersonal behavior.* Stanford: Stanford University Press, 1958.

Thibaut, J. S., and Kelley, H. H.  *The social psychology of groups.* New York: Wiley, 1959.

# PEER INFLUENCES ON ADOLESCENT EDUCATIONAL ASPIRATIONS AND ATTAINMENTS

C. NORMAN ALEXANDER, JR. AND ERNEST Q. CAMPBELL

An individual depends on communication with significant others for the consensual validation necessary to maintain stable and consistent attitudes toward social objects. Recently, there has been a widespread convergence of social psychological theories dealing with such normative reference group processes.[1] In general, these theories involve some concept of interpersonal balance, or strain-reducing tendencies toward a perceived symmetry between one's own evaluation of a cognitive object and its evaluation by an attractive other. These hypothesized tendencies toward balance direct the researcher to consider the interaction between an individual's attitude and the attitudes of those in his communication network — in short, to study his attitudes in the context of his position as the nexus of a structure of interpersonal relationships.

To deal with consensus in collectivities of mutual attraction — as well as with intrapersonal tendencies toward perceived symmetry — Newcomb has proposed the A-B-X model.[2] Intrapersonally, the model predicts that a condition of strain is produced when a person, A, perceives a discrepancy or lack of symmetry between his own attitude toward X (an object of perceived common relevance) and his perception of B's attitude toward the same object. The magnitude of strain is a direct function of the degree of his positive attraction to B and of the importance of X. So long as X remains of importance and perceived common relevance, A's condition of strain persists. Thus, if other factors were irrelevant, and if X were of sufficient importance, we should

Reprinted with abridgement from the *American Sociological Review*, Vol. 29, No. 4 (August 1964), pp. 568–575, by permission of the American Sociological Association and the authors.

Based on data secured during conduct of Grants M-04302 and MH-08489, National Institute of Mental Health, Ernest Q. Campbell, Principal Investigator. The Graduate Fellowship Program, National Science Foundation, freed the time of the first author for work on this paper, an assistance gratefully acknowledged.

observe either that A comes to perceive symmetry between his own and B's attitudes toward X or that he ceases to be positively attracted to B.

On the basis of such an intrapersonal system of orientation as outlined above, we predict that — given positive attraction to B and the importance and *perceived* common relevance of X — A will tend to eliminate any perceived discrepancy between his own and B's attitudes toward X. When an interpersonal system of orientation exists — when B is also attracted to A and regards X as important and of common relevance — Newcomb postulates that actual disagreement produces a condition of "imbalance." He then hypothesizes that, through mutually adjustive communication, a condition of actual, rather than merely perceived consensus tends to result.[3] Within this general theoretical framework the present paper deals with high school seniors' educational goals and their attainment as these are influenced by peers.

The balance model leads us to expect, for example, that an individual's plans regarding college attendance will be similar to those of his best friend and that similarity between them will be greater if his best friend reciprocates the choice. This implies that, if his best friend plans to go to college, a student is more likely to plan to go when the choice is reciprocated than when it is not; but if his best friend *does not* plan to go, the student is more likely to expect to attend when his choice is *not* reciprocated than when it is reciprocated. Reciprocation, as an indication of more extensive communication between the individual and his choice, should increase pressures toward consensus if college attendance is a relevant and important object of communication.

Aspects of the substantive situation, however, suggest that this straightforward, balance theory expectation needs qualification. First it seems reasonable to expect that the relevance of the issue varies according to whether or not the student's friend plans to attend college. Because college attendance is socially valued and personally rewarding, a college-bound student is likely to exert positive influence on his friend to attend. On the other hand, it seems unlikely that a student not planning college would actively discourage his friends from attending; whatever influence he exerted would be more indirect, that is, he would not contribute positively to his friends' educational aspirations. This leads us to expect that the effects of reciprocation on the chooser's college plans will be considerably stronger when his friend is college-bound than when he does not plan to attend.

314     *Peer Influences on Adolescent Educational Aspirations*

Furthermore, variables associated with reciprocation itself may also complicate these relationships. Those whose choices are reciprocated are generally more popular among their peers; and popularity is positively associated with intelligence and with the likelihood of college attendance, independently of socio-economic status.[4] Thus, students whose choices are reciprocated should be more likely to plan and go to college than those whose choices are not reciprocated. This association supports the balance expectations of differences by reciprocation when the friend plans to go to college, but operates in the opposite direction when he does not. These factors are best eliminated by holding reciprocation constant and examining the differential strength of the relations between the student's and his friend's college plans.

Actual expectations of attending college are subject to a number of reality demands apart from tendencies toward consensus with attractive others and the importance attached to obtaining a higher education. But whether or not one *expects* to attend college presumably exerts a considerable influence on one's attitudes toward the desirability of attending. Thus, we shall also examine the hypotheses that the college plans and choice-reciprocation of the student's best friend will affect (1) the strength of his desire to attend college, *if he plans to go*, and (2) *even though he does not expect to go*, how strongly he would like to attend college, given the opportunity. Again, we shall remove the direct effects of his own status. For those who plan to go to college, we shall also ask what effect his friend's plans and the realization of these plans have on the individual's actual college attendance. Finally, for those who actually entered college and whose friends also attended, we shall relate the *specific* college they attended to the particular college attended by their best friend.

The balance model leads us to expect that individuals will tend, through communication, to become more similar with regard to important behaviors, attitudes and values of common relevance. The model also predicts, however, that individuals are more likely to choose as associates others with whom they already agree. Given only our aspiration data, we are unable to estimate either the extent to which an individual initially selects as friends those who are similar to him or the extent to which friends, once selected, influence him to become more similar to them. Undoubtedly, both processes are involved; but longitudinal data are needed to determine whether peers' plans help shape adolescent aspirations or whether the adolescent tends to select friends who have similar aspirations. Our data on the actualization of college plans are of this type.

## Data Analysis

In connection with a larger study,[5] questionnaires were administered to 1,410 male seniors in 30 high schools in the Eastern and Piedmont sections of North Carolina. Each respondent was asked the following question: "What students here in school *of your own sex* do you go around with most often?" A choice is considered codable if directed to another member of the high school senior class who returned a signed questionnaire. The individual's first-listed, codable choice is considered to be his "best friend." If that choice chooses the chooser as one of his first three codable choices, the choice is defined as "reciprocal."[6]

The status of an individual is determined by classification into one of five levels of parental educational attainment:[7]

I.   Both parents went to college
II.  Only one parent attended college
III. Both parents graduated from high school, but neither attended college
IV.  Only one parent graduated from high school and he did not attend college
V.   Neither parent graduated from high school

We say that the student expects to attend college if he responds, "Yes, definitely," to the question: "Realistically, do you expect to go to college *this coming Fall?*" His chosen friend's plans are determined by that friend's response to the same question.

Our first hypothesis is that a student at a given status level is more likely to plan to go to college if his best friend does rather than does not plan to go, and that this relationship is stronger when the choice is rather than is not reciprocated. Table 1 presents relevant data in percentages.

To evaluate the extent to which the data support expectations — in terms of both the direction and size of the differences — we computed the values of Yule's Q at each status level for the relevant comparisons;[8] then we averaged these five Q values to obtain a mean Q. An association is assigned a positive value if it is in the expected direction and

TABLE 1. PER CENT OF STUDENTS WHO DEFINITELY EXPECT TO GO TO COLLEGE—
BY PERSONAL STATUS LEVEL, COLLEGE PLANS AND RECIPROCATION OF FIRST CHOICE*

| Personal Status Level | Reciprocates | | Does Not Reciprocate | |
|---|---|---|---|---|
| | Choice Plans to Attend | Choice Doesn't Plan to Attend | Choice Plans to Attend | Choice Doesn't Plan to Attend |
| I (High) | 96.9 | 64.0 | 81.5 | 62.5 |
| | (97) | (25) | (54) | (16) |
| II | 78.1 | 39.6 | 69.0 | 41.2 |
| | (73) | (48) | (58) | (34) |
| III | 75.9 | 22.2 | 70.6 | 43.2 |
| | (54) | (45) | (34) | (37) |
| IV | 53.3 | 24.3 | 53.1 | 20.4 |
| | (60) | (74) | (49) | (54) |
| V (Low) | 51.0 | 5.3 | 25.5 | 7.0 |
| | (49) | (152) | (51) | (114) |

* Numbers in parentheses in all tables are the base from which the percentage derives, e.g., in the upper left-hand cell, 96.9 per cent of the 97 cases of high personal status, whose best friend reciprocates the choice and is college-bound, expect to attend college.

a negative value if it is contrary to expectations. The higher the mean Q values, the stronger the association in the expected direction.

The average Q value for the association between the student's and his friend's college plans is .777 when the choice is reciprocated and .327 when it is not. The association is in the expected direction and is much stronger under conditions of reciprocation; the data thus support the hypothesis that a student and his best friend tend to be similar in college plans and that the extent of similarity is greater when the choice is reciprocated.

Since actual expectations of college attendance depend on other factors as well as the desire to attend — e.g., intelligence, income, college proximity — less "reality-bound" attitudes toward college attendance are perhaps more appropriate to the theory. When we consider less realistic wishes or desires to go to college, however, it is obvious that these are greatly influenced by the subject's plans to attend or his expectations of being able to attend. To examine further the hypothesized influences of an individual's chosen friend and of the reciprocation of his friendship choice, we shall hold constant his *expectations* of college attendance while examining other aspects of his college plans.

Among those at a given status level who expect definitely to attend college, we expect a student to be more likely to desire strongly to go to college when his best friend plans to go. The relationship should be stronger when the friendship choice is reciprocated.

Again, we compute average Q values for the relation between the student's desire to attend college and his friend's plans, holding reciprocation of friendship choice constant. The summary measure of association is .474 when the choice is reciprocated and .319 when it is not, indicating substantial support for the hypothesis. We conclude, then, that friend's college plans affect the strength of the desire to attend college, especially among those whose choice is reciprocated.

Those who said that they did not plan to go to college were asked, "If you had a chance to go on to college next year, would you *like* to go?" Those who replied, "Yes, definitely," are said to wish to attend.

Our model leads us to expect that a student whose best friend is college-bound is more likely to *want* to go to college even though he does not expect to attend and that this association increases in strength when the choice is reciprocated. The average Q value for the hypothesized association is .451 when the choice is reciprocated and .098 when it is not. Thus, the college plans of their best friends tend to make students want to attend even when they do not have the opportunity to do so.

We have shown that his best friend's expectations of college attendance and reciprocation of friendship choice are closely related to a high school senior's educational aspirations. We now inquire whether his best friend's behaviors are associated with the actual college attendance of the student who had planned to attend. And if he did enroll in some college, we want to know whether his best friend influenced his selection of that particular college. We anticipate that the student who plans to attend college is more likely to get there when his best friend also plans to attend; and that, among those whose best friend does plan to attend, the proportion actually attending is higher when the best friend actually attends. Finally, we expect that a student and his friend are more likely to attend the same college if they initially agreed on where they planned to go, and if the student's friend either follows through with his plans when they initially agreed, or does not follow through when they initially disagreed. All of these predicted relationships should be stronger when the choice is reciprocated. Examination of *specific* college plans and their realization permits a more crucial examination of the predictive utility of the balance model than is possible with more general aspirations.

An extensive effort was made to locate all students who said that

TABLE 2. PER CENT OF COLLEGE-BOUND STUDENTS ACTUALLY ATTENDING—BY PERSONAL STATUS LEVEL, COLLEGE PLANS AND RECIPROCATION OF BEST FRIEND

| Personal Status Level | Reciprocates | | Does Not Reciprocate | |
|---|---|---|---|---|
| | Choice Plans to Attend | Choice Doesn't Plan to Attend | Choice Plans to Attend | Choice Doesn't Plan to Attend |
| I (High) | 93.8 (97) | 78.9 (19) | 100.0 (51) | 83.3 (12) |
| II | 91.8 (73) | 69.4 (36) | 91.1 (45) | 61.9 (21) |
| III | 89.1 (46) | 72.2 (18) | 83.3 (30) | 66.7 (21) |
| IV | 79.1 (43) | 65.7 (35) | 85.7 (28) | 72.2 (18) |
| V (Low) | 75.0 (36) | 46.2 (26) | 66.7 (24) | 46.4 (28) |

they expected to attend college. There were 707 respondents who made at least one codable choice, could be classified on relevant independent variables, expected to attend a legitimate college or university (not a barber college, mortuary school, etc.), and provided information necessary to permit a follow-up attempt — name, college intended, and supplemental questionnaire. We were able to ascertain the whereabouts of 653 and to determine definitely whether they did or did not attend college. There is little to indicate that the remaining 54 did attend college, and, although we have no conclusive evidence that they did *not*, we include them in Table 2 among those who planned to go to college but failed to do so.[9]

Table 2 presents the percentage who attended college during the fall semester following graduation from high school — by parental education and the college plans and reciprocation of their first friendship choice. Our hypothesis is that a student at a given status level is more likely to attend college if his best friend expects to go and that this association is stronger when the choice is reciprocated. The average Q value is .534 when the choice is reciprocated and .589 when it is not. Thus, while the actual attendance of the student is positively associated with the college plans of his best friend, reciprocation of the friendship choice does not increase the strength of the association as expected.

To examine actual attendance of the student in terms of his choice's attendance we must eliminate from the analysis all students whose choices did not expect to attend or did not provide sufficient information to permit a follow-up attempt. The remaining number of students whose friends do not realize their plans to attend is too small to permit analysis by reciprocation of choice. Thus, we predict simply that a student is more likely to attend college when his best friend also attends. Table 3 supports the hypothesis: at each status level, a higher proportion attend college when the friend also attends.

Finally, we wish to consider only those cases who planned to and did attend and whose best friend also planned to and did attend an institution of higher learning. We expect a student and his friend to be more likely to attend the same college when they initially agreed on where they planned to go. If they did agree, they are more likely to attend the same college when the student's friend follows through with his intentions; but if they initially disagreed, attendance at the same college is more likely when the friend does not follow through with his plans. These relationships should be stronger when the choice is reciprocated than when it is not. Thus, our hypothesis is as follows: A student and his friend are more likely to attend the same college if (1) they planned to attend the same college while in high school, and (2) when their plans were the same, the friend does attend his chosen college, but (3) when their plans differed, the friend does *not* attend the chosen college, and (4) the above relationships are stronger when the friendship choice is reciprocated.

Table 4 presents the percentage of students who actually attended the same college as their best friend — by initial agreement with best friend on choice of college, best friend's realization of his college

TABLE 3. Per Cent of College-Bound Students
Actually Attending — by Personal Status
Level and College Attendance of
Best Friend

| Personal Status Level | Does Best Friend Attend? | |
|---|---|---|
| | Yes | No |
| I | 94.7 | 84.6 |
| | (151) | (13) |
| II | 90.6 | 81.3 |
| | (128) | (16) |
| III | 86.6 | 55.6 |
| | (82) | (9) |
| IV | 81.3 | 66.7 |
| | (75) | (15) |
| V | 71.4 | 57.1 |
| | (63) | (14) |

TABLE 4. PER CENT OF STUDENTS AND CHOICES ATTENDING THE SAME COLLEGE — BY INITIAL AGREEMENT, CHOICE'S REALIZATION OF PLANS AND RECIPROCATION

| Initial Agreement of Student and Choice on Specific College Plans | Reciprocation of Friendship Choice | | | |
| --- | --- | --- | --- | --- |
| | Reciprocated | | Non-Reciprocated | |
| | Did Choice Realize Plans? | | Did Choice Realize Plans? | |
| | Yes | No | Yes | No |
| Agree | 85.1 | 22.2 | 76.9 | 9.1 |
| | (47) | (27) | (26) | (11) |
| Disagree | 5.1 | 7.0 | 2.8 | 14.0 |
| | (117) | (71) | (71) | (50) |

plans, and reciprocation. Attendance at the same college is more likely when the student and his friend initially agreed on college plans, and the relationship is stronger when the choice is reciprocated; the average Q value is .781 when the choice is reciprocated and .371 when it is not. When the student and his friend agree, the friend's realization of his plans is positively associated with attendance at the same college, but the relationship is somewhat weaker when the choice is reciprocated; the Q value is .905 when the choice is reciprocated and .942 when it is not. Finally, when their plans differ, the friend's realization of his plans is negatively associated with their attending the same college. Although they support the hypothesized association, the Q values of .167 when the choice is reciprocated and .698 when it is not clearly refute the expectation that reciprocation would increase the strength of the relationship. Thus, the data support the first three sub-hypotheses, but reciprocation strengthens only the first relationship. The latter two relationships are stronger when the friendship choice is not reciprocated.

Two rather surprising aspects of these data are the extent of initial disagreement between the student and his friend, regardless of reciprocation, and the lack of change toward greater consensus. Only 28.2 per cent of those with reciprocated choices initially agreed on where they planned to go to college, and the corresponding figure for those with non-reciprocated choices is 23.4 per cent. Since 60.4 per cent of those who initially agreed and only 6.5 per cent of those initially disagreeing actually attend the same college, the extent of similarity actually decreases. Only 21.8 per cent of those with reciprocated choices and 19.0 per cent of those with non-reciprocated choices end up at the same college. Nevertheless, initial agreement between friends does contribute to the realization of plans to attend a specific college. While the student or his friend changed plans in 62.1 per cent of the cases where they initially disagreed, the corresponding figure among those who initially agreed is only 45.9 per cent. Whether or not an individual realizes his plans to attend a specific college appears to be influenced by agreement with his friend on where they plan to go.

The precise interpretation of these results is unclear. Balance theory predicts a tendency to change toward greater consensus, given constancy of the friendship relation. The assumption of friendship constancy during this period of great transition is a rather tenuous one, however, and we have no data to indicate whether boys who are best friends during the spring of their senior year are still best friends at the time of entry into college. Also, initial consensus refers to long-range plans, while final consensus is determined by actual behaviors; and we have already indicated that the effects of efforts to achieve balance should be most pronounced when non-attitudinal reality considerations are minimized. In any case, the fact that initial agreement and friend's realization of plans do predict relatively greater similarity supports the balance expectations, but the effects of reciprocation are not entirely consistent with the hypothesis.

SUMMARY AND CONCLUSIONS

Confirming hypothesized tendencies toward balance, we have observed that a student at a given status level is more likely to *expect* to attend college, to have a strong desire to go to college when he *does* expect to go, to *want* to go when he *does not* expect to, and actually to attend, when his best friend does rather than does not plan to go to college, these relationships are stronger when the choice is reciprocated. When the student and his friend both plan to go, he is more likely to attend if his best friend does. And, finally, given the fact that they both attend a college, the likelihood that they attend the same college is increased by initial agreement on specific college plans and by the friend's realization of his plans; reciprocation, however, has relatively little effect on actual attendance at the same college. Our findings suggest that communication among male high school seniors affects both college plans and attendance.

## REFERENCES

1. Fritz Heider, *The Psychology of Interpersonal Relations*, New York: Wiley, 1958. A variety of sociological and social psychological propositions are restated in terms of Heider's balance model by James A. Davis, "Structural Balance, Mechanical Solidarity, and Interpersonal Relations," *American Journal of Sociology*, 68 (January, 1963), pp. 444–462.

2. Theodore M. Newcomb, *The Acquaintance Process*, New York: Holt, Rinehart and Winston, 1961.

3. *Ibid.*, pp. 14–15.

4. C. N. Alexander, Jr., "Ordinal Position and Sociometric Status," *Sociometry*, 29 (March, 1966) pp. 41–51.

5. "Normative Controls and the Social Use of Alcohol," National Institute of Mental Health Grants M-4302 and MH-08489, under the direction of Ernest Q. Campbell.

6. An I.B.M. procedure for determining reciprocation is described in C. Norman Alexander, Jr., "A Method for Processing Sociometric Data," *Sociometry*, 26 (June, 1963), pp. 268–269.

7. When the education of only one parent was reported, the student was assigned a rank (either II, IV or V) based on that parent's educational attainment.

8. For example, in Table 1 the Q values at personal status level I compare the proportions expecting to attend college by reciprocation; the frequencies of those who do and those who do not plan college in columns 3 and 4 and columns 1 and 2, respectively, form the 2-x-2 table from which Q values are computed.

9. We tried to obtain information by campus visits, mail, or telephone, from parents, high school principals and guidance counsellors, college registrars and student directories, high school classmates and the student himself. We did not establish contact with any of the parents of these 54 unclassified students; parents' information would have been accepted as definitive. In most instances, at least one report, usually from the high school principal, indicated that the student was or had been attending a specific college or university, but when we checked with college registrars, student information centers, and where possible with peers from his high school who were attending the specific college, we found no trace of him. We feel reasonably certain that a substantial majority of these 54 did not attend college, so that classifying them as non-attenders is less erroneous than classifying them as "non-respondents."

# ABILITY AND SCHOOL ACHIEVEMENT

## JAMES S. COLEMAN

In every social context, certain activities are highly rewarded, while others are not. The activities which are rewarded are those for which there is strong competition, in which everyone with some ability will compete. In such activities, the persons who achieve most should be those with the greatest potential ability. In unrewarded activities, on the other hand, those who have the greatest ability may not be motivated to compete; consequently, those who achieve the most may be persons of lesser ability. Thus in a high school where basketball is important, nearly every boy who might be a good basketball player will go out for the sport, and the resulting basketball stars will probably be the boys with most ability. If in the same school volleyball does not bring the same status to those who star in it, few boys will go out for the sport, and those who end up as members of the team will not necessarily be the boys with the greatest potential ability.

Similarly with academic achievement: In a school where such achievement brings few social rewards, those who are motivated to "go out" for scholarly achievement will be few. The high performers, those who receive good grades, will not be the boys whose ability is greatest, but will be a more mediocre few. The "intellectuals" of such a society, those defined by themselves and others as the best students, will not in fact be those with most intellectual ability. The latter, knowing where the social rewards lie, will be off in other directions which bring social rewards.

On the basis of these ideas, the original research design[1] included the hypothesis that in systems where academic achievement was rewarded by the adolescent culture, the correlation between IQ and grades in school would be higher than in schools where academic achievement was not so rewarded. In carrying out the analysis, it

Excepted from James S. Coleman, *et al.*, *Social Climates in High Schools* (Cooperative Research Monograph No. 4, OE-33016, pp. 5–59), by permission of the United States Office of Education and the author.

TABLE 1. CORRELATION BETWEEN IQ AND FRESHMAN GRADES, AVERAGED OVER THE
4 YEARS, AND AVERAGE YEARLY CHANGE IN 10 SCHOOLS OF THE STUDY

| | Class average over 4 years | | | |
| | Boys | | Girls | |
| School | Correlation between freshman grades and IQ | Yearly change | Correlation between freshman grades and IQ | Yearly change |
| **1** | **2** | **3** | **4** | **5** |
| 0. Farmdale | 0.603 | +.029 | 0.607 | −.131 |
| 1. Marketville | .591 | +.097 | .504 | +.024 |
| 2. Elmtown | .516 | +.007 | .645 | +.054 |
| 3. Maple Grove | .620 | −.012 | .579 | −.017 |
| 4. Green Junction | .559 | +.043 | .583 | −.029 |
| 5. St. John's | .404 | −.046 | | |
| 6. Newlawn | .615 | −.053 | .603 | −.020 |
| 7. Millburg | .493 | +.007 | .446 | +.080 |
| 8. Midcity | .611 | −.026 | .571 | −.014 |
| 9. Executive Heights | .540 | −.030 | .682 | −.112 |

became evident that this correlation (within a given class) changed over the course of the years in school, usually decreasing, but sometimes increasing. With such data on changes, it was possible to add a supplementary hypothesis: In social systems where scholastic achievement is rewarded, the correlations either increase in time or decrease less than in the other schools. Data which allow examination of these hypotheses are present in Table 1. The correlation between IQ (tests ordinarily given in the eighth or ninth grade in all the schools except in Elmtown, where IQ's were not available for the present freshmen) and average freshmen grades is given for boys and girls separately. The correlation is averaged over the four classes, in each case using the freshman grades of that class.[2] The average yearly increase or decrease in the correlation is also given, based on the correlation between IQ and present grades minus the correlation between IQ and freshman grades. There were three such differences, one for each of the three upper grades, from which an average yearly change was computed.

If the data show any relationship to the variations in importance of scholastic achievement in the different schools, the relationship is an obscure or complex one. The schools where scholastic activity is more highly rewarded by the culture are not distinguishable from those where it is not; there do not even appear to be general differences between boys and girls. In short, it appears that the original hypotheses is not at all validated.

However, the reasoning on which the hypothesis was based related only to those at the top, those with highest ability. Thus at the intermediate and low levels of ability one would have no reason to expect a higher correlation in those climates which rewarded scholastic activity than in those which did not. The question is, *are* the high achievers the ones with the most ability?

To examine this, the IQ's of all boys whose average grades were 7 or 8 (A or A—) were compared to the IQ of the student body as a whole.[3] The variations are quite great in this: In one school (Marketville) the boys who made an A or A— average have IQ's 1.53 standard deviations above the school average; in another (Farmdale) their IQ's are only about a third this distance above the mean, 0.59.[4] Given this variation, the question can be asked: Do these variations in ability of the high performers correspond to variations in the social rewards for, or constraint against, being a good student?

Figure 1 shows the relation between the social rewards for academic excellence for the boys (that is, the frequency with which "good grades" was mentioned as a criterion for being in the leading crowd), and the ability of the high performers, measured in terms of the number of standard deviations of their average IQ above that of the rest of the boys in the school.

For the boys, the relation is extremely strong. St. John's (No. 5) is the only school that deviates to an appreciable degree. In this school many boys have their most important associations outside the school rather than in it, so that its student body constitutes far less of a social system, able to dispense social rewards and punishments, than do the other schools.

Similarly for the girls, in Figure 1 the IQ of high performers is presented as a function of the proportion of girls who say that it takes good grades to get into the leading crowd.[5] Unfortunately, most schools are closely bunched in the degree to which good grades are important among the girls, so that there is too little variation among them to examine this effect as fully as would be desirable. Elmtown (No. 2) is the one school which greatly deviates from the general relationship in regard to the girls.[6]

The effect of these value systems in letting academic ability express

FIGURE 1. Relation between social rewards for academic excellence (percent of students mentioning "good grades" as a requirement for membership in the leading crowd) and the average IQ of best students (in terms of number of standard deviations above their own school mean) in all 10 schools of the study.

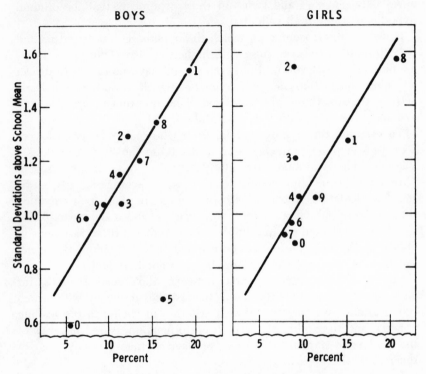

itself in high achievement is evident among the girls, as it is among the boys. It is important to realize that these effects are not merely due to the school facilities or social composition of the school. The two schools highest in the importance of scholastic achievement for both boys and girls are Marketville and Midcity, the first a small-town school of 350 students and the second a city school of 2,000 students. In both there are fewer students with white collar backgrounds than in Executive Heights, which is somewhere in the low middle in terms of the values its students place on academic achievement, but more of these students than in Millburg or Green Junction, which are also somewhere in the low middle. The highest expenditure per student was $695 per year (Executive Heights), and the lowest was little more than half that amount (Green Junction). These two schools are close together on the graph of Figure 1.

These results are consistent with an extensive unpublished Connecticut study using standard tests of achievement and ability. The study found no correlation between per pupil expenditure in a school and the achievement of its tenth-grade students relative to their ability. The effect shown in Figure 1 suggests that students with ability are led to achieve only when there are social rewards, primarily from their peers, for doing so.

It has been evident throughout this research that the variation among schools in the status of scholastic achievement is not nearly so striking as the fact that in all of them, academic achievement did not count as much as other activities in the school. In every school the boys named as best athletes and those named as most popular with girls were far more often mentioned as members of the leading crowd, and as someone to be like than were the boys named as best students. Similarly, in every school, the girls who were named as best dressed and those considered most popular with boys were far more often mentioned as being in the leading crowd and as someone to be like, than were the girls named as best students.

The relative unimportance of academic achievement together with the effects that have been shown, suggest that the adolescent subcultures in these schools exert a rather strong deterrent to academic achievement. In other words, in these adolescent societies, the students who are considered the "intellectuals" are not really those of highest intelligence, but only those who are willing to work hard at a relatively unrewarded activity.

The implications for American society as a whole are clear. When high schools allow the adolescent subcultures to divert energies into athletics, social activities, and the like, they recruit into adult intellectual activities many people with a rather mediocre level of ability and fail to attract many with high levels of ability.

## REFERENCES

1. See James Coleman, *The Adolescent Society* (New York: The Free Press, 1961) for a more complete account of the research.

2. This correlation was generally lower for seniors than for freshmen, probably due to the fact that dropouts were eliminated from the computation for later grades, making the population more homogeneous in both grades and IQ and thus tending to lower the correlation.

3. In each school but Maple Grove and Midcity, this constituted from 6 to 8

percent of the student body. In order to provide a correct test of the hypothesis, it was necessary to have the same fraction of the student body in each case (since IQ's of this group were being measured in terms of number of standard deviations above the total student body). To adjust the groups, enough 6's were added (each being assigned the average IQ of the total group of 6's) to bring the proportion up to 6 percent (from 3 percent in Maple Grove, 4 percent in Midcity).

4. Since the IQ tests differed from school to school, and since each school had its own mean IQ and its own variation around that mean, ability of the high performers was measured in terms of the number of standard deviations of their average IQ's above the mean. In this way, it was possible to see the high performers' ability in relation to the distribution of abilities in their school.

5. For the girls, only girls with a grade of 8 (that is, a straight A average) were included. Since girls get better grades than boys, this device was necessary in order to make the size of the "high performer" group roughly comparable for boys and for girls. Schools differed somewhat in the proportion of A students, about 6 percent in the small schools, about 3 percent in Newlawn and Millburg, 1 percent in Midcity, and 2 percent in Executive Heights. In Midcity and Executive Heights, enough girls were added and assigned the average IQ of the 7 (A—) group to bring the proportion to 3 percent, comparable with the other large schools. The difference remained, however, between the large and small schools.

6. The IQ's of the girls in Elmtown show a peculiar distribution. There were six girls whose IQ was listed in the office records as exactly 140, though no other girl in the school had an IQ listed above 130. Five of these six girls with an IQ of 140 had a grade average of 8. Of the 18 other girls whose IQ was listed as 120 or above, the grade average was far less: 5.9. It is hardly likely that this school contains 24 girls in the sophomore to senior classes with IQ's of 120 or greater; the IQ test undoubtedly overestimated the actual IQ's in this school. The test used in this school was the SRA Primary Mental Abilities, which has a top score of 140; six girls in the school had a raw score above this point and were given the top score.

C.

THE IMPACT OF MICRO-SOCIAL STRUCTURES:
THE STUDENT-TEACHER RELATIONSHIP

# DOCILITY, OR GIVING TEACHER WHAT SHE WANTS

JULES HENRY

This essay deals with one aspect of American character, the process whereby urban middle-class children in elementary school acquire the habit of giving their teachers the answers expected of them. Though it could hardly be said that I deal exhaustively with this matter, what I do discuss, using suggestions largely from psychoanalysis and communications theory, is the signaling process whereby children and teacher come to understand each other or, better, to pseudo-understand each other, within the limited framework of certain schoolroom situations.

I think it will be readily understood that such a study has intercultural significance and interesting biosocial implications. The smooth operation of human interaction, or "transaction," if one prefers the Dewey and Bentley decor, requires that in any culture much of the give and take of life be reduced to a conventional, parsimonious system of quickly decipherable messages and appropriate responses. These messages, however, are different in different cultures, because the give and take of life is different in different cultures. At a simple level, for example, a Pilaga Indian paints his face red when he is looking for a sexual affair with a woman, whereas were an American man to paint his face red, the significance of this to other Americans would be quite different. Behaviors that have been variously called signal, cue, and sign are as characteristic of the animal world as they are of the human, and in both groups tend to be highly specific both with respect to themselves (signs, signals, cues) and with respect to the behavior they release in those for whom they are intended. Since, furthermore, each culture tends to standardize these, it would seem that any study of such behaviors, or rather behavior systems, in humans in any culture would throw light on two problems:

Reprinted from the *Journal of Social Issues*, Vol. 2, No. 2 (1955), pp. 33–41, by permission of the author and the Society for the Psychological Study of Social Issues.

(1) What the signal-response system is; and (2) How humans learn the system.

Since in humans the mastery of a signal-response system often involves the emotional life, and since in this paper on docility I am dealing with urban American middle-class children, it will readily be seen that a study of the manner in which they learn the signal-response system called docility carries us toward an understanding of the character of these children.

When we say a human being is docile we mean that, without the use of external force, he performs relatively few acts as a function of personal choice as compared with the number of acts he performs as a function of the will of others. In a very real sense, we mean that he behaves mostly as others wish him to. In our culture this is thought undesirable, for nobody is supposed to like docile people. On the other hand, every culture must develop in its members forms of behavior that approximate docility; otherwise it could not conduct its business. Without obedience to traffic signals transportation in a large American city would be a mess. This is a dilemma of our culture: to be able to keep the streets uncluttered with automotive wrecks, and to fill our armies with fighting men who will obey orders, while at the same time we teach our citizens not to be docile.

It is to be supposed that, although the basic processes as outlined are universal, every culture has its own way of creating the mechanism of docility. It will be the purpose of the rest of this paper to examine the accomplishment of docility in some American middle-class schoolrooms. The study was carried out by several of my graduate students and me. Names of persons and places are withheld in order to give maximum protection to all concerned.

In the following examples I shall be concerned only with demonstrating that aspect of docility which has to do with the teacher's getting from the children the answers she wants; and I rely almost entirely on verbal behavior, for without cameras it is impossible to record non-verbal signals. The first example is from the second grade.

1. The children have been shown movies of birds. The first film ended with a picture of a baby bluebird.

Teacher: Did the last bird ever look like he would be blue?

The children did not seem to understand the slant of the question, and answered somewhat hesitantly: Yes.

Teacher: I think he looked more like a robin, didn't he?

Children, in chorus: Yes.

In this example one suspects that teacher's intonation on the word "ever" did not come through as a clear signal, for it did not create enough doubt in the children's minds to bring the right answer, "No." The teacher discovered that her signal had not been clear enough for these seven-year-olds, so she made it crystal clear the second time, and got the "right" response. Its correctness is demonstrated by the unanimity of the children's response, and the teacher's acceptance of it. Here the desire of the teacher, that the children shall acknowledge that a bird looks like a robin, is simple, and the children, after one false try, find the correct response.

In the next example we see the relation of signal to cultural values and context:

2a. A fourth grade art lesson. Teacher holds up a picture.

Teacher: Isn't Bobby getting a nice effect of moss and trees?

Ecstatic Ohs and Ahs from the children. . . .

2b. The art lesson is now over.

Teacher: How many enjoyed this?

Many hands go up.

Teacher: How many learned something?

Quite a number of hands come down.

Teacher: How many will do better next time?

Many hands go up.

Here the shifts in response are interesting. The word "nice" triggers a vigorously docile response, as does the word "enjoy." "Learned something," however, for a reason that is not quite clear, fails to produce the desired unanimity. On the other hand, the shibboleth, "better next time" gets the same response as "enjoyed." We see then that the precise triggering signal is related to important cultural values; and that the value-signal must be released in proper context. One suspects that the children's resistance to saying they had learned something occurred because "learned something" appeared out of context. On the other hand, it would be incorrect to describe these children as perfectly docile.

3. The children have just finished reading the story, "The Sun, Moon, and Stars Clock."

Teacher: What was the highest point of interest — the climax?

The children tell what they think it is. Teacher is aiming to get from them what she thinks it is, but the children give everything else but. At last Bobby says: When they capture the thieves.

Teacher: How many agree with Bobby?

Hands, hands, hands.

In this example the observer was not able to record all the verbal signals, for they came too fast. However, it is clear that hunting occurred, while the children waited for the teacher to give the clear signal, which was "(I) agree with Bobby."

In all the examples given thus far, the desired answer could be indicated rather clearly by the teacher, for the required response was relatively unambiguous. Even so, there was some trouble in obtaining most of the answers. In the example that follows, however, the entire situation becomes exceedingly ambiguous because emotional factors in the children make proper interpretation of teacher's signals difficult. The central issue is that teacher and children are seen to have requirements that are complementary on one level, because teacher wants the children to accept her point of view, and they want to be accepted by her; but these requirements are not complementary on a different level, because the children's emotional organization is different from the teacher's. Hence exact complementarity is never achieved, but rather a pseudo-complementarity which enables teachers and pupils to extricate themselves from a difficult situation. The example comes from a fifth-grade schoolroom:

4. This is a lesson on "healthy thoughts" for which the children have a special book that depicts specific conflictful events among children. There are appropriate illustrations and text, and the teacher is supposed to discuss each incident with the children in order to help them understand how to handle their emotions.

One of the illustrations is of two boys, one of whom is griping because his brother has been given something he wants himself — a football, I think. The other is saying his brother couldn't help being given it — they'll both play with it.

(Observer is saying that this sibling pair is illustrated by three boys: (1) The one who has received the ball. (2) The one who is imagined to react with displeasure. (3) The one who is imagined to react benignly and philosophically, by saying: My brother couldn't help being given the football; we'll use it together.)

Teacher: Do you believe it's easier to deal with your thoughts if you own up to them, Betty?

Betty: Yes it is, if you're not cross or angry.

Teacher: Have you any experience like this in the book, Alice?

Alice tells how her brother was given a watch and she envied him and wanted one too, but her mother said she wasn't to have one until she was fifteen, but now she has one anyway.

Teacher: How could you have helped — could you have changed your thinking? How could you have handled it? What could you do with mean feelings?

Alice seems stymied; she hems and haws.

Teacher: What did Susie (a character in the book) do?

Alice: She talked to her mother.

Teacher: If you talk to someone you often feel that 'It was foolish of me to feel that way. . . .'

Tommy: He says he had an experience like that. His cousin was given a bike, and he envied it. But he wasn't ugly about it. He asked if he might ride it, and his cousin let him, and then I got one myself; and I wasn't mean or ugly or jealous.

Here the process of signal development is intricate, and children and teacher do not quite manage to arrive at a mutually intelligible complex of signals and behavior. The stage is set by the presentation of a common, but culturally unacceptable situation: A child is pictured as envious of the good luck of his sibling. Since American culture cannot accept two of its commonest traits, sibling rivalry and envy, the children are asked by teacher to acknowledge that they are "bad," and to accept specific ways of dealing with these emotions. The children are thus asked to fly in the face of their own feelings, and, since this is impossible, the little pigeons never quite get home. This is because teacher and pupil wants are not complementary.

It will have been observed that at first Alice does well, for by docilely admitting that it is good to own up to evil, she correctly interprets the teacher's wish to hear her say that the ancient ritual of confession is still good for the soul; and she continues docile behavior by giving a story of her own envy. However, eventually she muffs the signal, for she says she was gratified anyway; she did get a watch. And the reason Alice muffs the signal is that her own impulses dominate over the signals coming in from the teacher. Teacher, however, does not reject Alice's story but tries, rather, to get Alice to say she could have "handled" her thoughts by "owning up" to them and talking them over with someone. Alice, however, stops dead because she cannot understand the teacher. Meanwhile Tommy has picked up the signal, only to be misled by it, just as Alice was. By this time, however, the matter has become more complex: Tommy thinks that because teacher did not reject Alice's story it is "correct." Teacher's apparent acceptance of Alice's story then becomes Tommy's signal; therefore he duplicates Alice's story almost exactly, except that a bike is substituted for a watch. Like Alice he is not "mean" or "ugly" or "jealous," not because he "dealt with" his thoughts in the culturally approved-but-impossible manner, but because he too got what he wanted. So far, the only part of the message that is getting through to the children from the teacher is that it is uncomfortable — not wrong — to be jealous, et cetera. Thus the emotions of the children filter out an important part of the message from the teacher.

We may summarize the hypotheses up to this point as follows:

1) By virtue of their visible goal-correcting behavior the pupils are trying hard to be docile with respect to the teacher.

2) They hunt for signals and try to direct their behavior accordingly.

3) The signals occur in a matrix of cultural value and immediate circumstance.

4) This fact at times makes interpretation and conversion into action difficult.

5) A basis in mutual understanding is sought, but not quite realized at times.

6) The children's internal signals sometimes conflict with external ones and thus "jam the receiver."

7) Both children and teacher want something. At present we may say that the children want acceptance by the teacher, and teacher wants acceptance by the children.

8) However, it is clear, because of the mix-up that may occur in interpreting signals, as in the lesson on healthy thoughts, that the desires of teacher and pupil are sometimes not quite complementary.

9) Teacher must avoid too many frustrating (painful) failures like that of Alice, otherwise lessons will break down.

As we proceed with this lesson, we shall see how teacher and pupils strive to "get on the same wave length," a condition never quite reached because of the different levels of organization of teacher and pupil; and the unawareness of this fact on the part of the teacher.

Two boys, the "dialogue team," now come to the front of the class and dramatize the football incident.

Teacher, to the class: Which boy do you think handled the problem in a better way?

Rupert: Billy did, because he didn't get angry . . . It was better to play together than to do nothing with the football.

Teacher: That's a good answer, Rupert. Has anything similar happened to you, Joan?

Joan can think of nothing.

(Observer notes: I do not approve of this business in action, though I have not yet thought it through. But I was intermittently uncomfortable, disapproving and rebellious at the time.)

Sylvester: I had an experience. My brother got a hat with his initials on it because he belongs to a fraternity, and I wanted one like it and couldn't have one; and his was too big for me to wear, and it ended up that I asked him if he could get me some letters with my initials, and he did.

Betty: My girl-friend got a bike that was 26-inch, and mine was only 24; and I asked my sister what I should do. Then my girl-friend came over and was real nice about it, and let me ride it.

Teacher approves of this, and says: Didn't it end up that they both had fun without unhappiness? (Observer notes: Constant questioning of class, with expectation of affirmative answers: that wasn't this the right way, the best way, etc., to do it?)

Here we note that the teacher herself has gone astray, for on the one hand her aim is to get instances from the children in which they themselves have been yielding and capable of resolving their own jealousy, etc., while on the other hand, in the instance given by Betty, it was not Betty who yielded but her friend. The child immediately following Betty imitated her since Betty had been praised by the teacher:

Matilde: My girl-friend got a 26-inch bike and mine was only 24; but she only let me ride it once a month. But for my birthday my mother's getting me a new one, probably (proudly) a "28." (Many children rush in with the information that "28" doesn't exist.) Matilde replies that she'll probably have to raise the seat then, for she's too big for a "26."

This instance suggests more clearly, perhaps, than the others, another possible factor in making the stories of the children end always with their getting what they want: the children may be afraid to lose face with their peers by acknowledging they did not get something they wanted.

As we go on with this lesson, we shall see how the children's need for substitute gratification and their inability to accept frustration prevent them from picking up the teacher's message. As we continue, we shall see how, in spite of the teacher's driving insistence on her point, the children continue to inject their conflicts into the lesson, while at the same time they gropingly try to find a way to gratify the teacher. They cannot give the right answers because of their conflicts; teacher cannot handle their conflicts because she cannot perceive them. The lesson goes on:

Teacher: I notice that some of you are only happy when you get your own way. (Observer noticed too, horrified.) You're not thinking this through, and I want you to. Think of an experience when you didn't get what you want. Think it through. (Observer wonders: Are the children volunteering because of expectations: making desperate efforts to meet the expectation, even though they do not quite understand it?)

Charlie: His ma was going to the movies and he wanted to go with her; and she wouldn't let him; and she went off to the movies; and he was mad; but then he went outside and there were some kids playing baseball, so he played baseball.

Teacher: But suppose you hadn't gotten to play baseball? You would have felt hurt because you didn't get what you wanted. We can't help feeling hurt when we are disappointed. What could you have done? How could you have handled it? (Observer notes: Teacher is not getting what she wants, but I am not sure the kids can understand. Is this a function of immaturity, or of spoiling by parents? Seems to me the continued effort to extract an idea they have not encompassed may be resulting in reinforcement for the one they have got — that you eventually get the watch, or the bicycle, or whatever.)

Charlie: So I can't go to the movies; so I can't play baseball; so I'll do something around the house.

Teacher: Now you're beginning to think! It takes courage to take disappointments. (Turning to the class) What did we learn? The helpful way. . . .

Class: is the healthy way!

Thus the lesson reaches this point on a note of triumphant docility, but of pseudo-complementarity. If the teacher had been able to perceive the underlying factors that made it impossible for these children to accept delayed gratification or total momentary frustration, and had handled that problem, instead of doggedly sticking to a text that required a stereotyped answer, she would have come closer to the children and would not have had to back out of the situation by extracting a parrot-like chorusing. The teacher had to get a "right" answer, and the children ended up giving her one, since that is what they are in school for. Thus on one level teacher and pupils were complementary, but on another they were widely divergent. This is the characteristic condition of the American middle-class schoolroom.

If we review all the verbal messages sent by the teacher, we will see how hard she has worked to get the answer she wants; how she has corrected and "improved" her signaling in response to the eager feedback from the children:

1) Do you believe it's easier to deal with your thoughts if you own up to them, Betty?

2) Have you any experience like this in the book, Alice?

3) What could you do with mean feelings?

4) What did Susie (in the book) do?

5) (Rupert says that Billy, the character in the book, handled the problem in the better way because he did not get angry.) That's a good answer, Rupert.

6) (Betty tells how nice her girl-friend was, letting her ride her bike.) Teacher approves of this and says: Didn't it end up that they both had fun without unhappiness?

7) I notice that some of you are happy only when you get your own way.

8) What could you have done (when you did not get your own way)?

9) Now you're beginning to think. It takes courage to take disappointments. What did we learn? The helpful way. . . . and the class responds, is the healthy way.


DISCUSSION AND CONCLUSIONS

This paper has been an effort to describe the mental docility of middle-class American children *in their classrooms*. It says nothing about the home or the play group. The analysis shows how children are taught to find the answer the teacher wants, and to give it to her. That they sometimes fail is beside the point, because their trying so hard is itself evidence of docility; and an understanding of the reasons for failure helps us to see why communication breaks down and pseudo-understanding takes its place. When communication breaks down it is often because complementarity between sender (teacher) and receivers (pupils) is not exact; and it is not exact because teacher and pupils are at different levels of emotional organization.

We may now ask: Why are these children, whose phantasies our unpublished research has found to contain so many hostile and anxious elements, so docile in the classroom? Why do they struggle so hard to gratify the teacher and try in so many ways, as our protocols show, to bring themselves to the teacher's attention?

We might, of course, start with the idea of the teacher as a parent-figure, and the children as siblings competing for teacher's favor. We could refer to the unresolved dependency needs of children of this age, which make them seek support in the teacher, who then manipulates this seeking and the children's sibling rivalry in order, as our unpublished research suggests, to pit the children against each other. Other important factors, however, that appear in the middle-class schoolrooms, ought to be taken into consideration. For example, our research shows the children's tendency to destructively criticize each other, and the teacher's repeated reinforcement of this tendency. We have taken note, in our research, of the anxiety in the children as illustrated in the stories they tell and observed that these very stories are subjected to carping criticism by other children, the consequence of which would be anything but an alleviation of that anxiety. Hence the schoolroom is a place in which the child's underlying anxiety may be heightened. In an effort to alleviate this he seeks approval of the teacher, by giving right answers, and by doing what teacher wants him to do under most circumstances. Finally, we cannot omit the teacher's need to be gratified by the attention-hungry behavior of the children.

A word is necessary about these classrooms in middle class. The novel *Blackboard Jungle*, by Evan Hunter, describes schoolroom behavior of lower-class children. There we see them solidly against the teacher, as representative of the middle-class. But in the classes we have observed we see the children against each other, with the teacher abetting the process. Thus, as the teacher in middle-class schools directs the hostility of the children toward one another (particularly in the form of criticism), and away from herself, she reinforces the competitive dynamics within the middle class itself. The teacher in the lower-class schools, on the other hand, appears to become the organizing stimulus for behavior that integrates the lower-class, as the children unite in expressing their hostility to the teacher.

In conclusion, it should be pointed out that the mental docility (or near docility) achieved in these middle-class schoolrooms is a peculiar middle-class kind of docility. It is not based on authoritarian control backed by fear of corporal punishment, but rather on fear of loss of love. More precisely, it rests on the need to bask in the sun of the teacher's acceptance. It is not fear of scolding or of physical pain that makes these children docile, but rather fear of finding oneself outside the warmth of the inner circle of teacher's sheltering acceptance. This kind of docility can be more than lethal than the other, for it does not breed rebellion and independence, as struggle against authoritarian controls may, but rather a kind of cloying paralysis; a sweet imprisonment without pain. Looking at the matter from another point of view, we might say that were these children not fearful of loss of love they would be indifferent to the teacher's messages. In a sense what the teacher's signals are really saying is: "This is the way to be loved by me; and this is the way I want you to love me."

# SOCIAL-CLASS VARIATIONS IN THE
# TEACHER-PUPIL RELATIONSHIP

HOWARD S. BECKER

The major problems of workers in the service occupations are likely
to be a function of their relationship to their clients or customers,
those for whom or on whom the occupational service is performed.[1]
Members of such occupations typically have some image of the
"ideal" client, and it is in terms of this fiction that they fashion their
conceptions of how their work ought to be performed, and their actual
work techniques. To the degree that actual clients approximate this
ideal the worker will have no "client problem."

In a highly differentiated urban society, however, clients will vary
greatly, and ordinarily only some fraction of the total of potential
clients will be "good" ones. Workers tend to classify clients in terms
of the way in which they vary from this ideal. The fact of client variation from the occupational ideal emphasizes the intimate relation of
the institution in which work is carried on to its environing society.
If that society does not prepare people to play their client roles in
the manner desired by the occupation's members there will be conflicts, and problems for the workers in the performance of their work.
One of the major factors affecting the production of suitable clients
is the cultural diversity of various social classes in the society. The
cultures of particular social-class groups may operate to produce
clients who make the worker's position extremely difficult.

We deal here with this problem as it appears in the experience of
the functionaries of a large urban educational institution, the Chicago
public school system, discussing the way in which teachers in this
system observe, classify and react to class-typed differences in the
behavior of the children with whom they work. The material to be
presented is thus relevant not only to problems of occupational organ-

Reprinted from the *Journal of Educational Sociology* (Vol. 25, 1952, pp. 451–465)
by permission of the publisher, the Kraus Reprint Corporation, and the author.
This paper is based on research done under a grant from the Committee on Education, Training, and Research in Race Relations of the University of Chicago.

ization but also to the problem of differences in the educational opportunities available to children of various social-classes. Warner,
Havighurst and Loeb[2] and Hollingshead[3] have demonstrated the
manner in which the schools tend to favor and select out children of
the middle classes. Allison Davis has pointed to those factors in the
class cultures involved which make lower-class children less and
middle-class children more adaptable to the work and behavioral
standards of the school.[4] This paper will contribute to knowledge in
this area by analyzing the manner in which the public school teacher
reacts to these cultural differences and, in so doing, perpetrates
the discrimination of our educational system against the lower-class
child.

The analysis is based on sixty interviews with teachers in the
Chicago system.[5] The interviews were oriented around the general
question of the problems of being a teacher and were not specifically
directed toward discovering feelings about social-class differences
among students. Since these differences created some of the teachers'
most pressing problems they were continually brought up by the
interviewees themselves. They typically distinguished three social-
class groups with which they, as teachers, came in contact: (1) a
bottom stratum, probably equivalent to the lower-lower and parts
of the upper-lower class; (2) an upper stratum, probably equivalent
to the upper-middle class; and (3) a middle stratum, probably equivalent to the lower-middle and parts of the upper-lower class. We will
adopt the convention of referring to these groups as lower, upper and
middle groups, but it should be understood that this terminology
refers to the teachers' classification of students and not to the ordinary
sociological description.

We will proceed by taking up the three problems that loomed
largest in the teachers' discussion of adjustment to their students: (1)
the problem of *teaching* itself, (2) the problem of *discipline*, and (3)
the problem of the *moral acceptability* of the students. In each case
the variation in the form of and adjustment to the problem by the
characteristics of the children of the various class groups distinguished
by teachers is discussed.

# I

A basic problem in any occupation is that of performing one's given
task successfully, and where this involves working with human beings

their qualities are a major variable affecting the ease with which the work can be done. The teacher considers that she has done her job adequately when she has brought about an observable change in the children's skills and knowledge which she can attribute to her own efforts:

> Well, I would say that a teacher is successful when she is putting the material across to the children, when she is getting some response from them. I'll tell you something. Teaching is a very rewarding line of work, because you can see these children grow under your hands. You can see the difference in them after you've had them for five months. You can see where they've started and where they've got to go. And it's all yours. It really is rewarding in that way, you can see results and know that it's your work that brought these results about.

She feels that she has a better chance of success in this area when her pupils are interested in attending and working hard in school, and are trained at home in such a way that they are bright and quick at school work. Her problems arise in teaching those groups who do not meet these specifications, for in these cases her teaching techniques, tailored to the "perfect" student, are inadequate to cope with the reality, and she is left with a feeling of having failed in performing her basic task.

Davis has described the orientations toward education in general, and schoolwork in particular, of the lower and middle classes:

> Thus, our educational system, which next to the family is the most effective agency in teaching good work habits to middle class people, is largely ineffective and unrealistic with underprivileged groups. Education fails to motivate such workers because our schools and our society both lack *real rewards* to offer underprivileged groups. Neither lower class children or adults will work hard in school or on the job just to please the teacher or boss. They are not going to learn to be ambitious, to be conscientious, and to study hard, as if school and work were a fine character-building game, which one plays just for the sake of playing. They can see, indeed, that those who work hard at school usually have families that already have the occupations, homes, and social acceptance that the school holds up as the rewards of education. The underprivileged workers can see also that the chances of their getting enough education to make their attainment of these rewards in the future at all probable is very slight. Since they can win the rewards of prestige and social acceptance in their own slum groups without much education, they do not take very seriously the motivation taught by the school. [6]

As these cultural differences produce variations from the image of the "ideal" student, teachers tend to use class terms in describing the children with whom they work.

Children of the lowest group, from slum areas, are characterized as the most difficult group to teach successfully, lacking in interest in school, learning ability, and outside training:

> They don't have the right kind of study habits. They can't seem to apply themselves as well. Of course, it's not their fault; they aren't brought up right. After all, the parents in a neighborhood like that really aren't interested. . . . But, as I say, those children don't learn very quickly. A great many of them don't seem to be really interested in getting an education. I don't think they are. It's hard to get anything done with children like that. They simply don't respond.

In definite contrast are the terms used to describe children of the upper group:

> In a neighborhood like this there's something about the children, you just feel like you're accomplishing so much more. You throw an idea out and you can see that it takes hold. The children know what you're talking about and they think about it. Then they come in with projects and pictures and additional information, and it just makes you feel good to see it. They go places and see things, and they know what you're talking about. For instance, you might be teaching social studies or geography. . . . You bring something up and a child says, "Oh, my parents took me to see that in the museum." You can just do more with material like that.

Ambivalent feelings are aroused by children of the middle group. While motivated to work hard in school they lack the proper out-of-school training:

> Well, they're very nice here, very nice. They're not hard to handle. You see, they're taught respect in the home and they're respectful to the teacher. They want to work and do well. . . . Of course, they're not too brilliant. You know what I mean. But they are very nice children and very easy to work with.

In short, the differences between groups make it possible for the teacher to feel successful at her job only with the top group; with the other groups she feels, in greater or lesser measure, that she has failed.

These differences in ability to do school work, as perceived by teachers, have important consequences. They lead, in the first place, to differences in actual teaching techniques. A young high school teacher contrasted the techniques used in "slum" schools with those used in "better" schools:

> At S————, there were a lot of guys who were just waiting till they were sixteen so they could get out of school. I————, everybody — well, a very large percentage, I'll say — was going on to secondary school, to college. That certainly made a difference in their classroom work. You had to teach differently at the different schools. For instance, at S————, if you had demonstrations in chemistry they had to be pretty flashy, lots of noise and smoke, before they'd get interested in it. That wasn't necessary at L————. Or at S———— if you were having electricity or something like that you had to get the static electricity machine out and have them all stand around and hold hands so that they'd all get a little jolt.

Further, the teacher feels that where these differences are recognized by her superiors there will be a corresponding variation in the amount of work she is expected to accomplish. She expects that the amount of work and effort required of her will vary inversely with the social status of her pupils. This teacher compared schools from the extremes of the class range:

> So you have to be on your toes and keep up to where you're supposed to be in the course of study. Now, in a school like the D———— [slum school] you're just not expected to complete all that work. It's almost impossible. For instance, in the second grade we're supposed to cover nine spelling words a week. Well, I can do that up here at the K———— ["better" school], they can take nine new words a week. But the best class I ever had at the D———— was only able to achieve six words a week and they had to work pretty hard to get that. So I never finished the year's work in spelling. I couldn't. And I really wasn't expected to.

One resultant of this situation — in which less is expected of those teachers whose students are more difficult to teach — is that the problem becomes more aggravated in each grade, as the gap between what the children should know and what they actually do know becomes wider and wider. A principal of such a school describes the degeneration there of the teaching problem into a struggle to get a few basic skills across, in a situation where this cumulative effect makes following the normal program of study impossible:

The children come into our upper grades with very poor reading ability. That means that all the way through our school everybody is concentrating on reading. It's not like at a school like S——— [middle group] where they have science and history and so on. At a school like that they figure that from first to fourth you learn to read and from fifth to eighth you read to learn. You use your reading to learn other material. Well, these children don't reach that second stage while they're with us. We have to plug along getting them to learn to read. Our teachers are pretty well satisfied if the children can read and do simple number work when they leave here. You'll find that they don't think very much of subjects like science, and so on. They haven't got any time for that. They're just trying to get these basic things over. . . . That's why our school is different from one like the S———.

Such consequences of teachers' differential reaction to various class groups obviously operate to further perpetuate those class-cultural characteristics to which they object in the first place.


II


Discipline is the second of the teacher's major problems with her students. Willard Waller pointed to its basis when he wrote that "Teacher and pupil confront each other in the school with an original conflict of desires, and however much that conflict may be reduced in amount, or however much it may be hidden, it still remains."[7] We must recognize that conflict, either actual or potential, is ever present in the teacher-pupil relationship, the teacher attempting to maintain her control against the children's efforts to break it.[8] This conflict is felt even with those children who present least difficulty; a teacher who considered her pupils models of good behavior nevertheless said:

But there's that tension all the time. Between you and the students. It's hard on your nerves. Teaching is fun, if you enjoy your subject, but it's the discipline that keeps your nerves on edge, you know what I mean? There's always that tension. Sometimes people say, "Oh, you teach school. That's an easy job, just sitting around all day long." They don't know what it's really like. It's hard on your nerves.

The teacher is tense because she fears that she will lose control, which she tends to define in terms of some line beyond which she will not allow the children to go. Wherever she may draw this line (and there is considerable variation), the teacher feels that she has a "discipline" problem when the children attempt to push beyond it. The form and intensity of this problem are felt to vary from one social-class group to another, as might be expected from Davis' description of class emphases on aggression:

> In general, middle-class aggression is taught to adolescents in the form of social and economic skills which will enable them to compete effectively at that level. . . . In lower-class families, physical aggression is as much a normal, socially approved and socially inculcated type of behavior as it is in frontier communities.[9]

These differences in child training are matched by variation in the teachers' reactions.

Children in "slum" schools are considered most difficult to control, being given to unrestrained behavior and physical violence. The interviews are filled with descriptions of such difficulties. Miriam Wagenschein, in a parallel study of the beginning school teacher, gave this summary of the experiences of these younger teachers in lower-class schools.

> The reports which these teachers give of what *can* be done by a group of children are nothing short of amazing. A young white teacher walked into her new classroom and was greeted with the comment, "Another damn white one." Another was "rushed" at her desk by the entire class when she tried to be extremely strict with them. Teachers report having been bitten, tripped, and pushed on the stairs. Another gave an account of a second grader throwing a milk bottle at the teacher and of a first grader having such a temper tantrum that it took the principal and two policemen to get him out of the room. In another school following a fight on the playground, the principal took thirty-two razor blades from children in a first grade room. Some teachers indicated fear that they might be attacked by irate persons in the neighborhoods in which they teach. Other teachers report that their pupils carry long pieces of glass and have been known to threaten other pupils with them while others jab each other with hypodermic needles. One boy got angry with his teacher and knocked in the fender of her car.[10]

In these schools a major part of the teacher's time must be devoted to discipline; as one said: "It's just a question of keeping them in line." This emphasis on discipline detracts from the school's primary function of teaching, thus discriminating, in terms of available educational opportunity, against the children of these schools.

Children of the middle group are thought of as docile, and with them the teacher has least difficulty with discipline:

> Those children were much quieter, easier to work with. When we'd play our little games there was never any commotion. That was a very nice school to work in. Everything was quite nice about it. The children were easy to work with. . . .

Children of the upper group are felt hard to handle in some respects, and are often termed "spoiled," "overindulged," or "neurotic;" they do not play the role of the child in the submissive manner teachers consider appropriate. One interviewee, speaking of this group, said:

> I think most teachers prefer not to teach in that type of school. The children are more pampered and, as we say, more inclined to run the school for themselves. The parents are very much at fault. The children are not used to taking orders at home and naturally they won't take them at school either.

Teachers develop methods of dealing with these discipline problems, and these tend to vary between social-class groups as do the problems themselves. The basic device used by successful disciplinarians is to establish authority clearly on the first meeting with the class:

> You can't ever let them get the upper hand on you or you're through. So I start out tough. The first day I get a new class in, I let them know who's boss. . . . You've got to start off tough, then you can ease up as you go along. If you start out easy-going, when you try to get tough they'll just look at you and laugh.

Having once established such a relation, it is considered important that the teacher be consistent in her behavior so that the children will continue to respect and obey her.

> I let them know I mean business. That's one thing you must do. Say nothing that you won't follow through on. Some teachers will say anything to keep kids quiet, they'll threaten anything. Then they can't or won't carry out their threats. Naturally, the children won't pay any attention to them after that. You must never say anything that you won't back up.

In the difficult "slum" schools, teachers feel the necessity of using stern measures, up to and including physical violence (nominally outlawed):

Technically you're not supposed to lay a hand on a kid. Well, they don't technically. But there are a lot of ways of handling a kid so that it doesn't show — and then it's the teacher's word against the kid's, so the kid hasn't got a chance. Like dear Mrs.————. She gets mad at a kid, she takes him out in the hall. She gets him stood up against the wall. Then she's got a way of chucking the kid under the chin, only hard, so that it knocks his head back against the wall. It doesn't leave a mark on him. But when he comes back in that room he can hardly see straight, he's so knocked out. It's really rough. There's a lot of little tricks like that that you learn about.

Where such devices are not used, there is recourse to violent punishment, "tongue lashings." All teachers, however, are not emotionally equipped for such behavior and must find other means:

The worst thing I can do is lose my temper and start raving. . . . You've got to believe in that kind of thing in order for it to work. . . . If you don't honestly believe it it shows up and the children know you don't mean it and it doesn't do any good anyway. . . . I try a different approach myself. Whenever they get too rowdy I go to the piano and . . . play something and we have rhythms or something until they sort of settle down. . . . That's what we call "softsoaping" them. It seems to work for me. It's about the only thing I can do.

Some teachers may also resort to calling in the parents, a device whose usefulness is limited by the fact that such summonses are most frequently ignored. The teacher's disciplinary power in such a school is also limited by her fear of retaliation by the students: "Those fellows are pretty big, and I just think it would take a bigger person than me to handle them. I certainly wouldn't like to try."

In the school with children of the middle group no strong sanctions are required, mild reprimands sufficing:

Now the children at Z———— here are quite nice to teach. They're pliable, yes, that's the word, they're pliable. They will go along with you on things and not fight you. You can take them any place and say to them, "I'm counting on you not to disgrace your school. Let's see that Z———— spirit." And they'll behave for you. . . . They can be frightened, they have fear in them. They're pliable, flexible, you can do things with them. They're afraid of their parents and what they'll do to them if they get into trouble at school. And they're afraid of the administration. They're afraid of being sent down to the principal. So that they can be handled.

Children of the upper group often act in a way which may be interpreted as "misbehavior" but which does not represent a conscious attack on the teacher's authority. Many teachers are able to disregard such activity by interpreting it as a natural concomitant of the "brightness" and "intelligence" of such children. Where such an interpretation is not possible the teachers feel hampered by a lack of effective sanctions.

> I try different things like keeping them out of a gym period or a recess period. But that doesn't always work. I have this one little boy who just didn't care when I used those punishments. He said he didn't like gym anyway. I don't know what I'm going to do with him.

The teacher's power in such schools is further limited by the fact that the children are able to mobilize their influential parents so as to exert a large degree of control over the actions of school personnel.

It should be noted, finally, that discipline problems tend to become less important as the length of the teacher's stay in a particular school makes it possible for her to build a reputation which coerces the children into behaving without attempting any test of strength.[11]

> I have no trouble with the children. Once you establish a reputation and they know what to expect, they respect you and you have no trouble. Of course, that's different for a new teacher, but when you're established that's no problem at all.

### III

The third area of problems has been termed that of *moral acceptability,* and arises from the fact that some actions of one's potential clients may be offensive in terms of some deeply felt set of moral standards; these clients are thus morally unacceptable. Teachers find that some of their pupils act in such a way as to make themselves unacceptable in terms of the moral values centered around health and cleanliness, sex and aggression, ambition and work, and the relations of age groups.

Children of the middle group present no problem at this level, being universally described as clean, well-dressed, moderate in their behavior, and hard working. Children from the "better" neighbor-

hoods are considered deficient in the important moral traits of politeness and respect for elders.

> Where the children come from wealthy homes. That's not so good
> either. They're not used to doing work at home. They have maids and
> servants of all kinds and they're used to having things done for them,
> instead of doing them themselves. . . . They won't do anything. For
> instance, if they drop a piece of cloth on the floor, they'll just let it
> lay, they wouldn't think of bending over to pick it up. That's janitor's
> work to them. As a matter of fact, one of them said to me once: "If I
> pick that up there wouldn't be any work for the janitor to do." Well,
> it's pretty difficult to deal with children like that.

Further, they are regarded as likely to transgress what the teachers
define as moral boundaries in the matter of smoking and drinking; it
is particularly shocking that such "nice" children should have such
vices.

It is, however, the "slum" child who most deeply offends the
teacher's moral sensibilities; in almost every area mentioned above
these children, by word, action or appearance, manage to give
teachers the feeling that they are immoral and not respectable. In
terms of physical appearance and condition they disgust and depress
the middle-class teacher. Even this young woman, whose emancipation from conventional morality is symbolized in her habitual use of
the argot of the jazz musician, was horrified by the absence of the
toothbrush from the lives of her lower-class students:

> It's just horribly depressing, you know. I mean, it just gets you down.
> I'll give you an example. A kid complained of a toothache one day.
> Well, I thought I could take a look and see if I could help him or some-
> thing so I told him to open his mouth. I almost wigged when I saw
> his mouth. His teeth were all rotten, every one of them. Just filthy
> and rotten. Man, I mean, I was really shocked, you know. I said,
> "Don't you have a toothbrush?" He said no, they were only his baby
> teeth and Ma said he didn't need a toothbrush for that. So I really
> got upset and looked in all their mouths. Man, I never saw anything
> like it. They were all like that, practically. I asked how many had
> toothbrushes, and about a quarter of them had them. Boy, that's ter-
> rible. And I don't dig that crap about baby teeth either, because they
> start getting molars when they're six, I know that. So I gave them a
> talking to, but what good does it do? The kid's mouth was just rotten.
> They never heard of a toothbrush or going to a dentist.

These children, too, are more apt than the other groups to be dishonest in some way that will get them into trouble with law enforcement officials. The early (by middle-class standards) sexual maturity of such children is quite upsetting to the teacher:

> One thing about these girls is, well, some of them are not very nice girls. One girl in my class I've had two years now. She makes her money on the side as a prostitute. She's had several children. . . . This was a disturbing influence on the rest of the class.

Many teachers reported great shock on finding that words which were innocent to them had obscene meanings for their lower-class students:

> I decided to read them a story one day. I started reading them "Puss in Boots" and they just burst out laughing. I couldn't understand what I had said that had made them burst out like that. I went back over the story and tried to find out what it might be. I couldn't see anything that would make them laugh. I couldn't see anything at all in the story. Later one of the teachers asked me what had happened. She was one of the older teachers. I told her that I didn't know; that I was just reading them a story and they thought it was extremely funny. She asked me what story I read them and I told her "Puss in the Boots." She said, "Oh, I should have warned you not to read that one." It seems that Puss means something else to them. It means something awful — I wouldn't even tell you what. It doesn't mean a thing to me.[12]

Warner, Havighurst and Loeb note that "unless the middle-class values change in America, we must expect the influence of the schools to favor the values of material success, individual striving, thrift, and social mobility."[13] Here again, the "slum" child violates the teacher's moral sense by failing to display these virtues:

> Many of these children don't realize the worth of an education. They have no desire to improve themselves. And they don't care much about school and schoolwork as a result. That makes it very difficult to teach them.
>
> That kind of problem is particularly bad in a school like ————. That's not a very privileged school. It's very under-privileged, as a matter of fact. So we have a pretty tough element there, a bunch of bums, I might as well say it. That kind you can't teach at all. They don't want to be there at all, and so you can't do anything with them. And even many of the others — they're simply indifferent to the advantages of education. So they're indifferent, they don't care about their homework.

This behavior of the lower-class child is all the more repellent to the teacher because she finds it incomprehensible; she cannot conceive that any normal human being would act in such a way. This teacher stresses the anxiety aroused in the inexperienced teacher by her inability to provide herself with a rational explanation for her pupils' behavior:

> We had one of the girls who just came to the school last year and she used to come and talk to me quite a bit. I know that it was just terrible for her. You know, I don't think she'd ever had anything to do with Negroes before she got there and she was just mystified, didn't know what to do. She was bewildered. She came to me one day almost in tears and said, "But they don't want to learn, they don't even want to learn. Why is that?" Well, she had me there.

It is worth noting that the behavior of the "better" children, even when morally unacceptable, is less distressing to the teacher, who feels that, in this case, she can produce a reasonable explanation for the behavior. An example of such an explanation is the following:

> I mean, they're spoiled, you know. A great many of them are only children. Naturally, they're used to having their own way and they don't like to be told what to do. Well, if a child is in a room that I'm teaching he's going to be told what to do, that's all there is to it. Or if they're not spoiled that way, they're the second child and they never got the affection the first one did, not that their mother didn't love them, but they didn't get as much affection, so they're not so easy to handle either.

## IV

We have shown that school teachers experience problems in working with their students to the degree that those students fail to exhibit in reality the qualities of the image of the ideal pupil which teachers hold. In a stratified urban society there are many groups whose life-style and culture produce children who do not meet the standards of this image, and who are thus impossible for teachers like these to work with effectively. Programs of action intended to increase the educational opportunities of the under-privileged in our society should take account of the manner in which teachers interpret and react to the cultural traits of this group, and the institutional consequences of their behavior.[14] Such programs might profitably aim at producing teachers who can cope effectively with the problems of teaching this group and not, by their reactions to class differences, perpetuate the existing inequities.

A more general statement of the findings is now in order. Professionals depend on their environing society to provide them with clients who meet the standards of their image of the ideal client. Social class cultures, among other factors, may operate to produce many clients who, in one way or another, fail to meet these specifications and therefore aggravate one or another of the basic problems of the worker-client relation (three were considered in this paper).

In attacking this problem we touch on one of the basic elements of the relation between institutions and society, for the differences between ideal and reality place in high relief the implicit assumptions which institutions, through their functionaries, make about the society around them. All institutions have embedded in them some set of assumptions about the nature of the society and the individuals with whom they deal, and we must get at these assumptions, and their embodiment in actual social interaction, in order fully to understand these organizations. We can, perhaps, best begin our work on this problem by studying those institutions which, like the school, make assumptions which have high visibility because of their variation from reality.

## REFERENCES

1. See Howard S. Becker, "The Professional Dance Musician and His Audience," *American Journal of Sociology*, LVII (September, 1951), pp. 136–144 for further discussion of this point.

2. W. L. Warner, R. J. Havighurst, and W. J. Loeb, *Who Shall Be Educated?* (New York: Harper and Bros., 1944).

3. August Hollingshead, *Elmtown's Youth* (New York: John Wiley & Sons, 1949).

4. Allison Davis, *Social-Class Influences Upon Learning* (Cambridge: Harvard University Press, 1950).

5. The entire research has been reported in Howard S. Becker, "Role and Career Problems of the Chicago Public School Teacher," (unpublished Ph. D. dissertation, University of Chicago, 1951).

6. Allison Davis, "The Motivation of the Underprivileged Worker," *Indus-*

*try and Society,* ed. William F. Whyte (New York: McGraw-Hill Book Co., 1947), p. 99.

7. Willard Waller, *Sociology of Teaching* (New York: John Wiley and Sons, 1932), p. 197.

8. Although all service occupations tend to have such problems of control over their clients, the problem is undoubtedly aggravated in situations like the school where those upon whom the service is being performed are not there of their own volition, but rather because of the wishes of some other group (the parents, in this case).

9. Allison Davis, *Social-Class Influence Upon Learning,* pp. 34–5.

10. Miriam Wagenschein, "Reality Shock" (Unpublished M. A. thesis, University of Chicago, 1950), pp. 58–9.

11. This is part of the process of job adjustment described in detail in Howard S. Becker, "The Career of the Chicago Public School Teacher," *American Journal of Sociology,* LVII (March, 1952).

12. Interview by Miriam Wagenschein. The lack of common meanings in this situation symbolizes the great cultural and moral distance between teacher and "slum" child.

13. *Op. cit.,* p. 172.

14. One of the important institutional consequences of these class preferences is a constant movement of teachers away from lower-class schools, which prevents these schools from retaining experienced teachers and from maintaining some continuity in teaching and administration.

# PART IV

Achievement in Occupational Settings:
Personality and Structural Factors

## INTRODUCTION

Many, if not all, societies today require more actual toil of their citizens than is exacted of Americans, but none surpass us in stressing the occupational setting as the appropriate domain for the pursuit of achievement. One may become an exemplary friend, spouse, kinsman, or parent — difficult tasks, all — and yet not be perceived as one who has achieved. Indeed, there are no broadly recognized criteria for honoring adults who excel as friends, as neighbors, as parents, or as adepts at any pursuits whatever aside from those of the work-a-day occupational world. For good or ill, "achievement" in the United States means achievement in work.

Because much work-achievement in the United States is assessed both by laymen and scholars, in terms of one's movement, upward or downward, in the occupational system, we devote a separate portion of the book to the topic of occupational mobility. In the present section, we are concerned with the processes, possibilities and problems of achievement in work, apart from the issue of mobility.

### ACHIEVEMENT IN ORGANIZATIONS

The key fact about work in present-day America is that it occurs for the most part in organizations of large size rather than in firms with few members or in one-man enterprises.[1] This means that achievement in work is affected by many more structural factors today than was the case earlier in our nation's history when firms of small size and the individual undertaking (including the independent family farm) were more prevalent as work settings. Accordingly, discovering orderly generalizations about achievement in work is a more difficult task now than in the relatively recent past. Acknowledging this fact, we seek to convey the complexity facing the student in this area, as well as reveal some order, by presenting four papers examining work achievement in quite diverse occupational settings.

In the first selection, Vroom demonstrates the impact of a personality characteristic — ego-involvement in the job — on one aspect of work achievement — performance on the job — among both white collar and blue collar industrial employees. The one structural variable studied, degree of autonomy in one's job, is found to enhance only slightly the relationship between ego-involvement and work performance. However, when the effect of autonomy on work performance is considered apart from ego-involvement, it becomes clear that the greater the autonomy the greater is the job performance.[2]

Next, Moore examines relationships between personality types and work achievement among corporate executives, stressing his belief that structural factors sharply inhibit the degree of achievement possible for the majority of corporate managers.

The immense contribution which structural factors may make to differential work achievement among organization members when bureaucratic controls are maximized is detailed by Davis. Although such an organization probably recruits a restricted range of personality types, it seems certain nevertheless that any variations in personality characteristics of members could not go far in affecting variations in the work achievement of members.

Finally, Roy shows how cooperative arrangements among workers devised to circumvent structural constraints imposed by management (said constraints, ironically, introduced to promote achievement) may sometimes enhance work achievement.

ACHIEVEMENT AND CREATIVITY

Discovering novel yet effective solutions to problems arising in work — whether in the efforts of the individual craftsman, artist, or scientist, in the operations of small groups or large scale organizations, or in the complex relations between machinery and men — is the essence of creativity in work. To the present, scholarly attention has been directed overwhelmingly to the creativity of individuals. Moreover, the great bulk of this literature has been concerned with the personality determinants of individual creativity rather than with the possible effects of social structural factors. Yet one may be confident that variations in social arrangements markedly enhance or impede the probability of creative work. Research in the coming decade will undoubtedly produce much greater understanding of structural factors in creativity than is now at hand. In the meantime, the reader should be aware that our selection of one report stressing personality factors and a second report stressing structural factors reflects the needs of this book rather than the current state of knowledge.

In the first selection, Mackinnon summarizes the knowledge he and his associates have gleaned from their intensive, ongoing studies of intrapersonal factors in individual creativity. Although data linking childhood socialization variables to the adult creativity of the men studied are not presented, the reader will note that the conditions described in earlier selections (see the papers by Biber and Minuchin, Rosen, and Hess and Shipman) as leading to the acquisition of competence, achievement motivation, and specific cognitive styles in children also seem well suited to produce a number of the characteristics possessed by the creative adults under study.

In the second selection, Bruner analyzes some social structural factors influencing a highly creative work group. As Bruner notes, none of the men in the group had been especially creative in their previous work-lives as individuals. Rather, factors emerging in group interaction lead to the group's signal accomplishments.

ACHIEVEMENT AND WOMEN

In this century, participation of women in the labor force has increased dramatically. Women comprised about one-sixth of the civilian labor force in 1890, but nearly one-third in 1956. Accompanying this change in the proportionate number of women working outside the home has been change in the types of women involved. The young, single woman dominated the scene in 1890, when 70 per cent of working women were single and half were under 25 years old. Today, single women comprise only about one-fourth of the female labor forces, while half of the working women are over 40 years of age. Of all married women, at least one in three now works outside the home; among mothers with school-aged children, about four in ten are now gainfully employed.[3]

This influx of young mothers and of married women of all ages into the labor force undoubtedly reflects the steady trend toward equality between the sexes which has marked our nation throughout this century. However, present evidence strongly indicates not only that nothing approaching full equality at work between men and women is likely in the foreseeable future, but also that most women themselves do not seek such equality.

On the first point, we note that the income gap between men and women in the labor force has been increasing rather than decreasing in recent years.[4] As the Simpsons[5] point out, this does not prove that women receive less pay than men for similar work; rather, such figures probably mean that women are typically employed in lower-ranking positions than are men in any given job category (e.g., operatives, semi-professions, etc.). Still, such a situation indicates unequal participation of men and women in the labor force; the Simpsons document this inequality fully in the case of the semi-professions.

Much of the evidence supporting the assertion that most women do not seek full equality with men in work is also reviewed by the Simpsons in the paper just cited. It is highly likely that this preference by women for a subordinate role in work is destined to prevail far into the future, since genuinely basic changes in American values and family arrangements would be necessary to affect significant change.[6]

Given the conditions sketched above, it is not surprising to find women underrepresented among those who attain eminence in work. Thus, Kiser and Schacter's[7] analysis of the 1948–49 edition of *Who's Who in America* showed that women accounted for only 6 per cent of the listings, and nearly half of the women listed were either educators or authors. And a study[8] of women holding higher-level business positions revealed women to be grossly underrepresented in such positions in comparison with the ratio of women to men among all employees of the firm studied.

We present two selections on women's achievement in work. In the first, Florence Kluckhohn traces the factors in our nation's history which have shaped the present state of affairs. In the second, Alice Rossi examines the current situation of women employed in the sciences, and offers some guidelines for promoting more equal participation of talented women in the scientific professions.

## REFERENCES

1. Robin Williams writes: "In 1951, firms having 1,000 or more employees employed about 40 per cent of all persons employed for pay — even though these firms were only 0.1 per cent of all firms. The top 5 per cent

of firms (those with over 20 employees) accounted for 75 per cent of the employees." Robin M. Williams, Jr., *American Society* (New York: Knopf, 1960), p. 165.

2. This relationship is not discussed by Vroom, but the reader may note it by reading down, rather than across, the data reported on Table 1, p. 374.

3. See National Manpower Council, *Womanpower* (New York: Columbia University Press, 1957), and the following publications of the Women's Bureau, U.S. Department of Labor: "Women's Jobs: Advance and Growth," *Bulletin 232* (Washington, D.C.: U.S. Government Printing Office, 1949); "Status of Women in the United States," *Bulletin 249* (1953); "Changes in Women's Occupations," *Bulletin 253* (1954); "1962 Handbook on Women Workers," *Bulletin 285* (1963).

4. *U.S. Census of Population: 1960, Final Report PC (1)-1C* (Washington, D.C.: U.S. Government Printing Office, 1962), Table 97, pp. 230–231, and Table 98, p. 232.

5. Richard L. Simpson and Ida Harper Simpson, "Women and Bureaucracy in the Semi-Professions," in Amitai Etzioni, editor, *The Semi-Professions* (forthcoming).

6. A 1960 survey involving over 400,000 high school students in grades 9 through 12 disclosed that girls in each of the four grade levels strongly preferred the occupation "housewife" over all others. Such preferences, laid down in the contemporary American family and reinforced in school, surely can be altered only through great changes in societal values and arrangements. See John C. Flanagan, *et al.*, *The American High School Student* (Pittsburgh, Project Talent Office, 1964).

7. Clyde V. Kiser and Nathalie L. Schacter, "Demographic Characteristics of Women in Who's Who," *Milbank Memorial Fund Quarterly*, 27 (October, 1949), 393–433.

8. Women's Bureau, U.S. Department of Labor, "Women in Higher-Level Positions," *Bulletin 236* (Washington, D.C.: U.S. Government Printing Office, 1950).

# A.

ACHIEVEMENT IN ORGANIZATIONS:
CONSTRAINTS AND ADAPTATIONS

# EGO-INVOLVEMENT, JOB SATISFACTION, AND
# JOB PERFORMANCE

### VICTOR H. VROOM

Psychologists interested in the relationship between motivation and work have typically dealt with three types of dependent variables: a) choices of occupations or jobs; b) satisfaction with, or attitudes toward, jobs; c) measures of performance or proficiency on jobs. While there has been no attempt to formulate a general theoretical framework capable of dealing in a coherent fashion with all three of these variables, they appear to have certain common characteristics. Each of them may be regarded as the outcome of interaction between characteristics of the person and characteristics of the work role.

While there are undoubtedly many different conceptual strategies for dealing with the implications of job content for job satisfaction and motivation for effective performance, it appears that the notion of the relationship between job content and individual self-conceptions utilized in occupational choice may prove useful. Job satisfaction may be viewed as determined, in part, by the extent to which the work role lowers or increases the worker's self-evaluation. Likewise, a person's motivation for effective performance in a task may be a function of the extent to which his self-evaluation is increased by high performance and decreased by low performance.

Two recent studies (Gurin, Veroff & Feld, 1960; Slater, 1959) have opened up certain aspects of the problems suggested by this point of view and should provide a basis for further investigation. Slater (1959) has studied the conditions associated with the internalization of motivation for occupational role performance. Motivation is defined as internalized to the extent that it is independent of externally-

Reprinted with abridgement from *Personnel Psychology* (Vol. 15, 1962, pp. 159–177) by permission of the publisher and the author.

This paper is based on data collected as part of the research of the Organizational Behavior and Organizational Change Programs of the Survey Research Center of the University of Michigan. The writer is indebted to Dr. Carol Slater for making the data available and for her constructive suggestions on the first draft.

mediated sanctions and is hypothesized to occur to the extent that role performance is relevant to the maintenance of an individual's self-identity. Among the factors found to be associated with internalization were management ratings of the amount of aptitude required in the employee's job and the employee's perceptions of the amount of self-determination on the job.

Gurin, Veroff and Feld (1960) refer to a similar variable in their concept of degree of personal involvement in the work role which they define as the "extent to which an individual seeks some expression and actualization of the self in his work." The degree of job involvement for a particular person was measured by his choice of "ego" rather than extrinsic factors in describing the sources of satisfaction and dissatisfaction on the job. Persons who were ego-involved in their jobs tended to be at the extremes on a scale of job satisfaction and to experience more problems connected with their work.

While it seems unlikely that a single dimension of job involvement or internalization will ultimately do justice to the ego relevant aspects of work motivation, it may suffice until further evidence is obtained concerning the value of such concepts in the explanation of behavior both within and outside the work situation. For purposes of the present research, a person will be described as ego-involved in a task or job to whatever extent his self-esteem is affected by his perceived level of performance. The present study will be concerned with the relevance of ego-involvement for job performance and job satisfaction.

Ego Involvement and Job Performance

Since, by definition, the self-esteem of persons who are ego-involved in their jobs is directly related to their evaluation of their level of performance, it seems reasonable to predict that on the average they would tend to be more highly motivated to perform effectively on their jobs than persons who are not ego-involved. Such motivation might be expected to be translated into effective job performance in the absence of barriers preventing the worker from attaining the desired level of performance. Such barriers might stem from properties of the person (e.g., lack of ability or knowledge) or environmental conditions (e.g., machine breakdowns, lack of needed cooperation from other persons, etc.). Where the worker had the necessary abilities to perform the job and had control over his own work pace, motivational variables like ego-involvement would be expected to be related to measures of job performance. On the other hand, where the worker lacked the requisite abilities, or where he lacked the freedom to set his work pace, no such relation would be predicted.

Support for the hypothesized interaction between ability and motivational variables has been obtained in studies by French (1957), Georgopoulos, Mahoney, and Jones (1957), and by Vroom (1960). No further replication of this observation will be attempted here. The second type of variable hypothesized to interact with motivation in the determination of job performance, autonomy in setting one's work pace, will be explored in the present study. The expected relationships between autonomy, ego-involvement and performance is stated in Hypothesis I.

> Hypothesis I. The greater the amount of autonomy afforded a person in his work role, the greater the positive relationship between the amount of his ego-involvement in his job and his level of job performance.

## EGO INVOLVEMENT AND JOB SATISFACTION

Gurin, Veroff and Feld's finding (1960), that individuals who are personally involved in their jobs are more frequently at the extremes of job satisfaction, suggests that ego-involvement may both facilitate and hinder satisfaction and adjustment, depending on the nature of the work performed by the person and the conditions of the work environment. Persons who are ego-involved in their jobs may be affected by certain environmental conditions to which those who are less ego-involved are indifferent.

There are a large number of aspects of the work role which have in past studies been found related to job satisfaction. While there is at present no adequate basis for the conceptualization of the work role in motivationally relevant terms, it is often assumed that the content of job is more "ego relevant" than are the social and physical characteristics of the work environment. Jobs which provide for the exercise of individual judgment and initiative, which provide for the use and development of aptitudes, and which permit some knowledge of the results of a person's performance are more "ego satisfying" than those which do not have these characteristics. For purposes of this paper, we will borrow from Super (1957) the concept of "opportunity for self-expression" to refer to a constellation of these factors.

The expected relationship between opportunity for self-expression, ego-involvement, and satisfaction is stated in Hypothesis II.

Hypothesis II. The more ego-involved a person is in his job the greater the positive relationship between the amount of his opportunity for self-expression in that job and his job satisfaction and adjustment.

## METHOD

Data relevant to the first hypothesis were obtained in a study of 94 supervisory and 305 nonsupervisory employees in a medium-sized electronics manufacturing company located in the southwestern United States. The second hypothesis was tested in a study of 489 hourly blue collar workers in a large Canadian oil refinery. The measures used in both studies are described below:

## EGO-INVOLVEMENT (BOTH STUDIES)

This variable was measured by means of the following question:

Q. If a problem comes up in your work and it isn't all settled by the time you go home, how likely is it that you will find yourself thinking about it after work?
\_\_\_\_ I am almost sure to think about it after work.
\_\_\_\_ There's a pretty good chance I'll think about it.
\_\_\_\_ I probably wouldn't think about it.
\_\_\_\_ I'm almost sure I wouldn't think about it after work.

In view of the importance attached to this single question throughout this study, a few words need to be said about the conceptual and empirical foundation for our assumption that it represents a measure of ego-involvement. Stemming from research by Zeigarnik (1938, pp. 300–314) and theoretical development by Lewin (1951), the intention to complete a task can be regarded as setting up a tension system within the person. If performance on the task is interrupted, the tension system persists and is reflected in a somewhat greater probability of recall of the incompleted task. While the evidence is not unequivocal, there is considerable support for the further proposition that the effects of interruption of a task or problem on the development of a tension system within the person is directly related to the extent to which the person is ego-involved in the performance of the task or problem. Zeigarnik (1938, pp. 300–314) reports, for example, that persons who are not "ambitious" and those who look on the tasks as a chore show no evidence of differential recall of completed and incompleted tasks. In a more recent experiment, Atkinson (1953) found that the tendency to recall a larger proportion of incompleted than completed tasks was a function of the amount of aroused achievement motivation, being greatest for subjects high in n achievement who perform the tasks under achievement-orienting instructions.

Empirical evidence supporting the validity of this assumption and the construct validity of this question as a measure of involvement has been presented by Slater (1959). Additional supporting evidence from the present study indicates that persons with high scores on the ego-involvement measure report that they are more highly involved in their jobs and more frequently report that they get the strongest satisfaction on the job from turning in a good performance than those with low scores.

### Job Satisfaction (Oil Refinery Study Only)

Sum of responses to the following three questions:

Q. 1. How do you feel about your supervisor?
____ Very well satisfied
____ Well satisfied
____ Satisfied
____ Not too well satisfied
____ Not at all satisfied

Q. 2. How do you feel about the kind of work that you do on your job?
____ Like it very much
____ Like it
____ Neither like it nor dislike it
____ Dislike it
____ Dislike it very much

Q. 3. All in all, how do you feel about your job?
____ Very satisfied
____ Satisfied
____ Neither satisfied nor dissatisfied
____ Not very well satisfied
____ Not at all satisfied

In addition to job satisfaction, measures of satisfaction with self, satisfaction with health, work-related tension and absences were obtained. While undoubtedly influenced by conditions outside the work situation, these four variables may be regarded as reflecting some aspects of the worker's adjustment to his job.

## Opportunity for Self-Expression in the Job (Oil Refinery Study Only)

Sum of responses to 9 questions concerning ego-relevant properties of job.

How much chance do you get
1. to do interesting work?
2. to try out your own ideas?
3. to do the kinds of things you are best at?
4. to feel at the end of the day that you've accomplished something?
5. to learn new things?
6. to finish things?
7. to do things your own way?
8. to work without feeling pushed?
9. to use the skills you have learned for this job?

Each question was answered on a five-point scale (a very good chance to no chance). An analysis of the intercorrelations between the 9 items for 489 cases indicated that all items are positively correlated with coefficients ranging from .26 to .57, with a median of .39.

## Job Performance (Electronics Manufacturing Study Only)

The sum of ratings of the employee by his supervisor on the following seven-point performance review scales:

_____ Quality of work
_____ Quantity of work
_____ Dependability
_____ Knowledge of job
_____ Judgment and common sense
_____ Personality
_____ Ability to learn
_____ Initiative

_____ Cooperation

_____ Industry and application

## AUTONOMY (ELECTRONICS MANUFACTURING STUDY ONLY)

Three different measures of autonomy were used:

1. *Self-report* — measured by the following question:

Q. 1. How free do you feel to set your own work pace?

_____ I have no freedom at all to set my own work pace

_____ I have little freedom

_____ I have some freedom

_____ I have quite a bit of freedom

_____ I am completely free to set my own work pace

2. *Supervisory — Nonsupervisory Classification* — Supervisors were assumed to be higher in autonomy than nonsupervisors.

3. *Departmental Membership* — Based on the assumption that the amount of autonomy afforded an individual in his work role varies with the centrality of his department to the productive process of the organization, respondents were classified into high, moderate, and low autonomy groups on the basis of their departmental membership.[1]

Central Research Department — High Autonomy

Engineering             — Moderate Autonomy

Manufacturing       — Low Autonomy

## RESULTS

Our first hypothesis, concerning the relationship between ego-involvement and job performance, was tested on data from the electronics manufacturing organization. A positive relationship was predicted between these two variables, with the magnitude of the relationship being a direct function of the amount of autonomy afforded the person. This hypothesis was tested in the electronics study by comparing the mean job performance scores of persons high in ego-involvement (almost sure to think about it) with those with lower scores on ego-involvement (pretty good chance — I'm almost sure I wouldn't think about it).[2] Separate comparisons were made for those at various levels of autonomy.

Table 1 shows a significant over-all difference in the predicted direction between the rated performance of employees high and low in

## TABLE 1

*Relationship Between Ego-Involvement and Rated Job Performance for Persons with Various Degrees of Work Autonomy*

(Electronics Study)

| | High Ego-Involvement | Low Ego-Involvement | Difference | $P_t$ |
|---|---|---|---|---|
| Total | 52.64 (N = 241) | 50.35 (N = 158) | 2.29 | .01 |
| High autonomy (supervisors) | 57.53 (N = 72) | 54.64 (N = 22) | 2.89 | ns |
| Low autonomy (nonsupervisors) | 50.56 (N = 169) | 49.66 (N = 136) | .90 | ns |
| High autonomy* (complete freedom to set own work pace) | 54.18 (N = 61) | 50.52 (N = 21) | 3.66 | ns |
| Moderate autonomy (quite a bit of freedom) | 52.51 (N = 136) | 50.68 (N = 100) | 1.83 | ns |
| Low autonomy (some, little, or no freedom) | 51.02 (N = 43) | 49.38 (N = 37) | 1.64 | ns |
| High autonomy** (Central Research) | 58.76 (N = 94) | 55.88 (N = 48) | 2.88 | .01 |
| Moderate autonomy (Engineering) | 51.12 (N = 43) | 49.22 (N = 36) | 1.90 | ns |
| Low autonomy (Manufacturing) | 44.20 (N = 46) | 43.50 (N = 38) | .70 | ns |

* One respondent failed to answer the question on work pace, leaving a total of 398 subjects for this analysis.

** 77 employees from central staff unit and 17 employees from a miscellaneous group are left out of this analysis.

ego-involvement. There is also some evidence in support of the hypothesis that the positive relationship between ego-involvement and performance is greater for persons with high autonomy. The differences between the mean scores on performance of persons high and low in ego-involvement are greater for supervisors than non-supervisors; greatest for persons reporting complete freedom to set own work pace and least for persons reporting the only some, little, or no freedom to set own work pace; and greatest for the department rated highest in autonomy (Central Research) and least for the department rated lowest in autonomy (Manufacturing). While all of these findings are in the predicted direction, none of the differences between autonomy groups are significant.

The second hypothesis, concerning differential effects of opportunity for self-expression in the job on the satisfaction and adjustment of persons with various degrees of ego-involvement in their jobs, was tested on data from the oil refinery study. Persons who are highly ego-involved in their jobs were predicted to be more affected by the amount of their opportunity for self-expression.

This hypothesis was tested by correlating the measure of opportunity for self-expression with measures of satisfaction and adjustment for persons high, moderate, and low in ego-involvement.[3] The results of this analysis are reported in Table 2.

For the total population, significant positive relationships were obtained between perceived opportunity for self-expression and job satisfaction, satisfaction with self, and satisfaction with health, and a significant negative relationship with work-related tension. Considerable support was also found for the prediction that opportunity for self-expression will have more effect on persons high in ego-involvement. Of the 15 differences between correlations, only one is in the opposite direction to the prediction. Two of the five differences be-

**TABLE 2**

*Relationship Between Perceived Opportunity for Self-Expression and Measures of Satisfaction and Adjustment Among Persons with High, Moderate and Low Ego-Involvement*

(Oil Refinery Study)

| Correlation Between Opportunity for Self-Expression in Job and: | Total (489) | Ego-Involvement | | | $P_{t(H-L)}$ | $P_{t(H-M)}$ | $P_{t(M-L)}$ |
|---|---|---|---|---|---|---|---|
| | | High (H) $(N = 121)$ | Moderate (M) $(N = 270)$ | Low (L) $(N = 98)$ | | | |
| Job satisfaction...... | .59 | .62 | .65 | .36 | .01* | ns | .01* |
| Satisfaction with self. | .14 | .30 | .15 | −.05 | .01* | ns | ns |
| Satisfaction with health............. | .16 | .20 | .16 | .09 | ns | ns | ns |
| Work-related tension. | −.21 | −.32 | −.20 | −.20 | ns | ns | ns |
| Absences............. | −.05 | −.14 | −.03 | .04 | ns | ns | ns |

* In the predicted direction.

tween the correlations for the high and low groups (on job satisfaction and satisfaction with self) are significant at the .01 level, while one of the differences between moderate and low groups reaches that level.

While the findings support Hypothesis II, at least for measures of job satisfaction and satisfaction with self, it is difficult to draw definitive conclusions from a field study such as this one concerning causal relations between specific variables. In addition to the ever present problem in inferring direction of causality, many variables remain uncontrolled in the typical field study. It is possible that the groups which we have termed high, moderate, and low in ego-involvement are also different in some other variable which could account for the results. An examination of the level of pay in the three ego-involvement groups indicated differences — with highly ego-involved persons the highest paid and those low in ego-involvement the lowest. In order to eliminate the possibility that the differences in correlations were due to pay or related differences in occupational level and not to ego-involvement, three new ego-involvement groups were selected from the same subjects but with identical distribution of scores on the pay variable. The correlations between opportunity for self-expression and both job satisfaction and satisfaction with self for these matched groups indicate that none of the correlations has been appreciably altered by controlling for pay and the differences between high and low ego-involvement groups remain.

Table 3 presents the correlations among the dependent variables used in the oil refinery study and ego-involvement. The measure of ego-involvement is not significantly related to any of the measures

TABLE 3

*Pearson Product-Moment Correlations Among Variables*
(Oil Refinery Study, $N$ = 489)

| | 2 | 3 | 4 | 5 | 6 |
|---|---|---|---|---|---|
| 1. Ego-involvement............... | .03 | −.08 | −.05 | −.01 | +.25* |
| 2. Job satisfaction................ | | .29* | .18* | −.07 | −.25* |
| 3. Satisfaction with self........... | | | .27* | −.04 | −.13* |
| 4. Satisfaction with health........ | | | | −.10 | −.09 |
| 5. Absences...................... | | | | | .03 |
| 6. Work-related tension........... | | | | | |

* Significant of the .01 level.

TABLE 4

*Mean Scores on Job Satisfaction for Persons with Different Degrees of Ego-Involvement and Perceived Opportunities for Self-Expression*

(Oil Refinery Study)

| Opportunity for Self-Expression | Ego-Involvement | | |
|---|---|---|---|
| | High ($N$ = 121) | Moderate ($N$ = 270) | Low ($N$ = 98) |
| High ($N$ = 152).................. | 13.39 | 13.40 | 12.78 |
| Moderate ($N$ = 182).............. | 12.31 | 11.90 | 12.14 |
| Low ($N$ = 155)................... | 10.65 | 10.25 | 11.14 |

of satisfaction, but it does show a significant positive correlation with job-related anxiety. This tendency for persons who are highly involved in their jobs to feel more anxious is consistent with the earlier results of Gurin, Veroff and Feld (1960).

While six of the ten correlations among the dependent variables are significant at the .01 level, the absence measure is not significantly related to any of the other dependent variables and the relationships among the other variables are not very large in magnitude. The largest correlation is .29 between job satisfaction and satisfaction with self. The fact that similar results are found using dependent variables which are relatively independent may be taken as adding further support to Hypothesis II.

The correlational analysis presented in Table 3 does not enable one to determine the relative amounts of satisfaction occurring with various degrees of ego-involvement and opportunity for self-expression. In Tables 4 and 5 the same data were used but they are presented in

TABLE 5

*Mean Scores on Satisfaction with Self for Persons with Different Degrees of Ego-Involvement and Perceived Opportunities for Self-Expression*

(Oil Refinery Study)

| Opportunity for Self-Expression | Ego-Involvement | | |
|---|---|---|---|
| | High ($N$ = 121) | Moderate ($N$ = 270) | Low ($N$ = 98) |
| High ($N$ = 152)................ | 3.94 | 4.04 | 4.04 |
| Moderate ($N$ = 182)........... | 3.78 | 3.75 | 3.67 |
| Low ($N$ = 155)................ | 3.43 | 3.79 | 4.00 |

somewhat different form. Mean scores on job satisfaction and satisfaction with self are given for persons with high, moderate, and low degrees of ego-involvement having various amounts of opportunity for self-expression.

It should be noted that persons who are high in ego-involvement with low opportunities for self-expression manifest the least amount of satisfaction with self and are next to the lowest in job satisfaction. Similar findings were obtained for the dependent variables not shown in Tables 4 and 5. Persons highly ego-involved in their work who are receiving little opportunities for self-expression also manifest the lowest satisfaction with their health, the greatest level of experienced tensions, and the highest frequency of absences. For persons low in opportunity for self-expression there is a marked tendency for satisfaction scores to increase and absence and anxiety scores to decrease with decreasing ego-involvement. The only exception to this occurs for job satisfaction where, as previously noted, the lowest mean score was obtained from moderately ego-involved persons.

The results under high opportunity for self-expression conditions are somewhat less clear-cut. On job satisfaction and satisfaction with self there is little variation between the mean scores of the three ego-involvement groups, with the low group having the lowest score on the job satisfaction measure and the high group having the lowest score on the satisfaction with self measure. There is, however, a consistent relationship between ego-involvement and satisfaction with health, tension, and absences which is similar in direction, if somewhat less in degree, than that which occurred under low opportunity for self-expression. There is an increase in the level of tension and in the frequency of absences, and a decrease in the amount of satisfaction with health, as one goes from low through moderate to high ego-involvement persons.

### Discussion of Results

This study has been directed at exploring some of the implications of ego-involvement in a work role for satisfaction with that role and performance within it. While the method used has been that of the field study with its attendant problems of control of variables, and while the measures have been far from precise, the results are generally in support of the hypotheses.

The finding that persons high in ego-involvement are rated higher in job performance than those low in ego-involvement derives from our conceptualizations of ego-involvement as the extent to which self-esteem is affected by level of performance. The results are consistent with Kausler's laboratory experiment (1951) demonstrating a higher level of performance on a learning task for subjects receiving ego-involving instructions than for those receiving task-oriented instructions.

Most attempts to explain the conditions under which persons will be motivated to perform effectively in a job have employed what has been termed a path-goal approach (Georgopoulos, Mahoney & Jones, 1957; Kahn, 1958). A person will be motivated to perform effectively on a task or job to the extent that performance is perceived to be instrumental to the attainment of certain extrinsic incentives. Motivation to produce is a function of the attractiveness of goals or incentives existing in the environment, e.g., money, promotion, acceptance by work group, and the worker's perceptions of the relative usefulness of productivity as a path to the attainment of these goals. The results of the present study suggest the limitations of this model. Persons may derive satisfaction from the performance of tasks independent of the externally-mediated consequences of this performance. An explanation of the conditions affecting motivation for effective performance must include the reward value of various levels of performance as well as the reward value of anticipated consequences of performance.

Although the present study sheds no light on this question, it seems reasonable to hypothesize on the basis of the available evidence that a person becomes ego-involved in the performance of a task to the extent to which performance is perceived to be relevant to certain aptitudes, abilities, or other attributes which are central to a person's self-conception. For example, if a person conceives of himself as intelligent, and if he perceives that performance on a particular task is related to intelligence, he will be ego-involved in performance of that task. A high level of performance under these conditions will be consonant with his self-conception whereas a low level of performance will produce cognitive dissonance (Festinger, 1957).

It seems likely that the constellation of variables which we and others have labeled opportunity for self-expression refers to the relevance of role performance for certain attributes which are likely to be part of the self-concept of most people. The more a task or occupation gives its occupant a chance to try out his own idea, or do the kind of thing that he is best at, the more likely role performance will be perceived by him to be relevant to dimensions which are central to his self-concept. This theoretical argument is given some support in Slater's finding that internalization of motivation for occupational role performance (another name for what we have termed ego-involvement) varies with management's rating of the amount of aptitude required in the job and the employee's perception of the amount of self-determination in his job (Slater, 1959).

The prediction that the relationship between ego-involvement and performance would be greater under conditions of high autonomy received only slight support from the data. While all of the findings are in the predicted direction, none of the differences between autonomy conditions is significant. This result is probably attributable to the rather gross nature of the autonomy variables. There are undoubtedly many other factors associated with each of the measures of autonomy which might have obscured the hypothesized interaction with ego-involvement. In addition to affording their incumbents greater freedom in setting their own pace, high autonomy jobs were generally more highly paying, higher in status, and higher in complexity. The effects of these confounding variables are probably indicated in the large differences between the rated job performance of persons at different levels on each of the autonomy measures (from Table 1). An adequate test of the "autonomy hypothesis" would seem to require a laboratory situation in which extraneous variables can be held constant.

The second finding, that the satisfaction of persons who are ego-involved in their jobs is more affected by the extent to which their jobs give them an opportunity for self-expression, was consistent with our hypothesis. If we make the assumption that ego-involvement in work increases with occupational level, these data also appear consistent with previous findings indicating that the nature of the work activity is less important to persons working at lower occupational levels than for those at higher levels (Centers, 1948; Morse & Weiss, 1955).

In accounting for these findings, we are assuming that persons vary in the extent to which they value and regard themselves as possessing work-related aptitudes and abilities. For some individuals the major components of the self-concept are attributes which are directly or potentially relevant to the work situation, while for others the most central components may relate to other spheres of activity, e.g., marriage, family, community etc. If work-related aptitudes and abilities are central to a person's self-concept, it seems likely that his satisfaction will be affected to a greater extent by the degree to which he has an opportunity to use them in the work situation than if they are peripheral to the self-concept.

It seems possible that, underlying our measure of ego-involvement and others' measures of occupational level, are differences in the centrality of the work-related attributes in the self-conception of the worker. Persons high in ego-involvement and occupying positions at higher occupational levels may be more likely both to value, and to regard themselves as possessing, abilities which are relevant to performance in work situations. Consequently one might expect the nature of the work, particularly those aspects of the work which are relevant to the abilities in question, to be more important in the determination of their satisfaction.

While relevance may be a necessary condition for ego satisfaction in work, it seems unlikely that it is a sufficient condition. Given a task or work role, performance in which is relevant to the worker's self-conception, satisfaction should also vary with level of performance. Cognition by the worker that he has not achieved a high level of performance should be dissonant with his self-conception and should be accompanied by dissatisfaction, while the cognition that he has succeeded in attaining a high level of performance should be consonant with this self-conception and be accompanied by satisfaction.

## SUMMARY

Data obtained from industrial workers in field studies conducted in an oil refinery and in an electronics manufacturing company support the following conclusions:

1) Persons who are ego-involved in their jobs are rated higher in job performance than those who are not ego-involved in their jobs. There is also some tendency for the relationship between ego-involvement and performance to be greater for persons who are high in autonomy, although the results are not significant.
2) The job satisfaction and satisfaction with self of persons who are ego-involved in their jobs is significantly more positively related to the amount of their opportunity for self-expression in their

jobs than is the case for persons low in ego-involvement. Similar but nonsignificant differences were also found for measures of satisfaction with health, reported feelings of tension, and frequency of absences.

## REFERENCES

1. A fourth department, Central Staff, was eliminated from this classification because of the diversity in positions represented, e.g., typists and top management.
2. The high-low breakdown on ego-involvement was chosen over some measure of association between ego-involvement and job performance because of the highly skewed distribution of scores of employees in the electronics organization on the involvement measure. Sixty per cent of the respondents selected the first alternative; 32% the second; 5% the third; and 3% the fourth alternative.
3. A three-way breakdown was made possible by a somewhat different distribution of responses on the ego-involvement measure from that in the electronics study. The 25% of the respondents choosing the first alternative were termed high in ego-involvement, the 55% choosing the second alternative were termed moderate in ego-involvement, while the remaining 20% distributed over the third and fourth alternatives were termed low in ego-involvement.

## REFERENCES

Atkinson, J. W. "The Achievement Motive and Recall of Interrupted and Completed Tasks." *Journal of Experimental Psychology*, XLVIII (1953), 381–390.

Centers, Richard. "Motivational Aspects of Occupational Stratification." *Journal of Social Psychology*, XXVIII (1948), 187–217.

Festinger, Leon. *A Theory of Cognitive Dissonance*. White Plains, New York: Row-Peterson, 1957.

French, E. G. "Effects of Interaction of Achievement, Motivation and Intelligence on Problem Solving Success." *American Psychologist*, XII (1957), 399–400 (Abstract).

Georgopoulos, B., Mahoney, G., and Jones, Nyle. "The Path-Goal Approach to Productivity." *Journal of Applied Psychology*, XLI (1957), 345–353.

Gurin, G., Veroff, J., and Feld, S. *Americans View Their Mental Health.* New York: Basic Books, Inc., 1960.

Kahn, R. L. "Human Relations on the Shop Floor." In E. M. Hugh-Jones (Editor), *Human Relations and Modern Management.* North-Holland, Amsterdam, 1958.

Kausler, Donald H. "A Study of the Relationship Between Ego-Involvement and Learning." *Journal of Psychology,* XXXII (1951), 225–230.

Lewin, Kurt. *Field Theory in Social Science.* New York: Harper and Brothers, 1951.

Morse, N. C. and Weiss, R. "The Function and Meaning of Work and the Job." *American Sociological Review,* XX (1955), 191–198.

Slater, C. W. "Some Factors Associated with Internalization of Motivation Towards Occupational Role Performance." Unpublished Ph.D. thesis, University of Michigan, 1959.

Super, Donald E. *The Psychology of Careers: An Introduction to Vocational Development.* New York: Harper and Brothers, 1957.

Vroom, V. H. *Some Personality Determinants of the Effects of Participation.* Englewood Cliffs, N. J.: Prentice-Hall, 1960.

Zeigarnik, B. "On Finished and Unfinished Tasks." In W. D. Ellis (Editor), *A Source Book of Gestalt Psychology.* New York: Harcourt-Brace, 1938.

# CLIMBERS, RIDERS, TREADERS

## WILBERT E. MOORE

To some of its employees the corporation provides jobs; to others it provides a succession of jobs constituting a "career." The notion of a career carries the connotation of success, of growth in wisdom and power, in rewards and respect. The hourly rated workman rarely has a career in that sense. He may change jobs and employers and improve his position with each change, but not much. He may be the exception who becomes a foreman, but his further advance is likely to be rather limited. He may fulfill the old wage-earner's dream and start his own small business. Whether that business succeeds, barely survives, or fails, this form of "mobility" involves too sharp a break to qualify for the usual meaning of career. Managerial employees and specialists of one sort or another may have careers that involve the slight progression from A to B, or they may travel both far and fast.

Far more is known about the social background and occupational histories of leading corporate executives than about their subordinates or the men who started but did not finish with them. In any statistical sense it is simply not true that there is always room at the top. If everyone in the corporation is aiming for the top, most are doomed to disappointment. Yet enough is known of the corporate environment to dispel some fables and to fill in the outlines of various kinds of careers.

The idea that managers can reasonably expect an orderly progression to higher responsibilities and rewards is clearly correct only for part of them. And for most of those, it is true only within the intersecting limits of personal capacities (or influence or luck) and objective opportunities. There is no reason to suppose that the coincidence of

Reprinted with abridgement from Wilbert E. Moore, *The Conduct of the Corporation*, Vintage Edition (New York: Random House, Inc., 1962) by permission of the publisher and the author.

capacities and opportunities is always neat and orderly, that chance plays no part in the outcome, or that mismatches do not occur.

Between the extremes of outstanding success and miserable failure lie many middle courses. In some of these the race is to the swift. In others, the prize is awarded for endurance or for mere persistence in the safe and steady pace. "He also serves, who only stands and waits."

## LADDERS AND ESCALATORS

The graded career consisting of a sequence of promotions through successive stages in the hierarchy of managerial authority is often called a ladder. For many persons in corporations the figure of speech is apt, as promotions do not come about automatically and for all aspirants. The triangular or pyramidal shape of the organization insures some selectivity, and the ideal of selection on the basis of performance normally requires effort. Thus climbing the ladder requires skill but also energy, a destination and a course of action.

Career ladders vary in length, the steps may be unevenly spaced, and the rate of ascent even for the same person may be uneven. Thus the language provides us with a variety of phrases descriptive of career differences. Certain career lines, which are potentially the longer ones, are called the "main line" or the "main stream." Others promise early arrival at a "dead end" or maroon people in some "backwater." The man who has reached a critical juncture in his career may be "bouncing his head against the ceiling," and his head may be less durable than the ceiling. Some individuals by some combination of merit and opportunity may have a "meteoric rise." By a kind of standing high-jump, an occasional contestant may skip several rungs of the ladder altogether. Others, after years of slight progress, may turn out to be "late bloomers." Still others, the "plodders," advance inch by painful inch, until age overtakes them at a fairly low level.

The ladder may be so short that the simile is questionable. First-line supervisors, normally recruited from the ranks of hourly-rated workers, are assured by higher management that they are on the bottom rung of the managerial ladder. This is normally deceitful, for the situation is that the ladder has at most one or two more steps, and often none at all. The foreman has mounted a platform rather than started a long climb.

Several large corporations have made much in their "institutional" advertising of the humble beginnings of their current top executives. Such advertising though certainly not false is certainly misleading. Current top executives started their careers and in fact completed much of their ascent prior to the extreme emphasis on higher education, general and technical, as a virtual prerequisite for a successful managerial career. If the presidents of large corporations started work as lathe operators, stock boys, or shipping clerks, it is quite unlikely that their successors will have started at ground level and virtually certain that their next-but-one successors will not have done so. Most current executives in fact had college educations, and the first company job was a brief "authenticating" apprenticeship.

The educational barrier in fact introduces a sharp discontinuity in types of careers. It is the principal reason for the low ceiling for supervisors. In the absence of precise data my guess is that the realistic horizon for a foreman in a large company stops at the level of assistant plant superintendent in a small plant or "general foreman" in a large one — in other words, two additional steps. Other managerial careers start with college diplomas and company training courses, perhaps followed by further apprenticeship in definitely non-supervisory positions. The man's first strictly managerial assignment, such as sales manager for a small and distant district or assistant production manager for a small unit in a manufacturing plant, is really the bottom step of his ladder. But he got on that ladder somewhere around the third or fourth rung. . . .

The competitive effort to fashion a career, each step won with a struggle, is clearly one form of career orientation. The men who are ambitious, who seek success in the new fashion of the administrative career rather than the old fashion of commerce or the individual enterprise, are the *strainers*. These are the men who keep alert, look smart, avoid missteps, and attempt to show up well on assignments or in group policy discussion. They have ideas if requested and otherwise find cogent reasons for supporting the wisdom of the boss's ideas. They learn golf, join the right clubs, think the right thoughts. Their wives are attractive but not brazen, entertain the right people, and suggest that John is brilliant as well as hard-working, a dedicated corporate servant but also a wonderful husband and father.

These strainers are widely depicted as typical of managerial folk.

To their competitive aspirations, their "status seeking," are attributed the competitiveness of their children, their conspicuous consumption, their political conservatism, their superficial religious conformity, and their latest struggles with crab grass.

I do not doubt the existence of strainers. Some of them are my neighbors and some of them are my friends. I do think their typicality is questionable. I question it because it seems to me that for many corporate careers the analogy of the ladder is scarcely appropriate. Some moderately successful people in corporations appear to be on escalators. Once they successfully mount the bottom step, it would take positive effort to avoid going to the next level.

To contrast with the strainers I offer the category of *secure mobiles*. Their lines of ascent may not reach to the dizzy heights attainable by some who struggle all the way. They do, however, provide assurance of modest progress not by doing nothing but also not by doing anything exceptional. Many staff positions have low ceilings from where the man starts, but that may be fairly high in the organization. The ceiling constitutes the level beyond which the man ceases to be a technician or professional, an information supplier, and becomes an administrator. That transition may be neither easy nor, to the occupationally committed employee, desirable. Short of that transition, the man may grow in value and rewards and possibly in autonomy of action by doing what he presumably likes to do — his job.

The secure mobiles are not lazy, but neither do they exhibit the anxious insecurity of the strainers. They may be ambitious but generally not for the power and position offered in a line career. They do not spurn money, but as payment for doing what they are doing and not for something else.

Some escalator riders, it is true, aspire to higher positions than can be achieved in their line of ascent. Thus to "upward" (and occasionally "downward") we must add the concept of "diagonal" mobility. The staff man who enters a managerial position has not just moved up but also across. He has entered a functionally different occupation and a different prospective career.

Over the relatively recent past the most common "diagonal" shift has been the transfer from engineering into administration. Many current engineering graduates are frank in their aspirations to start at their profession (generally at a higher initial salary than the liberal arts college graduate can command) but with no intention of making drawings and computing formulas all their lives. Their aim is to enter administration by the side door. My guess is that they are off-phase.

Such scattered evidence as I have been able to get leads me to a kind of "stage theory" of the primary talents sought in the executives of large corporations. Prior to the turn of the century, financial skills were paramount in assembling and organizing the capitalization of giant concerns. Public reaction and particularly "trust-busting" led to a brief ascendancy of lawyers. Financial operations and legal limits became more stabilized than technology, and with corporate success heavily dependent on technical change, the engineers had their day — that is just about to end. Their successors appear to be in high degree men concerned with organization as such, although this was a common minimum qualification for the others too. My guess is that the near future belongs to "relations experts," men concerned with the corporation's external environment, as that now seems to present the critical problems.

This kind of evolutionary pattern or any other pronounced shift in the demand for talents may not affect the majority of careers. For some, the changing structure of opportunities may be absolutely crucial. Some engineers may end up being engineers and some feeler of the public pulse may end up being president.

## The Rat Race and the Treadmill

Some corporate strainers refer to their work situations as the "rat race," some threaten to get some less demanding job and "live a little," and some in fact do. To the true believers in fighting the good fight, the drop-outs are battle casualties who couldn't stand the gaff and the company is better off without them. (Of course the elimination of competitors does not hurt the career chances of those who remain.) The man who drops out of the rat race may be treated with patronizing sympathy or open contempt. Yet of those who stay, only a few will run the complete maze and reach the cheese. The others are either doomed to frustration or they must find some rationale or rationalization for their positions.

The interplay between aspiration and achievement is an extremely complex one. It is symptomatic of a basic part of American ideology that this problem is nearly always discussed in terms of the handling of frustration. It is assumed that everyone aims for the top of whatever career he enters, and then, if his mental health remains in moderately good repair, he goes through a succession of reality adjustments as objective results fail to match subjective expectations. As a consequence of this ideological bias, almost no attention has been given to the man who has relatively limited expectations (leaving aside his Walter Mitty daydreams) and then succeeds well beyond those expectations (though perhaps still short of those wilder dreams).

For the man who is ambitious but somewhat realistic, expectations and achievements are periodically compared, and the expectations are inflated or deflated accordingly. Since every readjustment involves also an estimate of the future, there are ample opportunities for honest error as well as for neurotic failures in making a reasonable judgment of present reality or future prospects. The man who is "way off the pace" must, as time passes, invent bigger and bigger miracles. The line between this and insanity may become increasingly thin.

There is certainly some unknown incidence of acute frustration among the aspiring men in corporate employment. I think it would be easy to exaggerate the problem by starting from incorrect assumptions. The disparity between aspiration and achievement does not always carry a negative sign, as I just noted. Career choices radically delimit both the nature of the competition and the number of competitors, as the struggle for success is not "a war of each against all." Even the limits of rewards in money, power, or prestige are strongly conditioned by occupational characteristics.

It is particularly the strainers in the main stream, those on the long ladders that lead ultimately to positions carrying very high financial rewards, that raise the issue of frustration. The man who does not aspire to reach the top is unlikely to admit the fact, because he is "expected" to be ambitious. But surely the withdrawal from reality is not so general that most men expect to reach the uppermost ranks. As aspirations approach the quality of being realistic, the disparity between hopes and achievements becomes tolerably narrow.

One major element in limiting aspirations is that the rewards of success are not "free." Particularly in administrative careers, power carries responsibility, unless the organization is grossly unstable. The severity of the burden of responsibility naturally tends to increase with position and power. The time-and-energy demands are likely to grow, and accountability for the actions of others will certainly grow.

In talking with college students aiming for business careers I find them disbelieving that a man might choose to stop his career well short of the highest levels. With the confidence of the young they assume their future willingness to carry any responsibility and instead fix their eyes on the rewards. I think this attitude is partly ideological as well as simply inexperienced. In the American ideological baggage, the man who professes to be satisfied has "given up." He has left the rat race and entered the treadmill, where progress is foredoomed. Contentment is not a permissible goal; in fact, it is downright immoral. The notion that a man likes his job but would not like to replace his superior raises questions as to whether he is suitable for the job he has. I know a successful manager who succeeded too well. He actively dislikes his job, which he got because of his excellent record at the next lower level in a more technical assignment. He was afraid to refuse the appointment because he did not believe he would be permitted to keep the job he liked. He would, he believed, be put out of harm's way in a job even less to his liking than the one he accepted and hates.

Many men are protected against revealing their weakness of character, their dislike for devoting their lives exclusively to their job and for living dangerously. Others apparently enjoy the challenge and the rewards. Out of common human decency, one can hope that these men of a strong will are not far more numerous than the positions that need them.

# BUREAUCRATIC PATTERNS

## ARTHUR K. DAVIS

This paper concerns the sociology of occupations. Our specific hypothesis is: *the effective performance of the manifest functions of a military bureaucracy requires a certain type of occupational discipline and formal organization; these in turn tend to create inherent pressures toward recession of goals, occupational ritualism, and professional insulation; which in turn may alter the actor's definition of the situation so as to impair systematically his effectiveness in carrying out the manifest functions of the bureaucracy.*[1]

Concrete data for this paper, which in no way represents the official views of the Navy Department, are based on three years in the Naval Reserve as an Air Combat Intelligence Officer with two Fleet Air Wings. Observations are limited to four aspects of naval social organization: (1) the tendency to avoid responsibility; (2) legalism; (3) the Navy as an insulated occupation; (4) ceremonialism. These aspects are functionally related to each other and to the ideal (normative) pattern of military bureaucracy, whence they issue and upon which they profoundly react. This study relates the ideal pattern or "manifest structure" of a military bureaucracy to concrete social reality. It points to unintended "latent structures" which necessarily emerge from attempts to realize in practice an abstract ideal pattern.[2]

For scientific relevance participant-observer studies like this one depend on integration with a more highly generalized theoretical system. Empirical observation can thus gain support and validity from the body of older propositions, which in turn it may confirm or refine. In this way a series of such observations may form a significant element of cumulative, systematic and therefore compelling scientific knowledge, though each investigation by itself may provide merely plausible "post factum" sociological interpretations, "proving" nothing.[3]

Reprinted with abridgement from "Bureaucratic Patterns in the Navy Officer Corps" in *Social Forces* (Vol. 27, December 1948, pp. 143-153) by permission of the publisher and author.

This study is accordingly oriented to the work of Weber and Parsons on institutional structure and to the significant contributions made by Merton and Barnard in the field of large-scale organization.[4]

## I. THE NAVY AS A MILITARY VARIANT OF BUREAUCRACY

In terms of occupational functions the Navy corresponds to the general occupational pattern of modern industrial economies. On an ideal-typical level, this pattern may be conceived as large-scale organization, the upper and smaller division of which is a steep hierarchy of executive and technical-expert functions ("line" and "staff"), roughly equivalent to Weber's concept of bureaucracy. The lower division is a broad mass of easily learned "labor" roles (operatives, enlisted men), usually classified as skilled, semi-skilled, and unskilled. The "foreman" role (army noncom, navy Chief Petty Officer) is a subsidiary link between the two divisions.

Our present concern is with the upper division, the Navy Officer Corps, the social structure of which is highly bureaucratized. A label and not an epithet, bureaucracy denotes an integrated hierarchy of specialized offices defined by systematic rules — an impersonal routinized structure wherein legitimized authority rests in the office and not in the person of the incumbent. Founded on technical competence, the bureaucratic career begins with successful examination or appointment to office, and it proceeds by regular stages of promotion, often based largely on seniority, to honorable and pensioned retirement. Salary is better conceived as a means of maintaining requisite social status than as a wage for irksome labor. We do not "pay" military men to risk their lives in war. Rather, we give them high social status and tacitly invoke extraordinary service on the principle of *noblesse oblige*. Officers are gentlemen by common consent as well as by legal fiat, as is shown by their frequent admission to exclusive clubs regardless of their social origins.

Achieving any high occupational status usually involves a probationary ordeal which inculcates the requisite technical skills sometimes, and the necessary social attitudes and behavior patterns always. Examples are an Annapolis education or getting a Ph.D. Such apprenticeship devices are often ritual rather than rational.

The key to understanding the military variant of bureaucracy probably lies in (1) its ultimate purpose of winning battles; (2) the highly "seasonal" nature of combat operations; (3) the consequently acute problem of maintaining a battle organization during long stand-by periods. Sociologically, a Navy is a bureaucratic organization designed to operate under battle conditions which rarely occur. Civilian groups can usually operate in terms of probabilities calculated from their everyday experience. But in military groups the dire consequences of defeat preclude routines based to the same degree on the weight of experience, that is, on non-combat conditions. A Navy can never exist entirely in the present. It must keep in view a future moment which rarely comes, but which must be assumed as constantly impending. Hence it builds its routines on the abnormal, its expectations on the unexpected. This procedure affords a rational technique for war and an equally necessary rationale for peacetime.

The extreme uncertainty of the battle situation directly affects the social organization of the Navy. Size alone would impose the bureaucratic pattern on Naval organization. Coordination of masses of men and material clearly requires those properties of precision, impersonality, and reliability which make bureaucracy the most efficient form of large-scale organization. The battle premise greatly intensifies the need for those same qualities. This pressure is met by an extraordinary emphasis on authority and tradition which also serves the need for peacetime self-maintenance.

The essence of any military organization is its structure of authority, the ultimate source of which is the enormous file of written regulations. Military groups carry the normal bureaucratic stress on authority to its extreme development. It is the function of a multitude of practices — drills, musters, inspections, deference to superiors — to minimize uncertainty by instilling habits of automatic response that will survive the distractions of combat and the *ennui* of peace. Reducing the jobs of officers and men to the simplest possible operations permits rapid substitution of personnel on the principle of the interchangeability of standardized parts. Uniforms and insignia, by "telegraphing" the wearer's status in the hierarchy of authority and his job in the division of labor, facilitate communication, coordination and impersonality.

Against the hazards of sea and battle, a mass of rules is designed for every possible occasion. Men must come to attention at the approach of an officer. This is partly because he may announce an emergency wherein split-second response is the only alternative to destruction. Such a consideration will be irrelevant 999 times, but navies are more prone than other groups to take the thousandth chance as their norm. The other 999 cases symbolically reaffirm and "exercise" the Navy's basic social structure — its system of authority. Both as rehearsal for battle and as a device for self-perpetuation of the organization, deference is an instrumental pattern. Yet its endless repetition tends to build up the pattern as an end in itself so that hierarchy comes to be an ultimate value far beyond its instrumental requirements.

Carrying out his prime function of military command may require a line officer to order men to death. Impersonality is often a prerequisite to maximum efficiency both in issuing and obeying the order; hence the institutionalizing of the "caste line" between officers and enlisted men. Within the Officer Corps the danger from particularism is minimized partly by the secondary caste lines which exist between all commissioned ranks, especially between Ensign and Lieutenant (junior grade) between Lieutenant-Commander and Commander, and between Captain and Flag Offiers. It is also restricted by the Navy's pervasive formality and ritual, both vocational and social. But even more important in reinforcing impersonality is the intensive indoctrination of the Officer Corps with the idea of duty — with such sentiments as "Don't give up the ship." The instrument of this indoctrination is the 4-year Annapolis course. On the enlisted level there is nothing corresponding to this indoctrination. Petty Officers have less need of it since they merely administer the hazardous orders which commissioned officers issue.

The military variant of bureaucracy may thus be viewed as a skewing of Weber's ideal type by the situational elements of uncertainty and standing by. Detailed description of the Navy's "blueprint" organization would tell us how the Navy ought to work without always showing how it actually does work. We turn therefore to some concrete material. Clearly our analysis must be far from comprehensive. The limited empirical uniformities described below, since they are recurrent, may be conceived as structural pressures or tendencies — sometimes overt, sometimes latent — subject in any particular instance to modification by other basic tendencies, by local circumstances, and by the effect of individual personalities. Attention is focused on the Regular Officer Corps. Although by 1945 there were more than five times as many Reserve Officers as there were Regulars, the latter defined the situation to which the others were indoctrinated to conform.

## II. SOME CHARACTERISTICS OF NAVAL ORGANIZATION

A. *Avoiding responsibility: the philosophy of do-the-least.* So pervasive a tendency must be explained primarily in terms of social organization and only secondarily on the basis of particular personalities and local conditions. The "buck-passing" pattern includes (a) minimizing responsibility for making decisions, especially those for which no precedent exists; (b) getting out of doing work (carrying out decisions). Responsibility tends to be passed upward; work, downward. Whenever it is practiced in primary groups, whether in the context of large-scale organization or not, it is generally sanctioned by the primary group as a whole. Sentiments of solidarity together with informal sanctions like ridicule usually keep the members in line. The basic explanation of avoiding responsibility must therefore lie outside the informal organization. It must be sought in the pressures generated by the formal organization or by the situation. Five propositions are submitted.

1. Shunting responsibility upward stems partly from the universal fact that a functionary's area of responsibility invariably exceeds that of his control. No official can direct or even recognize all the complex social, personal, and technical factors operating in his department. Yet he is generally accountable for whatever befalls there, and most strictly and necessarily so in military organizations. For adequate performance and a successful career the official must rely heavily upon favorable attitudes on the part of his superiors. Consequently he is strongly tempted to slide his problems into his superior's lap by asking advice, requesting instructions, securing approval in advance. And he will accept for decision some of his subordinates' problems to minimize uncertainty in his own sphere of accountability. Responsibility for making decisions tends to move upward. This does not apply to authority to carry out decisions. Interference by superiors in the routine execution of work is strongly resented.

The discrepancy between control and responsibility makes for avoiding responsibility particularly in the lower and middle levels of a bureaucracy. For the man at the top there is no such escape from the strains of decision except by a do-nothing policy. Another pressure on top executives is to find subordinates who will get things done.

2. A second incentive for buck-passing is the latent conflict between authority and specialization. When organizations involve elements as

dynamic as science and technology, officials sometimes lack the specialized knowledge prerequisite to making adequate decisions. The temptation is strong to get rid of such problems as soon as possible. The rapidity of wartime technological and organizational changes made for an extraordinary circulation of these hot potatoes among military units.

The two tendencies just outlined are in some degree common to all bureaucratic hierarchies. Business corporations partly counteract these pressures by making status and rewards depend heavily on individual initiative. These incentives and sanctions are less available to the Navy, where seniority is primary and competition often operates negatively. Officer personnel are seldom dismissed, and then usually for offences against discipline rather than for incompetence. "Misfits" are often transferred to posts where they can do no harm. In military organizations the rewards for assuming responsibility and the penalties for failing to do so seem less extreme than in the business world.

Moreover cost reduction is a constant pressure in modern capitalism. No such compulsion operates on military organizations, whose competition for income is lobbying for a larger share of the federal budget. Lobbying is confined to a few top officers, whereas the cost-consciousness of many business firms permeates their entire hierarchy.

3. Bureaucracies often develop an *esprit de corps* which congeals individual initiative. They present two conflicting goal-orientations: (a) the tangible and intangible rewards for efficient performance in the formally defined role; (b) the informal social satisfactions from harmonious in-group relations, which are prerequisite to (a) yet incompatible with the invidious sentiments aroused by (a). For the "eager beaver" often appears to his fellows as a threat to their status and self-esteem. Epithets such as "sucking around" and "brown-nosing" operate as informal sanctions.[5] The resultant *esprit* protects in-group solidarity by restraining competition and resists change by intrenching vested interests.

The "sucker philosophy" of the Armed Forces grew partly from this conflict. The widespread sentiments against volunteering for special tasks were tacitly recognized and conciliated by "compulsory volunteering" ("Three volunteers — you and you and you!"). Enlisted men seeking commissions were observed to conceal the fact from their fellows, although they discussed it freely with their officers. Trainees at the Quonset Officers Indoctrination School were invariably eager beavers until they got out on a billet. The zeal of trainees at the Navy Air Combat Intelligence School contrasted sharply with the later indifference of the same officers back for a refresher course. Instructors without field experience loaded graduating student officers with intelligence publications. But instructors who had seen field duty advised the graduates to stow such paraphernalia in the nearest furnace and to carry whisky instead. It was the writer's observation that the latter advice was the more functional.

4. Structuralized discrepancies between individual effort and reward in military systems restrain initiative in both war and peace, though for different reasons. The wartime Services expanded so rapidly that they could attend only to categories and not to individuals. The imputed needs of the organization at the moment determined the disposition of resources. Most of the individual's vital interests — his work, friends, rewards, punishments — were largely outside his control. Uncertainty evokes many responses, including "griping," scapegoating, magic, and religious conversion. Here we will indicate only its relation to buck-passing.

Zeal could bring undesirable results as often as not. An "eager beaver" might be held overseas or in rank longer than less valuable personnel. Sudden transfer to another unit could deprive a man of the fruits of prestige hard-earned in his old outfit. Unearned rewards might fall into his lap. Everyone knew of such cases if he did not experience them himself. Many basic needs which are major incentives in civilian occupations are furnished automatically in the Service. All this contributed to fatalism and inertia. The individual naturally sought refuge in his primary-group relationships. If clique behavior did not modify one's formal situation, it did at least make it more endurable.

Competitive achievement officially counted for promotion in the Army Officer Corps but not in the Navy except for rare "spot" promotions and for ranks above Lieutenant Commander. But the Army system aroused more discontent. Its capriciousness was due to (1) the exigencies of the organization; (2) lack of standardized competitive criteria; (3) invidiousness aroused by competition. And non-competitive criteria (e.g. seniority) drew resentment because they contradicted official ideology. Navy promotions, based on seniority, evoked less resistance, although the fact that some incompetents went up with everyone else was disliked because of the implied downward levelling.

In time of peace unpredictability is minimized, but a ritualism stemming from minute observance of routine and regulation submerges initiative more than ever. Military organizations between wars, in terms of their wartime *raison d'etre*, are relatively lacking in manifest functions. To maintain their organization they must fall back on routine for its own sake. Security and every possible comfort are provided, unhampered by wartime hazards and improvisations. The philosophy of Do-the-least rules unchallenged.[6]

5. The unofficial conception of a Regular Navy career often minimizes assumption of responsibility. Promotions below and to Lieutenant Commander are *en bloc*, based on seniority, examination, and quotas authorized by Congress. Higher appointments are filled by individual selection. Elaborate "fitness reports" on each officer are periodically filed with the Navy Department by his superior. During the war these examination and quota rules were suspended, and mass promotions in the junior grades became in effect automatic on completion of the specified months in rank. The ranks above Lieutenant Commander continued to be filled by individual selection. Despite the large element of seniority the naval career is competitive in important respects, and it thus conforms roughly to the basic occupational pattern of the United States. In peacetime the "up or out" principle is applied to all ranks.

But this is often a negative competition to avoid departure from precedent. If an officer makes a decision unsupported by regulation or custom he is sticking out his neck, because he is officially responsible for his acts and nothing will save him if things go wrong. Deviation from routine may pull down his fitness report and cause him to be passed over years later by the Selection Board. It is difficult indeed to escape indoctrination with a psychology of affirm-and-conform. Minimizing responsibility is simply playing it safe. This is reinforced by the inherent exaltation of authority-obedience relationships in military organizations, by the relatively greater role of seniority in the early and formative stages of the career, and by strong tendencies toward ritualism and legalism.

An apparent exception to the buck-passing philosophy was the Construction (Seabee) Branch. Its slogan, "Can Do," seems to have been a realistic index of attitudes toward work and responsibility. Instances on Okinawa were observed where Seabee outfits consistently volunteered for additional *routine* tasks — a sharp contrast to the atmosphere in the writer's own attachment, a relatively elite combat command. A partial explanation may be the fact that the Seabees were drawn from the construction industry with a minimum of occupational reorientation. They could give maximum scope to the industry's best traditions of visible achievement and ingenious improvisation.

B. *Legalism: the psychology of affirm-and-conform.* This results from the characteristic bureaucratic tendency toward displacement or recession of goals whereby instrumental patterns become ends in themselves. A Navy's hierarchy of authority is necessarily overemphasized because of (a) the primacy of authority-obedience relationships in military groups; (b) the necessity for bureaucracies to proliferate and to refine rule-systems so as to minimize role-conflict; (c) the prevalence of the "play-it-safe" attitude toward the naval career. Regulation becomes a sacred cow.

The minimizing of role-conflicts in a complex organization requires a clear definition of jurisdictions. Because of the need for standardization, new situations bring a ceaseless flow of new regulations. *Navy Regulations* specifies detailed behavior for thousands of situations. If trouble results from failure to observe these directions, responsibility can be pinned on someone. Against the pressure of authority from above, the sole defense of the individual lies in strictly observing regulations — an outcome reinforced by the endless routine in naval life.[7]

Bureaucratic personnel suffer from chronic status-anxiety. Everyone focuses his attention on his superior, whose slightest display of pleasure or displeasure is magnified and distorted downward. The mildest criticism from a superior is often viewed by the recipient as a crushing attack. Praise may bring an accusation of "brown-nosing" from one's colleagues. To counteract both these tensions is one function of the Navy's extraordinarily emphasized norm of "loyalty upward."

Combining legalism and avoidance of unnecessary responsibility, we arrive at the golden rule for the professional military career: Follow the book or pass the buck.

C. *The navy as an insulated occupation.* To some extent every bureaucracy and occupation draws its members into common interaction, though not intensively. But in the Regular Navy Officer Corps both workaday routine and out-of-hours social life are concentrated largely within the profession. Unusual insulation is a structural feature of the naval occupation.

(1) The separation between place of work and residence characteristic of urban occupations is minimized in the Navy. At sea officers

are thrown together both on and off duty. On shore stations during peacetime, senior officers with their families occupy quarters on the compound. Families living off the station have many interests aboard — the commissary sells food to naval personnel at low cost, free medical care is available, and the well-appointed but inexpensive Officers' Club is the social center for everyone. Whereas Navy families spend most of their time on guarded compounds, other occupations are widely dispersed about the community, subject to a rough class — rather than a strict occupational segregation. One function of the extraordinary formality of Navy routine and social life is to maintain the requisite professional impersonality in the face of this unusually close contact.

(2) The geographic mobility of Navy families needs no emphasis here. The systematic rotation of duty afloat and ashore in different parts of the world reduces local ties, while the fund of common experience in the same places is a significant occupational bond.

(3) The non-political tradition of the American military further reduces participation in the civil community. Whatever an officer would say about professional matters is restricted to communication by the chain of command. Speaking out on non-professional public issues is prevented by the conception of the Forces as nonpartisan servants of the State — a device to avert praetorian tendencies.

(4) A more positive occupational tie is the heavy demand made on officers by social and ritual activities. Formal calls, the extensive use of visiting cards,[8] and similar indispensables of polite social life are legitimized obligations. Unlike other professional or business occupations, the Navy wife must be a "lady" with an unusual mastery of the delicate arts of status-exhibition and status-deference. A working Navy wife would be distressing less for her lack of lady-like tone than for her lack of leisure to do justice to the subtle and intricate expressions of social punctilio.

Numerous other Service customs, some of which the women of Navy families participate in or observe, also act as in-group occupational ties — commissioning ceremonies, visits to ships in port, formal receptions, the impress of training and rituals at Annapolis.[9] Above all must be stressed the wearing of uniforms and the lore and lingo of Navy life. A unique occupational vocabulary serves both utilitarian and symbolic purposes. It provides essential nomenclature, thereby setting the group apart in its specialized knowledge; and it verbalizes in-group attitudes, thus strengthening them and performing the same latent function as ritual.[10] Few other occupations are knit by such ancient traditions or by so much symbolism.

The margin of personal choice in out-of-hours social life is much smaller in the Navy than in most other occupations. In the latter one is generally free to accept or decline a relatively larger proportion of whatever social participation is accessible. In the Regular Navy there is a definite pecking order according to the husbands' dates of rank. References to a wife usually specify the husband's rank: "Mrs. X, wife of Commander X." Invitations from higher ranking officers or their wives have the force and often the form of positive orders. Little time is left for social ties outside Navy circles, even if such were desired.

(5) Another way to indicate the Navy's insulation is to refer to its strong *esprit de corps,* some ingredients of which have just been outlined. *Esprit* is based on common traditions, symbols, shared routines and goal-orientations — in brief, an integrated way of life. The forces segregating naval personnel contribute to their morale and their in-group cohesiveness with results both functional and disfunctional for the system. Strong *esprit* helps the organization to survive battle crises: it has written famous sagas in our naval history. But it also hampers adjustment to the external situation by developing parochialism. The few Regular Officers observed by the writer in two theatres knew little or nothing about the places they visited, despite their global travels. Their experience had been limited to the Officers' Clubs at Pearl, the big Shanghai hotels, the British Officers' Club on Repulse Bay. The Regular Navy is probably the most travelled and least cosmopolitan of American occupational groups. This is a function of occupational ethnocentrism.

D. *Ceremonialism: the conspicuous consumption of military systems.* If regulation is the sacred cow of a military system, ritual is its golden calf. An essential aid in exercising bureaucratic authority, ritual is symbolic behavior more important for its latent functions than for its manifest objectives. In time of peace military groups more than other bureaucratic types exist on routine. Ritual helps to provide the goal-orientation and motivation needed to maintain organization.

Ceremonialism may be viewed as the conspicuous consumption of power hierarchies. The Navy's cocked hats and swords are archaic survivals which have become functionally autonomous, significant chiefly for in-group solidarity. The 1947 Navy Department budget proposed $97,000 (deleted by Congress) for officers' silver-plated finger bowls, properly engraved for each rank. As he gains in rank an officer acquires a larger ceremonial due, symbolizing his professional success. Though not highly paid he is a "gentleman," and must exhibit proper gentility. He learns that it is unseemly to carry bundles. Pye and Shea devote much attention to servants.[11] They strongly advise owning a car,[12] and name the monthly amount ($30) a young officer should put aside for one. An unusually large proportion of an officer's income must go for uniforms, whereas but a minor part of a civilian family's clothing budget is spent on the head of the household.

One function of differential rewards is to provide incentives for assuming responsibility. Higher ranks receive more deference, better quarters, more money. Another function is to give officers the public status and prestige necessary to exercise authority. So essential is this instrumental pattern that it is often subject to disfunctional over-emphasis. Two cases are cited.

1. Awards and citations, theoretically given for extraordinary service beyond the call of duty, could legally be granted to many persons not morally entitled to them. Under the "strike-flight" system of aviation awards adopted late in 1944, 5 operational flights in areas where enemy action was "expected" automatically won an Air Medal, and 20 missions won a Distinguished Flying Cross. Formerly awarded very charily for heroism, these medals were now passed out profusely. Some strike-flight awards represented real hazards, but about three-quarters of the thousand-odd citations processed by the writer during a three-month period did not. Some strenuous ribbon-hunting developed. The ribbon rather than the achievement it symbolized became the conscious goal.

Among high-ranking USN officers there is a well-defined pattern of awarding each other ribbons more by virtue of position than performance. Soon after D-Day Normandy, the Legion of Merit (a fairly high award) was given to a number of senior USN officers in the European theatre. Though many were in charge of rear echelons doing routine work but indirectly significant for the invasion, their citations all mentioned D-Day — the ostensible occasion of the awards. Since senior officers receive a disproportionate share of the medals, especially of the higher ones, awards may be viewed sociologically as a perquisite of high rank. A chestful of ribbons does not mean that the wearer is a super-hero.[13] It is an infallible sign of only one fact — that he is a high-ranking Regular Navy officer. Regular officers received a greater proportion of awards than Reservists did, and officers in general were favored over enlisted men.

2. The "caste system" is popularly used as an epithet to suggest excessive discrepancy between the privileges of officers and men. The epithet indicates a problem but poses it inexactly. Stratification and differential privileges are recognized even by the rank-and-file as prerequisites of any legitimized structure of authority. Hence mere stratification can hardly be the source of the intense antagonism felt by many GI's toward the military hierarchy.

If differential privileges are necessary to clothe high status with moral authority, the principle of *noblesse oblige* is equally essential, at least on the public level, to get the rank-and-file to acquiesce in differential privileges. *Noblesse oblige* legitimizes the expectation that the higher the status, the greater the obligations and the severer the punishment for failing to live up to those obligations.[14] The rub comes in implementing this principle in practice. Violation of the norms of expected competence and self-restraint of officers arouses moral indignation. Failure to punish officer violations intensifies the sense of outrage, further reinforced by the vague American tradition of egalitarianism. This abuse of rank rather than stratification itself probably explains GI hostility to military hierarchy.

Differential privilege and punishment (*noblesse oblige*) are legitimized, but differential implementation of the law is not. With minimum friction the law can favor the powerful, as we may assume it always does, but only while the powerful do not publicly abuse their privileges so as to make the protective ideology of *noblesse oblige* an unrealistic myth.

This may help us to understand the reluctance of military systems to punish their officers. A public trial is a threat to the charisma of the uniform and to the whole structure of authority, because it destroys the basic premise that the King will do no wrong. Apart from possible guilt-feelings, the hierarchy is caught between the demand for justice and the need of the system for (public) inviolability. The latter pressure is usually the stronger because of the primacy of authority in military structures. Hence military organizations resist admitting that an officer can commit a crime, and they thereby compound the offense in the eyes of the rank-and-file.

III. CONCLUSION

We may conclude that there is considerable evidence from the Navy Officer Corps affirming the hypothesis stated at the head of this paper. Avoiding responsibility, legalism, insulation, and ceremonialism can be found in all bureaucratic organizations; they are especially prominent in military bureaucracies. Other pressures may and often do counteract them. This study is not a comprehensive analysis of the Navy or of any other bureaucracy.

Beginning with Weber's ideal bureaucratic type, we have discussed the military variant of bureaucracy chiefly in terms of its special emphasis on authority and tradition. These elements require such emphasis because of the situational pressures of uncertainty and organizational self-maintenance. Devices for meeting those pressures were shown to be disfunctional at times as well as functional for the organization. Significant latent structures, such as those making for legalism and avoidance of responsibility, were outlined. Points of articulation between this paper and other studies of large-scale organization, particularly those by Merton and Barnard, were indicated as part of the generalized theoretical system upon which the present observations depend for much of their scientific relevance.

This study suggests the great plasticity of individual behavior in response to occupational discipline. What was it that almost overnight made us all buckpassers? that steeped us in a psychology of affirm-and-conform? The answer — in this case bureaucracy — may be sought in the structure of the action situation. In industrial society the occupational pattern is a primary aspect of that situation.

Further light would be shed on the problems of this paper by investigation of the following hypothesis: the effectiveness of military leaders tends to vary inversely with their exposure to a conventionally routinized military career. Some outstanding military leaders were men who (1) had had experience in non-military occupations; or (2) rose with phenomenal rapidity through the ranks; or (3) belonged to military organizations newly created or renovated — e.g. the German and Soviet armies and the several air forces. Conventional career soldiers on the other hand have frequently resisted essential innovations like automatic firearms in the nineteenth century, tanks in World War I, the modern conception of air power, the unified command.

## REFERENCES

1. Sociological inquiry into the structural strains in bureaucratic organization was begun by Robert K. Merton, "Bureaucratic Structure and Personality," *Social Forces*, XVIII (1940), 561–568. The present writer found this paper invaluable for understanding the Navy as a social system.

2. The terms *manifest structure* and *latent structure*, credit for which belongs to Professor Marion Levy of Princeton University, resemble Merton's well-known concepts of manifest and latent function. In this study latent structure is viewed as an emergent property of the manifest structure. Manifest structure is the abstract formal organization consciously taken as a model or normative ideal pattern to realize the manifest (intended) functions of a group. Latent structure is that structure, originally unintended but prone to become increasingly "manifest" over time, which results from the concrete activation of the manifest structure, by virtue of the influence of other elements in the situation not foreseen or not provided for in the manifest structure. Structure of course cannot be equated with function, since a given structure may serve several functions.

3. Cf. Merton, "Sociological Theory," *American Journal of Sociology*, L (1945), 467–473.

4. Cf. Weber, *Theory of Social and Economic Organization* (New York: Oxford University Press, 1947); and *Essays in Sociology* (New York: Oxford University Press, 1946), ch. 8; Parsons, *Structure of Social Action* (New York: McGraw-Hill, 1937), and miscellaneous papers (bibliography in *Psychiatry*, X, May, 1947); Merton, "Bureaucratic Structure and Personality," *loc. cit.*, and "Role of the Intellectual in Public Bureaucracy," *Social Forces*, XXIII (1945), 504–515; Barnard, *Functions of the Executive* (Cambridge: Harvard University Press, 1938), and "Functions and Pathology of Status Systems in Formal Organizations," in W. F. Whyte, ed., *Industry and Society* (New York: McGraw-Hill, 1946), 46–83.

5. These epithets are primarily related to the violation of universalistic norms, but rationalization easily distorts others' success into unfair competition. The "sucker philosophy" is also closely linked to other aspects of naval organization such as legalism and wartime fatalism. It is not a simple function of the conflict between manifest and latent functions of formal and informal organizations.

6. Cf. E. Larrabee, "The Peacetime Army: Warriors Need Not Apply," *Harper's* (March, 1947), pp. 240–247.

7. In wartime the predominance of Reservists and the pressure of situational necessities resulted in systematic rule-breaking. This could be done safely

where in-group solidarity and/or approval of superiors gave such practices a secondary or *ad hoc* institutionalization. Their contribution to winning the war was probably very great, although there were disfunctional aspects too.

8. Even after three years of war the Quonset Indoctrination School included in its curriculum the advice to lay in a supply of these cards to take to the western Pacific beachheads.

9. Summarized in A. B. Pye and N. Shea, *The Navy Wife* (N. Y.: Harper's, 1942).

10. E.g. "all Navy" and "4.0" are approving phrases. "Lubber" and "civilian" connote contempt. Neutral words like "topside" and "scuttlebutt" are solidary influences because their knowledge and use are confined to *the* in-group. For glossaries of occupational terms, see Pye and Shea, *op cit.*, pp. 308–325; Lovette, *op. cit.*, pp. 207–270; F. W. Cottrell, *The Railroader* (Stanford University Press, 1940), pp. 117–139.

11. *Ibid.*, pp. 28–29, 33–34, 41, 58, 60, 276, 296, 299. Acknowledging that ensigns and lieutenants cannot always afford servants, they suggest that "it is not unusual" for young wives to cook dinner themselves, hiring a waiter to serve it to the guests, p. 176.

12. ". . . the Navy family usually owns a fairly good one even if the home is a one-room apartment," — *Ibid*, 148. For the Army version of ceremonialism, see *The Officer's Guide* (Harrisburg: Military Service Publishing Co., (1942), pp. 323–344.

13. Of course it does not preclude that possibility either. It is not very likely, however, in the writer's estimation.

14. Cf. the 95th Article of War: "Any officer or cadet who is convicted of conduct unbecoming an officer and a gentleman shall be dismissed from the Service" — *United States Code* (Washington: Government Printing Office, 1941), I, 625. Also the first Article of the Navy: ". . . commanders are required to show in themselves a good example of virtue, honor, patriotism, and subordination; . . . any commander who offends against this article shall be punished as a court-martial may direct" — *Navy Regulations, loc. cit.* No such extraordinary demands are made on enlisted men. I am indebted here to A. K. Cohen, Differential Implementation of the Criminal Law, unpub. Master's thesis, Indiana University, 1942.

# EFFICIENCY AND "THE FIX": INFORMAL INTERGROUP RELATIONS IN A PIECEWORK MACHINE SHOP

DONALD ROY

As part of a broader examination and appraisal of the application of piecework incentive to the production line of an American factory this paper essays the simple but largely neglected task of exploring the network of intergroup relations in which the work activity of machine operatives is imbedded. Exploration will be restricted to a limited sector of the total web of interaction in one shop; description will center upon those relationships that provide support to the operator group in its resistance to and subversion of formally instituted managerial controls on production. It is hoped that observations reported here not only will bear upon the practical problem of industrial efficiency but will also contribute to the more general study of institutional dynamics.

This could be considered the third in a series of attempts to make more careful discriminations in an area of research that has been characteristically productive of sweeping generalizations, blanket conceptualizations, or algebraic gymnastics that tend to halt inquiry at the same time that they lay a fog over otherwise easily discerned reality. Data for all three papers were acquired in an investigation of a single work situation by a single technique of social inquiry, participant observation. The writer was employed for nearly a year as radial-drill operator in one of the machine shops of a steel-processing plant, and he kept a daily record of his observations and experiences relating to work activity and social interaction in the shop. His major interest lay in the phenomenon of restriction of output, or "systematic soldiering," the practice of which various sociological soundings have revealed in the lower depths of our industrial organization. To complete the analogy: the writer donned a diving suit and went down to see what it looked like on the bottom.

One conclusion has already been set forth,[1] namely, that the usual view of output restriction is grossly undifferentiating. Different kinds of "institutionalized underworking" were practiced, each with its characteristic pattern of antecedents and consequences. The blanket term "restriction" was found to cloak all-important contrarieties of work behavior. Machine operatives not only held back effort; sometimes they worked hard. The very common failure to note such contrarieties has tended, of course, to impede the progress of research by checking consideration of the specific conditions under which differences in behavior occur.

A second finding was the discovery of complexity where simple lines of relationship had generally been assumed to exist.[2] When inconsistencies in the operator's behavior seemed to contradict the hypothesis that variations in application of economic incentive could account for the variations in work effort, a more intensive examination of response to piecework was undertaken. This disclosed that piecework incentive was not equivalent to economic incentive and that attainment of piecework "quotas" afforded machine operators a complex of rewards in which the strictly economic might or might not play a part.

The third set of observations, to be here discussed, again exhibits complication in a picture that has come to be accepted as simple in design. Here the focus of interest is the structure of "informal" intergroup connections that bear directly upon work behavior at the machine level. The material will not deny the hypothesis that the willingness of operatives to put forth effort is a function of their relationship with management or the widely held affirmation that this relationship is mediated by the organization of operatives into "informal groups." It will indicate, however, that further advances in the understanding of work behavior in the factory may involve attention to minor as well as major axes of intergroup relations. It will show that the relevant constituents of problematic production situations may include "lateral" lines of interaction between subgroups of the work force as well as "vertical" connections between managerial and worker groups.

It will be seen, in other words, that the interaction of two groups in an industrial organization takes place within and is conditioned by a larger intergroup network of reciprocal influences. Whyte has called attention to the limitations of studying groups in "isolation," without regard for the "perspectives of large institutional structures."[3]  A second warning might be: The larger institutional structures form networks of interacting groups.

As a bona fide member of an informal group of machine operatives the writer had an opportunity to observe and experience management–work group conflict in its day-to-day and blow-by-blow particulars. Also, he participated in another kind of social process, intergroup co-operation. Not only did workers on the "drill line" co-operate with each other as fellow-members of a combat team at war with management; they also received considerable aid and abetment from other groups of the shop. This intergroup co-operation was particularly evident when operators were trying to "make out," or attain "quota" production, on piecework jobs.

It has been noted in another connection that machine operators characteristically evinced no reluctance to put forth effort when they felt that their group-defined piecework quotas were attainable. It might seem, at first glance, that the supporting of operators during intensive application to "getting the work out" would represent co-operation *with* and not *against* management. However, the truth is that operators and their "allies" joined forces in certain situations in a manner not only unmistakably at variance with the carefully prepared designs of staff experts but even in flagrant violation of strongly held managerial "moral principles" of shop behavior. In short, machine operators resorted to "cheating" to attain their quotas; and since this often involved the collusion of other shop groups, not as mere "accessories after the fact" but as deeply entangled accomplices, any managerial suspicion that swindling and conniving, as well as loafing, were going on all the time was well founded. If the workers' conviction that the echelons of management were packed with men addicted to the "dirty deal" be additionally considered, it might appear that the shop was fairly overrun with crooks. The kind of effort made by operators and their aids to expedite production, when they did try to expedite it, was actually in many respects in conflict with management.

One belief, universally accepted in the work group, may be phrased thus: "You can't 'make out' if you do things the way management wants them done." This gem of shop wisdom thus negatively put is hardly a prescription for action, but its obverse, "You've got to figure the angles," gave all hands plenty to do.

According to Al McCann (all names used are fictitious), the "Fagan" of the drill line, "They time jobs to give you just base rates. It's up to you to figure out how to fool them so you can make out. You can't make any money if you run the job the way it's timed."

We machine operators did "figure the angles"; we developed an impressive repertoire of angles to play and devoted ourselves to crossing the expectations of formal organization with perseverance, artistry, and organizing ability of our own. For instance, job timing was a "battle all the way" between operators and time-study men. The objective of the operators was good piecework prices, and that end justified any old means that would work. One cardinal principle of operator job-timing was that cutting tools be run at lower speeds and "feeds" than the maximums possible on subsequent production, and there were various ways of encouraging the institution of adequate differentials. Also, operators deemed it essential to embellish the timing performance with movements only apparently functional in relation to the production of goods: little reachings, liftings, adjustings, dustings, and other special attentions to conscientious machine operation and good housekeeping that could be dropped instanter with the departure of the time-study man.

However, the sophistication of the time-study men usually matched the strategy employed against them. The canniest operators often gave of their best in timing duels only to get "hopeless prices" for their pains:

> Gus Schmidt was timed early in the evening on a job, and given a price of $1.00 per 100 for reaming one hole, chamfering both sides of three holes, and filing burrs on one end of one hole. All that for one cent!
> "To hell with them," said Gus.

This is not to say that the "hopeless price" was always truly hopeless. Since the maintenance of an effective control over job-timing and hence price-setting was an uncertain, often disheartening matter, operators were forced to develop skills for turning bad into good. Under the shaping hands of the "angle-applicators" surprising metamorphoses sometimes took place. Like the proverbial ugly duckling that finally feathered out into a beautiful swan, piecework jobs originally classified in operator vernacular as "stinkers" came to give off the delightful aroma of "gravy." Without going into the particulars of the various types of operation, one might say that jobs were "streamlined." This streamlining was, of course, at times "rough on the tools" and adverse in its effects on the quality of output. The jettisoning of quality called, necessarily, for a corresponding attention to ways and means of shielding supervisors and inspectors from discovering the sacrifices and consequently brought into further play the social graces of equivocation, subterfuge, and prestidigitation.

Still, the adroitness of the machine operators, inventing, scheming, and conniving unto themselves to make quotas attainable, was not enough. Many "stinkers" would not yield before the whitest heat of intelligence or the most cavalier disregard for company property. An appreciable incidence of failure should not be surprising when it is kept in mind that the black arts of "making out" were not only responses to challenge from management but also stimulations, in circular interaction, to the development of more effective countermagic in the timing process. It would be hard to overestimate the wizardry of the time-study men with pencil and paper in computing "angle-tight" piecework prices. During the latter months of his employment, months that marked the peak of his machine performance, the writer was able to achieve quota earnings approximately half the time that piecework jobs were offered. If this experience is roughly representative of the fortunes of the drill-line group, the battle with the stop-watch men was nip and tuck.

It is to be expected that a group of resourceful operatives, working with persistent intent to "make out" at quota levels, and relying heavily upon illegal practices, would be alert to possibilities of assistance from groups that were able and willing to give it and would not hesitate at further flouting the rules and regulations in cultivating it. It is also to be expected that the upholders of a managerial rational and moral order would attempt to prevent corruptive connections and would take action to stamp out whatever subversive organization did develop. During the eleven-month study, machine operators, including the drill-line men, were enjoying the co-operation of several other shop groups in an illegal facilitation of the "make-out" process. This intergroup network effectively modified certain formally established shop routines, a too close attachment to which would handicap the operators. The "syndicate" also proved adequate in circumventing each of a series of "new rules" and "new systems" introduced by management to expurgate all modifications and improvisations and force a strict adherence to the rules.

The shop groups that conspired with the operators were, namely, the inspectors, the tool-crib men, the time-checkers, the stockmen, and the setup men. With a single exception, these "service" groups stemmed from lines of authority distinct from the one for which the operators formed the base. The one exception was the setup group; it was subordinate to the same set of officials in the "production" line of authority that controlled the operators. A brief description of the duties of each of these service groups and a rough tracing of the sequences of interaction involved in the prescribed work routine of the drill men will indicate the formal pattern of intergroup relations within which informally instituted variations were woven.

## The Setup Men

A chief function of the setup men was to assist machine operators in the "setting-up" of jigs and fixtures preparatory to operation of machines in the processing of materials. It included the giving of preliminary aid and advice at the beginning of the production process, at which time the setup men would customarily "run the first piece" to show operators how to do it and to indicate that the setup was adequate to meet work specifications. The duties of the setup men also included "trouble-shooting" on occasions when operators encountered difficulties that effected a lowering of the quality of output below inspection standards or a reduction of the rate of output unsatisfactory to operators or supervisors.

## The Inspectors

The chief function of the inspectors was to pass judgment on the quality of the output of the machine operators, either accepting or rejecting work turned out, according to blueprint specifications. Their appraisals came at the beginning of operations, when especially thorough examinations of the first pieces processed were made, and subsequently at varying intervals during the course of a job.

## The Tool-Crib Men

The tool-crib attendants served the operators as dispensers of jigs, fixtures, cutting tools, blueprints, gauges, and miscellaneous items of equipment needed to supplement basic machinery and operator-owned hand tools in the processing of materials. They worked inside a special inclosure conveniently located along one of the main arterials of shop traffic and did most of their dispensing across the wide sill of a "window," an aperture which served, incidentally, as locus of various and sundry transactions and communications not immediately relevant to tool-dispensing. There were two other openings into the crib, a door, two steps from the window, and a wide gate, farther down the corridor.

## THE STOCKMEN

The stockmen were responsible for conducting a steady flow of materials to the machines for processing. Their work called for the removal of finished work as well as the moving-up of fresh stock and involved a division of labor into two specializations "stock-chasing" and "trucking." The chief duties of the stock-chasers were to "locate" unprocessed materials in the various storage areas, when operators called for stock, and to direct the activities of the truckers, who attended to the physical transportation.

## THE TIME-CHECKERS

The time-checkers worked in another special inclosure, a small "time cage," from which they distributed to the operators the work orders "lined up" by the schedulemen of the Planning Department and within which they registered the starting and completion times of each job. There were four time-registering operations for every work order. First, upon presenting an operator with a work-order slip, the checker would "punch" him "on setup" by stamping a separate order card with a clocking mechanism that registered the hours in tenths. Later, when the operator would call at the cage window to announce completion of all preparatory arrangements for the actual processing of materials, the checker would punch him "off setup" and "on production." Finally, following another operator announcement, the checker would clock the termination of the machining process with a fourth punch. At the time of his terminal punch the operator would report the number of "pieces" completed on the job just concluded and would receive a new work order to start the cycle over again. And, since the terminal punch on the completed job would be registered at the same time as the initial punch on the new one, hours on shift would be completely accounted for.

## OPERATOR INTERACTION WITH SERVICE GROUPS

The machine operator's performance of each individual job or order assigned to him involved formal relationships with service groups in well-defined sequences or routines.

First, the operator would receive his work order from the time-checker. Next, he would present the work order to a tool-crib attendant at the crib window as a requisite to receiving blueprints, jigs, cutting tools, and gauges. At the same time, that is, immediately before or after approaching the crib attendant, sometimes while waiting for crib service, the operator would show his work order to a stock-chaser as a requisite to receiving materials to work on. The stock-chaser, after perusing the order slip, occasionally with additional reference to the blueprint, would hail a trucker to bring the necessary stock to the operator's machine. If there were no delay in contacting a stock-chaser or in locating and moving up the stock, a load of materials would await the operator upon his arrival at his machine with equipment from the tool crib.

Upon returning to his machine, the operator would proceed with the work of "setting up" the job, usually with the assistance of a setup man, who would stay with him until a piece was turned out whose quality of workmanship would satisfy an inspector. In appraising a finished piece, the inspector would consult the blueprint brought from the crib for work specifications and then perform operations of measurement with rules, gauges, micrometers, or more elaborate equipment. The inspector might or might not "accept" the first piece presented for his judgment. At any rate, his approval was requisite to the next step in the operator's formal interactional routine, namely, contacting the time-checker to punch "off setup" and "on production."

The operator would ordinarily have further "business" contact with a setup man during the course of production. Even if the job did not "go sour" and require the services of a "trouble-shooter," the setup man would drop around of his own accord to see how the work was progressing. Likewise, the operator would have further formal contact during the course of his job with inspectors and tool-crib attendants. Each inspector would make periodic "quality checks" at the machines on his "line"; and the operator might have to make trips to the tool crib to get tools ground or to pick up additional tools or gauges. He might also have to contact a stock-chaser or truckers for additional materials.

Upon completion of the last piece of his order the operator would tear down his setup, return his tools to the tool crib, and make a final report to the time-checker. Should the job be uncompleted at the close of a shift, the operator would merely report the number of pieces finished to a checker, and the latter would register a final punchout. The setup would be left intact for the use of the operator coming in to work the next shift.

## Major Job Categories

Certain variations in types of jobs assigned to operators are pertinent to a discussion of intergroup collusion to modify formal work routines. These variations could be classified into four categories: (1) piecework; (2) time study; (3) rework; and (4) setup.

Each piecework job carried a price per 100 pieces, determined by the timing operations mentioned earlier. Time-study and rework jobs carried no prices. The time-study category included (a) new jobs that had not yet been timed and (b) jobs that had once carried a piecework price. As the label indicates, rework jobs involved the refinishing of pieces rejected either by inspectors or in the assembly process but considered salvageable by reprocessing.

Since time-study and rework jobs carried no piecework prices, operators engaged in these two types of work were paid "day rate," that is, according to an hourly base rate determined in collective bargaining. The base rates represented minimal wage guaranties that not only applied to "day work" but also covered piecework as well. If an operator on piecework failed to exceed his base rate in average hourly earnings on a particular job on a particular day, he would be paid his base rate. Failure to produce at base rate or above on the first day of a piecework job did not penalize an operator in his efforts to earn premium pay on the second day; nor did failure to attain base rate on one piecework job on a given day reduce premiums earned on a second job performed that day.

Not a fourth type of job, but measured separately in time and payment units, were the setup operations. Piecework jobs always carried piecework setups; failure to equal or exceed base rate on setup did not jeopardize chances to earn premium on "production," and vice versa. Time-study jobs frequently carried piecework setups; rework never.

Obviously, these formal work routines may easily be modified to fit the perceived needs of machine operators. Possibilities for the development of "make-out angles" should be immediately apparent in a work situation characterized by job repertoires that included piecework and day-work operations; minimum-wage guaranties uniform for all work done; and separate payment computations by jobs and days worked. If, for instance, time formally clocked as day work could be used to gain a "head start" on subsequent piecework operations, such a transferral might mean the difference between earning and not earning premiums on doubtful piecework jobs. Similarly, time on "hopeless" piecework jobs might be applied to more promising operations; and the otherwise "free time" gained on "gravy" jobs might be consumed in productive anticipation of the formal receipt of ordinarily unrewarding piecework. Especially lush "gravy" jobs might even contribute extra time enough to convert "stinkers" into temporary "money-makers." Realization of such possibilities in any given case would necessarily involve obtaining, without a work order, the following: (1) identification of future operations as listed in sequence on the schedule board inside the time cage; (2) jigs, blueprints, and cutting tools appropriate to the work contemplated; (3) stock to work on; (4) setup help and advice; (5) inspection service; and (6) "trouble-shooting" assistance as needed. Obviously, this sequence of accomplishments would call for the support of one or more service groups at each step. That the required assistance was actually provided with such regularity that it came to be taken for granted, the writer discovered by observation and personal experience.

The following diary recording of interaction between the writer and a time-checker may be indicative of the extent to which service-group collaboration with the operators in perverting the formal system of work routine had become systematized:

> When I came to punch off the rework, the time-cage girl said, "You don't want to punch off rework yet, do you?" — suggesting that I should get a start on the next job before punching off rework.

Even line foremen, who, in regard to intergroup collusion preferred the role of silent "accessory after the fact," became upset to the point of actual attempted interference with formal rules and regulations when the naïve neophyte failed to meet the expectations of his own informal system.

Acceptance of such subversive practices did not extend, however, to groups in management other than local shop supervision. The writer was solemnly and repeatedly warned that time-study men, the true hatchet men of upper management, were disposed to bring chiselers to speedy justice.

## New Rules and New Systems

During the near-year that he spent in the shop the writer felt the impact of several attempts to stamp out intergroup irregularities and enforce conformity to managerial designs of procedure. He coincidentally participated in an upholding of the maxim: "Plus ça change, plus c'est la même chose."

Attempts to tighten controls came in a series of "new rules" or "new systems" promulgated by bulletin-board edicts.

The first new rule during this study was designed to tighten controls in the tool-crib sector, where attendants had not only been passing out setups ahead of time but allowing operators or their setup men to enter the toolroom to make the advance pickups themselves. An aim of the new rule was also to curb the operators' practice of keeping "main setups" at the machines instead of turning them in at the completion of operations.

> A new crib ruling went into effect today. A memorandum by Bricker [superintendent] was posted on the side of the crib window. Those who check out tools and jigs must sign a slip in triplicate, keeping the pink one and turning it in with the tools in exchange for the white original, which would constitute proof that the tools had been returned. No new setups would be issued until the old ones had been turned in.

An optimistic perception of the new procedures was expressed by young Jonesy, a tool-crib attendant and otherwise willing conniver with the operators: "Tools are scattered all over the shop. This way we'll have them all in order in the crib, and the fellows can get them anytime they need them."

But multiple-drill operator Hanks, old-timer on the line, drew upon his lengthy experience with managerial efficiency measures and saw the situation differently:

> Hanks commented unfavorably on the new ruling. He and the day man [his machine partner on the other shift] had been keeping the tools for their main setups at their bench, or, rather, under it. This practice, according to Hanks, was to insure their setting up promptly without inordinate waste of time and to insure their having all the tools needed. Hanks said that on a previous occasion he was told to turn in one of his main setups, which included over a dozen drills, reamers, taps, etc., of varying sizes. He did so, but, when he needed this setup again, the crib man couldn't locate all the tools. He asked Hanks to come back in the crib and help him find them. Hanks refused. After several hours of futile search, Hanks was finally induced to "come back and find his tools." He did so on condition that it would not be on his own time. The foreman agreed to this.
>
> "The same thing is going to happen again," predicted Hanks. "And I'm not going back there to find my tools they scatter all over, on my own time."

Though the operators went through the formality of an exchange of slips when they exchanged setups, the new procedures did not modify the practice of getting setups from the crib ahead of time. Appreciable effects of the new ruling included making more paper work for crib attendants at the same time that more work at assembling setups was thrust upon them. Jonesy's happy prediction did not materialize: the tools were not "always in order." Subsequent events confirmed Hanks's gloomy forebodings.

Included in the new ruling was a stipulation that blueprints and gauges be turned in by the operators at the end of each shift, though setup paraphernalia other than prints and gauges were to be left at the machines as long as jobs were in operation. Calling for prints and gauges at the beginning of the shift, waiting at the crib window in the line that naturally formed, even when these items were "located" immediately, consumed operator time.

Four months later the new crib ruling was modified by another that canceled the stipulation regarding the turning-in of blueprints and gauges and called for changes in the paper work of operator-crib-attendant relations. These changes were featured by a new kind of work order, duplicates of which became involved in tool-crib book-keeping. The change reduced the waste of operator time at the start of shifts, but to the burden of the crib attendants paper-work irritations were now added.

> When I punched in on the rework and asked Walt [crib attendant] for a print, he fumed a bit as he sought a duplicate of my new-type yellow work order in a new file of his.
> "I haven't been able to find more than one in five duplicates so far," he said. "And there's supposed to be a duplicate for every one."

The "new system" did operate to handicap operators in that they were not to receive new setups from the crib until they received the new yellow work orders from the time cage to check with the duplicates in the crib. However, setup men roamed at will in the toolroom, grinding tools and fixing jigs, and were able to help the operators by picking up setups ahead of time for them. Their detailed knowledge of the various setups made it possible for them to assemble the necessary tools without the use of setup cards.

> "This is a good job," I said to McCann [now setup man]. "I wish I could get it set up ahead of time, but I guess it's no use trying. I can't get the setup now from the toolroom until I get the new work order from the time girls."
> McCann thought a moment. "Maybe I can get the jig and tools out of the crib for you."
> McCann did get the jig and tools, and I got a half-hour's head start on the job.

The writer had found Ted, a stock-chaser, and his truckers, George and Louie, willing connivers in the time-chiseling process. They moved up stock ahead of time, even after the new system made presentation of the new work order to the stock-chaser a prerequisite to getting stock. Contrary to first impressions, for all practical purposes the situation was unchanged under the new system.

The new system also included complication of operator-inspector relations. Inspectors were now to "sign off" operators from completed jobs before new work orders could be issued at the time booth. The "signing-off" process included notation by the inspector of the time of operation completion, a double check on the time-checker's "punch out." This added, of course, to the paper work of inspectors.

Drill-man Hanks's first response to this feature of the new system was "individualistic":

Hanks commented on the new system tonight. He thinks that its chief purpose is to keep the operators from getting ahead on an operation and starting the next job on saved time. He said that the inspector checked him off a job tonight at 4:40, and he was not due to punch in on the next one until 6:10. He changed the time recorded by the inspector on his work slip to 6:10 and went ahead as usual. If he had not done so, there would have been a "gap" of an hour and a half unaccounted for in the records.

The writer found himself "stymied" at first but soon discovered that the new obstacle could be overcome without engaging in such a hazardous practice as "forging."

It was ten o'clock when we were ready to punch off setup, and Johnny [setup man] asked Sam [inspector] to sign me off setup earlier, so that I could make out on setup.

"Punch me off at nine o'clock," I said, not expecting Sam to check me off earlier, and purposely exaggerating Johnny's request.

Sam refused. "I can't do that! If I do that for you, I'll have to do it for everybody!"

Sam seemed somewhat agitated in making the refusal.

A few minutes later he said to Johnny, "Why did you ask me to do that when Hanks was standing there?"

Hanks had been standing by my machine, watching us set up.

"I can't take you off an hour back. Go find out when you punched in on this job in the first place."

Johnny consulted the time-cage girl as to the time I punched on the job, later talked to Sam at Sam's bench while I was working, and came to me with the announcement that it was "fixed up" so that I made out on setup and was credited with starting production at 9:30. This gave me an hour and a half of "gravy."

By the time the "new system" was a month old, Sam was not only doing this for everybody but actually taking the initiative.

No sooner had the shop employees adjusted to this "new system" and settled down to normal informal routine than they were shocked by a new pronunciamento that barred admittance to the toolroom to all save superintendents and toolroom employees. The rule seemed to be enforced.

Johnny, the setup man, predicted that the new ruling would be "tough on" the tool-crib employees, not on setup men.

Johnny says that the new rule is going to be tough on grinders and crib attendants, because setup men and foremen have been doing much of the grinding and have made it easier for them by coming in to help themselves to tools, jigs, etc.

Johnny says that the new rule suits him fine. Now he can just stand at the window and holler and let the toolroom employees do the work.

The line foremen seemed to take offense at the new "exclusion act" and threatened reprisals to the crib attendants.

At quitting time I noticed Gil [line foreman] talking to Walt at the crib window. Gil seemed very serious; Walt was waving his arms and otherwise gesturing in a manner indicating rejection of responsibility. I didn't catch any words but gathered that Gil was voicing disapproval or warning, and after Gil left I said to Walt, "Looks like you're behind the eight-ball now!"

I noticed that Walt's hair was mussed, and he looked a little wild. He denied that he was in any trouble whatsover; nor was he worried about anything whatsover.

"I'm just working here!" he exclaimed. "I just go by the cards, and beyond that I've got no responsibility!"

I was curious as to what Gil had told him and asked Johnny later, on the way home. I had noticed that Johnny was standing near by when Gil was talking to Walt. Johnny said that Gil was telling Walt that from now on the crib was going to be charged with every minute of tool delay to the operators — that, if there was any waiting for tools, Gil was going to make out allowance cards charging these delays to the crib.

Contrary to Hanks's prediction, the new rule did "last out the week," and crowds milled around the crib window.

It was at this time that Jonesy, erstwhile optimist and regarded by shop employees as the most efficient of the crib attendants, decided that he had "had enough." He transferred to the quiet backroom retreat of toolgrinding. But several days later, just ten days since the new rule was promulgated, the sun began to break through the dark clouds of managerial efficiency. Hanks's prediction was off by four days.

While I was waiting for tools at the crib window tonight, I noticed the jockey [turret-lathe man] dash into the tool crib through a door that was left ajar; he was followed soon after by Gil. Later, when the door was closed, Paul shook it and shouted to the attendant, "Let me in!" He was admitted.

Steve [superintendent] called out, "Hey!" when he saw the jockey go into the crib. When the jockey came out, he spoke to him, and the jockey joshed him back. Steve did not seem to be particularly put out about it.

Soon the boys were going in and out of the crib again, almost at will, and setup men were getting setups ahead of time for operators, ignored by the crib attendants.

"So much for Faulkner's order!" The "fix" was "on" again, and operators and their service-group allies conducted business as usual for the remaining weeks of the writer's employment.


CONCLUSIONS

This rough sketch of the operation of one shop "syndicate" has been no more than indicative of the existence of intergroup co-operation in the lower reaches of factory social structure. No attempt has been made here to account for the aid extended by service groups, though suggestion that this assistance might be part of a larger system of reciprocal obligations has been implicit. It is apparent, for instance, that tool-crib attendants benefited from their practice of admitting operators and setup men to the toolroom to seek and pick up equipment.

A more complete picture of intergroup relations would include conflict, as well as co-operation, between operators and the various service groups. It could be shown, if space permitted, that changes in relationship accompanied, in cyclical fashion, changes in basic conditions of work.

Furthermore, attention has not been drawn to intragroup role and personality variations in intergroup relations. Such additional discriminations and the questions that they might raise in regard to the study of institutional dynamics must be left for future discussion.

As for their possible bearing on practical industrial administration, materials presented here seem to challenge the view held in some research circles that the "human" problem of industrial efficiency lies in faulty communication between an economically "rational" or "logical" management and "nonrational" or "nonlogical" work groups. While nothing has been offered to deny linkage between communication and efficiency, observations reported here suggest examination of the stereotypes of the two parties.[4] And questioning the fitness of the stereotypes may lead to a more fruitful conceptualization of the process that is reputedly in need of attention: communication.

Do we see, in the situation studied, an economically "rational" management and an economically "nonrational" work group? Would not a reversal of the labels, if such labels be used, find justification? Does it not appear that operatives and their allies resisted managerial "logics of efficiency" because application of those "logics" tended to produce something considerably less than "efficiency"? Did not worker groups connive to circumvent managerial ukase in order to "get the work out"? Did not Walt, for instance, break the rules "to keep the boys on production"? May not the common query of industrial workers, "What in the hell are they trying to do up there?" be not merely reflective of faulty communication but also based on real managerial inadequacy, quite apart from a failure in "explanation"? May it not be assumed that managerial inefficiency is and has been for some time a serious problem to those who labor?

If managerial directives are not the guides to efficient action that they are claimed to be, then, perhaps, "logics of efficiency" would be better designated as "sentiments of efficiency." When failure to "explain" is additionally considered, perhaps bulletin-board pronunciamentos might properly be classified with the various exorcisms, conjurations, and miscellaneous esoteric monkey-business of our primitive contemporaries.

If we conceive of "logical" behavior not as self-contained ratiocinative exercises but as intellectual operations in continuous reciprocal interplay with concrete experience, machine operators and their service-group allies would appear the real holders of "logics of efficiency." Like big-city machine politicians, they develop plans for action that, under given conditions of situational pressures, "work."

But this rejection of commonly held stereotypes cannot lead to mere reversal of invidious distinctions; the situation is far too complex for that. The group life that the writer shared was by no means devoid of "sentiments." To the contrary, operator interaction was rich in shared feelings, attitudes, and practices not only of doubtful bearing on getting the work out but often undeniably preventing production maximization. Nor can it be maintained that management, in applying its "sentiments of efficiency," was always ineffective. Perhaps solution to the human problem of industrial efficiency would best be expedited by abandoning altogether the use of contrasted caricatures handed down to us from a preindustrial social class structure. Instead of concerning ourselves with such blind-alley issues as who is "rational" and who is not, we might recognize with John Dewey that both intellectual and emotional activity are essentials of goal-directed behavior[5] and that the development of effective communication focusing on production goals is a matter of instituting interactional processes that engender ideas, sentiments, and plans for action held in common.


## REFERENCES

1. Donald Roy, "Quota Restriction and Goldbricking in a Machine Shop," *American Journal of Sociology*, LVII (March, 1952), 427–42.

2. Donald F. Roy, "Work Satisfaction and Social Reward in Quota Achievement: An Analysis of Piecework Incentive," *American Sociological Review*, 5 (October, 1953), 507–514.

3. William F. Whyte, "Small Groups and Large Organizations," in *Social Psychology at the Crossroads*, ed. John R. Rohrer and Muzafer Sherif (New York: Harper & Bros., 1951), pp. 297–312.

4. William F. Whyte, "Semantics and Industrial Relations," *Human Organization*, VIII (Spring, 1949), 1–7.

5. John Dewey, *Art as Experience* (New York: Minton, Balch & Co., 1934), p. 55.

# B.

## ACHIEVEMENT AND CREATIVITY

# WHAT MAKES A PERSON CREATIVE?

## DONALD W. MacKINNON

Six years ago, a group of psychologists began a nationwide study of human creativity. They wanted the scientific answers to the mystery of human personality, biology, intelligence, and intuition that makes some persons more creative than others.

Working under a grant by the Carnegie Corporation of New York, the researchers were faced with the usual stereotypes that picture the highly creative person as a genius with an I.Q. far above average, an eccentric not only in thinking but in appearance, dress, and behavior, a Bohemian, an egghead, a longhair. According to these unproved stereotypes, he was not only introverted but a true neurotic, withdrawn from society, inept in his relations with others, totally unable to carry on a conversation with others less gifted than himself. Still others held that the creative person might be profound but that his intelligence was highly one-sided, in a rather narrow channel, and that he was emotionally unstable. Indeed, one of the most commonly held of these images was that he lived just this side of madness.

The psychological researchers who sought a more precise picture of the creative person conducted their investigations on the Berkeley campus of the University of California in the Institute of Personality Assessment and Research. At the Institute, the persons to be studied have been brought together, usually ten at a time, for several days, most often a three-day weekend. There they have been examined by a variety of means — by the broad problem posed by the assessment situation itself, by problem-solving experiments, by tests designed to discover what a person does not know or is unable to reveal about himself, by tests and questionnaires that permit a person to manifest various aspects of his personality and to express his attitudes, interests, and values, by searching interviews.

The professional groups whose creative members were chosen for

Reprinted from the *Saturday Review* (February 10, 1962) by permission of the publisher and the author.

study were writers, architects, research workers in the physical sciences and engineering, and mathematicians. In no instance did the psychological assessors decide which highly creative persons should be studied. Rather, they were nominated by experts in their own fields; and to insure that the traits found to characterize the highly creative were related to their creativity rather than indigenous to all members of the profession, a wider, more representative sample of persons in each of the professional groups was also chosen, though for somewhat less intensive study. All told, some 600 persons participated.

As the study has progressed it has become abundantly clear that creative persons seldom represent fully any of the common stereotypes, and yet in some respects and to some degree there are likenesses. It is not that such images of the creative person are fantastic but that they are caricatures rather than characterizations, heightening and sharpening traits and dispositions so as to yield a picture recognizable, yet still out of accord with reality. There are, of course, some stereotypes that reflect only error, but more often the distortion of the reality would seem to be less complete.

As for intellectual capacity, it will come as no surprise that highly creative persons have been found to be, in the main, well above average. But the relation between intelligence and creativity is not as clear-cut as this would suggest, if for no other reason than that intelligence is a many-faceted thing. There is no single psychological process to which the term "intelligence" applies; rather, there are many types of intellective functioning. There is verbal intelligence, and on a well-known test of this factor creative writers on the average score higher than any of the other groups. But there is also spatial intelligence — the capacity to perceive and to deal with spatial arrangements — and on a test of this aspect of intelligence creative writers as a group earn the lowest average score, while creative architects as a group are the star performers. There are, of course, many elements of intelligence in addition to these two.

If for the moment we ignore those patterns of intellective functioning which clearly and most interestingly differentiate one creative group from another, there are some more general observations that may be noted. It is quite apparent that creative persons have an unusual capacity to record and retain and have readily available the experiences of their life history. They are discerning, which is to say that they are observant in a differentiated fashion; they are alert, capable of concentrating attention readily and shifting it appropriately; they are fluent in scanning thoughts and producing those that serve to solve the problems they undertake; and, characteristically, they have a wide range of information at their command. As in the case of any intelligent person, the items of information which creative persons possess may readily enter into combinations, and the number of possible combinations is increased for such persons because of both a greater range of information and a greater fluency of combination. Since true creativity is defined by the adaptiveness of a response as well as its unusualness, it is apparent that intelligence alone will tend to produce creativity. The more combinations that are found, the more likely it is on purely statistical grounds that some of them will be creative.

Yet intelligence alone does not guarantee creativity. On a difficult, high-level test of the more general aspects of intelligence, creative persons score well above average, but their individual scores range widely, and in several of the creative groups the correlation of intelligence as measured by this test and creativity as rated by the experts is essentially zero.

Certainly this does not mean that over the whole range of creative endeavor there is no relation between general intelligence and creativity. No feeble-minded persons appeared in any of the creative groups. Clearly a certain degree of intelligence, and in general a rather high degree, is required for creativity, but above that point the degree of intelligence does not seem to determine the level of one's creativeness. In some fields of endeavor, mathematics and theoretical physics for example, the requisite intelligence for highly creative achievement is obviously high. But it does not follow that the theoretical physicist of very superior I.Q. will necessarily be creative, and in many fields of significant creative endeavor it is not necessary that a person be outstanding in intelligence to be recognized as highly creative, at least as intelligence is measured by intelligence tests.

Regardless of the level of his measured intelligence, what seems to characterize the creative person — and this is especially so for the artistically creative — is a relative absence of repression and suppression as mechanisms for the control of impulse and imagery. Repression operates against creativity, regardless of how intelligent a person may be, because it makes unavailable to the individual large aspects of his own experience, particularly the life of impulse and experience which gets assimilated to the symbols of aggression and sexuality. Dissociated items of experience cannot combine with one another;

there are barriers to communication among different systems of experience. The creative person, given to expression rather than suppression or repression, thus has fuller access to his own experience, both conscious and unconscious. Furthermore, because the unconscious operates more by symbols than by logic, the creative person is more open to the perception of complex equivalences in experience, facility in metaphor being one specific consequence of the creative person's greater openness to his own depths.

This openness to experience is one of the most striking characteristics of the highly creative person, and it reveals itself in many forms. It may be observed, for example, in the realm of sexual identifications and interests, where creative males give more expression to the feminine side of their nature than do less creative men. On a number of tests of masculinity-femininity, creative men score relatively high on femininity, and this despite the fact that, as a group, they do not present an effeminate appearance or give evidence of increased homosexual interests or experiences. Their elevated scores on femininity indicate rather an openness to their feelings and emotions, a sensitive intellect and understanding self-awarness, and wide-ranging interests including many which in the American culture are thought of as more feminine, and these traits are observed and confirmed by other techniques of assessment. If one were to use the language of the Swiss psychiatrist C. G. Jung, it might be said that creative persons are not so completely identified with their masculine *persona* roles as to blind themselves to or deny expression to the more feminine traits of the *anima*. For some, of course, the balance between masculine and feminine traits, interests, and identifications is a precarious one, and for several it would appear that their presently achieved reconciliation of these opposites of their nature has been barely achieved and only after considerable psychic stress and turmoil.

It is the creative person's openness to experience and his relative lack of self-defensiveness that make it possible for him to speak frankly and critically about his childhood and family, and equally openly about himself and his problems as an adult.

One gets the impression that by and large those persons who as adults are widely recognized for their creative achievements have had rather favorable early life circumstances, and yet they often recall their childhood as not having been especially happy.

In studying adult creative persons, one is dependent upon their own reports for the picture they give of their early years. Although they may often describe their early family life as less harmonious and happy than that of their peers, one cannot know for certain what the true state of affairs was. In reality the situation in their homes may not have been appreciably different from that of their peers. The differences may reside mainly in their perceptions and memories of childhood experiences, and it seems the more likely since one of the most striking things to be noted about creative persons is their unwillingness to deny or to repress things that are unpleasant or troubling.

The theme of remembered unhappiness in childhood is so recurrent that one is led to speculate about its role in fostering creative potential. In the absence of a sensitive awareness of one's own experience and of the world around one, without considerable development of and attention to one's own inner life, and lacking an interest in ideational, imaginal, and symbolic processes, highly creative responses can hardly be expected to occur. Something less than complete satisfaction with oneself and one's situation in childhood, if not a prerequisite for the development of a rich inner life and a concern for things of the mind and spirit, may nevertheless play an important contributory role.

There is no doubt, too, that some of the highly creative persons had, as children, endured rather cruel treatment at the hands of their fathers. These, to be sure, constitute the minority, but they appear today to be no less creative than those who could more easily identify with their fathers. There is some evidence, however, that those who were harshly treated in childhood have not been so effective or so successful in the financial and business (masculine) aspects of their profession as the others. There is in these persons more than a hint that they have had some difficulty in assuming an aggressive professional role because, through fear of their fathers, their masculine identifications were inhibited.

Both in psychiatric interviews that survey the individual's history and present psychological status, and in clinical tests of personality, creative persons tend to reveal a considerable amount of psychic turbulence. By and large they freely admit the existence of psychological problems and they speak frankly about their symptoms and complaints. But the manner in which they describe their problems is less suggestive of disabling psychopathology than of good intellect, richness and complexity of personality, and a general candor in self-description.

They reveal clearly what clinical psychologists have long contended: that personal soundness is not an absence of problems but a way of reacting to them.

We may resort again to Jung's theory of the psychological functions and types of personality as an aid in depicting the psychology of the creative person. According to this view it might be said that whenever a person uses his mind for any purpose he either perceives (becomes aware of something) or he judges (comes to a conclusion about something). Everyone perceives and judges, but the creative person tends to prefer perceiving to judging. Where a judging person emphasizes the control and regulation of experience, the perceptive creative person is inclined to be more interested and curious, more open and receptive, seeking to experience life to the full. Indeed, the more perceptive a person is, the more creative he tends to be.

In his perceptions, both of the outer world and of inner experience, one may focus upon what is presented to his senses, upon the facts as they are, or he may seek to see, through intuition, their deeper meanings and possibilities. One would not expect creative persons in their perceptions to be bound to the presented stimulus or object but rather to be intuitively alert to that which is capable of occurring, to that which is not yet realized; this capacity is, in fact, especially characteristic of the creative person.

One judges or evaluates experience with thought or with feeling, thinking being a logical process aimed at an impersonal analysis of the facts, feeling, on the other hand, being a process of appreciation and evaluation of things which gives them a personal and subjective value. The creative person's preference for thinking or for feeling in his making of judgments is less related to his creativeness as such than it is to the type of material or concepts with which he deals. Artists, in general, show a preference for feeling, scientists and engineers a preference for thinking, while architects are more divided in their preference for one or the other of these two functions.

Everyone, of course, perceives and judges, senses and intuits, thinks and feels. It is not a matter of using one of the opposed functions to the exclusion of the other. It is rather a question of which of them is preferred, which gets emphasized, and which is most often used. So also is it with introversion and extroversion of interest, but two-thirds or more of each of the creative groups which have participated in the study have shown a rather clear tendency toward introversion.

Yet, interestingly enough, extroverts, though they are in the minority in our samples, are rated as high on creativity as the introverts.

Whether introvert or extrovert, the creative individual is an impressive person, and he is so because he has to such a large degree realized his potentialities. He has become in great measure the person he was capable of becoming. Since he is not preoccupied with the impression he makes on others, and is not overconcerned with their opinion of him, he is freer than most to be himself. To say that he is relatively free from conventional restraints and inhibitions might seem to suggest that he is to some degree socially irresponsible. He may seem to be, and in some instances he doubtless is if judged by the conventional standards of society, since his behavior is dictated more by his own set of values and by ethical standards that may not be precisely those of others around him.

The highly creative are not conformists in their ideas, but on the other hand they are not deliberate nonconformists, either. Instead, they are genuinely independent. They are often, in fact, quite conventional in matters and in actions that are not central to their areas of creative endeavor. It is in their creative striving that their independence of thought and autonomy of action are revealed. Indeed, it is characteristic of the highly creative person that he is strongly motivated to achieve in situations in which independence in thought and action are called for, but much less inclined to strive for achievement in situations where conforming behavior is expected or required. Flexibility with respect to means and goals is a striking characteristic of the groups we have studied.

On a test that measures the similarity of a person's expressed interests with the known interests of individuals successful in a variety of occupations and professions, creative persons reveal themselves as having interests similar to those of psychologists, architects, artists, writers, physicists, and musicians, and quite unlike those of purchasing agents, office men, bankers, farmers, carpenters, policemen, and morticians. These similarities and dissimilarities of interest are in themselves less significant than the abstractions and inferences that may be drawn from them. They suggest strongly that creative persons are relatively less interested in small details, in facts as such, and more concerned with their meanings and implications, possessed of considerable cognitive flexibility, verbally skilful, eager to communicate with others with nicety and precision, open to experience, and relatively uninterested in policing either their own impulses and images or those of others.

With respect to philosophical values — the theoretical, economic, esthetic, social, political, and religious as measured on one of our tests — there are two values most emphasized by all the creative groups. They are the theoretical and esthetic. One might think that there is some incompatibility and conflict between a cognitive and rational concern with truth and an emotional concern with form and beauty. If this is so, it would appear that the creative person has the capacity to tolerate the tension created in him by opposing strong values, and in his life and work he effects some reconciliation of them. Perhaps a less dramatic and more cautious interpretation of the simultaneous high valuing of the theoretical and the esthetic would be that for the truly creative person the solution of a problem is not sufficient; there is the further demand that it be elegant. The esthetic viewpoint permeates all of a creative person's work. He seeks not only truth but also beauty.

Closely allied to his strong theoretical and esthetic values is another pervasive trait of the creative, his preference for complexity, his delight in the challenging and unfinished, which evoke in him an urge, indeed a need, to discover unifying principles for ordering and integrating multiplicity.

In so brief a report, emphasis has had to be placed upon the generality of research findings. What needs to be equally emphasized is that there are many paths along which persons travel toward the full development and expression of their creative potential, and that there is no single mold into which all who are creative will fit. The full and complete picturing of the creative person will require many images. But if, despite this caution, one still insists on asking what most generally characterizes the creative individual as he has revealed himself in the Berkeley studies, it is his high level of effective intelligence, his openness to experience, his freedom from crippling restraints and impoverishing inhibitions, his esthetic sensitivity, his cognitive flexibility, his independence in thought and action, his high level of creative energy, his unquestioning commitment to creative endeavor, and his unceasing striving for solutions to the ever more difficult problems that he constantly sets for himself.

# THE CONDITIONS
# OF CREATIVITY

JEROME S. BRUNER

## I

There is, alas, a shrillness to our contemporary concern with creativity, and of this I would like to say a little. Man's search for the sources of his dignity changes with the pattern of his times. In periods during which man saw himself in the image of God, the creation of works *ad majorem Dei gloriam* could provide a sufficient rationale for the dignity of the artist, the artisan, the creative man. But in an age whose dominant value is a pragmatic one and whose massive achievement is an intricate technological order, it is not sufficient to be merely useful. For the servant can pattern himself on the master — and so he did when God was master and man. His servant creating works in His Glory — but the machine is the servant of man, and to pattern one's function on the machine provides no measure for dignity. The machine is useful, the system in terms of which the machines gain their use is efficient, but what is man?

The artist, the writer, and to a new degree the scientist seek an answer in the nature of their acts. They create or they seek to create, and this in itself endows the process with dignity. There is "creative" writing and "pure" science, each justifying the work of its producer in its own right. It is implied, I think, that the act of one creating is the act of a whole man, that it is this almost rather than the product that makes it good and worthy. So whoever seeks to proclaim his wholeness turns to the new slogan. There is creative advertising, creative engineering, creative problem solving — all lively entries in the struggle for dignity in our time.

Edited especially for this volume. Reprinted from Howard Gruber, ed., *Contemporary Approaches to Creative Thinking*, by permission of the author and publishers, Atherton Press. Copyright © 1962, Atherton Press, New York. All rights reserved. The author was assisted in this research by Dr. Jean MacKenzie Pool.

## II

We had best begin with some minimum working definition that will permit us at least to look at the same set of things. An act that produces *effective surprise* — this I shall take as the hallmark of a creative enterprise. The content of the surprise can be as various as the enterprises upon which men are engaged. It may express itself in one's dealing with children, in making love, in carrying on a business, in formulating physical theory, in painting a picture. I could not care less about the person's intention, whether he intended to create. The road to banality is paved with creative intentions. Surprise is not easily defined. It is the unexpected that strikes one with wonder or astonishment. What is curious about effective surprise is that it need not be rare or infrequent or bizarre and is often none of these things. Effective surprises, and we shall spell the matter out in a moment, seem rather to have the quality of obviousness to them when they occur, producing a shock of recognition, following which there is no longer astonishment. It is like this with great formulae, as in the formula for the conservation of energy or for the brilliant insight that makes chemistry possible, the conservation of mass. The stunning condensation of all falling bodies into Galileo's $S = \frac{1}{2} gt^2$ is of this order. It is also a self-evident surprise, after Agamemnon awards the arms of Achilles to Odysseus and not to Ajax, that Ajax's effort to kill himself on his own sword should be thwarted at first by the refusal of his sword to impale him. The maddened hero must thrust it into his heart through his vulnerable armpit.

I think it is possible to specify three kinds of effectiveness, three forms of self-evidence implicit in surprise of the kind we have been considering. The first is *predictive effectiveness*. It is the kind of surprise that yields high predictive value in its wake — as in the instance of the formula for falling bodies, or in any good theoretical reformulation in science. One may well argue that predictive effectiveness does not always come through surprise, but out of the slow accretion of knowledge, and urge, like Newton, *hypothesis non fingo*. I will reply by agreeing and specifying simply that whether the result of intuitive insight or of slow accretion, I will accept it within my definition. The surprise may only come when we look back and see whence we have come.

A second form of effectiveness is best called *formal*, and its most usual place is in mathematics and logic — possibly in music. One of the most beautiful descriptions of the phenomenon is to be found in Hardy's engaging *A Mathematician's Apology* (1941). It consists of an ordering of elements in such a way that one sees relationships that were not evident before, groupings that were before not present, ways of putting things together not before within reach. Consistency or harmony or depth of relationship is the result. One of the most beautiful and penetrating essays ever written on the subject is, of course, Poincaré's — in his *Science and Hypothesis* (1905). He speaks of making combinations that "reveal to us unsuspected kinship between . . . facts, long known, but wrongly believed to be strangers to one another." It was this kinship that he found on the famous trip he and his unconscious took from Caen to Coutances upon arrival at which there was the surprise of finding the continuity of transformations in Fuchsian functions and those in non-Euclidean geometry.

Of the final form of effectiveness in surprise it is more difficult to write. I shall call it *metaphorical effectiveness*. It, too, is effective by connecting domains of experience that were before apart, but with the form of connectedness that is art.

It is effective surprise that produces what Melville (1850) celebrated as the shock of recognition. Jung (1933) speaks of art that can produce such metaphoric connectedness as "visionary" in contrast to the merely psychological. It is, for example, Eliot's achievement in bringing into a single compass the experience of compassion and contempt in his *Prufrock* (1917), or in the achievement of the unknown Renaissance sculptor whose *Santa Maria Alba* brings to a single expression in sculpture the faces of woman as virgin, strumpet, flirt, daughter, wife, and mother. It is the connecting of diverse experiences by the mediation of symbol and metaphor and image. Experience in literal terms is a categorizing, a placing in a syntax of concepts. Metaphoric combination leaps beyond systematic placement, explores connections that before were unsuspected.[1]

### III

I propose that all the forms of effective surprise are the resultant of combinatorial activity — a placing of things in new perspectives. But it is somehow not simply that, not a taking of known elements and running them together by algorithm into a welter of permutations

One could design a calculator to do that, but it would be with embarrassment, for this is stupid even for a calculator, and Simon can show us much more interesting computer models than that.[2] "To create consists precisely in not making useless combinations and making those which are useful and which are only a small minority. Invention is discernment, choice." If not an algorithm, then it must be a heuristic that guides one to fruitful combinations. What is the heuristic? Poincaré (1905) urges that it is an emotional sensibility: "the feeling of mathematical beauty, of the harmony of numbers and forms, of geometric elegance." It is this that guides one in making combinations in mathematics. But this is surely not enough. One hears physicists speak of "physical intuition" as distinguishing the good theorist from the mere formalist, the mathematician. I suspect that in each empirical field there is developed in the creating scientist a kind of "intuitive familiarity," to use a term that L. J. Henderson was fond of, that gives him a sense of which combinations are likely to have predictive effectiveness and which are absurd. What precisely this kind of heuristic consists of is probably difficult to specify without reference to the nature of the field in question, which is not to say that the working models are utterly different in different areas of empirical endeavor, for there is obviously some generality, too.

One final point about the combinatorial acts that produce effective surprise. They almost always succeed through the exercise of technique. Henry Moore, who is unusually articulate both as craftsman and as artist, tells us (Ghiselin, 1952) that he was driven to the use of holes in his sculpture by the technical problem of giving a sense of three dimensionality to solid forms — "the hole connects one side to the other, making it immediately more three-dimensional," a discovery made while fretting over the puzzle of how to avoid relief carving on brittle material like stone. Consider Joseph Conrad and Ford Madox Ford, sitting before a scene, trying to describe it to each other in the most economical terms possible; Katherine Ann Porter on a campstool before a landscape trying to jot down everything before her — and finally deciding that she could not train her memory that way; Poincaré's endless struggle with his Fuchsian transformations. My young daughter once skated up to Dick Button, the great figure skater, who had just been doing some beautiful free figures on the Harvard rink, and asked him how she could learn to do that. His answer was as correct as it was sweet: "Janey, practice, practice,

practice, practice!" Technique, then, and how shall we combine it eventually with the doctrine of inspiration?

## IV

Let me now examine some of the conditions that affect the creative process. I have two objects in view. The first is to explore. More directly, however, I should like later to apply whatever notions we may come upon to a group of inventors whose behavior I studied for a year, participating with them as a member of an Invention-Design Group at a famous firm of consulting engineers.

As soon as one turns to a consideration of the conditions of creativity, one is immediately met by paradox and antinomy. A "determinant" suggests itself, and in the next pulse its opposite is suggested. I shall honor these antinomies and what I will have to say will, as a result, seem at times paradoxical.

*Detachment and Commitment.* A willingness to divorce oneself from the obvious is surely a prerequisite for the fresh combinatorial act that produces effective surprise. There must be as a necessary, if not a sufficient, condition a detachment from the forms as they exist.

But it is a detachment of commitment. For there is about it a caring, a deep need to understand something, to master a technique, to re-render a meaning. So while the poet, the mathematician, the scientist must each achieve detachment, they do it in the interest of commitment. And at one stroke they, the creative ones, are disengaged from that which exists conventionally, and are engaged deeply in what they construct in order to replace it.

*Passion and Decorum.* By passion I understand a willingness and ability to let one's impulses express themselves in one's life through one's work. I use it in the sense, "He has a passion for painting," or "She has a passion for cooking." I do not wish to raise or explore the Bohemian dilemma — whether the condition for passion in work is its expression in other forms of life. I happen to believe that Freud's fixed-quantity of libido (express it here and it must be withdrawn from there) is a kind of first-order nonsense. Passion, like taste, grows on its expression. You more likely do yourself into feeling rather than feel yourself into doing. In any case, it is true of the creative man that he is not indifferent to what he does; he has a passion for it. For the artist, if not for the scientist, there is a tapping of sources of imagery and symbolism that would otherwise not be available — as in the beautiful refrain line of Rimbaud's *Les Illumina-tions* (1953): "J'ai seul le clef de cette parade sauvage" (I alone hold the key to this wild parade). As for the scientist and the scholar, it is perhaps the eighteenth century French philosopher, Helvétius, who, in his *Treatise on Man* (1795–1796), has put it best: ". . . a man without passions is incapable of that degree of attention to which a superior judgment is annexed: a superiority that is perhaps less the effect of an extraordinary effort than an habitual attention. . . ."

But again a paradox. It is not all passion and vitality. There is a decorum in creative activity: a love of form, an etiquette toward the object of our efforts, a respect for materials. Rimbaud's wild beasts in the end are caged. For all that *Lord Jim* (Conrad, 1900) is a passionate book, full of the range of human impulse, it succeeds in the decorum that is provided by the dispassionate, gentlemanly narrator, Marlowe. Hercules of the myth was not a hairy ape ex-pressing mastery indiscriminately: his shrewd trickery is the de-corum. The wild flood of ideas that mathematicians like Hardy (1941) and Poincaré (1905) have described is eventually expressed in the courtesy of equations.

So both are necessary, and there must surely be a subtle matter of timing — when the impulse, when the taming.

*Freedom to Be Dominated by the Object.* You begin to write a poem. Before long, it, the poem, begins to develop metrical, stanzaic, symbolical requirements. You, as the writer of the poem, are serving it — it seems. Or you are pursuing the task of building a formal model to represent the known properties of single nerve fibers and their synapses: soon the model takes over. Or we say of an experiment in mid-stream that *it* needs another control group really to clinch the effect. It is at this point that one gets one's creative "second wind," at the point when the object takes over. I have asked about a dozen of my most creative and productive friends whether they knew what I meant as far as their own work was concerned. All of them replied with one or another form of timidity, most of them commenting that one usually did not talk about *this* kind of personal thing. The one psychologist among my informants was reminded of the Zeigarnik completion tendency, suggesting that when the watershed was reached, the task then had a structure that began to require completeness.

I have used the expression "freedom to be dominated" by the object being created. It is a strange choice of words, and I should like to explain it. To be dominated by an object of one's own creation — and its extreme is Pygmalion dominated by Galatea — is to be free of the defenses that keep us hidden from ourselves. And so as the object takes over and demands to be completed "in its own terms," it is temptation to express a style and an individuality. As one friend put it, "If it doesn't take over and you are foolish enough to go on, what you end up with is contrived and alien."

*Deferral and Immediacy.* There is an immediacy to creating a thing, a sense of direction, an objective, a general idea, a feel. Yet the immediacy is anything but a quick orgasm of completion. Completion is deferred.

This is not to say that there is not the occasional good luck, the piece that comes off "lickety-split" and finished, the theory hit upon at first fire.

I have read a good many journals and diaries by writers and have rather come to the conclusion that the principal guard against precocious completion, in writing at least, is boredom. I have little doubt that the same protection avails the scientist. It is the boredom of conflict, knowing deep down what one wishes to say and knowing that one has not said it. One acts on the impulse to exploit an idea, to begin. One also acts on the impulse of boredom, to defer.

*The Internal Drama.* There is within each person a cast of characters, his own cast of characters — an ascetic, and perhaps a glutton, a prig, a frightened child, a little man, even an on-looker, sometimes a Renaissance man.

As in the drama, so too a life can be described as a script, constantly rewritten, guiding the unfolding internal drama. It surely does not do to limit the drama to the stiff characters of the Freudian morality play — the undaunted ego, the brutish id, the censorious and punitive superego. Is the internal cast a reflection of the identifications to which we have been committed? I do not think it is as simple as that. It is a way of grouping our internal demands and there are idealized models over and beyond those with whom we have special identification — figures in myth, in the comics, in history, creations of fantasy.

There are some scripts that are more interesting than others. In some, there is a pre-empting protagonist in the center of the stage, constantly proclaiming, save for those moments when there are screamed intrusions from offstage, at which point the declaimer apologizes by pointing out that the voices are not really in the play. In others there is a richness, an inevitability of relationship, a gripping and constant exchange — or perhaps one should call it "inchange." These are dramatic personalities, surprise producers. I suppose it can be said that the first place where we may look for creativity is in the nature of the internal drama, the moving human being.

I would like to suggest that it is in the working out of conflict and coalition within the set of identities composing the person that one finds the source of many of the richest and most surprising combinations. It is not merely the artist and the writer, but the inventor, too, who is the beneficiary.

*The Dilemma of Abilities.* In the preceding pages we have looked at some of the paradoxical conditions that one might assume would affect the production of effective surprises — creativity. Nothing has been said about ability, or abilities. What shall we say of energy level, of combinational zest, of intelligence, of alertness, of perseverance? I shall say nothing about them. They are obviously important, but from a deeper point of view they are also trivial. For at any level of energy or intelligence there can be more or less of creating in our sense. Stupid people create for each other as well as benefiting from what comes from afar. So, too, do slothful and torpid people. I have been speaking of creativity, not of genius.

## V

I must say something now about my inventors, the Group. The Group with which we are concerned is as unique and full of idiosyncrasy as any other person or entity whose creative efforts we might study. It operates as a group, aloud, even noisily. Its deliberations are recorded and the sketches its members make are on huge sheets of paper rather than on a blackboard. We may go back and hear and look again, unquestionably an advantage. The hope was that in an externalized colloquy one might be able to acquire cues as to the manner in which the process of discovery and invention progressed, what things blocked the progress, what things swelled it. Perhaps because the members had to talk to share their notions with their tightly knit little community we would be able to catch more on the visible or audible wing. I have no illusions about this. In the end, there is still the question of how some members had fruitful things to propose and others were barren. But perhaps even here it was possible to find out something. For there were places and situations where the barren became useful and the fruitful were silent.

It is a Group that belongs to an engineering consulting firm of the kind that designs dams for India, atomic reactors for the government, and the rest. They work apart from the rest of the firm, physically and intellectually. It is the leader of the Group, not the personnel office, that hires the members. The Group that year consisted of six members, including the writer, and a highly skilled shop technician. The offices of the company front on a lake in a midwestern city that boasts a fine university which is situated close by. Behind the main building, chastely modern in design, there is a rather scuffed building that earlier served as a shop and drafting center. It is there that the Group works. Its quarters, a suite of rather ramshackle offices letting on to the beautifully equipped shop, have the air of a boys' club. There are models around, a half-finished sculpture, a large, barn-like room with old bookcases and redone couches, the walls hung with cellulose soundproofing that reminds one of attic space under the rafters on rainy afternoons in childhood. The windows give out upon a parking lot. The dress of the members is studiedly casual, from tweeds to turtlenecks. The two secretaries are part of the culture: clever, somewhat sardonic girls, educated at eastern colleges.

The members of the Group are in no conventional sense engineers. Their backgrounds are various and their job histories somewhat too checkered with changes to leave a conventional personnel office happy. There is a young man, an ex-Navy flier, who as an undergraduate at Brown studied linguistics and acoustics.[3] Another has worked as a designer of furniture with a certain success. He is a new member. One of the older members, approaching fifty, was an architect and works a bit at it still. The man closest to the leader of the Group, a somewhat religious man, was trained in paleontology. The architect and paleontologist are men of independent means, of good families, descended from New England gentry. So too is the furniture designer, though from a less established background. The ex-flier, who also paints rather well in oils, comes from humble immigrant origins. The shopman is a taciturn "Minnesota Swede."

The leader of the Group and its founder, the man who sold the idea to the engineering firm nearly ten years ago, is a flamboyant, wittily noisy, easy laughing man-about-town. He is short, rounded square with a rolling gait, crew cut, bushy eyebrows: a more muscular Henry VIII. He is a contrast to his own contemporaries who are tall, handsome, solidly lithesome, conventionally groomed. The ex-flier is slight, with a transparent skin and a somewhat watery aspect. The leader had studied some mathematics and philosophy as an undergraduate at Dartmouth. He too is independently well-off, a fine skier and swimmer, a born clowner, a man with a distinguished but ambiguous war record, a physically timid man in spite of his physical exploits.

The Group is very close in its relations. All of them had either been psychoanalyzed or had had some contact with psychiatry. They are psychoanalytic in outlook, and candid about it. They work hard and they are paid "when actually employed," as the personnel records say. The work is varied: jobs are sent their way from the research and development section of the company — the unconventional jobs that either fall outside the scope of the "main office" or relate to something the Group has worked on before. But mostly the jobs come from outside: from business, the armed services, and civilian agencies of the government. The Group thinks of itself as a court of last resort — the jobs they take on are ones that have already stumped others. Failure, then, is no great sin.

Let me give a picture of the mode of work on a job. The job, let us say, is to design a prototype model or models of solar energy units for small homes, ones that can be used for generating electricity to be stored in accumulator batteries. It has been screened first by the Group leader, determining whether they would take it on, whether it is general enough and interesting enough. The Group meets, it is nine o'clock in the boys' club room, the excellent tape recorder is turned on. This is almost a ritual. Walt (I shall call the Group leader that) leads in some literate and bawdy wisecracking as the equipment is being put in order. Then Walt will begin the presentation, and this is carefully done. It will consist of skirting the specific problem, talking about the general case. In this instance it may be the general question, "How do you catch light or heat?" or even, "What is something that is radiant?" This is the Group's ideology and the members do not feel "left out." Walt will enliven the presentation with his usual style of literate bawdiness: "Let us not begin by making little wee-wee holes in the snow. What gives with radiation and how do you capture as much of it as possible? and for Christ's sake, no zippers please" (referring to the tendency to come up with gadgets before they have the problem in the broad).

Likely as not, the Group will get under way through the impetus of somebody's metaphor, and in this company, the metaphors at the outset are almost sure to be organic. "What does a person radiate?" And somebody will say, "Glances?" And then, "Well, how do you catch a glance?" Or, "A dog's in heat, how do all the mutts in the neighborhood find out?" After a while, Walt will become a bit more specific. "Hey, knuckleheads, how do we get out of this one, if it's radiant energy like the sun? Maybe get some blonde cuties to lie out in the sun to lure it down, huh? Get Minsky to design them." Gradually, the problem emerges until it is all there, and for a while Walt and the others will attempt to keep the touch light with, "Wish we could do this one sitting on the beach in Acapulco," or "I can't think of sun without my bikini."

After an hour or an hour and a half, somebody will ask for the tapes to be played back, and the Group will sit and listen, until somebody picks up a compelling cue, urging that "the voices be turned off." The playback has a striking function in allowing the Group to re-examine its ideas with a sense of distance and detachment, and it is very often the case that one hears things in these playbacks, good ideas, that went unheard in the din and commitment of the original event. At any given point, a member may come forth with, "By god, I have the solution," and the others will stop and listen with some appropriate preliminary remark like, "Duck, here comes the cannon ball express again," for quick solutions are distrusted good-humoredly. The session will come to an end after two and a half or three hours, with breaks in between (in the room) for coffee. People drift in and out in the sagging middle period to make a phone call, but not often. Up to a dozen such meetings will be held before the project is completed, the times between being spent in tracking facts in the literature, going to talk to somebody about an expert matter, mocking up models, consulting the client. Sometimes the subject will be dropped for several weeks on the plea of getting nowhere, or of boredom. Along the way, ideas will come up for the new design of a pressure cooker, or a draftproof sleeping bag, or a new way to scrimshaw a boat's fixtures — byproducts of the main concern. These are not pursued for more than a few minutes: "They'll keep on the tape," or "OK, Bruner, you won't forget it, you would-be millionaire."

Very early one notices an interlocking set of identities, the meshing of several casts of characters, each brought by a different member. One, in a flamboyant mood, will parade his wild ideas, addressing them to another who, that day or in general, acts as tamer, counting on the tamer to bring him to earth at the appropriate moment. Another pair will reinforce each other with one being concerned about convenience and comfort in the product, the other with ease of production. And perhaps most important, all the members share in a community where elegance and generality are a standard — a set of Renaissance self-images that all reinforce in each other as a means of keeping the ubiquitous pragmatist at bay until needed. Beneath the surface other identities clash.

As the project moves to a close, as models are constructed and contempt is heaped upon all prior efforts outside the Group to deal "muddily" with the problem, the roles become stabilized. The architect may come to act more exclusively like one, the fringe of fantasy suppressed. By now the models and the emerged idea will have taken over. *It* dominates, and you may see the Group standing around the drawing board or around the model, talking about "it" needing this or that. Reference to "I," such as "I think we need to do so-and-so," begins to drop out. Walt will say to the furniture designer, "Leave the goddamned thing alone; stop hanging things on it, or it will end up like a fisherman's hat."

There is much talk in the Group, in pauses, about the process that they use. The members are self-conscious, they write memoranda about it, eagerly try to sell it to their clients, several of whom have, indeed, set up groups within their own companies to use much the same procedure on recalcitrant or off-beat problems.

This will do for a sketch. What has this to do with what went before?

## VI

Let me say, first, that the Group has produced nothing that is likely to revolutionize the life of either consumers or producers. They have obviously succeeded in producing things that are more imaginative than what comes out of the run-of-the-mill research departments of clients.

The creativity of the Group comes in considerable measure, let me say in the spirit of hypothesis, from the following factors:

*Detachment and Commitment.* Detachment for this Group comes in a variety of ways, crucial ways. Being "out back," away from the company, operating in a kind of den — this surely helps. The literate and aesthetic quality of the little culture marks it off from the "square-headed engineers" who couldn't solve the problem at hand with their conventional methods. "Experts you want to call in on this one yet! Go see them in the woodwork and pick their termite brains. Then let's see what we can do." It matters greatly that the image the Group has of itself is that of elegant generalists, not wedded to any particular way of proceeding. The members identify more with the university community than with the firm which, they feel, would cheerfully get rid of them were they not doing such a "terrific" job.

Minimizing the cost in self-esteem for error and wildness of hypothesis also increases detachment from the conventional, and in a major way. Both the "last resort" psychology of the Group and the manner in which unfit ideas are rejected reinforce this cost reduction. Rejection of ideas is never conventionally polite, but it is warm and direct. To Walt somebody will say, "How can such an occasionally intelligent character like you come up with such a turkey! Go out and take a pep pill, boy." Or, "Look, the reason that idea is no good, aside from the fact that it doesn't work, is that you got it from a pterodactyl, and they're extinct."

It is also by the use of the general formulation, the worship of the general case, that the members achieve detachment from conventional procedure — "zipper methods." In a sense, their pride is in doing it differently, more simply, in a way that is not trivial and one-shot.

The commitment comes with these men (and I believe this is their weakness) out of the sense that their operation is what marks them as creative men — a status that none of them has achieved on his own. They have an image of themselves as humdrum without the Group as a mode of expression. It makes for a certain preciousness, a certain overly-long lingering on body imagery and organic metaphor.

Yet, for all this, there is no question that as a product development grows, the Group becomes committed to it, pursues it, takes pride in it. There are few instances of an injured sense of priority about ideas. Walt goes out of his way to give everybody credit — both within the Group and with the clients. And what has become quite interesting recently is that there is a sense of pride in parentage — that others have picked up the idea of this kind of free-wheeling, not-expert group.

*Passion and Decorum.* I have never seen a work group in which there was such a wide latitude for the expression of impulse in connection with work. From the point of view of efficiency, it is wasteful, I rather suspect. Of only one thing is the Group especially wary, and of this they are not always consciously aware. When a member proposes metaphoric notions over a series of meetings that seem to be expressing an acting-out of personal troubles in his life, there is a growing access of politeness, and the usual camaraderie of idea-rejection freezes into measured protectiveness. Yet there are areas in which metaphors do not occur, where ideas are not exploited. There is a taboo, unwritten, on mention of homosexuality, for the working relationship is too close for that. No reference is made to relations with wives, and it is as well since several of the wives feel the Group to be too dominant in the lives of their husbands, too dependency-making. But in general, almost anything goes, provided it can be transformed into the grammar of the problem.

The principal source of decorum is in the adoration of elegance and generality: let the hypotheses be wild, the solution must be as elegant and generalized as possible. The sense of the Group's identity depends upon this idea, of course, for it is in this respect that they see themselves as intellectuals rather than drones, inventors rather than amateur engineers. But there is something more, too. It is interesting that, to a man, the members have a sense of the goodness and the fitness of materials. It comes partly from the fact that before a problem ever reaches the material stage, likely as not it has been hammered out in terms of what kind of materials are required. So the material, on the whole, is deduced. And when it fills the requirements, it is treated as an ally.

*Autonomy of the Object.* The Group is quite self-conscious on this score. "It's on the tape," or "Get Elaine to bring in that bunch of sketches from the time before last," are typical comments in the early stages. At the later stages, models take over, and when they do, there is a notable reduction in strain. The most extreme example is a can opener of a revolutionary design, a closely guarded trade secret, that lives a magical life of its own. There is about some of the members a quality of unquenched adolescence that includes a real passion for externalized models, and it helps.

*The Internal and the External Cast.* Unfortunately, space does not permit a proper account of the manner in which the Group interacts in a way to bring out the diversity of each member's cast. For to describe the matter in appropriate detail would take more by way of description of personalities and the situations in which they express their complex identities than can be accomplished here.

In general, it seems to me, one can make the following points about this subtle matter. First, the Group provides a matrix of relations that for virtually every member permits expression of a wider range of identities than one normally finds in a work setting. Having provided the condition for more of each member's cast to be onstage, it then provides a focus of work for their expression, a passion for whatever enterprise is on the board. So while the Group may be lacking in expertise, it is not lacking in rich hypotheses for guiding the members to information as they need it.


## VII

At the outset I proposed that we define the creative act as effective surprise — the production of novelty. It is reasonable to suppose that one will some day devise a proper theoretical model capable of understanding and predicting such arts.

Often it is the poet who grasps these matters most firmly and communicates them most concisely. Perhaps it is our conceit that there is only one way of understanding a phenomenon. I have urged that just as there is predictive effectiveness, so is there metaphoric effectiveness. Our patience may be tested as scientists before we are through. For the while, at least, we may have to live with a metaphoric understanding of creativity, hoping that in time we may be able to tame our metaphors to a useful predictiveness.


### FOOTNOTES

1. Herbert Simon points out quite rightly that there is an interesting parallel between the three forms of effectiveness I have noted and the three modes of evaluating symbol systems proposed some years ago by Charles Morris (1938): formal effectiveness being the province of syntactics, predictive effectiveness the domain of semantics, and metaphoric effectiveness

being closely related to pragmatics. The parallel is anything but trivial. The formal, the empirical, and the aesthetic — these are the three principal expressions of cognitive functioning and each generates its own criterion of effectiveness, even of truth. It is worth a note in passing that the three modes have at least one thing in common: at the frontiers of their respective excellence, they all seem to fit a common criterion of beauty.

2. J. T. Culbertson has elucidated the interesting, if stupidly inefficient, properties of such an algorithmic computing problem-solver, and if the reader is interested in pursuing the matter, he is referred to Culbertson's paper in *Automata Studies* (1956).

3. The reader will recognize, of course, that appropriate disguises are being introduced to protect the anonymity of the Group and its members. Yet, though details have been changed, I hope that I have retained the spirit.

## REFERENCES

Culbertson, J. T., "Some Uneconomical Robots," in *Automata Studies*, No. 34, eds. G. E. Shannon and J. McCarthy (Princeton, N. J.: Princeton University Press, 1956).

Eliot, T. S., *The Love Song of J. Alfred Prufrock* (New York: Harcourt, Brace, 1917).

Ghiselin, B., ed., *The Creative Process* (Berkeley: University of California Press, 1952).

Hardy, G. H., *A Mathematician's Apology* (Cambridge, England: Cambridge University Press, 1941).

Jung, C. J., *Modern Man in Search of a Soul*, trans. W. S. Dell and C. F. Baynes (New York: Harcourt, Brace, 1933).

Melville, H., "Hawthorne and His Mosses," *Literary World* (August 17 and 24, 1850).

Morris, C. W., *Foundations of the Theory of Signs* (Chicago: University of Chicago Press, 1938).

Poincaré, H., *Science and Hypothesis* (London: Scott, 1905).

# C.

## ACHIEVEMENT AND WOMEN

# AMERICAN WOMEN AND
# AMERICAN VALUES

## FLORENCE ROCKWOOD KLUCKHOHN

Four distinguishable aspects of the present-day feminine role have been stated by Professor Talcott Parsons of Harvard University.[1] First is the domestic component, which, though once a unitary whole, is now noticeably split into the two ill-fitting parts of *mother-wife* and *housewife*. Being a mother has real merit; but whenever a woman is heard to remark, "Oh, I am *just* a housewife," she is voicing a doubt as to the importance of her work. Second is the *career* or job component, which is looming larger and larger in the lives of many women. Third is that aspect which can best be called the *glamour girl* component. For many women this specific role is important before marriage; for some it continues to be of importance for many — perhaps too many — years thereafter. The fourth aspect Professor Parsons labels the humanistic component. I prefer to call it the *culture bearer* component, meaning by culture in this instance all the refinements, the aesthetic, intellectual and moral interests, which busy men often see as the "embroidery" of American life, an embroidery which women can take care of in the spare time that men themselves do not have. Cross-cutting all these components and hence not so clearly distinguishable is a fifth and most important one which I would add to the list, woman as the husband's or father's *status symbol*.

The history of the feminine role is really a history of these components, and it is far from being the uniform, straight-line evolution that can be, and has been, traced by the noting of only the changes in women's political status, or the rights women have won before the law. Legal and political status are not the whole of social status,

Edited especially for this volume. Reprinted with abridgement from Lyman Bryson, ed., *Facing the Future's Risks*. Copyright 1953 by Mutual Insurance 200th Anniversary Committee. Reprinted by permission of Harper & Row, publishers, and the author.

453

and sometimes not even the most important part. This is particularly the case when conflicting values are present in what is expected or allowed by law, and that which is required by more pervasive social customs. Indeed, most of the strains and tensions which so many women feel today arise from the discrepancies in values the several components are expressing. Some of these components are in accord with general, or dominant, American values; others are not. Thus, even today in the year 1952, women can be said to be participating only partially, or indirectly, in those activities for which are reserved the most highly prized symbols of prestige and the most sought-after rewards. These activities are chiefly, of course, those of the business and professional world.

The term "value" has many meanings, and no doubt there is already some question about what is being referred to as basic American values. Core values, some would call them. I much prefer the term "value orientations," and mean by it the basic assumptions or tenets which are expressed in the total philosophy of one people as differentiated from another. For, if social science has taught us anything in recent years, it is that not all peoples have the same views as to the right and proper way to solve the several universal or broadly human problems. Although I believe that it can be shown that there are definite limits to the possible variations in views, it is of the greatest significance that people do differ. They differ widely in what they deem to be the right and proper way of relating man to other men, and in the conception of man's relationship to the natural world in which he lives. They also vary in the types of personality and activities they value highly. They treat the problem of time variously and differ again in what they define basic human nature to be.

An emphasis upon individualistic human relationships, a belief that natural forces are to be exploited, or at least harnessed, by man for his own use, a great stress upon an action or accomplishment type of personality, a firm conviction that it is always the future to which one must look and strive for, and a conception of human nature as being in need of perfection through self-control — these are in a brief phrasing the solid core of value orientations in the American way of life. Or, at least they are the core of what is dominantly and ideally the American way of life.

Most Americans take these value orientations as so much given, so definitely what is and must be, that they seldom call any of them into question. In the minds of many they are deeply embedded at unconscious levels of thought; hence tend to be considered as absolute values, the *only* right and proper ones. This is a chief reason why misunderstanding so frequently arises between Americans and the peoples of the many nations with whom there is now, because of international crises, a necessarily constant contact. It is also a reason why it is difficult to recognize and acknowledge the fact that some persons within our own borders are not full participants in those parts of national life which best express these central values.

But even though not well recognized, the differences exist. I want to describe the variations in three of these orientations for the light they throw on masculine and feminine role differences. First, the view of man's relations to other men. Typically, the American view is that of an individualistic relationship. Cooperation is believed to be essential and a good thing in itself, but first and foremost must come the goals and aims of individuals acting as free and autonomous persons. For example, while it certainly is expected that the business or professional man who is a member of an organization will have a positive attitude toward the aims and purposes of that organization, and will cooperate with his fellow workers, who but the rare person would expect him to turn down an offer of a better job elsewhere and sacrifice personal advancement just because of attachments to the goals of one organization? It happens, of course, that some men do just that, but there is no requirement that they do so and no terrific social sanctions if they do not.

Yet in other societies this is what is required. The first order emphasis must be on group goals and all individual ones are conceived to be subordinate to them. The individual is not autonomous and not free to make his own way on his own initiative. Instead he is considered a representative of a fixed group whose goals he must always put ahead of his own.

I have phrased this difference as between countries to sharpen the contrast. It is always, however, also found *within* countries. One of the marked dissimilarities in the role of men and women in the United States is precisely this one. Men, in their main sphere of activity, the occupational world, are autonomous; women, in their domestic role, that is, as wives, mothers, housewives, are primarily representatives from whom a dedication to group goals is expected behavior. This is a tremendous difference in a country that ideally stands for an equality of the sexes. A central issue for years has been that of her right to an individualistic type of self-expression.

The second of the values we need to note is that of the valued personality type, or, if one wishes to put it another way, the kinds of activities for which individuals receive the greatest approval. That the generalized American view of this is a preference for the person of action, a type I have called the *doing* personality, is, or should be, evident to everyone. "Getting things done," and finding the way "to do something about it" are stock American phrases. Furthermore, "What does he do," or "What can or will be accomplished?" are almost always the ranking questions in any scale of appraisal of persons. One writer,[2] in a whimsical discussion of how it felt to be the husband of a suffragette in the year 1915, expressed the view in these words: "It is far more important that a man *make good* than *be good*, and this applies with special force to husbands."

Yet evident as it may be that men of action are the American preference, it is not equally apparent that other peoples place their value emphasis upon different personality types. In some countries the preference is for the spontaneous personality which has small concern with achievement of any sort. Mexicans, among whom I have lived from time to time, have such a preference, and most action-oriented United States Americans call them lazy. In other places it is the reflective personality devoted to a self-realization through intellectual, aesthetic, and religious activities that is most highly valued.

Where one finds these alternative preferences it is more often the scholar, the statesman, or even the man of leisure who represents the ideal. In sharp contrast, the American ideal is the businessman, practical, hard-headed, and efficient. Scholars in the United States have usually been called "long-hairs" and statesmen mere politicians, because neither the affairs of the mind nor matters of government have a significance or a prestige comparable to that found in the business world.

Yet many Americans have never been easy in their minds about the definiteness of this preference. Not infrequently there are uncomfortable reactions when someone asks, as Nehru is reported to have done at a luncheon in one of our universities, "Is it really true that Americans have no time for reflection and do not know how to meditate?" A partial answer was to make women responsible for all those pursuits which men tend to consider the embroidery of the American life, desirable embroidery certainly, but embroidery nonetheless.

The preferred or favored time dimension is the third of the basic values which have a bearing upon masculine and feminine role differences. The American choice in this value orientation is clearly that of *future time*. The typically good citizen is the one who always looks ahead and strives hard for a future which is certain to be both bigger and better, if only he will work hard, plan well, and save. Americans recognize a past and are sometimes deeply sentimental about parts of it, but the respect for true traditionalism, which is so often a dominant value in other countries, is small indeed. As for evaluation of the present, there is something immoral about those of us, and there are many, who choose to live from day to day with little regard for either the past or the future.

But relative to this value, too, it is chiefly men who are supposed to be actively future oriented. For the most part, though not entirely, daughters and wives are limited to a vicarious participation. They are often praised for the help and encouragement they give to an advancing man and sometimes verbally lashed or ridiculed for their nagging and prodding, but the fact remains that a majority of the achievements of future promise are those of fathers, husbands, or sons. The glory which comes from mounting success is largely a man's glory, the light from which is, for women, merely reflective.

In all these respects, a woman's role, in some of its component parts and time phases, is markedly at variance with the dominant American values which are much better and more often expressed in the role of the man. The role is a variant role, patterned in accord with variant values, whereas the masculine role, mainly an occupational one, is a dominant role expressing dominant values. Therefore, the roles of American men and women are not really complementary. The existent variation has created a gap between the interests and aims of husbands and wives which widens with each passing year. Few feel free to admit or discuss this gap because there is a concept of ideal marriage which says it should not be there.

The question is why this variance developed and has been maintained so long in spite of great efforts to break it down. Complete answers to questions of this magnitude are seldom, and never easily, found. But if one looks thoughtfully into the history of the feminine role, into all the trends and countertrends which have gone into the making of its five component parts, one can find sufficient clarification to undertake a cogent reasoning as to what may be expected or can, perhaps, be effected in the years ahead.

Of all the components in the feminine role, the domestic one is certainly the oldest. For a long time, all during the American colonial period, certainly, custom decreed it to be the only right and proper one for almost all women whether in the North or the South. "Women was indeed a sweet sex," writes one historian, "but her sphere was narrow." The training of women for anything other than domestic virtue was almost universally conceived to be a waste of time and substance; worse still, it endangered their minds. Puritan friends did not search long or far for causes when the wife of one Massachusetts governor became insane. "Had she not gone out of her way and calling to meddle in such things as are proper for men, whose minds are stronger, she had kept her wits and might have improved them usefully and honorably in the place God set her."

This concept of woman's work retained much of its content as long as the United States remained a predominantly rural nation. It lingers still as a total concept, that is, as a unitary domestic component composed of both a wife-mother role and a housewife role. But what a hollow concept the latter part is today for many women, especially those in cities and of the middle class! One has only to glance over the advertisements in the many current magazines to realize that the home as a house to be managed is pictured constantly as a mild variety of penal institution. Work in it must be reduced to a minimum, say all these advertisements for all kinds of gadgets and household equipment, the washing machines, eggbeaters, dishwashers, and vacuum cleaners. If dishes must be washed by hand, one must certainly be sure to use a type of soap which will ensure against dishpan hands. For feminine glamour must be preserved! If meals must be prepared, they can go into an automatic cookstove which has the mechanical sense to cook whole meals in empty houses.

There is not a thing wrong, morally or otherwise, with either the gadgets or the saving of time. I most emphatically do not agree with the two authors of a book entitled *Modern Woman the Lost Sex* when they suggest as one solution for present-day difficulties in the feminine role a removal of all or most household aids. One might as well expect a farmer to store his tractor and buy back his team of horses. We cannot have a technological era and limit the use of the conveniences it provides to the masculine half of the population. This would be but one more illustration of women's partial participation in our type of society.

It is something far more significant than mere gadgetry that all the advertisements for the household aids are conveying. Almost every one of them is tacitly saying that household tasks are menial, a drudgery, and hence provide few significant rewards or satisfactions. They lack the worth of true accomplishment. This is the basic difference between the attitude toward the tractor and the automatic dishwasher. It is still a good thing to get the fields plowed and the crops cultivated; it is only a necessity that the dishes be washed. Would it not seem obvious that one place in which constructive alteration can be made in the feminine role is in the attitudes which housewives themselves, and all others as well, have regarding household tasks?

Although it is true that not all colonial women were as I have pictured them, that there were many who can more easily be likened to stalwart trees than hyacinths for all the work they did in numerous occupations, it is still a fact that woman's role was little changed until the nineteenth century. It is in the history of the nineteenth century that one can see so clearly the changes effected in the feminine role by these events and trends: industrialization; a romantic movement borrowed from Europe; the feminist movement; the development of a definite middle-class ideology in the society as a whole; a shattering Civil War. Each of these had its marked but often different effect upon the evolution of woman's role. Indeed, much of the present-day confusion concerning her role has stemmed fairly directly from the numerous contradictions which the frequently opposing nineteenth-century trends produced.

The rapid industrialization of the country alone brought about changes of different kinds. For the first time in history, a large number of women attempted to combine their domestic role with an occupational one for which money wages were paid. The immediate effects of the employment of women, chiefly in factories, were sorry ones. Family life was disrupted by a mother's long hours away from home. All too frequently both women and children were hired because they were cheap labor and the legal rights of women were still too few for them to protest or make demands on their own behalf. In most places women still were not permitted by law any control over their own earnings.

Indeed, to make a long story short, many of the workingwomen of the nineteenth century were much exploited both by employers and by the men at home, fathers, husbands, and even brothers and sons. One young millworker has left this statement of her own and other girls' reasons for their long hours at a textile loom:

> The most prevailing incentive to our labor was to secure the means of education for some male member of the family. To make a gentleman of a brother or son, to give him a college education, was the dominant thought in the minds of a great many of these provident girls.

Eventually there were more favorable results which derived in part at least from woman's entrance into the industrial world, but they were slow in coming. A partial cause of the slowness was the quickly growing countertrend which was bringing about an idealization of the women of another economic group, the women who were the wives and daughters of men of means and substance. It was these women to whom Pearl Buck had reference when she wrote of the nineteenth century era of the "angel on the pedestal," for there certainly was no pedestal standing beside the weaver's loom.

Obviously the number of ladies of fashion in the country as a whole was not large. Yet their influence was great, for they were the models for all other women to admire or envy and emulate. They were, however, only one type of woman and were representative of only a little of what was happening. Contemporary with the genteel lady, and with the factory worker as well, was the feminist who was busy making history in a remarkably different way. Even though the origins of the woman's rights movement lie far back in time, the movement as a movement is usually considered to be both American and nineteenth century.

Under the leadership of such forceful and able persons as Susan B. Anthony, Elizabeth Cady Stanton and Lucy Stone, many women went on the march and did their marching in a bloomer brigade. For rebellion against restrictions had gone beyond the legal rules first attacked, and extended even to modes of dress. In some quarters the clamor was terrific, but let it be said for Americans that they almost always find something to laugh at, even in what they deplore. And certainly that costume, which one person has described as a smother of clothes which had mainly the advantage of revealing woman to be a biped, was an easy target for humor as well as outrage. Indeed, for a period the bloomer costume was the chief symbol of the whole suffrage movement.

Eventually the suffragettes reluctantly abandoned their bloomers. They had proved too much an issue and were becoming too serious a handicap in achieving the main goals of the woman's rights movement. But a return to feminine dress did not at all dampen the ardor of the women for their campaign. The fight went on and extended, as all know, into the twentieth century. It goes on yet. As the movement went over the line between the centuries and neared achievement of some of its stated goals, the arguments on both sides became more blunt and forceful. On the side of the opposition there were many statements such as these an irate congressman is reported to have voiced:[3]

> I do not believe that there is a red blooded man in the world who in his heart believes in woman's suffrage. I think every man who favors it should be made to wear a dress . . . I have seen them here in the Capitol. The suffragettes and a little hen pecked fellow crawling along beside her; that is her husband. She is a suffragette, and he is mortal suffering yet.

In voices made firm by years of effort against just such opposition as this, the women took a forceful stand. Some pushed the claims of equality to limits which greatly obscured, when they did not obliterate altogether, the fact that there are basic differences between the sexes which inevitably make for some variation in the role each must play. Thus it was that, while benefits to women, such as the vote, gains in legal rights and educational opportunities, came from the woman's rights movement, problems also were created. It is chiefly due to the suffrage movement that modern woman has inherited what a writer as long ago as 1922 called the vicious alternative, marriage *or* career. Many of the problems which educators find today in the methods of training women also stem from it, for it was the feminists who insisted that women be educated exactly as men were educated.

There was yet another type of nineteenth-century woman who was influential in altering woman's role. This was the pioneer woman of the American frontier. More than any other of the women described, this woman has been well enshrined in the sentiments of all Americans.

The pioneer women were indeed persons of great courage, and to do what was required of them they had to have daring, resourcefulness, and fortitude in large measure. When persons have these qualities, and also live in groups which are unstructured and fluid, they do not argue about equality; they assume it. In so far as their status was concerned, it was also to the advantage of pioneer women that they were few in number. As has been frequently remarked, any woman, no matter how unattractive, could be assured a wide range of choice in marriage partners if only she had the daring to venture out on the frontier and the strength to withstand its terrors. And, once married, she assumed a position of authority within the family that no other women of the time had.

There is irony in the fact that many of the symbols of recognition so dear to the hearts of the feminists were won more easily and earlier on the plains of the West than on the feminists' own eastern battleground. The first seven of the states to vote in woman's suffrage, for example, were western states, and all of these, except Kansas, far western ones.

But these frontier women were not feminists arguing a cause to the extreme, and in some ways they had an effect upon woman's role which did not accord well with feminist aims. The demands that women be made the equals of men in the occupational world were only faintly echoed in the family life of the West. The spheres of the two sexes were still distinctly and differently defined. Indeed, if one were to single out but one major contribution of frontier family life to the feminine role it would certainly be the enormous strengthening of the authority of woman within the home. In it one finds the main source of the all-powerful mother-child relationship in the present-day American family.

Pioneer women, feminists, genteel ladies, and factory workers — each of these kinds of women, and the processes they represented, were creating new designs for woman's role. Some parts of these designs were similar, but others were radically different. As a total assortment of parts to be fitted into the structure of the whole role, they offered small promise of any consistency in expectations or requirements. Yet some ordering of all the pieces was essential if there was ever to be any consensus in the conception of woman's roles as seen in the South, North, East and West, in cities and rural areas, or in the different economic classes.

Although the contradictions in the role are still numerous, there has been some ordering of its parts in the past fifty to seventy-five years. And of all the agents responsible for the ordering process the most effective were probably America's three large-scale wars: the Civil War in the nineteenth century and the two world wars in the twentieth.

It was during the Civil War, or War Between the States, that women in large numbers were for the first time called on to help meet a national emergency. In both the North and the South, women of all kinds took over the work that fighting men had had to forsake. Most of these women displayed in all that they did a courage and a level of ability which was astonishing to both themselves and others.

To the nation as a whole this may have been just another case of women responding well to an emergency situation. For many women it was significantly more than this. They found in war work a sense of usefulness and personal satisfaction hitherto unknown to them, and they viewed a return to their former way of life with anxious reluctance.

Some of the women thus affected sought a new way of life by pushing their way into business and the professions. The census of 1870 was the first in American history to list employed persons by sex. It was also only after the Civil War that nursing was recognized as a profession. However, the number of women who did any of these things was small, for the resistance to having women in the occupations, other than as factory workers, was still strong even among women themselves.

Many more women found yet another solution for the restlessness they had come to feel. This was the organized woman's club, the first two of which were founded in 1868. No one needs to be reminded of the variety of things the women of America have attempted to do, often most successfully, through their organized groups. Most persons today are equally aware of the fact that women have more and more taken over the volunteer work in community organizations, most especially in the residential suburbs which are chiefly women's communities inhabited by commuting men only intermittently.

But much as this type of work has meant to some women, its appeal has never been generalized to all. There have always been those, today a growing number, who have felt that what could be accomplished by women, organized apart from men, in groups which pursued first one goal and then another, was not comparable to the opportunities for achievement which the business world afforded.

Even in the early years of this century, the number of women on the lists of the gainfully employed was gradually increasing. Then came World War I with its demand that women once more move into the work posts left vacant by suddenly mobilized men. As in the Civil War, most of the women workers performed well and were warmly commended for having done their share in winning a war. But this time mere praise was not sufficient. Many women, for a variety of reasons, preferred to stay on the job, and did. By 1930 one-fourth of all women 16 years and over were in the labor force. Although not exactly a revolt, this certainly was the beginning of an invasion.

Going to work was not, however, the only or even the most evident sign of women's growing demand for independence and the right to be individuals in an individualistic society. The woman of the "roaring twenties" made herself into a flapper and smashed hard at some of the nineteenth-century conceptions of womanly ways. There were two main directions in which the flapper moved, and neither was entirely new, although it is to be suspected she herself thought they were. As we look back upon all her efforts to flatten breasts, streamline hips, shorten hair, and her striving to prove her ability to compete successfully with men on playing fields and in classrooms, we often call her radical. But was she so radical in this emulation of the masculine? There was much in all these aspects of her behavior which was clearly reminiscent of feminism.

Perhaps the failure to see the similarity comes from the fact that the flapper had so many other ways of behaving which tended to maximize rather than minimize sex differences. It was relative to the flapper that the term "sex appeal" first came into common usage, and it was she who made glamour a practical if not entirely proper means for feminine achievement. This concept, which is still with us and perhaps better accepted now that it has been tempered with time, was as clear cut in its separation of the spheres of the sexes as were many nineteenth-century ideas. It differed from them mainly in that it included and openly acknowledged sexuality as a legitimate feminine interest. The decorative and pampered "doll" of nineteenth-century fame may have had sex appeal, but she dared not flaunt it or use it openly as a means to success.

The flapper died, of course, after a brief day in a brief period of ostentation of many another kind than hers.

But even though her life was short she accomplished much. She dealt a death blow to the notion of the genteel lady, blurred the line between the "good" woman and the "bad," and raised to prominent position the glamour component of the feminine role. Simultaneously she aided the newly employed woman in forcing a recognition of woman's right to participate in many more activities as man's equal.

The evidence that some of these changes were substantial ones is found in the manner in which women were mobilized for World War II. The newspapers of ten years ago did not hesitate to use captions which declared "THIS IS A WOMAN'S WAR TOO." For the first time women were marshaled into the armed services and had meted out to them many more tasks and responsibilities than those of nursing. Complicated technical work was turned over to women, and people everywhere became accustomed to seeing women perform service functions which only men had done before. There were approximately 16 million women in the labor force when World War II ended. In 1951, as has been mentioned before, the figure stood well above the 18 million mark, and of greater significance than the actual increase is the fact that it is the employment of married women which mainly accounts for it. There are now over 10 million married women in the occupations without counting farm wives, many of whom would certainly call themselves employed women.

The vicious alternative of extreme feminism, marriage *or* career, has been changed by modern women to marriage *and* career, or at least marriage and the job. The switch of conjunctions is a meaningful one, and the issue as now phrased will undoubtedly be recorded in future history of the feminine role as the major one of the mid-twentieth century. This prediction is, however, general and does not state which of several possible phrasings will finally be given to the issue. Certainly, to some extent, both the final phrasing and the effects it may have for family life and the whole society will depend upon what thoughtful men and women think and do in the near future. A trend once started may be difficult to stay, but few Americans submit to the view that human beings can have no say in the direction trends will take.

Being myself a majority American, I would like, in conclusion, to summarize briefly the three factors which I believe to be the main reasons for the formulation of this current issue.

The three main factors in the order of their importance are: the changes which have come in the wife-mother role; woman's growing dissatisfaction with typically feminine activities outside the home; the character of woman's education.

There is little reason to doubt that for a vast majority of American women the wife-mother role is still the dominant component in the total role. Although there are women who refuse to become wives and mothers because they believe the marital state hampering to self-expression, they are few. Most of America's single women are not single by choice. They either failed to find and attract a man who also attracted, or they gave him up for reasons of pride or duty to others.

The idealization of the American woman is primarily an idealization of her motherhood. As one writer has caustically remarked, American men more often seek mothers in their marriages than wives. It is also as mothers that women are most often self-consciously critical of themselves. And of all family relational bonds, the mother-child relationship has the greatest emotional strength and depth. Although it was real insight which led an English anthropologist to label Mother's Day an American rite of atonement, we all know that there is a profound attitude of devotion underlying the commercialized sentimentality about mothers which fills American magazines in the month of May.

No, there certainly is not much danger that women either are developing or will develop completely negative attitudes toward their wife-mother role. I see no substantial evidence for the argument that women, in their desire to seek self-fulfillment outside family life, are the main cause of increases in delinquency and divorce rates and the mounting list of neurotic symptoms discovered in both children and adults. All these various symptoms are related and to some extent have a common origin, but rather than say simply that the cause is woman's wish for self-expression, it would seem more logical and accurate to place this wish, too, on the list of symptoms. But even though I cannot agree with those who blame women so much, I concur in the opinion that a majority of women now find, and will continue to find, it difficult to be both adequate wives and mothers and also successful competitors in the occupations. Why, then, if it is so difficult, are so many women already attempting to do both, others expressing the wish that they could, and still others showing signs of frustrations because they do not or cannot?

The changes in the wife-mother role itself provide part of the answer to the question. However important the role may still be, it has lost both meaning and scope in recent years. Meaning is undeniably lost when the role is separated in the minds of men and women alike from its inevitable counterpart, the housewife role, and the tasks of that counterpart greatly demeaned in value. Work which is done because one has to do it, and which does not have a value worthy of an adequate training for it, is not apt to be rewarding. Moreover, the negative attitudes can so easily lead to the expression, either consciously formulated or unconsciously made known in behavior, of a belief that mother deserves much because she has given up so much and done so many things she did not really enjoy.

The scope of the role has been narrowed because modern families are both small in size and share so many of their functions with a host of other organizations. Not only is the mother of today freed from many of the worrisome problems that colonial women always faced, she is also all too soon out of a mother's job.

In an action oriented, future time-minded society, having no job to do engenders a feeling of uselessness which in turn creates emotional disturbance. Most of us have witnessed the disoriented behavior and emotional stress of women whose children have grown up and gone. Some respond by clinging to children, others try desperately to fit into jobs with the outmoded skills they learned and used years ago; others become unnecessarily fussy housewives; some are merely restless.

There would be many fewer occurrences of any of these responses if the evaluation of women's activities outside the home was sufficiently high to provide the needed feelings of usefulness and accomplishment. But such is not the case; hence we have the second of the reasons why more and more women are trying to combine marriage with a career.

In whatever part of the history of woman's role we look, we note that being a status symbol, a glamour girl, especially an *old* glamour girl, or even a culture bearer, does not bring many badges of merit in our kind of society. Not even in community work are there many satisfactions left for women today. Here again men have damaged the value of the work by often adopting an attitude that it, too, is secondary to business and safely left in the hands of women until conditions become really bad or the issues extreme. Then, of course, they plan to step in and put things on a businesslike basis.

But more than the attitudes of men, it has been the professionalization of community activities which has deflated women's interest in them. It is the way of Americans to organize and professionalize everything which becomes important. Welfare work, many community services, and even recreational programs in cities of any size are now large scale and important. The formulation of their policies and their administration are, therefore, matters which require professional competence. What is left to the well-intentioned but untrained woman who must work part time and as a volunteer is neither much nor very important. Sometimes volunteer services are not accepted at all. More than a few of my former students report a refusal of their services in any capacity. They are told, kindly enough, to go back to school, obtain the necessary degree, and then apply for a paid position.

This situation is enough to discourage women in their efforts to play their variant role. It is worsened, however, by the kind of education these women have had, a training which I have elsewhere labeled a *contingency education.* Educational opportunities are no longer refused women, although in some colleges there are still some professors who let it be known that they consider a higher education for women both a nuisance and a waste of time. Nor is the education girls receive different from that given to boys. Throughout childhood and youth the girl child goes to school with boys and is trained in accord with masculine patterns. From babyhood on, she learns the ways of being independent and autonomous. Even though little sister still finds a doll in a carriage under the Christmas tree while brother has a train for his or father's amusement, she is expected to learn to look after herself all through adolescence and beyond, even forever if need be. The hope is expressed that she will not have to remain independent and therefore need not use much of what she has learned. Instead, and this is the great problem, she is expected, upon her marriage or certainly after children are born, to give her attention to other things for which she has not been well trained.

These are the powerful factors which are making women look to the occupations for the means of becoming dominant Americans. I find it difficult to criticize any woman for what she either does or does not do as long as she is left so much in doubt as to what is expected of her.

## REFERENCES

1. Talcott Parsons, *Essays in Sociological Theory Pure and Applied,* Chap. I. Glencoe, Ill.: Free Press, 1949.
2. By Him, *How It Feels to Be the Husband of a Suffragette.* New York: George H. Doran Co., 1915.
3. Eugene A. Hecker, *A Short History of Women's Rights.* New York: G. P. Putnam's Sons, 1914.

# WOMEN IN SCIENCE: WHY SO FEW?

## ALICE S. ROSSI

Where women are concerned, the late 1940's and the 1950's were marked by a national mood of domesticity demonstrated by the rapid rise in the birth rate and the flight of families to the suburbs. It was a period of high praise for woman's domestic role. That mood has shifted in the 1960's. Educators, employers, government officials, and manpower specialists are urging women to enter more fully into the occupational life of the nation. A President's Commission on the Status of Women has recently issued a set of wide-ranging recommendations to this end (1). Particular stress has been put on the need for women in fields in which there is a critical shortage of manpower — teaching, science, and engineering — and conferences on women in science have been held under federal auspices, at Marymount College in 1963 and at the Massachusetts Institute of Technology in 1964.

What can we expect as a result of this campaign? Working women in the industrial, service, and clerical occupations will probably experience an improvement in status. The implementation of the Equal Pay Act and the retraining possible under the Manpower Development and Training Act will be of help to such women, as will all attempts to improve community childcare and housekeeping facilities, increased tax deductions for families including a working mother, and the like. A steady supply of older, married women secretaries, clerks, machine tenders, and technicians seems assured.

A second group directly benefiting from the campaign consists of women residents of the national and state capitals. There is a renewal of optimism among women in government employment, and some indications that in Washington itself their opportunities for advancement may be increasing. But a very large proportion of women in all grades of the Civil Service are unmarried, and a very large proportion of those who are married have no children (2).

Most college-educated women in this country are married and living with their husbands and children. Whether we are interested in the status of women or in the needs of science or both, I do not think we can expect any appreciable increase in the representation of women in the top professions unless that fact is taken into account. As long as it is mostly spinsters or widows who are appointed or elected or promoted to a college presidency, a national commission, a senatorship, or a high post in a government agency or scientific institute, we cannot consider that a solution has been found to the problem of women's status in American society. Marriage, parenthood, and meaningful work are major experiences in the adventure of life. No society can consider that the disadvantages of women have been overcome so long as the pursuit of a career exacts a personal deprivation of marriage and parenthood, or the pursuit of happiness in marriage and family life robs a woman of fulfillment in meaningful work.

## THE PRESENT SITUATION

How many women are there in the fields of science and engineering in the United States, and what are their characteristics? The latest figures available are from the 1960 Census. In 1960 (3), only 9 percent of the employed natural scientists and less than 1 percent of the engineers were women (see Table 1). Within these broad fields, there was considerable variation: from 2 percent in the earth sciences and 4 percent in physics to 26 percent in mathematics and 27 percent in the biological sciences (4). Women lost rather than gained ground in the sciences between 1950 and 1960, for although they appeared in greater absolute numbers in 1960, the rate of increase was much lower than that of men. Thus while there was a 209 percent increase in the number of women mathematicians, the number of male mathematicians increased 428 percent, so that the proportion of women actually declined from 38 percent to 26 percent in that decade. Hiestand (5) has shown that this is a characteristic of all occupations undergoing an accelerated rate of growth. The majority group in the labor force is white men, and it is their growth pattern which defines the rapidly growing fields. Since women constitute a far smaller proportion of the total labor force, they can usually provide

seniors of the class of 1961 by the National Opinion Research Center
(9), indicates no new trend toward more women physicists and engineers, although there is an increase of women headed for the biological sciences. Among college seniors planning graduate work in
physics 8 percent were female, in engineering 1 percent, in chemistry 20 percent, in mathematics 28 percent, in all biological sciences
43 percent. Furthermore, some of these women will become secondary
school science teachers rather than practicing scientists. A follow-up
study one year after graduation showed that among those actually
enrolled in graduate school, the percent female in the physical sciences was 16, in the biological sciences 34 (10). If the pattern
shown in Table 2 holds for this younger group of women, by 1965
about half of them will have voluntarily withdrawn at least temporarily from advanced training or jobs in science.

Several questions emerge from the foregoing review. Why are
there so few women in science? Why are they less apt to get advanced degrees than men? Why are they less apt to marry? Why do
they withdraw from their fields?

## THE PRIORITY OF MARRIAGE

What a man "does" defines his status, but whom she marries defines
a woman's. In meeting strangers, one can "place" a man socially by
asking what he does, a woman by asking what her husband does.
This is particularly true for the top professional and technical strata
of American society. Only small proportions of the wives of doctors,
scientists, engineers, and lawyers are employed, ranging (in 1960)
from a low of 16 percent of doctors' wives to a high of 25 percent
of scientists' wives (7, table 12). In contrast, 44 to 47 percent of the
wives of librarians, social workers, and school teachers are employed.

This has decided implications for the paths young women see as
open to them for success in American life. A man must express his
intelligence and ambition in the occupational sphere. A woman's
ambition can find an outlet in marriage or in work, seldom in both.
If a woman has a successful husband, there are no cultural pressures
upon her to use her intelligence or training in the work of the world.
In fact her husband may resist a desire on her part for such a separate
career, for a wife with leisure is one symbol of his success, and a wife's

career might require him to carry some of the parental responsibilities his wife has carried for him.

I think it is the awareness that marriage and careers are not now compatible for women in the upper middle class (despite protestations to the contrary in recent years) that lies behind the often pathetic vacillations of high school and college girls between the pursuit of social popularity (a route to successful marriage) and excellence in scholarship (a route to successful careers). Surely it plays a role in the different concerns parents have for their adolescent boys and girls — the educational goals of their sons and the dating patterns of their daughters.

A sample of women college graduates 3 years beyond graduation were asked the following question (11): "An American woman can be very successful in a variety of ways. Which of the following would you most like to be yourself?" The most frequent answers were: to be the mother of several accomplished children and to be the wife of a prominent man. Yet some echoes of earlier aspirations and the imprint of their college education are found in their responses to the further question, "Which of the following do you personally admire very much?" Four out of five chose winners of scientific, scholarly, or artistic awards. They admire the minority within their sex who have careers, but choose themselves to live in the shadows of their husbands' and children's accomplishments.

Unless there are changes in the organization of professional and technical work or in the attitudes of men toward women's roles, it seems likely that fewer rather than more college-trained women will pursue serious careers in the future, for there has been a steady increase in the proportion of the male labor force found in the top occupations. This is not to say that wives of such men will not work. They will, particularly early in the marriage when their earnings supplement university stipends to support the graduate training of their husbands. And we shall hear from these women again when they reach their forties. As long as their husbands are not "too" successful, they may become social workers, teachers, computer programmers, professional or technical aides in laboratories or offices. Only rarely will they become doctors, lawyers, scientists or engineers. Harriet Martineau's observation in 1834 that the "prosperity of America is a circumstance unfavorable to its women," meaning women are not "put to the proof as to what they are capable of thinking and doing" (*12*), is as true for the upper middle class in 1964 as it was when she compared America with England on her first visit to the young nation.

It is ironic that with a life span now long enough to experience many and varied adventures of the mind, the spirit, and the senses, the major life experiences of marriage and parenthood and the intellectual excitement of advanced study are compressed into the same narrow few years of early adulthood. Instead of savoring each to the full and in their turn, we feast upon all three simultaneously as on a triple decker sandwich. This quickened pace of life and the earlier age at which marriage, parenthood, and occupational success take place play an important role in lowering the career aspirations of women and in deflecting them from the pursuit of such goals as they have. There is not enough time in late adolescence for young women to evolve a value system of their own and a sense of direction toward an individual goal, for they are committing themselves prematurely to marriage and adapting to the goals of their husbands at the expense of their own emotional and intellectual growth.

Men are more conservative than women concerning the role of careers in the lives of women. Much larger proportions of college-trained men than women in the NORC career development study (*11*) believed women should not choose a career difficult to combine with child-rearing, and disapproved of women's working when they have preschool children. The same men were between two and three times more likely than the women to say there was "no need at all" for the major recommendations made by the President's Commission on the Status of Women — increased child-care facilities, equal opportunity in hiring and promotion, and encouraging more women to enter the professions and national political office.

Women see the sharp differences between their own views and those of "most men." Women in the NORC sample were given a brief account of a hypothetical family conflict and asked how they themselves would resolve it, and how they thought "most wives" and "most husbands" would resolve it. In the story, a woman graduated from college with honors in biology, married, and held a teaching job while her husband completed law school. Now he has a degree and a good job. Both wish to have children, but she would like to take an advanced degree in biology and eventually pursue a career in biological research. The respondents were asked what decision the couple should make: to start a family and have the wife get the degree later; to start a family and give up the wife's career goal; to postpone child-bearing and let the wife get the degree now; or carry out both wishes simultaneously. Only one-fourth of the women thought the couple should start the family now, with the wife either giving up or postponing her training and career plans; but half of them believed these two decisions would be favored by "most wives," and three-fourths that it would be favored by "most husbands."

In actual fact, most women do as they say most husbands would prefer: they are less apt to complete any advanced training, highly likely to work after marriage and then withdraw for the child-bearing and -rearing years. The typical pattern of work for American women shows two peaks of employment, the first in their early twenties, the second in the 40 to 55 age group. As seen in Table 2, this withdrawal in the 25 to 44 age group is particularly high for women in the sciences. Thus in their expressed attitudes, women are less conservative than men, but their actual behavior reflects an adaptation to the views of men.

EFFECT OF INTERRUPTION OF CAREER

During the last 5 years there has been a mushrooming of centers for counseling and retraining older women who wish to return to professional employment. I think there is a danger that by thus institutionalizing the withdrawal-and-return pattern of college-educated women, we may reduce even further the likelihood that women will enter the top professions. Older women who have not worked for many years may be retrained and contribute significantly to personnel shortages at the lower professional levels as laboratory assistants, technical writers, nurses, and school teachers, but only rarely as doctors, full-fledged scientists, and engineers. Not only is training for such fields a long and difficult process, but the pace of technological and scientific knowledge has been so rapid that even those who remain in these fields have difficulty keeping up, let alone those who return to advanced training after a 10-year break.

Even more fundamental, however, is the effect on potential creativity of withdrawal precisely during early adulthood. Lehman's researches into the relation between age and achievement (13) have shown that the quality of intellectual output is strongly related to age, and that in the sciences the peak of creative work is reached in the late twenties and early thirties. The small number of women included in his samples showed their most creative years to be no different from those of the men. They were making their major contributions during the very years when most American women withdraw and devote a decade or more to home and family.

If more women are to choose science and remain active in science, it must be possible for them to do so without lengthy interruption of their careers during their potentially most creative years. There has to be a better balance between marital, parental, and career obligations and pleasures for both sexes; work must be *less* dominant than it is in the lives of men in order for it to be *more* dominant in the lives of women.

## New View of the Maternal Role

Women will not be strongly motivated to remain active professionally during the early years of child-rearing simply out of concern for the effect of withdrawal upon their intellectual creativity. The development of their children is a concern equal to if not greater than their own work. Until very recently, there was a widely held belief that any separation of the mother and the child would have dire consequences for the emotional development of the child, and many women who worked throughout their children's early years did so with considerable anxiety about the effect of their daily absence upon their children. It is only very recently that this myth has been laid to rest. A current volume of some 22 empirical studies on the employed mother (*14*) has shown that maternal employment has no unfavorable effects upon children. Of much greater importance than employment per se are the mother's reasons for working, the quality of the care the child receives in her absence, and the attitudes of her husband. In the last few years, social scientists have begun to stress the desirable rather than the unfavorable consequences of maternal employment (*15*, p. 615).

There is a second body of research on child development that reflects a further shift in the concept of the maternal role. For years psychologists focused rather exclusively on the mother's feelings toward and physical care and training of the child. Now there is increasing emphasis on the role of mothers in their children's cognitive development. It has been found that how well the child takes to his early school experiences is strongly related to whether he has had stimulating experience with language and ideas during his pre-school years. The better educated the mother, the greater will this stimulation of the child tend to be. There is research currently under way testing the hypothesis that it is the lack of cognitive stimulation that contributes most heavily to poor school performance among lower-working-class children (16).

The implications for social action in behalf of children in culturally deprived homes are clear: enrich the environment of the very young child by means of child-care facilities designed to provide such cognitive stimulation (17). The implications as regards children of college-educated parents are less clear-cut. Some child specialists may say that the mother is more necessary at home than ever, not only to love and care for the child but to stimulate the growing mind of the child. This is to stress the role of the mother as a *teacher*. She may be even more effective, however, as an *example* to the child. If she is utilizing her education in a professional job which keeps her alert and involved with things of the mind, she may transmit far more zest for learning than the educated mother who shelves her books along with her diploma. With the view that maternal employment will harm the child now shown to be unfounded, younger women are potentially free of one source of anxiety if they choose to pursue a profession.

WOMEN AND SCIENCE: INCOMPATIBLE?

What is there about women on the one hand, and science on the other, that leads to such a very low affinity between them in American society? What are the major characteristics of the scientist, and why are women in our society less apt to have these characteristics than men?

The following thumbnail sketch of the scientist is based largely on the intensive research of Roe (18) on eminent physicists and biologists. Two caveats must be noted. First, there have been no detailed psychological studies of women scientists in any way comparable to those of men scientists. Some studies suggest that differences in students' interests and values are more closely related to their fields of study than to sex differences, but in drawing a portrait of the characteristics of the scientist it is an assumption rather than an empirically established fact that women scientists do not differ from men scientists in the major characteristics relevant to their occupational role. Secondly, Roe's studies of scientists were conducted in the 1940's with men largely in their fifties at that time. Whether younger men entering the considerably changed world of science in the 1960's and 1970's will differ we do not know, though a comparison of physics students with the physics faculty at a major university in the 1950's shows such striking similarity in personality and social traits as to suggest little change from generation to generation (*19*).

The four characteristics Roe found most typical of outstanding natural scientists are the following:

1) *High intellectual ability,* particularly spatial and mathematical.

2) *Persistence in work;* intense channeling of energy in work such that the greatest personal satisfaction was experienced when working.

3) *Extreme independence,* showing itself in childhood as a preference for a few close friends rather than extensive or organized social groups, and preference for working alone; in adulthood as a marked independence of intense relations with others and a preference for being free of all supervision.

4) *Apartness from others;* low interest in social activities, with neither preference for an active social life nor guilt concerning such tendencies toward social withdrawal.

All four characteristics manifest themselves early in life; hence a predisposition toward science as a career goal is established long before the college student makes a formal commitment to a "major." Furthermore, these are all characteristics girls in American society are considerably less apt to have than boys. Both at home and at school, girls are socialized in directions least likely to predispose them toward science as a career. What are these sex differences during the formative years?

INTELLECTUAL ABILITY

For many years it was assumed that there were practically no sex differences in intelligence, for studies relying on the Stanford-Binet intelligence test showed almost no difference between boys and girls. It had somehow been forgotten that, in standardizing this test, items which revealed consistent sex differences were discarded so that the scores of boys and girls could be evaluated against the same norms. During more recent years, as specific tests were constructed to measure different dimensions of intellectual and creative ability, consistent sex differences began to emerge.

These differences may be summarized as follows (20): Girls talk at younger ages, put words together into sentences somewhat sooner, and learn to read more easily than boys. After the fifth or sixth grade, however, boys do as well as girls in reading comprehension, though girls show somewhat greater verbal fluency. In mathematical skills there are no sex differences during the early school years, but during high school boys begin to excel, and by the time they take the Scholastic Aptitude Tests the boys score an average of 50 points higher on the mathematical portion, while girls score only 8 or 10 points higher on the verbal portion. Throughout school boys do better on spatial tests (for example, detecting a simple figure embedded in a more complex one), which suggests that "boys perceive more analytically, while the girls are more global, more influenced by all the elements of the field together" (20, p. 29).

Thus girls develop cognitive abilities along somewhat different lines than boys, and enter adolescence with a style of thinking less appropriate to scientific work. Any final interpretation of this sex difference awaits further research, but what is known to date is that one key lies in the kind and degree of training in independence the child receives. Bing (21) found that high verbal ability is fostered by close relationship with a demanding and somewhat intrusive mother, while high mathematical abilities were enhanced by allowing a child a considerable degree of freedom to experiment on his own. Children whose scores on standard intelligence tests rise between their 6th and 10th years are highly likely to have been six-year-olds who were "competitive, self-assertive, independent and dominant in interactions with other children," while those who showed declining scores were "passive, shy and dependent" youngsters at six. (20, p. 33).

## EARLY FAMILY INFLUENCES

If we look more closely at the family environment of the young child, we can guess at some of the sources of this difference in cognitive style between boys and girls. The scientist's characteristics of independence, persistence in work, and social isolation are mirrored in significant differences between the father and the mother as seen through the eyes of the child. No matter what the father works at, the child sees him leave the family to pursue it; it is a normal part of every day's expectation that father will not be present. Mother, in contrast, is usually at home and instantly available, someone who takes care of the thousand details of home and family life, none of them so important that she cannot be easily interrupted. Even when he is at home, father may be far less "available" than mother.

It is easy for the child to conclude from daily observation that men work for long stretches of time at something important, and that men are less involved with people than women are. There is a consistency between these observations of the parents and the characteristics of young children. Very young girls have a greater interest in other people than boys have and are influenced to a greater extent by what other people think of them. Coleman (22) has found that in adolescence, girls are far more often involved in same-sex cliques than boys, who are more often independent loners. Girls comply with the demands of social situations more than boys do, whether at home in doing what parents ask of them or at school in doing what teachers ask. In short, by the example of their parents boys receive encouragement to stand on their own, to be alone, to aim high, and girls are encouraged to be cooperative and responsive to people and to minister to their needs.

The result of these early influences is a marked contrast between men and women in the values that underlie their career choices. Rosenberg (23) and more recently Davis (24) have indicated that the occupational value which most sharply differentiates the career choices of women from those of men has to do with the orientation toward people. Women strongly prefer fields in which they work with people rather than things, and hence we find college-trained women most heavily represented in the humanities, the applied aspects of the social sciences, education, and the health professions. Some of these differences persist even among men and women who have chosen the same occupational field. Women are more often found teaching science than doing science. Women college teachers mention as most satisfying about their campus jobs "good students" and "desirable colleagues," whereas men teachers stress "opportunity to do research" and "freedom and independence" (25).

For most American women, growing up has meant shifting from being taken care of in a well-peopled social environment to taking care of others. If we want more women to enter science, not only as teachers of science but as scientists, some quite basic changes must take place in the ways girls are reared. If girls are to develop the analytic and mathematical abilities science requires, parents and teachers must encourage them in independence and self-reliance instead of pleasing feminine submission; stimulate and reward girls' efforts to satisfy their curiosity about the world as they do those of boys; encourage in girls not unthinking conformity but alert intelligence that asks why and rejects the easy answers. A childhood model of the quiet, good, sweet girl will not produce many women scientists or scholars, doctors or engineers. It will produce the competent, loyal laboratory assistant "who will not operate so readily on her own," as Pollard wrote recently in describing his preference for a female rather than a male laboratory assistant (26).

## SUMMARY AND CONCLUSIONS

American society has prided itself on its concern for the fullest development of each individual's creative potential. As a nation, we have become sensitive to the social handicaps of race and class but have remained quite insensitive to those imposed because of sex. Those women who have entered the top professional fields have had to have extraordinary motivation, thick skins, exceptional ability, and some unusual pattern of socialization in order to reach their occupational destinations. In their backgrounds one is likely to find a professional mother, an unusually supportive father, or dedicated and stimulating teachers.

If we want more women scientists, there are several big tasks ahead:

1) We must educate boys and girls for all their major adult roles — as parents, spouses, workers, and creatures of leisure. This means giving more stress in education, at home and at school, to the future family roles of boys and the future occupational roles of girls. Women will not stop viewing work as a stopgap until meaningful work is taken for granted in the lives of women as it is in the lives of men.

2) We must stop restricting and lowering the occupational goals of girls on the pretext of counseling them to be "realistic." If women have difficulty handling the triple roles of member of a profession,

wife, and mother, their difficulties should be recognized as a social problem to be dealt with by social engineering rather than be left to each individual woman to solve as best she can. Conflicts and difficulties are not necessarily a social evil to be avoided; they can be a spur to creative social change.

3) We must apply our technological skill to a rationalization of home maintenance (15). The domestic responsibilities of employed women and their husbands would be considerably lightened if there were house-care service firms, for example, with teams of trained male and female workers making the rounds of client households, accomplishing in a few hours per home and with more thoroughness what the single domestic servant does poorly in two days of work at a barely living wage.

4) We must encourage men to be more articulate about themselves as males and about women. Three out of five married women doctors and engineers have husbands in their own or related fields. The views of young and able women concerning marriage and careers could be changed far more effectively by the men who have found marriage to professional women a satisfying experience than by exhortations of professional women, or of manpower specialists and family-living instructors whose own wives are homemakers.

The physiological differences between male and female are sufficiently clear and so fundamental to self-definition that no change in the direction of greater similarity between male and female social roles is going to disturb the sex identity of children or adults. No one would be confused if men were more tender and expressive and women more aggressive and intellectual. If anything, greater similarity in family and occupational roles would add zest and vitality to the relations between men and women and minimize the social segregation of the sexes. An increase in the number of women scientists would be only one of many desirable outcomes to the social changes that I have here urged.

## REFERENCES

1. *American Women: Report of the President's Commission on the Status of Women, 1963* (Government Printing Office, Washington, D.C., 1963).
2. *Report of the Committee on Federal Employment to the President's*

*Commission on the Status of Women* (Government Printing Office, Washington, D.C., 1963), pp. 104–105.

3. *1960 Census of Population* (Government Printing Office, Washington D.C.), vol. 1, pt. 1. Table 202.

4. Scientific personnel in government employment do not show so high a proportion of women in the biological sciences: the proportion female by major scientific field among those federally employed is 8 percent for physical sciences, 4 percent for biological sciences, 1 percent for engineering (*2*, Appendix D).

5. D. Hiestand, *Economic Growth and Employment Opportunities for Minorities* (Columbia Univ. Press, New York, 1964).

6. 1962 National Register data, reported in *Physics: Education, Employment, Financial Support, A Statistical Handbook* (American Institute of Physics, New York, 1964).

7. *1960 Census of Population: Characteristics of Professional Workers* (Government Printing Office, Washington, D.C.).

8. *Ibid.*, rates calculated from data in Tables 3 and 6.

9. J. Davis, *Great Aspirations: The Graduate School Plans of America's College Seniors* (Aldine, Chicago, 1964), pp. 154–155.

10. N. Miller, "One year after commencement," *National Opinion Research Center, Chicago, Report No. 92* (1963), pp. 125–126.

11. Preliminary results of a recent questionnaire sent to the same sample as in Davis (*9*).

12. H. Martineau, *Society in America*, S. M. Lipset, Ed. (Doubleday, New York, abridged ed., 1962), p. 295.

13. H. Lehman, *Age and Achievement* (Princeton Univ. Press, Princeton, N.J., 1953).

14. A. Rossi, *Daedalus* 93, 615 (1964).

15. F. I. Nye and L. W. Hoffman, *The Employed Mother in America* (Rand McNally, Chicago, 1963).

16. R. Hess, *J. Marriage and the Family* 26, 422 (1964).

17. One experimental day-care center in Syracuse, New York, will test the effect of an optimal environment for 6-month-to-3-year-old children on learning readiness at school age. B. M. Caldwell and J. B. Richmond, *ibid.*, p. 481.

18. A. Roe, "A psychological study of eminent biologists," *Psychol. Monograph No. 65* (1951), p. 331: "A psychological study of physical scientists," *Genet. Psychol. Monograph No. 43* (1951): "Psychological study of research scientists," *Psychol. Monograph No. 67* (1953), p. 2; "Crucial life experiences in the development of scientists," in *Talent and Education*,

E. Torrance, Ed. (Univ. of Minnesota Press, Minneapolis, 1960); *The Making of a Scientist* (Dodd, Mead, New York, 1963).

19. G. Stern, M. Stein, B. Bloom, *Methods in Personality Assessment* (Free Press, Glencoe, Ill., 1956).

20. E. Maccoby, "Woman's intellect," in *The Potential of Women*, S. Farber and R. Wilson, Eds. (McGraw-Hill, New York, 1963), gives a more detailed summary of sex differences in intellectual ability.

21. E. Bing, *Child Development* 34, 631 (1963).

22. J. Coleman, *The Adolescent Society* (Free Press, Glencoe, Ill., 1961).

23. M. Rosenberg, *Occupations and Values* (Free Press, Glencoe, Ill., 1957).

24. J. Davis, *Undergraduate Career Decisions*, in press.

25. R. Eckert and J. Stecklein, "Job motivations and satisfactions of college teachers," *U.S. Office of Education Coop. Res. Monograph No. 7* (1961).

26. E. Pollard, *Science* 145, 1018 (1964).

# PART V

Achievement and Social Mobility:
Personality and Structural Factors

## INTRODUCTION

Upward movement in the occupational system is a basic way in which contemporary Americans assess their own and others' achievements. Whether one consults the proverbial man-in-the-street, novelists, social scientists, or other intellectuals, it is clear that achievement via occupational mobility remains a crucial concern in the United States today.[1] Given the American emphasis upon activity, practicality, and like values, it could hardly be otherwise. Thus, in the United States today, having a job higher in prestige (whether or not in actual "skill" required) than that of one's father is generally seen to be an "achievement"; similarly, holding a job considerably higher in prestige at the apex of one's job career than that held at the beginning of one's work-life is generally counted an "achievement."

While some upwardly mobile persons — whether the comparison is with the position of their fathers or with their own work-life beginnings — may experience subjectively little sense of accomplishment, we believe that most upwardly mobile men are deeply gratified by such occupational movement. Certainly great variation may occur between one's own sense of achievement and the degree of achievement "objectively" assigned one's performance by others. A man judged to be highly successful, both by his peers at work and by laymen (especially relatives and friends), may remain terribly disappointed with his own accomplishments; another man judged to be only slightly successful by peers and others may nevertheless sustain a strong personal sense of accomplishment. However, one of the best-documented generalizations of modern social psychology is that assessments of self are much more likely to merge through time toward assessments provided by peers than to remain distinctly different from, or move further away from, the judgments of peers.

Achievement honors are accorded, then, both to others and to oneself, on the basis of comparisons of present occupation either with that of one's father or with that first held by oneself at the start of the work-life career.

### DIFFERENTIAL OCCUPATIONAL MOBILITY

Any discussion of occupational mobility as achievement must take account of the changing nature of opportunities in the job market. For example, the proportion of white collar occupations in our total labor force has risen steadily in this century, due to fundamental changes in technology. At the same time, birth rates among white collar workers have not been sufficient to provide replacements for the white collar jobs vacated by older workers and created by technological change. Hence, many sons from blue collar origins are constrained to enter white collar jobs, if they are to work at all. Shall we count such movements as "achievements," required as they are by the shift in the nature of the occupational system itself? This question highlights the importance of "differential occupational mobility" for our purposes. While it is true that changes in the occupational system in this century require many more white collar workers today than were needed in the past, many blue collar positions remain to be filled. Hence, while upward movement into white collar occupations is constrained for some fraction of the sons of blue collar workers and farmers, such movement is not constrained for any particular person. In turn, while some fraction of the sons of white collar workers must remain in white collar positions, no particular son of a white collar worker is guaranteed white collar status. Upward movement, then, is an indicator of individual achievement among persons starting from similar origins.[2]

### POSSIBILITIES FOR OCCUPATIONAL ACHIEVEMENT

For a given time-period, much occupational movement (both upward and downward) in a society indicates considerable opportunity for occupational advancement. To assess changes towards more or less opportunity, rates of mobility at different points in time must be studied.

Using national sample data gathered in 1957, Jackson and Crockett[3] found that 70 per cent of the American men studied held occupations either notably higher or lower than the occupations of their fathers. It was estimated that 27 per cent of the movement was necessitated by changes in the distributions of occupations between the generations;

specifically, many sons of farmers were constrained to enter nonfarm jobs due to the disappearance of farm positions. However, 43 per cent of the movement was not "forced" in this manner, but represented "true" mobility wherein persons gained higher or lower ranking positions than those of their fathers for reasons other than those imposed by the varying occupational distributions. Comparing the 1957 data with results from several earlier studies, the authors found no evidence of a trend toward diminishing opportunities for occupational achievement.

Results largely supporting the above findings are reported by Duncan[4] for a national sample of men interviewed in 1962. Containing materials on both work-life mobility and intergenerational mobility, this is the most comprehensive study of mobility trends in the United States to date. Duncan's[5] concluding comments summarize succinctly current knowledge regarding the possibilities for occupational achievement in the United States:

> As of 1962, there was little immediate cause for anxiety about whether the American occupational structure was providing more restricted opportunities. But it is well to remember that the . . . data refer to a historical experience in which the transition to complete industrialization was rapidly nearing its end. If the movement off farms has been a major factor inducing upward mobility from nonfarm origins in the past, it is not clear what its counterpart may be in an era when few persons originate on farms. American sociology may be approaching another period of concern about tendencies producing rigidification. Repeated readings of the trends will be required.

## DETERMINANTS OF OCCUPATIONAL ACHIEVEMENT

A resurgence of scholarly interest in social mobility, a subject first treated comprehensively by Sorokin[6] in 1927, was marked and given focus by the appearance of Lipset and Bendix'[7] *Social Mobility in Industrial Society* in 1959. Even within the short span of eight years since 1959, fundamental advances in both substantive knowledge and research methodology in the subject area have been made. Especially provocative are studies of the determinants of occupational mobility. Though definitive knowledge cannot be claimed at present, results obtained from studies using a wide variety of research procedures among divergent types of samples display an encouraging number of common threads. We have stressed these commonalities in selecting materials for this section. Recognizing that some of the findings reported will be modified or found untenable as research proceeds, and that other variables than the ones considered here will emerge as important ones in the future, we have nonetheless chosen to take advantage of the good fortune of convergent results in the rapidly growing body of knowledge in this area.

Some basic factors affecting occupational achievement between generations are first examined by Blau and Duncan, whose national sample data represent not only the most recent but also the most comprehensive materials on the matter yet collected in the United States. Of all the factors assessed, level of education has much the greatest impact on occupational achievement. Those with the most education, other things equal, show the highest rates of upward mobility. Positive effects on occupational achievement are also reported for the following variables: being white rather than nonwhite; growing up in a metropolis rather than in smaller cities or on farms; moving away from one's place of origin rather than remaining in the same community; growing up in a small family rather than a large one; being an only, oldest, or youngest son rather than a middle son. These findings substantially confirm results previously reported in the literature. They also set the stage for studying differential mobility: Why do some persons sharing a given characteristic or set of characteristics (e.g., the age-cohort of men who are white, native-born, high school graduate, reared in large cities) achieve occupationally while others do not?

The second selection is primarily concerned with this question. It offers a speculative, though empirically based, account of the interactive effects of individuals' values and motives on occupational achievement. The general thesis is that variation in personality characteristics conducive to mobility will be more predictive of occupational achievement among persons reared in lower social strata than among those reared in higher strata. This is so because extra-individual factors (e.g., financial support from parents, social connections, social class expectations) assist persons reared in higher strata, but not those reared in lower strata, to achieve occupationally quite apart from their own personality characteristics.

This line of thought is supported in the next paper, which deals with the early occupational achievements of a cohort of men entering a large Midwestern university in 1952. Education is again shown to be the most powerful predictor of upward mobility, in that those who graduate from college attain higher occupations than the non-graduates. Even men from Working class origins of low measured ability who manage to graduate from college do better occupationally than do non-graduate Middle class men of high ability. Among the non-graduates, however, the motivational component becomes important. For these men, while measured ability is not associated with occupational achievement, social class of origin does affect such achievement. We infer, then that class-linked values, motives, understandings and "connections" are more important than intellectual capacity in the occupational achievement of the non-graduate college man.

Next we turn from studies of actual occupational achievement to a study of persons destined for exceptional upward mobility, namely, Working class men enrolled in a high-prestige university. Even among the most intellectually able Working class boys, only a small fraction ever go to college. How do these few Working class youths find their way to college, and hence on to marked occupational achievement? Ellis and Lane's account stresses two factors: a family setting characterized by a dominant mother and a relatively weak father, and the influence of non-family, middle class adults. The subtle but pervading influence of personality factors may again be noted here by asking why these particular Working class students, but not others equally able, were aided by influential adults to obtain a high quality education. As Lipset and Bendix[8] have suggested, the answer probably is that these Working class youths displayed, along with high academic ability, many personality traits and habits which were highly prized by their Middle class benefactors.

Many of the themes of the preceding papers are found again in the next selection, Warner and Abegglen's report of big business leaders in America. These men tend to be highly educated, highly mobile geographically, and to possess distinctive personality characteristics in comparison with other men from similar social backgrounds. Although not discussed in their present paper, the larger study from which this report is drawn also stresses the importance of the mother-dominant family described by Ellis and Lane in the previous selection. It is remarkable also that the same factors found by Blau and Duncan to be significant in the occupational achievement of a national sample of American men recur here in the case of eminent businessmen.

The final paper in this section calls into question the degree to which intrapersonal variables, such as enduring motives, contribute to occupational achievement. The paper reminds us that differential occupational mobility must not be attributed exclusively to personality factors — indeed, differential occupational achievement may be less attributable in the end to systematic differences in underlying personality factors than to systematic differences in adult work-life experiences.

## REFERENCES

1. The evidence is unambiguous that for at least the past 35 years a common conception of the prestige of various occupations has been shared by Americans in practically all social strata. See Robert W. Hodge, Paul M. Siegel, and Peter H. Rossi, "Occupational Prestige in the United States, 1925–63," *American Journal of Sociology*, 70 (November, 1964), 286–302. While not as extensive, evidence also indicates that attainment of higher prestige occupations is commonly viewed as "achievement." Data on both issues are reviewed in Harry J. Crockett, Jr., "The Achievement Motive and Differential Occupational Mobility in the United States," *American Sociological Review*, 27 (April, 1962), 194–195.

2. Although we have used an intergenerational comparison to illustrate our point concerning differential mobility, an intragenerational comparison would have served equally well. For example, among men commencing their work lives as laborers, those who become semi-skilled or skilled craftsmen, foremen, or move into white collar positions have shown differential upward movement relative to those who remain laborers — they have "achieved" occupationally.

3. Elton F. Jackson and Harry J. Crockett, Jr., "Occupational Mobility in the United States: A Point Estimate and Trend Comparison," *American Sociological Review*, 29 (February, 1964), 5–15.

4. Otis Dudley Duncan, "The Trend of Occupational Mobility in the United States," *American Sociological Review*, 30 (August, 1965), 491–498.

5. *Ibid.*, p. 498.

6. Pitirim A. Sorokin, *Social Mobility* (New York: Harper and Brothers, 1927).

7. Seymour Martin Lipset and Reinhard Bendix, *Social Mobility in Industrial Society* (Berkeley: University of California Press, 1959).

8. *Ibid.*, p. 258.

# SOME PRELIMINARY FINDINGS ON
# SOCIAL STRATIFICATION IN THE UNITED STATES

PETER M. BLAU AND OTIS DUDLEY DUNCAN

This is a preliminary report from a study of occupational mobility in the United States. The objectives of the study are to describe the patterns of social mobility in some detail, to estimate the influence of various factors on occupational life chances, and to ascertain a few consequences of socio-economic status and mobility, such as their implications for fertility. The present paper reports selected findings pertaining to factors affecting occupational achievement and the chances to move away from one's social origins. In particular, we shall examine the significance for occupational attainment of education, ethnic background, community size, migration, and parental family.

In addition to presenting preliminary substantive findings from our research, this paper also provides an opportunity for illustrating the analytical procedures we have used. The analysis relies to a large extent on the regression approach. Two major advantages of this approach which prompted our decision to adopt it are that it is a very efficient method of large-scale data reduction and that it permits, consequently, the simultaneous examination of the interrelations of fairly large numbers of variables, especially if computers are used. Contingency tables containing half a dozen or more variables and many hundreds of cells are too complex to be analyzed by inspection, whereas the regression method permits the analysis of these interrelations. To be sure, a limitation of regression analysis is that it makes restrictive assumptions about linearity and the absence of interaction effects, but the assumptions can be taken into account and hence removed in more complex analytical models. Simpler methods we use,

Reprinted with abridgement from *Acta Sociologica* (Vol. 9, Fasc. 1-2, 1965, pp. 4-24) by permission of the publisher and the authors.

We gratefully acknowledge grant number G-16233 from the National Science Foundation, which enabled us to carry out this research.

such as comparisons of mean scores of occupational status, are complemented by regression analysis to determine not only the gross effects of various factors on socio-economic status but also the net effects with other variables held constant.

RESEARCH PROCEDURES

The data for this research were collected by the U.S. Bureau of the Census in March, 1962, partly in the course of its regular "Current Population Survey" interview, and partly in a supplementary self-administered questionnaire specifically designed for the purpose of our research. The sample of 20,700 American men between the ages of 20 and 65 represents the 45 million men in this age group who are in the "civilian noninstitutional population," that is, who are neither in the Armed Forces nor in institutions. A subsample of those respondents who failed initially to return the supplementary questionnaire by mail was interviewed and appropriately weighted to make the sample highly representative. The present analysis, however, is confined to men whose fathers were *not* in farming occupations, which excludes a quarter of the total group.[1] In brief, the data derive from a representative sample of the 33 million American men with nonfarm backgrounds between 20 and 65 years old who are not in military service and do not live in institutions.[2]

Respondent's occupation and that of his father when the respondent was 16 years old were transformed into SES (socio-economic status) scores. The score, which ranges from 0 to 96, is based on the proportion of men in a specific occupation ("detailed occupational classification") who were, at least, high school graduates and the proportion reporting an income of over $3,500 in 1949, making adjustments for differences in age distribution between occupations.[3] The multiple correlation between these two predictors — the education and the income of the men in an occupation — and the N.O.R.C. prestige rating[4] for the 45 occupations that could be matched is +.91, and the regression equation that expresses this multiple correlation is used to determine the SES scores for all 446 detailed occupations. Respondent's education was transformed into an arbitrary score ranging from 0 to 8 which takes into account the special significance graduation from a given school level has.[5] Whereas socio-economic status and education are assumed to be continuous quantitative variables, no such assumption is made concerning the other factors used in the analysis, which are treated as qualitative attributes in terms of which individuals are classified into discrete categories.

To convey the meaning of the SES scores, the average scores of the conventional major groups of nonfarm occupations are presented below:

| | |
|---|---:|
| Professionals and technicians | 75 |
| Managers, proprietors, and officials | 57 |
| Sales and clerical occupations | 47 |
| Skilled workers and foremen | 31 |
| Semiskilled workers | 18 |
| Unskilled workers | 7 |

The average difference between two adjacent categories is 13.6. Hence, the finding that an attribute affects the SES score by four or five points implies that, on the average, one third of the men with this attribute are one full step higher in this rank order (for example, are skilled rather than semiskilled workers) than those without this attribute. Fairly small differences in score are, therefore, of substantive significance, and given our large number of cases such small differences also are statistically significant.[6]

EDUCATION AND ETHNIC BACKGROUND

The over-all correlation between father's and son's occupational status is $+.38$. This indicates that there is much occupational mobility in the United States; only one seventh of the variance in socio-economic status is attributable to the influence of father's socio-economic status.

To examine the relative importance of social origins and of education for occupational attainments, the (nonfarm background) sample is first divided into five cohorts, providing a control for age (20–24, 25–34, 35–44, 45–54, 55–64). The multiple correlation of education and father's socio-economic status on son's SES increases from $+.51$ for the youngest group to $+.66$ for those 25–34 years old and then decreases again to $+.59$ for the oldest group (Table 1, row 1). This nonmonotonic relationship with age suggests that the influences of social background and of education on a man's career extend beyond its early phases and become increasingly pronounced for some years but that

Table 1. *Correlation analysis: Respondent's occupational SES on education and father's SES, for American men with nonfarm backgrounds, age 20 to 64, 1962.*

| Item | 20–24 years | 25–34 years | 35–44 years | 45–54 years | 55–64 years |
|---|---|---|---|---|---|
| 1. Multiple correlations (SES on education and father's SES) ........ | .51 | .66 | .65 | .61 | .59 |
| a. *Beta* coefficient, education .... | .46 | .61 | .57 | .53 | .52 |
| b. *Beta* coefficinet, father's SES .. | .09 | .12 | .15 | .16 | .13 |
| 2. Zero order correlation, SES and father's SES ................. Components*) | .29 | .37 | .40 | .38 | .34 |
| a. Independent of education .... | .09 | .12 | .15 | .16 | .13 |
| b. Mediated through education .. | .20 | .25 | .25 | .22 | .21 |

* For method of calculation, see O. D. Duncan and R. W. Hodge, "Education and Occupational Mobility: A Regression Analysis," *American Journal of Sociology*, 68 (May, 1963), 629–44.

the significance of these factors eventually declines as they recede in time. An alternative explanation of this finding is that the influence of education has become increasingly important since the beginning of this century although a decline may now be under way. There has probably been little change in the significance of father's occupational SES for that of his son in this century.[7] The *beta* coefficients indicate that the net influence of education is at a maximum at about age thirty and then decreases, whereas that of father's SES continues to increase until about age fifty (rows 1a and 1b). Taking these partial regression coefficients in standard form (*beta* coefficients) as indications of the relative significance of the two antecedents, the data also show that the impact on occupational status of education independent of social origin is considerably greater than that of social origin independent of education.[8]

This finding implies that the influence of father's socio-economic status on son's status is largely mediated in the United States by education. A man's chances of occupational advancement depend on his education (zero-order correlation, +.61), which, in turn, depends to a considerable degree on the socio-economic status of his father (+.41). These relationships can be further clarified by restating them in a slightly different way. Instead of asking how SES is affected by education and by father's SES separately, as we did above, we take now the (zero-order) correlation between father's and son's SES (Table 1, row 2) and ask to which extent this influence of father's SES on son's status is mediated through education (row 2b) and to which extent it is independent of education and thus due to other factors (row 2a). It is apparent from the data that education is the major means by which fathers affect the occupational chances of their sons. It should not be ignored, however, that social origins also have a definite effect on occupational opportunities that has nothing to do with educational qualifications.

Negroes have, of course, far less educational opportunity than whites in the United States. Whereas 18 per cent of the native whites have no more than eight years of schooling, fully 37 per cent of the nonwhites do.[9] The education of the second-generation Americans hardly differs from that of other native whites (21 per cent), but the foreign born are nearly as poorly educated as the Negroes, with 35 per cent not having gone beyond the eight years of elementary school. It is interesting that age affects educational attainment to an even greater extent than race. Among the native whites with native parents, only 8 per cent of the men 20–24 years old have no more than eight years of schooling, as compared with 39 per cent of those 55–64 years old. Among the Negroes, similarly, 22 per cent of the youngest age cohort in contrast to 70 per cent of the oldest one have not gone beyond elementary school. Discrimination notwithstanding, young Negroes in today's nonfarm population are better educated than old whites. Negroes, nevertheless, continue to suffer serious educational handicaps, and these are, moreover, not the only handicaps that impede their occupational opportunities.

To ascertain the impact of various attributes, such as ethnic background, on occupational chances, the following procedure is used. The mean SES score for each age cohort is determined, and so are the deviations from this mean in various subgroups under consideration. Differences between these deviations from the mean indicate the gross effect of the attribute on SES, for example, the gross effect of being a Negro rather than a white with a given education on occupational status. The net effects the same attribute has on SES when father's SES is held constant are derived from a regression equation.[10] These net effects can be considered approximate indications of occupational mobility in the sense that they refer to average occupational achievements of groups whose point of social origin has been standardized. An interesting over-all finding that emerges from our analysis is that controlling for father's occupation reduces the influence of various attributes but hardly ever alters the patterns of influence observed. In other words, the same factors that are associated with differential occupational status are also associated with differential achievements independent of level of origin.

Even when education is held constant, the occupational status of Negroes is far inferior to that of whites in the United States. Twenty independent comparisons between native whites of native parentage and nonwhites can be made in Table 2 (four educational groups in each of the five age cohorts). In all twenty, the score of whites is higher, and the average difference is 12.1, nearly a full step in the rank order of major occupational classes. This is a clear indication of the serious discrimination Negroes with the same educational qualifications as whites suffer in the employment market.[11] Moreover, controlling for father's occupation does not wipe out this difference. All twenty net effects favor the whites, an average of 10.2, notwithstanding the fact that Negroes, due to past discrimination, have much lower social origins than whites. In sum, Negroes are handicapped by having less education and by having lower social origins than whites. But even if these handicaps are controlled statistically — asking, in effect, what the chances of Negroes would be if they had the same education and social origins as whites — the occupational attainments of Negroes are still considerably inferior to those of whites.

Foreign-born Americans and their children, the second-generation Americans, in sharp contrast to Negroes, do not differ in occupational attainments from the native whites of native parentage on the same educational levels. The twenty comparisons of gross effects between native whites of native parentage and native whites of foreign parentage are inconsistent (averaging —1.1), and so are the twenty comparisons between the former and the foreign born (averaging 0.8). The various white ethnic groups in the United States apparently achieve occupational positions commensurate with their education. Whatever occupational discrimination may exist against some of these ethnic groups must be compensated for by other factors since it does not find expression in their over-all occupational chances.

Another perspective on the disadvantaged situation of the American Negro can be gained by examining the rewards he obtains for given educational investments compared to those a white person obtains. The average difference for the five age groups between native whites of native parentage who have some college education and those who have only an elementary school education is 33.0, whereas the corre-

Table 2. *Ethnic background, education, and occupational SES of American men with non-farm background, age 20 to 64.*

| Ethnicity by Education | 20–24 years | 25–34 years | 35–44 years | 45–54 years | 55–64 years |
|---|---|---|---|---|---|
| Grand Mean, All Groups | 31.5 | 41.0 | 42.6 | 40.1 | 40.0 |
| | | *Gross Effects* | | | |
| **Native white, native parentage** | | | | | |
| 8 years of schooling or less .......... | −12.9 | −18.1 | −18.7 | −13.8 | −10.6 |
| 9 to 11 years of schooling .......... | − 8.7 | −13.6 | −11.1 | − 5.6 | 0.3 |
| High school graduate .............. | 0.2 | − 3.1 | 1.7 | 3.0 | 8.0 |
| 1 year of college or more .......... | 8.3 | 20.1 | 22.2 | 19.3 | 20.9 |
| **Native white, foreign parentage** | | | | | |
| 8 years of schooling or less .......... | −12.9* | −18.0 | −18.1 | −14.6 | − 9.0 |
| 9 to 11 years of schooling .......... | 2.5* | −11.6 | −14.3 | − 6.6 | − 0.9 |
| High school graduate .............. | 4.7 | − 3.0 | − 0.8 | 6.4 | 6.7 |
| 1 year of college or more .......... | 12.3 | 21.2 | 20.3 | 24.1 | 21.2 |
| **Foreign-born white** | | | | | |
| 8 years of schooling or less .......... | −12.9* | −15.5* | −19.4 | −13.8 | −10.8 |
| 9 to 11 years of schooling .......... | 0.3* | − 9.6* | −12.8* | − 3.0 | 1.5 |
| High school graduate .............. | 1.1* | −13.2* | 3.8 | − 2.9 | 4.9 |
| 1 year of college or more .......... | 5.4* | 19.3 | 12.9 | 17.0 | 19.6 |
| **Nonwhite** | | | | | |
| 8 years of schooling or less .......... | −20.3 | −25.3 | −23.8 | −21.0 | −19.5 |
| 9 to 11 years of schooling .......... | −13.5 | −23.4 | −20.9 | −17.7 | −20.6 |
| High school graduate .............. | − 7.5 | −19.0 | −18.3 | −18.3 | − 2.8* |
| 1 year of college or more .......... | − 1.4* | 9.7 | 5.4 | − 3.9* | 8.1* |
| | | *Net Effects*** | | | |
| **Native white, native parentage** | | | | | |
| 8 years of schooling or less .......... | −12.0 | −16.8 | −16.8 | −12.1 | − 9.4 |
| 9 to 11 years of schooling .......... | − 8.0 | −12.9 | −10.4 | − 5.6 | (−)0.0 |
| High school graduate .............. | 0.1 | − 3.0 | 1.3 | 2.4 | 6.4 |
| 1 year of college or more .......... | 7.6 | 18.6 | 18.9 | 16.3 | 18.9 |
| **Native white, foreign parentage** | | | | | |
| 8 years of schooling or less .......... | −12.2* | −17.2 | −15.8 | −12.8 | − 8.0 |
| 9 to 11 years of schooling .......... | 2.9* | −10.2 | −12.8 | − 5.2 | − 0.7 |
| High school graduate .............. | 4.8 | − 2.6 | − 0.2 | 6.3 | 6.3 |
| 1 year of college or more .......... | 11.6 | 20.2 | 20.2 | 21.7 | 20.0 |
| **Foreign-born white** | | | | | |
| 8 years of schooling or less .......... | −12.4* | 14.8* | −17.9 | −12.1 | −10.0 |
| 9 to 11 years of schooling .......... | 0.5* | −10.6* | −13.2* | − 1.7* | 1.7 |
| High school graduate .............. | 0.7* | −13.4* | 3.8 | − 2.6 | 3.7 |
| 1 year of college or more .......... | 4.8* | 17.5 | 12.2 | 15.0 | 18.3 |
| **Nonwhite** | | | | | |
| 8 years of schooling or less .......... | −18.8 | −23.8 | −20.6 | −18.3 | −17.5 |
| 9 to 11 years of schooling .......... | −12.1 | −21.7 | −17.9 | −15.4 | −19.4 |
| High school graduate .............. | − 6.2 | −17.8 | −16.5 | −16.2 | − 4.9* |
| 1 year of college or more .......... | − 0.5* | 10.0 | 6.8 | − 1.7* | 12.5* |

\* The cell frequency on which this value is based is less than 100.
\*\* Father's occupational SES held constant.

sponding average difference for Negroes is 25.6. In other words, roughly the same amount of educational investment has one and one third times as much payoff for a white man as for a Negro. The fact that Negroes obtain comparatively little reward for their educational investments, which robs them of incentives to incur these costs, might help explain why Negroes often manifest only weak motivation to pursue their education. The early school leaving that results from this lack of motivation further intensifies the disadvantaged position of the Negro in the labor market.

## CITY SIZE AND MIGRATION

The discussion of the relationships between size of place, migration, and occupational opportunities will concentrate upon the urban areas, since the present analysis is confined to men whose fathers were not in farming occupations. Although data for nonfarm rural areas will be presented too, these must be interpreted with great caution, inasmuch as all the sons of farmers living in these areas are excluded from consideration.[12] It should also be remembered that the large number of migrants from farms to cities is not reflected in the data that are now being analyzed.

The findings on size of community reveal few surprises. People who live in the urban fringe of cities have somewhat higher socio-economic status than those who live in the central cities, and this difference persists if their father's SES is controlled. Of the 15 possible comparisons (three city sizes by five age cohorts), 14 of the gross differences favor the fringe over the central city, an average of 4.1 points, and 12 of the net differences do so, an average of 2.7. The socio-economic status of men who live in suburbs is directly related to the size of the central city, at least for younger men, but the status of the inhabitants of the central cities is not monotonically related to city size.

Within the central city, socio-economic status is highest in cities with between one quarter and one million inhabitants. It is somewhat lower in the largest cities of over one million (an average difference of 3.3 points from the former), as well as in the medium cities with 50,000 to 250,000 inhabitants (2.5) and in the small towns with 2,500 to 50,000 inhabitants (2.1). The average socio-economic status in the smallest American towns, however, is still higher than that in rural areas even when farm workers and their sons are excluded from the comparison (2.8). All these differences persist in slightly attenuated form when social origins are controlled. In short, occupational opportunities are poorest in rural areas and best in fairly large cities, and they differ little on the average in the very large cities and those that are medium or small.

The question arises whether this pattern of differences is the result of migration. The answer appears to be that although migration plays a role the basic pattern has not been produced by it. Table 3 presents the data on socio-economic status, again as derivations from the means, by size of present place of residence and by the community where the respondent lived at age 16. The socio-economic status of the nonmigrants — the men who reached adolescence in the same community where they live now — reveals a pattern similar to that previously encountered for the total population. For all five age groups of nonmigrants, as the first row in each section shows, average SES is higher in cities of at least medium size than in small towns (an average difference of 5.2), and it is higher in small towns than in rural areas (3.6), and the same is true for the net differences when father's SES is held constant (4.4 and 2.6). Since all cities with more than 50,000 inhabitants were combined for this analysis, as were the central cities and their urban fringe, it is not possible to determine whether all specific differences observed in the total populations are reflected in parallel differences among nonmigrants. But the evidence does show that the over-all pattern is the same and that migration cannot account for the status differences between fairly large cities and small ones and between the latter and rural regions.

The socio-economic status of urban migrants is clearly superior to that of nonmigrants, though rural migrants are not superior to nonmigrants. In order to isolate the significance of migration as such from that of either living now or having lived previously in a certain environment, nonmigrants will be compared with only those migrants who reside at present in communities of the same size and who also lived as adolescents in communities of about the same size, that is, with those migrants who moved from as well as into communities of approximately the same size. (The cell entries being compared for this analysis are connected by arrows in Table 3.) In all ten comparisons of urban nonmigrants with migrants who came from and are now in the same environment (two city sizes for five age cohorts), the socio-economic status of the migrants is superior, an average of 7.0

Table 3.   *Geographic mobility and occupational SES of American men with nonfarm background, age 20 to 64.*

| Community at Age 16 | Age and Present Residence | | |
|---|---|---|---|
| | City over 50,000 and Fringe ("urbanized area") | Town under 50,000 ("other urban") | Rural |
| **20 to 24 years (mean, 31.5)** | | | |
| Same as present .......... | 1.3 | −2.5 | −5.4 |
| Different from present | | | |
|   Large city & fringe ...... | 4.2 | 5.0* | 1.9 |
|   Small town ........... | 0.6 | 5.8 | |
|   Rural area ............. | −3.0 | −3.1 | −7.8 |
| **25 to 34 years (mean, 41.0)** | | | |
| Same as present .......... | −1.4 | −7.9 | −10.7 |
| Different from present | | | |
|   Large city & fringe ...... | 7.6 | 12.1 | 3.5 |
|   Small town ........... | 6.2 | 7.2 | |
|   Rural area ............. | 4.3 | −7.8 | −2.3 |
| **35 to 44 years (mean, 42.6)** | | | |
| Same as present .......... | −0.6 | −7.1 | −7.1 |
| Different from present | | | |
|   Large city & fringe ...... | 5.7 | 11.6 | 2.1 |
|   Small town ........... | 2.5 | 2.8 | |
|   Rural area ............. | −4.4 | −6.2 | −9.2 |
| **45 to 54 years (mean, 40.1)** | | | |
| Same as present .......... | 0.4 | −3.8 | −11.7 |
| Different from present | | | |
|   Large city & fringe ...... | 5.7 | 10.8 | 1.5 |
|   Small town ............. | 3.2 | 2.9 | |
|   Rural area ............. | −9.5 | 1.1* | −7.8 |
| **55 to 64 years (mean, 40.0)** | | | |
| Same as present .......... | 2.2 | −2.8 | −7.4 |
| Different from present | | | |
|   Large city & fringe ...... | 5.0 | 5.8* | −0.4 |
|   Small town ........... | 1.1 | 1.3 | |
|   Rural area ............. | −5.5 | −4.8* | −12.3 |

* The cell frequency on which this value is based is less than 100.

** The data for migrants to rural areas who come from cities of different sizes have been combined.

Table 3.  Geographic mobility and occupational SES of American men
with nonfarm background, age 20 to 64 (continued).

| Community at Age 16 | City over 50,000 and Fringe ("urbanized area") | Town under 50,000 ("other urban") | Rural |
|---|---|---|---|
| *Age and Present Residence* | | | |
| **20 to 24 years (mean, 31.5)** | | | |
| Same as present ......... | 0.7 | −2.0 | −4.6 |
| Different from present | | | |
| Large city & fringe ...... | 2.6 | 5.2° | 2.6 |
| Small town ........... | 1.1 | 5.3 | |
| Rural area ............ | −1.0 | −3.3 | 4.5 |
| **25 to 34 years (mean, 41.0)** | | | |
| Same as present ......... | −1.3 | −6.4 | −8.3 |
| Different from present | | | |
| Large city & fringe ...... | 5.4 | 9.8 | 1.9 |
| Small town ........... | 4.8 | 8.0 | |
| Rural area ............ | −2.4 | −2.9 | −0.4 |
| **35 to 44 years (mean, 42.6)** | | | |
| Same as present ......... | −0.7 | −6.2 | −4.5 |
| Different from present | | | |
| Large city & fringe ...... | 4.5 | 9.1 | 1.1 |
| Small town ........... | 1.8 | 1.4 | |
| Rural area ............ | −1.8 | −3.1 | −6.9 |
| **45 to 54 years (mean, 40.1)** | | | |
| Same as present ......... | 0.8 | −3.4 | −9.8 |
| Different from present | | | |
| Large city & fringe ...... | 4.2 | 6.2 | 0.4 |
| Small town ........... | 2.6 | 1.9 | |
| Rural area ............ | −7.1 | 3.4° | −4.8 |
| **55 to 64 years (mean, 40.0)** | | | |
| Same as present ......... | 2.5 | −2.1 | −5.8 |
| Different from present | | | |
| Large city & fringe ...... | 3.3 | 5.2° | −0.8 |
| Small town ........... | 0.6 | −1.1 | |
| Rural area ............ | −3.0 | −3.8° | −9.9 |

° The cell frequency on which this value is based is less than 100.
°° The data for migrants to rural areas who come from cities of different sizes have been combined.

(net of father's SES, 5.4). The five comparisons between nonfarm rural migrants and nonmigrants yield no consistent results — two going in one and three in the other direction — and the average difference is very small (0.6; net, 1.3). Migrants within urban areas, then, tend to occupy superior occupational positions and enjoy higher achievements relative to their social origins than their nonmigrant counterparts, but there are no corresponding differences between the migrants within rural areas and the nonmigrants in these areas. These differences cannot be primarily due to the fact that migrants frequently move from smaller to larger communities where occupational opportunities are superior, because the influence of city size has been roughly controlled in this analysis. The inference therefore is that intra-urban migration is selective of men predisposed to occupational success, whereas this is not the case for intra-rural migration.

We turn now to examine the significance of the change in environment migration produces, which is the very factor we attempted to control in the preceding analysis of the significance of migration itself. What are the implications of the migrant's area of destination for his occupational chances? Regardless of geographical origins, men who move into urban areas tend to achieve higher socio-economic status than those who move into rural areas. Most pronounced is the difference between migrants to small cities and those to rural regions, with nine of ten comparisons indicating a higher SES for the men who moved to small cities, the average difference being 4.2 (and 3.5 if father's SES is held constant).[13] This difference parallels that between nonmigrants in small cities and rural areas. When cities over 50,000 are compared with smaller ones, however, the findings assume quite another pattern. Here point of origin makes a difference, and the situation of migrants differs from that of nonmigrants in the same type of place. Whereas nonmigrants tend to achieve *higher* occupational status in the relatively larger cities than in small ones, the status of migrants from rural areas does not differ consistently in the two localities, and migrants from other urban areas achieve lower status in the larger than in the small cities. Comparison of columns 1 and 2 in Table 3 shows that the SES of nonmigrants is *higher* in the larger than in the smaller cities in five instances out of five, the average difference being +5.2 (net, +4.4), but the SES of migrants from urban areas (rows 2 and 3) is *lower* in the larger than in the smaller cities in nine cases out of ten, the average difference being —2.3 (net, —2.0).

It seems paradoxical that the occupational chances of urban migrants are worse, and those of rural migrants are no better, in larger
cities than in smaller ones, while the occupational opportunities of
the natives are better in the larger than in the smaller cities. It must
be remembered that the urban migrants to larger cities are somewhat
superior in socio-economic status to the nonmigrants there, but their
superiority is not as great as that of migrants over nonmigrants in
small cities. One possible explanation of these findings is that the migrants to larger cities constitute a more heterogeneous group than
those to smaller towns, including not only disproportionate numbers
with good occupational qualifications but also very many with extremely poor qualifications. Thus the migrants who stream into the
large Northern cities from the South can frequently only obtain the
least desirable occupational positions, and these migrants take the
place at the bottom of the industrial hierarchy that was once occupied
by the recent immigrants from Europe. Another reason for the lesser
superiority of migrants over nonmigrants in larger cities might be that
being raised in large cities gives the natives an advantage in the
struggle for occupational success that compensates for some of the
other advantages the migrants have. The comparison of men reared
in places of different size supports this interpretation.

Migrants who lived in larger cities when they were 16 years old
tend to be superior in socio-economic status to those raised in smaller
cities, and the latter tend to be superior to those who grew up in rural
areas (Table 3, rows 2, 3, and 4). Of ten comparisons between migrants coming from larger and those coming from smaller cities, nine
show that the former have a higher SES, the average difference being
4.0 (net, 2.9), and of 15 comparisons between migrants raised in small
cities and those raised in rural areas, 14 show that the former have
higher SES, the average difference being 8.6 (net, 5.5). The same
difference is reflected in the finding that the SES of nonmigrants is
directly related to the size of their present community, since in the
case of nonmigrants the present community is, of course, identical
with the place where they lived at age 16. Whether a man is a migrant or not, therefore, and regardless of the size of the community
where he now works, the larger the community where he grew up,
the better are his chances to achieve occupational success and to move
up from the status of his father.

Since growing up in a large city is an occupational advantage, and
so is being a migrant to a small city, the highest occupational status

is achieved by migrants from larger to small cities, whose status is, on the average, 9.1 points above the mean (net, 7.1 points). One might speculate why men raised in large cities have greater chances of success in their careers. The advantage of the urban over the rural environment is undoubtedly in large part due to the superior educational facilities in the former, but it is questionable whether the superiority of the large-city environment over that in small cities can be attributed to differences in the educational system. It may be that at least part of this superiority is due to the greater sophistication about the labor market and occupational life generally that boys growing up in large cities tend to acquire.

PARENTAL FAMILY

A man's occupational chances are strongly affected by the size of his parents' family. The socio-economic status of men with three or fewer siblings is considerably superior to that of men with four or more siblings. The data in Table 4 permit 20 independent comparisons between men from small and from large families (excluding only children). All 20 indicate that the SES of men from smaller families is superior, the average difference being 8.0. Some of this difference is due to the fact that poorer couples tend to have larger families rather than to the influence of family size on the occupational chances of sons. But even if the former factor is controlled by holding father's socio-economic status constant, the socio-economic status of men from smaller families continues to be higher than that of men from larger families in all 20 comparisons, an average of 5.2 points. This net effect shows that a man's chances of occupational success are impeded by many siblings. Although in strictly economic terms only children must have an advantage over others, since they do not have to share their parents' financial resources with anybody, this economic advantage is not reflected in their careers. Only children do not achieve higher occupational positions than those from small families; the differences between the two groups are inconsistent, and the average approximates zero.

Sibling position as well as number of siblings influences occupational attainments. There are no consistent differences between oldest and youngest children, but the SES of both tends to be superior to that of middle children. Ten independent comparisons can be made between oldest children and middle children with an older brother (two sizes for five age cohorts). Eight of these indicate that the oldest child has a higher status, one that the middle child has, and one reveals no difference. The average difference is 3.7, which is reduced to 2.7 if father's SES is controlled. When youngest children are compared to middle children with an older brother, the youngest are seen to have superior SES in all ten cases, the average difference being 4.3, and this difference persists if father's SES is controlled (net, 4.0). (Comparisons with middle children without an older brother yield essentially the same results.) Both oldest and youngest children gain advantages from their positions compared to middle children, but perhaps for different reasons. The fact that the occupational advantages of oldest children depend in part on the socio-economic status of their fathers while those of youngest children do not suggests that the latter are due to socio-psychological rather than economic factors. It may be that the occupational success of youngest children is primarily due to the greater social and emotional support they receive in their families rather than to the fact that their education pre-empts the economic resources of their parents.

Middle children with and without an older brother have been separated in order to examine the implications of having an older brother for occupational chances. The significance of an older brother for careers appears to be slight and confined to small families. Four of the five comparisons in small families (Table 4, rows 6 and 7) indicate that middle children without an older brother have higher SES than those with one, with an average difference of +2.3, but four of the five comparisons in large families go in the opposite direction and the average difference is zero. If father's SES is controlled, the difference in small families is +2.0 and that in large ones is −0.5. Having no older brother is a slight advantage for middle children in small families but not in large ones.

The bottom third of Table 4 presents the residual effects of size of parental family and sibling position when not only father's SES but also a number of other factors are controlled, namely, respondent's education, his first job, his ethnic background, the region where he was born and where he lives at present, the size of his place of birth and of his present community, and migration status. It is evident from the table that the residual effects of parental family on socio-economic status that remain after all these conditions have been held constant are small. This does not mean, however, that the effects of number of

Table 4.    Parental family and occupational SES of American men
with nonfarm background, age 20 to 64.

| Sibling Position and Number of Siblings | 20–24 years | 25–34 years | 35–44 years | 45–54 years | 55–64 years |
|---|---|---|---|---|---|
| Grand Mean ..................... | 31.5 | 41.0 | 42.6 | 40.1 | 40.0 |
| | *Gross Effects* | | | | |
| 1. Only child, no siblings .......... | 5.1 | 6.0 | 4.1 | 7.0 | 3.0 |
| 2. Oldest, 1 to 3 siblings ......... | 3.6 | 6.4 | 6.1 | 4.7 | 7.0 |
| 3. Oldest, 4 or more siblings ...... | −2.1 | −6.0 | −6.0 | −4.8 | −0.3 |
| 4. Youngest, 1 to 3 siblings ....... | 5.3 | 3.6 | 6.5 | 5.3 | 5.6 |
| 5. Youngest, 4 or more siblings .... | −2.3 | −2.4 | −2.5 | −2.3 | −1.6 |
| 6. Middle, 2–3 s's, no older brother.. | −2.1 | 0.6 | 4.7 | 0.3 | 10.2 |
| 7. Middle, 2–3 s's, older brother ... | −2.3 | −0.8 | 3.7 | 1.5 | −0.1 |
| 8. Middle, 4+ s's, no older brother . | −7.3 | −4.3 | −8.2 | −4.8 | −5.4 |
| 9. Middle, 4+ s's, older brother ... | −6.3 | −7.6 | −7.5 | −3.6 | −5.1 |
| | *Net Effects** | | | | |
| 1. Only child, no siblings .......... | 3.8 | 3.9 | 2.9 | 4.2 | 3.0 |
| 2. Oldest, 1 to 3 siblings ......... | 2.6 | 4.0 | 4.2 | 2.6 | 4.4 |
| 3. Oldest, 4 or more siblings ...... | −1.8 | −4.5 | −4.0 | −3.1 | 0.8 |
| 4. Youngest, 1 to 3 siblings ....... | 4.4 | 2.3 | 4.0 | 3.5 | 4.6 |
| 5. Youngest, 4 or more siblings .... | 0.1 | −0.4 | 0.7 | −0.6 | −0.2 |
| 6. Middle, 2–3 s's, no older brother.. | −3.0 | −0.1 | 3.8 | 0.3 | 8.4 |
| 7. Middle, 2–3 s's, older brother ... | −2.3 | −0.5 | 1.9 | 1.1 | −0.7 |
| 8. Middle, 4+ s's, no older brother . | −5.6 | −2.6 | −7.1 | −4.6 | −3.8 |
| 9. Middle, 4+ s's, older brother ... | −4.5 | −5.1 | −5.3 | −1.9 | −4.5 |
| | *Residual Effects*** | | | | |
| 1. Only child, no siblings .......... | 1.5 | −1.2 | −1.3 | 0.5 | −0.9 |
| 2. Oldest, 1 to 3 siblings ......... | 1.0 | 1.0 | 1.4 | 0.5 | 1.3 |
| 3. Oldest, 4 or more siblings ...... | 0.3 | −0.3 | 0.2 | −0.8 | 1.7 |
| 4. Youngest, 1 to 3 siblings ....... | 2.4 | −0.3 | 0.6 | 0.6 | 1.4 |
| 5. Youngest, 4 or more siblings .... | 0.3 | 0.9 | 2.4 | −2.5 | 0.5 |
| 6. Middle, 2–3 s's, no older brother.. | −2.7 | 0.5 | 2.0 | −1.0 | 6.5 |
| 7. Middle, 2–3 s's, older brother ... | −3.4 | −0.8 | 1.8 | 1.5 | −1.2 |
| 8. Middle, 4+ s's, no older brother . | −3.3 | 0.5 | −3.2 | −0.2 | −1.1 |
| 9. Middle, 4+ s's, older brother ... | −1.0 | 0.0 | −1.7 | 0.2 | −1.7 |

Note: No cell frequency is less than 100 and only one – youngest in large families for cohort
20–24 years – is less than 200.

   * Father's occupational SES held constant.

  ** First job, education, father's occupational SES, ethnic classification, region and place
of birth and residence, and geographic mobility held constant.

siblings and sibling position previously observed were spurious, because the factors that are now being controlled are not independent of a man's parental family. Some of these control factors are directly determined by the family into which a man is born, such as his ethnic affiliation and the area where he grows up, and others are strongly affected by the size of his family and his position in it, such as his education and his first job. The reduction in effects produced by the introduction of these controls indicates, by and large, the degree to which the initial effects of parental family were mediated by various social and economic conditions, for example, the training and experience a man obtained and the opportunities existing in the area where he was raised. If the initial (gross) effects are little reduced by introducing the controls, it suggests that they are not primarily due to the economic advantages children gain from their families, directly or indirectly, but to other, socio-psychological forces in the family.

Whereas the gross effects on SES of sibling position are considerably smaller than those of sib size, the former persist to a greater degree than the latter when economic conditions are controlled. Instituting these controls reduces the impact of family size on SES very much, it reduces the influence of sibling position a great deal, though not as much, and it reduces the interaction effect of having no older brother in small families hardly at all. The average gross difference in SES between men from small and from large families of 8.0 points is reduced to a residual average difference of merely 1.1 points in Table 4. In contrast to this decrease to one seventh of the original difference, instituting controls decreases the effects of sibling position on SES considerably less, only to about one third of their original size, from 4.3 to 1.3 for youngest (vs. middle) and from 3.7 to 1.3 for oldest (vs. middle) children. The case is more extreme for the interaction effect of having no older brother and family size on SES. The gross differences in SES between middle children with no older brother and those with an older brother are +2.3 in small families and 0.0 in large ones, and the residual differences are +1.5 in small and −0.6 in large families. Hence, the difference between these differences, which indicates the interaction effect, is virtually not affected by introducing controls, being 2.3 originally and still 2.1 for the residuals. Although the residual effects are very small, the reduction in gross differences effected by introducing controls varies so greatly that we are tempted to hazard some interpretations based on these variations.

The superior occupational achievements of children from small families are largely accounted for by the better economic conditions in which they find themselves compared to children from large families. The superior occupational achievements of oldest and youngest children relative to those of middle children, on the other hand, seem to be due to a combination of economic and psychological factors. The distinctive position the oldest and the youngest child occupy in the family may not only have the result that parents devote disproportionate resources to their training but also make it likely that these children receive more social and emotional support from other members of the family than do middle children. (Since the residual effects for oldest and for youngest child do not differ, we had to modify here an interpretation advanced earlier that distinguished the situation of the youngest from that of the oldest.)

The occupational advantages middle children without older brothers have in small families but not in large ones are apparently not due to economic factors. A possible explanation of this interaction effect is that an older brother is more likely to be the oldest child in a small than in a large family, and oldest children occupy, as we have seen, privileged positions, which means that not having a brother who is an oldest child is an advantage. One might also speculate whether older sisters are protective and supportive of younger brothers and thereby strengthen their potential for subsequent occupational success. If older sisters actually have such a beneficial influence on their younger brothers, it would explain the observed interaction effect, because the middle child without an older brother necessarily has an older sister, and the middle child with an older brother in a small family is unlikely to have also an older sister but in a large family he is likely to have also an older sister.

CONCLUSIONS

We have illustrated our procedures as well as some preliminary findings from our research in this paper. The complexity of the analysis required when several factors influence occupational success has undoubtedly become evident. Since the condensed discussion may well have been difficult to follow at various points, it might be useful to summarize in conclusion the main substantive findings.

There is much intergenerational occupational mobility in the United

States, though probably not much more than in other Western countries such as Sweden and Britain. The correlation between father's and son's SES is $+.38$. The influence of father's on son's status is largely mediated through education, in apparent contrast to the situation in some other countries, but socio-economic origins also influence career chances independent of education.

It hardly comes as a surprise that racial discrimination in the United States is reflected in the Negro's inferior chances of occupational success, although the extent to which Negroes with the same amount of education as whites remain behind in the struggle for desirable occupations is striking. Negroes receive much less occupational return for their educational investments than whites do, and their consequent lesser incentive to acquire an education further disadvantages them in the labor market. What may be surprising, however, is that white ethnic minorities, on the average, appear to have as good occupational chances as the majority group. At least, the occupational achievements of foreign-born and second-generation Americans are no worse than those of native whites of native parentage with the same amount of education.

Urban migrants are more likely to occupy desirable occupational positions and to have moved up from the socio-economic status of their fathers than nonmigrants. Migration to urban areas brings occupational success more often than migration to rural areas (for the nonfarm population here under consideration), and migration from urban areas to small cities is particularly advantageous. The larger the place where a migrant grew up, the greater are the chances of his occupational success, regardless of the type of place where he ends up working. Indeed, for nonmigrants as well as migrants, there is a direct correlation between the size of the place where a man was reared and his occupational achievement.

Size of parental family and sibling position affect careers. The occupational attainments of men with many siblings, with whom they had to share parental resources, are inferior to those of men with few siblings, but only children do not achieve higher socio-economic positions than men from small families. Oldest and youngest children tend to have more successful careers than middle ones. In small families, though not in large ones, finally, having no older brothers appears to give a middle child a slight advantage in the struggle for occupational success, which suggests that older sisters improve future life chances.

REFERENCES

1. We plan, of course, to analyze the farm population in the future, with particular attention to the patterns of geographical and occupational mobility into urban sectors.

2. All frequencies in the original tables, from which the analytical tables presented in this report are derived, refer to the estimated actual population in the United States in the given categories, reported in 1000's. The sampling ratio is, on the average, 1:2,173. To obtain the approximate numbers of actual cases from whom data were collected, therefore, the numbers reported in 1000's should be divided by 2.2.

3. See Otis Dudley Duncan, *A Socio-Economic Index for All Occupations* in Albert J. Reiss, Jr., Occupations and Social Status, New York: Free Press, 1961. (This score was derived from the 1950 U.S. Census of Population, not from our sample.)

4. National Opinion Research Center, *Jobs and Occupations*, Opinion News, vol. 9 (1947), pp. 3–13.

5. Education is scored by the following system, which takes into account the special significance of graduation from one of the three main levels of schooling:

0    No school
1    Elementary, 1 to 4 years
2    Elementary, 5 to 7 years
3    Elementary, 8 years
4    High school, 1 to 3 years
5    High School, 4 years
6    College, 1 to 3 years
7    College, 4 years
8    Graduate school, 1 year or more

6. The complex nature of the weighted sample makes it difficult to determine levels of statistical significance accurately, but the following conservative estimates may serve as an approximate guide: All differences between specific pairs of cells of 1.5 or more are significant on the .05 level unless the reported number in one of the two cells involved in the comparison is less than 200. All those differences of 2.0 and above are significant unless one of the reported frequencies is less than 100. Any difference of 5.0 or more is significant. When nearly all of several independent comparisons are in the same direction, the chance that an average difference of a given size is not statistically significant is further reduced. Cells where the reported number is less than 100 are indicated by an asterisk in the tables.

7. Although we plan to investigate the problem of estimating time trends more thoroughly in the future, a re-analysis of Rogoff's data for the city

of Indianapolis by Duncan indicates that there is no change in the father-son correlation between 1910 and 1940.

8. Since the index used to score the status of an occupation is based on the amount of education and the amount of income that prevailed in the occupation, it is necessarily related to education to some degree. Experimentation with an alternative index of occupational SES, not based explicitly on education levels, however, shows that the results are not dependent on the specific form of SES index used here.

9. Our data actually refer to "nonwhites" but 92 per cent of all nonwhites in the United States are Negroes.

10. For an explanation of the statistical model used, see Otis Dudley Duncan, *Farm Background and Differential Fertility*, paper presented to the Population Association of America at its June 1964 annual meeting. For a published discussion, see T. P. Hill, *An Analysis of the Distribution of Wages and Salaries in Great Britain*, Econometrics, vol. 27 (July, 1959), pp. 355–381.

11. It should be noted that some of the difference between Negroes and whites, though hardly all of it, may be due to the fact that holding constant the amount of education for the two groups does actually not hold constant their educational qualifications, since many of the schools to which Negroes go are inferior to those whites attend. Moreover, our broad categories do not even hold the amount of education fully constant, since, given the lower educational attainments of Negroes, there are undoubtedly fewer Negroes than whites near the upper end of the distribution within each category; for example, within the category, "one year of college or more", the proportion of college graduates is slightly smaller for Negroes than for whites.

12. Since the criterion of nonfarm background is whether a man designated his father's occupation as being in farming, not whether he lives on a farm, there are a few farm residents in this nonfarm population. Wherever possible, these have been excluded from this analysis, but this was not possible in all cases. However, the numbers involved are so small that it is unlikely that these farm residents affect the results substantially.

13. Since only one value for migrants from the two urban to rural areas is given, the unweighted average of the two values for the migrants to small towns from large cities and those from small towns was used in computing the differences. In case of the youngest age group, for instance, 1.9 was subtracted from 5.4 (the average of 5.8 and 5.0).

# B.

## INTERACTION OF PERSONALITY AND
## STRUCTURAL FACTORS IN DIFFERENTIAL MOBILITY

# SOCIAL CLASS, EDUCATION, AND MOTIVE TO ACHIEVE
# IN DIFFERENTIAL OCCUPATIONAL MOBILITY

HARRY J. CROCKETT, JR.

Recent works by Anderson and by Carlsson challenge the widely held notion that education exercises a dominant influence on inter-generational occupational mobility.[1] Both studies do find that extended formal education markedly enhances the probability of upward movement for sons originating in lower status levels, and that the lack of extended formal education increases the probability of downward movement for sons originating in higher status levels. But these reports stress the finding that much mobility occurs beyond that attributable to the influence of education.

In searching for additional understanding of the contribution of education and other variables to the mobility process, it is possible to focus either on the determinants of the amount of mobility taking place in a society or on the determinants of mobility among persons sharing similar opportunities. The papers cited above are more concerned with the former question, while differential mobility will be the prime concern of this report.

An ubiquitous finding in mobility studies is that movement across the nonmanual-manual line is notably less than movement within the two broad occupational groupings. This fact, coupled with the relatively great differences in proportions with college training invariably reported for the two groups, is a major source for the widely held notion already cited concerning the potency of education in the mobility process. It is now clear, however, that status level of parent (or social class background of respondent) affects mobility directly, that is, separately from the influence of social class background on son's education.[2] Measures of variables associated with social class background, other than occupation of father and education of son, are not available in the present data. However, inferences regarding class-

Reprinted from *Sociological Quarterly* (Vol. 4, Summer 1964, pp. 231–242) by permission of the publisher and the author.

linked variables supported by an extensive literature and consistent with the data will be introduced in the analysis.

A separate order of potential determinants of differential mobility, conceptually distinct from both education-level of son and his social class background, is observable in the personality characteristics of sons. Anderson has recently suggested that "ability, whether hereditary or not, and associated motivation, varying independently of schooling, plays a powerful role in generating mobility."[3] Empirical research testing the contribution of personality factors to mobility is scarce. To my knowledge, such research utilizing national sample data is to be found in only two studies. First, intelligence — specifically, generational disparities in intelligence — has been estimated to exert strong influence on mobility by Anderson, Brown, and Bowman.[4] Second, in a previous paper I have shown strength of achievement motive to be positively associated with upward mobility among men reared in lower social strata, but not among men reared in higher social strata.[5] The study also examined affiliative and power motives, finding neither to be consistently related to mobility.

The present paper cannot offer findings concerning the contribution of intelligence to mobility. Rather, the paper will present findings which provide additional understanding of how social class background factors, education level, and strength of achievement motive may interact to influence mobility.

Since the theoretical relevance of achievement motivation to occupational mobility was set forth in detail in the earlier paper, it may be sufficient here to state only the principal points examined in that discussion. The achievement motive is defined as a disposition to strive for success when performance is to be evaluated in relation to some standard of excellence. The motive is presumed to be learned, and to be relatively enduring through time. A theory of achievement motivation developed by Atkinson predicts that in achievement-relevant situations persons with strong achievement motive, as compared to persons with weak achievement motive, will put forth more persistent effort, and will strive toward more realistic goals.[6] The properties essential for the use of the theory are shown to be present in the occupational domain. The theory, then, clearly predicts that greater upward and less downward mobility will be shown by persons with strong achievement motive as compared with persons having weak achievement motive.

Although measures of intelligence are not present in the data at hand, discussion of intelligence in relation to achievement motivation seems relevant. As noted above, the achievement motive is not presumed to be genetically given but rather is seen to be acquired through learning experiences in the process of socialization. To the extent that intelligence is genetically given, then, variation in level of intelligence and strength of achievement motive should occur. One kind of evidence bearing upon this question is offered by studies examining the relationship of achievement motive to performance with intelligence controlled;[7] some, but not all, of these studies find that strength of achievement motive affects performance (on diverse tasks) independent of intelligence (measured by diverse tests). It seems legitimate to infer from these conflicting results that the achievement motive is not identical with intelligence as measured by current IQ tests as well as that intelligence sometimes has effects on performance which obscure the effects of achievement motive.

Performance on IQ tests, however, may well be a function of ability and skills *plus* the motivation to learn and to do well on tests. This hypothesis was tested by Kagan *et al.* among a sample of youths whose IQ scores were roughly similar (all were above 115).[8] A significant positive relationship between strength of achievement motive (measured for most youths at ages eleven and twelve) and increase in IQ test score from the ages six to ten was obtained. In a subsequent study, Kagan and Moss report further that while initial intellectual capacity (as measured at age three) was significantly related to measured intelligence at age six, change in IQ score from the ages six to ten was *not* related to initial intellectual capacity.[9] It is inferred from these longitudinal studies that strength of achievement motive is not identical with measured intelligence but rather seems to be one of the determinants of increases in measured intelligence. Hence, while it is not doubted that intelligence will prove on empirical study to be important for mobility, it does not seem likely that results concerning strength of achievement motive and mobility will be vitiated at that time.

## DATA AND PROCEDURES

Data reported here are taken from a national sample survey conducted in the United States in 1957. In keeping with common practice in analysis of survey materials which lack detailed data relevant to social class placement, nonmanual occupations are presumed to indicate middle-class status, manual occupations are presumed to indicate working-class status. To assess movement within these broad class groups as well as across class boundaries, mobility is measured in terms of occupational prestige. Difficulties in assessing the prestige of farm occupations, and hence in measuring mobility, preclude use of respondents whose fathers were farmers. Using the North and Hatt prestige assignments as a base,[10] four prestige categories are constituted: 1. (high) scores of 78–93; 2. scores of 69–77; 3. scores of 61–68; and 4 (low) scores of 33–60.[11] Thus, a respondent whose occupation falls in a category different from that of the occupation of his father is considered to have been mobile, whether or not the mobility involves crossing the middle-class–working-class boundary. To facilitate analysis further, upper and lower groups are differentiated within each social class: the upper middle class includes all nonmanual occupations classified in prestige categories 1 or 2; the lower middle class includes all nonmanual occupations classified in prestige categories 3 or 4; the upper working class includes all manual occupations classified in categories 2 or 3; and the lower working class includes all manual occupations classified in category 4. The achievement motive is measured by the thematic apperceptive technique developed by McClelland and his co-workers.[12] A total of 367 adult men, representing all those in the original national sample for whom satisfactory measures of achievement motive strength, education level, and occupation of self and father were obtained, form the sample. In evaluating the data, one-tailed probability values computed from a significance of difference between proportions test corrected for the effects of cluster sampling are used when the $N$'s being compared are around 25 or greater. Consistency of predicted differences is also stressed in the analysis.

## ANALYSIS

The primary concern of this analysis is with the interactive effects on mobility of social class background factors, education level, and strength of achievement motive. It is necessary to begin, however, with discussion of the separate relationships between education level and mobility, and between strength of achievement motive and mobility.

Table 1. Education and Occupational Mobility by
Social Class Background

| Social Class Background | Education | N (367) | Occupation Prestige Category of Respondent in Relation to That of Father | | | |
|---|---|---|---|---|---|---|
| | | | Below | Same | Above | |
| Upper Middle | Any College | (52) | 21% | 46% | 33% | |
| | | | | p < .002 | | p < .05 |
| | Non-college | (51) | 67 | 28 | 6 | |
| Lower Middle | Any College | (18) | 6 | 17 | 78 | |
| | | | | p < .09 | | p < .004 |
| | Non-college | (23) | 30 | 39 | 30 | |
| Upper Working | Any College | (24) | 17 | 25 | 58 | |
| | | | | N.S. | | p < .01 |
| | Non-college | (88) | 28 | 49 | 23 | |
| Lower Working | Any College | (18) | | 22 | 78 | |
| | | | | | | p < .03 |
| | Non-college | (93) | | 51 | 49 | |

The effects of education on occupational mobility within social class groups are displayed in Table 1. Persons with extended formal education, at each class level of origin, are much more likely to rise and much less likely to fall than persons lacking such training. Non-college-educated groups from each social class of origin except the upper middle class, however, do contain sizable fractions of upwardly mobile persons. Moreover, of all upwardly mobile persons, less than half (44 per cent) are in the college-educated group. These data clearly support the position of Anderson and Carlsson noted earlier: while higher education has a marked effect on differential mobility, much upward mobility does occur which is not attributable to higher education.

Relationships between strength of achievement motive and occupational mobility within social class groups of origin are shown in Table 2. The data are puzzling. For persons reared in either the lower middle class or the lower working class, those high in achievement motive,[13] move up much more frequently and down much less frequently than do those low in achievement motive. But among persons reared in the upper working class, while those high in achievement motive do move up more frequently and down less frequently than do those low in achievement motive, the trend is not marked.

TABLE 2. STRENGTH OF ACHIEVEMENT MOTIVE AND OCCUPATIONAL
MOBILITY, BY SOCIAL CLASS BACKGROUND

| Social Class Background | Strength of Achievement Motive | N (367) | Occupational Prestige Category of Respondent in Relation to That of Father | | |
|---|---|---|---|---|---|
| | | | Below | Same | Above |
| Upper Middle | High | (58) | 45% | 36% | 19% |
| | Low | (45) | 42 | 38 | 20 |
| Lower Middle | High | (23) | 9 | 26 | 65 |
| | | | $p < .10$ | | $p < .04$ |
| | Low | (18) | 33 | 33 | 33 |
| Upper Working | High | (63) | 24 | 41 | 35 |
| | | | N.S. | | N.S. |
| | Low | (49) | 29 | 47 | 25 |
| Lower Working | High | (52) | | 35 | 65 |
| | | | | | $p < .09$ |
| | Low | (59) | | 56 | 44 |

And among persons in the upper middle class, strength of achievement motive is essentially unrelated to mobility.

Comparative study of the data in Tables 1 and 2 might suggest the hypothesis that the college-educated are evenly distributed between motive groups in both the upper middle and upper working classes, and disproportionately represented in the high achievement motive group in the lower middle and lower working classes. If the hypothesis were true, relationships between strength of achievement motive and mobility might turn out to be spurious — merely functions of education. The data of Table 3, however, while sustaining the hypothesis, do not support the conclusion.

As the hypothesis predicts, the percentages of college-educated persons in the high and low motive groups are practically identical for those reared in both the upper middle class (50 per cent *versus* 51 per cent) and the upper working class (22 per cent *versus* 20 per cent); and the high motive groups do show higher percentages of college-educated persons than the low motive groups in both the lower middle class (57 per cent *versus* 28 per cent) and the lower working class (21 per cent *versus* 12 per cent). With education controlled, however, the data still show greater upward mobility in high rather than low motive groups in six of eight comparisons, and less downward mobility in high rather than low motive groups in five of six comparisons. And, looking only at the non-college group comparisons — where $N$'s are generally larger — upward mobility of persons high in achievement motive exceeds that of persons low in achievement motive by 10 percentage points in the upper middle class, 17 percentage points in the lower middle class, 14 percentage points in the upper working class, and 21 percentage points in the lower working class.[14]

It appears, then, that a positive relationship between strength of achievement motive and mobility, which is not explained by the relationship between education and strength of achievement motive, is present. Let us proceed now to discussion of interaction between social class, education, and achievement motive in the determination of mobility.

First, consider the middle class groups. In the upper middle class, persons low in achievement motive are as likely to have attended college as are persons high in achievement motive. Data from a number of studies support the following inferences here: (1) Parents in this group want their sons to attend college, have the means to send them to college, and exert pressure on them to go to college; (2) From the point of view of the sons in the upper middle class, attend-

TABLE 3. EDUCATION, STRENGTH OF ACHIEVEMENT MOTIVE, AND OCCUPATIONAL MOBILITY, BY SOCIAL CLASS BACKGROUND

| Social Class Background | Education | Strength of Achievement Motive | N (367) | Occupational Prestige Category of Respondent in Relation to That of Father | | | | |
|---|---|---|---|---|---|---|---|---|
| | | | | Below | | Same | Above | |
| Upper Middle | Any College | High | (29) | 24% | | 48% | 28% | |
| | | Low | (23) | 17 | | 44 | 39 | |
| | Non-college | High | (29) | 66 | N.S. | 24 | 10 | N.S. |
| | | Low | (22) | 68 | | 32 | 0 | |
| Lower Middle | Any College | High | (13) | 0 | | 15 | 85 | |
| | | Low | ( 5) | 20 | | 20 | 60 | |
| | Non-college | High | (10) | 20 | | 40 | 40 | |
| | | Low | (13) | 39 | | 39 | 23 | |
| Upper Working | Any College | High | (14) | 14 | | 29 | 57 | |
| | | Low | (10) | 20 | | 20 | 60 | |
| | Non-college | High | (49) | 27 | | 45 | 29 | |
| | | Low | (39) | 31 | N.S. | 54 | 15 | p < .19 |
| Lower Working | Any College | High | (11) | | | 18 | 82 | |
| | | Low | ( 7) | | | 29 | 71 | |
| | Non-college | High | (41) | | | 39 | 61 | p < .09 |
| | | Low | (52) | | | 60 | 40 | |

ing college is undoubtedly strongly influenced by social class values and norms: they go to college because it is the accepted and expected thing for young persons in their class to do.

Now the picture of factors important to college attendance among persons in the lower middle class contrasts sharply with that among persons from upper middle class backgrounds. It will be recalled that strength of achievement motive is markedly more related to college attendance among the lower middle class than in any other group of respondents: 57 per cent of persons high in achievement motive, as compared with 28 per cent of those low in achievement motive, have had some college education. The emphasis upon the desirability of a college education is no doubt as pervasive in the lower middle class as in the upper middle class. In all likelihood, however, lower middle class parents do not have the financial resources to make it easy for their sons to attend college. In order for sons from lower middle class backgrounds to go to college, strong individual effort and persistence (as in part-time jobs and summer work, as well as in diligent study for those on scholarships) is no doubt generally essential. Strong motive to achieve, it is suggested, is therefore an important determinant of the acquisition of college training for these respondents, while it does not appear as an important determinant among persons reared in the upper middle class. In turn, this differential acquisition of college training permits those with strong achievement motive in the lower middle class to exhibit appreciably more upward mobility than those with weak achievement motive.

If the above reasoning be granted, then an explanation is at hand for the different relationships observed between achievement motive and mobility in the two middle class groups. The majority of occupations carrying high prestige in the middle class require a college education; some of these occupations may be secured solely through the possession of wealth and social connections; and relatively few are open to persons with great talent who lack both college training and a privileged social position at the outset. When college training is assured to sons with even marginal capacities by parents — as probably occurs frequently in the upper middle class — then strength of achievement motive should not be related to mobility. Irrespective of achievement motive strength, the more talented sons and those with the more privileged connections will maintain or enhance their positions, while the less talented and privileged will fall. But when college training is itself secured through the diligent effort of sons — as probably occurs frequently in the lower middle class — then strength of achievement motive will be strongly related to acquisition of a college education and, hence, to upward mobility.

Turning now to persons reared in the working class, the remarkable effect of social class background on acquisition of higher education is to be noted. Only 19 per cent of working class sons (as compared with 49 per cent of middle class sons) have had any college training. Moreover, within the working class, persons high in achievement motive do not attend college in markedly greater proportions than do those low in achievement motive (22 per cent *versus* 16 per cent). This result is fully congruent with the line of argument developed, and evidence cited, above. Persons reared in the working class, irrespective of achievement motive strength, are not likely to have acquired a high evaluation of a college education. As Rosen [15] has pointed out, strong achievement motive assures persistent effort toward only those goals which the person's values and experience define as appropriate. Hence, strength of motive to achieve would not be expected to differentiate sharply between the college-educated and the non-college-educated among persons reared in the working class. But strength of achievement motive does contribute noticeably to upward mobility in this group, especially among persons reared in the lower working class (Table 3). For these persons, many occupations notably higher in prestige in comparison with the occupation of their fathers may be attained without benefit of college training.

The differential effect of strength of achievement motive and factors associated with social class background on the acquisition of college education, and hence on mobility, may be further highlighted by comparison of persons from lower middle class backgrounds with persons from upper working class backgrounds. In the two groups, the ability of parents to provide financial assistance toward a college education for sons is roughly equal and relatively slight. Yet 44 per cent of persons from lower middle class backgrounds but only 22 per cent of persons from upper working class backgrounds have had some college education. As noted above, strength of achievement motive is strongly related to the acquisition of higher education among persons from lower middle-class backgrounds but not among persons from upper working-class backgrounds. The inference to be drawn is clear. Middle class norms which stress the desirability of higher status, "white collar" jobs, that are usually attainable only through higher education, strongly influence persons in the lower middle class but not persons reared in the upper working class. The mobility differences between these two groups of respondents shown in Table 3 are fully consistent with these inferred relationships between strength of achievement motive, social class values and norms, and attainment of some college education. If persons reared in the upper working class are to be upwardly mobile, they must ordinarily acquire some college training. But the values of their social class do not stress college education. Two consequences would seem to follow: (1) These persons are as a group substantially less upwardly mobile than are persons reared in the lower middle class (30 per cent as compared with 51 per cent, $p. < .08$); and (2) upwardly mobile respondents are much less sharply differentiated by strength of achievement motive among persons from upper working class backgrounds than among persons from lower middle class backgrounds.

SUMMARY

This paper has examined effects on mobility of education level, social class background, and strength of achievement motive. The attainment of some college education is shown to enhance greatly the likelihood of upward mobility and reduce the likelihood of downward mobility. However, much mobility is not attributable to the factor of education. Strength of achievement motive is shown to exert noticeable influence, on upward mobility especially, among persons who lack any college training. An analysis of the interaction of factors associated with social class background, strength of achievement motive, and level of education in the determination of mobility is offered; the analysis rationalizes both the absence of expected relationships between strength of achievement motive and mobility among persons from upper middle class backgrounds, and the presence of such relationships among persons from the other social class groups. The correctness of this latter analysis will, of course, turn upon the results of future research in which more refined measures of social class variables are used.

REFERENCES

1. C. Arnold Anderson, "A Skeptical Note on the Relation of Vertical Mobility to Education," *American Journal of Sociology*, 66:560–70 (May, 1961); Gösta Carlsson, *Social Mobility and Class Structure* (Lund, Sweden: C.W.K. Gleerup, 1958).

2. Anderson, *op. cit.;* Carlsson, *op. cit.;* Seymour M. Lipset and Reinhard Bendix, *Social Mobility in Industrial Society* (Berkeley: University of California Press, 1959), pp. 98–99.

3. Anderson, *op. cit.,* p. 569.

4. C. Arnold Anderson, James C. Brown, and Mary Jean Bowman, "Intelligence and Occupational Mobility," *Journal of Political Economy*, 60:218–239 (1952).

5. Harry J. Crockett, Jr., "The Achievement Motive and Differential Occupational Mobility in the United States," *American Sociological Review*, 27:191–204 (Apr., 1962).

6. John W. Atkinson, "Motivational Determinants of Risk-Taking Behavior," *Psychological Review*, 64:359–72 (Nov., 1957).

7. John W. Atkinson and Walter R. Reitman, "Performance as a Function of Motive Strength and Expectancy of Goal Attainment," in John W. Atkinson (ed.), *Motives in Fantasy, Action, and Society* (Princeton, N.J.: Van Nostrand, 1958), pp. 596–616; David C. McClelland, John W. Atkinson, Russell A. Clark, and Edward A. Lowell, *The Achievement Motive* (New York: Appleton-Century-Crofts, 1953), pp. 229–42.

8. Jerome Kagan, L. W. Sontag, C. T. Baker and Virginia L. Nelson, "Personality and IQ Change," *Journal of Abnormal and Social Psychology*, 56: 261–66 (1958).

9. Jerome Kagan and Howard A. Moss, "Stability and Validity of Achievement Fantasy," *Journal of Abnormal and Social Psychology*, 58:357–64 (1959); see also Jerome Kagan and Howard A. Moss, *Birth to Maturity* (New York: Wiley, 1962), pp. 148–52.

10. National Opinion Research Center, "Jobs and Occupations: A Popular Evaluation," in Reinhard Bendix and Seymour M. Lipset, *Class, Status, and Power* (Glencoe, Ill.: Free Press, 1953), pp. 411–26.

11. Data attesting to the reliability and validity of the coding procedures employed are to be found in Harry J. Crockett, Jr., "Achievement Motivation and Occupational Mobility in the United States." Unpublished doctoral dissertation, University of Michigan, 1960.

12. For an assessment of the use of this technique in the national sample survey providing the data for the present paper, see Joseph Veroff, John W.

Atkinson, Sheila Feld and Gerald Gurin, "The Use of Thematic Apperception to Assess Motivation in a Nationwide Interview Study," *Psychological
Monographs*, vol. 74 (No. 499), pp. 1–32 (1960).

13. "High" and "low" achievement motive groups are formed by cutting the
distribution of motive scores at the median. The numbers of respondents in
the two groups for the present sample are unequal because the median for
all respondents giving adequate motive protocols in the original study is
used here.

14. These results would not be changed if finer distinctions of education
level within the non-college group were to be made. Both the proportions of
high school graduates and of persons with some high school education are
greater for the low-motive group than for the high-motive group, while the
proportion of persons who did not reach high school is greater among the
high-motive group than among the low-motive group.

15. Bernard C. Rosen, "The Achievement Syndrome," *American Sociological
Review*, 21:203–11 (Apr., 1956).

# ACADEMIC ABILITY, HIGHER EDUCATION, AND OCCUPATIONAL MOBILITY

BRUCE K. ECKLAND

The literature on vertical mobility makes it clear that we know very little about the part that ability plays in the movement of persons through the class structure. The functional theory of social stratification suggests that industrial societies must provide a relatively open contest for mobility, so that talent, randomly dispersed at birth, is redistributed in such a way that "the most important positions are filled by the most 'qualified' personnel."[1] In this allocating process, the formal institutions of education supposedly serve as the primary selectors and sorters of talent for later assignment to occupational roles.[2] Little systematic empirical evidence exists, however, as to how the supply of talent is really distributed, especially after students leave the school system.

Although ability contributes to achievement at all levels of education, all students do not have equal educational opportunities. Location in the class structure is an important determinant of achievement in the primary and secondary grades, and a particularly strong determinant of who goes to college.[3] This imperfect association between ability and education might be amended, in effect, after students leave school and enter the occupational world: some observers have suggested that ability is perhaps the dominant factor influencing mobility, and that it accounts for occupational achievement quite independently of the amount of formal education attained.[4] On the other hand, past research[5] indicates that ascriptive elements affecting education may be carried over into the allocation of jobs, particularly among the professions and other white-collar occupations. Unfortunately, none of the published studies provides evidence of the separate effects of

Reprinted with abridgement from the *American Sociological Review* (Vol. 30, No. 5, October 1965, pp. 735–746) by permission of the American Sociological Association and the author.

533

ability and education upon mobility. Is the high correlation between education and occupation largely incidental to the ability of the students who had succeeded in the school system, or is formal education, independent of ability, really the crucial variable? Moreover, if education is the crucial variable, do such effects as ability has operate directly on occupation or are they primarily mediated through the school system?

The present study investigated these questions with reference to the occupational achievement of college dropouts and graduates. The *ideal* design for gauging the full impact of ability and education might be to administer a test of native intelligence to a random sample of the pre-school-age population, and then trace their academic and occupational careers for the next 30 or 40 years. But since psychological testing has not yet developed an instrument to isolate the innate characteristics of IQ and long-term surveys are expensive, this study was limited to a more modest approach. The data, nevertheless, provided a rare opportunity to investigate the general relations between *academic* ability, higher education, and social mobility.

THE STUDY SAMPLE

The sample consists of all 1,332 men born in 1934 who were residents of the state, had no previous college experience, and enrolled at the Urbana campus of the University of Illinois in the fall of 1952 as full-time freshmen in degree-granting programs. Most of the data were obtained from a questionnaire mailed during the late spring and early summer of 1962, or ten years after the sample's matriculation in college. Because many addresses were out of date,[6] 192 questionnaires were returned by the post office on the first mailing. An extensive search[7] reduced this number to 73, which meant that only 5 per cent of the sample was permanently lost while the remaining 1,259 students presumably received our mail.

The first three mailings produced a 67 per cent response from these students. Following the third wave, we placed over one thousand telephone calls to the non-respondents in a further effort to elicit returns. If the subject could not be reached by phone, or if after a telephone contact a questionnaire was not returned within a reasonable waiting period, a certified letter was mailed as our final effort.

These methods yielded 1,180 usable returns, or responses from 94 per cent of all students to whom questionnaires were delivered.[8]

For the purposes of the analysis to follow, sample size was reduced by 6 per cent, from 1,180 to 1,107, because high school percentile ranks were not available for 73 cases. There is no evidence that excluding these cases has introduced bias.[9] On the contrary the evidence is substantial that the Illinois sample is fairly representative of the students at most state universities during the period of this study, although certainly it does not represent the full range of college student populations. A relatively unrestricted admissions policy at the University in 1952 provided a diversity of talent; e.g., while nearly half of the students ranked in the top quarter of their high school classes, about one out of four ranked in the bottom half. As in most student bodies, social background played an important part in the pre-college selection process; yet their fathers' occupational distribution indicates that we have sampled from a sufficiently broad range of class origins to obtain some measure of its impact on the student's occupational achievement. All major fields of study are included among the curricula in which the respondents were enrolled, with concentrations in engineering, liberal arts and science, commerce, and agriculture.

METHOD OF ANALYSIS

The data are presented in contingency tables as well as in a multiple regression analysis. In the contingency tables, the traditional multiple cross-tabulation procedure was used and most variables were collapsed, forming conceptually-appropriate trichotomies so as to retain fairly large cell entries. The multiple regression technique is used primarily to compare the effects of the independent variables on the dependent variable and to describe the paths through which they operate. The regression equation, which predicts the value of the dependent variable on the basis of a number of factors simultaneously, employs the full range of scores on each variable rather than trichotomies. Interval-scale measurement and linearity of regressions are assumed, except in the case of subject-fields (see footnote 29) which have been expanded into a set of categoric, or binary-coded, predictor variables.

In addition to simple zero-order correlations, use is made of R, the unbiased correlation ratio, which is derived from the multiple regression model, $Y = a + b_1X_1 + b_2X_2 + b_3X_3$. R is defined as $\sqrt{1}$ minus the ratio of within-class mean square variance to total mean square variance.[10]

From this model, two forms of within-class variance are derived. The first is based on the sum of squares due to the total regression, from which a conventional multiple coefficient is derived. The second is based on the difference between the sum of squares of a full model and that of a reduced model. This difference estimates the prediction of one independent variable that is not included in its intercorrelation with the remaining independent variables.[11] I shall refer to this estimation as the "partial association," since it is analogous to a conventional partial correlation.

MEASUREMENT

Two measures of ability were initially employed: high-school rank (HSR) and scores from the American Council on Education Psychological Examination (ACE) which was administered to all freshmen at the time of matriculation. Either of these methods should be used to operationalize ability only with considerable caution. High-school performance certainly is an inseparable mixture of intelligence and social processes. The ACE examination, probably the most widely used test of its kind in American colleges and universities in 1952, also reflects social factors. And apart from the difficulty of isolating intellectual characteristics, both indices are at best only approximations of the gross concept of talent. Proficiency in many occupational roles, including the professions, may require a number of personal attributes, however acquired, that are quite distinct from a student's scholastic aptitude. Both HSR and the ACE, then, are basically measures of *academic* ability, which presumably is only one component of talent.

Unfortunately, some peculiarities of the data made it unfeasible to collapse HSR and ACE into a single index of ability or introduce them simultaneously in the multiple regressions.[12] In the first place, ACE test scores were available for fewer than two-thirds of the respondents. More critical, however, than the large reduction that would occur in sample size was the systematic bias that this loss would introduce — it would remove, among others, all 248 of the commerce students.[13] Furthermore, the available ACE scores were in the form of decile ranks based on norms fixed separately for the students in each college of the University, so that the rank, for example, of a freshman entering engineering was relative to other engineers only and not to the entire freshman class. The raw scores that would have made it possible to reestablish an all-freshman norm were unavailable. High-school rank alone will be used in the following analysis.

Both indices yield substantially similar correlations with occupational achievement. Of the two, however, high-school rank is a better predictor of graduation, or of college grades, which are the criteria usually employed in attrition studies. In the subsample for which both HSR and ACE scores were available, their correlations with first-semester grade averages were .53 and .36, respectively. These correlations are entirely consistent with an abundance of studies on academic predictors in college and suggest that high-school rank is a valid measure of academic ability.

The regression analysis is based on decile ability ranks (0 to 9), while the percentages involve low, medium, and high ability levels, designating ranks below the median, in the second quarter, and in the first quarter, respectively, of high-school graduating class.

By June, 1962, 762 respondents had obtained bachelor's degrees and 345 had not. Degrees not earned at the University of Illinois, initially identified from the questionnaire information supplied by each respondent, were verified through correspondence with the 71 colleges and universities from which 23 per cent of the graduates reported having received them. The figures indicate that the rate of graduation is about 69 per cent, considerably higher than what past research at either local or national levels would have predicted. The present study departs from past research by taking account of the transfer students, the dropouts who later returned to graduate, and the otherwise prolonged nature of college careers, and the rate reported here actually may typify the achievement of a very large proportion of the American college-going men who initially enter state universities.[14]

Social class origin was determined by using the first digit of Duncan's Index of Socioeconomic Status (SES) as applied to the father's usual occupation when the student was growing up. Again, the regression analysis employs a full range of values from 0 to 9, while the contingency tables divide the subects into three groups, low, medium, and high, depending on whether the father's occupation was classified in the 0–3, 4–6, or 7–9 range of SES scores derived by Duncan from estimates of the income and educational levels of all persons employed in each of some 446 occupations in the 1950 labor force.[15] The cutting point (3.5) at which *low-* has been differentiated from *medium-* and *high-*status parallels the customary manual-nonmanual occupational dichotomy.[16] *High-*status occupations as we defined them are held by less than 10 per cent of the national male labor force,[17] but the pre-college selection process is such that 23 per cent of our respondents originate in this class. Similarly, over 70 per cent of the national labor force is in the *low-*status category, compared with about 39 percent of the students, by origin.

In an earlier report, I excluded all students with farm origins from the analysis of these data,[18] because the SES index assigns low scores to most farm occupations.[19] The fathers of these students were, on the whole, the more prosperous farmers in a state where farm incomes, to begin with, were well above average.[20] Excluding the farm students, however, caused a 15 per cent loss in sample size and a significant change in the character of the population. To retain the farm sample in this investigation and yet conform to the intent of the scale, I adjusted the index values by computing the median SES for each income category in our non-farm sample and assigning these scores on an individual basis, by income, to the farmers.[21]

Occupational achievement, the main dependent variable, also utilizes the SES index, applied in this case to the respondent's present occupation.[22] Again, the regression analysis employs index values from 0 to 9, and the contingency tables use the same tripartite division as above, with the same cutting points.[23] Only 3 per cent of the respondents were employed in farm occupations; their scores were adjusted as described above.

FINDINGS

Observe in Figure 1 that social class and high school rank *in this study sample* are not positively related. The following explanation seems worth considering. Class origin and academic ability are strong determinants of *where* one goes to college, and the state university probably draws a larger-than-average proportion of its students from the middle ranks of both dimensions. To the extent that the extremes actually are under-represented, correlations between class and ability will be low. In addition to attracting the modal students, however,

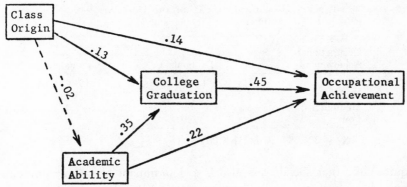

FIGURE 1.   ZERO-ORDER CORRELATIONS OF CAUSAL VARIABLES ASSOCIATED WITH
OCCUPATIONAL ACHIEVEMENT

the state university attracts many for whom these factors do not
coincide. Its open doors provide an opportunity for middle and upper-
middle class students who do *poor* work in high school to go, if not to
the "best," at least to a "respectable," essentially middle-class school.
At the same time, the large state-supported university is accessible and
attractive to working-class students with middle-class aspirations who
do reasonably *well* in high school. If this reasoning is accurate, then
strong correlations between class and ability are not likely to occur
in *any* sample drawn from a single institution. At the most and at the
least selective schools, the social and intellectual composition of the
student body will be uniformly high or low, but at most state universities, any dependence of ability on class origin will be concealed
by the presence of incongruent combinations. In effect, then, any
dependence of academic ability on the origin of our respondents has
inadvertently been controlled in our sample.

Treating college graduation as the dependent variable, observe that
its zero-order correlation with HSR is considerably larger than its
correlation with social class (see Figure 1). That high-school rank
should predict college performance certainly was not unanticipated,
but even the low correlation between class origin and graduation is
inconsistent with the equivocal findings of earlier studies on college
attrition. Previous investigators, apparently, did not trace the academic careers of the many college dropouts whose eventual return
and graduation, we found, actually depends as much on class origin
as ability. A re-examination of past research, coupled with a more
elaborate examination of our data than I am reporting here, made it

TABLE 1. COLLEGE GRADUATION AND OCCUPATIONAL
ACHIEVEMENT (in percentages)

| Occupational | College | |
| Achievement | Dropouts | Graduates |
| --- | --- | --- |
| (N) | (345) | (762) |
| High | 21 | 66 |
| Medium | 59 | 30 |
| Low | 20 | 4 |

$X^2 = 204.994$, 2 d.f., $p < .001$.

quite clear that social class also is a determinant of college graduation.[24]

*Graduation and Occupational Achievement.* The very strong association between graduation and early occupational careers is shown in Table 1 (and by the .45 zero-order correlation in Figure 1). That 66 per cent of the graduates, compared with 21 per cent of the dropouts, obtained high-ranking jobs suggests that a young man who leaves college with a degree is reasonably more certain than others to obtain a fairly high-status nonmanual position. But is it the degree that accounts for his success, or rather the effects of the academic ability and class origin that helped him earn the degree in the first place?

The effects of ability and class are partialled out in Table 2. Most notable is the marked influence that graduation has on occupational achievement quite apart from the separate effects of social origin and academic ability, especially among the students from working-class (low-status) homes. In fact, the few (22) low-status, low-ability students who managed to attain a college degree were apparently more successful after leaving school than the (even fewer) high-status, high-ability men who failed to graduate (compare Columns 1 and 9).

Holding ability and class constant, the partial association between occupational achievement and college graduation, .39, is only slightly lower than the zero-order correlation shown in Figure 1. Little of the effect of graduation can be accounted for by its dependence on either class or ability.

*Class Origin and Occupational Achievement.* The difference between the father's occupation and the son's may be a reasonably good indicator of *individual* mobility between generations, even when the two statuses are compared at different points in the individuals' occupational careers. That is, the difference between the father's age and the son's at the time when their respective positions were estab-

TABLE 2. ACADEMIC ABILITY, CLASS ORIGIN, AND COLLEGE GRADUATION AS
INFLUENCING OCCUPATIONAL ACHIEVEMENT
(in percentages)

| Occupational Achievement: | Low-Status Origin | | | Medium-Status Origin | | | High-Status Origin | | |
|---|---|---|---|---|---|---|---|---|---|
| | 1 Low Ability | 2 Medium Ability | 3 High Ability | 4 Low Ability | 5 Medium Ability | 6 High Ability | 7 Low Ability | 8 Medium Ability | 9 High Ability |
| (A) *Graduates* | (22)[a] | (50) | (118) | (72) | (104) | (199) | (34) | (61) | (102) |
| High | 55 | 64 | 79 | 60 | 61 | 65 | 50 | 59 | 76 |
| Medium | 36 | 34 | 17 | 32 | 38 | 29 | 47 | 41 | 23 |
| Low | 9 | 2 | 4 | 8 | 2 | 6 | 3 | 0 | 1 |
| (B) *Dropouts* | (46) | (42) | (31) | (67) | (53) | (44) | (35) | (15) | (12) |
| High | 15 | 10 | 23 | 21 | 26 | 20 | 40 | 13 | 25 |
| Medium | 59 | 67 | 39 | 66 | 53 | 61 | 49 | 73 | 75 |
| Low | 26 | 24 | 39 | 13 | 21 | 18 | 11 | 13 | 0 |

[a] Numbers in parentheses are base N's.

Graduation and Achievement

| | | Col. | $X^2$ | df | $p <$ |
|---|---|---|---|---|---|
| (A) | (B) | 1 | 11.756 | 2 | .01 |
| (A) | (B) | 2 | 31.396 | 2 | .001 |
| (A) | (B) | 3 | 42.502 | 2 | .001 |
| (A) | (B) | 4 | 21.800 | 2 | .001 |
| (A) | (B) | 5 | 25.307 | 2 | .001 |
| (A) | (B) | 6 | 30.760 | 2 | .001 |
| (A) | (B) | 7 | 2.095 | 2 | .50 |
| (A) | (B) | 8 | 15.933 | 2 | .001 |
| (A) | (B) | 9 | 14.631 | 2 | .001 |

Class and Achievement

| | Col. | | | $X^2$ | df | $p <$ |
|---|---|---|---|---|---|---|
| (A) | 1 | 4 | 7 | 2.955 | 4 | .70 |
| (A) | 2 | 5 | 8 | 1.657 | 4 | .80 |
| (A) | 3 | 6 | 9 | 10.315 | 4 | .05 |
| (B) | 1 | 4 | 7 | 10.076 | 4 | .05 |
| (B) | 2 | 5 | 8 | 5.655 | 4 | .30 |
| (B) | 3 | 6 | 9 | 9.310 | 4 | .10 |

Ability and Achievement

| | Col. | | | $X^2$ | df | $p <$ |
|---|---|---|---|---|---|---|
| (A) | 1 | 2 | 3 | 9.949 | 4 | .05 |
| (A) | 4 | 5 | 6 | 5.507 | 4 | .30 |
| (A) | 7 | 8 | 9 | 12.001 | 4 | .05 |
| (B) | 1 | 2 | 3 | 6.102 | 4 | .20 |
| (B) | 4 | 5 | 6 | 2.305 | 4 | .70 |
| (B) | 7 | 8 | 9 | 5.743 | 4 | .30 |

TABLE 3.    CLASS ORIGIN AND OCCUPATIONAL ACHIEVEMENT
(in percentages)

| Occupational Achievement | Class Origin | | |
|---|---|---|---|
| | Low | Medium | High |
| (N) | (309) | (539) | (259) |
| High | 50 | 51 | 58 |
| Medium | 36 | 41 | 39 |
| Low | 14 | 9 | 3 |

$X^2 = 20.899$, 4 d.f., p<.001

lished should tend to be offset by the general shifts in the labor force
that have occurred during the same period as a result of technological
change.[25] Whereas the youth of the respondents, averaging about 28
years old, leads one to underestimate their achievement relative to
their fathers', the structural changes that have upgraded the whole
occupational distribution cause one to overestimate the respondents'
achievement relative to their fathers'. If the youth of the respondents
does offset the effects of technological change, then Table 3 indicates
that 86 per cent of the low-status students were upwardly mobile,
and 42 per cent of the high-status students were downwardly mobile,
although only a few (3 per cent) fell into the lowest (manual)
stratum. While a slight majority of the medium-status students moved
upward, most of those who did not maintained their class position.

In a sample limited to college students, however, only the select
few who have reached college from the lower stratum are included,
and their rate of upward movement is far greater than that of a
normal population. Table 3, then, simply shows that class origin had
a significant bearing on the occupational achievement of these students. Yet, at precisely what point does class origin have its effect?
Is it entirely antecedent to graduation or does it continue to affect the
student's achievement after he leaves school and enters the job
market?

The zero-order association between class origin and occupational
achievement (Figure 1) may be considered as having two components,
i.e., the direct effect represented by the partial association between
occupation and class, controlling for graduation, and the indirect effect
mediated through graduation (estimated by the difference between
the partial and zero-order associations between occupation and class).
These figures were .10 and .04, respectively. Apparently, social class

makes a significant contribution to occupational achievement independently of its effect on the student's college career.

The data in Table 2, however, suggest that the validity of this proposition may depend on whether the student obtains his degree. For men of about equal ability who have graduated from college (upper panel), class origin does not appear to affect occupational achievement.[26] In fact, the partial association between the graduate's occupational achievement and his class origin, holding academic ability constant, was an insignificant .002.

Still, these observations do not demonstrate that a system of full equality of opportunity exists, since class origin initially determines who goes to college and who graduates. Furthermore, differences in occupational achievement that can be ascribed to class origin continue to appear among the *dropouts*, especially in terms of low achievement. The proportion of college dropouts from low-status backgrounds who remained in the lower stratum was two to three times larger than the proportion of dropouts from high-status backgrounds who fell into the lower stratum (lower panel of Table 2). Moreover, the correlation between class and occupational achievement for the dropouts, with or without holding ability constant, was .24. A high-status youth who does not graduate from college, irrespective of his ability, apparently is protected from falling too far.

*Academic Ability and Occupational Achievement.* Although high-school rank had a strong influence on college graduation, its effect on the students' subsequent occupational achievement is less important (Figure 1). Moreover, the main effect of academic ability (see Table 4) tends to be confined to the upper end of the scale, with over half again as many high-ability as low-ability students achieving high-ranking jobs. To what extent is even this correlation simply a function

TABLE 4.   ACADEMIC ABILITY AND OCCUPATIONAL
ACHIEVEMENT (PERCENTAGES)

| Occupational Achievement | Ability | | |
|---|---|---|---|
| | Low | Medium | High |
| (N) | (276) | (325) | (506) |
| High | 39 | 46 | 63 |
| Medium | 49 | 46 | 29 |
| Low | 12 | 8 | 7 |

$X^2 = 51.159$, 4 d.f., $p < .001$

of the fact that the high-ability youths were more successful *in* college?

The direct effect of high-school rank on occupation is smaller than the effects produced by its indirect influence through graduation: whereas the partial association, holding graduation constant, was .09, the difference between the zero-order and partial associations was .13. Graduation from college, therefore, accounts for a large share of such effect as ability has on occupational achievement. (Note, in addition, that the partial association of academic ability with occupation, independent of graduation [.09], is very similar to that of class origin with occupation [.10].)

Graduates and dropouts should again be distinguished, however, for Table 2 shows that academic ability appears to have played no direct part in the occupational success of the dropouts, whereas among the *graduates* it continued to contribute to occupational success. Confirming this pattern were the separate zero-order correlations between occupational achievement and HSR for the graduates and dropouts, .18 and −.06, respectively.[27] Without a diploma, then, academic ability could not alter a man's status. The graduate's status, on the other hand, clearly was modified by this factor.

One should not overlook the distinct possibility that the effect of the graduates' HSR on their occupational status is due primarily to their postgraduate education and the field in which they took their degrees. That is, the success of the ablest graduates may only reflect the fact that they were more likely to have attained an advanced degree or to have taken a degree in a professionally-oriented field. The graduate and professional schools at which 26 per cent of the graduates had received advanced degrees must have admitted these men partly on the basis of academic ability, which, in turn, may account for the occupational success of the highest achievers. Too, the field of study in which the student graduates, such as engineering or medicine, is certainly an important predictor of occupation and, to the extent that the choice of fields depends initially on academic ability, it also may account for part of such effects as ability has.

Our suspicion that the effects of academic ability on the graduates' occupational achievement are mediated mainly through features indigenous to the formal system of higher education appears to be justified: controlling for advanced degrees,[28] the partial association between HSR and occupation was .11, or less than the .18 zero-order correlation. Moreover, when both advanced degrees and subject-field[29] were held constant, the partial association was reduced to a statistically insignificant .06. Apart from the selection processes operating within the school system, then, academic ability has as little direct effect on the graduates' occupational achievement as it does on that of the dropouts.

## SUMMARY AND COMMENT

Qualified by the limitations of this study, my summary conclusions with respect to the early occupational careers of contemporary college students are:

1. Employment in a nonmanual occupation is almost guaranteed by the attainment of a college diploma, quite independently of either academic ability or class background, thus assuring the upward mobility of graduates from manual origins and the stability of graduates from nonmanual origins.

2. Without a diploma, occupational achievement is not altered by academic ability, although it is significantly affected by class origin; the downward mobility of failing students whose fathers are in nonmanual occupations is likely to be arrested.

3. A graduate's achievement is not altered by either class origin or academic ability, except to the extent that ability affects his choice of fields and the extent and nature of his postgraduate education.

4. Thus, while academic ability is associated with occupational achievement, its effects apparently operate wholly within the school system, especially as a determinant of graduation.

What do these findings suggest about the notion that college is a vehicle for social mobility in an open society that rewards the ablest and not the inept? Three general conditions, each of which must be present, underlie the capacity of higher education to function as a vehicle for social mobility: the sorting mechanisms, such as graduation, must be variable; a substantial part of this variation must be accounted for by individual ability; and the relevant variables must contribute to achievement in the occupational stucture.

If all college entrants graduated, for example, graduation obviously would have no differentiating effect. Having gone to college would be equivalent to having a degree. Such a situation, in fact, *tends* to characterize higher education in the English[30] and Soviet[31] systems, where as many as 80 to 90 per cent of the students graduate. The 40 to 70 per cent rates characteristic of the U.S. signify that the sorting function may be operating to a larger extent in American colleges. Screening devices in the English and Soviet school systems instead effectively remove the inept student before he reaches the university which, in part, explains why American colleges devote so many of their resources to developing and administering examinations to weed out less-qualified entrants.[32]

Given a pool of students at diverse ability levels, as a second condition, the college must actually accomplish the task of removing the inept while retaining the apt. Although the formal institutions of higher education originally were not designed for this job, it has been thrust upon them with the need to alleviate pressures for expansion and to maintain academic standards in the face of mass enrollments, especially at the public or tax-supported schools. As most other research on college attrition has found, ability has a significant influence on graduation and perhaps on other sorting mechanisms in the school system as well. But, in addition to a large majority of the ablest students, a rather significant portion of the least-qualified in this sample graduated,[33] raising some doubt about how assortative colleges of this kind really are.

No matter how effectively colleges weed out less able students as they compete for degrees, the sorting function is not complete unless jobs are allocated on the assumption that the colleges have done their part. Our evidence suggests that this is the strongest link in the process, for even the low-ability graduate generally was far more successful in finding high-status employment than was the high-ability dropout. A college degree is evidently so crucial that jobs are allocated with little regard for the likelihood that colleges perform only moderately well as sorters of talent. (Perhaps Turner was correct when he noted that in a system of contest mobility, victory tends to be won by those who exert the most effort and not necessarily by the most able.[34])

This is not to suggest that maximizing the correlation between college education and occupational status is entirely disadvantageous for the occupational system. Regardless of his native ability or even his academic learning, the graduate may be presumed to have developed social skills, work habits, loyalties, or other attributes required for performance of many roles in modern industrial organizations. A fruitful line of inquiry may lie in clarifying this connection between college and work experience.

Selection by talent, of course, may also operate at other points in the higher education system, in addition to the selection of the ablest students for postgraduate programs and professionally-oriented fields.[35] *Where* a student goes to college may affect mobility increasingly, as the intellectual diversity of the college-going population grows, and as the mass system of higher education develops specialized institutions in which the intellectual character of each student body is set farther apart. But even the cumulative effect of these sorting mechanisms is unlikely to provide completely equal educational opportunities for college students with similar capabilities. Class origin affects the student's choice of college and his admission to the college of his choice; the schools whose admissions policies are the most restrictive academically continue to be the same schools whose students come from higher socioeconomic backgrounds.[36] In part this reflects the association between social class and achievement in the primary and secondary school system, but in part it lies in the subtle prerequisites of the privately-endowed university. Among many of the best schools in the country, the number of applicants who qualify on academic grounds far exceeds the number who can be admitted without expanding the school's facilities. This pressure not only permits but requires them to employ subjective, and perhaps ascriptive, criteria in the selection process.

## REFERENCES

1. Wilbert E. Moore, "But Some Are More Equal Than Others," *American Sociological Review*, 28 (1963), pp. 13–18.

2. Ralph H. Turner, "Sponsored and Contest Mobility and the School System," *American Sociological Review*, 25 (1960), pp. 855–867.

3. Dael Wolfle, *America's Resources of Specialized Talent*, New York: Harper, 1954, pp. 158–169; Ralph F. Berdie, *After High School — What?*, Minneapolis: University of Minnesota Press, 1954; Byron S. Hollinshead, Robert J. Havighurst, and Robert R. Rodgers, *Who Should Go to College*, New York: Columbia University Press, 1952; W. Lloyd Warner, Robert J. Havighurst, and Martin Loeb, *Who Shall Be Educated?*, New York: Harper, 1944; and R. Clyde White, *These Will Go to College*, Cleveland: Press of Western Reserve University, 1952, pp. 34–59.

4. C. Arnold Anderson, "A Skeptical Note on the Relation of Vertical Mobility to Education," *American Journal of Sociology*, 66 (1961), pp. 560–570; and C. A. Anderson, J. C. Brown, and M. J. Bowman, "Intelligence and Occupational Mobility," *The Journal of Political Economy*, 40 (1952), pp. 218–239. See also Gunner Boalt, "Social Mobility in Stockholm: A Pilot Investigation," in *Transactions of the Second World Congress of Sociology*, London: International Sociological Association, 1954, Vol. II, pp. 67–69.

5. Seymour Martin Lipset and Reinhard Bendix, *Social Mobility in Industrial Society*, Berkeley: University of California Press, 1959, pp. 91–101; and Otis Dudley Duncan and Robert W. Hodge, "Education and Occupational Mobility: A Regression Analysis," *American Journal of Sociology*, 68 (1963), pp. 629–644.

6. About 38 per cent of the respondents were no longer residents of Illinois but were scattered throughout 45 states and 17 foreign countries. (The eight-page questionnaire required about one hour to complete.)

7. Most effective of the techniques employed to locate these "missing persons" was a state-wide telephone search. This usually involved placing calls to phone listings closely corresponding to the student's name that appeared in directories from the area of the state in which he was last known to reside. A series of such calls very often led to the student, or to a relative who knew his whereabouts. Cost was made nonprohibitive by the evening use of university phones on an unlimited intra-state contract.

8. The contribution that this high return made toward achieving a representative mail sample, and the failure of our prodding devices to adversely affect the veracity of the data, are discussed in Bruce K. Eckland, "Effects of Prodding to Increase Mail-Back Returns," *Journal of Applied Psychology*, 49 (1965), pp. 165–169.

9. The only other instances of incomplete data involved the occupations of ten fathers and four sons. Rather than excluding these cases, they were assigned mean values on the appropriate scales. With respect to the comparative strength of two of our independent variables, removing the unascertained cases on the ability index (which is based on high school rank) tends to maximize the effects that later will be measured statistically. On the other hand, assigning mean values to the cases whose class origins (based on occupation) were unascertained, and retaining them in the correlations, yields something short of the maximum effects that class origin may actually have. Errors of this kind, however, are negligible beside other errors that undoubtedly weaken the observed magnitude of these associations.

10. For a full description of this measure see Charles C. Peters and Walter R. VanVoorhis, *Statistical Procedures and Their Mathematical Bases*, New York: McGraw-Hill, 1940, pp. 323, 325, 337 ff.

11. Unless specified otherwise, the coefficients for all zero-order and partial

associations reported here are statistically significant above the .05 level of confidence. (The second sum of squares was used to test the sub-hypothesis that $B_r = B_r^*$ [r<p] where $B_r^*$ is a null vector.) For a full description of the computer program used, see Richard Galyon Ames, "Multiple Regression Analysis for Categoric Data," Computation Center Programming Note 109, University of North Carolina, Chapel Hill, 1963.

12. Previously I used both variables together in contingency tables where college graduation was the dependent variable; in that analysis, however, ability was not one of the major independent variables. See Bruce K. Eckland, "Social Class and College Graduation: Some Misconceptions Corrected," *American Journal of Sociology,* 70 (1964), pp. 36–50.

13. The testing bureau at Illinois inadvertently had discarded their 1952 data, but a records search in the administrative offices of each of the separate colleges in the University produced scores for nearly all freshmen entering engineering, liberal arts, and agriculture. No scores were found for commerce, fine arts, or physical education majors.

14. Although only 27 per cent of the 1952 male entrants graduated from the University by June, 1956 (i.e., in normal progression) 50 per cent had graduated there by June, 1962, and 71 per cent would eventually attain a college degree somewhere. In the long run, most dropouts return to college and most returnees graduate. A discussion of the extent to which these findings may be generalized is presented in Bruce K. Eckland, "College Dropouts Who Came Back," *Harvard Educational Review,* 34 (1964), pp. 402–420. Also, see Nathan Young, David Riesman, Joseph Gusfield, and Robert E. Ifferts' comments on "College Dropouts Who Came Back" *Harvard Educational Review,* 34 (1964), pp. 580–587.

15. The components of Duncan's index — income and education — make it especially sensitive to status variations among white-collar occupations which are otherwise lost in the U. S. Census classification of major occupations (see Albert J. Reiss, Jr., Otis Dudley Duncan, Paul K. Hatt, and Cecil C. North, *Occupations and Social Status,* New York: The Free Press of Glencoe, 1961, Appendix B.) Thus, the index enabled us to stratify the already upwardly-skewed class origins of our college-going population and thereby measure small, yet significant increments of intergenerational mobility.

16. The parallel is not precise, since 17.7 per cent of all non-farm workers are misclassified when a manual-nonmanual split is located at this point. This figure is somewhat higher than the 11.6 per cent reported by Duncan as the proportion of workers in the national labor force who were misclassified when an index value of 38.5 was used as the optimum cutting point on a 96-point scale (see *ibid.,* p. 159). Since the cutting points were very nearly the same, the difference simply may reflect a somewhat larger proportion of workers in our sample whose SES scores are very close to the cutting point.

17. *Ibid.,* p. 147.

18. Eckland, "Social Class . . . ," *op. cit.*

19. Reiss, *et al., op. cit.,* p. 131.

20. The median income of all Illinois farmers during the relevant period was 66 per cent higher than the national farm average and apparently was exceeded only by the Iowa farm income. The farmers in this study, all of whom sent their sons to the state University, reportedly earned over two and one-half times the average for Illinois farmers. In fact, the average earnings of the farm students' fathers differed little from those of non-farm fathers: $6,500 and $7,600, respectively. See the *1950 Census of Population,* Vol. II, Pt. 13, p. 294 and Vol. IV, Pt. 1, Ch. B, p. 183.)

21. This procedure raised the scores of most farmers from the dubious value of 1 (those classified mainly as "owners and tenants" in the original index) to values of 3, 5, and 6, with 49, 70, and 57 of the farmers, respectively, receiving these scores. The resulting similarity between the median SES for the non-farm sample, 6.1, and the median of the adjusted scores for the farm sample, 5.5, is consistent with the actual income differences.

22. The subject's *last* job was used if he had returned to college as either a full-time undergraduate or a postgraduate student (11 per cent of the sample), or if he were temporarily on active duty in the military service, including those recalled during the Berlin crisis (3 per cent of the sample). This procedure underrates somewhat the eventual occupational achievement of students still attending college. It may be noted, however, that on the SES index the *last* jobs of the graduates who had returned to college ranked well above the *current* jobs of graduates who had not received an advanced degree and were not presently working toward one. Since most of the current enrollments (seven out of ten) involved returning graduates, rather than returning dropouts, the underratings are not a serious limitation here.

23. Mainly because the distribution was upwardly skewed, far fewer misclassifications arise in the SES scores of sons (4.2 per cent of non-farm workers) when a manual-nonmanual split is located at the *low*-status cutting point.

24. Eckland, "Social Class . . ." *op. cit.*

25. Joseph A. Kahl, *The American Class Structure,* New York: Rinehart, 1957, pp. 251–268.

26. This finding is similar to the results of other investigations. For example, see the report on the 1958 college graduates in the National Science Foundation's *Two Years After the College Degree,* Washington: U. S. Government Printing Office, 1963, pp. 53–54.

27. These correlations did not differ from the partial associations controlling for class origin.

28. Graduates without advanced degrees were assigned a score of zero, holders of master's degrees, one, and holders of doctoral degrees, three. About 14 per cent of the graduates had not obtained an advanced degree but were presently working toward one, and about 40 per cent of those with graduate degrees were still engaged in part- or full-time academic programs. (On the other hand, another 9 per cent had taken some postgraduate work but apparently had terminated it without a degree.) The correlations with postgraduate education presented here are thus of rather uncertain stability.

29. To introduce subject-fields into the regression equation, we used a set of categoric predictors (so-called "dummy variables") whereby each major field took the value of one if it was the one in which the student had received his *last* degree, and zero if it was not. (Consequently, no restrictive assumption about the linearity of the effect of subject-field was required in this equation.)

30. Turner, *op. cit.*, p. 863.

31. Alexander G. Korol, *Soviet Education for Science and Technology*, Cambridge: Massachusetts Institute of Technology, 1957, pp. 193–197.

32. Of course, the entrants to some of the more prestigeful and therefore selective American colleges graduate at a rate at least comparable to that of the entrants to the best English universities.

33. Our data showed that of the entrants who ranked in the upper quarter of their high-school graduating class and scored In the highest three ACE deciles, well over nine out of ten would someday graduate. Yet, better than one out of three of the entrants who ranked in the bottom half of their high school class and scored in the lowest five ACE deciles would graduate too.

34. Turner, *op. cit.*

35. A more elaborate analysis of these and a number of other such mechanisms will be reported elsewhere.

36. Warner, *et. al.*, *op. cit.*, pp. 71–72; David Reisman and Christopher Jencks, "The Viability of the American College," in Nevitt Sanford (ed.), *The American College*, New York: John Wiley, 1962, pp. 74–192; Burton R. Clark, *The Open Door College*, New York: McGraw-Hill, 1960, p. 54; and White, *op. cit.*, p. 48.

# STRUCTURAL SUPPORTS FOR UPWARD MOBILITY

ROBERT A. ELLIS AND W. CLAYTON LANE

Research of the past decade has brought us much closer to understanding the factors that lead a substantial, if small, proportion of lower-status youth to avail themselves of the opportunity for a higher education.[1] The answer in part lies in the internal variables of intelligence and motivation.[2] It is also evident that social mobility does not occur in a social vacuum. Generally, lower-class youth find themselves confronted by an environment in which going to college is the exception, not the rule, and in which strong counterpressures may be mounted against those who seek to deviate from prevailing cultural norms. Consequently, if college goals are to emerge among lower-class youth, some substitute channels must exist for transmitting information about college — information that is traditionally handed down to children in the more favored classes. In addition, the negative pressures of the environment require that some intermediate social support be available to sustain the mobile individual when the occasion arises for him to sever ties with age mates of his acquaintance who do not possess educational aspirations to match his own.

The part the nuclear family plays in the mobility process still remains far from clear. Early investigators largely discounted the family's significance, premising instead that clique associates in high school or school teachers are chiefly responsible for stimulating and patterning the mobility aspirations of adolescents.[3]

Recently the family's contribution to educational mobility has become a focus of attention. Kahl, the chief exponent of this position, pointedly rejects the possibility that an "encouraging and sympathetic"

Reprinted with abridgement from the *American Sociological Review* (Vol. 28, No. 5, October 1963, pp. 743–756) by permission of the American Sociological Association and the authors.

This research has been supported by grants from the Society for the Investigation of Human Ecology, the Social Science Research Council, Stanford University Faculty Research Funds, and the National Institute of Mental Health (M–4968).

teacher might have been instrumental in setting "common man boys" on the path to college. In addition, he relegates to the peer group the passive role of reinforcing college ambitions, not of initiating them. He finds that the attitudes of the parents — and particularly of the father — represent the pre-eminent factor differentiating intellectually capable lower-class boys who aspire to go to college from those who do not. The father, disappointed with his own life accomplishment, "teaches his son that the next step up demands more education." Furthermore, it is in such families that parents apply the continual pressure necessary to insure the boy's doing well in school.[4]

Despite widespread acceptance of Kahl's general thesis, an extensive body of findings suggests that his emphasis on the father's role in the mobility process may be misplaced.[5] This evidence indicates that a distinctive feature of upward mobility is that the mother's educational or occupational attainments outrank those of the father. The reversal of parental authority implied by these data does not necessarily rule out the factor of paternal dissatisfaction; but it does cast its significance in a new light, suggesting a symptom more than a cause of the structural conditions precipitating upward mobility. The father may be dissatisfied with his attainments; but this later evidence suggests that the dissatisfaction stems from the presence of a wife who is all too willing to remind him of his failure to measure up to her standards of attainment.

One difficulty in reconciling these divergent viewpoints is that the evidence is largely confined to high school students hopeful of going on to college. The intention of going to college is by no means a guarantee of attendance, particularly in the lower strata where as many as 50 per cent of the students who expect to continue their education beyond high school fail to do so.[6]

Another limitation of these studies is the failure to differentiate among the college goals held by students. Despite the diversity of higher education in our society, going to college has been equated automatically with social mobility. Yet, many students from lower social backgrounds go to junior college or community college where they frequently receive vocational training that is only an extension of the training obtained in high school. Furthermore, they live at home cloistered from the influence of a middle-class undergraduate environment. It is doubtful that such an educational encounter provides a real social transition either in terms of status experiences or in terms of status opportunities.[7]

The present paper focuses on lower-status youth entering the West Coast coeducational equivalent of an Ivy League university. Like other students in the university, those from the lower strata have been screened for personal characteristics (defined according to middle-class values) as well as for ability and motivation to do college-level work. Thus, the combined factors of self and institutional selection enable us to locate individuals unequivocally enmeshed in the process of using higher education as an avenue for mobility.

## RESEARCH PROCEDURES

*Sampling.* The data are taken from a four-year panel research designed to give information on the social and behavioral consequences of upward mobility.[8] The initial panel consisted of 194 matriculants at Stanford University. Two samples were used for their selection:

1. A probability sample was taken of one out of every six first-year freshmen entering this institution in the fall of 1958 (N=160). This sample, which we shall refer to as the Regular Sample, is used to describe the general characteristics of Stanford undergraduates.[9]

2. To compensate for the underrepresentation of lower-status students in the Stanford setting, an oversample was taken of all remaining lower and lower-middle class freshmen not originally included in the Regular Sample. The oversample (N=34) is added to the Regular Sample whenever the factor of social class is analyzed.

All 194 subjects included in these two samples actually participated in the study. They were initially interviewed a month after matriculation and, so long as they remained at college, again at the end of their freshman, sophomore, and senior years.

*Research variables.* Social class was measured by an Index of Class Position developed and validated for the present research.[10] It is derived from two component scales: (1) the rating assigned to the student's father on Hollingshead's 7-point scale of occupational prestige[11] and (2) the class rating the student gives his family in response to Centers' class identification question (modified to permit a tripartite division of the middle class[12]). These ratings are combined to yield a six-point scale of class position, as follows:

| Social Class | Nominal Designation |
|---|---|
| I | Upper |
| II | Upper-Middle |
| III | Middle-Middle |
| IV | Lower-Middle |
| V | Upper-Lower |
| VI | Lower-Lower |

Information on mobility influences was collected at the start of the freshman year. Students were instructed to specify on a check list the persons who had been "important in helping . . . [them] decide to come to college." The list contained the following categories of individuals: (1) father, (2) mother, (3) siblings, (4) other relatives, (5) school friends, (6) persons connected with the church, (7) school teachers, (8) adult club leaders, and (9) any other persons not already mentioned. After responding affirmatively or negatively to each of these categories, the students were asked to designate which specific individual had been the most important influence.[13]

## THE INFLUENCE OF THE FAMILY

Like other Stanford undergraduates, the lower-class student's decision to go to college is made with the approval and support of his family. Ninety-six per cent of class V and VI freshmen view at least one, and usually both, of their parents as having influenced them to continue their schooling beyond high school. Moreover, they are no less likely than other freshmen to report being influenced by other members of the family. About half the students mention an older sibling who had been to college; others mention a more distant relative — an aunt, an uncle, or a cousin. When we consider that 59 per cent of these upwardly mobile students specifically single out one parent as the person most important in influencing their college decision, it seems abundantly clear that these lower-status families are actively involved in the mobility plans of their offspring.

What pattern of parental influence prevails among these mobile individuals? Is it, as Kahl's research indicates, the father who exerts the dominant pressure for mobility? Our evidence suggests the reverse. For males, the frequency with which the father is considered an important influence tends to decline with class, especially in the lower strata. Only 19 per cent of class V and VI students report their father as the major person influencing them to go to college, in contrast to 51 per cent of the Regular Sample. In the lower strata, the mother is more apt to be mentioned, though the effect of maternal dominance is somewhat obscured by the competing tendency of lower-class subjects to name neither parent as the primary influence. But for those cases where a parent is considered most important, the results firmly establish a sharp reversal of parental dominance in the lower classes. For Stanford undergraduates generally, the main source of parental support for going to college is the father. In classes V and VI, the mother is singled out as the dominant influence by 75 per cent of the students.

The tendency to identify with mothers rather than fathers in seeking college direction suggests that distinctive authority patterns may characterize the lower-status homes from which the upwardly mobile come. This inference is supported by the fact that the mother's education is markedly superior to the father's in 37 per cent of the class V and VI families as compared to 9 per cent of the families from the Regular Sample. Moreover, among the ten cases where the balance of education clearly favors the mother, not one student designated the father as the major person influencing his college plans.[14] Seven of the ten perceived the mother as the dominant influence, while the remaining three named a high school teacher.

In the lower class, these parental influences are regarded as only part of a more general pattern of mobility expectations. This is brought out by data on the parents' post-college expectations for male students. Male students from classes V and VI report long-range parental ambitions in which a college education is but the first step toward an anticipated upper-middle class career. These students see their parents as expecting them to embark upon a professional career that will bring them respect and deference in the community and, at least so far as mothers are concerned, to be outstanding in their chosen occupations. Not unexpectedly, lower-class parents differ from other Stanford parents in their emphasis on the son's entering a profession and in their greater tendency to expect the son to have a better job than his father.

## Influences Outside the Family

Students from all social levels credit persons outside the family with a significant role in their decision to come to college. Though girls are somewhat more likely than boys to mention the importance of nonfamilial influences, for both sexes it is the students from lower social backgrounds who report the greatest number of nonfamilial influences. Clearly, upwardly mobile individuals range more freely beyond their families for reinforcement of their plans to attend college than do their socially privileged counterparts.[15] However, to be a girl as well as a member of the lower class constitutes a double handicap so far as one's college chances are concerned:[16] it is not surprising to find that the number of nonfamilial influences reported reaches its maximum among lower-status girls.

*High school teachers.*[17] Of the nonfamilial influences, the high school teacher turns out to be the most significant, especially in the lower strata. Some 85 per cent of Class V and VI students mention a high school teacher as having played an important part in helping them decide upon college, and 33 per cent nominate a high school teacher as the person chiefly influencing that decision. Hence, an important structural support for social mobility is provided within the formal framework of the public secondary school, even to the extent that the influence of a school teacher may supersede that of the parent.

Undoubtedly, the considerable talents of these youngsters help bring them to the attention of their teachers.[18] On the other hand, mobile individuals apparently must gain adult encouragement and guidance if their aspirations are to be implemented effectively. If our interpretation is correct, the teacher's significance in the mobility process largely stems from the lower-class parents' inability to give effective direction to the aspirations they have stimulated in their children.

Support for the latter conclusion is furnished by data collected at later stages of the research on social influences governing the students' choice of an undergraduate major. Compared to other undergraduates at Stanford, students from the lower classes are far more likely to depend upon their high school teacher for guidance in making this decision. Sixty-eight per cent of the students from classes V and VI, but only 39 per cent of those in the Regular Sample, mention the high school teacher. This is apt testimony to the role these teachers have played in shaping the college plans of the upwardly mobile students. Even more germane to our thesis is the fact that in the lower classes teachers are twice as likely as parents to have an important role in influencing the students' choice of major, while in the general population, parents reportedly exercise as much influence as the teachers.

*Other adults.* That the upwardly mobile need auxiliary adult support is further confirmed by data on references made to "other adults" as important influences on their coming to college. This category encompasses ministers, family friends, previous employers, family physicians, etc. Students in classes V and VI are almost twice as likely as those in the Regular Sample to mention those individuals; but outside adults do not play as significant a role as high school teachers in guiding the decisions made by upwardly mobile students once they are in college — at least so far as these are represented by their choice of an undergraduate major.

*Peers.* Peer influences are more evenly distributed by class. Nevertheless, a substantial proportion of lower-class freshmen mention high school friends as an important factor in their own decision to go to college and in their subsequent choice of a college major.

Even though high school peers do not directly exercise the influence that, for example, high school teachers do, they may nevertheless have a latent function in the mobility process: either, as Kahl has emphasized, by providing reinforcement for the mobility goals held by the lower-class youth[19] or by providing informal training in the varied motives, attitudes, and social skills needed to make the shift to a middle-class reference group a behavioral reality.[20] Data on class V and VI students in the Stanford sample indicate that close peer-group ties with the middle class were formed in high school. Two-thirds of them took a prominent role in high school extracurricular activities, where they undoubtedly had frequent opportunities to be drawn into close association with students of higher social status.[21] Moreover, they belonged to high school cliques in which the majority of their close friends were college-bound — one third of these to major four-year institutions.

*Travel and work experiences.* The findings also underscore the special advantage upper- and upper-middle class students have in planning their college careers. To a much greater degree than persons from the middle or lower classes, they have had travel and work experiences which later guide their choice of a major. Thirty-nine per cent of class I and II students specifically refer to the important bearing such experiences had on their choice of a major, while only 20 per cent of the students from classes III and IV and 17 per cent of those from classes V and VI do so.

Thus, students from lower status circumstances encounter a second handicap in their quest for social mobility. Lower-class parents are not only less able to give direct guidance to students' career plans, but they are also less able to create for them the intermediate learning opportunities by which students from more favored backgrounds are prepared for their future roles.

CONCLUSIONS

Our findings emphasize the collateral role that both parents and adults outside the family play in the mobility process. They show that:

1. The impetus for mobility has its roots in the nuclear family; but, contrary to Kahl's thesis, it is the mother more often than the father whose reaction to the family's status in life is the catalyst for mobility.[22]

2. While the family may provide the initial leverage to propel the lower-class youth toward college, mobile youth must also gain outside social support and direction for their college plans.[23]

3. The chief source of outside support is the school teacher, often overlooked as a factor in mobility.[24] While in a general sense it may be true that the public school system does not radically alter the status hierarchy, teachers may nevertheless be instrumental in helping some of the more talented youth in the lower class realize their mobility potential. Comments made by students during the interviews indicate that the public school system did bring these intellectually able youngsters from the lower class into close and friendly contact with individual teachers with whom they could discuss their plans for the future and gain the incentives and encouragement needed to sustain their motivation for higher education. Here, the teacher reinforces the mobility strivings instilled by the parents and conveys information about the educational system that is not ordinarily available in the lower-class home.

4. The teacher, however, is not the only middle-class role model for

upwardly mobile youngsters. These youth also turn to other adults in the community for the additional outside support needed to overcome the handicaps of their class background.

5. High school peers have a less direct role in the mobility process. Rather than influencing the lower-class youth in their college goals, they provide a middle-class learning environment where the mobile individual is exposed to the norms and behavioral traits successful mobility requires.

6. The continuing reliance of these lower-class youth on extra-familial support gives some confirmation for Merton's hypothesis of the *disassociative* consequences of social mobility.[25] The need to turn to outside adults for help and guidance implies a gradual weakening of dependence upon the family.[26] Since, as Merton points out, "membership in a group which has involved deep-seated attachments and sentiments cannot be easily abandoned without psychological residue,"[27] the result is very likely to be a strong ambivalence toward the parents that the student may find difficult to face at a conscious level. Thus these findings offer clues to further study of the incipient stresses and strains that may accompany social mobility.

## REFERENCES

1. An excellent summary of the extensive literature bearing on this problem is found in Chapter IX, "Intelligence and Motivation," of Seymour Martin Lipset and Reinhard Bendix, *Social Mobility in Industrial Society*, Berkeley and Los Angeles, California: University of California Press, 1960, pp. 227–259.

2. Burton R. Clark, *Educating the Expert Society*, San Francisco: Chandler Publishing Co., 1962, pp. 44 and 84; Robert J. Havighurst and Bernice L. Neugarten, *Society and Education*, Boston: Allyn & Bacon, 1957, pp. 221–260; Byron S. Hollinshead, *Who Should Go to College*, New York: Columbia University Press, 1952, pp. 31–39; Dael Wolfle, *American Resources of Specialized Talent*, New York: Harper & Bros., 1954, pp. 158–163.

3. August B. Hollingshead, *Elmtown's Youth*, New York: John Wiley & Sons, 1949, pp. 446–447; Robert J. Havighurst and Robert R. Rodgers, "The Role of Motivation in Attendance at Post-High School Educational Institutions," Appendix to *Who Should Go to College*, by Byron S. Hollinshead, *op. cit.*, pp. 135–165.

4. Joseph A. Kahl, "Educational and Occupational Aspirations of 'Common Man' Boys," *Harvard Educational Review*, 23 (Summer, 1953), pp. 186–

203; Joseph A. Kahl, *The American Class Structure*, New York: Rinehart, 1957, pp. 281–289. Also see David J. Bordua, "Educational Aspirations and Parental Stress on College," *Social Forces*, 38 (March, 1960), pp. 262–269.

5. Lipset and Bendix, *op. cit.*, pp. 238, 249–250; Fred L. Strodtbeck, "Family Interaction, Values, and Achievement," in D. C. McClelland (ed.), *Talent and Society*, Princeton, N.J.: D. Van Nostrand, 1958, pp. 181–184, 189–191; W. Lloyd Warner and James C. Abegglen, *Big Business Leaders in America*, New York: Atheneum, pp. 77–78.

6. R. C. White, *These Will Go to College*, Cleveland: Western Reserve University Press, 1952, p. 45; Phillips Cutright, "Students' Decision to Attend College," *Journal of Educational Sociology*, 33 (February, 1960), pp. 292–299.

7. Cf., Burton R. Clark, *The Open Door College: A Case Study*, New York: McGraw-Hill, 1960, pp. 51–61; Havighurst and Neugarten, *op. cit.*, pp. 251–257; David Riesman and Christopher Jencks, "The Viability of the American College," in Nevitt Sanford (ed.), *The American College: A Psychological and Social Interpretation of the Higher Learning*, New York: John Wiley & Sons, 1962, pp. 74–192.

8. For a fairly concise statement of the research goals and procedures, see Robert A. Ellis, "Stanford Study of Social Differences in the Academic Success of College Undergraduates," in Charles E. Bidwell (ed.), *The American College and Student Personality: Report of a Conference on College Influences on Personality*, Andover, Mass.: Social Science Research Council Committee on Personality Development in Youth, 1960, pp. 15–16.

9. The representativeness of the Regular Sample was checked against known parameters of the population from which it was drawn, with uniformly positive results. Comparison of the Regular Sample with an identically drawn sample of male freshmen entering Stanford the previous year showed a high degree of stability in students' social characteristics, as well as in the various attitudes and values to which they adhered. The comparison, however, did sustain the evidence of gradual rise in intellectual capacity found in most selective institutions around the country.

10. See Robert A. Ellis, W. Clayton Lane, and Virginia Olesen, "The Index of Class Position: An Improved Intercommunity Measure of Stratification," *American Sociological Review*, 28 (April, 1963), pp. 271–277.

11. August B. Hollingshead and Frederick C. Redlich, *Social Class and Mental Illness: A Community Study*, New York: John Wiley & Sons, 1958, pp. 390–391.

12. Following Kahl and Davis, we instructed those respondents who placed their family in the middle class to indicate whether their family was in the upper-middle, middle-middle, or lower-middle class. See Richard Centers, *The Psychology of Social Classes*, Princeton, N.J.: Princeton University

Press, 1949; Ellis, Lane, and Olesen, *op. cit.;* Joseph A. Kahl and James A. Davis, "A Comparison of Indexes of Socio-Economic Status," *American Sociological Review,* 20 (June, 1955), pp. 317–325.

13. These data are obviously no better than the respondents' ability and willingness to recall pertinent information. Accuracy of recall was abetted by the date of the interviews, which was sufficiently soon after matriculation for the events leading up to college to be fresh in the students' minds. The students' willingness to impart this information cannot be so easily assessed, though the reliability and validity of data gained in other segments of the interviews indicate that the majority had cooperated fully in the research.

14. Mother's education is defined as markedly superior to the father's when: (1) she has had college training, while the father has had no more than a high school education; or (2) she has graduated from high school, while the father has not gone beyond ninth grade.

15. The possibility that a response set of "productivity" contaminated these results is ruled out by collateral data on students' reasons for coming to college. Here, in contrast to the findings on non-familial influences, the number of highly important reasons cited consistently declines with class position. See Lee J. Cronbach, "Response Sets and Test Validity," *Educational and Psychological Measurement,* 6 (Winter, 1946), pp. 475–494; E. R. Smith, Ralph W. Tyler, *et al.,* "Appraising and Recording Student Progress," *Adventure in Education* (Vol. III), New York: Harper & Bros., 1942, pp. 80–111, 180–190.

16. David F. Aberle and Kaspar D. Naegele, "Middle Class Fathers' Occupational Role and Attitudes Toward Children," *American Journal of Orthopsychiatry,* 22 (April, 1952), pp. 366–378; Havighurst and Neugarten, *op. cit.,* p. 243; Samuel A. Stouffer, *Social Research to Test Ideas,* New York: The Free Press of Glencoe, 1962, pp. 228–230.

17. When the teacher mentioned was also a relative, priority was always given to kinship in classifying the student's answer.

18. Unlike lower-class adolescents in the general population, those at Stanford excelled in all criteria used to measure academic potential. For example, their College Board test scores were, on the average, some twenty points higher than those obtained for the Regular Sample. The median three-year high school grade point average for lower-class boys was 3.89; for the girls, 3.92.

19. Kahl, "Educational and Occupational Aspirations of 'Common Man' Boys," *op. cit.*

20. Cf. Merton's treatment of the function of anticipatory socialization in the mobility process. Robert K. Merton, *Social Theory and Social Structure* (rev. ed.), Glencoe, Ill.: Free Press, 1957, pp. 260–271.

21. This is consistent with Beilin's evidence that a high level of extracurricular participation in high school typifies college-bound boys from the lower

class but not those who do not plan to go to college. See Harry Beilin, "The Pattern of Postponability and Its Relation to Social Class Mobility," *Journal of Social Psychology*, 44 (August, 1956), p. 42.

22. Other evidence indicates that a "strong mother-weak father" family structure is especially conducive to upward mobility. See Bendix and Lipset, *op. cit.*, pp. 249–250, 255–256. (This same familial authority pattern is inordinately prevalent among individuals suffering from severe mental illness. See Melvin L. Kohn and John A. Clausen, "Parental Authority Behavior and Schizophrenia," *American Journal of Orthopsychiatry*, 26 [April, 1956], pp. 297–313.)

23. Simpson reaches similar conclusions on the need for auxiliary supports in upward mobility in his recent study of the differential effect of parental and peer-group influences on "mobile" and "non-mobile" working-class boys in high school. Richard L. Simpson, "Parental Influence, Anticipatory Socialization, and Social Mobility," *American Sociological Review*, 27 (August, 1962), pp. 517–522.

24. Brookover and Warner and Abegglen stand out as exceptions among sociologists in their willingness to give credence to the teacher's part in fostering upward mobility among children from lower socio-economic backgrounds. See Wilbur B. Brookover, *A Sociology of Education*, New York: American Book Co., 1955, pp. 107–115; Warner and Abegglen, *op. cit.*, p. 79. For a more typically negative view of the teacher's role, see Neal Gross, "A Critique of 'Social Class Structure in American Education'," *Harvard Educational Review*, 23 (Fall, 1953), pp. 316–318.

25. Robert K. Merton, *op. cit.*, pp. 269–275, 293–294, 302–304, and 329–330.

26. A recent nation-wide sample of high school boys provides evidence that college aspirants from the lower social strata are, when compared to those from the same background who do not plan to go to college: (1) significantly less likely to nominate a family member as an "adult ideal," (2) somewhat more predisposed to affirm that "friendship can be as intimate as a family tie," and (3) more apt to report disagreements with their parents. While the authors interpret their data in psychological terms as the development of autonomy interests among the socially mobile, the results also fit the sociological hypothesis of familial disassociation. See Elizabeth Douvan and Carol Kaye, "Motivation Factors in College Entrance," in Nevitt Sanford (ed.), *op. cit.*, pp. 209–212.

For additional evidence on the disassociative consequences of upward mobility, see Gene Norman Levine and Leila A. Sussman, "Social Class and Sociability in Fraternity Pledging," *The American Journal of Sociology* (January, 1960), pp. 391–399; Warner and Abegglen, *op. cit.*, pp. 59–64, 70–83.

27. Merton, *op. cit.*, p. 294.

# EXECUTIVE CAREERS TODAY: WHO GETS TO THE TOP?

## W. LLOYD WARNER AND JAMES C. ABEGGLEN

It is often said, nowadays, that the "American Dream" of climbing from the bottom to top positions of power can no longer be realized. Many Americans are convinced that the seats at the top are now permanently reserved for the sons and families of those who are already there, and that ambitious men born to low position, even if they have the necessary pluck, will-to-do, and ability to accumulate, can no longer work their way to the top. Yesterday American society was fluid and open and invited men of strong will and brains to pour their energies into the economic life of the nation, encouraging them by rewards of prestige, power, wealth, and position. But today, it is believed, our country has closed the doors to advancement and mobility up from the lower ranks to high position.

Do the facts justify this belief? The question is of vital concern to those who manage big business as well as to those who aspire to the managerial jobs. The present authors set out to find the answer, and many facts along the way, in a study[1] of 8,000 top executives of large business and industry all over the United States. From questionnaires completed by all of them we learned what the occupation and education of their fathers and paternal grandfathers had been, in what kind of place they were born, what their education had been, when they had started working, what their wives and families were like, what kinds of jobs they had held, etc. We personally interviewed a carefully selected sample and their wives, using psychological tests and depth interviewing to determine the personality factors in the success of the leaders and the kind of women they had married.

We used two criteria for our selection of business leaders — (1) that they be in the highest executive positions: chairmen of the board, presidents, vice presidents, and in no position below treasurer; and

Reprinted with abridgement from *Management Review* (Vol. 45, February 1956, pp. 83–94) by permission of the American Management Association, Inc., and the authors.

(2) that they be in big business enterprises, which we established by determining each industry's proportional contribution to Gross National Product and then selecting the largest companies in each type of industry.

Our study attempted to discover how many of these leaders were born to position, how many were mobile — and how they were mobile and why — and how these proportions compared with those of a former period. We were fortunate in having the results of an earlier study to use for comparison. In 1928 Professors F. W. Taussig and C. S. Joslyn of Harvard University, in *American Business Leaders,* reported on a nation-wide research study of thousands of business leaders. In their conclusions they predicted that by the middle of the century occupational advancement from lower levels into the business elite would have largely disappeared and declared, "It is entirely possible that by the middle of the century more than two-thirds of the successful business men in the United States will be recruited from the sons of business owners (large or small) and business executives (major or minor)."

The incomplete evidence we had before we began our study strongly suggested that the Taussig-Joslyn predictions were probably coming true, that top positions in American business and industry were increasingly occupied by the sons of business leaders, and that only limited numbers of capable and well-trained men could rise from low levels of origin to the top of the management hierarchy. To maintain accurate comparison with the earlier period, we designed our research on the Taussig-Joslyn study.

## Where The Leaders Come From

Of the men who hold top positions today, about two-thirds are sons of owners or executives of business firms and professional men and the remaining third primarily from white-collar and laboring backgrounds; a few come from farms and other occupations. Since the proportions for the general population are just the reverse, it looked as if the land of equal opportunity were indeed a fiction. But we found that the movement of men into top business positions does not always take place in one generation. Occupations of paternal grandfathers, for example, showed that, whereas few business leaders were sons of farmers, over a third were the grandsons of farmers. Mobility

TABLE 1

ORIGINS OF BUSINESS LEADERS OF 1928 AND 1952

( IN PERCENTAGES )

| Occupation of Father | 1928 | 1952 | Difference |
|---|---|---|---|
| Unskilled or semi-skilled laborer .......... | 2 | 5 | 3 |
| Skilled laborer ......................... | 9 | 10 | 1 |
| Clerk or salesman ...................... | 5 | 8 | 3 |
| Minor executive and foreman ............ | 7 | 11 | 4 |
| Major executive ....................... | 17 | 15 | −2 |
| Owner small business ................... | 20 | 18 | −2 |
| Owner large business ................... | 14 | 8 | −6 |
| Professional .......................... | 13 | 14 | 1 |
| Farmer ............................... | 12 | 9 | −3 |
| Other ................................ | 1 | 2 | 1 |
| TOTAL ......................... | 100 | 100 | |

involves leaving the farm; as the fathers of our present business leaders moved to the city they made their way in almost every kind of occupation. Only half as many grandfathers as fathers were major executives or large owners.

The mobility figures for today don't look very optimistic until they are compared with those for the period covered by the Taussig-Joslyn study, when it becomes clear that present business leaders include many more men from lower-level occupations. In both periods most business leaders are sons of business men, but the proportion is smaller now, while the proportion of sons of laborers, white-collar workers, and farmers has increased (see Table 1).

Although our system has not changed much in a generation, the trend is towards greater mobility and increased recruitment of business leaders from lower occupational levels. There is increasing opportunity today for men from the bottom to reach the top.

EDUCATION: ROYAL ROAD TO ADVANCEMENT

Since almost anyone in this country who really wants and has the capacity for a higher education can get it, education has become a great leavening force. What kind of education did our business leaders have? Did those starting at lower occupational levels require a type of training not needed by the sons of executives?

Three-fourths of the business leaders in our study at least attended college, over half of all of them graduated, and a third of these went on to postgraduate work. This leaves only one-fourth who did not go to college. The great differences between the business group and the general population are at the extremes (see Table 2).

Since it is possible for so many to get an education at public expense, what motivated the business leaders to get a higher education in eight times the proportion for the general population? And the group that achieved business success with no college education — what kinds of men were these, what kinds of families did they come from, what regions and communities?

Over half of the business leaders born to skilled or unskilled laborers went to college or graduated. This proportion increases steadily up the occupational scale: three-fourths of the sons of small owners, almost that proportion of the sons of white-collar workers and of farmers, and nine of every 10 sons of big business and professional men had some college or graduated. At all levels college graduates predominate; and as we go down the scale, from college graduate to less than high school, the percentages drop rapidly for every group but the unskilled workers. Apparently, business leaders have been motivated to achievement throughout their careers. They have been ambitious to get an education whether it was easy or not; and ambition has continued to drive them on to higher and higher goals in the business world. A proof of this is that so many of those who started college stayed to finish: of all those who started, only one-fourth did not graduate.

Does the education of the father make a difference in the education of the son? Our study found that the two generations reversed the educational scale: whereas over half of the sons had graduated from college, over half of the fathers had only some high school, or less

TABLE 2

Education of Business Leaders in 1952 and of the
General Population in 1950 (in percentages)

|  | U.S. Adult Males (30 years and over) | Business Leaders |
|---|---|---|
| Less than high school | 55 | 4 |
| Some high school | 16 | 9 |
| High school graduates | 16 | 11 |
| Some college | 6 | 19 |
| College graduates | 7 | 57 |
| TOTAL | 100 | 100 |

than high school. Three-fourths of the sons had gone to college or graduated, as against slightly over one-fourth of the fathers. But the fathers were much better educated than the general population of their time.

College-educated fathers had the largest proportion of college-educated sons — 91 per cent. But fathers with less than college education also had large percentages of college-educated sons, and the other groups followed the expected proportions.

That two-thirds of the sons of men with less than high school education would go to college shows again that other factors motivate these men, often against great financial odds and against the behavior pattern of their group. Combining the occupational and educational backgrounds of the fathers, and also of the grandfathers, accented the findings. Space does not permit us to present these findings here. One example, however: 18 per cent of the business leaders are sons of college graduates who were mostly professional and big business men; but more than twice as many are sons of men with less than high school education, many of them skilled and unskilled laborers, farmers, and small owners. Many of our present business leaders had a long way to travel to make good. And higher education is doing a tremendous job boosting them up.

EDUCATION AND FREEDOM TO MOVE AHEAD

Because education loomed so large in the careers of the business leaders, and because it varies so markedly in type and quality among the various regions of the country, it was important to look at educational achievement against region of origin. We found little variation among the regions at any educational level. Since there is considerable variation by region in the education of the general male adult population, in contrast with that of the business leaders, it is apparent that business leaders from some areas overcame many obstacles in advancing their careers.

From regional differences within the country, we went on to possible differences between native-born leaders and those of foreign birth. The largest proportion of college-educated men was in the category of business leaders whose fathers, grandfathers, and possibly other generations were American-born; this proportion decreased through the various categories to that of foreign-born business leaders who are least likely to have gone to college; but business leaders whose fathers were American-born have the same educational average as the entire group.

Actually the proportions of college-educated business leaders who were foreign-born or of foreign parentage are only one and two percentage points lower than the high old-American average. That people from other countries can come to the United States and find higher education attainable as a possible route to business success shows the extent to which we offer our resources to others and, in turn, benefit from what these newcomers have to give us. Of course, for this situation to exist, it is not enough for the resources of society to be available: the individuals must be motivated to use them.

To achieve business leadership, it is necessary to move not only in the business hierarchy but, for many, territorially as well.

> The business leaders, like the nation whose commerce they direct, are men on the move. Changes in location and residence are a dimension of their lives no less meaningful than the changes in social position they have experienced, and this spatial mobility plays an important part in determining the nature and patterns of occupational mobility in American business. To a large extent, these leaders are determined by geographic factors, working with factors of social background. [2]

Does education affect this important territorial movement? Do those with higher education, for example, move more often from their place of birth, and how do they move and where? Generally, movements between states are longer and socially more significant than those within a state. The business leaders with less than college education tended to stay within their home states; those who had graduated went out of their states in higher proportions. Education seemed stronger than all other factors — high or low status, city or country background — in determining how much these business leaders have moved.

Perhaps the college-educated man, mobile from the bottom, can gain advantages from territorial movement because he has the equipment to operate in more kinds of situations, while the mobile man with less education stays in the familiar place where he feels more secure.

Business men today are much more highly educated than a generation ago, and the increase is much greater than for the population as a whole. It is often said today that a business career requires college preparation. In the month of January, 1954, more than 600 large companies sent representatives to the nation's colleges in search of potential managerial talent. The search is among liberal-arts graduates — for "liberally schooled, broad-gauge executives, many-faceted men, for the highest posts."

The changes in educational achievement during the past generation have been enormous. Smaller proportions of leaders from the lowest occupational backgrounds get minimum education now than sons of large owners and executives did a generation ago, and the proportion of college graduates is almost double. If this is a point in a trend, as it may well be, then today's young men will have to be even more highly educated to become the business leaders of tomorrow.

What colleges do the job of training our business leaders? From the great variety of colleges in this country — ranging from small sectarian institutions to large state universities, "cow colleges," and the Ivy League — which ones were favored by these business leaders, and how did the occupation and education of the fathers affect the sons' choice of colleges?

A random sample of 505 college graduates from among our business leaders had gone to 194 different colleges and universities, both here and abroad, but almost one-half of them had gone to only 14 different colleges. And these same 14 colleges were mentioned 87 times as the second college attended, either for graduate work or as a transfer college. So we see a high concentration among a few most favored colleges. Almost one-third of those listing one of these colleges first went to Harvard or Yale; together, these two colleges accounted for exactly one-third of both first and second mentions.

A sizable number of our sample went to another select group of 10 colleges. These institutions were mentioned first 62 times and second 17, in the following order: Northwestern University, Pennsylvania State, Stanford University, the University of Wisconsin, Western Reserve, Dartmouth, and the Universities of Washington, North Carolina, Pittsburgh, and Texas.

The large New England men's colleges, Northwestern in the Midwest, and Stanford in the West, had the highest proportions of sons of major executives: almost half of the leaders going to these colleges were of this background. The small private Eastern colleges, like Amherst and Colgate, were next with one-fourth. Every college group had a fair proportion of sons of professional men except Northwestern and Stanford, where there was a fairly large proportion of sons of white-collar workers, exceeded only by Pennsylvania University and Penn State.

Of the business leaders going to Harvard, more than three-fourths were from top occupational backgrounds and only 12 percent from the lowest occupational groups. A sizable proportion, too, had grandfathers in the business elite. Among all the large New England colleges, and at Northwestern and Stanford as well, there was not one son of a laborer. Not only were most of the fathers of Harvard men members of the professional and business elite; over one-third were college graduates. Yet over half had only high school education; here is a sizable group of successful men who had risen to the top in the previous generation without the benefit of college education.

We know that slightly over half of the business leaders of laborer background either graduated from college or had some college education, but we have seen them represented in the most favored colleges only in the smallest proportions. What colleges are doing the job of educating these men and making it possible for our society to maintain, and even increase, the elasticity of status lines? The large city universities, the state universities in the Big Ten, the Big Seven, and also in the South and West, the specialized universities — M.I.T., Carnegie Tech., I.I.T. — and the University of Pennsylvania and Penn State all educated more sons of laborers than the others.

## Geographical Origins

In view of the large proportion of business leaders graduating from the big Eastern colleges, one might expect them to come from all parts of the country — especially since most of these colleges have attempted to spread their geographical and social base through fortified scholarship programs and nation-wide public relations efforts. Actually, however, the geographical base in our sample seems quite narrow. Almost one-third of the leaders graduating from the most favored colleges were from the Middle Atlantic states, over one-fourth from New England, one-fifth from the East North Central states, and one-tenth from the West North Central region. Stanford and the Western state universities drew students from the Western area and, to some extent, from the South. The universities in the Big Ten and the Big Seven, Northwestern and Stanford, and the state universities of the South — all drew heavily from their local areas.

Many of those who went to college not only acquired A.B.'s but went on to higher degrees, including doctorates. An additional and striking fact is that so many, unsatisfied with college or even graduate training, continue to equip themselves through adult education with the special knowledge necessary for their advancement: comprehensive courses, business school training, and commercial training within a college or university. The sons of men from lower occupational levels are most likely to make this extra effort, yet about half of the sons of big business and professional men also take specialized training.

> Men who have been ambitious to succeed apparently do not lose this ambition nor their ability to translate it into many forms of self-improvement that continue to enlarge their capacities and increase their skills and abilities. Since the demands made upon a top executive by a large organization are not confined within the company or even the industry but often are ramified by the community, the resources of the business leader may be great, but never enough.
> . . . The measurable characteristic shared by our group of business leaders to the highest degree is the amount of their education. They have become, to a large extent, a professional class which demands formal training and preparation, over a broad field of knowledge as well as in technical areas, as prerequisites to a successful career. Education has become the royal road to positions of power and prestige in American business and industry. That this royal road is open to all men is given ample testimony by the large number of educated men from the bottom social layers who appear in our sample.[3]

Many of the latter went to college on scholarships for which they qualified by their records in high school. Others were "late developers" who went to college through their own efforts and began only at this level to demonstrate what they could do.

The two kinds of movement of the American people — spatial movement, from place to place, and social movement, from one social position to another — are interrelated in various ways. A man's place of birth, as well as the social level of his parents, helps to determine the position he will occupy in his career. Not all parts of the nation produce business leaders in equal proportion. The Yankee and the Southerner, the small-town boy and the city boy, the native-born and the foreign-born (who play a special role) — all share differently in the opportunity of American business. The highly industrialized group of states, extending from the Eastern seaboard through the Great Lakes area, produced over half of our business leaders. Birthplace for many is only a point of departure. New England produces more leaders than it retains, while the Pacific Coast has twice as many leaders as it produces. These gains and losses reflect the commercial and industrial growth of the areas.

Some argue that the small-town boy has a greater chance to be mobile because he comes in contact with the life of all groups in his community, whereas the urban boy is likely to know only the life of his own class, or ethnic or religious community. This argument, however, does not seem to hold for the business elite. The typical business leader is born not in a small town but in a large city (the larger the community, the greater the probability of business success), in the North or Midwest, the son of a business or professional man. Most rare in the group is the Southern small-town or country boy, son of a laborer or farmer. But they do happen.

## The Kinds of Men Who Move Up

The effect of geographic movement on social mobility is seen most dramatically in the foreign-born. The disadvantage of foreign birth in a business career is shown by the fact that the proportion of foreign-born business leaders (5 per cent) is only half that for the general population. But this disadvantage does not continue long, for the sons of foreign-born make up the same proportion (one-fifth) of business elite and general population. In a single generation the disadvantage of foreign birth in achieving top business position disappears — and this in spite of the fact that the occupational background is lower than the average for the group. Somehow sons of immigrants move to top-level positions in business in larger proportion than do the sons of old Americans from lower-status backgrounds.

From this unexpected and apparently puzzling fact it is possible to get a better understanding of what social mobility consists of and the meaning of geographic movement in the process. To be mobile, a person has to sever the many emotional and social ties and obligations that hold an individual to his place of birth. Consider the man born in a small community, the home of his family for generations. The house he lives in, the streets he walks, the parish he belongs to, his neighbors, his occupation — in short, the entire pattern of his life — most intimately intertwine the past with the present and future.

If we put aside all questions of ambition, talent, and opportunity and look simply at the movement itself — its nature and the difficulties it presents — we see the place of spatial movement in the mobility process. The son of the immigrant is that man least engaged with the past. He is to an extreme degree disengaged. To become a part of American society he must turn his manner from that of his father, who in turn had undergone the experience of shattering the web of relations holding men to their social positions as he migrated to America. Wherever they might go, whatever their social destination, the sons of immigrants are *par excellence* men on the move, whether they will it or not. The preconditions for movement upward in the social system are established for these men. To a degree this same condition of potential social mobility exists for all persons in American society. To the extent that this is a restless nation, where men move from place to place easily, and children learn to accept such movement as a part of their normal life experience, the conditions are established upon which the factors of emotional need, ambition and motivation, talents and techniques which make up the mobility process may operate.[4]

The unique rationalization and impersonalization of action and outlook that seem to differentiate the men in American business management from those of other nations no doubt are due in large part to this freedom from unquestioned custom. By their geographic mobility these men are in many ways independent of the past; entering new situations — new communities, new companies, new people — they can adopt sets of attitudes towards these situations unencumbered by the traditions of their early training and environment. Separation from the past in social and physical space enables mobile men to act as innovators and to accept and put in motion new ideas and methods. Much of the unique strength of American business management is due in part to geographic mobility.

But the effect is not all good, for sometimes these men tend to view themselves as the products only of their own ambition and training. Yet today we recognize that the concept of the self-made man rests on a fallacy. No social being is really self-made; the successful mobile business leader is a product of his society as surely as his mediocre counterparts, the failures, and all the rest. The notion of self-made men may, too, carry unpleasant implications. Men who regard themselves as self-made often tend to feel that they owe no debts to their fellows, their community, or their subordinates — and they are not likely to preserve the values of the past when working for the future.

## SUCCESS IN BIG AND SMALL BUSINESS

In studying the career patterns of business leaders and their relation to the larger business world, many factors were considered. Were some types of business and industry more favorable, for example, to the mobile man, and how was this affected by his occupational background and education? Our findings are too complex for inclusion here, but the following facts are suggestive: In investment banking, and the general category of brokers and dealers, over half of the leaders were sons of big business and professional men (as compared with an average percentage of 38 for all businesses) and almost three-fourths were college graduates. This category represents least the ideal of an "open" economy. We found that rapidly expanding businesses were most available to leaders with the least education in our group, that certain industries were dominated by men from certain geographic regions, that sons of laborers make up a larger proportion (one-fourth) of the total leadership of railroad and highway transportation companies than of any other kind of business. By classifying business and industry in a number of ways in terms of size, type, rate of expansion, etc., we were able to see how the patterns of movement in them were affected by the leaders' occupational backgrounds, regions of birth, and educational levels.

The giant corporations are of particular interest because of their dominance of the business scene. How do they affect the mobility process? We found that the proportion of sons of major executives and owners of large businesses is substantially smaller in the larger businesses than in the smaller ones. Fourteen per cent of the business leaders in firms with less than $10 million annual gross are sons of laborers, and 30 per cent are sons of big business men. In the larger firms — those with a gross of more than $250 million — 16 per cent of the leaders are sons of laborers and only 19 per cent sons of big business men. The bigger the business, the greater the opportunity to rise.

We found that the higher business positions are occupied in proportionately larger numbers by sons of big business men. They occupy more than one-third of all chief-executive positions studied. It is the larger firms that are more often led by men from lower-status backgrounds. But, for the most part, the sons of laborers appear in positions of secretary, treasurer, and controller rather than in the vice-president group. Mobility takes place to all levels of business positions, but less often to the topmost.

## The Boss's Daughter?

We studied the length of time required by our business leaders to achieve top position from the time they entered their business careers, and whether this was affected by marriage or kind of education; whether they had relatives or friends in the firm; whether they had received financial help; what kind of jobs they held — and found much significance among these factors. Money, we found, doesn't buy success; nor does there appear to be justification for the current adage: "It isn't what you know but who you know."

Another popular notion that found no verification in our study is that position is secured by marrying the boss's daughter. If our figures prove anything, it takes longer for the mobile man to reach the top if he marries the boss's daughter than if he marries at his own level.

Women play an important role in the careers of business leaders. The occupational and educational backgrounds of the wives were related to those of their husbands to see how the men of the various backgrounds married. When we conducted personal interviews with the selected sample of business leaders we also interviewed their wives, in their homes, to gain another insight into their lives and personalities.

Many of the business leaders married at their own social level, but a considerable number married above or below, indicating that there is fluidity in present American society and that upward movement is possible not only through occupational advancement but by marriage — and, for the children, by descent. Thus it is true to say that, while for some families it is only two generations from shirtsleeves to shirtsleeves, for others it is but two or less from shirtsleeves to dinner jacket.

Especially important to the business leader is his family's ability to adjust to new situations, to move with him to whatever new environments his career may take him. They must learn and unlearn easily, fit themselves into many social and cultural situations which cluster around the job and life of the community, and relate to each other in their ever-changing world.

## REFERENCES

1. The entire research, financed by Chicago business men and the Hill Foundation, is reported on in two books: *Occupational Mobility in American Business and Industry* (University of Minnesota Press, 1955) which is a comprehensive presentation of the facts and findings of the study, illustrated with many charts and tables, a volume designed primarily for the professional social scientist; and *Big Business Leaders in America* (Harper and Brothers, 1955), a more popular presentation of the same material. The latter book also examines the personality factors having to do with the success of the men, as well as the role of their wives in helping, or hindering, their careers.

2. *Big Business Leaders in America*, p. 178.

3. *Ibid.*, pp. 56–57.

4. *Ibid.*, pp. 193–194.

# C.

## STRUCTURAL FACTORS
## IN DIFFERENTIAL MOBILITY

# SOCIAL ORIGINS, OCCUPATIONAL ADVICE, OCCUPATIONAL VALUES, AND WORK CAREERS

## RICHARD L. SIMPSON AND IDA HARPER SIMPSON

Three major generalizations sum up much of the research on factors affecting occupational careers. First, despite the net upward mobility which prevails in industrial societies, there is some tendency for men to inherit the occupational status levels of their fathers.[1] Second, people are strongly influenced by the advice of significant others when they select jobs and choose occupational aspiration levels.[2] Third, the general values which people hold are systematically related to their aspiration levels and to the kinds of occupations they choose.[3] It has been shown that these factors are interrelated. The inheritance of occupational level is not due entirely to external limitations on mobility; not only the objective life-chances of the poor, but also their aspiration levels are usually low.[4] Moreover, personal influences on occupational preference vary by social class.[5]

Despite the ample documentation of the points mentioned above, the existing research on occupational choice and mobility leaves some gaps which suggest directions for further study. Most of the research on personal influence and values has dealt with the aspirations of students rather than with the actual careers of workers,[6] and most of it has treated either personal influences or values alone (or sometimes in conjunction with social class) as the independent variable which explains career aspirations. The interrelationships of class origins, personal influences, values, and occupational plans and accomplishments are still in need of systematic study.[7]

In this paper we try to answer, at least in a preliminary way, some

Reprinted from *Social Forces* (Vol. 40, No. 3, March 1962, pp. 264–271) by permission of the University of North Carolina Press and the authors.

The research reported herein was performed pursuant to a contract with the United States Office of Education, Department of Health, Education, and Welfare. It was also supported by a grant from the Ford Foundation to the Urban Studies Program, Institute for Research in Social Science, University of North Carolina.

general questions about the joint relationships of these variables; these are indicated below.

1. Lipset and Bendix suggest that one of the advantages possessed by boys in the higher social classes is the access to superior advice about the labor market, and they present evidence that boys who receive occupational advice from numerous sources are relatively likely to begin their work careers at the higher occupational levels.[8] We will test this hypothesis in a different type of community setting from the one they studied, by seeing whether the number of sources of occupational advice is positively related to the beginning job levels of workers entering the labor force.

2. Still following the general reasoning of Lipset and Bendix, one might expect that parents, especially working-class parents, will usually be ill-equipped to give sound occupational advice because of their own limited occupational perspectives. It is also reasonable to expect that occupational advisers outside the family are likely to be experts or people who know about specific job or career possibilities. We are therefore hypothesizing that the status level of a worker's first job tends to be high when his main occupational adviser has been someone outside his family.

3. Most research on values and occupational choice has focused on values as they relate to the type or situs of work chosen. One would also expect values to be related to the status levels of the occupations which workers choose. Specifically, we are hypothesizing that values indicating positive attraction to work are characteristic of workers entering the labor force at the higher levels, and values unrelated to the nature of the work or the work career are characteristic of workers entering the labor force at the lower levels. The association of positive work values with higher status levels could mean either (1) that the chance to realize work-related values is greatest in the higher-status jobs and therefore people who initially hold such values strive harder to achieve high occupational status, or (2) that the process of considering a job at a given status level evokes a limited range of values from among the full repertoire of values which are latent in all workers. More simply put, by the first of these interpretations the values characterize the individual and motivate him to seek a given job level; by the second interpretation the values characterize the job-seeking situation, to be seized upon by any worker who for whatever reason finds himself in the situation, so that the status level of a

job determines the standards by which the individual evaluates it. These alternative interpretations are dealt with in hypothesis 5, below.

4. If the first three hypotheses are all borne out, this might simply mean that different patterns of occupational advice-seeking and values are the outcomes of different class backgrounds. In this case the advice and values per se could conceivably have no independent relationship to first-job level, and we might feel that workers from high-status backgrounds would have obtained good jobs no matter what their advice and value patterns had been. It is reasonable to suppose, however, that superior advice and strong work-oriented values have independent effects. Hypothesis 4 is that occupational advice and values are related to the status levels of workers' first jobs even when workers' family backgrounds are controlled.

5. As mentioned earlier, if these predicted relationships are found, they might reflect the effects of motives of the individual worker on his work career or, alternatively, they might reflect the effects of the normative standards evoked by the immediate job-seeking situation on the advice and value patterns of the individual.[9] Evidence for the first of these interpretations — that general motives have long-term effects on work careers — has been presented by Crockett, who reports that "achievement motivation" is related to upward occupational mobility.[10] We can put this general hypothesis to a further test. If the "individual motivation" hypothesis is correct, we would expect that workers who obtain superior advice and reveal work-oriented values when choosing their first jobs will not only tend to obtain high-status first jobs, but will also tend more than others to be upward mobile during their later careers, on the ground that the advice and value patterns brought to bear in choosing the first job tell us something about the person's general career motivation. If on the other hand the situation tends to evoke the advice and value patterns rather than to be determined by them, we would not expect to find any relationship between first-job advice and value patterns and subsequent career mobility.

6. So far we have been discussing workers' advice-seeking and occupational values when they choose their first jobs. We also want to know what advice and value patterns prevail when they choose later jobs. Hypothesis 6 is that the same relationships of advice and values to job status levels prevail when workers choose later jobs as when they choose their first jobs.

The data are from semistructured interviews with 380 workers in two middle-sized southern cities. The potential sample included all adult white males in the labor force living in randomly selected blocks in the two cities in the summer of 1959.[11] One city was primarily industrial and the other was primarily commercial and governmental; the two communities rather than only one of them were studied to obtain a diversified occupational distribution. Defining the sample as all known white male labor force members in all blocks where any interviewing was done, completed and usable interviews amounted to 380 in a sample of 541, or 70 percent. Findings reported elsewhere indicate that the sample is fairly representative of the white male populations in the communities studied, and that the over-all mobility patterns parallel those found in other studies conducted nationally and in other communities.[12]

The hypotheses involve four variables: job level, number of advisers, main adviser, and occupational value.

*Job level,* obtained from occupational histories of the respondents, was measured with the Hollingshead Index of Occupational Status. In this paper we group Hollingshead's seven occupational strata into two white-collar and two blue-collar levels. Upper white-collar jobs include those of executives and business managers, proprietors of large and medium-sized businesses, and major and middle professionals. Lower white-collar jobs are those of clerical, sales, and lesser administrative personnel, technicians and minor professionals, and small businessmen. Upper blue-collar jobs are those of skilled manual employees and foremen. Lower blue-collar jobs are those of semi-skilled and unskilled manual and service workers.[13] The two white-collar and two blue-collar strata are combined in some of the analysis, but all four levels are used in tabulations involving mobility, which is defined as movement from one to another of the four levels.

*Number of advisers* was obtained from an interview question which asked, "Before you took your first regular full-time job, what people gave you advice or information about your future work career?"

The question on *main adviser* was, "What three people had the strongest influence on your plans for a work career, before you actually started working on your first regular full-time job? Who had the most influence. . . .?" Tabulations refer to the first-ranked adviser only.[14]

The question on *occupational value* was, "Why did you go into this kind of work (take this job) instead of some other kind of work (job)?" The first reason given was classified as indicating either positive attraction to the work itself or the career it offered (enjoy the work, self-expression, serve humanity, good income, chance for advancement, etc.) or a negative, uninterested approach which stressed extrinsic considerations more than the work itself or its career possibilities (only job available, someone suggested it to me, had friends who did that kind of work, place of employment was near home, etc.).

## FINDINGS: ADVICE, VALUES, AND FIRST JOBS

It has long been known that the occupational status of workers' fathers is highly predictive of the status levels of the workers' own first jobs. Table 1 shows this familiar status-inheritance pattern for our sample and also the relationships of first-job level to number of advisers, main adviser, and occupational value. The figures support the first three of our hypotheses.

### 1. Number of Advisers

Part B of Table 1 supports the hypothesis that the number of advisers is positively related to the status level of the first job. Of the men who had three or more advisers before taking their first jobs, 57.2 percent had white-collar first jobs including 19.9 percent with upper white-collar first jobs. The comparable figures for men with two or fewer advisers are 35.6 percent in the combined white-collar category and only 11.1 percent in the upper white-collar level.

### 2. Main Adviser

Part C of Table 1 shows that among workers who could name some individual as main adviser, those with nonfamily main advisers tended

TABLE 1.   LEVEL OF FIRST JOB BY FATHER'S OCCUPATIONAL STATUS, NUMBER OF
ADVISERS, MAIN ADVISER, AND OCCUPATIONAL VALUE

| Characteristic | Level of First Job | | |
| --- | --- | --- | --- |
| | Upper White-Collar | Lower White-Collar | Blue-Collar |
| | *Percent* | *Percent* | *Percent* |
| A.  Father's Status | | | |
| White-collar (N = 168) | 28.6 | 38.1 | 33.4 |
| Blue-collar (N = 191) | 3.1 | 22.5 | 74.3 |
| B.  Number of Advisers | | | |
| 3 or more (N = 161) | 19.9 | 37.3 | 43.8 |
| 0 to 2 (N = 216) | 11.1 | 24.5 | 64.4 |
| C.  Main Adviser | | | |
| Nonfamily (N = 86) | 30.2 | 38.4 | 31.4 |
| Family (N = 184) | 13.6 | 27.2 | 59.3 |
| D.  Occupational Value | | | |
| Positive (N = 157) | 27.4 | 31.2 | 41.4 |
| Negative (N = 220) | 5.9 | 29.1 | 65.0 |

Chi-square with the two white-collar groups combined, so that d.f. = 1 in each instance: Part A, 60.79, $p < .001$; Part B, 17.24, $p < .001$; Part C, 18.18, $p < .001$; Part D, 20.63, $p < .001$.

to have higher-ranking first jobs than those whose main advisers were family members. Of the workers with nonfamily main advisers, 68.6 percent began their careers in one of the white-collar levels including 30.2 percent in upper white-collar jobs. The comparable percentages for workers with family members as main advisers were 40.8 percent in the combined white-collar category and 13.6 percent in upper white-collar jobs. (Workers with no main adviser at all, who are omitted from this section of the table, tended to have the lowest-ranking first jobs of all.) These findings are as predicted.

### 3. *Occupational Value*

Part D of Table 1 supports the hypothesis that values indicating positive attraction to work would go with high-status first jobs. Of the workers citing positive work values as reasons for taking their first jobs, 58.6 percent had white-collar first jobs including 27.4 percent in the upper white-collar level, but of those with negative values, only 35.0 percent began their careers in white-collar work including 5.9 percent in upper white-collar jobs.

## 4. Independent Relationships with Level of First Job

It has been shown that advice and values were related to first-job level. Conceivably, however, advice and values might merely be correlates of the father's status and give no independent explanation of first-job level apart from effects of father's status. It therefore becomes necessary to ask whether the various relationships are independent of each other.

Table 2 deals with this question by cross-tabulating father's occupational level, occupational value, number of advisers, and level of first job.[15] By observing four comparisons — row 1 with row 2, 3 with 4, 5 with 6 and 7 with 8 — the relationship of number of advisers to level of first job, with father's status and occupational value controlled, can be seen. In all four comparisons, men with three or more advisers

TABLE 2. LEVEL OF FIRST JOB BY CROSS-TABULATION OF FATHER'S STATUS, OCCUPATIONAL VALUE, AND NUMBER OF ADVISERS

| Father's Status, Occupational Value and Number of Advisers | Level of First Job* | | |
|---|---|---|---|
| | Upper White-Collar | Lower White-Collar | Blue-Collar |
| | Percent | Percent | Percent |
| Father white-collar: | | | |
| Positive value: | | | |
| 1. 3 or more advisers (N = 49) | 46.9 | 34.7 | 18.4 |
| 2. 0 to 2 advisers (N = 41) | 34.1 | 43.9 | 22.0 |
| Negative value: | | | |
| 3. 3 or more advisers (N = 33) | 18.2 | 51.5 | 30.3 |
| 4. 0 to 2 advisers (N = 50) | 12.0 | 30.0 | 58.0 |
| Father blue-collar: | | | |
| Positive value: | | | |
| 5. 3 or more advisers (N = 31) | 35.5 | | 64.5 |
| 6. 0 to 2 advisers (N = 33) | 21.2 | | 78.8 |
| Negative value: | | | |
| 7. 3 or more advisers (N = 48) | 37.5 | | 62.5 |
| 8. 0 to 2 advisers (N = 82) | 19.5 | | 80.5 |

* White-collar first-job categories combined if father was blue-collar, because of small N's.

Chi-squares for comparisons of rows within "father white-collar" category, d.f. = 2 in each instance, two-tail tests: row 1 vs. row 2, 1.54, p < .50; row 3 vs. row 4, 6.17, p < .05; row 1 vs. row 3, 13.24, p. < .01; row 2 vs. row 4, 7.17, p < .05. Chi-squares for comparison, d.f. = 1 in each instance, one-tail tests: row 5 vs. row 6, 1.61, p < .15; row 7 vs. row 8, 5.07, p. < .05; row 5 vs. row 7, .04, p < .45; row 6 vs. row 8, .03, p < .45.

tended to have higher-level first jobs than men with two or fewer advisers. The relationship is statistically significant at the .05 level, however, only in the two comparisons where the occupational values were negative. If a man held negative work values, having a large number of advisers greatly improved his chances of beginning with a white-collar job, whether his father's status was high or low, as is seen in comparing row 3 with row 4 and row 7 with row 8.

The relationship of occupational value to level of first job, with father's status and number of advisers controlled, appears in the comparisons of row 1 with 3, 2 with 4, 5 with 7, and 6 with 8. In the first two of these four comparisons, involving men with white-collar fathers, men with positive occupational values were significantly more likely (p < .05) to have high-ranking first jobs than were men with negative values, as the hypothesis predicted. Among workers with blue-collar fathers, however, occupational value had little or no relationship to level of first job when number of advisers was controlled. This suggests that more light can be thrown on the relation of advice to level of first job, among men from blue-collar family backgrounds, by ignoring values altogether among this group of workers. When this is done, the picture is clear. Figures combined from those shown in Table 2 indicate that of the 79 workers with blue-collar fathers and three or more advisers, 36.7 percent began their careers in white-collar work, but of the 115 with blue-collar fathers and two or fewer advisers, only 20.0 percent began in white-collar work (p < .01).

From the above it can be said that in some subgroups of workers, occupational advice and values were related to first-job levels independently of the status levels of workers' fathers. Advice seemed to have an independent effect when values were negative, and values seemed to have an independent effect among workers from white-collar family backgrounds.[16]

FINDINGS: ADVICE, VALUES, AND CAREER PATTERNS

5. *Career motivations and mobility*

These relationships of advice and values to first-job levels could be interpreted in two ways, one involving motivational characteristics of the individual job-seeker and the other involving characteristic advice-seeking and value patterns evoked by different job-seeking situations,

TABLE 3.  PERCENT UPWARD MOBILE DURING CAREER, BY NUMBER OF ADVISERS, MAIN ADVISER, AND OCCUPATIONAL VALUE WITH RESPECT TO FIRST JOB*

| Advice and Values | First Job Lower White-Collar | | First Job Blue-Collar | |
|---|---|---|---|---|
| | Percent Mobile | Total N† | Percent Mobile | Total N† |
| Number of Advisers | | | | |
| 3 or more | 44.2 | (43) | 47.0 | (66) |
| 0 to 2 | 51.2 | (41) | 42.9 | (126) |
| Main Adviser | | | | |
| Nonfamily | 47.8 | (23) | 52.0 | (25) |
| Family | 43.6 | (39) | 41.7 | (103) |
| Occupational Value | | | | |
| Positive | 45.9 | (37) | 42.6 | (61) |
| Negative | 47.7 | (44) | 44.6 | (130) |

* Workers who had held only one job, workers whose first job was upper white-collar, and workers who had been downward mobile from lower white-collar to blue-collar jobs are omitted from tabulations. A worker is defined as mobile if his first job was lower white-collar, or if his first job was blue-collar and his present job is white-collar.

† Total N refers to base for percentage.

Chi-square test reveals no difference in predicted direction significant at better than .15 level using a one-tail test, and no difference in either direction significant at better than .30 level using a two-tail test.

regardless of the initial motives of the worker. If the first or "individual motivation" hypothesis is correct, we would reason that the advice and value pattern brought to bear in choosing the first job should tell us something about the characteristic motives of the worker and therefore predict not only his first-job level, but also his subsequent career.

Pertinent figures are shown in Table 3, and they do not support the individual motivation hypothesis. From the hypothesis we would predict more upward career mobility among workers who had many advisers, nonfamily main advisers, and positive work values when they chose their first jobs, but these predictions are not borne out. In neither of the two relevant groups of workers — those whose first jobs were at the lower white-collar level and those whose first jobs were manual — were those with "favorable" first-job advice or values significantly more likely to be mobile into higher levels in their later careers. Three of the six comparisons in Table 3 show relationships in the predicted direction, but the other three show relationships in the opposite direction, and none of the six relationships is significant at better than the .15 level.[17]

Thus the individual motivation hypothesis is not supported. We will be in a better position to assess the alternative, "situational" interpretation after testing hypothesis 6, which deals with advice and value patterns in connection with the workers' choice of their most recent jobs.

## 6. *Advice, values, and present job levels*

Table 4 classifies workers by advice and value patterns with respect to the most recent job change, and shows for each group the percentage whose present jobs were in the white-collar levels. The questions on advice and values were similar to those asked about the choice of the first job. Workers who had held only one job are excluded from the tabulations. As expected, workers with three or more advisers, with nonfamily main advisers and with positive work values were somewhat concentrated in the white-collar group; but of these relationships, only the one between main adviser and present-job level was significant at the .05 level and the others reached only the .10 level using a one-tail test of significance.

Table 5 is an attempt to see whether favorable advice and value patterns were especially prevalent among workers whose present jobs represented upward mobility from the levels of their immediately

TABLE 4.  PERCENT CURRENTLY IN WHITE-COLLAR JOBS, BY NUMBER OF ADVISERS, MAIN ADVISER, AND OCCUPATIONAL VALUE WITH RESPECT TO MOST RECENT JOB CHANGE*

| Advice and Values | Current Job White-Collar |
|---|---|
|  | *Percent* |
| Number of Advisers: |  |
|   3 or more(N = 163) ................ | 66.3 |
|   0 to 2 (N = 165) .................. | 57.6 |
| Main Adviser: |  |
|   Nonfamily (N = 67) ............... | 73.1 |
|   Family (N = 261) ................. | 59.0 |
| Occupational Value: |  |
|   Positive (N = 189) ............... | 64.6 |
|   Negative (N = 128) ............... | 55.5 |

\* Workers who had held only one job are omitted from tabulations.

Chi-squares, d.f. = 1, one-tail tests: number of advisers, 2.62, $p < .10$; main adviser, 4.51, $p < .05$; occupational value, 2.65, $p < .10$.

TABLE 5. PERCENT UPWARD MOBILE FROM PREVIOUS TO CUR-
RENT JOBS, BY NUMBER OF ADVISERS, MAIN ADVISER, AND OCCU-
PATIONAL VALUE WITH RESPECT TO MOST RECENT JOB CHANGE*

| Advice and Values | Upward Mobile |
|---|---|
| | *Percent* |
| Number of Advisers: | |
| 3 or more (N = 138) ............... | 42.0 |
| 0 to 2 (N = 144) ................. | 40.3 |
| Main Adviser: | |
| Nonfamily (N = 53) ................ | 52.8 |
| Family or none (N = 229) .......... | 38.4 |
| Occupational Value: | |
| Positive (N = 165) ............... | 47.3 |
| Negative (N = 113) ............... | 31.0 |

* Workers who had held only one job, and workers whose
previous job was upper white-collar, are omitted from
tabulations.

Chi-squares, d.f. = 1, one-tail tests: number of advisers, .10,
$p < .40$; main adviser, 3.69, $p < .05$; occupational value, 7.38,
$p < .01$.

preceding jobs. All three comparisons show differences in the expected
direction; the difference with respect to number of advisers is so small
as to be meaningless, but the differences with respect to main adviser
and occupational value are significant beyond the .05 level.[18]

Thus hypothesis 6, that the relationships found in connection with
the choice of first jobs would also be found in connection with the
choice of the most recent job, receives general support, though not
all of the relationships found are statistically significant at the .05
level.

## SUMMARY

Interview data from 380 workers in two cities show that when these
workers chose their first jobs, those who received occupational advice from numerous sources, whose main occupational advisers were
persons outside their families, and whose stated reasons for taking
the jobs they took indicated positive orientations to work were more
likely than others to obtain high-ranking first jobs. The relationship
of occupational advice to status level of first job was independent of
the worker's class background among workers with negative work
values, and the relationship of occupational values to first-job level

was independent of advice among workers from white-collar family backgrounds.

These same relationships of advice and value to status level of job chosen held up in general, though not with complete consistency, when workers chose their most recent jobs; yet the advice and value patterns which workers brought to bear when choosing their first jobs were not significantly related to their subsequent career mobility patterns. In conjunction these findings strongly suggest, though they cannot prove, that the underlying occupational motives of individuals have less effect on the status levels of the jobs they will obtain than the status levels of the jobs chosen have on the advice-seeking and value patterns which will be brought to bear. By this interpretation the status level of the job evokes characteristic normative standards which influence the way in which the individual decides whether to take the job, no matter what his underlying motives may be. This interpretation is consistent with Foote's "situational" theory of motivation, part of which in simple form states that interpersonal situations determine motives more than the other way around.

## REFERENCES

1. See, for example, Percy E. Davidson and H. Dewey Anderson, *Occupational Mobility in an American Community* (Stanford, Calif.: Stanford University Press, 1937); Natalie Rogoff, *Recent Trends in Occupational Mobility* (Glencoe, Ill.: Free Press, 1953); Joseph A. Kahl, *The American Class Structure* (New York: Rinehart, 1957), pp. 251–275, which has a general discussion and reworks data from National Opinion Research Center, "Jobs and Occupations: A Popular Evaluation," *Opinion News*, 9 (September 1, 1947), pp. 3–13; Raymond W. Mack, Linton C. Freeman, and Seymour Yellin, *Thirty Years of Research and Theory* (Syracuse: Syracuse University Press, 1957), an annotated bibliography of articles on social mobility in American sociological journals from 1924 to 1953; and Seymour Martin Lipset and Reinhard Bendix, *Social Mobility in Industrial Society* (Berkeley and Los Angeles: University of California Press, 1959), esp. ch. II, by Lipset and Hans L. Zetterberg, which summarizes research on intergenerational mobility and gives extensive bibliography.

2. Joseph A. Kahl, "Educational and Occupational Aspirations of 'Common-Man' Boys," *Harvard Educational Review*, 23 (Summer 1953), pp. 186–203; Jean E. Floud (editor), A. H. Halsey, and F. M. Martin, *Social Class and Educational Opportunity* (London: Heinemann, 1956), pp. 93–95, 107–108;

Lipset and Bendix, *op. cit.*, pp. 194–195, 229, 237; David J. Bordua, "Educational Aspirations and Parental Stress on College," *Social Forces,* 38 (March 1960), pp. 262–269; Richard L. Simpson, "Parental Influence, Anticipatory Socialization, and Social Mobility," *American Sociological Review,* forthcoming.

3. Morris Rosenberg, with the assistance of Edward A. Suchman and Rose K. Goldsen, *Occupations and Values* (Glencoe, Ill.: Free Press, 1957); Harry K. Schwarzweller, "Value Orientations in Educational and Occupational Choices," *Rural Sociology,* 24 (September 1959), pp. 246–256; Harry K. Schwarzweller, "Values and Occupational Choice," *Social Forces,* 39 (December 1960), pp. 126–135.

4. R. A. Mulligan, "Socio-Economic Background and College Enrollment," *American Sociological Review,* 16 (April 1951), pp. 188–196; Ely Chinoy, "The Tradition of Opportunity and the Aspirations of Automobile Workers," *American Journal of Sociology,* 57 (March 1952), pp. 453–459; Leonard Reissman, "Levels of Aspiration and Social Class," *American Sociological Review,* 18 (June 1953), pp. 233–242; Genevieve Knupfer, "Portrait of the Underdog," and Herbert H. Hyman, "The Value Systems of Different Classes," in Reinhard Bendix and Seymour Martin Lipset, editors, *Class, Status, and Power* (Glencoe, Ill.: Free Press, 1953), pp. 255–263, 426–442; Robert H. Guest, "Work Careers and Aspirations of Automobile Workers," *American Sociological Review,* 19 (April 1954), pp. 155–163; LaMar T. Empey, "Social Class and Occupational Ambition," *American Sociological Review,* 21 (December 1956), pp. 703–709; Archie O. Haller and William H. Sewell, "Farm Residence and Levels of Educational and Occupational Aspiration," *American Journal of Sociology,* 62 (January 1957), pp. 407–411; William H. Sewell, Archie O. Haller, and Murray A. Straus, "Social Status and Educational and Occupational Aspiration," *American Sociological Review,* 22 (February 1957), pp. 67–73; Jackson Toby, "Orientation to Education as a Factor in School Maladjustment of Lower-Class Children," *Social Forces,* 35 (March 1957), pp. 259–266; J. Kenneth Morland, "Educational and Occupational Aspirations of Mill and Town Children in a Southern Community," *Social Forces,* 39 (December 1960), pp. 169–175; N. F. Dufty, "Occupational Status, Job Satisfaction and Levels of Aspiration," *British Journal of Sociology,* 11 (December 1960), pp. 348–355.

5. Lipset and Bendix, *op. cit.*, pp. 194–196.

6. The studies cited above by Chinoy, Reissman, Knupfer, Hyman, Guest, and Dufty deal with aspirations and use adults as subjects, but of these, only the Chinoy, Reissman, Guest, and Dufty studies treat specifically occupational aspirations.

7. For a systematic attempt to work both personal influences and values into a common frame of reference, see Peter M. Blau, John W. Gustad,

Richard Jessor, Herbert S. Parnes, and Richard C. Wilcock, "Occupational Choice: A Conceptual Framework," *Industrial and Labor Relations Review,* 9 (July 1956), pp. 531–543. See also Richard L. Simpson and Ida Harper Simpson, "Values, Personal Influence, and Occupational Choice," *Social Forces,* 39 (December 1960), pp. 116–125.

8. Lipset and Bendix, *op. cit.,* pp. 194–196.

9. The notion that values are evoked by situations rather than simply brought to situations is consistent with the motivational theory presented in Nelson N. Foote, "Identification as the Basis for a Theory of Motivation," *American Sociological Review,* 16 (February 1951), pp. 14–21.

10. Harry J. Crockett, Jr., "The Achievement Motive and Social Mobility in the United States," *American Sociological Review,* 27 (April, 1962), pp. 191–204; Harry J. Crockett, Jr., "Level of Education and Strength of Achievement Motive as Determinants of Occupational Mobility," *Sociological Quarterly,* 4 (Summer, 1964) pp. 231–242. So far as we can discover, Crockett's study is the only one relating achievement motivation to actual careers rather than to student aspirations. For studies on the achievement motive see David C. McClelland, John W. Atkinson, Russell A. Clark, and Edgar L. Lowell, *The Achievement Motive* (New York: Appleton-Century-Crofts, 1953); David C. McClelland, *Studies in Motivation* (New York: Appleton-Century-Crofts, 1955); David C. McClelland, *Report of Committee on Identification of Talent* (New York: Social Science Research Council, 1956); Bernard C. Rosen, "The Achievement Syndrome," *American Sociological Review,* 21 (April 1956), pp. 203–211; David C. McClelland, Alfred L. Baldwin, Urie Bronfenbrenner, and Fred L. Strodtbeck, *Talent and Society* (Princeton, N. J.: D. Van Nostrand, 1958); Bernard C. Rosen, "Race, Ethnicity, and the Achievement Syndrome," *American Sociological Review,* 24 (February 1959), pp. 47–60; Bernard C. Rosen and Roy D'Andrade, "The Psychosocial Origins of Achievement Motivation," *Sociometry,* 22 (September 1959), pp. 185–218; James V. Pierce and Paul H. Bowman, "Motivation Patterns of Superior High School Students," in *The Gifted Student: Research Projects Concerning Elementary and Secondary School Students,* U. S. Department of Health, Education, and Welfare, Office of Education, Cooperative Research Monograph No. 2 (Washington: Government Printing Office, 1960), pp. 33–66; and Bernard C. Rosen, "Family Structure and Achievement Motivation," *American Sociological Review,* 26 (August 1961), pp. 574–585.

11. The sampling procedure as it applies in rural areas is described in Walter L. Slocum and Carol L. Stone, "A Design for Area Probability Sampling," *Rural Sociology,* 24 (June 1959), pp. 176–177.

12. For sample representativeness in one of the two communities see David R. Norsworthy, "Mobility Effects of Industrial Growth," unpublished Ph.D. dissertation, University of North Carolina, 1961. For some of the main find-

ings on mobility patterns, see Richard L. Simpson, "Occupational Choice and Mobility," ch. XII in F. Stuart Chapin, Jr. and Shirley F. Weiss, editors, *Urban Growth Dynamics* (New York: Wiley, forthcoming).

13. The Index of Occupational Status is one of two components, the other being years of education completed, in Hollingshead's Two-Factor Index of Social Position, whose validation and utility are described in August B. Hollingshead and Frederick C. Redlich, *Social Class and Mental Illness* (New York: Wiley, 1958), pp. 359–368. We classified workers' fathers who owned farms of 100 acres or more as lower white-collar, other farm owners as upper blue-collar, and farm tenants and laborers as lower blue-collar. Our sample was entirely urban but some workers' fathers were farmers.

14. These and other personal influence questions used in this study were adapted from items used in Howard S. Gall, "The Functions of Multi-Group Sanctions in the Academic Decisions of Adolescents," unpublished M.A. thesis, University of North Carolina, 1955. For suggestive (though not conclusive) evidence that the answers the respondents gave to questions about their first jobs are sufficiently valid for analytical purposes, see Richard L. Simpson, David R. Norsworthy, and H. Max Miller, "Occupational Choice and Mobility in the Urbanizing Piedmont of North Carolina," unpublished report submitted to the United States Office of Education by the Institute for Research in Social Science, University of North Carolina, 1960, pp. 126–127.

15. Number of advisers instead of main adviser was used for this cross-tabulation because number of advisers was more independent of father's status.

16. When workers are matched on their fathers' and their own job levels, there are no significant relationships between number of advisers and occupational value.

17. The figures in Table 3 exclude workers whose first jobs were at the upper white-collar level and workers who had held only one job, since by definition these could not be mobile. The relatively few downward mobile workers are also omitted. Similar omissions are made from other tables, as described in footnotes to the tables.

18. When Tables 4 and 5 were rerun in the subsample of workers who had migrated across county lines to take their current jobs, the results showed no important differences from those reported here for the total sample. The migrants were analyzed separately on the supposition that a worker who migrates to take a new job might behave more like a worker choosing his first job than a nonmigrant would, but this turned out not to be the case so far as our advice and value variables were concerned.

# PART VI

Developing Achievement

## INTRODUCTION

This book has assembled under one cover a record of empirical knowledge regarding the achievement process in the United States. In concluding, we go a step beyond reports describing and analyzing existing phenomena to consider the problem of fundamental goals and the means to their attainment. We shall not advance alternatives to the basic American value which holds that achievement should be judged almost exclusively in terms of occupational performance. Rather, in keeping with the empirical orientation of this book, we shall take the contemporary value-position as given, and raise questions within its framework.

Every industrial society distributes rewards unevenly among its citizens. Democratic societies justify the reward system by stressing equality of opportunity for all members. But the data reviewed disclose staggering disadvantages are suffered by most children growing up in low status families. The slum home, the slum school and the slum environment generally (including, of course, the "rural slum") provide experiences which severely thwart rather than advance the child's development. Unless one clings to the discredited Social Darwinist position discussed at the beginning of the book, public intervention on behalf of these children is required. Deutsch's paper reviews evidence on this matter and offers specific proposals for action programs to offset these conditions. Some of the proposals made are already being tried out by governmental agencies (e.g., as in the Headstart program). If intensive intervention on a broad scale becomes the norm, future research on achievement in the United States should reveal a decline in the currently strong relationship between status position of family of origin and adult achievement.

Another feature of modern industrial society is the pervasive influence of large scale organizations on the achievement process. Not only does the modern society require a highly literate, technically proficient labor force, it also demands increasingly a labor force imbued with interpersonal skills. For as the numbers of persons in a given work-setting increase, the complexity of interaction leading to the organization's product expands enormously, and the costs of interpersonal conflict among organization members rise precipitously. Hence, organizations — whether they be industrial plants, commercial establishments, hospitals or universities — tend to discourage idio-syncratic (including innovative) behavior among members while re-warding non-disruptive, routinized, socially harmonious behavior.

In keeping with these conditions of adult work-life (and in an unknown but doubtless important degree in response to these con-ditions), the American system of education holds out its greatest rewards to students who are both academically proficient and socially tractable. The dominant goals of the school system thus harmonize with presumed basic requirements of the economy.

Of course, this sketch of complementary relations between school and economy is over-stated. Some large scale organizations are de-voted to innovation, while others permit greater innovative activity than the sketch implies. Some schools, from the elementary level to the graduate school level, stress capacities other than the narrowly academic and socially conforming. Yet the sketch, as a forecast of an emerging reality, is alarming.

This problem is taken up in the final selection of the book. McClelland describes how our educational system stresses the capac-ities indexed by I.Q. score and high academic performance as bases both for selecting those who will enter, and for determining those who will succeed, in college. He argues, then, that the criteria for selecting and sorting in higher education should be broadened to include such other attributes as curiosity, creativity, motivation to achieve, and interpersonal sensitivity. Allowing these attributes some place in determining who enters and graduates from college would, McClelland asserts, enrich the learning process — both for students and professors — in college. While not reducing materially the supply of technically proficient persons, such a development would infuse the nation's life — at work, at home, and in the community — with a leaven of innovative, risk-taking, sensitive citizens. Achievement in the United States, then, might come to be assessed in far broader terms than the current focus on success in work.

# A.

## THE PROBLEM OF METHODS

# FACILITATING DEVELOPMENT IN THE PRE-SCHOOL CHILD: SOCIAL AND PSYCHOLOGICAL PERSPECTIVES

MARTIN DEUTSCH

A large portion of the following discussion will be the examination of some of the psycho-social highways that criss-cross the early life of the child, and how socio-educational engineering might provide the most facilitating architecture for maximizing human achievement.

Massive evidence makes it clear that a child's social experience is a very influential factor in his development; yet it is also obvious that the relationship between experience and development is an extremely complex one. A basic assumption of the approach to be presented in this paper is that there is a continual and influential interpenetration of environmental experience and psychological development along a broad front, and that therefore simple cause-effect models can be accurate on only the grossest level.

In a sense, our current social dilemma has the usual contradictions that every period feels are unique to its particular time. Historically, the present era may or may not have more contradictions than other periods. But the rapid development of automated, highly skilled, labor-reducing techniques does have revolutionary consequences for man's relationship to the social order, to work and leisure, and to intellectual activity. Further, the level of our technology, particularly in the field of communication, creates conditions in which these new techniques are rapidly disseminated. Thus, the time within which institutional and structural adjustments can take place is greatly reduced. This necessitates the deliberate and planned manipulation of social conditions in order to avoid, or at least attenuate, the sometimes invidious consequences of rapid change.

In a society of abundance, there is an amazingly large segment of our population living in a subsociety of social, economic, and educational impoverishment. The estimates range from 20 to 40 per cent

Reprinted from the *Merrill-Palmer Quarterly* (Vol. 10, No. 3, July 1964, pp. 249-263) by permission of the publisher and the author.

of our population, depending on criteria. (For example see Harrington, 1963.) The problems associated with marginal employment and crowded, dehumanizing living conditions are, of course, characteristic of the lives of most of the peoples of the world. But here in this country we have the facilities, the productive capacity, and at least some of the knowledge required consciously to reorient social development. A necessary focus for such orientation should be the child, so that he can develop the requisite basic skills for the new technology and changing social institutions.

A thesis presented in this paper is that the behavioral scientist and the educator can facilitate the evolution of the educational institution so that it will be capable of preparing all children for optimal social participation, as the racial, social class, and sex gatekeepers become inoperative. The contemporary problems of education are to some extent a reflection of current technological, racial and urban conflicts inherent in accelerated social change. At the same time, the human sciences (though beset by similar problems) could become major instrumentalities for the resolution of social conflict, since they are among the few systems oriented toward change. For example, the intervention concepts in social psychology and psychiatry are relatively quite new. These disciplines can thus be seen as possible agents for the construction of blueprints to harmonize human needs with cultural transformations.

In general, the human sciences are moving from social and individual diagnosis to remedial therapies. Those sciences are now, in some of the more advanced thinking, concerned with primary prevention, ranging from mental illness and juvenile delinquency to disabilities in learning and socialization. To speculate on a possible avenue of future development, it might be that from this stage an orientation will develop toward assisting the individual to potentiate his intrinsic capacities for productive living and full individual realization.

This is by no means meant to minimize the importance of activities in other disciplines; rather, it is an attempt to specify the potential role and contribution of the human sciences. It must also be remarked that the knowledge available in the combined human sciences is still quite limited, and that too frequently formulas have been presented which are insufficiently related to scientific knowledge.

While to a major degree the behavioral sciences and education have run parallel courses, they have insufficiently interacted with and enriched each other. What better place is there to investigate meaningfully the development of learning processes — or of attitudes or of mental health — than in longitudinal studies in the context of the school, from the nursery school through college? It is always surprising to us how many educators are not aware of the exciting investigations of socialization, learning, and cognitive processes in the field of child development. On the other hand, too many social scientists look upon education and work in the educational field as "applied," "atheoretical," and somehow unrelated to the growth of a child into an adult. Just as medicine is the application of physiology, biochemistry, and similar sciences to human problems, so too could education be the application of the human sciences. As medicine discovers principles and laws that are continually being circulated back to its basic sciences, so could education not only evaluate and validate the principles which it derives from the human sciences, but also could lead toward the genesis of methods of influencing and accelerating individual growth.

In order to achieve such integration, a crucial historical difference between education and psychiatry, sociology, and psychology must be recognized. While the latter have the impetus coming from both their newness and their response to challenge, education has the disadvantage of a long and encumbering history. In a sense, the institution of education — the school — is the status quo. Often it must operate through politically oriented bureaucracies that continually inhibit its potential for change and for developing strategies to meet social crises such as those inherent in the new urban America. These bureaucracies are often so large that introduction of meaningful change, even when agreed on by the higher echelons, is limited by the clogging of communication channels with paper, red tape, and assorted other artifacts, and by the constraints under which the average classroom teacher operates.

Somehow, this great gap in the educational hierarchy, separating the educator and his concept from the classroom teacher with her idea, creates a discontinuity that results in much wasted energy and distortion of effort. A clear educational philosophy can come best from educators who are free enough from bureaucracy to communicate with the classroom teacher as a full professional, and to attenuate the burden of the past while setting up new relationships with the human sciences. Inherent in this approach is the necessity for effective cooperation between educators and behavioral scientists, so as to incorporate the growing knowledge of the socio-psychological development of the child into educational procedures in the interests of facilitating realization of his greatest intellectual and social potential.

The children most in need of help are from the economically and socially marginal and quasi-marginal segments of the community. These groups are the ones most caught in the technological and social changes; in many of our metropolitan areas they are becoming the majority of the center city population. It is in these groups that we find the highest proportion of unemployment, welfare support, and broken families. And it is in their children that we see the highest proportion of learning disabilities and school dropouts. While in the past it was possible to absorb most of such youth in unskilled, low-paying jobs, now the current adult generation is increasingly being replaced in such jobs by machines. With the number of unskilled and semi-skilled jobs decreasing, in order to find any place in the job market youth must now learn more complex functions, for which a successful educational experience is a prerequisite. This is a central problem for the total community, and a challenge for education. How it is met has wide ramifications for other underdeveloped areas outside our large cities and national boundaries.

There are various avenues of approach to the problem of both preventing learning disabilities and facilitating intellectual growth.

In recent years, there have been major curriculum renovations, enrichment programs, new systems for teaching mathematics and the sciences, programmed courses and teaching machines, as well as a multiplicity of new methods for teaching reading. However, in the disadvantaged, underdeveloped areas of our communities, where there is the large proportion of underachievers, these new methods are probably least applicable, being most often based on an assumption that the child has reached a particular level in skills which underlie them. As will be pointed out later, for the disadvantaged child this is an unwarranted assumption. For the most part, it is a correct assumption for the middle-class child; but here there are other problems. Too often, new methods are seen mainly as more effective techniques to help the child get into college and achieve occupation status goals, and the aim of education along with its innovations becomes narrowly pragmatic. This is not to say that new methods should not be devised and attempted, but rather, that they might be seen neither as solutions to underachievement nor as substitutions for the development and encouragement of intrinsic motivation toward intellectual mastery and scholastic achievement.

An approach that combines the preventive with the facilitating — and which would establish a basis for the absorption of new methods — is that of planned intervention at the earlier periods of development of the various components of the intellectual spectrum. Evidence which is accumulating points more and more to the influence of background variables on the patterns of language and cognitive development of the child, and a subsequent diffusion of the effects of such patterns into all areas of the child's academic and psychological performance. Deprived backgrounds thus lead to the inadequacy of such patterns. What is proposed is that experiential inadequacies in the social background can be compensated for by a planned enrichment, channeled through improved schools.

Reference has been made to the constellation of factors in lower-class life which are associated with a limited range of experiential variability available to the child. Of course, there are probably differing clusters of economic, social, and family factors associated with greater or lesser retardation. But the fact remains that lower social class status apparently predisposes to scholastic retardation, even though not all children are equally affected. Therefore, before discussing learning processes in the school it might be helpful to delineate some of the major features of urban slum life.

Geographically, there are crowded and dilapidated tenements quite at variance with the TV image of how people live. If the people are Negro, Puerto Rican, or Mexican-American, or poor mountain white, life is in a more-or-less segregated community. There are likely to be extremely crowded apartments, high rates of unemployment, chronic economic insecurity, a disproportionate number of broken families, and (particularly in the case of the Negro) continual exposure to denigration and social ostracism of varying degrees. The educational level of the adults tends to be quite limited. In the homes, there is likely to be a nearly complete absence of books, relatively few toys, and, in many instances, nothing except a few normal home-objects which may be adapted as playthings. In addition — particularly but not exclusively where relatively new in-migrants are concerned — there is a great deal of horizontal mobility. The result is a pattern of life that exposes a child to a minimum of direct contacts with the central channels of our culture. The conditions of social inequality, the absence of an accessible opportunity structure, and the frequent non-availability of successful adult male models create an atmosphere that is just not facilitating to individual development. Moreover, the everyday problems of living, particularly those of economic insecurity and a multiplicity of children, leave minimum time for the adults who may be present to assist the child in exploring the world, to reward him for successful completion of tasks, or to help him in the development of a differentiated self-concept. Even in homes which are not broken, the practical manifestations of economic marginality result in the father sometimes holding two jobs and having little time for interaction with the child. We have found in various studies that children from these circumstances have relatively few shared or planned family activities, again resulting in a narrowing of experience.

The implications of these environmental conditions for the development of the child can be appreciated in terms of Hunt's (1961) discussion of Piaget's developmental theories. He points out that, according to Piaget, ". . . the rate of development is in substantial part, but certainly not wholly, a function of environmental circumstances. Change in circumstances is required to force the accommodative modifications of schemata that constitute development. Thus, the greater the variety of situations to which the child must accommodate his behavioral structures, the more differentiated and mobile they become. Thus, the more new things a child has seen and the more he has heard, the more things he is interested in seeing and hearing. Moreover, the more variation in reality with which he has coped, the greater is his capacity for coping" (pp. 258–259). In essence, it is this richness and variety which a compensatory enrichment program must provide.

Previously, I have said that emphasis on the importance of variety in the environment implies the detrimental effects of lack of variety (Deutsch, 1963). I then postulated that a child from any circumstance, who has been deprived of a substantial portion of the variety of stimuli to which he is maturationally capable of responding, is likely to be deficient in the equipment required for school learning. This does not necessarily imply restriction in the quantity of stimulation; rather, it refers to a restriction in variety — i.e., restriction to only a segment of the spectrum of stimulation potentially available. In addition to such restriction in variety, from the description of the slum environment, it might be postulated that the segments made available to children from that background tend to have poorer and less systematic ordering of stimulation sequences, thereby being less useful to the growth and activation of cognitive potential.

The most promising agency for providing environmental compensations is the school. It is through this institution, which reaches every child, that the requisite stimulation for facilitating learning, psychological maturation, and acculturation can be most efficiently organized and programmed. Yet it is now estimated that up to 60 per cent of lower-class children are retarded two years or more in reading, by the time they leave the elementary school.

Before we place the entire responsibility on the school, however, an important fact must be noted. The overwhelming finding of studies on the relationship between social class and learning, school performance, and the like is that children from backgrounds of social marginality enter the first grade already behind their middle-class counterparts in a number of skills highly related to scholastic achievement. They are simply less prepared to meet the demands of the school and the classroom situation. Conversely, though, the school has failed to prepare to meet their needs. The failure of the educational institution to overcome the children's environmentally determined handicaps too often results in early failure, increasing alienation, and an increasingly greater gap between the lower-class and middle-class youngsters as they progress through school. In other words, intellectual and achievement differences between lower-class and middle-class children are smallest at the first grade level, and tend to increase through the elementary school years. It is here where the interaction between school and early environment, instead of having a facilitating influence, has a negative effect. While the school does not contribute to the initial problem (except through its effects on the previous generation), neither does it contribute to the overcoming of the initial handicaps.

It would seem quite reasonable, in the light of this discussion and its supporting evidence, to better prepare the child to meet the school's demands before he enters the first grade, and before there has been an accumulation of failure experiences and maladaptive behavior. It would also seem eminently reasonable that the school should accept this responsibility. At the same time, it does not seem reasonable that an institution which so far has generally failed to meet its responsibility to this group should simply be given a mandate, without the incorporation of new and appropriate knowledge and techniques. Here is where the knowledge from the behavioral sciences can be put to its most effective use.

For example, all peoples have difficulties in spanning cultural discontinuities, and the entrance of the child into school for the first time places him in an environment which, in many respects, is discontinuous with his home. This discontinuity is minimal for the middle-class child, who is likely to have had the importance of school imprinted in his consciousness from the earliest possible age. For him, therefore, the school is very central and is continuous with the totality of his life experiences. As a result there are few incongruities between his school experiences and any others he is likely to have had, and there are intrinsic motivating and molding properties in the school situation to which he has been highly sensitized. Further, there is more likely to be contiguity in the school-faculty orientation with his home-family orientation. Failure can be interpreted to him in appropriate and familiar terms, and methods of coping with it can be incorporated, increasing the motivation or offering the necessary rewards, goals, or punishments to effect the desired change in performance.

For the lower-class child there is not the same contiguity or continuity. He does not have the same coping mechanisms for internalizing success or psychologically surviving failure in the formal learning setting. If the lower-class child starts to fail, he does not have the same kinds of operationally significant and functionally relevant support from his family or community — or from the school. Further, because of the differences in preparation, he is more likely to experience failure.

In this context, let us consider White's concept of competence motivation as a primary drive. The middle-class child comes to school prepared, for the most part, to meet the demands made on him. The expectations of his teachers are that he will succeed. As he confronts material that is congruent with his underlying skills, he is able to succeed; and thus he achieves the feeling of efficacy which White (1959) points out is so necessary to the "effectance motivation" which promotes continuing positive interaction with the environment. The lower-class child, on the other hand, experiences the middle-class-oriented school as discontinuous with his home environment, and further, comes to it unprepared in the basic skills on which the curriculum is founded. The school becomes a place which makes puzzling demands, and where failure is frequent and feelings of competence are subsequently not generated. Motivation decreases, and the school loses its effectiveness.

It is in the transitional years from the pre-school period through the elementary school years that the child is first subject to the influence and the requirements of the broader culture. It is then that two environments are always present for him: the home environment and the school environment. But it is also in these transitional (and especially in the pre-transitional) years that the young organism is most malleable. Thus, that is the point at which efforts might best be initiated to provide a third — an intervention — environment to aid in the reconciliation of the first two. Such reconciliation is required because, especially for the child from a disadvantaged background, there are wide discrepancies between the home and school milieus. In the intervention environment, preventive and remedial measures can be applied to eliminate or overcome the negative effects of the discontinuities.

The importance of early intervention is underlined in the summary by Fowler (1962) of findings on cognitive learning in infancy and early childhood. He points out that seemingly minimal cognitive stimulation in the pre-school years, when organized appropriately to the capabilities of the child, can be highly effective in accelerating the development of intellectual functions.

Critical and optimal time periods for many aspects of development and learning in both humans and animals have long been studied. These concepts are always related to stimulation or interaction between the organism and the environment, and thus represent an important additional dimension when we discuss influences on development and behavior. Apparently, it is not sufficient merely to provide particular stimulation for the growing individual; it must be supplied at a special time, or within particular time limits, if it is to have the most desired effect. Thus, a program intended to compensate for environmental deprivation would be most effective if supplied at a particular stage in the life of the child.

Scott's (1962) summary of the relevant research information on critical stages in development indicates that the period of greatest plasticity is during the time of initial socialization. Since the bulk of the literature in this area is on animals, generalizations must be carefully confined. But seemingly, as one ascends the phylogenetic scale, there are greater ranges of time during which the organism has high levels of plasticity and receptivity. There is an insufficient body of data to hypothesize a most critical period for learning in the human child, and there are probably different critical or optimal periods for different functions. However, at about three or four years of age there is a period which would roughly coincide with the early part of what Piaget calls the "preoperational stage." It is then that the child is going through the later stages of early socialization; that he is required to focus his attention and monitor auditory and visual stimuli; and that he learn through language to handle simple symbolic representations. It is at this three- to four-year-old level that organized and systematic stimulation, through a structured and articulated learning program, might most successfully prepare the child for the more formal and demanding structure of the school. It is here, at this early age, that we can postulate that compensation for prior deprivation can most meaningfully be introduced. And, most important, there is considerably less that has to be compensated for at this age than exists when, as a far more complex and at least somewhat less plastic organism, the child gets to the first grade.

This position and its implications for specially organized early stimulation of the child find support in a recent article by Bruner (1961) on cognitive consequences of sensory deprivation. He says: "Not only does early deprivation rob the organism of the opportunity of constructing models of the environment, it also prevents the development of efficient strategies for evaluating information — for digging out what leads to what and with what likelihood. Robbed of development in this sphere, it becomes the more difficult to utilize probable rather than certain cues, the former requiring a more efficient strategy than the latter" (pp. 202–203). Bruner goes on to a discussion of nonspecific transfer of training in which, I think, he provides the most incontrovertible foundation for a structured, systematic pre-school enrichment and retraining program which would compensate, or attempt to compensate, for the deficiencies in the slum environment. His discussion is not of slums or compensation, but in his pointing up the importance of the "normally rich" environment, the serious cognitive consequences of the deprived environment are thrown into relief. Bruner says, ". . . nonspecific or generic transfer involves the learning of general rules and strategies for coping with highly common features of the environment" (p. 203). After pointing out that Piaget ". . . remarks upon the fact that cognitive growth consists of learning how to handle the great informational transformations like reversibility, class identity, and the like" and that Piaget speaks of these as "strategies for dealing with or, better for creating usable information," Bruner proposes: ". . . that exposure to normally rich environments makes the development of such strategies possible by providing intervening opportunity for strategic trial and error" (p. 203).

What Bruner talks about under "trial and error" requires a certain level of motivation and exploratory efforts. I have previously discussed the possible role of early failure experiences in influencing the motivational and goal orientations, and the self-expectancies, of the lower-class child. When the lower-class child gets into first grade, too frequently his cognitive, sensory, and language skills are insufficiently developed to cope with what for him are the complex and confusing stimuli offered by the school. It is the interaction of these motivational and maturational dynamics that makes it extremely important for society, through institutions such as the school, to offer the lower-class child an organized and reasonably orderly program of stimulation, at as early an age as possible, to compensate for possible cognitive deficit.

The focus has been on deficit because of the general hypothesis that the experiential deprivations associated with poverty are disintegrative and subtractive from normative growth expectancies. The extent of academic failure and reading retardation associated with lower-class status — and especially with minority group membership within the lower class — makes it imperative that we study the operational relationship between social conditions and these deficits, and the subsequent failure of the school to reverse the tendency toward cumulative retardation in the primary grades.

Our work has been directed particularly toward delineating the effects of conditions of life on cognitive structures. For an understanding of these relationships and the scientific development of enrichment programs, we have emphasized the role of specific social attributes and experiences in the development of language and verbal behavior, of concept formation and organization, of visual and auditory discrimination, of general environmental orientation, and of self-concepts and motivation; and of all of this to school performance. It is the areas mentioned which apparently are essential to the acquisition of scholastic skills, and around which a basic curriculum for early childhood should be developed. Pragmatically, this must be a program which successfully teaches disadvantaged children.

*Examination of the literature yields no explanation or justification for any child with an intact brain, and who is not severely disturbed, not to learn all the basic scholastic skills. The failure of such children to learn is the failure of the schools to develop curricula consistent with the environmental experiences of the children and their subsequent initial abilities and disabilities.*

As has been emphasized previously in this paper, a compensatory program for children, starting at three or four years of age, might provide the maximum opportunity for prevention of future disabilities and for remediation of current skill deficiencies. In addition, such a program might serve to minimize the effect of the discontinuity between the home and school environments, thereby enhancing the child's functional adjustment to school requirements.

For an early enrichment program, one model available is that developed by Maria Montessori (1959) in the slums of Italy. Though her theoretical system need not be critically evaluated here, there is much in her technology that could productively be re-examined and incorporated in compensatory programs. Basically, this includes the organization of perceptual stimuli in the classroom, so that singular properties become more observable, one at a time, without the distraction of competing, overly complex elements. For example, materials used to convey and illustrate the concept of size and size differential are all the same color and shape. This maximizes the attentional properties of size, and minimizes competing elements. Use of such materials should make it possible for size discriminations to be learned more easily. This method is, of course, carried over to many fields, and the availability of such stimuli under the Montessori system gives the child an opportunity to select materials consistent with his own developmental capabilities. This makes possible success experience, positive reinforcement, and subsequent enhancement of involvement and motivation. The attention to the minutiae of learning, and the systematic exposure to new learning elements based on prior experience, could allow for the development of individualized learning profiles. This would be particularly appropriate for a compensatory program, where there is a great deal of variation in individual needs.

There is, however, a major variable which is apparently inadequately handled by this method, and that is language.

Language can be thought of as a crucial ingredient in concept formation, problem-solving, and in the relating to and interpretation of the environment. Current data available to the author and his co-workers tend to indicate that class differences in perceptual abilities and general environmental orientation decrease with chronological age, while language differences tend to increase.

In a social-class-related language analysis, Bernstein (1960), an English sociologist, has pointed out that the lower class tends to use informal language and mainly to convey concrete needs and immediate consequences, while the middle-class usage tends to be more formal and to emphasize the relating of concepts.[1] This difference between these two milieus, then, might explain the finding in some of our recent research that the middle-class fifth grade child has an advantage over the lower-class fifth grader in tasks where precise and somewhat abstract language is required for solution. Further, Bernstein's reasoning would again emphasize the communication gap which can exist between the middle-class teacher and the lower-class child.

One can postulate that the absence of well-structured routine and activity in the home is reflected in the difficulty that the lower-class child has in structuring language. The implication of this for curriculum in the kindergarten and nursery school would be that these children should be offered a great deal of verbalized routine and regulation, so that positive expectations can be built up in the child and then met. It can also be postulated that differences in verbal usage are directly attributable to the level of interaction of the child with the adult, and at this age to a lesser extent, with peers.

In observations of lower-class homes, it appears that speech sequences seem to be temporally very limited and poorly structured syntactically. It is thus not surprising to find that a major focus of deficit in the children's language development is syntactical organization and subject continuity. But in analysis of expressive and receptive language data on samples of middle- and lower-class children at the first and fifth grade levels, there are indications that the lower-class child has more expressive language ability than is generally recognized or than emerges in the classroom. The main differences between the social classes seem to lie in the level of syntactical organization. If, as is indicated in this research, with proper stimulation a surprisingly high level of expressive language functioning is available to the same children who show syntactical deficits, then we might conclude that the language variables we are dealing with here are by-products of social experience rather than indices of basic ability or intellectual level. This again suggests a vital area to be included in any pre-school enrichment program: training in the use of word sequences to relate and unify cognitions.

A language training program would require the creation of a rich, individualized language environment, where words are repeatedly placed in a meaningful context, and where the child is allowed multiple opportunities for expressive language demonstrations as well as for receiving language stimuli under optimal conditions and being encouraged to make appropriate responses. More specifically, stress could be placed on the following areas: orienting feedback, so that if the child says "give me the ——" or "where is ——," the teacher consciously instructs him in a complete sentence as to direction, location, placement, context, etc.; the systematic attempt to increase vocabulary; allowing the child to sort symbols, pictures, and artifacts with letters and words; verbal labelling practice; relating objects and experiences verbally, for example, constructing stories using specified objects and events; every child completing differently incomplete stories suggested by the teacher; reinforcing and encouraging the simultaneous articulation of motor behavior. Through the verbal area it is also possible to train memory, to some extent to train auditory discrimination, and to improve environmental orientation. However, it is not the purpose of this paper to go into a detailed description of potential enrichment procedures.

Working out compensatory programs is based on the assumption that retardation in achievement results from the interaction of inadequately prepared children with inadequate schools and insufficient curricula. This in turn is based on the contention that this large proportion of children is not failing because of inferior innate resources. Also implied is the assumption that one does not sit by and wait for children to "unfold," either on the intellectual or behavioral levels. Rather, it is asserted that growth requires guidance of stimulation, and that this is particularly valid with regard to the child who does not receive the functional prerequisites for school learning in the home. Hunt (1961) points out that ". . . the counsel from experts on child-rearing during the third and much of the fourth decades of the twentieth century to let children be while they grow and to avoid excessive stimulation was highly unfortunate" (p. 362). This is particularly true with regard to lower-class children. We have found that, controlling for socio-economic status, children with some preschool experience have significantly higher intelligence test scores at the fifth grade than do children with no pre-school experience (Deutsch and Brown, 1964).

But it is not necessary to consider special education programs only on the pre-school level, even though that is what has been emphasized here. Rather, to assure stability of progress, it would be desirable to continue special programs for several more years. The construction of a pre-school program does not absolve a community or a school system from the responsibility to construct an effective strategy for teaching the marginal youngster from kindergarten on. In fact, if there is to be a reversal of some of the sequelae associated with poverty discussed in this paper, programs must have continuity, at least through the period of the establishment of the basic scholastic learning skills. This means that it is necessary for the community to support kinder-gartens with reasonable enrollments and adequate equipment, as well as specialized training of staff. As far as the primary grades are con-cerned, the continuation of special programming through establish-ment of basic skills would involve probably the time through the third grade year. This level is used, because there is empirical reason to believe that levels of achievement for different social classes start their greatest divergence here. This is probably so because here the work begins to become less concrete and more abstract, more dependent on language symbolization, and, probably most important, more related to good reading skills. For these reasons, it would seem that the child from the pre-school and enriched kindergarten classes might best remain in a special ungraded sequence through the third grade level, a period in which he could be saturated with basic skill training, and not be allowed to move on until he has attained basic competence in the skills required by the higher grades. Such an ungraded school would also be of considerable interest theoretically, inasmuch as the child would be in its program through the preoperational stage de-lineated by Piaget. This should make it possible to devise a systematic curriculum that is consistent with the actual developmental levels of the child during the early childhood period.

Fowler (1962) points out that —

Few systematic methods have been devised for educating young children, especially in complicated subject matter. We have in mind methods for simplifying and organizing the presentation of cognitive stimuli. Equally important, methods must be sufficiently flexible and play oriented to be adaptable to the primary learning levels and personality organization char-acteristic of the infant and young child.

The advantages of utilizing the now relatively untapped "preschool" years for cognitive education are, of course, manifest. Most obvious, is the availability of more years of childhood to absorb the increasingly complex technology of modern society, a technology already requiring many of the more productive years of development to acquire. A second is the less evident but more crucial possibility that conceptual learning sets, habit patterns, and interest areas, may well be more favorably established at early than at later stages of the developmental cycle (pp. 145–146).

There are those people who seem to fear the word "cognitive," sometimes correctly, because they are reacting to the over-stringent mechanical models of the past. These models are not what is meant. The potentiation of human resources through the stimulation of cognitive growth could represent a primary therapeutic method for developing positive self-attitudes and a meaningful self-realization. For the lower-class child especially, I would postulate that time is extremely valuable if the deficits are not to be cumulative and to permeate the entire functioning of the child.

The overgeneralized influence on some sections of early childhood education of the emphasis in the child guidance movement upon protecting the child from stress, creating a supportive environment, and resolving emotional conflicts has done more to misdirect and retard the fields of child care, guidance, and development than any other single influence. The effect has especially operated to make these fields ineffective in responding to the problems of integrating and educating the non-white urban child. These orientations have conceived of the child as being always on the verge of some disease process, and have assigned to themselves the role of protecting the child in the same manner that a zoo-keeper arranges for the survival of his charges. Too frequently a philosophy of protectiveness that asks only about possible dangers has prevailed over any question of potential stimulation of development. The attitude that perhaps helped to create this policy of protectionism can also be seen in the suburban "mom-ism" that so many sociologists and psychoanalysts have commented on. The child is a far healthier and stronger little organism, with more intrinsic motivation for variegated experience and learning, than the over-protectionists have traditionally given him credit for.

As Fowler (1961) states further —

Much if not most of the energy in child psychology and development in late years has been concentrated on the child's personality, perceptual motor, and socioemotional functioning and development. Originating primarily as a reaction to historically inadequate and stringent methods, fears have generalized to encompass early cognitive learning per se as intrinsically hazardous to development. As legitimate areas of study, the contributions of studies on perceptual-motor and socio-emotional problems are obvious. But in the field of child guidance, interest in these areas has come to permeate and dominate work in child development almost to the exclusion of work on cognitive learning. In harking constantly to the dangers of premature cognitive training, the image of the "happy," socially adjusted child has tended to expunge the image of the thoughtful and intellectually educated child. Inevitably, in this atmosphere, research (and education) in cognition has lagged badly, especially since the 1930's, not only for the early years of childhood but for all ages (p. 145).

And as Hunt (1961) says: "The problem for the management of child development is to find out how to govern the encounters that children have with their environments to foster both an optimally rapid rate of intellectual development and a satisifying life" (pp. 362–363).

A curriculum as discussed here should serve both for the primary prevention of the social deviancies associated with deprivation and for the stimulation of healthy growth and utilization of individual resources. This orientation would represent one effective method of offering opportunities to all peoples to overcome and break the chains of social and historical limitations that have been externally imposed on them. This of course has immediate significance to the current critical questions in both race relations and education in America.

## REFERENCE

1. In a recent discussion, Bernstein indicated that he was replacing the terms "public" and "formal" with the terms "elaborated" and "restricted." He feels that the latter offer better analytic distinctions and operate at a higher level of abstraction.

## BIBLIOGRAPHY

Bernstein, B. Language and social class. *Brit. J. Sociol.*, 1960, **11**, 271–276.

Bruner, J. S. The cognitive consequences of early sensory deprivation. In P. Solomon (Ed.), *Sensory deprivation*. Cambridge: Harvard Univ. Press, 1961. Pp. 195–207.

Deutsch, M. The disadvantaged child and the learning process. In A. H. Passow (Ed.), *Education in depressed areas*. New York: Bur. Pub., Teach. Coll., Columbia Univer., 1963. Pp. 163–179.

Deutsch, M. Minority group and class status as related to social and personality factors in scholastic achievement. *Monogr. Society for Applied Anthropology*, 1960, No. 2.

Deutsch, M. & Brown, B. Social influences in Negro-White intelligence differences. *J. soc. Issues*, April, 1964, 24–35.

Fowler, W. Cognitive learning in infancy and early childhood. *Psychol. Bull.*, 1962, **59,** 116–152.

Harrington, M. *The other America.* New York: Macmillan Company, 1962.

Hunt, J. McV. *Intelligence and experience.* New York: Ronald Press, 1961.

Montessori, Maria. *Education for a new world.* Wheaton, Ill.: Theosophical Press, 1959.

Scott, J. P. Critical periods in behavioral development. *Science*, 1962, **138,** 949–955.

White, R. Motivation reconsidered: The concept of competence. *Psychol. Rev.*, 1959, **66,** 297–333.

# B.

## THE PROBLEM OF GOALS

# ENCOURAGING EXCELLENCE

## DAVID C. McCLELLAND

Americans have already discovered, and are pursuing with alarming vigor, a system for encouraging excellence. It may be summed up briefly in the following formula: *the best boys should go to the best schools and then on to the best jobs.* The implications of the formula are eminently practical: the nation engages in a country-wide talent search to discover by means of objective psychological tests who the ablest youngsters are. The tests identify the ablest students regardless of race, creed, color, economic condition, or teacher's opinion. Once discovered, these students ideally go to the best schools. In order to facilitate the process, the schools, in their turn, participate in the talent search and encourage the best students to apply. Since many of the colleges currently defined as best are in the expensive Ivy League, National Merit Scholarships are provided so that the ablest young people can attend them. Once they are in the best colleges, the students, if they continue to do their academic best, can look forward to being recruited by professional schools or business for the most important positions in developing and serving the nation.

The American formula for encouraging excellence involves a single upward mobility ladder based on academic performance and running from West Redwing, Minnesota, to Harvard, to President of the United States or General Dynamics. The formula is an attractive one and has always appealed to important American values — like belief in achievement and in giving everyone a fair chance to get ahead according to his merit. Only recently, however, have we been in a position to put it into effect with any real efficiency. We have

Reprinted from *Daedalus* (Vol. 90, No. 4, Fall 1961, "Excellence and Leadership in a Democracy"), published by the American Academy of Arts and Sciences (Boston, Massachusetts), copyright © 1961 by the American Academy of Arts and Sciences, by permission of the publisher and the author. Copyright © 1962 by the Columbia University Press in Graubard and Holton, *Excellence and Leadership.*

developed objective psychological tests that can be and have been administered to tens of thousands, if not millions of students, so that we can discover the ablest ones quickly and within small margins of error. We have begun to get better organized in providing nation-wide scholarship competitions administered by some of the better universities or independently. Mass communication networks — the radio, the press, TV — have knit the country together so that the talented boy in West Redwing has a better chance of knowing than he did a generation ago that Ivy League colleges exist and that in the rankings of institutions for academic merit, they stand at the top. Shouldn't he, as the ablest boy in his town, go to the place where he can get the best education and have the greatest chance to realize his own potential and be of most use to his country? Isn't this the model of success most Americans have in mind when they think about "encouraging excellence" today? To be sure, local considerations still apply — alumni bring pressure to admit a quarterback, or Alabamans may not want their sons to go out of the state to school, but such events may be viewed as unfortunate imperfections in the idealized, rational model in terms of which most thinking people are planning the future of the nation.

In fact, to raise any questions about the rational model is a little like being against virtue. It is so obviously practical, efficient, democratic, and nonauthoritarian. For, after all, no one is forcing anybody to do anything. In fact, the model calls only for creating a climate of per-suasion in which excellence is defined, identified, and encouraged to go to the top. Why, then, does it make us slightly uneasy? Why does it positively give John Hersey the shivers in *The Child Buyer?* His Orwellian nightmare revolves precisely around what happens when the ablest boy in a small town is offered the "best" kind of edu-cation (though it is considerably different from Harvard's!) in order to maximize his own potentialities and his contribution to his country. Why does Jerome S. Bruner state with some concern that "the danger signs of meritocracy and a new form of competitiveness are already in evidence"?[1] What has led Dael Wolfle of the American Associa-tion for the Advancement of Science to insist on the diversity of talent?[2]

Let us look at the balance sheet for a moment: what do we gain by such a system and what do we lose? On the credit side, it has certainly helped to set uniformly high academic standards everywhere and to provide an upward channel of mobility for talented youngsters no matter what their social class or racial background may be. Not even Texans can argue for the superiority of their academic institutions if their students regularly score lower on scholastic achievement tests. And no one can deny that a high test score and a National Merit Scholarship have given many an underprivileged boy or girl a break they would never otherwise have had. These are important matters: we believe in an open society with rewards given for uniformly high standards of achievement and, to a very considerable extent, we have created one. Access to high-level positions in our society probably depends less on social class background and more on individual merit than in any other country today.[3] Why complain? We do indeed have a great deal to be proud of, and a long way to go in introducing the academic merit system everywhere in the country, yet we must also look ahead lest such a system lead us into a kind of overspecialized excellence that would be as fatal in the long run as the overspecialization of the dinosaur.

If we restrict ourselves to the better colleges, or what are called more euphemistically the "preferred" colleges, the debit side of the merit system is also impressive though less obvious. Consider the extreme case: suppose the better colleges should admit only the academically talented — those whose grades and scores in scholastic aptitude tests are high. The supposition is not unreal for many of them; the Directors of Admissions can proudly report annually that a higher and higher proportion of the freshmen are from the top quarter of their secondary-school classes. What is wrong with such a method of encouraging or rewarding excellence?

The core of the problem lies in the definition of excellence implicit in our current nation-wide attempts to recognize and encourage talent. Ability means, for the purposes of these tests, academic excellence, skill in taking examinations, in following instructions and finding solutions to problems set by others. This is an extraordinarily important type of excellence. It can be discovered by techniques already well developed. It is related to success in many different types of occupations. It deserves and needs encouragement, particularly in lower-class areas as yet untouched by the general American recognition of the importance of academic achievement. But it is not the only type of excellence. It just happens to be the only one that we psychologists can measure at the present time with any degree of certainty, and, therefore, it tends to get more than its share of attention.

If the better colleges go on admitting solely or primarily on this basis, everyone will lose in the long run. The better colleges will lose because they are excluding students whose excellence, though not so obvious, can contribute much to making a college experience more educational for all concerned. Society will lose because young people with very important nonacademic talents will not be exposed to the most liberalizing kind of education. Most importantly, the students themselves will lose — both those admitted and those not admitted — because the system tells them that there is *only one kind of excellence that really counts:* the ability to take examinations and get good grades in school. A single standard of success is being promoted, which, in Riesman's telling phrase, tends to homogenize our cultural value system. Americans all too often, anyway, end up wanting exactly the same thing: the same car, the same standard of living, the same toothpaste, the same wife — all as promoted on television or in the newspapers. Now they must all want the same education — so long as it is the *best* (like the best toothpaste, which is like every other toothpaste only more so) and so long as they can demonstrate what they got out of it, all in exactly the same way, by getting good grades and being promoted upward on the identical ladder of success in the system. So the boy who does not "make" it, who does not get good grades, or get into the "best" college, may well define himself as a failure in terms of the only norm that seems to count. What satisfaction can he get out of alternative paths of life, even out of an alternative kind of education, particularly when he knows that education at a "good" college is increasingly a necessity for leadership in our society? If he is a boy with political talents, and mediocre academic ones, is it likely any more that he can be President of the United States like Harry Truman without a college degree? How can he feel that he can contribute importantly to society if he does not make the academic grade? Or if, on the other side of the picture, a girl happens to have excellent academic talent, how can she feel that she can contribute to society if she marries and has a family, which prevents her from following the professional career that the merit system tells her is the one thing she is ideally suited for? Overstressing academic merit can discourage young people with types of talent that are very important for our society and can create in them a discontent and sense of frustration that lasts a lifetime. Must we not encourage other varieties of excellence along with the ability to do well in course work?

To be sure, there have always been those who have insisted on the importance of musical and artistic talents or athletic prowess. I even know of a case in which a college director of admissions admitted an excellent 'cello player with a "C" average prediction to complete the college string quartet, though nowadays in one of the better colleges he would have been most embarrassed to admit publicly that he had given similar preference to a quarterback. But with all due respect for such visible talents, I should like to focus attention for a moment on less visible, more intangible types of excellence. For the fact of the matter is that Americans are "rating and ranking happy." What they can see and measure on a scale of excellence, they will encourage. They can recognize musical and athletic talent early and, therefore, they find ways of giving youngsters with these talents the encouragement and rewards they deserve. But my concern is with important types of excellence that are not so readily recognizable or so obviously meriting reward.

Let me give three brief illustrations of what I have in mind. For over a dozen years now, I have been concerned as a professional psychologist with understanding the nature of a particular human motive called the "need for Achievement," the desire to do a good job of work. In a crude sort of way, we can measure it, and by now we have developed a pretty fair understanding of what people are like in whom such a need is very strong.[4] To oversimplify a little, they seem characterized by "the entrepreneurial spirit," by a desire and a capacity to do well in situations which challenge their ingenuity and resourcefulness. They are particularly apt to be successful in business, rather than the professions, and wherever a large number of them collect in a particular country at a particular time, the country has tended to show rapid economic development. In short, these men represent a valuable national resource, a type of excellence that should be encouraged. In a very real sense, it is on them that the future economic well-being of everyone in the country rests. Yet their need for Achievement does not lead them to do particularly well in school. Perhaps the reason lies partly in the fact that they like to solve problems set by themselves, rather than those set for them by others; but the fact remains that whatever the reason, they are not likely to be viewed with particular approval by their teachers or selected for help by present tests of academic excellence. Where do they fit in the current system for encouraging excellence?

Or consider another example — curiosity. My colleague Richard Alpert and his students want to measure this important human characteristic and to discover how it can be encouraged by the educational process. But note how it requires a type of behavior in a sense directly opposed to the academic excellence so feverishly promoted by our testing and grading systems. That is, curiosity may be defined as a desire to know, or as the knowledge of, things one is not supposed to know; whereas academic excellence is defined as knowing what one is supposed to know or has been taught. To test for curiosity, one might have to inquire into matters that the student had not been taught at all or that he could not be expected to know because of insufficient background in his previous training or in the test item itself. Such procedures might be unfair to the good and conscientious student, but they tap a type of excellence not currently identifiable or assisted in any way. Let me say again: I do not want to discourage academic excellence or unduly praise curiosity. For the moment I want merely to argue that curiosity is an important type of excellence that we should be concerned with developing.

Finally, let us consider briefly the problem of excellence in the other half of the human race, women. Ours is a male-oriented society. It is so male-oriented that the women, particularly the better educated ones, have tended to accept male definitions of excellence and have felt unhappy about not being able to achieve great success in terms of such standards. A recent nation-wide survey has clearly shown that women are unhappier and worry more than men.[5] They ought to. They are caught up in a system which does not encourage or recognize the types of excellence at which they are best. They enter the competition in academic skill just as the boys do. They receive National Merit Scholarships. They go to the best colleges; but there the system is apt to break down. Their superior academic performance suits them much less for their future role in life than it does the boys. They do not become President of the United States or of General Dynamics, or even very often Nobel-prize-winning scientists. It is small wonder that many of them feel frustrated and unhappy over lost opportunities. They have been gulled. They have swallowed the male definition of excellence, in terms of full-time work, visible achievements, measurable results (e.g., money earned), the manipulation of nature, etc. There are other types of human excellence without which life would hardly be worth living, and I do not mean sewing or the art of polite conversation. I do mean such characteristics as sensitivity to other human beings, compassion, richness and variety of imaginative life, or a lifelong concern for a particular scientific problem, whether one is paid to work on it or not. These are less visible and less measurable types of human excellence, but nonetheless important for all that.

Here we encounter a problem that will shock some and amuse others. Should these qualities be measured? Should we psychologists try to find ways of discovering who are the young people with the highest need for Achievement, the greatest curiosity, the most social sensitivity, or the greatest imaginativeness? The romantic answer is "no." Must we, after all, bring even these human qualities into the same "rating and ranking" competition that currently marks the field of academic competence? The practical answer, I am afraid, is "yes," for two reasons. On the one hand, no one can stop the psychologists; they are already developing crude measures of many such qualities outside the strictly academic sphere and are likely to be increasingly successful at it in the years to come.[6] On the other hand, a very good case can be made for the use of such other measures in defense against the exclusive use of academic criteria in deciding what kind of excellence to encourage.

Careful studies have repeatedly shown that, despite the fact that most human judges insist on taking other factors into account in making selections of any kind, their final decisions are almost perfectly correlated with the single quantitative score that they have, namely, some form of academic achievement or aptitude test score.[7] They like to think that they are taking other factors into account, but in actuality they do not, and the reason is simple: the other factors are not expressed in quantitative terms, but come in the form of vague verbal descriptions or recommendations that are very hard to compare in making final choices. So the choices are made in terms of the one available quantitative measure: for academic promise. If we want to encourage a concern for other types of excellence in this merit-oriented society of ours, we may have to develop measures of other types of excellence.

But suppose they can be identified. How are they to be encouraged? Does it mean the schools should teach and grade curiosity, the need for Achievement, imaginativeness, and sensitivity? That way lies certain disaster. It is caricatured by those educators who have argued that everyone must be good at something and that therefore the schools must discover and teach that something, whether it be cooperativeness in play or preparation for happiness in marriage. Cultivating other types of excellence need bring no changes in the curriculum of the schools, though it may require a change in the attitude of some teachers. Teachers still have to teach content — geology, English, mathematics, or social science — but they can encourage human beings. They can teach in ways that show a genuine respect for curiosity or the entrepreneurial spirit. The schools have always feared that concern for other types of excellence than academic performance would lower standards. Why should it? Suppose a student of algebra is curious and spends so much time picking up odd bits of information about mathematics that he does not learn his algebra. Should he be given an "A" for his curiosity? Certainly not, because he has not learned his algebra. However, it does not follow that the teacher should not encourage curiosity, admire the student's willingness to go off on his own, or perhaps even change the way he teaches mathematics so as to engage the student's curiosity more. The teacher-student relation should not be limited strictly to the grade-giving function, nor should the grade come to summarize all that a student has learned in college or high school.

As a matter of fact, the human qualities we are speaking of do not develop by formal teaching nor do they require the external rewards of grades. How can a student be taught to be curious in the usual way? A contradiction is involved. Can he be taught that he is supposed to learn what he is not supposed to learn? Certain "progressive" schools have come to grief precisely by trying to give instruction in such matters as creativity and curiosity, which almost by definition defy formal instruction, because they involve a student's doing things on his own that are different from what he is expected to do. Or consider the need for Achievement, the desire to do a good job in a situation involving personal challenge. At the present time we do not know how to increase it by formal instruction, nor are we sure that we would want to even if we could. Would it not make the intense competitiveness of the country even worse? Furthermore, research has shown that external rewards, such as grades, are not only meaningless for such people, they may actually be disconcerting. A person with a strong need to achieve works best when left alone to pursue his own goals. Offering him special incentives or rewards only serves to put him off his stride, unlike the person with a low need for Achievement, who needs such rewards to spur him on.

If the usual methods of encouraging excellence — by teaching and grading — do not work for such qualities, what does? Unfortunately, psychologists have only just begun to work on such problems. Their efforts to date have been almost wholly directed to identifying various types of academic talent and measuring the effects of various methods of teaching and grading it. Only a few mavericks have strayed into studying the nonacademic effects of education. However, one conclusion is already fairly well established, even at this early stage in the research. Schools and colleges tend to develop distinctive "personalities," distinctive and persistent climates of opinion that have rather marked effects on students attending them. R. H. Knapp and H. B. Goodrich have noted this in demonstrating that certain undergraduate colleges excelled in the production of scientists, whereas others produced more humanists, or lawyers.[8] P. E. Jacob has surveyed studies of value attitudes in various colleges and come up with some similar findings.[9] Certain values are more common on some campuses than others. At Haverford the students are more community-minded, at Wesleyan they express a stronger ethical-religious concern, at state universities they are more often interested in promoting their careers than in a general liberal-arts education.

More recent research has pinpointed some of these influences more precisely. For example, academically talented boys were brought together from high schools all over New Hampshire for a six-week summer session at one of the state's oldest and most distinguished private schools for boys. The summer program almost certainly enriched their education in the formal sense, but it also had important effects on their values and outlook on life. For example, before they arrived they had viewed authority as bad, arbitrary, and ineffective. After the summer school experience, they viewed authority as good, strong, and impersonal. They also were more concerned about problems of impulse control or discipline and had developed a sophisticated suspiciousness of the world not characteristic of their fellow classmates who had remained behind in the high schools.[10] Now none of these attitudes or personal qualities was consciously taught by the masters at the private school or consciously learned by the bright students attending it. Yet the effects were very marked, and in the long run they may be more important in the future lives of the boys than the extra amount of mathematics and biology they picked up during the summer.

A somewhat similar study has been started at Harvard University. Preliminary results suggest that Harvard may be having an effect on its students very much like the one people have been claiming it has had for over a hundred years. It turns out students who tend to feel indifferent, superior, and slightly disillusioned. There are very few "committed romantics" among its graduates. Henry Adams' description of the Class of 1858 is still amazingly accurate in 1960: [11]

> Free from meannesses, jealousies, intrigues, enthusiasms, and passions; not exceptionally quick; not consciously skeptical; singularly indifferent to display, artifice, florid expression, but not hostile to it when it amused them; distrustful of themselves, but little disposed to trust anyone else; with not much humor of their own, but full of readiness to enjoy the humor of others; negative to a degree that in the long run became positive and triumphant. Not harsh in manners or judgment, rather liberal and open-minded, they were still as a body the most formidable critics one would care to meet, in a long life exposed to criticism.

This is the Harvard style — a type of excellence, if you will, that is strongly encouraged among students who attend Harvard. Not all of them acquire it, of course, but its very existence points a moral. Educational institutions can and do have important influences on the human qualities we have been talking about, in subtle ways that are not as yet understood. Should we not, therefore, encourage varieties of excellence among such institutions as a means of promoting a similar variety in the characteristics of students who attend them? Harvard may promote "objectivity" and a kind of critical sophistication, while Texas produces unashamed enthusiasts. College X may be a haven for the curious, and College Y, a woman's college, may stress the life of the mind, the world of the imagination. Why should it not be so?

There are certain to be those at Harvard who will object to its style, who will think that it should turn out more committed people. But why should a college or any educational institution be all things to all students, or, what is worse, be like every other institution? Harvard encourages a certain type of excellence. Let other colleges encourage other types. It means, of course, that not all the best brains in the country should go to Harvard, however good it may be academically. Society needs brainy romantics as well as brainy critics. The most serious weakness in the argument that the best students should go to the best schools is the naive assumption that the best schools academically can be the "best," too, in the effects they have on character and personality, in shaping other types of human excellence. But let this not be an excuse for easy local pride. No college or university can lay a serious claim to the best students in its area if it is all things to all men and has developed no distinctive excellence of its own.

Varieties of excellence in individuals, therefore, can be encouraged by varieties of excellence in the educational institutions they attend; but one more step is necessary for such a system to work. The institutions must avoid admitting students solely in terms of one type of excellence, namely, academic promise or performance. That is, if our new model provides for a variety of types of excellence encouraged in a variety of excellent ways, then one type of excellence must be prevented from becoming a monopoly and placing a strong restraint on "trade." Academic excellence has very nearly reached a monopoly position, despite the protests of admissions officers that they are still operating in terms of "other criteria." They are fighting a losing battle. The logic is inexorable. Students with the highest predicted grade-point averages are increasingly the ones admitted to any school or college. The last bastion in the Ivy League colleges of the East is about to crumble: alumni sons can no longer receive preference. Sons of Harvard professors have received some preference in the past in being admitted to Harvard, but a recent report on admissions at Harvard has demonstrated that on the average they do less well academically than do boys who are admitted solely on the basis of their academic performance. The report therefore recommends the abolition of the preference for sons of Harvard professors.

Now I hold no particular brief for the sons of alumni or Harvard professors; but I strongly object to the stranglehold that academic performance is getting on the admissions process. So long as there were other means of getting into our better colleges, at least there was a chance of admitting some students who were not marching in tune to the academic lock-step. A Franklin D. Roosevelt or a Chief Justice Harlan Stone might slip in through the side door as a son of an alumnus or graduate of a distinguished private school — though on the basis of academic performance neither could get in the front door today. Yet they represent for me a type of excellence that deserves an education in one of the "preferred" colleges. Yet even if they got in today, they would not stay long, if a practice tried out at Amherst College (where Justice Stone was an undergraduate) spreads. There for a time a student had to live up to his predicted grade-point average or he was expelled, even though he was earning passing grades. Here is concern with one type of excellence with a vengeance. The Amherst professors argue that if a student who should be getting "A's" is only getting "C's," he could better cultivate his curiosity, his need for Achievement, or the life of the mind somewhere else, say, at home watching television or working in the local gas station. Anyway, he is a bad influence on the other boys, who must keep up their performance in the academic lock-step.

It is difficult not to be misunderstood on this point. Academic excellence is a wonderful thing. As a teacher, I much prefer to have conscientious people in my classes who do what they are told, read their assignments, and turn in interesting papers on time. I am annoyed by that boy in the back of the room who comes late to class, never participates in the discussion, and appears to be listening only half-heartedly to the pearls of wisdom I am dropping before him, and I certainly will give him a low grade — but is that all there is to education? Am I or his college having no influence on him except in terms of what is represented in that grade? Does it mean nothing for the future of the country that the scion of one of our great fortunes received such a ribbing from a sociology professor at Yale that it is alleged to have changed his whole outlook on life? He did not graduate, and, probably, with the greater efficiency of our academic predictors today, he would not have been admitted; but is that all there is to the story?

The clock is certainly not going to be turned back. The old leisurely, relaxed, admissions procedures cannot be reinstated with the competitive pressure for entrance into college growing year by year. What can be done, practically speaking? I have a dream about a new type of admissions procedure that I would at least like to see tried out at one of our better colleges. First, the admissions office would set a floor for predicted academic performance. It should not be set too high. For the sake of argument, let us say that it is set at "C," a passing grade at most colleges. Only those boys who on the basis of the usual academic test had a predicted average grade of "C" would be further considered for admission. Then, within that group, quotas should be set up for various types of excellence. For example, the one hundred boys with the highest academic prediction should be admitted, then the one hundred with the most curiosity, another hundred with the highest need for Achievement, one hundred with the greatest imaginativeness or the most political ability, and so on down the list. The professors would be sure to protest, and perhaps they should get the quota of the academically talented up to fifty percent, but at least the principle would be established that other types of excellence deserve the kind of education that college is giving. For the professors should not have the exclusive say as to who should be educated. Quite naturally they like people who are like themselves, but they do not represent the only type of excellence in the country that is important or needs encouragement. What a revolution in values it would bring if only a few National Merit Scholarships were given for the highest scores on tests of curiosity, creativity, or imaginativeness! I shudder to think of the difficulties of developing such tests and trying to keep the schools and parents from figuring out ways to get round them, but frankly, I see no other effective way in the long run of breaking the stranglehold that academic excellence is getting over the American educational system and the American hierarchy of values. Perhaps some first-rate college will be brave enough to try it out in the short run on a smaller and less public scale.

Our national problem is that we have tended to focus increasingly on encouraging one type of excellence, and a practical, measurable, action-oriented type of excellence at that. Other types of human excellence exist, particularly those involving character and the inner life, and the world of imagination and human sensitivity. They can be measured, if necessary, to combat the stress on academic performance. They, too, need encouragement, and they can be encouraged by less stress on the purely academic side of life and more stress on the unique styles of educational institutions that most influence such other human qualities.

## REFERENCES

1. Jerome S. Bruner, *The Process of Education.* Cambridge: Harvard University Press, 1960.

2. Dael Wolfle, "Diversity of Talent," *American Psychologist,* 1960, *15:* 535–545.

3. See for example: W. L. Warner and J. C. Abegglen, *Occupational Mobility in American Business and Industry.* Minneapolis: University of Minnesota Press, 1955. David C. McClelland, *The Achieving Society.* Princeton: D. Van Nostrand, 1961; chapter 7.

4. See for example: David C. McClelland, J. W. Atkinson, R. A. Clark, and E. L. Lowell, *The Achievement Motive.* New York: Appleton-Century-

Crofts, 1953. D. C. McClelland, *The Achieving Society.* Princeton: D. Van Nostrand, 1961.

5. Gerald Gurin, Joseph Veroff, and Sheila Feld, *Americans View Their Mental Health.* New York: Basic Books, 1960.

6. See for example: D. C. McClelland, A. L. Baldwin, U. Bronfenbrenner, and F. L. Strodtbeck, *Talent and Society.* Princeton: D. Van Nostrand, 1958. J. W. Getzels and P. W. Jackson, "Career Aspirations of Highly Intelligent and Highly Creative Adolescents," *Journal of Abnormal Social Psychology,* 1960, *1:* 119–123.

7. See the Technical Reports of the research on Fellowship Selection Techniques, supported by the National Science Foundation, Office of Scientific Personnel, National Academy of Sciences, National Research Council, Washington, D. C.

8. R. H. Knapp and H. B. Goodrich, *Origins of American Scientists.* Chicago: University of Chicago Press, 1952.

9. P. E. Jacob, *Changing Values in College.* New York, Harper & Brothers, 1957.

10. See D. G. Winter, Personality Effects of a Summer Advanced Studies Program. Unpublished honors thesis, Department of Social Relations, Harvard University, 1960.

11. Reprinted by permission from Henry Adams, *The Education of Henry Adams* (Boston-New York: published for the Massachusetts Historical Society by Houghton Mifflin, 1918), p. 56.

# SELECTED ANNOTATED REFERENCES

## I. ACHIEVEMENT: THE SOCIAL CONTEXT

DENNIS W. BROGAN, *The American Character* (New York: Knopf, 1944). A friendly, but firm portrait of the American in which some of the origins of our concern with achievement are examined.

MARGARET MEAD, *And Keep Your Powder Dry* (New York: William Morrow and Company, 1943). An eminent anthropologist examines the American character and points out its strong emphasis on achievement.

DAVID C. MCCLELLAND, ALFRED L. BALDWIN, URIE BRONFENBRENNER, and FRED L. STRODTBECK, *Talent and Society* (New York: Van Nostrand, 1958). Contains a series of papers and research reports on the need for and means of identifying talent in American society.

MYRON WEINER, *Modernization* (New York: Basic Books, 1966). A number of distinguished social scientists examine the causes and effects of modernization, and ways in which individual achievement affects this process.

## II. ORIGINS OF ACHIEVEMENT

### The Family

VAUGHN CRANDALL, W. KATKOVSKY, and ANNE PRESTON, "A Conceptual Formulation of Some Research on Children's Achievement Development," *Child Development, 31* (1960), 787–797. The paper defines achievement behavior and the various parameters of achievement standards, and then suggests research problems on parental attitudes and behavior in relation to the child's achievement.

ELIZABETH G. COHEN, "Parental Factors in Educational Mobility," *Sociology of Education, 38* (1965), 404–425. A study of a working class sample of boys and their parents. Attention is given to the son's educational mobility and such parental characteristics as social class differences of mother and father and favorable attitudes toward college.

DAVID C. MCCLELLAND, *The Achieving Society* (New York: D. Van Nostrand Co., 1961). Includes a summary of the child-rearing literature related to achievement motive strength through 1960.

BERNARD C. ROSEN, "Family Structure and Achievement Motivation," *American Sociological Review, 26* (August, 1961), 574–585. This study tests hypotheses regarding family size, ordinal position, mother's age, and social class and their relation to the son's achievement motivation.

Such associations do appear but interact with each other in a complex fashion.

RALPH H. TURNER, *The Social Context of Ambition* (San Francisco: Chandler Publishing Co., 1964). A study of high school seniors in Los Angeles which explores social structural factors (familial and scholastic) related to educational, occupation, and material ambitions. Includes valuable data on sex differences in ambition and factors related to ambition.

MICHAEL ARGYLE and PETER ROBINSON, "Two Origins of Achievement Motivation," *British Journal of Social and Clinical Psychology, 1* (June, 1962), 107–120. A study that finds identification with parents, particularly when the parents have high achievement tendencies, and guilt positively associated with achievement motivation.

### Race, Ethnicity, and Social Class

DAVID J. BORDUA, "Educational Aspirations and Parental Stress on College," *Social Forces, 38* (1960), 262–269. This study found in a Boston sample of high school students that middle class more than lower class parents stressed the importance of college attendance. Religious differences were also found, with social class held constant.

JOSEPH A. KAHL, "Educational and Occupational Aspirations of 'Common Man' Boys," *Harvard Educational Review, 23* (1953), 186–203. A report of data drawn from the Harvard Mobility Project, which attests to the crucial role that parental influence plays in shaping the son's aspirations. Notes particularly the sizable proportion of working class boys who show typically middle class aspirations.

MURRAY A. STRAUSS, "Deferred Gratification, Social Class, and the Achievement Syndrome," *American Sociological Review, 27* (June, 1962), 326–335. A study of 338 high school upper classmen which found that there was a tendency for adolescents to defer certain needs and that this deferment was related to performance of achievement roles, but deferred gratification did not appear to be related to social class.

JAMES W. SWINEHART, "Socio-Economic Level, Status Aspiration, and Maternal Role," *American Sociological Review, 28* (June, 1963), 391–399. Using interviews and questionnaires with 252 mothers matched on several family characteristics, the study explores social class differences in performance of the maternal role and what consequence this might have on the mother's aspirations for her children.

### III. ACHIEVEMENT IN ACADEMIC SETTINGS

### The School as a Social System

A. H. HALSEY, JEAN FLOUD, and C. ARNOLD ANDERSON, editors, *Education, Economy and Society* (Glencoe, Ill.: The Free Press, 1961). A collection of readings, dealing with education and its relation to the larger society. Includes papers on education and social mobility, educational selection in light of the social class structure, and some social factors in educational achievement.

C. WAYNE GORDON, *The Social System of the High School* (Glencoe, Ill.: The Free Press, 1957). One of the earliest and best studies of a high school as a social system, noting in particular that the informal peer group exerts great influence on students and their behavior in school.

PATRICIA C. SEXTON, *Education and Income* (New York: The Viking Press, 1964). A study of elementary and high schools in a large midwestern city. Major attention is given to differential education opportunity and its relation to social class (income).

ALAN B. WILSON, "Social Stratification and Academic Achievement," in A. Harry Passow, editor, *Education in Depressed Areas* (New York: Bureau of Publications, Teachers College, Columbia University, 1963), 217–235. Explores the homogenizing effects of the differential social class composition of schools on academic achievement and finds such an effect present, among other related findings.

JAMES S. COLEMAN, *et al.*, *Equality of Educational Opportunity* (Washington, D.C.: Government Printing Office, 1966). A nationwide study of 4,000 schools which represents the most definitive work on educational opportunity to date. It contradicts many popular beliefs about Negro-white differences in school facilities, teachers' qualifications, and students' motivations and learning. New insights into equality of educational opportunity are provided in abundance.

### The Peer Group

JAMES S. COLEMAN, *The Adolescent Society* (Glencoe, Ill.: The Free Press, 1961). The most intensive study of student culture and its significance for academic achievement. Evidence reveals an overwhelming athletic-popularity emphasis and an under-emphasis of scholastic goals.

EDWARD L. McDILL and JAMES S. COLEMAN, "Family and Peer Influence in College Plans of High School Students," *Sociology of Education*, 38 (Winter, 1965), 112–126. A study of students at six midwestern high schools, which found that by the end of the senior year in school, status in the school social system explained more of the variation in college plans than did the parent's education.

WALTER L. WALLACE, "Institutional and Life-cycle Socialization of College Freshmen," *American Journal of Sociology*, 70 (November, 1964), 303–318. Using somewhat different techniques than those of Coleman, Wallace found essentially the same powerful peer group effect operating at the college level to influence attitudes, aspirations, and achievement.

EVERETT C. HUGHES, HOWARD S. BECKER, and BLANCHE GEER, "Student Culture and Academic Effort," in NEVITT SANFORD, editor, *The American*

*College* (New York: John Wiley and Sons, Inc., 1962), 515–530. Shows the medical student culture adversely affecting maximal academic output.

## The Student-Teacher Relationship

N. L. COGAN, "The Behavior of Teachers and the Productive Behavior of Their Pupils: A 'Perception' Analysis," *Journal of Experimental Education*, 27 (1958), 90–105. A study of 987 eighth graders in five junior high schools in Boston revealing some of the teacher behaviors related to high level of student performance.

N. L. GAGE, editor, *Handbook of Research on Teaching* (Chicago: Rand McNally and Co., 1963). A comprehensive survey and summary of the research on a wide range of factors relevant to the teacher's role as a socializer of academic talent, including social interactions in the classroom, personality characteristics of teachers, and social backgrounds of teachers.

HARON J. BATTLE, "Relation Between Personal Values and Scholastic Achievement," *Journal of Experimental Education*, 26 (1957), 27–41. Found that with age, sex, and aptitude controlled, student-teacher value congruence was predictive of higher grades, even when these values were not directly relevant to the task.

VIRGINIA C. CRANDALL, SUZANNE GOOD, and VAUGHN J. CRANDALL, "Reinforcement Effects of Adult Reactions and Nonreactions on Children's Achievement Expectations: A Replication Study," *Child Development*, 35 (1964), 485–497. An experimental study of adult verbal reactions (positive and negative) and nonreactions (silence) and their effects on children's achievement expectations. Found nonreactions produced results opposite to those of preceding verbal reactions, positive or negative.

## IV. ACHIEVEMENT IN OCCUPATIONAL SETTINGS: PERSONALITY AND STRUCTURAL FACTORS

### Achievement in Organizations: Constraints and Adaptations

PETER M. BLAU, *Bureaucracy in Modern Society* (New York: Random House, 1956). The starting point for acquiring insight into work in industrial society.

ROBERT BLAUNER, *Alienation and Freedom* (Chicago: University of Chicago Press, 1964). Analyzes work-performance and satisfaction in technologically diverse types of work-settings, disclosing the immense influence of social structural arrangements on possibilities for achievement in work.

ROBERT DUBIN, GEORGE C. HOMANS, FLOYD C. MANN and DELBERT C. MILLER, *Leadership and Productivity: Some Facts of Industrial Life* (San Francisco: Chandler Publishing Co., 1965). Essays by four leading scholars on many issues relevant to this book.

AMITAI ETZIONI, "Organizational Control Structure," in James G. March, editor, *Handbook of Organizations* (Chicago: Rand McNally & Company, 1965). Systematically presents numerous propositions regarding worker behavior in the context of the author's valuable theoretical scheme.

FREDERICK HERZBERG, BERNARD MAUSNER and BARBARA B. SNYDERMAN, *The Motivation to Work* (New York: John Wiley & Sons, 1959). A careful study of factors affecting job satisfaction and achievement among professional employees of large organizations.

EVERETT C. HUGHES, *Men and Their Work* (Glencoe, Illinois: The Free Press, 1958). A collection of papers by a pioneer in the study of work.

W. RICHARD SCOTT, "Theory of Organizations," in Robert E. L. Faris, editor, *Handbook of Modern Sociology* (Chicago: Rand McNally & Company, 1964), 485–529. A comprehensive assessment of current knowledge about organizations.

## Achievement and Creativity

HARVEY C. LEHMAN, *Age and Achievement* (Princeton, New Jersey: Princeton University Press, 1953). Reports the author's extensive studies of creativity in relation to age, showing different patterns for members of various professions.

ANNE ROE, "Psychological Study of Research Scientists," *Psychology Monographs*, 67, No. 2, 1953. One of the author's numerous pioneering papers on creativity among scientists, showing diverse personality characteristics accompanying eminent achievement in different scientific disciplines.

MORRIS I. STEIN and SHIRLEY J. HEINZE, *Creativity and the Individual: Summaries of Selected Literature in Psychology and Psychiatry* (Glencoe, Illinois: The Free Press, 1960). Valuable annotations of the vast literature on intrapersonal factors in creativity.

GARY A. STEINER, editor, *The Creative Organization* (Chicago: University of Chicago Press, 1965). Report of a symposium on creativity in organizations presenting the current thinking of many leading psychologists and sociologists.

## Achievement and Women

JESSIE BERNARD, *Academic Women* (University Park, Pennsylvania: Pennsylvania State University Press, 1964). A comprehensive assessment of women's achievements in academia by one of the most eminent of academic women.

JACQUELINE A. MATTFELD and CAROL G. VAN AKEN, editors, *Women in the Scientific Professions* (Cambridge, Massachusetts: M.I.T. Press, 1965). Presents conference papers reviewing the problems, achievements and prospects of women in the sciences.

MARY CROWLEY MULVEY, "Psychological and Sociological Factors in Prediction of Career Patterns of Women," *Genetic Psychology Monographs*,

*68* (November, 1963), 309–386. The best study of occupational mobility among women.

U. S. DEPARTMENT OF LABOR, Women's Bureau, Bulletin No. 285, 1962, *Handbook on Women Workers* (Washington, D. C.: U. S. Government Printing Office, 1963). Presents basic data on women in the labor force.

## V. ACHIEVEMENT AND SOCIAL MOBILITY

OTIS DUDLEY DUNCAN, "The Trend of Occupational Mobility in the United States," *American Sociological Review, 30* (August, 1965), 491–498. The most recent, and most methodologically refined, assessment of mobility trends in the United States.

SEYMOUR MARTIN LIPSET and REINHARD BENDIX, *Social Mobility in Industrial Society* (Berkeley: University of California Press, 1959). A landmark in the contemporary study of mobility, presenting the most comprehensive materials available from other industrial nations as well as the United States.

NEIL J. SMELSER and SEYMOUR MARTIN LIPSET, editors, *Social Structure and Mobility in Economic Development* (Chicago: Aldine, 1966). Presents a number of valuable papers on various aspects of mobility, including theoretical statements, methodological studies, and assessments of the consequences of mobility and of personality factors in mobility.

PITIRIM A. SOROKIN, *Social Mobility* (New York: Harper and Brothers, 1927). The classic American work on mobility.

FRANK W. TAUSSIG and C. S. JOSLYN, *American Business Leaders* (New York: Macmillan, 1932). An invaluable early study of the business elite.

W. LLOYD WARNER and JAMES C. ABEGGLEN, *Occupational Mobility in American Business* (Minneapolis: University of Minnesota Press, 1955), and *Big Business Leaders in America* (New York: Harper and Brothers, 1955). These books provide the most extensive recent materials on mobility in the business world. They are especially valuable in that the study from which they are drawn was designed to yield information comparable to that reported by Taussig and Joslyn in 1932.

## VI. DEVELOPING ACHIEVEMENT

JOHN W. GARDNER, *Excellence: Can We Be Equal and Excellent Too?* (New York: Harper and Row, Publishers, 1961). A prominent American discusses the worthiness of maximizing excellence in American society and the problems of accomplishing this end in a democratic society.

MARY JANE ASCHNER and CHARLES E. BISH, editors, *Productive Thinking in Education* (The National Education Association and the Carnegie Corporation of New York, 1965). A series of papers, commentaries, and

643 Selected Annotated References

discussions of implications for teaching creative thinking contributed by some of the leading authorities of the field.

WILBERT J. McKEACHIE, "Students, Groups, and Teaching Methods," *American Psychologist, 13* (1958), 580–584. Reviews a series of experiments that investigate the effects of teaching methods, which incorporate different degrees of control and social interaction, on the student's performance. Some attention is given to the interactive effects of methods and the student's strength of achievement motive and anxiety.

B. J. BLOOM, ALLISON DAVIS, and ROBERT HESS, *Compensatory Education for Cultural Deprivation* (New York: Holt, Rinehart and Winston, Inc., 1965). A series of working papers from a "conference on education and cultural deprivation." The purpose of the conference was to review evidence, make recommendations for change, and suggest problems for future research.

MERRILL-PALMER QUARTERLY, *10* (July, 1964), 207–309. Entire issue of papers from the Arden House Conference on Pre-school Enrichment.

A. HARRY PASSOW, editor, *Education in Depressed Areas* (New York: Columbia University, Bureau of Publications, 1963). A collection of papers that explore the social and psychological aspects of education in urban depressed areas. Attention is given to implications of these facts for a more effective educational system in depressed areas.

# INDEX

Ability
  academic, and occupational achieve-
    ment, 543–546
  and class standing, 288
  collective, 20–21
  defined, 625
  as factor in the economy, 18–19
  improving levels of, 22–24
  inhibited by culture, 26–27
  research in, and development of,
    28–30
  social rewards, and school achieve-
    ment, 323–327
Achievement
  academic
    effect of diverse pressures, 91–94
    and socialization process, 87–88
  attitudes related to, 100–101
  broken homes and, 176
  consumption as mark of, 14–15
  defined, 12
  as dominant focus of business success,
    13–14, 15
  efforts, of grade school children,
    96–97
  intellectual, and social activities, 327
  and intellectual stimulation, 96–98
  inter-level
    and intra-level, and social class,
      234 n.4
    and social structural variables, 230
  and intervention in environment, 97–
    98
  intra-level, and personality variables,
    230
  occupational, 360–361
    and academic ability, 543–546
    and college graduation, 540, 545–
      546
    determinants of, 491–494
    and education and ethnic back-
      ground, 514–515
    possibilities for, 490–491
    women and, 361–362
  via occupational mobility, 489

  parent-child relationship affecting,
    106
  personal excellence distinguished
    from, 13
  rewards and, 56
  scholastic, 245–247
  and social class origin, 541–543, 545–
    547
  student peer group influencing, 231–
    232
  teacher-student relations and, 232–
    233
  traditional explanations of, 3–7
Achievement behavior, defined, 95
Achievement motivation
  autonomy index, 71
  categories of, 62-63
  and delayed gratification, 99
  defined, 95–96, 133–134
  experimental tasks, 52–62
  findings in, 81–84
  in girls, 102–103
  and I.Q., 100
  and national economic growth, 627
  origins of, 96
  and parent-child interaction, 69–70
  parental involvement as basis for,
    105–106
  and parental profiles, 72–77
  and parental role relationship, 77–81
  and self-reliance training, 70–71
  sex differences in, 280
  and social mobility, 138–140
  social values influencing, 183
  and standards of excellence, 55, 64–
    67
Achievement orientation, components
  of, 132
Achievement value orientations, of
  racial and ethnic groups, 140–
  145
Achievement process
  acceleration of, in school programs,
    599
  large scale industry and, 599–600

645

Achievement training, 55–56; and social
mobility, 137–138
Achievement Syndrome, 132
Achieving children
acceleratory mothers, 104–106
compliance with parental values, 92,
93, 99
development of hostility, 93–99
interdependence among, 103–104
motivation in girls, 102–103
parental influence, 104–106
personality characteristics, 88–90, 98–
100
relation of expectancy to performance,
100–101
Adolescent
deviant behavior, 155, 158–172
experimentation with unacceptable
patterns, 255
group, position
and educational norms and goals,
158–172
and parental expectations, 163–166
*see also* peer group; youth culture
Adults
achieving, best working environment,
630
extrafamilial, influencing upward mobility, 558–559
Aggression, in different social classes,
348
Ambition
and family attitudes, 113
and family size, 122–123
and family structure, 120–123
findings about, 126–127
and parental education, 115–120
and sibling position, 123–126
socioeconomic background and, 112–
113
and stress in family, 121
types, 114
and undesirable parent-child relationship, 121–122
Anti-intellectualism, in youth culture,
250
Anxiety
about competence and school performance, 279 n.9
alleviated by teacher approval, 340
job related, 376–377
Apprenticeship
devices, 392

executive, 386
Aspiration
boundary, 27–28
educational
influenced by student body, 233–
234 n.2
and social mobility, 145–149
learning, destructive effect of school,
26
levels, and intelligence, 183
and social mobility, 112
Attitude
and achievement, 100–101
effect on intelligence, 25–26
Autonomy
in child training, 56
in job situation, 373
Autonomy index, in achievement motivation, 71

Balance model, 312–315
Behavior, basic assumptions about, 86–
87
Bureaucracy
apprenticeship devices, 392
in educational institutions, 605
impersonality in, 394
*see also* navy
Business
access to executive positions, 625
achievement motivation in, and national economic growth, 626
*see also* career; industry; job
Business executives
apprenticeship, 386
class origins, 565–566
colleges contributing largest numbers
of, 570–571
geographic mobility of, 571–574
geographic origins, 571–573
wives, background of, 576
Business success, achievement as dominant focus of, 13–14, 15

Career
aspiration and achievement, 388–
390
changing, opportunity structure, 388
diagonal mobility group, 367–368
differentiated from job, 384
educational barrier to, 386
factors affecting, 581, 591–592
graded, 385–386

patterns, motivations and mobility in, 589–591, 592
secure mobile group, 367
and status of first job, 585–588
status inheritance pattern, 585–586, 588
upward mobile group, 386–387
values affected by social class, 582–583
women and, 470–478
Career advice, influenced by social class, 582–583
Career motivation, and class values, 582–583
*Child Buyer, The* (Hersey), 624
Child development
ignorance about, in education, 605
importance of early influence, 611
Hunt, J. McV., on, 619
and social experience, 603
and variety of stimuli, 607–608, 612
working mother affecting, 478–479
Child training
for achievement and independence, 55–56
autonomy, 56
City size, and occupational opportunity, 504–510
Class *see* school class; social class
Cognitive growth
conditions inhibiting, 194–209
and language, 194–195
Collective ability, 20–21
College
graduation and occupational achievement, 543–546
overstressing of academic merit, 625–626
"personality" of (affecting students, 631–632
Colleges, contributing largest number of executives, 570–571
Communication
on factory production goals, 424
mother-child, and cognitive growth, 194–195
restricted or elaborated, 194–195
Community influence
on school performance, 285–286, 290–294
on upward mobility, 558, 559, 560
Competence
anxiety about, 279 *n*.9

defined, 265
and divergent thinking, 262–263
Competence feelings
and motivation, in traditional and changing schools, 273–277, 278 *n*.8
Competence motivation
as primary drive in middle and lower class children, 610–611
traditional and modern views, 266–267
Consumption, as mark of achievement, 14–15
Creative personality
deferral and immediacy, 441
detachment and commitment, 439, 447–448
dominated by creative object, 440–441, 448
early family life, 430–431
independence, 433
intellectual capacities, 428, 429
interests, 433–434
internal resources, 441–442, 449
introversion, 432–433
lack of repression, 429–430
masculinity-femininity, 430
need to order and integrate complexity, 434
passion and restraint, 439–440
perceptivity, 434
psychological problems, 431–432
stereotypes of, 427–428
values, 434
Creative process
and effective surprise, 436–438
and technique, 438–439
Creative research group
creative factors in, 447–449
described, 442–444
working methods, 447–449
Creativity, 360–361; in traditional and modern school, 264
Curiosity
and academic excellence, 627–628
teaching for, 630

Delayed gratification, 99
Delinquency, and upgraded educational processes, 250–251
Deprivation *see* social deprivation
Deprived, lack of rewards for, 344
Discipline, in classroom, 347–351

Economic success, 13–14
Education
　affecting ability levels, 23–24
　as barrier to career, 386
　and geographic movement, 569
　middle and lower class orientation toward, 344
　and occupational achievement, 514–515, 540, 545–547
　and occupational mobility, 566–568, 572
　and occupational opportunity, 499–504
　sequence of, 264–265
　as sorting-out process, 35–36
Educational aspirations
　influenced by student body, 233–234 *n.*2
　and social mobility, 145–149
Educational norms and goals, and adolescent group position, 158–172
Educators, and behavioral scientists, 605–606
Ego involvement
　and job performance, 368–369, 373–375, 379–381
　and job satisfaction, 369–370, 375–376, 378
　measuring, 370–371
Enrichment program
　expansion of, 616–617
　language training in, 615–616
　Montessori, 614
　pre-school, verbalized routine in, 615
Ethnic background
　education, and occupational achievement, 514–515
　and occupational opportunity, 499–504
　and vocational aspiration, 149–150
　*see also* Greeks; French Canadians; Jews; Negroes
Ethnic cultures
　achievement values of, 140–145
　tendency to survive, 138
Excellence
　curiosity and, 627–628
　encouraging variety of, 633–635
　non-academic, 625–626
　systematic encouragement of, 623–624, 629–630
　in women, 628
Executives *see* business executives

Extra-family influences
　and career advice, 582–583
　and upward mobility, 558–559
Extra-school experiences, and upward mobility, 558–559

Factory
　communication in, 424
　intergroup cooperation, 409–412, 416–422
　intergroup relations, 407, 422–424
　managerial inefficiency, 423
　restriction of output, 407–408, 423
　work procedure, 412–415
Failure, and environmental deprivation, 612–613
Family
　and ambition, 27, 120–125
　inhibiting cognitive growth, 194
　and intelligence of children, 25
　and occupational mobility, 510–514, 515
　and school performance, 284–286
　social-status oriented *vs.* person-oriented, 195–198
　socio-educational status, and continuing education, 288
　stress in, and ambition, 121
　and upward mobility, 555–556
Fowler, W., on preschool education, 617–618, 618–619
French Canadians, 150–151
　achievement motivation, 139–140
　achievement training, 137–138
　achievement values, 141–145
　educational aspiration levels, 146–149
　effect of social structure on, 131–132

Girls, achievement motivation in, 102–103
Goals, reflecting social values, 12
Greeks, 150–151
　achievement motivation, 139–140
　achievement values, 141–145
　educational aspiration levels, 146–149
　effect of social structure on, 131–132

Harvard University, effect on students' personalities, 631–632, 633
Hereditary career status, 585–586, 588
Hereditary social status, 13
Hersey, John, *The Child Buyer,* 624
Hostility, in achieving children, 93, 99

Hunt, J. McV., on child development, 619

Independence, 99
in achieving children, 103–104
and creative personality, 433
on entering school, 242
Independence training, 55–56; and social mobility, 135–136, 138
Industry, and achievement process, 599–600
Italians, Southern, 150–151
achievement motivation, 139–140
achievement training, 137–138
achievement values, 141–145
educational aspiration levels, 146–149
Intelligence
aspiration levels, social status and, 183, 189–190
attitude affecting, 25–26
of creative personalities, 428, 429
development of, 606
factors affecting, 25–26
stimulation of, and achievement, 96–98
Intelligence quotient (I.Q.)
and achievement, 90, 100
and desire to quit school, 167
effect on educational norms and goals, 158–172
influenced by family background, 25
personality characteristics of "ascenders," 98–99
regression of, 94 *n*.2
scores
and achievement, 6–7
and socio-economic status, 616
tests
cultural bias of, 221–222
performance factors in, 523
Intervention
influencing achievement, 97–98
concepts, 604
in school programs, 599
*see also* enrichment program
Invention, rate of, 20
Involvement, parental, and achievement, 105–106

Jews, 150–151
achievement motivation, 138–140
achievement training, 137

achievement values, 141–145
educational aspiration levels, 146–149
effect of social structure on, 131–132
Job
and anxiety, 376–377
autonomy in, 373
and career, 384
performance, and ego involvement, 368–369, 373–375, 379–381
and upward mobility, 558–559
Job satisfaction
and ego involvement, 369–370, 375–376, 378
measuring, 371–373
and self satisfaction, 376–378, 381–382
Juvenile delinquency, and ungraded educational processes, 250–251

Language
difficulties, in disturbed socialization patterns, 90–91
in lower and middle classes, 614–615
restricted or elaborated, 194–195
in social status and person-oriented families, 195–198
training program, 615–616
Learning abilities, development of, 606
Learning aspiration, destructive effect of schools on, 26
Learning theory, insufficiently explored, 85–86
Lower class
pre-school environment compensation, 609
orientation toward school, 216–217, 220–224, 344
and scholastic retardation, 606–607
slum conditions described, 607–608
Lower class children
lack of competence motivation, 610–611
discipline problem, 348–350
moral traits, 352–354
unprepared for school, 609

Marriage rates, and propinquity, 302
Masculinity-femininity, in creative personality, 430
Mastery, school approach to, 262–263
Middle class
child
competence motivation, 610–611

*Middle class, child (cont.)*
    discipline of, 349, 350, 354
    family structure, 113
    orientation toward school, 217–220, 221, 224, 344
Migration, and occupational opportunity, 504–510
Mobility
    and aspiration, 112
    in career, 583
    channeled by educational system, 624–625
    divergent viewpoints on, 552–553
    extra-familial adults influencing, 558, 559, 560
    and family influence, 555–559
    peer group influencing, 558, 560
    teacher influencing, 557–558, 559
    travel and work experience and, 558–559
*see also* occupational mobility
Montessori, early enrichment program described, 614
Mother
    acceleratory, 104, 106 and cognitive growth of child, 194–195
    teaching styles and social status, 205
    and upward mobility, 559
    working, and child development, 478–479
Motivation
    internalized, 367–368
    and lack of rewards, 344
    and unattainable goals, 409

National Merit Scholarships, 623, 625
Navy
    avoidance of responsibility in, 395–399
    ceremonialism in, 401–402
    competition restrained in, 396–397
    conflict between authority and specialization in, 395–396
    function of routine, 398
    incompetence in, 396
    initiative restrained in, 397
    as insulated occupation, 399–401
    legalism in, 399
    promotions in, 398
    rewards in, 402–403
    social mobility of officers, 392
    as variant of bureaucracy, 392–394, 404

Negroes, 150–151
    achievement motivation, 139–140
    achievement training, 137–138
    achievement values, 141–145
    educational norms and goals, 146–149, 172
    effects of chronic stress on, 175
    occupational opportunity for, 499–504, 514–515
    parental educational expectations, 165–166
    slum conditions and, 607–608
    social structure and, 131–132
    in socialization of cognitive modes study, 194–209
    students, attitudes of teachers toward, 175

Occupational achievement *see* achievement, occupational
Occupational mobility, 489, 490
    of business leaders, 565–566, 571–576
    colleges contributing most executives, 570–571
    education and, 566–568, 572
    and geographic movement, 569
    foreign birth and, 573–574
    in large and small business, 575–576
    within social class groups
        achievement motivation and, 525–527
        effect of education on, 525
        interaction of education and achievement motivation, 527–530
Occupational opportunities
    city size and migration, 504–510
    for Negroes, 499–504, 514–515
    parental family affecting, 510–514, 515

Parent-child relationship
    and achievement motivation, 69–70
    undesirable
        and achievement, 106
        and ambition, 121–122
Parental achievement, and motivation of child, 65–69
Parents
    and career advice, 582, 583
    education of, influencing ambition, 115–120, 123–125

influencing educational expectations, 163, 166

involvement of, and achieving children, 105–106

profiles of, and achievement motivation, 72–77

role relationship and achievement motivation, 77–81

as socializing agents, 90

vocational ambitions influenced by, 27

Peer group, 297–300, 306–307

attitudes of, 309–310

balance model, 312–315

college-bound child and, 254

continuity of, 305–306

emotional dependency on, 254

formation, conditions for, 300–304

homogeneity of, 308

and impetus to perform, 267

influence on achievement, 231–232

influence on educational aspiration, 316–321

isolation of, 308–309

in larger colleges, 313

size of, 307–308

and upward mobility, 558, 560

and youth culture functions, 254–255

Personality

of achieving child, 88–90, 98–100

ideal, 456

of school, 631

Pre-school enrichment program

Montessori. 614

verbalized routine in, 615

Propinquity, and interpersonal relationships, 302–303

Protestants, 150–151

achievement motivation, 139–140

achievement values, 135, 141–145

educational aspiration levels, 146–149

Racial groups, achievement values of, 140–145

*see also* Negroes

Regression method, of test analysis, 497–499

Rewards

and achievement, 56

in Navy, 402–403

social, and school achievement, 323–327

Roman Catholics, 150–151

achievement motivation, 139–140

achievement values, 135, 141–145

School

ability, and further education, 288

achievement in, 245–247, 323–327

anxiety, relieved by teacher, 340

atmosphere, and motivation and competence feelings, 278 *n.*8

bureaucracy in, 605

changes in educational structure of, 262

as channel of selection, 241, 256–257

child's attitude toward, 216–217

cooperative functioning of, 270–271

cultural discontinuity with home, 609–610

desire to quit, 166–171

destructive influence on learning aspiration, 26

docility training in, 332, 339–341

effect on individual performance, 284, 286

environmental compensations in, 608–609

evolution of, 604

failure of curricula, 613

grade lag in, 347–348

and intellectual mastery, 262–263

lower-class orientation toward, 216–217

middle-class orientation toward, 217–220, 221, 224, 344

orientation of toward middle class values, 178–179

need for compensatory programs in, 614

performance, and anxiety, 279 *n.*9

"personality" of, affecting students, 631

sequence of education, 264–265

signal, cue and sign behavior in, 331

socializing influence of, 176–177, 180

stress on competence and divergent thinking, 262–263

traditional and modern, 244–245, 246

approach to creativity, 264

competence motivation in, 266–267

and competence feelings, 267–268

motivation and competence feelings, 273–277

*School, traditional and modern (cont.)*
   teaching of skills, 265–266
   test-taking in, 270–271
   thinking processes affected by,
      268–272
   ungraded, 617
School class
   ability and class standing, 288
   effects of cross pressures in, 249–250
   discipline in, 347–351
   elementary
      socialization and selection in, 247–
         251
      structure of, 243–245
   secondary, differentiation and selec-
      tion in, 251–256
   selection of college and non-college
      program students in, 241–243
   socialization in, 239–240, 247–248
   status system in, 248
Scientists, characteristics of, 480
Seashore, Carl E., on musical ability,
      21–22
Self-concept, and job performance, 380–
      381
Self-reliance training, 70–71
Sibling position, and ambition, 123–
      125
Signal, cue and sign behavior, 331–332
   and cultural values, 333
   signal development in, 333–339
Slum conditions, 607–608
Social activities, detracting from in-
      tellectual achievement, 327
Social class
   and achievement motivation, 139
   career advice influenced by, 582, 583
   and career values, 582–583
   and classroom discipline, 347–351
   and educational aspiration, 147
   educational opportunities of, 343
   groups
      effect of education on, 525
      factors in mobility within, 527–530
   and inter- and intra-level achieve-
      ment, 243 *n.*4
   low, and scholastic retardation, 606–
      607
   and occupational achievement, 545–
      547
   as pattern of experience, 194
   status, and education, 283
   syntactical organization levels, 615

and vocational aspiration, 149–150
Social deprivation
   compensating for, 607
   early, effects of, 612
   family context inhibiting cognitive
      growth, 194
   inadequate school accommodations,
      178–179
   need for early intervention, 611
   need for educational help, 606–607
Socially deprived
   and overcrowding, 177–178
   reinforcement of by teacher, 177
Social experience, of child, and develop-
      ment, 603
Social mobility
   achievement motivation and, 138–140
   achievement orientation of racial and
      ethnic groups and, 131–132,
      140–145
   achievement training and, 137–138
   and geographic movement of foreign-
      born, 573
   educational aspiration levels of ethnic
      groups and, 145–149
   and independence training, 135–136,
      138
   research procedures in, 133–134
   and vocational aspiration levels of
      ethnic groups, 149–150
Social status
   and achievement process, 599
   differences in and concept utilization,
      202–205
   educational and occupational aspira-
      tions and, 183–190
   and heredity, 13
   and intelligence, 183
   and maternal teaching styles, 205–
      209
   and teaching techniques, 346–347
   and use of restricted or elaborated
      verbal codes, 199–202
Social strata in youth system, 253
Social values, affecting individual goals,
      12
Socialization
   and academic achievement, 87–88
   augmenting influence of school, 176–
      177
   of behavior, leading to poverty, 194,
      209
   critical stage in, 611–612

defined, 240
and effect of diverse pressures on students, 91–94
parents as primary agents of, 90
in school class, 239–240, 247–248
Socio-economic status
and ambition, 112–113
classifications, 112
educational norms and goals, 158–172
Stress, in family, and ambition, 121
Student
high status-low ability, 257 *n.*3
Negro, attitude of teacher toward, 175
*see also* adolescent; peer group; youth culture

Talent
demand for, 34
development of, 37–41
*see also* ability
Teacher
discipline affected by social class of pupils, 347–351
female, providing emotional support, 247
lower-class hostility toward, 340
male, beneficial role, 179
and middle class competitive dynamics, 340
as model of learning attitudes, 267
and Negro students, 175
and non-academic excellence, 630
reaction to pupil class-differences, 342, 345–347, 356 *n.*14
reinforcement of socially deprived, 177
relationship with student, 267; and achievement, 232–233
signal, cue and sign behavior, 331–339
teaching techniques in various schools, 346–347
upward mobility influenced by, 557–558, 559
values of, affecting lower class students, 213–216
Test taking, in modern schools, 270–271
Truancy, 156–157

Unemployment, and lack of aptitude, 20

Upper-class children
discipline of, 348–351
moral traits, 352–353

Value system
in American society, 154, 454–457
parental, child's acceptance of, 92, 93
success *vs.* achievement in, 14
Vocational aspiration levels of ethnic groups, 149–150

Weber, Max, 135
Women
American basic values and, 454–457
career interruptions, 477–478
early family influences, 481–483
educating for scientific career, 483–484
employed mother and child development, 478–479
excellence in, 628–629
individualistic self-expression, 455
intellectual ability, 480–481
lack of affinity to science, 479–480
modern attitudes toward domesticity, 458–469
modern role, 453
occupational achievement, 361–362
preferred occupation, 363 *n.*6
priority of marriage over profession, 474–477
professional status of, 470–471
proportion of in labor force, 471–472
upgraded education as agent of socialization, 256
withdrawal from profession, 473–474
Work, as motive for leaving school, 170–171
Work role, personal involvement with, 368
Work situation, present day, 359

Youth culture
anti-intellectualism in, 250
foreshadowing family formation, 255–256
selective function of stratification in, 253–254
shifts in pattern, 253–254
*see also* adolescent; peer group